P9-BYU-986

Königsberg

Danzig

EAST PRUSSIA

P R U S S I A

N

W   E

S

Oder
River

Breslau

S I L E S I A

GERMANY · 1919-1933

BUCTEL

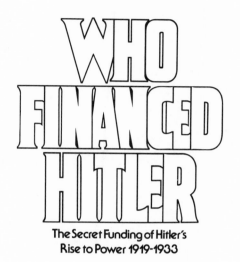

WHO FINANCED HITLER

The Secret Funding of Hitler's
Rise to Power 1919-1933

James Pool &
Suzanne Pool

WHO FINANCED HITLER

The Secret Funding of Hitler's Rise to Power 1919-1933

The Dial Press
New York

Published by
The Dial Press
1 Dag Hammarskjold Plaza
New York, New York 10017

Copyright © 1978 by James E. Pool III and Suzanne Pool

All rights reserved. No part of this book may be reproduced or transmitted in any form or by any means, electronic or mechanical, including photocopying, recording or by any information storage and retrieval system, without the written permission of the Publisher, except where permitted by law.

Manufactured in the United States of America

First printing

Library of Congress Cataloging in Publication Data

Pool, James, 1948–
    Who financed Hitler.

    Bibliography: p.
    Includes index.
    1. Hitler, Adolf, 1889–1945. 3. Finance. I. Pool, Suzanne, 1953–   joint author. II. Title.
    2. Germany—Politics and government—1918–1933.
DD247.H5 P63   320.9'43'086   78-15978
ISBN 0-8037-9039-2

To our parents

Many of those who have contributed valuable information wish to remain anonymous for reasons which are easily understood. Although we can not mention everyone individually, we would like to express our sincere gratitude to all of those who have assisted in making this book possible.

If money go before,
all ways do lie open.
—Shakespeare

Preface

Adolf Hitler did not come to power easily. He began his political career in 1919 and did not become Chancellor until fourteen years later in 1933. During this time it took a tremendous sum of money to support the Nazi Party. Where it came from, who provided it, and why, are the topics of this book.

There have been many books written on the Nazi period, but this most important aspect of Hitler's activity—one of the very keys to his success—has never been dealt with. One reason is that much of the information about financial contributions has only recently come to light, but the primary reason is an understandable reluctance to acknowledge the ease with which money can subvert the democratic process.

History is replete with unsavory tales of political financing, and there is a serious question whether democratic principles can ever ultimately be upheld in an atmosphere of unsupervised and unpublicized political fund raising. Perhaps the newly created German democracy was more vulnerable than most free societies, yet the story of how Hitler found the necessary money to undermine the Weimar Republic has universal implications.

In Germany from 1919 to 1933, political parties were little more than tools for powerful interest groups. Hitler was quick to recognize this and turn his formidable and nefarious talents to the task of fund raising. His methods were unscrupulous. At first he courted the powerful; then as his party grew in size and strength, he was perfectly willing to use blackmail and bribery to gain his ends. But it must be admitted that he knew the value of money:

that it could purchase almost all the necessary resources of politics, such as propaganda campaigns, newspaper coverage, full-time staff, etc. In short, Hitler knew that money meant power.

It is even partly true that Hitler was able to sell an evil idea like anti-Semitism simply because he had the support of wealthy contributors. By continuous propaganda even the greatest untruth will be believed by some people. There were many anti-Semites in Germany long before Hitler, but they belonged to small splinter parties that were ineffective because of their endless squabbling. Large donations provided Hitler with the needed tools to organize these fringe elements and turn them into a major political force.

Discovering the exact sums of contributions and the identity of contributors is not an easy task. Money moves silently as well as easily. Cash leaves no tracks. Checks can be laundered—passed through intermediaries and false corporations—to obscure the original source of funds. But, despite the difficulties, the search is worthwhile. Money is the tracer element in the study of political power. Light thrown upon transactions involving financing illuminates the flow of both influence and power.

Hitler was launched on his political career by a wealthy and powerful secret society, none of whose members were big businessmen. Other funds came from the most unexpected sources. Germany's most important Jewish industrialist even gave to the Nazis—to make them dependent on his money in hopes of eventually disrupting them. Hitler got some of his biggest "contributions" by first discovering the corrupt dealings between certain big industrialists and prominent liberal politicians, and then blackmailing the industrialists with threats of exposure.

Hitler's fund raising gave birth to many of the techniques of covert funding and dirty tricks that later became the stock-in-trade of most major governments. The double subsidiary corporations through which Captain Ernst Röhm channeled army funds to Hitler were so secret in their operations that, even after the government became aware of the missing money, the corporations were able to continue functioning undetected for about a year.

One of the most important and unexpected discoveries of this study is the importance of foreign financing in bringing Hitler to power. Hitler received money from Austria, Britain, Czechoslovakia, Finland, France, Italy, Holland, Hungary, Switzerland, Sweden, and the United States. It is true that some money came from Germans living in these countries, but most of it came from prominent foreign citizens. Their motives varied: Henry Ford wanted to spread his anti-Semitic philosophy, Mussolini hoped to encourage German fascism, Grand Duchess Victoria of Russia wanted to support anti-Communism, Sir Henri Deterding aimed to get back his oil interests confiscated by the Communists, etc.

Those who financed Hitler, both Germans and the foreigners, are just as responsible for his coming to power as the active Nazis who spread anti-Semitic propaganda or fought in the streets. Yet, because of their influence and the power of money, few of them were prosecuted at Nuremberg. Many are now exposed here for the first time.

1
A MYSTERIOUS
BEGINNING

In the first week of January 1931 an important dinner party was held at Hermann Göring's residence outside of Berlin. The hostess was Göring's beautiful and charming wife Carin, a Swedish baroness by birth. Among the guests were Adolf Hitler, the Prince and Princess zu Wied; Fritz Thyssen, a multimillionaire industrialist who was chairman of the board of Germany's largest firm, the United Steel Works; Ernst Tengelmann, the wealthy director of an important Ruhr coal mining company; and Dr. Hjalmar Schacht and his wife.

Dr. Schacht, a prominent banker, was generally regarded as Germany's financial wizard. In 1923 he had been appointed Special Commissioner to stabilize the inflated mark. Shortly after his outstanding success, he became president of the Reichsbank (Germany's national bank). Politically, Schacht was a moderate liberal who had been one of the founders of the German Democratic Party, but when the Allies continued to force Germany to pay heavy reparations, Schacht resigned his office in disgust. He was, however, still a great power in the financial world and sat on the boards of several important banks and corporations.

Schacht had never met Hitler before and although he was curious about the man, he was skeptical. "After the many rumors that we had heard about Hitler," wrote Schacht, "and the published criticisms we had read of him, we were pleasantly impressed."[1] The Nazi leader arrived wearing dark trousers, the brown uniform jacket of the Party, a white shirt, and dark tie. "His appearance," said Schacht, "was neither pretentious nor affected."[2]

The meal was a rather simple but wholesome one: pea soup, pork, potatoes and vegetables, and for dessert Swedish apple tart with vanilla ice cream. After dinner the guests retired to the drawing room. Hitler sat near Carin Göring, who was resting on the couch because of her weak heart condition. He was in a jovial mood and entertained the ladies with some amusing stories.

A little later Göring, Hitler, Thyssen, Schacht, and some of the other men went into the library for a long discussion. "Our talk quickly turned to political and economic problems," said Schacht. "His [Hitler's] skill in exposition was most striking. Everything he said he stated as incontrovertible truth: nevertheless, his ideas were not unreasonable."[3]

The next day Carin Göring wrote to her mother, Baroness von Fock: "I could tell from Hermann's positively beatific smile that it was a most successful party."[4]

The description of Hitler given by Schacht and most other people who met him personally contrasts very noticeably with the way he is portrayed by present-day biographers. For instance, Alan Bullock has described Hitler's physical appearance as "plebeian through and through."[5]

Although Hitler was known for his ability as a speaker, some authors seem to contend that he was at a total loss with individuals or small groups. "A quiet conversation with him was impossible," said Hermann Rauschning. "Either he was silent or took complete charge of the discussion."[6] Hitler was "unable to argue coolly," Alan Bullock tells us; ". . . his one resort was to shout his opponent down. The questioning of his assumptions or of his facts rattled him."[7] Above all, he would have found it almost impossible to talk with businessmen, industrialists, or bankers because, as William Shirer reported, "economics . . . bored Hitler and he never bothered to try to learn something about it."[8]

If Hitler behaved in such a fashion, he could hardly have persuaded wealthy, well-educated people to contribute great sums of money to his party. But he had two different sides to his character. The ranting bully of the beerhall could be very charming and persuasive when he wanted to be. It is a dangerous mistake to underestimate the ability and intelligence of an enemy. In fact, to a certain extent, Hitler succeeded because he was dismissed as being more ridiculous than dangerous. The man who shouted crude anti-Semitic slogans in public could, to the amazement of those who met him in private, discuss complex political and economic issues with logic and penetrating insight. He was able to convince his financiers that he was not a rabble-rouser at heart but had to act that way to attract the masses away from the Communists.

In 1919 when his political career began, Hitler's manners were not as polished as they were when Dr. Schacht met him in 1931, nor were his ideas on political or economic policy as fully developed. However, even in 1918 Hitler was not to be underrated. Throughout his youth he had been a keen student of history. In Vienna he had observed and studied the rise of modern mass political movements, especially Marxism, with the thoroughness of a political scientist.[9] He never let his prejudices prevent him from realistically appraising his opponents. Although he was largely self-educated, by the end of the war he was more widely read than most university graduates.[10]

On September 12, 1919, with orders from his commanding officer, Hitler attended a political meeting of a group called the German Workers' Party in Munich's Sterneckerbräu beerhall. His mission was to report back on what was said because the Reichswehr (Army), which was very inquisitive about politics, wanted to have more exact information about the little group which seemed to be "well intentioned."[11] Very few people had ever heard of the German Workers' Party, one of about fifty different political groups and parties which existed in Munich at this turbulent time. The Party had been founded nine months earlier by Anton Drexler, a thirty-five-year-old railway locksmith, and its members were mostly his fellow workers from the railway yards. Its program was radical, anti-Semitic, and nationalistic.

Dressed in civilian clothes, Hitler was inconspicuous among the audience of some fifty people. By his own account he went purely as an observer, with no intention of speaking. However, during the discussion period a professor named Baumann made a speech advocating the separation of Bavaria from Germany and its linking up with Austria to form a new south German state. Destesting the idea of separatism, Hitler stood up on the spur of the moment and made a fiery speech rebutting the arguments of the professor and advocating the unity of all Germans. Then he turned and walked out.[12]

Anton Drexler came running down the aisle after him and

handed him a pamphlet entitled "My Political Awakening." Although quite pedestrian in style, the pamphlet, written by Drexler himself, expressed some of the very same ideas about a nationalistic workers' party that Hitler had been pondering for a long time. Before Hitler had a chance to consider the little party further, he received a postcard informing him that he had been accepted as a member. He thought it was a curious way of enrolling members and didn't know whether to laugh or be irritated. "I had no intention of joining an existing party," he said, "but wanted to found one of my own."[13] Nevertheless, he attended a committee meeting and two days later made what he called "the most crucial decision of my life" when he signed up as a member.

"This absurd little group with its handful of members," he wrote, "seemed to me to have the advantage that it was not petrified into an 'organization,' but offered the individual an opportunity for truly personal activity."[14] There was another reason Hitler joined, one which he neglected to mention in *Mein Kampf*. Despite this tiny party's many weaknesses, it had one outstanding strength. Behind the German Workers' Party stood its founder, protector, and financial sponsor: the Thule Society, the most powerful secret organization in Germany.* Outwardly, this mysterious group passed as a literary circle devoted to studying ancient German history and customs. Its name was taken from the mythological land of the north, the ancient Ultima Thule, believed to be the original home of the Germanic race. The Munich branch had been founded during the war by a Baron Rudolf von Sebottendorff, a shadowy individual who enlisted over 250 members from the city and 1,500 throughout Bavaria.[17] The significance of the membership, however, was not to be found in its quantity but its quality. Among the group's members were lawyers, judges, university professors, police officials, aristocratic members of the royal entourage of the Wittelsbachs, leading industrialists, surgeons, physicians, scientists, as well as rich businessmen like the proprietor of the elegant Four Seasons Hotel in Munich where the society had its headquarters.

Only those who could prove their racial purity for at least three generations were admitted to this organization, whose motto

---

*Originally, the organization was an offshoot of the Germanen Orden, another powerful secret society whose branches through the country were patterned on Masonic lodges.[16]

was: "Remember that you are a German! Keep your blood pure!"[18] The symbol of the Thule Society was the swastika. Its letterheads and literature displayed the emblem, and large swastika flags decorated its plush meeting rooms and offices. Many of the themes and slogans of the group were later repeated by Hitler almost word for word.

Like many other *völkisch* (racial, nationalist) movements in Germany, the ostensible objective of the Thule Society was the establishment of a Pan-German state of unsurpassed power and grandeur. There were also mystical aspects to the association involving bardic ritual and occult ceremonies. On the practical political level, the society espoused German racial superiority, anti-Semitism, and violent anti-Communism.

During World War I, the Thule members were busy fighting "treason" and advocating the most extreme Pan-German views. But with the Communist instigated uprisings at the end of the war,* things became more serious. On November 9, 1918, Sebottendorff spoke before a meeting of the entire membership to issue a call to arms against "Judah."[19] The Thule offices became a center of activities for the counterrevolutionary underground. A secret intelligence network was set up and caches of arms were assembled. Early in December, Sebottendorff planned to kidnap Eisner, the president of the Bavarian Soviet government, but something went wrong at the last moment and the action was called off.

Operating simultaneously with these covert activities was a more or less open anti-Communist propaganda campaign that involved the distribution of hundreds of thousands of anti-Semitic pamphlets. The society's propaganda posters were stuck up during the night and leaflets were hurled into crowds from speeding automobiles. A determined effort was made to win over the masses of the population, especially the workers "poisoned with the Jewish ideas of communism and internationalism." Unlike most other conservative nationalists, the Thule Society was aware of the danger presented by the widening gap between the officer class and the workers. It became one of the society's

---

*The revolution developed from a series of uprisings throughout Germany at the end of the war which were led by Communists. From November 1918 to May 1919 Bavaria was ruled by a Soviet government. But the beginning of the end for the Communists came when the Free Corps troops crushed the Spartacist (Communist) uprising in Berlin.

primary objectives to bring the working man back into the nationalist camp.

Thule member Karl Harrer was instructed to form a "Workers Political Circle."[20] However, neither Harrer, who was a journalist, nor any of the other upper-middle-class or aristocratic members of the society knew anything about the politically minded workers. Given the existing sentiments of class hostility, the Thule program would be automatically rejected by the masses if proposed by someone of a privileged class. The circle needed to be directed, nominally at least, by a manual worker. Harrer decided to back Anton Drexler, who was both a Pan-German anti-Semite and a proletarian. In the last years of the war, Drexler had written an article, published in Harrer's newspaper, which urged the workers to rally behind the Army.

Shortly after the revolution of November 9, 1918, Drexler and Harrer drew up a general program for a nationalist workers' party. On January 5, 1919, Drexler invited some of his patriotic fellow workers to the first "public meeting," and the German Workers' Party was officially founded.[21] Drexler was probably aware that the Thule Society was supporting his efforts, but such a simple man could hardly have understood the extent of the organization's power and influence. But was Hitler aware at the time he joined that the German Workers' Party was backed by the Thule Society?

A few days before the liberation of Munich by the Free Corps troops, the Communists raided the hotel headquarters of the Thule Society and took seven members hostage. On May 1, 1919, as the anti-Communist Free Corps units tightened the ring around the city, the hostages were stood up against a wall in the courtyard of the Luitpold High School and shot. Of the seven Thule members killed, four were titled aristocrats, including the beautiful young secretary of the society, Countess Heila von Westarp, and Prince Gustave von Thurnund Taxis, who was related to several European royal families.[22]

Not only Germany but the entire world was shocked by the murders of such respectable people. The London *Times's* headline read, "Shooting of Hostages . . . Munich Savagery."[23] Everyone in Munich was now aware of the Thule Society's existence and that it had some very important members. Considering Hitler's position as an Army agent and his interest in nationalist anti-Semitic politics, it is likely that he was aware of the society's backing this new little movement called the German Workers' Party. If Hitler had such information it would explain why he chose this small party from the many other nationalist groups which were in existence at the time.

Outwardly, it did not seem as if the German Workers' Party was supported by anyone with power, influence, or money. In *Mein Kampf* Hitler described with utmost disdain his first impressions of the Party: The members assembled in the dimly-lit back room of a beerhall and discussed political ideas they did not understand. They wrote letters to other patriotic movements in Lubeck, Hanover, and elsewhere, and discussed the answers received. The total funds of the Party amounted to seven marks and fifty pfennigs.[24] As far as property was concerned, the movement did not even own a rubber stamp. The members were afraid to hold public meetings because they might irritate their opponents, the Social Democrats and Communists.

Hitler urged the Party committee to court publicity or else the movement would never become known. But Harrer and the others felt they were not ready to become known. They first wanted to jointly discover "the truth" in order to "get things clear in their own minds." After tedious and exhausting discussions Hitler finally persuaded his comrades to risk a public meeting. Invitations were typed or written out by hand and then dropped into the mailboxes of prospective individuals. Hitler himself walked through the deserted streets of Munich before dawn distributing eighty invitations. But when the long-expected evening arrived, only the seven party committee members turned up; not another soul. The next few meetings were only slightly more successful.

The Party finally placed a notice for one of their gatherings in the *Völkischer Beobachter (The Racial Observer)*, an extreme nationalist newspaper owned by the Thule Society. Hitler claimed that the "poor devils" who were the members of the Party paid for this advertisement themselves.[25] The meeting was to be held in a cellar room of the Hofbräuhaus, the most famous beerhall in Munich. The room would hold about 130 people, a number which seemed enormous to Hitler and his comrades. Hitler had the "unshakable conviction" that if only people would come and listen he could win them over to his cause. The advertisement drew 111, the largest audience the German Workers' Party had ever had and the collection taken at the end of the speech netted 300 marks (about nine U.S. dollars).

It is difficult to determine exactly how much financial assistance the Thule Society gave during this early period, but most likely it was very little. The Thule Society had more important projects. For a long time the society had been subsidizing the Free Corps Oberland, a fully armed regiment of about 2,000 men.[26] Naturally this required considerable funds and, although there is no complete record of donations, one account mentions frequent contributions in the neighborhood of 30,000 to 70,000 marks.[27] The society also spent a considerable amount on its own activities, for one of its executives, Herr Töpfer, complained that banquets seemed the chief activity.[28] Moreover, neither Harrer nor any of the Thule Society had any idea of how to form a mass party. If Hitler wanted a political movement of the common man to rival the Communists, he would have to build it himself. The most significant assistance he would get from the Thule Society for the time being was protection from police prosecution thanks to Thule members in the Bavarian government. But as the German Workers' Party would begin to grow and develop under Hitler's guidance, able and intelligent Thule sympathizers and members would join it and be of the utmost value to Hitler. Eventually the child of the masses would outgrow its secret society parent. In the meantime, the most important help Hitler received was from his employer, the Army.

The seemingly slow, snaillike progress of the German Workers' Party was particularly painful to Hitler because he was not engaging in politics merely for his own satisfaction. He was participating with the consent and, in part, by the orders of his superiors at the Army District Headquarters. He was still on the full-time payroll of the Reichswehr as a political agent.[29] The Army was looking for a mass political party on which it could rely as a patriotic alternative to Communism, but it would not wait forever.

One day an officer who worked with Hitler took him to a meeting of the Iron Fist.[30] There he met the organization's commander, Captain Ernst Röhm, who almost immediately recognized a certain ability in Hitler. In its blunt militarylike way, the Iron Fist was an important patriotic group in Munich in 1919. Röhm and his men, mostly tough young officers and a few loyal troops, would march into a beerhall, and every quarter of an hour they would have the band play a patriotic song. When the tune was blared out, everyone stood up. Those of Marxist sympathies or anyone else who remained seated was soon confronted by a rough figure in military uniform. A silent glance was usually enough, but if the unfortunate individual did not immediately rise to his feet, he just barely lived to regret his error.

Officially the officer "in charge of press and propaganda" for the Bavarian Reichswehr, Röhm's influence was much greater than his rank of captain indicated.[31] Unofficially, the generals took his advice on all political matters; he organized new paramilitary Free Corps units and he directed the clandestine movement of arms to secret hiding places out of the reach of the Allied Control Commission. Under his supervision thousands of rifles, machine guns, and mortars were stockpiled in remote forests and deserted villas. Röhm's activities made him a key figure in the so-called "black" Reichswehr, the surreptitious reserve of the reduced legitimate Army, which was limited to 100,000 men by the Versailles Treaty.

Within a short time after their first meeting, Röhm became so convinced of Hitler's talent as a political agitator that he joined the German Workers' Party and began to attend its meetings regularly. He greatly strengthened the little party by recruiting new members from among his troops and the younger officers,[32] men who were all hardened veterans of the trenches, seething with hatred against the Weimar Republic. They supplied the strength and muscle Hitler needed to defend his young party against the Marxists in the streets. Röhm also siphoned certain Army funds into Hitler's movement.[33] Yet very little money actually changed hands. Instead, Röhm arranged things so that Hitler's men could list Party bills as Free Corps expenses and could obtain various government services to which the Army was entitled. "Röhm," said Hitler's close associate Kurt Lüdecke, "was of decisive importance to the (Nazi) Party, finding money, arms, and men at the most critical times."[34]

The fact that Captain Röhm treated Hitler as a social equal automatically gave Hitler a certain status among Röhm's fellow officers. But social distinctions were of little importance for Röhm. If a man was a veteran of the trenches and was opposed to Communism, that was enough for him. Röhm himself was not exactly a figure of gentlemanly military elegance. He was a short bulky man whose face was marked with dueling scars and bullet wounds. In his blunt, aggressive manner there was also a hint of brutality. But this was just the kind of man Hitler needed to help him secure the leadership of the German Workers' Party away from the cautious, conservative Harrer who was wary of anything bolder than pedantic back-room discussions.[35]

Hitler, setting his hopes on drawing larger audiences, insisted on renting a bigger hall, and, in hopes of attracting more soldiers, he chose a tavern called Zum Deutschen Reich on Dachauerstrasse, close to the barracks of the List Regiment. The results were disappointing and expectations were far from being met; only about 140 people came. The Party executive committee was discouraged and frightened; Harrer argued that Hitler would ruin the Party with such wreckless aggressiveness. Finally Hitler succeeded in convincing Drexler and the others that they were bound to succeed if only they persisted. One of Hitler's obvious strengths was this determination, persistence, and self-confidence even in the face of defeat. The next meeting held at the Zum Deutschen Reich drew slightly more than 200 people. Another meeting attracted 270 listeners, and the fourth was attended by over 400. Hitler was on his way.

Making the rounds of the beerhalls and restaurants of Munich, he searched for a headquarters for the Party, whose total equipment at that point consisted of a cigar box to hold its funds and a few envelopes for correspondence. He found a dark back room available in the Sterneckerbräu where the rent was fifty marks a month (about 95 cents in U.S. currency). This was regarded as an exorbitant sum by the Party committee. As one of the cosigners of the lease, Hitler gave his occupation as "artist," probably to throw off any suspicion of Army support.

The new headquarters had only one small window, which faced an alley so narrow that hardly any sunlight entered. "The room," said Hitler, "had more the look of a funeral vault than an office." A table and a few borrowed chairs were obtained, then a telephone installed, and finally a safe for the Party's membership cards and the treasury, which did not have much money in it.

The first Party treasurer was a one-armed former poacher named Meir.[36] Being of a humble background with little formal education, his only qualification for the job was his honesty. As the Party grew in size and the role of treasurer became more important, Meir was succeeded by a Herr Singer, a lesser official in the Bavarian state government. Hitler later described Singer as "a fine man" whose talents were "exactly what suited us at that time."[37] With the inflation eating away the purchasing power of the mark, Singer's regular salary was not sufficient to permit him to make even a small donation to the Party, so he took a part-time job in the evenings as a guard at the Bavarian National Museum in order to be a regular monthly contributor.

The collections at all Party meetings were directed by Singer, who would stuff the money received into a small tin trunk, which he then lugged home under his arm. A Party member who walked home with him one evening remembered watching Singer empty the pile of dirty inflation marks onto his dining room table and start carefully counting and sorting them. There was an unpleasant, damp chill in the unheated room where the "treasurer" worked. Sometimes Singer's wife helped him, but on this occasion it was very late and she had long since retired to the warmth of the bedroom. As in most Munich homes during that desperately cold winter of 1920, only one room was warmed by a small stove. These were the humble beginnings of the Nazi treasury.

Hitler once mentioned three men as "important" early financial supporters: Josef Füss and Herr Gahr (both jewelers) and Herr Pöschl (a small businessman).[38] None of these men could be considered wealthy. At the most they contributed their savings and the income from their businesses.

Gahr was one of Hitler's oldest and most devoted followers. A clean-cut, good-looking man about fifty, he was once described as "the true type of the old-style honest craftsman."[39] With a modest, quiet, and dignified personality, Gahr reflected the narrow but sound culture of the master guildsman of a traditional society. Hitler entrusted Gahr's jewelry firm with the execution of his design for a standard for the first Storm Troops. In Hitler's presence Gahr's behavior was always a bit reserved, but he looked up to the young Party leader with boundless respect. Although Josef Füss, who was also a goldsmith, was not quite as close to Hitler as Gahr, he was just as strong a supporter of the Party as his colleague. Füss's firm produced the first swastika emblem in the form of a gold and enamel lapel pin.[40] Herr Pöschl was not as active in everyday Party affairs as Gahr or Füss, but his loyalty to

Hitler and the movement was no less.

There were several other men, most of them shop owners, who gave regularly and generously to the Party in the early days. Once or twice a week Hitler used to visit Quirin Diestl, the owner of a stationery shop which was located near the Regina Hotel. Frau Diestl was a great admirer of Hitler and always made the best black coffee and cakes for him. Diestl was a feisty little man with red hair and a red mustache trimmed like Hitler's. Whenever Hitler came by, he always managed to scrape together a little money for him. Diestl however was more than just a financial supporter. He never missed a Party meeting and was always ready to lend a hand in a fight with hecklers.[41]

Oscar Koerner, a middle-aged man who owned a small toy shop, was one of the original founders of the Party. He gave everything he had to the movement and later was even to give his life. (Koerner was killed in the Nazi putsch, November 9, 1923.) Koerner was always eager and enthusiastic for every new project Hitler had in mind and on many occasions he would be the first to give a few marks to see that the project was carried out. With his quick, vivacious temperament, Koerner was also one of the activists of the Party who frequently defended his beliefs with his fists.[42]

Those who were the Party's best contributors were invited to attend the Monday evening *Stammtisch* at the Café Neumaier, an old-fashioned coffeehouse on the corner of the Petersplatz and the Viktualien Market. The interior of the cafe, which had space for about a hundred people, was one long irregular room, with built-in benches and wood-paneled walls. Here every Monday night Hitler would meet informally with his most devoted financial supporters. Many of them were middle-aged, married couples who had come to have their dinner with Hitler and usually ended up paying for his as well. None of these people were rich; every mark they gave meant a personal sacrifice. Those present on Monday night were usually the first, other than the Party officials, to hear Hitler's newest ideas. After dinner Hitler would sit for hours discussing politics in a friendly, conversational manner.

Usually present on Monday evenings were other faithful donors to Hitler's cause. There was a family named Lauböck. The father, a man in his sixties, was a high railway official at the East

Station, who gave a part of his salary regularly. The son Fritz
Lauböck, who was about eighteen, served as Hitler's secretary. A
furrier named Wutz, who was known to have handed Hitler
money on various occasions, was also present, sometimes with
his wife, a singer who took somewhat of a fancy to Hitler. The
wealthiest person in attendance was probably Theodor Heuss, a
local paper manufacturer who was a leading member and financier of the Thule Society. Occasionally Dr. Friedrich Krohn,
another Thule Society member from Starnberg, took part in the
Monday evening gathering; Krohn, a dentist, gave frequently and
helped design the party's swastika flag.[43]

The Party's financial subsistence was, however, made possible
not just by the donations of the most generous contributors, but
by the day-to-day income from the average members. Every
member of the Party was expected to pay his dues of one mark a
month and give whatever his means would permit, but since
many of them were unemployed there was very little surplus
income. "You have no idea," Hitler later told Gregor Strasser,
"what a problem it was in those days to find the money to buy my
ticket when I wanted to deliver a speech at Nuremberg."[44]

Even though the dues of impoverished Party members and the
donations of small shopkeepers may not seem like very much,
they were "important" in the early days of the German Workers'
Party, as Hitler rightly pointed out. By being able to get regular
donations out of such people, Hitler demonstrated to the Army
and other potential big financiers his talent as a fund raiser. No
other political party had such a spirit of dedication and willingness to contribute among its rank-and-file members.[45] The shopkeepers and small businessmen who gave to the German Workers' Party were a desperate group. Unlike the people who supported the traditional German parties and took politics lightly,
those who donated to the German Workers' Party believed it was a
question of life or death. They felt squeezed by Marxist labor on
one hand and "monopoly capitalism" on the other. The inflation
was rapidly eating away their savings and the old middle-class
virtues of thrift and hard work seemed to be suddenly worthless.
These people were Hitler's most sincere supporters. They gave
their money without asking for anything in return. As "true
believers," they accepted every point of the Nazi philosophy without question, and it must be remembered that they grew up in a

provincial, traditional culture where anti-Semitism was commonplace. They lived through World War I when the most extreme nationalist hatreds were encouraged, and then the bloody excesses of the 1918 revolution made them ripe for someone like Hitler. None of them really understood what the results of their actions would be. They willingly accepted everything Hitler said and their personal respect for him as the spokesman of their cause was one of the key factors on which he based his strength within the Party.

Hitler continued to press for ever larger public meetings, but Harrer refused. However, by this time the Party executive committee was on Hitler's side. Harrer resigned his post as first chairman of the Party and was succeeded by Anton Drexler.[46] It would be a mistake to think Harrer's resignation indicated that the Thule Society was giving up on the German Workers' Party. They had simply come to the conclusion that, in view of the little party's rapid growth, the task was now beyond a man of Harrer's ability. More capable members of the society would have to become involved if an influence on the Party and its amazing propaganda director Adolf Hitler was to be maintained.

Hitler transformed the German Workers' Party from a directionless back-room discussion club into a genuine political force. It is unlikely that at this stage he saw himself as the prospective dictator of Germany, but his imagination was already obsessed with the idea of a "Germanic Revolution" that would sweep away the Communists, Jews, and Social Democrats who had "betrayed" the Fatherland in November of 1918. He proclaimed himself as the drummer of this coming revolution. The key to it was that nationalism and patriotism must spread beyond the upper middle class. The masses, Hitler insisted, were capable of being as patriotic as anyone else. He was fond of citing how the appeal to patriotism had had an overwhelming effect on the workers at the outbreak of the war in 1914. If a new party wanted to rekindle similar mass patriotism, it would have to convince the workers that they were a valuable part of the national community. The common man, Hitler argued, was in return entitled to social justice, a decent wage, and a secure livelihood.[47] Hitler had the right policy; the only difficulty was presenting it to the people.

Traditional nationalist meetings had tended to be dull and academic. Hitler deliberately made his meetings exciting and provocative. He practiced and developed his natural gift for oratory. What he had learned about propaganda in Vienna during the war and during the revolution now paid its dividends. Neglecting no technique that might improve his speaking, he spoke at meetings both in the afternoon and evening to see when the emotions of the audience could be more easily aroused. He went to almost every beerhall and public meeting room in Munich to study the acoustics and "atmosphere." Above all, he learned to get the "feeling" of his audience, to tell what they were thinking, and what they wanted.

Perhaps the most compelling and for that very reason the most diabolical thing about Hitler's speeches was their air of sincerity. He was the voice from the trenches, the unknown young war veteran with the Iron Cross who expressed himself so passionately. Although he wore civilian clothes, his stiff bearing, his narrow mustache, and his mannerisms were typical of the non commissioned officer. Standing stiffly at attention with his chin up, he would begin to speak in a low voice. When he caught the attention of his audience, his voice became deeper and increased in volume. As he relaxed and got the "feel" of his speech, he would begin to use gestures. His right forefinger would point out the evils Germany faced; then a sweeping gesture of the left arm would wipe them away. With variations in pace and style he could keep an audience enraptured for an hour or even two. Sometimes he spoke in an imaginary dialogue in which he stated an opponent's case and then completely demolished it with his rebuttal. He planted questioners in the audience to "feed" him and help create the right mood. It was really a kind of dramatic performance. From observation, experience, and instinct, he learned how to arouse and control peoples' emotions. It is, however, a mistake to think that his arguments made no sense. A progressive logical development was one of the strongest points of a Hitler speech.[48] Toward the conclusion his gestures would become more dramatic and his voice would break with passion as he worked up to the peroration. He finished with a call to arms that had the sting of a lash: "Germany Awake!"

The passion and conviction with which Hitler spoke had a particularly strong effect on women. He realized this and took advantage of it by always directing a special appeal to the women in the audience, who were voting for the first time in the 1920s.

"Many a time," reported an early Nazi, "I have seen him face a hall plentifully sprinkled with opponents ready to heckle and interrupt, and in his search for the first body of support, make a remark about food shortages or domestic difficulties or the sound instinct of his female listeners, which would produce the first bravos. And time and again these came from women. That would break the ice."[49] He prided himself on his ability "to play on feminine sentiments"; even his words would be carefully chosen for their appeal. In describing the difficulties of the housewife without enough money to buy the food her family needed, he would produce just the phrases she would have used herself to describe the predicament, if she had been able to formulate them.

Some of the largest contributions at early Party meetings came from women. A Fräulein Dornberg who once made a donation of 300 marks was one of the first of many women to succumb to Hitler's oratory and open their purses to his cause.[50] Whenever Hitler was scheduled to speak there were many females in the audience who, one Party member said, "responded even more enthusiastically—and generously—than the men. Frankly, I did not fail to note that some of these devoted females were of the hysterical type, who found an emotional ecstasy in surrender to the man on the platform. He could twitch their very nerves with his forcefulness. But many of the women were as intelligently interested as the men, and without their financial aid the Party's early years would have been much more difficult. . . . I was present when a woman of perhaps fifty years came to the Party's office and offered all of an inheritance she had just received. And she was one of slight means."[51]

Night after night Hitler spoke to ever-growing crowds in the beerhalls of Munich and his followers multiplied. In light of his success, more important members of the Thule Society began to join the German Workers' Party to carry on where Harrer had left off. One of them, Dietrich Eckart, came to exert a tremendously powerful personal influence on Hitler.[52]

Born of well-to-do parents in a little town of northern Bavaria, Eckart had been a failure as a law student because he drank too much and worked too little. Even when he was in his forties in Berlin, he led the life of a poor writer and a vagrant, lodging in flophouses and sleeping on park benches. He blamed the Jews for blocking the success of his works. He had written plays and, like the Marquis de Sade, staged some of them in an insane asylum, using the inmates as actors. His poetry and writing was generally about Nordic and mystical themes. Finally he became a success as a writer. His translation of Ibsen's *Peer Gynt* was brilliant and became the standard German version, bringing him a steady income from royalties, and his writings on Norse mythology became widely read, especially in nationalist circles. Before the war he was for a time the feuilleton editor of the well-known conservative Berlin newspaper the *Lokal-Anzeiger*. By the early twenties he was the editor and publisher of *Auf gut Deutsch (In Plain German)*, a satirical Munich periodical that had a fairly large circulation and was anti-Semitic, Pan-German in viewpoint.[53]

To the political philosophy of the Thule Society, Eckart brought the idea that the hour for a great charismatic leader had struck. In 1919, before anyone had ever heard of Adolf Hitler, he composed a bardic verse in which the coming of a national redeemer was prophesied, a leader "familiar and foreign at the same time, a nameless one." In a cafe he once described in plainer language the man he thought was needed to save Germany: "We must have a fellow as a leader who won't wince at the rattle of a machine gun. The rabble must be given a damned good fright. An officer wouldn't do; the people don't respect them any more. Best of all would be a worker, a former soldier who could speak. He needn't be very brainy; politics is the most stupid business in the world and every market-woman in Munich knows as much as the men in Weimar. I'd rather have a stupid vain Jackanapes who can give the Reds a juicy answer and not run away whenever a chair-leg is aimed at him than a dozen learned professors who sit trembling in wet pants." The final requirement was: "He must be a bachelor! Then we'll get the women."[54]

Adolf Hitler met most of Eckart's specifications, and the two soon became close friends. Although usually contemptuous and hostile to intellectuals, Hitler found in Eckart a kindred spirit with whom he felt at ease. In spite of his social background, university degree, and works published, Eckart was, like Hitler, essentially a rootless revolutionary. The two men made an odd pair, for outwardly Eckart was very different from Hitler. He was a big stout man with an imposing bald head and rather small eyes.

Gregarious, with a boisterious humor, he loved to spend his time in cafes and beerhalls.

Taking a personal interest in Hitler, Eckart began to groom his young friend for the role of a political leader.[55] Having grown up in a lower-middle-class atmosphere in a provincial town and having been poor most of his adult life, Hitler lacked a certain social style and breeding. He had never been in a formal drawing room nor dined in a first-class restaurant. In order to be able to deal with members of the upper class without their taking a condescending attitude toward him, it would be necessary to polish up his manners, looks, and dress. Eckart gave him his first trench coat and persuaded him to trim his mustache. He began to take Hitler around with him to the better cafes and restaurants of Munich.

Picking up Hitler's check in the cafes and taking him out to dinner in a good restaurant were only some minor services Eckart did for the emerging political leader. He gave Hitler his first introduction to better society and, what is more important, to people who were financial backers of the Thule Society. These were people who would one day render similar services for the Nazi Party. Although Eckart was not really a wealthy man himself, he was never short of money and contributed generously to the Party treasury.[56] His activities as a Party member were also of great value to Hitler. His writing ability and flair for strong, colorful language made him an excellent propagandist. The feverish battle song of the Nazi movement, "Storm! Storm! Storm!" was one of his works.

Yet another of the early collaborators who helped provide funds for Hitler's new party was Alfred Rosenberg, a member of the Thule Society who in 1918 was only a penniless emigré. Rosenberg, a Baltic German, came to Munich as a refugee from Reval in 1918. The Russian Revolution had aroused his interests in politics when he was in his mid-twenties, and it had turned him into a fanatical anti-Communist and anti-Semite. Although a well-educated man with a doctorate in architecture, Rosenberg was at first unable to find employment in Munich and survived on the charity soup kitchen of the Relief Committee.

One day his interest in anti-Communist politics led him to pay a visit to the office of Dietrich Eckart. The first thing Rosenberg said to Eckart was, "Can you use a fighter against Jerusalem?" Eckart laughed, "Certainly!"[57] Then he asked whether Rosenberg had ever written anything. Rosenberg had not only done so, but he had brought it with him. The article, published under the title "The Russian-Jewish Revolution," described the excesses of the "destructive forces" of Judaism and Communism in Russia. The theme was perfect for the propaganda series on the Jewish plan to dominate the world which Eckart was publishing in his newspaper.

Thereafter, Rosenberg frequently wrote articles for Eckart's paper and the two collaborated on several anti-Semitic booklets. In the meantime, Rosenberg became a member of the Thule Society. When the revolution broke out in Munich in November of 1918 both Eckart and Rosenberg opposed it and eventually had to flee for their lives.

In the autumn of 1919 Rosenberg and Hitler met for the first time in the home of Dietrich Eckart. They discussed how Marxism was undermining the state "the same way that Christianity had corroded the Roman Empire." A few days later Rosenberg attended one of Hitler's speeches: "Here I saw a German front-line soldier," said Rosenberg, "embarking on this struggle in a manner as clear as it was convincing, counting on himself alone with the courage of a free man. It was that which after the first fifteen minutes drew me to Adolf Hitler."[58] Toward the end of 1919 Rosenberg became a member of the German Workers' Party. He was assigned the task of researching the role of the Jews in Communism.

Speaking Russian fluently and knowing the country well, Rosenberg had no difficulty becoming the Party's expert on the East. It was a time of confused fighting on Germany's eastern frontiers, which had not been finally determined by the Treaty of Versailles. Munich was full of White Russians who hoped that the German Free Corps in the Baltic, or possibly a reactionary German government, if one came to power in Berlin, might march into Russia and throw out the Communists. Many of the White Russians had money, and money was one of the essential needs of the struggling German Workers' Party. Thus the impoverished refugee Rosenberg became the first contact man between Hitler and the wealthy Russian emigrés.

As the Party's expert on the Jewish question, it was Rosenberg who first showed Hitler a booklet entitled *The Protocols of the Learned Elders of Zion*, the most important propaganda document of the White Russian anti-Semites.[59]. The booklet, said to be the minutes of a secret meeting of Jewish leaders in 1897, the year of the first International Zionist Congress, revealed a terrible plot to undermine European society and overthrow all governments. The principal weapons to be used in the accomplishment of this conspiracy were to be Marxist revolution and international financial manipulations.

Hitler was fascinated with the *Protocols* and immediately recognized their propaganda value. The Thule Society arranged to have the *Protocols* printed in German by the Ludwig Müller publishing firm. The success was extraordinary. Edition followed edition. Interestingly, historian Konrad Heiden, who was then living in Munich, reported: "The little volume was given away and widely distributed; the good cause found backers who preferred to remain anonymous."[60]

It has been said that Eckart, Rosenberg, and other members of the Thule Society conducted spiritualistic neopagan séances with an entourage of White Russian emigrés. Certainly many of the upper-class Russian exiles were interested in such phenomena because Czar Nicholas II and his wife had been avid spiritualists.[61] It is difficult, however, to obtain precise information on the mystical activities of the Thule Society. Within the society itself there were several different schools of thought. There was Pan-German propaganda put out by the society for mass consumption, various intermediate levels of involvement in mystical activities, and a supposed inner circle who gained higher levels of initiation through the practice of neopagan ritual. No one group clearly predominated. For example, in 1918 Baron Sebottendorff had delivered a lecture on "divining rods" that was strongly objected to by Johannes Hering, also an official of the society, because he thought "such occult nonsense" was ruining the public image of the group.[62]

It is not certain whether the mysticism was simply a cover for semi-illegal political activity or whether the political propaganda was intended to shroud the occult rituals of a wealthy powerful group. A colorful, even if slightly exaggerated, description of the deeply hidden knowledge of the innermost strata of the Thule Society is given by the authors Pauwels and Bergier in their book *The Morning of the Magicians:* "The legend of Thule is as old as the Germanic race. It was supposed to be an island that had disappeared somewhere in the extreme North. Off Greenland? or Labrador? Like Atlantis, Thule was thought to have been the magic center of a vanished civilization. Eckart and his friends believed that not all the secrets of Thule had perished. Beings intermediate between man and other intelligent beings from Beyond would place at the disposal of the Initiates a reservoir of forces which could be drawn on to enable Germany to dominate the world again and be the cradle of the race of Supermen which would result from mutations of the human species. One day her legions would set out to annihilate everything that had stood in the way of the spiritual destiny of the Earth, and their leaders would be men who knew everything, deriving their strength from the very fountain-head of energy and guided by the Great Ones of the Ancient World. Such were the myths on which the Aryan doctrine of Eckart and Rosenberg was founded."[63]

While Eckart was involved in mysticism and Rosenberg was courting aristocratic Russian anti-Semites, Hitler was busy with his propaganda campaign to win mass support for the movement. Throughout the winter of 1919–1920 he remained in the Army as an instructor teaching short political courses to soldiers about to be demobilized, but most of his energy was spent working for the German Workers' Party. By now he realized that if the Party was to grow larger it would have to have an official program. After a number of meetings held in the humble atmosphere of Drexler's kitchen, Hitler and Drexler succeeded in drawing up a twenty-five point program for the Party. Eckart made a few improvements in style and by February 6, 1920, the program assumed its final form.

Hitler thought the proclamation of the new Party's program would be an ideal occasion to give his adherents their first baptism of fire. He needed a large hall and a large audience, preferably one that would include a good percentage of Communists. From his years of studying propaganda tactics he knew that a speech would be remembered more vividly if its advocates put up a fight for its defense. The conservative parties only gave the impression of cowardice when they closed down their meetings because of Communist disruptions. Instead, Hitler and his followers planned to stand and fight and in doing so win the admiration of the audience.

After renting the main hall of the Hofbräuhaus for the evening of February 24, Hitler and his comrades put up bright red posters all over Munich advertising the meeting.[64] This irritated the Communists who claimed red was the color of the workers, so they decided to put an end to such "reactionary tricks." At 7:30 on the night of the twenty-fourth the hall was filled to capacity with over 2,000 people present, many of them Communists determined to break up the meeting. The chairman of the evening, Marc Sesselmann, a member of both the Thule Society and the German Workers' Party, opened the ceremonies.

The first speaker was Dr. Johannes Dingfelder, a conservative nationalist of the traditional school. He said the salvation of the Fatherland depended on work, order, and sacrifice. Sensing that trouble was brewing in the audience, he avoided any reference to the Jews in his speech. He concluded with pious abstractions and the customary sort of quotations from Goethe. Herr Sesselmann thanked the speaker and then thanked the Communists in the audience for keeping quiet during the speech. Their quiet probably indicated boredom more than tolerance and in any case they were saving their strength for the next speaker.

The tone of the meeting was no longer polite when Hitler reached the speaker's stand. He attacked the government in Berlin, accusing it of direct responsibility for the mounting inflation which was already eating away hard-earned savings. There was loud applause, because most Bavarians blamed the Berlin government for all their problems. Then Hitler began to denounce the Jews. Most all Communist leaders were Jews, he said. They were responsible for the 1918 revolution and Germany's defeat. Class hatred served only their interests; they had sold the nation into the slavery of the Versailles Treaty.

An uproar began before he could go any further. The Communists and socialists interrupted him with organized chants and catcalls. However, the Marxists were not the only ones who were organized. Hitler and Röhm had seen to it that "faithful war comrades and other adherents" were strategically grouped throughout the hall. Violent clashes occurred but within a few minutes order was restored.

Then Hitler took up the subject of the new Party program and presented it to the audience point by point. Applause began to drown out the interruptions. By the time Hitler concluded, most of the audience was on his side; he was confident this was a historic moment of victory.

From all outward indications, the program was designed to appeal to the masses and not to the Party's financial backers. Despite the strong emotional language used in almost all of its twenty-five points, the program was not simply a piece of demagoguery nor so empty of constructive proposals as has sometimes been represented. Combined with an anti-Semitic racist ideology was a determination to eliminate the abuses of capitalism, to overcome sentiments of class hostility, to offer immediate assistance to the hard-pressed lower middle class, and to bring about the reconciliation of all interest groups in a united national community.

Of the points dealing with economic issues, some would be harmful only to Jewish businessmen. For example, Point 16 called for large department stores to be turned over to the communities, divided up, and rented out "at low rates" to small shopkeepers. Other points, however, would directly affect the interests of almost the entire upper class. All income not earned by work was to be confiscated (Point 11) as well as all war profits (Point 12). Point 14 called for a profit-sharing plan for large industries. A vague proposal for land reform was presented in Point 17 along with a demand for a ban on land speculation.[65]

The program as a whole contained the germ of future National Socialist doctrine. Included were widely accepted platitudes that could ultimately be made the basis of a totalitarian state; for instance: Common good takes precedence over the good of the individual. On the matter of foreign policy there were points demanding the abrogation of the Versailles Treaty and the union of all German-speaking people into one Reich.

By incorporating anticapitalist points in the Party program, it seems unlikely that Hitler could hope for contributions from the upper class. In fact, everything about his presentation at the Hofbräuhaus—the propaganda, the violence, the vicious anti-Semitism, and the fire-breathing oratory—would seem to have discouraged respectable support. However, there was still a great danger of a Communist revolution in Germany at the time, and if the Communist forces in all the industrial centers of Germany rose up at once, the Army, which simply did not have enough troops, would have difficulty in suppressing them.[66] The Generals and the upper class needed a new nationalist party that would appeal to the workers and win them away from the Marxists. Very few members of the upper class would want to join such a party, but because of Hitler's method of responding to Communist violence with counterviolence it would be a useful ally. Naturally, they did not want to have violence at the meetings of their conservative parties, but if a Communist revolution were to break out they would need a patriotic workers' party that was willing to fight. Hitler's strategy could hardly fail; he offered both the masses and the German power elite what they wanted at the same time. But the upper class did not rush to embrace this "tribune of the people." Irritated at the hostility of high society, Hitler would ask, "What have they got against me? That I have no title, that I am not a doctor or a first lieutenant! That they can never forgive me." On another occasion he declared that they were not resentful of him just because of his political views, but primarily because he was a "poor devil" who had nevertheless ventured to open his mouth.

Hitler was not a popular guest in Munich society. In spite of Eckart's help, the drawing rooms remained closed to him. It is sometimes thought that Frau Carola Hofmann, who lived in a suburban villa, was an exception to the general disdain Hitler received from "good" society.[67] She heard him speak for the first time early in 1920 and was captivated. In a sense, this sixty-one-year-old woman began to take the place of the mother he missed so much. She was present for some of the early beerhall brawls of the movement, started a local Party group in her neighborhood, and, for a time, her country house was an unofficial headquarters for the Party. However, Frau Hofmann, the widow of a headmaster, was neither socially prominent nor wealthy. She lived comfortably on her husband's savings, and though she frequently gave money to the Party, these were very small sums. Her gifts to Hitler were more often home-baked cakes and cookies than cash.

A week after the meeting at the Hofbräuhaus, the German Workers' Party, at Hitler's urging, changed its name to the National Socialist German Workers' Party (NSDAP). But the change in the Party's name did little to alter its always desperate economic situation. Although people of all classes were joining the movement, by far the majority were poor. An early member who gave much of his time described some of the monetary problems that Hitler's men faced in those days: "The Nazi organization itself lived from day to day financially, with no treasury to draw on for lecture-hall rentals, printing costs, or the other thousand-and-one expenses which threatened to swamp us. The only funds we could count on were membership dues, which were small, merely a drop in the bucket. Collections at mass meetings were sometimes large, but not to be relied on. Once in a while, a Nazi sympathizer would make a special contribution, and in a few cases these gifts were really substantial. But we never had money enough. Everything demanded outlays that were, compared with our exchequer, colossal. Many a time, posting the placards for some world-shaking meeting, we lacked money to pay for the paste.

"Instead of receiving salaries for the work we did, most of us had to give to the Party in order to carry on. Clerks and officers, except for a very few, got no pay, and the majority of members pursued their usual occupations during the day as a livelihood. Consequently, those who gave full time to Party work were a miscellaneous crew, including only two or three who had sufficient means to support themselves. The rest were chiefly recruited from the jobless men who would work for their meals."[69] Somehow Hitler always seemed to manage to find enough money to keep the movement going from one day to the next.

On March 13, 1920, extreme reactionary circles in Berlin attempted a coup. Headed by a little-known Prussian civil servant, Dr. Kapp, they were supported by the Ehrhardt Free Corps Brigade which conducted the military part of the operation and forced President Ebert and his cabinet to flee to Dresden. The coup had virtually no popular support except for the extreme right wing of the Nationalist Party, and moreover, the German upper class was against the venture. The leading industrialists condemned it and the High Command of the Army refused to take part.[70] The Social Democratic Party then called a general strike, and due to the political ineptitude of Dr. Kapp and his Free Corps friends, the rebel regime began to collapse.

In Munich, the conservative supporters of the Wittelsbach monarchy, who wanted a more independent Bavarian state, decided to take advantage of the situation in Berlin and carry out a coup of their own. On the night of the thirteenth, the Bavarian military authorities presented the Social Democratic government of Johannes Hoffmann with an ultimatum to reign peacefully or be suppressed. The new government, backed by the military, was headed by Ritter Gustav von Kahr, a reactionary monarchist from a family that had served the Bavarian kings for generations.

Although the Bavarian monarchists had no wish to unite forces with Berlin's new Kapp government, they did decide to send a liaison officer to Berlin to keep in touch with the regime there. Surprisingly, the choice fell on Hitler and Dietrich Eckart.[71] A military plane was put at their disposal and they immediately flew north in spite of bad weather. The pilot lost his way in the storm and was forced down at Jüterbog, forty miles southwest of Berlin. The strikers had set up barricades along the roads; no trains were running. If the real purpose of their mission became known, Hitler and Eckart would have been arrested and shot. Eckart claimed to be a paper merchant and Hitler, disguised with a goatee, said he was Eckart's accountant. Allowed to continue their flight, they arrived in Berlin just as the Kapp regime collapsed five days after taking office.

Even though the liaison mission to the Kapp government proved futile, the trip to Berlin turned out to be very advantageous for Hitler. He made contact with north German right-wing circles that had access to financial support from major industrialists like the locomotive manufacturer von Borsig. He was introduced to Free Corps leaders and officials of powerful nationalist groups like the Stahlhelm (steel helmet), a reactionary veterans' association supported by the Junkers (Prussian landed aristocrats) and extreme right-wing big business interests. The most exciting moment of Hitler's visit must have been when he was introduced to General Ludendorff, who had been the second highest ranking general in World War I and was now looked on as the senior officer of the patriotic camp. That a general like Ludendorff would shake hands with a corporal was a sign of Hitler's increasing political importance.

Dietrich Eckart, who had entree to the higher levels of Berlin society because he had once been a drama critic for a conservative newspaper there, was also a great help in putting Hitler forward. He presented him in the homes of several wealthy upper-class families. One of the ladies who received Hitler in her salon, Frau Helene Bechstein, the wife of the piano manufacturer Carl Bechstein, was particularly struck by him.

Hitler was a bit ill at ease when he first arrived at the Bechstein residence, a great monstrosity of a house in the center of the city, built in the 1870s. The interior and furnishings were all very pretentious in the style of the Berlin *haute bourgeoisie.* Frau Bechstein, who was wearing diamonds as big as cherries strung around her neck and wrist, greeted Hitler with a friendly smile. A vivacious, self-confident woman, she was intrigued by his initial shyness and tried to draw him out. As soon as the conversation turned to politics Hitler warmed up and began to speak. Before the evening was over he had found his first socially prominent supporter. With Frau Bechstein's patronage Hitler would eventually be accepted socially in the highest circles. More important, Helene Bechstein was soon to give him sizeable contributions and urge her friends to do likewise.

Hitler returned to Munich on March 31, 1920. The next day he finally decided to leave the Army. He collected his back pay and signed out of the barracks for the last time. What is important is not simply that Hitler had supported himself on an Army salary during his first year in politics, but that he was an Army representative, working under orders from his commanders. As such, he received assistance and protection from the most powerful institution in Germany. Simply because he quit being a soldier does not indicate that any break took place with his former employer. Actually, Hitler's action was of mutual benefit to both himself and the military. Because of his recent success, people were beginning to take an interest in him and there was always a danger that he might be labeled an Army puppet.

Henceforth, Hitler was on his own; he could now devote himself entirely to political work. He rented an apartment at No. 41 Thierschstrasse, near the Isar River. He spent most of his time at Party headquarters, although he took no salary in order to avoid being listed as a Party employee. What he lived on was a mystery and his enemies within the Party were soon to raise this question.[73]

Under closer scrutiny, however, the mystery disappears. Hitler was able to get along without a salary only because his life style was so spartan. His "apartment" would be described as dingy at best. He had one room and the use of an entrance hall as the subtenant of a Frau Reichert. Hitler's room itself was tiny, hardly nine feet wide. His simple iron military bed was too wide for its corner and projected over the one small window. The floor was covered with a cheap worn linoleum and two threadbare rugs. On the wall opposite the bed there was a makeshift bookshelf that was weighted down with heavy volumes which seemed almost out of place in these extremely humble surroundings. The only pieces of furniture in the room, with the exception of the bed, were a chair and a heavy old table. The room would have been unbearably bleak if it had not been for Hitler's drawings and watercolors, a few of which were on each wall.[74]

Members of the Party who had jobs often took turns inviting him to dinner. Later, when reminiscing with some of his comrades, Hitler said: "It's crazy what economies we had to make." Small stallkeepers at the market who were sympathizers of the Party used to bring him a couple of eggs. In the autumn he lived on practically nothing but Tyrolean apples because they were so cheap during that season. Occasionally he did make a little money by speaking for a small fee/ at the meetings of other patriotic groups or by doing some occasional intelligence work for Army headquarters. But even when he did get some money, he spent it only on the bare necessities for himself. "Every mark," he said, "was saved for the Party."[75]

It was not long before Hitler allowed himself one luxury—an automobile. There were very few cars in Munich at the time, but getting one was almost an obsession with him. Frequently he would be seen in the automobile showrooms around Munich looking at second-hand cars. He said the Party needed to buy an auto for him to get around to meetings more quickly. A car would also gave him a head start on the Marxists who still went on foot or by tram. He finally obtained an old vehicle that looked like a dismantled horsecab without a top; it was all that could be afforded at the moment. Within a short time, however, Hitler purchased a second-hand Selve with funds that one Party member said "he had drummed up in a mysterious way from someone."[76] This car was not much better than the first; it was a rattling monster. Those who saw it said each end of the car looked as if it were going a different way at the same time. Nevertheless, Hitler thought that having an automobile conferred a certain dignity on himself and the Party and never again was he seen taking a tram or bus.

In the summer of 1920 Hitler introduced the swastika as the Party symbol. When mounted in a white circle on a blood-red flag, the swastika had an eye-arresting vividness. On the occasion of the flag's first public appearance, Hitler wrote: "It was wonderfully suited for the young movement. . . . No one had ever seen it before; it was like a blazing torch."[77] He took such matters as the design of flags, insignias, and uniforms very seriously for he believed that the success of a movement depended to a considerable extent on the use of symbols immediately comprehensible to the people. No one in the Party could argue with Hitler's methods, for they were obviously working; by the late summer of 1920 the Nazis had hundreds of members and several thousand supporters.

On December 18, 1920, the National Socialist Party took a step that marked its emergence from the circles of fringe movements into a viable political force: It obtained its own newspaper, the *Völkischer Beobachter.* The paper did not have a very large circulation and it was deep in debt. This was the first occasion Hitler received a donation of a large sum of money, part of it from the Army's secret funds, and more importantly, part of it from an industrialist. The major stockholders of the *Völkischer Beobachter* represented the Thule Society, so the purchase of the paper indicated that the National Socialist Party was overtaking the Thule Society in importance.

From 1918 through 1920 the *Völkischer Beobachter* was controlled by the Thule Society and was looked upon as the leading right-wing, anti-Semitic paper in Bavaria.[78] The principal stockholder was Fräulein Käthe Bierbaumer, who was mistress and financial backer of Rudolf von Sebottendorff, the Thule Society leader. Frau Dora Kunze, Sebottendorff's sister, was a minority stockholder. In the early months of 1920 the newspaper accumulated new debts and required a new infusion of capital. Some of this money came from members of the National Socialist Party and its sympathizers. The register of the Munich Corporation Court lists the stockholders and the amount of their capital participation as of March 20, 1920:[79]

Käthe Bierbaumer	RM*46,500
Franz Freiherr von Feilitzsche	RM 20,000
Dora Kunze	RM 10,000
Franz Eder	RM 10,000
Gottfried Feder [Nazi]	RM 10,000
Dr. Wilhelm Gutberlet [Nazi]	RM 10,000
Theodor Heuss [Nazi]	RM 10,000
Karl Braum	RM 3,500[80]

*Reichsmark.

By December the paper was on the brink of bankruptcy, with its income dwindling and its debts mounting. There was a scramble for money among the right-wing groups of Munich to get control of the paper before it fell into separatist hands. The climax of the financial struggle came when Dietrich Eckart succeeded in obtaining a loan from General Ritter von Epp for RM 60,000. It is assumed that this money came from secret Army funds. Eckart pledged repayment in a personal note given to von Epp dated December 17, 1920.[81]

The total purchase price of the newspaper was RM120,000 and a contract was signed for the assumption of debts amounting to 250,000. But Eckart had received only 60,000 from General von Epp. Where did the other RM 60,000 come from?

On December 17, Hitler made a personal appeal to Dr. Gottfried Grandel, an industrialist from Augsburg, Bavaria, who had recently made a few moderate contributions to the Party. Surprisingly, Grandel agreed to help. He and Simon Eckart, an official of the Hansa Bank, advanced part of the purchase money and pledged their credit to consummate the deal. Not long after the transaction had taken place, Fräulein Bierbaumer and Frau Kunze came to Grandel for payment in full and received a total of RM 56,500.[82] Although the bulk of the necessary money was supplied by Grandel and von Epp, others also contributed. For example, Dr. Gutberlet made Hitler a present of shares valued at RM 5,000 and Dietrich Eckart probably put in a small amount of his own money.[83]

A small announcement appeared in the *Völkischer Beobachter* on Christmas day stating that the Nazi Party had taken over the paper at great sacrifice "in order to develop it into a relentless weapon for Germanism." The "great sacrifice" was Grandel's and the Army's. The acquisition of a newspaper with a circulation of about 7,000 represented an enormous gain for a new party which hardly had 1,000 members. However, the fact that Hitler could obtain such large sums of money for its purchase was even more significant. It had taken a great persuasive ability for the young agitator of a small radical group to convince an industrialist like Grandel to contribute 60,000, even if the Army was putting up an equal sum. Normally, industrialists and businessmen gave financial backing only to the established "reliable" parties, but increasing signs of another Communist uprising in Germany undoubtedly made the wealthy more sensitive to Hitler's appeal.

According to Hitler's own account, not long after the Party had acquired the *Völkischer Beobachter*, he was walking along a busy street in the center of Munich when he met Max Amann, who had been his regiment's sergeant-major in the Army and whom he had not seen since the end of the war. Amann was not particularly interested in politics, but at Hitler's prompting he attended a Nazi meeting and soon afterward became a Party member. He was a strong, active-looking little man with a heavy head set on a short neck that was almost invisible between his shoulders. His physical appearance gave no hint of Amann's intelligence. He was a former law student and after the war had obtained a good job in a mortgage bank.

Hitler proposed to Amann that he should give up his job and become full-time Party business manager. According to Hitler, Amann at first thought to reject the offer. He had secure career prospects and a pension to look forward to at the bank, while employment by the little Nazi Party would mean a substantial cut in salary and an uncertain future. Hitler exercised his powers of persuasion on him for two hours. "What good will your pension be if someday the Bolsheviks string you up from a lamppost?" Amann pondered for three days and then finally accepted the job.

Hitler made an excellent choice in Amann. Efficient, parsimonious, incorruptible, and without personal political ambition, Amann was exactly the right man for the job. He brought a commonsense business approach to Party affairs. His motto was "Make propaganda pay its own way." Hitler later praised Amann in particular for his financial management of the Party newspaper: "The fact that I was able to keep the *Völkischer Beobachter* on its feet throughout the period of our struggle—and in spite of the three failures it had suffered before I took it over—I owe first and foremost to . . . Amann. He as an intelligent businessman refused to accept responsibility for an enterprise if it did not possess the economic prerequisites of potential success."[84]

Max Amann was a member of the Thule Society.[85] Everyone who belonged to the society was aware of Hitler's activities and it is hardly possible that Hitler would have failed to notice one of his old Army comrades among the Thule members. Certainly it is not likely that Hitler's offer was made to Amann on the spur of the moment or that Amann had much difficulty deciding whether or not to accept it. When the Thule Society turned the *Völkischer Beobachter* over to the Nazi Party, it must have been specified in the deal that a Thule member (Amann) would remain in charge of the newspaper's funds and, moreover, would be appointed "Party business manager" with control over all Party money.

However, this is not to say that Amann was not an excellent business manager for Hitler. In fact, because of his Thule Society connections, he was able to obtain short-term credit for the Party when no one else could have. In more than one instance Amann was able to get an extension on a debt when it meant the difference between survival or bankruptcy for the *Völkischer Beobachter*. With Amann as Party business manager, Eckart as editor of the Party newspaper, and Rosenberg as assistant editor, the Thule Society's involvement with the Nazis was stronger than ever. But since the basic ideology of the Thule Society and the Nazi Party were the same, these men could be loyal Nazis as well as members of the society.

The membership of the National Socialist Party had risen to 3,000 by the summer of 1921. In July of that year Hitler went to Berlin to spend six weeks conferring with north German right-wing leaders. He stayed in the plush Bechstein villa and took elocution lessons every afternoon from a dramatics instructor in order to remedy his Austrian dialect and strengthen his voice. He met the prominent nationalist leader Count Reventlow, whose French wife, the former Baroness d'Allemont, introduced him to the Free Corps leader Walther Stennes (who was soon to join the Nazis). He also met Count Yorck von Wartenburg, who recognized that the movement could be useful in case of a Communist revolution. Von Wartenburg urged Hitler to transfer the headquarters to Berlin and offered financial assistance if he decided to do so.

Dr. Emil Gansser, a Nazi sympathizer with important connections among wealthy Protestants and a friend of Dietrich Eckart, was of considerable help.[86] An executive of the firm Siemens & Halske, Gansser was well educated and cut an imposing figure. He wore stiff white collars, starched shirts, and always dressed in a black coat and striped trousers. Gansser was able to arrange for Hitler to speak at the prestigious National Club of Berlin. The impression made upon his audience of Junkers, officers, and businessmen was a generally favorable one. Only a very few, however, were particularly impressed; but among them was Admiral Schröder, the former commander of the German Marine Corps.

The next day Hitler was taken to the Officers Club. Here again he met Schröder who, Hitler said, "made the best impression on me."[87] At that time the radical Nazi program filled most respectable people with alarm. As Hitler himself admitted: "They were even terrified lest people should know they had even heard of it!" Conservatives were particularly frightened by Nazi demands for government welfare measures, the abolition of freedom of the press, and anti-Semitism. But, said Hitler, Admiral Schröder "accepted the whole thing without further ado."[88] Schröder became the first real Nazi supporter in top military circles. This was quite a triumph for Hitler. In a military oriented society like Germany it meant considerable prestige for a small new party to have a high-ranking officer among its supporters. Moreover, the Admiral was of great help in propagating Hitler's views among the Prussian upper class.

Perhaps it seems a bit strange that after all the support the Army gave Hitler, the first high officer to join his Party would be an admiral. But it is not, given the secret connection between the German Navy and the Thule Society. The Bavarian Army and the Thule Society were *not* allies backing Hitler for the same ideological reason.[89] New evidence indicates that they were actually rivals, each backing Hitler in order to exercise an influence on him and make use of him for their own objectives.

With Germany beset by political difficulties, the old rivalry between Bavaria and Prussia grew intense once again. Ideas of separatism were very popular in Bavarian conservative circles in the early 1920s.[90] It was even hoped that the Wittelsbach monarchy might be restored and Bavaria become an independent state. France had hinted that Bavaria, once independent from Germany, might be free from the restrictions of the Versailles Treaty. Most all the higher officers of the Bavarian Army, such as General von Lossow, were Bavarians first and Germans second. They took their orders from the government in Munich, not Berlin.

The Thule Society on the other hand was a fanatically nationalistic organization opposed to Bavarian separatism,[91] and consequently did not want to see Hitler become too dependent on the Bavarian Army. However, in spite of its ideological opposition to the Weimar Republic, the Thule Society had a secret link with the central government in Berlin. According to Baron Sebottendorff, J. F. Lehmann, *the* official book publisher for the German Navy, was "the most active" member of the society and one of its biggest financiers.

Before the Thule Society rented their own offices in the Four Seasons Hotel, they held their meetings in the rooms of the Naval Officers Club in the same hotel.[93] The Thule Society supported and later sheltered many of the officers and men of the Ehrhardt Brigade, a naval unit, after the Kapp putsch failed. The commander of the Navy at this time was Admiral von Trotha, an extreme nationalist, anti-Communist, and strong supporter of the Ehrhardt Brigade. It is very possible that some naval funds may have gone to Hitler through Lehmann and the Thule Society.

Whatever the ideological beliefs of its commanders, the German Navy was totally committed to maintaining a united German state. Most naval officers were from north Germany and had absolutely no sympathy for Bavarian separatism. Of course, this was also true for the majority of Army officers, who were Prussians; but the Army was divided in two. The Bavarian regiments were stationed in Bavaria and commanded by Bavarian officers. If it had become known that the Army High Command in Berlin had interferred in Bavarian affairs by supporting nationalist groups like the Nazis, the Bavarian Army and government would have regarded it as an invasion of their territory. The Navy on the other hand could operate freely in Bavaria, for there were no separate Bavarian naval units. Naval officers could come and go anywhere in the state without arousing any suspicion or hostility. Thus, the Navy was the perfect instrument by which the central government could keep in contact with nationalist groups in separatist Bavaria.

And so a struggle developed for influence over Adolf Hitler and his rapidly growing movement. On the one side were the Bavarian conservatives and Bavarian Army, represented by men like von Kahr and General von Lossow, who made little effort to conceal their separatist statements. They hoped to be able to use the anti-Communist Hitler movement against the Marxist Social Democrats in Berlin when Bavaria made her move for independence. On the other side was the nationalist Thule Society, linked closely to the German Navy and to the central government in

Berlin, which was determined to keep Bavaria in the Reich at all costs.

This might explain why the German government didn't suppress the Nazi Party. Movements that were ideologically nationalist like Hitler's and the Free Corps Oberland—both financed by the Thule Society—could pose a continual threat to Bavarian separatist ambitions. Perhaps it is not too Machiavellian to think that moderate Social Democrats, like President Ebert, would cooperate with men who were their political enemies when the survival of Germany was at stake. After all, Ebert and the moderates had cooperated with the Free Corps in 1918–1919. Later, in 1924, when it was proposed in the Bavarian Parliament that Hitler be deported on the grounds that he was not a German citizen, the leaders of the conservative Catholic Bavarian Peoples' Party and all the other principal Bavarian parties were in favor of deportation; but the matter had to be dropped, because the leader of the Social Democratic Party in Bavaria, Erhard Auer, objected.[94] According to the traditional interpretation, Auer was opposed to an arbitrary infringement of anyone's political freedom, even Hitler's; but since the Social Democratic Party in Bavaria actually took their orders from the party's national leadership in Berlin, it is far more likely that Auer was carrying out the wishes of the central government when he permitted Hitler to remain in Bavaria as a thorn in the side of the separatists.

While Hitler was in Berlin conferring with Admiral Schröder and getting promises of north German support, a factional revolt directed against him erupted within the Party. Some of the original members of the executive committee, who were resentful of being disregarded while Hitler ran the Party as he saw fit, circulated an anonymous leaflet against him.[95] It called him a demagogue with a "lust for power" who was trying to mislead the German people and wreck the Party. The leaflet also charged that there was something unsavory in the way he supported himself, since he never answered questions on this subject but only went "into a fit of rage and excitement." The rebels wanted to know where he got the money for his "excessive association with women." It was strongly implied that he was acting as a tool for obscure financial backers. Three thousand of these leaflets were circulated and it was printed in two Munich newspapers.

Hitler returned from Berlin at once, promptly sued the

newspapers, and submitted his resignation to the Party, confident that it would be rejected. Without him the Party would probably shrink back to the insignificant state it was in before he brought it publicity, members, and money. Moreover, he controlled the movement's newspaper, the *Völkischer Beobachter*, which was edited by Eckart. In addition, all the important supporters of the movement, such as Ernst Röhm, were on his side. When Drexler and the committee realized Hitler had the upper hand and yielded, Hitler immediately revised the structure of the Party along authoritarian lines.[96] All provisions for majority rule and parliamentary process were disregarded. He became "First Chairman,"or president, with almost absolute powers. Henceforth, his decisions would be acted upon without question.

2
BILLIONS

Early in 1923 Hitler was contacted by a certain Herr Schaffer who offered to sell him an arsenal of weapons. Hitler thought the moment "opportune" for such a deal, so a meeting was arranged to take place in the little town of Dachau outside of Munich. Hermann Göring accompanied Hitler to the designated rendez-vous. At first they thought they had fallen into a bandit's lair. Armed men asked them for the password and then led them into the presence of a woman with a short, mannish haircut, Schaffer's wife. She was surrounded by a group of men who seemed to be mostly criminal types. Hitler later remarked that they all had the faces of "gallows birds."[1]

The bargaining began. Hitler warned Frau Schaffer that he wouldn't hand any money over to her until the weapons were in his possession. Finally an agreement was reached. Then Hitler and Göring were taken to a deserted military airfield at Schleissheim where the weapons were stored. There were thousands of rifles, seventeen pieces of light field artillery of various calibers, and other assorted equipment like mess tins and haversacks. Hitler said that, after it had all been put into working order, "there would be enough to equip a regiment."[2] As soon as the payment was made, the Nazis began to cart away the arms. Then Hitler went to see General von Lossow, the Commander-in-Chief of the Army in Bavaria and turned the entire stockpile of weapons over to him. He asked the General to take care of the weapons and promised that the Nazis would make no use of them "except in the event of a show-down with Communism. It was thus solemnly agreed," said Hitler, "that the material would remain in the hands of the Reichswehr as long as this eventuality did not arise."[3]

To have made such a purchase his funds must have been abundant indeed, for he always considered weapons of secondary importance to political propaganda. Obviously he was no longer an employee of the army, but rather he was dealing with General von Lossow as an equal. Was the Bavarian Army Command conspiring along with Hitler in a plot to overthrow the Weimar Republic, or was their alliance only a temporary one motivated by practical purposes as each worked toward a different goal? In order to purchase a stockpile of weapons and be able to negotiate a deal with the commanding general of the Army in Bavaria, Hitler must have had the backing and support of powerful, wealthy men. Who were they?

After he had acquired his own Party newspaper, the *Völkischer Beobachter,* Hitler intensified his recruiting drive. The times were ideal for such a campaign. There were violent strikes, Communist uprisings, and general disorder throughout the country. The rate of unemployment remained high and wages were low. Many former soldiers were still unable to find jobs and fit themselves into an orderly civilian society.

The German economy labored under the weight of the reparations payments which the Treaty of Versailles required Germany to make to the victorious powers. The impoverished country found it impossible to meet these large payments since the Versailles Treaty also blocked Germany out of most export markets.[4] In addition to the international problems, the inflation was already underway. The German mark, normally valued at four to the U.S. dollar, had begun to fall; by the summer of 1921 it had dropped to seventy-five to the dollar. Personal savings of a lifetime were rapidly becoming valueless. Fixed incomes no longer sufficed to pay for vital necessities. Many small businesses were going bankrupt. The middle class was desperate.

As Hitler's following increased in size, the Marxist parties became alarmed. They warned the workers to stay away from Nazi public meetings. However, Hitler's ranting denunciations of the Versailles Treaty, the inflation, and Germany's humiliation by the Allies were too compelling to miss hearing. So workers, artisans, shopkeepers, and the unemployed came to hear him in spite of all threats and warnings. Violence erupted at Hitler's meetings. He organized Nazi "defense squads" to silence hecklers and beat up disrupters. It was not long before Nazis and Communists were fighting in the streets. Important rightist leaders watched this developing struggle carefully. Hitler's party looked like the only nationalist movement capable of winning over the lower classes. If it could hold its own against the Communists, it would prove itself a party worthy of considerable financial support.

The Nazi Party's "defense squads" were a poorly disciplined group of volunteer brawlers, until they were reorganized in the summer of 1921 under the camouflage name "Gymnastic and Sports division." On October 5, 1921, they were officially named the Sturmalteilung (Storm Troopers) from which the title S.A. came. The S.A. uniform, the brown shirt, was somewhat acciden-tal; it originated when the Party was able to purchase cheaply a surplus lot of khaki Army shirts once intended to have been worn in Africa. Outwardly the structure of the S.A. was based on the tradition of the Free Corps units of ex-servicemen which in the years after 1918 had banded themselves together to put down the Communist revolution. But the Free Corps were vague in their political objectives beyond a general dislike for revolutionaries, whereas the S.A. were followers of Hitler's anti-Semitic ideology.

Naturally, equipping and arming a paramilitary unit like the S.A. cost a great deal of money. Since many of the members were unemployed, they often had to be provided with food and shelter as well. Uniforms, flags, and above all weapons had to be pur-chased. Rent had to be paid for meeting halls and headquarters. There were transportation costs whenever the S.A. units traveled as a group. The Party itself could not supply such funds, for it needed every available cent for its own upkeep and propaganda costs. Who then financed the S.A. ? Fortunately Kurt Lüdecke, the man who subsidized one of the first elite Storm Troop com-panies, wrote a detailed account of his activities.[5]

Lüdecke had joined the National Socialists on August 12, 1922, the day after his friend Count Ernst Reventlow had taken him to hear one of Hitler's speeches. After being a Party member for a short time he became aware of the lack of military discipline in the S.A. At that time, he said the Storm Troopers "were little better than gangs." They still regarded themselves as ordinary

Party members rather than Storm Troopers. He felt there was a need to instill into these men a pride in their special function as the Party's defense squads. If he could form one elite, well-disciplined company of Storm Troopers, he thought that their example might prove an inspiration to the rest of the S.A. "Hitler listened to my plan," said Lüdecke, "and told me to go ahead and form a troop, if that was what I wanted."[6]

Lüdecke began recruiting, accepting only the toughest and most able-bodied men who had either served in the war or had some military training. Two former Army officers were appointed as platoon leaders. A number of young students began to join the troop. A band with four drummers and four fifers was organized. Drills were held regularly. Every Wednesday night the entire company would assemble in a room Lüdecke had rented in a cafe on Schoenfeldstrasse, where he lectured his men on the political aims of the Nazi Party. Every new member took an oath of allegiance on the swastika flag and pledged loyalty to Hitler.

In order to have a regular headquarters, Lüdecke leased a large apartment which had several bedrooms and an "enormous" studio. Immediately it became a meeting place for the men and "a sort of armory." Lüdecke's valet cooked for the men and, as his employer reported, "used up the most appalling quantities of fancy groceries" doing so. Lüdecke also bought the uniforms and other equipment for the men. Soon one whole room was reserved for tunics, Army boots, steel helmets, etc. Every man was completely outfitted with full Army gear.

Except for a few small details, the appearance of Lüdecke's men was almost indistinguishable from regular Army troops. Their uniform consisted of Army tunic, military breeches, Austrian ski-caps, leggings, and combat boots. Each man also wore a leather belt, without side arms, and of course a swastika armband.

Most of the equipment of Lüdecke's troop was stored in the apartment. Although it was war surplus material, all of it was in fine condition. Since the bearing of arms, or even the possession and concealment of them, was severely punishable, usually by several years' imprisonment, it was not easy to obtain them and keep them in secret.[7] True, there were plenty of old Army rifles that could be had for a price, but less than 10 percent of them were undamaged and in working order. "I solved the problem," said Lüdecke, "by keeping two Jewish dealers constantly on the lookout for what we needed."[8]

Why would Jewish arms dealers supply weapons to the Nazis? On the one hand they could have been unaware that Lüdecke was a Nazi. But on the other hand they may have known of his Nazi affiliations and yet been willing to sell to him because Hitler's anti-Semitic vituperations were not taken seriously at the time.

By the end of December 1922 about one hundred men had enlisted in Lüdecke's company, and over forty regular Army soldiers had pledged their loyalty in secret. All the men possessed complete combat gear and field outfits. In addition, Lüdecke had managed to secure and hide outside Munich fifteen heavy Maxim guns, more than two hundred hand grenades, one hundred and seventy-five perfect rifles, and thousands of rounds of ammunition. He quite correctly termed this "a real arsenal."

Every Saturday and Sunday morning the unit would assemble on the outskirts of Munich and drill along the country roads leading into the forests. The tall evergreen woods which were usually dark and quiet suddenly rang with the cracking of military commands and the roll of drums. "When bad weather prevented outdoor drill," said Lüdecke, "I was able through my connections with certain Reichswehr officers to gain the privilege of using the drill-hall of the Second Bavarian Regiment."[9]

One night in early January, Hitler paid an inspection visit to Lüdecke's apartment headquarters. He went into the studio, an immense room with skylights, comfortably furnished, decorated with swastika banners hanging on the walls. "Beautiful . . . ,"Hitler commented, as he walked around. "Exactly what I've always wanted to have. I love this place."[10] Hitler and Lüdecke began to talk about various problems in organizing the S.A. Then the discussion turned to the matter of Party funds which, according to Lüdecke, "were still a serious problem." Lüdecke's opinion on the Party's financial situation is to be taken seriously, for he acknowledged he "was giving money to Hitler . . . in addition to the large sums the troop was costing."[11] Lieutenant Klintzsch, the S.A. commander, and some of his company commanders, said Lüdecke, also "frequently came to me for aid and got it. Several times I gave them foreign notes, including some . . . French money."[12]

Kurt Lüdecke was not a big businessman, industrialist, or landowner. True, he was from a respectable background, could speak several foreign languages, had traveled widely, and was at ease in the best social circles; yet he had relatively little money of his own. Having only one servant, a valet, and occupying a bedroom in the apartment which he also used as his S.A. company headquarters, he was far from living in splendor. His only extravagances were having his suits tailor-made in London and dining out frequently at the Walterspiel, one of Munich's best restaurants. According to Lüdecke's own account, he earned the money to finance his S.A. troop by selling treadless tires to the Russian government while he was in Reval, Estonia. But, he was spending at least ten times as much money on the Party as he was on himself, and it is somewhat questionable if he would have parted with this hard-earned money so freely.

In addition to being the leader of a Storm Troop company, Kurt Lüdecke also performed another function for the Nazi Party about which he was more reticent: He worked as a Party fund raiser. Hitler had originally asked him to confer on his behalf with the leaders of other German nationalist groups in an attempt to gain their support. "It was just the sort of confidential work I wanted," said Lüdecke.[13] The job of being Hitler's representative in high society was not an easy one. Lüdecke later recalled that his efforts to gain the support of wealthy and educated men "brought many headaches and few results." It was easier to win over a hundred common men than to convert a single gentleman. "The more educated the man, the greater his academic resistance to the 'impossible' and 'undignified' program advocated by 'that uncultivated . . . radical.' " Even though he was unable to get any influential men to "sign up" as Party members, Lüdecke was certainly successful in being received by the right people. He had lengthy interviews with such important personalities as Count Fugger and the famous war ace Udet, but found them all reluctant to join the movement or give it their "open" moral support. Although many of the men to whom Lüdecke spoke regarded Hitler with "a sort of detached benevolence," they did not think the time had come for them to rally round a single nationalist leader. Furthermore, they feared the socialist side of the Nazi program.

Through his acquaintance with Princess Joachim, widow of

the Kaiser's youngest son, Lüdecke met her younger brother, the Duke of Anhalt. Since he was only twenty years old, impressionable, and one of the richest princes in Germany, Lüdecke naturally made every effort to convince him of Hitler's merit. Incognito, the Duke accompanied Lüdecke to two of Hitler's beerhall mass meetings. The young nobleman, however, decided such intimate contact with the rough masses was beneath his dignity.

A question remains to be answered: Did the Duke of Anhalt, Count Fugger, or any of the other wealthy men to whom Lüdecke talked see fit to contribute to the Nazi treasury secretly, even though they were reluctant to declare their support for the Party openly? Lüdecke wrote only that "after several weeks of futile interviews, it became clear that nothing could come—except in a few rare cases—from conferences with men of position."[14]Unfortunately, Lüdecke did not say who the "few rare cases" were nor how much they contributed.

One of the principal sources of money and equipment for the S.A. was the secret Army funds originally set up to finance Free Corps units and military intelligence work. However, up to now historians have incorrectly assumed that assistance was given to Hitler on the orders of the High Command of the Bavarian Army.[15] Actually most of the aid was given to Hitler on the initiative of one officer, Captain Ernst Röhm, without the knowledge or approval of his superiors.

The technique Röhm used to channel Army money and material to Hitler was one that has become very popular in recent decades. Two privately owned corporations were created, one dependent on the other. The basic corporation, the very existence of which was top secret, was the Feldzeugmeisterei, directed by Ernst Röhm. The other, the dependent corporation, was the Faber Motor Vehicle Rental Service, operated openly as a business by Major Wilhelm Faber, who was under Röhm's command. Röhm had the initial approval of his military superiors in setting up these corporations because they were an ideal cover for concealing extra armaments and vehicles forbidden by the Versailles Treaty. The corporations also served the purpose of making this illegal equipment available to the clandestine reserve Army—the Free Corps units. The Nazi S.A. as one of the many Free Corps regiments was entitled to occasionally use some of this equipment and receive a few small subsidies from Röhm's corporations. But as the year 1922 went on, Röhm began to channel more and more money, equipment, arms and even trucks and cars to the Nazis through the Faber Motor Vehicle Rental Service, Inc.

At first the senior officers of the Bavarian Army were not aware of the increased amount of aid being given to Hitler because Röhm's corporations functioned so secretly that even the Army Command received no reports of their activities. It was not until 1923 that the Army Commander, General von Lossow, and the Bavarian government discovered the extent of Röhm's activities. But even then it was some time before they could actually slow down the flow of aid to the Nazis, because Röhm's "corporations" were staffed by men whose primary loyalty was to him personally rather than to the Army. In addition, Röhm's companies functioned legally as independent business entities and were not technically subject to the authority of the Army.

The reason the Army did not simply arrest Röhm for stealing government property was that Röhm, as liaison officer with the Free Corps and Black Reichswehr, had many influential friends, and so it would have been impossible to get rid of him without an outcry of public protest and a full-scale investigation. Such an investigation, however, would have revealed that the Army itself was violating the Versailles Treaty and thus was out of the question.

The year 1922 saw the German mark fall to 400 to the U.S. dollar; the runaway inflation was beginning. Every day meant an increase in prices. Resentment against the government spread. The discontented middle class began to swell the ranks of Hitler's movement. As the German economic situation grew worse, the financial position of the National Socialist Party grew stronger. More Party members meant more dues, and bigger audiences at meetings meant a larger sum when the hat was passed. In November of 1921 the Party had moved into a new and larger headquarters and by April of the following year it already had thirteen full-time salaried employees. A central archive and filing system was developed under the direction of the Party "business manager" Max Amann.

On the evening of November 22, 1922, a Harvard graduate, Ernst (Putzi) Hanfstaengl, whose mother was American and whose cultivated, wealthy family owned an art-publishing business in Munich, attended one of Hitler's speeches on the advice of Captain Truman Smith, the assistant military attaché of the United States.[16] Opposed to Communism and appalled by Germany's present weaknesses, Hanfstaengl was captivated with Hitler's oratory. A few days later he joined the Party. The six-foot four-inch Hanfstaengl, whose nickname Putzi ironically meant 'little fellow' in Bavarian dialect, shared Hitler's interest in art and music and became his frequent companion.

One night as they were walking home together from the Café Neumaier after several hours of discussion with devoted Party followers, Hitler turned to Hanfstaengl and said: "You must not feel disappointed if I limit myself in these evening talks to comparatively simple subjects. Political agitation must be primitive. That is the trouble with all the other [non-Marxist] parties. They have become . . . too academic. The ordinary man in the street cannot follow and, sooner or later, falls a victim to the slap-bang methods of Communist propaganda."[17]

Agreeing wholeheartedly, Hanfstaengl told Hitler that one of the things which gave him the most confidence in the Party's eventual success was his (Hitler's) ability to speak in everyday language with "real punch" behind his words. Hanfstaengl went on to say that in some ways he reminded him of the American President Theodore Roosevelt who had a vigor and courage, a vitality and familiarity with all kinds of people, and a direct style of action and speaking that endeared him to the average citizen. "People in Munich say that all you and your party stand for is tumult and shouting, brutality and violence," Hanfstaengl continued. "It may console you to know that all those things were said about Roosevelt, but he did not listen and carried the country with him."[18]

"You are absolutely right," Hitler replied. "But how can I hammer my ideas into the German people without a press? The newspapers ignore me utterly. How can I follow up my successes as a speaker with our miserable four-page *Völkischer Beobachter* once a week? We'll get nowhere until it appears as a daily."[19] Hitler then told of the great plans he had for the Party newspaper if only he could find the funds.

"It must have been that evening," Hanfstaengl later wrote, "that I decided to render more substantial help."[20] About this time Hanfstaengl received partial payment for his share of the family art gallery in New York which had been closed during the war. The money came to only $1,500, but that represented an absolute fortune when converted into depreciated marks. There were two American rotary presses for sale; if their purchase could be financed, it would mean that the Nazi Party newspaper could come out as a daily in a full-size format.

"I learned," said Hanfstaengl, "that a thousand of my dollars would make up the required sum, incredible as it may seem, and one morning I went down and handed it over to Amann in greenbacks, on the understanding that it was an interest-free loan. He and Hitler were beside themselves."[21]

"Such generosity," Hitler exclaimed. "Hanfstaengl, we shall never forget this. Wonderful!"[22] Hanfstaengl was rather pleased with himself. His loan, however, was not made simply from altruistic reasons, as he pretended in his autobiography; actually he hoped to increase his own influence over the newspaper and guide it in a more conservative direction. He may have even hoped to succeed Dietrich Eckart, whose health was failing, as editor of the paper, because when Hitler later appointed Alfred Rosenberg to that position Hanfstaengl was very bitter about the Fuhrer's "divide-and-rule tactics."[23]

Hanfstaengl's motives had probably been building up over a long period of time. He had not served in World War I, and, haunted by a guilty conscience for not fulfilling his patriotic duty, he compensated by supporting the most extreme nationalist party he could find—the Nazis. To account for his behavior, he offered two rather feeble excuses. He tried to justify himself for overlooking the racist policy of the Nazis with the claim that there was no way for him to know if Hitler's anti-Semitism was sincere or just a propaganda tactic. By contributing money and introducing Hitler to good society, he contended that he hoped to gradually moderate the Nazi leader.

From Hitler's own style of living there was little indication that the Party was growing and finding new sources of financial support. The life of the Nazi Party's leader was not that of a dashing mercenary captain with plenty of champagne, caviar, and beautiful women. Conservative industrialists were not going to fling their hard-earned money at the first adventurer who came along with a strong voice. Before investing a large sum in the very risky venture of trying to destroy Marxism, they considered for a long time whether an understanding with Marxism could not be worked out more cheaply. So, for the present, Hitler continued to wear the same old trench coat and cheap blue suit. Every night after his work was finished he went back to the same dingy one-room apartment. The only sign of his growing importance as a political figure was that he was now accompanied everywhere by a bodyguard, a tough beerhall fighter named Ulrich Graf.

Putzi Hanfstaengl's comfortable and cultivated upper-class home was the first house of its kind in Munich to open its doors to Hitler. He seemed to feel at ease with Hanfstaengl's pretty wife and children. Putzi could play Wagner beautifully, and Hitler, who loved music, considered Wagner his favorite composer. After a while Hanfstaengl made himself a sort of social secretary to Hitler, zealously introducing him to Munich hostesses. Hitler still had an air of shyness in the presence of those of wealth and social position, yet his naiveté in social matters tempted hostesses to invite him. Frequently he would sit in silence until the topic of politics was introduced and then dominate the conversation. However, it is a mistake to think he was so rude as to shout down the other guests or shock them with his most extreme opinions. In many instances, even though people disagreed with his anti-Semitic views, they would find themselves "amused" by his "quite witty" criticisms of the Jews.[24] He always made a point of leaving a party before the company broke up, so that the other guests would be left behind to talk about him and thus deepen their own impression.

Hanfstaengl introduced Hitler to William Bayard Hale, who had been a friend of President Wilson at Princeton and for years chief European correspondent of the Hearst newspapers. Hale had more or less retired in Munich but he was still an avid observer of world affairs. He talked with Hitler in his suite in the luxurious Hotel Bayrischer Hof, where he was living. Through Putzi, Hitler also met a German-American artist of considerable talent, Wilhelm Funk, who had a lavishly equipped studio furnished with exquisite Renaissance furniture and tapestries. Funk had something of a salon, which included Prince Henckel-Donnersmarck and a number of wealthy nationalist businessmen. Hitler was invited a number of times, but when they made veiled suggestions about a political alliance he shied away. "I know these people," he told Hanfstaengl. "Their own meetings are empty and they want me to come along and fill the hall for them and then split the proceeds. We National Socialists have our own program and they can join up with us if they like, but I will not come in as a subordinate ally."[25]

There were good reasons for Hitler's attitude of independence. Increasing numbers of people were turning away from the traditional political parties which seemed unable to solve the mounting crisis. In January 1923, on the pretext that the Germans were 100,000 telegraph poles short in reparations deliveries, the French Army occupied the Ruhr. With only the small army permitted by the Versailles Treaty, Germany was incapable of defending itself, so the government ordered a campaign of "passive resistance." This involved the shutting down of all factories in the Ruhr, Germany's most highly industrialized region. During a dispute at the Krupp factory in Essen, the French opened fire on the workers with machine guns, killing thirteen men.

Along with the French occupation of the Ruhr came the total collapse of the German currency. The government had to pour financial support into the Ruhr for the hundreds of thousands whom passive resistance had put out of work; in order to meet this enormous obligation, more money was printed. It is often incorrectly assumed that this was the beginning of the inflation. Actually, the inflation began during the war. In England, war expenses had been financed by increased taxation, but in Germany mounting expenditures were met by printing more currency. The process was accelerated after the war. First prices doubled, then tripled. The government told the people the inflation was an economic process over which no one had any control. In reality, however, the inflation was the method chosen by the German financial elite to escape their obligations and push off the burden onto the middle class.[26]

When prices doubled because more currency was being circulated, the real value of savings accounts, pensions, and bonds were cut in half, but few people realized it at the time. Financing the passive resistance in the Ruhr provided the government with the excuse it needed to begin the runaway inflation. The mark fell to 10,000 to the dollar and then to 50,000. Prices began to rise daily and then twice a day.

The hardest hit were the good, solid middle-class citizens who had saved for the future and suddenly saw all they had worked for wiped out overnight. Bills of increasingly higher denomination were printed. Factories began paying twice a week because the value of the money diminished so much from Monday to Saturday. On paydays the wives of the workers waited outside the factory gates. As soon as the men were paid, they rushed out and gave the money to the women who hurried off to the nearest store to buy things before the value of the money went down further. But at least the pay of industrial workers, most of whom belonged to unions, was adjusted somewhat to the declining value of the mark. The middle class was harder hit. More than a few professional men found it impossible to support themselves on incomes eroded by the inflation. They were forced to take jobs at night as cab drivers and waiters in order to survive.

Many people driven to the wall by the inflation put their property up for sale at a stated price according to the value of the mark at the time. But when the legal formalities were completed and the deal closed, the worth of the mark had further deteriorated to the point where the purchaser acquired a home worth $20,000 for the equivalent of $1,000. Financiers and large companies with unlimited credit took advantage of these conditions to accumulate vast holdings at very little cost.[27] A small factory might be purchased for 50 million marks on a six-month's basis. When the six months had elapsed and it was time to pay, the 50 million marks was hardly enough to buy an automobile. Big business found the inflation extremely profitable; mortgages were paid off, bonds retired, and debts wiped out with inflated marks worth only a fraction of their former real value.

"Believe me, our misery will increase," Hitler warned the people. "The scoundrel will get by. But the decent, solid businessman who doesn't speculate will be completely crushed; first the little fellow on the bottom, but in the end the big fellow on top too. But the scoundrel and the swindler will remain, top and bottom. The reason: because the state itself has become the biggest swindler and crook. A robbers' state!"

"You have defrauded us, you rogues and swindlers," he shouted against the government. "We don't care a fig for your paper money. Give us something of value—gold!" And then Hitler told his audience that although they had thousands and even millions of marks in their pockets they would soon be starving, because the farmer would stop selling his produce. "When you offer him your million [marks] scraps of paper with which he will only be able to cover the walls of his out-house, can you wonder that he will say, 'Keep your millions and I will keep my corn and my butter.' "[28]

Hitler was one of the few politicians who correctly assessed the inflation as a deliberate campaign to defraud the middle class of their savings. Representatives of the established political parties were always telling the people no one had any control over the inflation, but to have confidence and the mark would not fall any lower. When Hitler's predictions about the inflation began to come true, his speeches attracted bigger and bigger audiences. Because he exposed this one fraud, many people thought he was a man of honesty and sincerity. Since savings had never meant anything to him personally, he was probably just using the inflation as an issue to win popularity. Nevertheless, as the value of the mark went down, the membership in the National Socialist Party went up.

Almost nothing is known about the man who was the most important fund raiser for the Nazi Party—Max Erwin von Scheubner-Richter. There is confusion about his background, his profession, and his activities during World War I.[29] Even during his life, Scheubner-Richter was always a man of mystery. He took great pains never to appear in the limelight and always shrouded his activities in secret. Yet there is no doubt about his importance. According to a note in an official file, he succeeded in raising "enormous sums of money" for the Nazi Party.[30] By 1923 his influence over Hitler was considerable and the Party was dependent on him for most of its contacts in high society. In the putsch of November 9, 1923, he marched in the front rank of Nazi leaders, arm in arm with Hitler; when he was hit by a bullet, his fall dislocated Hitler's shoulder. Extremely disturbed by the death of Scheubner-Richter, Hitler commented, "All the others are replaceable but not he."[31]

In 1884 a child baptized Maxmillian Erwin was born into an upper-middle-class German Baltic family named Richter. As a student he was a member of the aristocratic Rubonia fraternity in Riga. During the 1905 revolution he fought for the Imperial Russian government as a young cavalry officer in a Cossack regiment and helped organize the German settlers' self-defense units against the insurgents. He later married the daughter of a manufacturer, Mathilde von Scheubner, whose factory his regiment had guarded. Since the industrialist von Scheubner had no sons, Max Erwin joined his wife's noble name to his own as was the custom at the time.[32]

Scheubner-Richter went to Munich in 1910 to study engineering. While there he joined an aristocratic Bavarian regiment, the *Chevaux légers,* and became a German citizen. His only real political belief during this period was a strong nationalist sentiment. During World War I he fought gallantly both on the western front and in the Middle East. In view of his linguistic abilities and his interest in the more subtle aspects of political manipulation, he was appointed German consul in Erzerum, Turkey, in the latter part of the war. While a diplomat, he personally participated in several perilous expeditions to the Kurds and other oppressed national minorities in the Caucasus. His experiences and knowledge of the political intrigues of this oil rich region were later to be a great asset to him.

Considered an expert on Russia, Scheubner-Richter was summoned in late 1917 to the German Army headquarters in the Baltic countries to take charge of the Bureau of Press and Public Information in Riga. The position of the German units on the eastern front had changed very little after the Russian Revolution, so in 1918 there was a great reluctance to give up the conquered territories. A firm opponent of Communism, Scheubner-Richter tried to indoctrinate the German soldiers with nationalism and make them immune to Bolshevik influence through several patriotic publications, including the newspaper *Das Neues Deutschland.* However, he was only moderately successful; under pressure of the Red Army and the newly independent Latvians, the Germans were forced to retreat.

Scheubner-Richter returned to Germany convinced both by personal background and wartime experience not only that Communism was a great danger to Europe but that anti-Communism could be profitable. In Königsberg in 1919 he became the political advisor of August Winning, the Reichkommissar for the eastern territories still under German protection. He remained deeply involved in anti-Communist politics as the director of a propaganda agency known as the Home Office for Eastern Germans which disseminated warnings against the "dangers" of the Bolsheviks and the Poles. At the same time he held a financially

important post as business manager of the right-wing parliamentary group in Danzig.[33] In this capacity he met many East Prussian landlords and businessmen. Like many other right-wing
leaders in East Prussia, Scheubner-Richter became involved in
the Kapp conspiracy in 1920. When the Kapp putsch took place,
he went to Berlin to act as Kapp's "press chief." The putsch
collapsed soon after he reached the capital and a few days later he
fled to Munich.

While in East Prussia, Scheubner-Richter had made plans and
laid the groundwork for an economic cooperation scheme between the White Russian government (which then controlled
about one-half of Russia) and Germany. His old friend Alfred
Rosenberg, who was a member of the Thule Society and now
Hitler's lieutenant, had contacted him and told him about his
(Rosenberg's) negotiations with some large Bavarian companies
wanting to make contact with General Wrangel, whose anti-
Communist government was established in southern Russia.
The German businessmen wanted exclusive trading rights with
the territory under Wrangel's control and in return were willing to
extend economic assistance. Scheubner-Richter, with his many
connections and fluent Russian, seemed to be the right man to
negotiate with General Wrangel and act as liaison officer with the
White armies, and he soon succeeded in interesting a group of
German industrialists in the possibility of exchanging German
war-surplus weapons and manufactured goods for Ukrainian
wheat.[34] Along with two German businessmen and some White
Russian officers, he went to the Crimea and held talks with
General Wrangel. Scheubner-Richter and some of his German
business associates formed what they called the Europe-Asia
Company, which was granted a virtual monopoly on all trade
between Germany and the White Russian territory. But then
came the collapse of the White armies and all was lost. Ultimately, however, Scheubner-Richter profited from all this because he had established contact and friendships with some of
the most important south German industrialists and the leading
White Russians.

Failure did not dim Scheubner-Richter's enthusiasm for continued cooperation between right-wing Russians and Germans
against the Bolsheviks in Moscow and the Social Democrats in
Berlin. He soon learned, through Alfred Rosenberg, of the exis-

tence of the rapidly growing National Socialist Party, and in October of 1920 he met Hitler for the first time. On November 22, he attended a Party meeting and heard Hitler speak. The hypnotic power radiating from this lower-class ex-corporal impressed him so much that he described him as "the prophet of the new Germany."[35] Hitler's virulent anti-Communism and anti-Semitism, and his large working-class following, led Scheubner-Richter to think he had found the party that would one day destroy Marxism. Before the year was over he and his wife joined the Nazi Party.

The *grand seigneur* who moved easily in all spheres of society made a very favorable impression on Hitler. True, he was not an ideologist like Rosenberg or a hardened professional soldier like Röhm, but Scheubner-Richter had the personality of a first-rate diplomat. Along with his aristocratic manners and appearance was a certain charm and seeming warmth of character that made it easy for him to make friends and to use his influence effectively. He was not a very good public speaker, but Hitler needed little help in that respect. What he needed, and what only Scheubner-Richter offered, was a respectable, upper-class public relations man who believed in the ideas of the Party, who was a capable organizer, and who had influential political connections with the traditional right-wing parties.

Of even greater importance was Scheubner-Richter's talent for getting donations for the movement. He was a genius at procuring funds even during this time of economic crisis when money was not easy to come by in Germany. He approached Bavarian aristocrats, big businessmen, bankers, and leaders of heavy industry, such as Thyssen and Paul Reusch. Unlike other members of the Nazi Party, Scheubner-Richter was a wealthy man in his own right and since he did not ask for money for himself but for what he thought was a worthy political cause, he did it with perfect ease and notable success. He was even said to have received a contribution from the house of Wittelsbach, but, considering their separatist ambitions, it is doubtful.[36] Scheubner-Richter was also a close personal friend of General Ludendorff and on several occasions the General channeled money to him from industrialists.

Much of Scheubner-Richter's time and energy was spent working with the White Russian emigrés. He received large contributions from Russian industrialists, especially the oil men who had been able to transfer some part of their fortunes to Germany. Listed among those who gave to Hitler's Party through Scheubner-Richter were such names as Gukasov, Baron Koeppen, Lenison, Nobel, and the Duke of Leuchtenberg.[37] Along with Scheubner-Richter's activities came an increasingly close cooperation between the right-wing Russian emigrés and the Nazis. Each group saw the other not only as an anti-Communist, anti-Semitic ideological companion but as a source of money. The Whites still hoped to be able to reconquer Russia if only they could get German help. Apparently they contributed to the Nazi Party, a rapidly growing anti-Bolshevik mass movement, because Scheubner-Richter convinced them that Hitler's movement would soon have a great influence on the German government and would see that they got the necessary funds and equipment to march east.

In 1910–1921 there were good reasons why the White emigrés refused to accept their defeat and exile as final. Millions of people were starving in Russia, industry was at a standstill, and chaos reigned throughout the countryside.[38] It was possible that the Soviet government might be overthrown from within, or collapse as a result of its own incapacity.

In the town of Bad Reichenhall, which was a fairy-tale mountain resort nestled on the Bavarian border about twelve miles southwest of Salzburg, a large number of White Russians began to gather during the last week in May 1921 for a great monarchist congress. This would be the most ambitious attempt ever launched to bring the Russian Right together under one platform. Although he kept in the background, Scheubner-Richter was the main organizer of this event.[39]

The participants and their elegantly dressed wives assembled in the main dining hall of the Post Hotel in front of a green-garlanded podium flanked by the red-white-and-blue Imperial Russian flag on one side and the white-yellow-and-black banner of the monarchists on the other. A large photograph of Czar Nicholas looked down on the proceedings as Scheubner-Richter welcomed the delegates. After his short speech, several Russian representatives warmly commended the work of his Munich association for economic cooperation between Germany and (White) Russia. Scheubner-Richter then retired from the scene leaving the delegates to iron out their own problems in the hope that they would find common ground. The doors of the dining hall remained closed and guarded for the next few days to the puzzlement of the non-Russian guests of the hotel.

Although the Russians had plenty of money, they did not pay for the Reichenhall Congress. A group of south German industrialists were persuaded by Scheubner-Richter to cover all the expenses. Among the German sponsors were several well-known politicians including Cramer-Klett, who was known to represent the interests of the Vatican, and Hofrat Aman of the Bavarian People's Party. There were businessmen and industrialists from Munich, Rogensburg, and Augsburg. Most interestingly, there was General Ludendorff and a certain Colonel Bauer, who had been one of Ludendorff's staff officers during the war and now headed a semiprivate intelligence service that sometimes carried out assignments for the German government in which the latter could not afford to become involved. Bauer's backing was supposed to be a secret, but it became known in informed circles.[40]

These German "sympathizers" did not finance the Reichenhall Congress simply out of ideological loyalty to monarchy. Their openly acknowledged aim was to restore the old Russian-German alliance. It was rumored, however, that the generous cooperation of the German Right was actually an ambitious attempt to capture the political allegiance of the White Russians to prevent them from turning to France for aid. Whatever their real aim, the influence of Scheubner-Richter's circle of supporters was attested to by the generally favorable accounts of the congress carried in almost all of the south German newspapers.[41]

The Reichenhall Congress marked a high point in the history of White Russian politics. The Russian Right did not unite as was hoped, but Scheubner-Richter was successful in convincing most of them of the necessity to join forces with Hitler's movement. After the congress he founded a new German-Russian political-economic association, which published a periodical entitled *Aufbau (Reconstruction)*. It was really a right-wing, united-front alliance of various political groups including some very respectable Bavarian politicians such as Cramer-Klett. Through this association Scheubner-Richter was able to gradually acquaint many respectable people with Hitler who would never have thought of supporting the Nazi Party, and although there is no actual proof of it, he was probably able to siphon funds from this organization to Hitler because all the key positions in the association were held by pro-Naƶis.

Scheubner-Richter also used his activities with the White Russians to spread pro-Nazi propaganda to the general public. The Jews, he said, were responsible for the Bolshevik Revolution. Communism must be wiped out as Mussolini was doing in Italy. He expressed the hope that a movement like Italian Fascism would take over in Germany too. But the traditional German right-wingers were not militant enough for this task, so he urged them to accept new leadership that would carry out a march on Berlin "to save Germany from the Red terror.[42] *Aufbau,* which was financed by both wealthy Germans and Russians, predicted that only Adolf Hitler could achieve something. His struggle would decide the fate not only of Germany but of Europe: "This struggle will be waged under the slogan of the Soviet star versus the Swastika. And the Swastika will prevail."[43]

The efforts of Scheubner-Richter were the beginning of real cooperation between the leading White Russians and their German anti-Semitic friends, based not only on mutual political hatred of the Jews, Communists, and liberals, but also on a desperate need for funds and political support which each thought the other would supply. Wealthy Russians were giving money to Hitler and in turn having their anti-Semitic and anti-Communist ideas propagated to the German masses. But how could the White Russians expect to get any significant sums from the Nazis or even Scheubner-Richter and his friends? True, Scheubner-Richter had persuaded a few German industrialists to finance the Reichenhall meetings, but this was nothing compared to the kind of sums that the emigrés would need to finance their reconquest of Russia. Were the White Russians naive for thinking they might get the support and money they needed through men like Scheubner-Richter? Not at all.

Since 1920 the German Foreign Office had taken a keen interest in the politics of the right-wing emigrés. Although they had refused to support General Wrangel during the civil war in Russia, the officials of the Wilhelmstrasse (Foreign Ministry) were impressed by Scheubner-Richter's lengthy report on his mission to southern Russia and his ideas on overthrowing the Soviets. Noting that the right-wing Russians were friendly to

Germany, Behrendt of the Foreign Office said that "they should be supported in some way, secretly if not publicly."[44]

The German Foreign Office viewed the various Russian exiled political groupings in terms of their orientation toward either Germany or the Allied powers. Because of their close cooperation with the French, the liberals and socialists were not worth consideration; there remained either the Russian extreme Right or the Soviets as the only possibilities. White Russian leaders, for example, denounced the Versailles Treaty as "an insult to mankind."[45] For this reason the German government continued to show an interest in the right-wing Russian movement at the same time they were working toward closer relations with the Soviet government in preparation for the Treaty of Rapallo.

Since it was far from certain that the Communists would be able to remain in power, the German government had to maintain ties with the White Russians, just in case. Through Scheubner-Richter and right-wing parties like the Nazis, the German government could keep in contact with the Whites secretly, and be prepared for any eventuality, while they negotiated with the Soviets openly. Scheubner-Richter's connections with the German Foreign Office were very advantageous for Hitler because they gave the White Russians an exaggerated idea of the Nazi Party's influence on the German government.

One of the most important right-wing Russians to give his unqualified support to Hitler was General Vasili Biskupsky. Not only did he play a leading part in emigré politics, but he also acted as intermediary between Hitler and various financial backers, some of them beyond the White Russian circle. A handsome, dashing man, Biskupsky had the reputation of an able officer and even better gambler. When the revolution broke out, he was one of the youngest generals in the Russian Army, in command of the Third Corps in Odessa. After the evacuation of the Ukraine by the White forces, he made his way to Berlin. There he was a frequent visitor at the home of General Max Hoffmann, who had the financial backing of Sir Henri Deterding, the British-Dutch oil tycoon.[46] Together Biskupsky and Hoffmann plotted various schemes to reconquer the Caucasus oil field, but for the time being nothing came of them.

After the Kapp putsch, in which he was involved, Biskupsky fled to Munich and began to seek out new allies in the struggle against Communism. He was introduced to Scheubner-Richter who urged him to look into the activities of a promising new party called the National Socialists. One evening out of curiosity Biskupsky and a friend went to a Nazi meeting in a Munich beerhall where Hitler was speaking. He gave the two Russians the impression of being "a strong man" who had great influence over those around him. Hitler was just the kind of popular leader Biskupsky thought was needed to draw the common man away from Marxism. The two men got to know each other and became fairly close friends. On one occasion Hitler hid from the police in Biskupsky's house, and the General's wife, a well-known singer, is said to have pawned some of her pearls to enable him to escape. A man of remarkable cunning, Biskupsky was a grand schemer always involved in some major financial or political intrigue. He and Scheubner-Richter made an ideal team as fund raisers for the Nazi and anti-Communist cause.

In 1922 Biskupsky declared his support for Grand Duke Cyril, Romanov pretender to the Russian throne, and was appointed as Cyril's "prime minister." It was in this capacity that Biskupsky performed his greatest service for the Nazi movement. Grand Duke Cyril was a first cousin to Czar Nicholas II and therefore a rightful heir to the crown. There were, however, many monarchists who did not recognize Cyril and bitter debates took place between his supporters and those of Grand Duke Nikolai Nikolaevich in Paris. General Biskupsky argued that Cyril's enemies were suspected of democratic and constitutional leanings and were puppets of the French.

A rather unassuming man, Cyril had served without notable distinction in the Russian Navy during the war, went to Finland with his family after the revolution, then to Switzerland, and, in 1921, to the south of France where they held court at the Château Fabron. Although their marital relationship was not a happy one, Cyril's strong-willed wife, Grand Duchess Victoria,* was nevertheless his closest political confidante and probably the real driving force behind his claim to the Imperial throne. In 1922 Cyril and his wife moved to Coburg, Germany, where Victoria's family had its possessions. Here they lived in seclusion in the

---

*Grand Duchess Victoria was the granddaughter of Queen Victoria of England and the sister of Queen Marie of Romania.

palatial Villa Edinburgh.

Cyril was no stranger to Germany, for his mother was the Princess of Mecklenburg, Maria Pavlovna, and as a young man he was surrounded by German maids, tutors, and relatives; years later he recalled that his aunt, Grand Duchess Alix of Saxe-Altenburg, "always spoke German to us."[47]

At Coburg, the Grand Duke Cyril, who was very handsome and somewhat of a playboy, indulged his passions for hunting, motor cars, beautiful women, and political intrigue, but his circle of followers was small and isolated. Even Cyril's most loyal publicist in Munich, Nikolai Snessarev, often had trouble getting to see Cyril, since his wife and friends formed a barrier to filter out any unwanted visitors. Cyril often left important decisions to his wife, and in fact, Victoria managed to obtain from abroad some of the funds needed for her husband's political activities; but she also collected for the Nazi Party. It is said that she was even more active in her support of the National Socialists than her husband. Scheubner-Richter and his wife became close personal friends of the Grand Duke and Duchess, and the Grand Duchess Victoria and Scheubner-Richter's wife Mathilde would often watch the S.A. drill in a Munich suburb and attend Nazi meetings and parades together.[48] Attracted to the Nazis' anti-Communism and anti-Semitism, Victoria soon contributed some of her valuables to them.[49]

Most of Cyril's support was largely limited to the pro-German, radical rightist, Russian emigrés who were concentrated in Bavaria. His supporters, such as Count Bobrinsky and General Biskupsky wrote manifestos which proclaimed Cyril's right to the throne and underlined the need for future cooperation between monarchist, agricultural Russia and industrial Germany, but not being a very intelligent man, Cyril became more of a political object to be manipulated by General Biskupsky and his German friends for their private purposes than an exiled leader in his own right.

All the White Russians around the Grand Duke, and even Cyril himself, were anti-Semites and were in fact more fanatically anti-Communist and anti-Semitic than many of the Nazis themselves. Many of those in Cyril's circle, such as G. V. Nemirovich-Danchenko, were also avid supporters of the Nazis and contributed articles to the *Völkischer Beobachter*. The movement to restore the Grand Duke to the throne had a program (later described as racist-nationalist) which was very similar to the Nazi program. In the spring of 1923, Cyril's men in Munich organized their own monarchist journal called the *Messenger of the Russian Monarchist Union,* which had an unchanging theme: Cyril was the legal heir to the Imperial Russian throne and behind the evils of the modern world stood the "mercantile morality" of the Jews.[50]

Once Hitler's cause was taken up by Russian grand dukes, counts, and generals, he automatically became more acceptable in the eyes of the upper-class Germans. When Frau Bechstein came to Munich, she and her husband invited Hitler to dinner in their luxurious hotel suite. Frau Bechstein was dressed in a long, formal evening gown and covered with jewels; her husband wore a dinner jacket. "I felt quite embarrassed in my blue suit," Hitler later told a friend. "The servants were all in livery and we drank nothing but champagne before the meal."[51] That evening Frau Bechstein convinced Hitler that he was now important enough to acquire a dinner jacket, starched shirts, and patent leather shoes.

A domineering and possessive woman, Frau Bechstein thought she could tell the shy, retiring Hitler how to dress, behave, and even how to conduct his political affairs. But she, like so many women after her, made the mistake of underestimating his determination and independence. He would sit alone with her for hours explaining his political ideas. In return for her generous donations he was even willing to let her call him "my little wolf." However, the rumors that there was a clandestine romance between them are probably false. Frau Bechstein was considerably older than Hitler, and she was satisfied as long as he smiled at her, kissed her hand, and complimented her on her appearance.

In society Hitler behaved in a somewhat awkward but not unpleasant fashion. Contrary to the stories printed in several Munich newspapers, Hitler did not throw fits in private or have the manners of a gangster. Many people, especially women, were charmed by him. Usually he would present his hostess with an extravagantly large bouquet of roses, and bow to kiss her hand in the dramatic old Viennese fashion. He was careful never to sit down before they were seated. Even his voice changed when speaking with women; its often harsh, guttural tone was replaced with a certain melodious quality. He spoke to them with the accent, vocabulary, and warmth that characterized many Austrians. When talking to a woman he was able to give her the impression that he was totally interested in her and her alone. Finding themselves confronted by such a charmer instead of the crude character they had expected, most women were overcome by speechless amazement and intense delight. "I felt myself melt in his presence," said one wealthy lady. "I would have done anything for him," affirmed another who knew him well.[52]

Frau Elsa Bruckmann, the wife of the well-known publisher Hugo Bruckmann, was also one of Hitler's early supporters. Her husband's company had a great deal of influence in right-wing circles and published the books of Houston Stewart Chamberlain, one of the most popular nationalist authors at the time. Frau Bruckmann, who was born Princess Cantacuzene of Romania, had a great deal of money and was known to frequently give Hitler contributions. In return, however, she was very demanding of his attention. Years later, in commenting on the strange effect he had on women, Hitler said: "One day I detected an unexpected reaction even in Frau Bruckmann. She had invited to her house, at the same time as myself, a very pretty woman of Munich society. As we were taking our leave, Frau Bruckmann perceived in her female guest's manner a sign of interest [in me]. . . . The consequence was that she never again invited us both at once. As I've said, the woman was beautiful, and perhaps she felt some interest in me—nothing more."[53]

Frau Winifred Wagner, the English-born wife of Siegfried Wagner, Richard Wagner's son, was one of the first few hundred to join the Nazi party.[54] She became one of Hitler's personal friends and a contributor to his cause. Moreover, she used the influence of her name wherever possible to help get money for the Party.

Two Finnish ladies living in Munich were persuaded by Rosenberg and Scheubner-Richter to subsidize what they assumed to be Hitler's anti-Communist crusade.[55] A lady of a noble Baltic family, Frau Gertrud von Seidlitz, gave a considerable sum of money to help the Party purchase its new printing press. In 1924, after the collapse of Hitler's putsch, Frau von Seidlitz admitted to the Munich police that she had helped Hitler financially for some time, but would not disclose any exact sums. With considerable pride she went on to mention that she had also persuaded others both in Germany and abroad to contribute to the Nazi cause.[56]

On April 3, 1923, the *Munich Post* carried a story about women who were "infatuated with Hitler" and lent or gave him money.[57] In many instances their contributions did not take the form of cash; instead, wealthy patrons presented him with valuable objets d'art and jewelry to dispose of as he saw fit. Frau Helene Bechstein stated that in addition to the regular financial support given by her husband to the leader of the National Socialist Party, she herself had made sizeable contributions, "not, however, in the form of money, but rather of a few objets d'art which I told him he could sell or do anything he liked with. The objets d'art in question were all of the more valuable sort."[58]

Usually Hitler would raise loans on the valuables presented to him by his admirers, and spend the money to support his Munich headquarters. A loan and transfer agreement concluded between Hitler and a merchant, Richard Frank, of the firm Korn-Frank of Berlin in the summer of 1923, provides an example of the type of valuables in question: "As security for the loan (of 60,000 Swiss francs) Herr Adolf Hitler will turn over to Herr Richard Frank the undermentioned property presently in the keeping of Heinrich Eckert, Bankers of Munich. . . . A platinum pendant set with an emerald and diamonds on a platinum chain. . . . A platinum ring set with ruby and diamonds. . . . A platinum ring set with a sapphire and diamonds. . . . A diamond ring (solitaire), a 14-carat gold ring with diamonds set in silver. . . . A piece of *grosspointe de Venise,* hand-stitched, six and a half metres long and eleven and a half centimetres wide (seventeenth century). . . . A Spanish red silk piano runner with gold embroidery."[59]

At first Hitler had considerable respect for the upper-class people he met in soliciting contributions. Germany was the most class-conscious country in western Europe and being from lower-middle-class origins himself Hitler was careful to address aristocrats and officers with all ceremonial politeness. In high society his naiveté was an asset as well as a drawback. "I can still see Frau Bruckmann's eyes shining," wrote Kurt Lüdecke, "as she described Hitler's truly touching dismay before an artichoke. 'But madam,' he had said in his softest voice, 'you must tell me how to eat this thing. I never saw one before.' "[60]

In the fall of 1922 an abrupt change in his attitude toward the upper class took place. A group of right-wing Bavarian parties and Free Corps units called the Fatherland Societies, to which the

Nazis belonged, planned a putsch to take over the government. The head of the organization was a Dr. Pittinger who was commander of one of the largest Free Corps units, the *Bund Bayern und Reich*. He was also commonly regarded as the unofficial representative of Crown Prince Rupprecht of Bavaria. But when the moment for the coup finally came and the Nazis and the Free Corps troops were ready to strike, Dr. Pittinger and his staff of officers and aristocrats got cold feet.

Hitler and his men were left in the lurch. He was furious: "No more Pittingers, no more Fatnerland societies!" he shouted; ". . . these *gentlemen* — these counts and generals — they won't do anything. *I* shall. I *alone*."[61] Up to this time Hitler had thought of himself simply as a sort of drummer or propagandist of the coming German reawakening that would be led by some nationalist general. But on that day of betrayal and disappointment in 1922, he began to think of himself as the "Führer." The disgraceful failure of the Pittinger putsch, said Kurt Lüdecke, "also altered his inner regard for the 'great' people toward whom he had previously shown a certain deference and humility. But his demeanor did not change. He had found that it worked to be naive and simple in a salon, to assume shyness. It was a useful pose, but now it covered scorn. These important people—who were they? Mediocrities! Cowards!"[62]

If Hitler was ready to lead, the time was certainly ripe. By 1923 the runaway inflation was leaving distress and chaos in its wake. Workers were making millions of marks a week and had to carry their salaries home in bags. But the price of food was rising faster than wages and people were beginning to go hungry. A middle-class professional man or doctor who thought he had a small fortune in the bank would receive a polite letter from the directors: "The bank deeply regrets that it can no longer administer your deposit of sixty-eight thousand marks since the costs are out of all proportion to the capital. We are, therefore, taking the liberty of returning your capital. Since we have no bank-notes in small enough denominations at our disposal, we have rounded out the sum to one million marks. Enclosure: one 1,000,000 mark bill."[63] On the outside of the envelope there was a canceled stamp for five million marks.

The savings of the middle class melted to nothing; the money they had invested before the war in bonds of the government, the

German states, and the municipalities was also lost. Financially the middle class was wiped out. The day that Hitler had foretold was coming to pass; the paper money was almost totally worthless now. More than 300 paper mills and over 2,000 printing presses were operating on a twenty-four-hour basis just to supply paper money, most of which had printing only on one side. The banks were actually using the blank side of the money for scratch paper because it was cheaper than purchasing scratch pads for the purpose.[64] A woman who took a wicker basket full of marks to the vegetable stand to buy a few potatoes sat the basket down and turned her back for a few moments while standing in line; when she turned around again the marks had been dumped on the sidewalk and the basket stolen.

Speaking about the inflation, Hitler described a process of destruction that had already been felt by many of those in his audience. "The government," he said "calmly goes on printing these scraps, because if it stopped, that would mean the end of the government. Because once the printing presses stopped— and that is the prerequisite for the stabilization of the mark—the swindle would at once be brought to light. For then the worker would realize that he is only making a third of what he made in peacetime, because two-thirds of his labor go for tribute to the enemy."[65]

Foreign observers were shocked when Hitler shouted from the speaker's platform that the Treaty of Versailles was only "a piece of paper." But those words were not so shocking to millions of Germans who had seen their money, their savings, and their contracts become nothing more than that. With his instinct for emotional reactions, Hitler knew his words would fill them with rage. He had chosen his expression very carefully.

The runaway inflation destroyed the people's confidence in the government. The Communist Party began to grow stronger; within a short time they had taken over power in the states of Saxony and Thuringia. The frightened upper class suddenly became more receptive to Hitler's pleas for money. He made several trips to Berlin to solicit contributions and in Munich he frequently made the rounds of prominent conservative citizens.

Sometimes he would take his friend Hanfstaengl along to give an added touch of respectability to these "begging expeditions." On one occasion they drove to Bernried on Lake Starnberg to see a wealthy retired consul-general named Scharrer, whose wife was a member of the prominent German-American Busch family of St. Louis. Their colossal estate was a typical nouveau riche sort of place, with the grounds full of peacocks and tame swans. Hitler noticed that the radiator of Scharrer's car was plated not in nickel but in gold, and in the house there was a lavatory with all gold fixtures. Frau Scharrer was an immense, fat woman whose hands were covered with rings so big that she could hardly move her fingers.[66] According to Hanfstaengl, Hitler got no money out of Scharrer "on that occasion," implying that he was more successful at some other time.[67]

Hanfstaengl, who was in a fairly good position to know about the Party revenues during this period, wrote: "The Party was permanently short of funds. In fact the conversion of the *Beobachter* into a daily, for all its propaganda value, had only made the financial situation worse in other respects, and Hitler was always on the lookout for other sources to tap. He seemed to think that I would be useful with my connections, but however interested and encouraging my friends were, they did not choose to dip into their pockets. . . . Some of the national-minded Bavarian industrialists were doubtlessly prodded into giving a check from time to time, but it was all hand to mouth stuff and there were always debts demanding payment and nothing to meet them with."[68]

Financial worries increased as the Party grew larger. The initial one thousand dollars which Hanfstaengl gave Hitler for the *Völkischer Beobachter* was an interest-free loan, not a gift.[69] Hitler had been obliged to pledge the entire plant of the *Völkischer Beobachter*—presses, office equipment, etc.—as security for the loan. The money was to be repaid on May 1, 1923, but of course Hitler was unable to do so. Hanfstaengl had little choice but to give him an extension until January 1, 1924. However, Putzi himself became in need of money, so he sold the claim against the paper to Christian Weber, a horse dealer and Nazi Party member.

Weber was a big, rough man of enormous girth, who liked plenty of good food, wine, and women. He had somewhat of an unsavory reputation. He was frequently seen in the company of "ladies of easy virtue" and it is said that he lived off their earnings. Later it was incorrectly reported that he had worked as a bouncer at a notorious Munich dive. The exact source of Weber's money is not clear, but only a small part of it could have come from buying and selling horses. Weber pressed Hitler to repay the money with all the tricks of a professional loan shark. He had the Party automobiles mortgaged in his favor and as one Nazi said, behaved "worse than a Jew." Such business worries were a continual irritation to Hitler, who remarked that he hoped to high heaven that the Party would one day be put on "a sound footing."

With the inflation growing more serious, Hitler was finally able to approach the conservative leaders of the Munich business community. At first they were cautious. Dr. Kuhlo, the director of the Association of Bavarian Industrialists, invited the Nazi leader to his office to ascertain his Party's intentions in regard to economic policy; also present at the meeting with Dr. Nöll and Hermann Aust, both officials of the Association of Bavarian Industrialists and prominent Munich businessmen. The conversation in Dr. Kuhlo's office led to the holding of a small meeting at the Munich Herren Club and later to a much larger meeting in the Merchants Hall. On both occasions the audiences were primarily composed of small businessmen. Hitler's speech on the aims of the National Socialist Party at the Merchants Hall received strong applause. Hermann Aust, who helped arrange the meeting, said that "several gentlemen, unacquainted with Hitler personally but who knew that I was acquainted with him, gave me donations for the movement with the request that I would hand the sums in question to Hitler himself."[70] Aust remembered that some of the money handed to him was in Swiss francs, but since he did not mention any large sum, it is probable that the donations were comparatively small.

Although Hitler received no large monetary contributions after his speeches to the Munich businessmen, his efforts were not wasted. Hermann Aust and Dr. Kuhlo and some of the other men he met on these occasions were very influential in local conservative circles. A few weeks later the most important of the city's conservative newspapers, the *Münchener Neueste Nachrichten,* which had been prodemocratic in the first years of the Weimar Republic, began to accord Hitler favorable publicity. At the same time the *Münchener Zeitung,* another respectable conservative paper, suddenly turned pro-Nazi.[71] Thus, men who had influence behind the scenes could contribute more important things than just cash.

There were three prominent businessmen who were particularly generous with their contributions in 1923: Gottfried Grandel of Augsburg, who had originally helped finance Hitler's purchase of the Party newspaper; a small manufacturer named Becker of Geislingen; and Richard Frank, a wealthy food distributor. Hitler had met Frank through Dr. Gansser and later commented that, if it had not been for Frank, he "wouldn't have been able to keep the *Beobachter* going in 1923."[72] Frank gave his money without any strings attached; in fact, he was such a fanatical Nazi that Hitler said he was "one of the greatest idealists I've known."[73] There were others who were willing to contribute to the Nazis, but only if they could in return exert an influence over the Party. Some would actually try to bring about a moderation in Hitler's policies, others would simply be concerned with their own economic interests.

By 1923, when the Nazi Party was in need of new and larger headquarters, Richard Frank tried to help Hitler raise the money. Together they went to see Dr. Kuhlo. If Frank was willing to pledge a certain sum of money as initial security for the venture, Dr. Kuhlo said he would try to form a syndicate with a few other public-minded businessmen to buy the Hotel Eden located near the station. The owners were demanding Swiss francs in payment, but within a surprisingly short time the financial arrangements were made and Hitler was invited to a meeting of the syndicate in the plush boardroom of a prominent Munich firm. As chairman of the syndicate, Dr. Kuhlo stood up and said he was pleased to announce that the hotel would be put at the Party's disposal for a modest rental fee. He then went on to suggest casually that the Party might suppress its program's article against Freemasonry. "I got up and said goodbye to these kindly philanthropists," Hitler recalled. "I'd fallen unawares into a nest of Freemasons! . . . It's by means of these continual blackmailings that they succeeded in acquiring the subterranean power that acts in all sectors."[74]

Although Hitler may have been able to avoid the influence of the Freemasons,* he was not able to remain independent of Swiss francs. Those who had access to stable foreign currency

---

*The Freemasons, who were opposed to tyranny and anti-Semitism, would undoubtedly have tried to exercise a moderating influence on Hitler.

could acquire staggering sums of German money for very little and consequently live like royalty. Ernest Hemingway, who was then a reporter in Europe, wrote of spending four days at a deluxe German resort hotel with a party of four. The bill, including tips, came to millions of marks—or twenty cents a day in American money. Germany was invaded by a host of inflation profiteers. Swiss, Dutch, Czech, Italian, and Austrian money circulated freely and possessed a high purchasing power when converted to inflation marks. Hitler, by obtaining these currencies, found an excellent way to help keep the Party financially afloat during this period. Comparatively small donations from sympathizers and Germans in other countries instantly became sums of importance when the stable foreign currencies were brought into inflation-torn Germany.

Switzerland was an excellent source of funds, and the Nazis played on every possible appeal to get a few Swiss francs: anti-Communism; the affinity of German-speaking cultures; anti-Semitism, etc. In 1923 Dr. Emil Gansser toured the country, canvassing, in particular, wealthy Swiss Protestants. On April 2, 1922, Gansser wrote from Munich to an evangelical mission inspector in Switzerland that he had "observed with keen delight on my last journey through Switzerland that among the influential German families Hitler's great ideological struggle is followed with far more attention and sympathy than in my own country . . . because this vigorous young movement has at the same time to wage a second and equally difficult conflict: namely, that against Roman Jesuitism, which is at the present day more active than ever behind the scenes. . . . Here in Munich the brother of the Empress Zita has resumed his treasonable activity and, with Papal-French support, continuously wages a frantic campaign against Protestant Prussia—in conjunction with attempts to establish a considerably enlarged Catholic Danube monarchy involving 'temporary' severance from Protestant Prussia. Here above all, then, there is twofold reason to welcome a movement which, under the leadership of a talented simple workman, Adolf Hitler, is striving to make Germany once more a respected factor, as a federal State under the leadership of Prussia."[75]

Hitler himself went on several fund-raising tours in Switzerland. On one occasion in Zurich in 1923 he was feted at a dinner that had over twelve courses. He returned from the trip "with a steamer trunk stuffed with Swiss francs and American dollars."[76]

Frequently Hitler spoke to German nationalist groups in Czechoslovakia and Austria. Though he received only a speaker's fee and a few small contributions, this money was worth a great deal back in Munich. When the *Völkischer Beobachter* became a daily newspaper in 1923 and moved into new and larger offices, Hitler, accompanied by Max Amann, went to buy office furniture in the old part of Munich. The clerk stared wide-eyed when Hitler, ready to pay, pulled out his wallet which was stuffed full of Czech money. Hitler noticed this. "The Ratsch-Kathel* . . ." he said, "are always wanting to know where we get our money from. You see where it comes from: the Germans in other countries all over the world send us foreign currency because they begin to cherish hopes for Germany again, since we appeared on the scene."[77]

There were contributions from Germans in Czechoslovakia, Austria, and Switzerland, from the White Russians, and from Bavarian businessmen and wealthy upper-class nationalists like the Bechsteins. When he was going on one of his fund-raising tours of Switzerland, Prince Ahrenberg insisted on personally driving him part of the way. The Prince, said Hitler, was "one of our earliest adherents."[78] Ahrenberg drove what Hitler said was one of the oldest Benz cars he had ever seen: "On the level the old car ran reasonably well; but at the slightest sign of a hill it blew its head off, and we were in grave danger of sticking fast. He had to change gear all the time, and so we trundled along hour after hour. At last we came to the downhill part of the journey, and there the car flew along at at least thirty miles an hour!"[79] Hitler could never quite understand why the Prince did not buy a new automobile for he knew him to be a "multimillionaire." It was also indicated by Hitler that Prince Ahrenberg was not so stingy about everything; but how much money he gave the Nazis is impossible to determine.

The two men became close personal friends. It was from Ahrenberg, who had been in Africa before the war, that Hitler formed his impression of what colonial policy should be. The Prince, said Hitler, "told me many interesting tales of pioneering days in our colonies. He was once sentenced to twelve years of penal servitude—and served six of them—for having killed a

---

*Ratsch-Kathel was a term of abuse for the Social Democratic paper, the *Munich Post*.

nigger who had attacked him!"[80] Hitler agreed with the Prince
that Germany would have had greater success with her colonies if
she had followed as strict a racist policy as Britain had.

Prince Ahrenberg was the outstanding exception to the rule,
for otherwise there were few aristocrats in the Nazi Party. There
were some right-wing nationalists, such as the Duke and
Duchess of Coburg (both related to the Grand Duchess Victoria,
Cyril's wife), Count Reventlow, and Baron von Dewitz (leader of
the Pomeranian Landbund), who were sympathetic toward the
National Socialists and were willing to help them occasionally.
Once when commenting on the attitude of the upper class toward
the Party, Hitler mentioned two noblemen, von der Pfordten and
Stransky, who were early members and especially valuable supporters.[81] But it was only among the aristocratic German emigrés
from the Baltic states that the Nazi cause was really popular: the
rest of the German nobility preferred their traditional right-wing
conservative parties.[82]

Besides the aristocrats, businessmen, and White Russians,
there remained one other group from which Hitler received
money: namely, Naval Intelligence. This is a most unexpected
source, partly because its motives were less obvious than those of
other contributors. One must recall that the German central
government had decided that the best method to thwart Bavarian
separatism was to use the Navy as an agency through which
support could be given to the nationalist movements in Bavaria,
such as the Nazis. This gave rise to one of the most complex and
mysterious cases of covert funding. Involved in this case was the
man who was later to become known as a leader of the German
resistance against Hitler, Admiral (then Lieutenant Commander)
Wilhelm Canaris. Since intelligence agencies are expert at covering up any traces of their activities, the evidence that remains is
rather sketchy. However, it is enough to definitely link Hitler, the
Organization Consul (a right-wing terrorist unit of former naval
officers), and funds of Naval Intelligence. This case is an excellent example of the dangers of unsupervised intelligence agencies.

After the Kapp putsch, when the government ordered Commander Ehrhardt's Second Marine Brigade to disband, Ehrhardt
and his men fled to Bavaria where they reorganized the unit
under the name Viking Bund. Although the unit accepted some

new recruits, the basic cadre still consisted of former naval officers and enlisted men. Historian Harold Gordon writes: "Bund Wiking (Viking Bund) was armed only with light weapons, most of which came from hidden arsenals of the organization, *although Lieutenant Commander Wilhelm Canaris, already active in naval intelligence and similar areas, provided further weapons and money when necessary.*"[83] (Author's italics.)

Unfortunately, Gordon does not carry his investigation any further. Although another officer was nominally in charge of the Viking Bund, Ehrhardt was the real commander and at the same time also commanded a more sinister unit, the Organization Consul. This group was a secret terrorist network made up primarily of Ehrhardt's naval officers from the Viking Bund. With Ehrhardt commanding both units and both staffed by the same officers, it is certain that the funds from Naval Intelligence which Canaris gave to Ehrhardt for the Viking Bund also financed the Organization Consul.

Naval officers of the Organization Consul were responsible for the assassinations of both Matthias Erzberger, the former Minister of Finance, and Walther Rathenau, Germany's brilliant Jewish Foreign Minister. In other words, money from Naval Intelligence financed the killing of government ministers.[84]

Irrefutable evidence closely connects Hitler with the Organization Consul, the Viking Bund, and Commander Ehrhardt. Hitler had subjected both Erzberger and Rathenau to a campaign of vicious public denunciation just before their assassinations.[85] During this period, armed members of the Organization Consul acted as Hitler's bodyguards instead of his own Storm Troopers, and O.C. men stood on guard outside his office at Party headquarters.[86] The commander of the Nazi Storm Troop units was Lieutenant Klintzsch, one of Ehrhardt's naval officers, as were a number of other key S.A. officers. The Viking Bund later was affiliated with the Kampfbund, of which Hitler was the political leader. When Hitler attempted his putsch to overthrow the government, the troops of the Viking Bund supported him. Both Lieutenant Kautter, chief of staff of the Viking Bund, and Hermann Göring later testified that Hitler's S.A. and the Viking Bund were "closely related."[87]

By mid-1923 German economic life was grinding to a standstill and many people were reverting to barter. Suicides were common among the middle class. Farmers were now refusing to sell their produce for the inflated paper money, as Hitler had predicted. Those who lived in cities were going hungry. The signs of malnutrition began to appear; increasing cases of scurvy were reported.[88] Mothers who could no longer feed their babies brought them to charitable institutions frequently wrapped, not in diapers, but in paper. There were widespread strikes and riots under Communist leadership in many industrial cities.[89] But most dangerous of all was that the Communists, who had gained control of the state governments in Saxony and Thuringia, were planning to launch a nationwide revolution from these bases.

The country, cried Hitler, "is on the brink of a hellish abyss." He alternately wept with the people in their despair and chided them for accepting it so passively. "The people are like a lot of children. You can only press million-mark notes into the hands of a childish public!" The size of the Nazi Party was multiplying so rapidly it was difficult to determine the exact extent of the membership. In the fall of 1922 it was a little over 10,000; less than a year later estimates ran between 35,000 and 200,000, with sympathizers of at least ten times this number.[90] If elections had been held at that time, the National Socialists would probably have been the second strongest party in Bavaria. It was even said that a majority of the Munich police were Nazi supporters, which is not too surprising considering that the head of the police, Dr. Ernst Pöhner, was a member of the Thule Society.

Hitler's popularity was so great that he was allowed an appointment with General von Lossow, the commander of the Army in Bavaria. At the time it was very unusual for a German general to meet formally with an ex-corporal; but, of course, Lossow knew Hitler had powerful backers and represented important interests. After their first conversation together the General was clearly impressed. Throughout the spring and summer of 1923 Hitler called on von Lossow almost daily. When General von Seeckt, the Supreme Commander of the Germany Army, came from Berlin on his official inspection tour, he sat in Lossow's office for an hour and a half listening to the man Lossow termed a "political prophet"—Adolf Hitler. A few years ago Hitler had been a poorly paid Army agent; now he was meeting the commanding generals as an equal. Hitler explained his plans for a union of all nationally-minded people, the formation of a huge militia under the S.A., the crushing of the Communists, and the expulsion of the French from the Ruhr. But Seeckt was not persuaded as easily as Lossow; he replied curtly to Hitler and that was all.

On September 25, after delivering a very persuasive two-and-a-half-hour speech, Hitler was appointed political leader of the Kampfbund—an organization of nationalist groups and Free Corps units. Historians incorrectly attribute Hitler's appointment to his powers of oratory alone; it is now known that all the principal organizations that made up the Kampfbund—the Free Corps Oberland, commanded by Dr. Friedrich Weber, the son-in-law of the Navy publisher and Thule Society leader L. E. Lehmann; the Free Corps Reichskriegsflagge, commanded by Captain Ernst Röhm, a Thule Society member; and the National Socialist Party—were all financed in part at least by the Thule Society. The Viking Bund, which was affiliated closely with the Kampfbund and the Nazi Party, was funded directly by Naval Intelligence and worked in close cooperation with the Thule Society leaders.[91] Significantly, the general business manager who was in charge of the funds of the Kampfbund was the Nazi leader Scheubner-Richter.[92] Like the Thule Society, all the organizations of the Kampfbund had nationalist political aims; they were not only anti-Communists, but were strongly opposed to Bavarian separatism.

Both the Nazi Party and the Free Corps units that belonged to the Kampfbund were growing at a feverish tempo. Of course, some of those who joined were opportunists. "Many people of wealth and social position," said one Nazi, "suddenly discovered their patriotic hearts and made common cause with us, in the belief that Hitler might, after all, come out on top and share the spoils with them. Many others gave money to the movement without actually joining it. Nazi and Kampfbund members were giving to the limit, sometimes literally sacrificing their last million marks for the cause."[93]

Certainly it is an error to think that Hitler's fund-raising efforts were concentrated solely on getting contributions from the wealthy. The Party itself was now producing a sizeable income.[94] An admittance fee was charged at all of Hitler's speeches and the collections taken afterward sometimes netted a fair amount. Each Party member paid his monthly dues and anyone who paid more belonged to the "sacrificial ring" and got a front seat when

Hitler was speaking. Hitler did not hesitate to tap his followers for the most trifling amounts, so there were always special collections for one thing or another. In 1923 the Party issued non-interest-bearing bonds, which bore an inscription stating that they would not be redeemed if presented by a Jew. The bonds sold quite well among the Nazi faithful.

In the fall of 1923 it was clear that something would have to happen soon. Hitler and Scheubner-Richter were plotting a coup d'etat. With the forces of the Kampfbund, which had the strength of a small army, they would take over the Bavarian government and then march on Berlin to finish off the Social Democrats and Communists while the Army remained neutral. However, von Kahr, the leader of the Bavarian government, was planning a coup of his own. He intended to use the runaway inflation and accompanying chaos as an excuse to declare Bavaria independent of Germany and then restore the Wittelsbach (Bavarian) monarchy. The forces of Hitler and von Kahr were both outwardly opposed to the Berlin government, but beneath the surface each was trying to outwit the other.

A few months before Hitler was made political head of the Kampfbund, he found the ideal commander for his 15,000 man S.A. unit,[95] — Hermann Göring. During the war Göring had been a fighter ace in the Richthofen Squadron and won the Pour le Mérite (Blue Max), Germany's highest decoration. Before the war was over, he succeeded his famous commander Baron von Richthofen (the Red Baron), and was himself appointed commander of the Richthofen Squadron.

Germany's defeat left Göring disillusioned. One evening in November of 1922 he attended one of Hitler's speeches and was almost instantly converted. The next day Göring sought out Hitler to volunteer his services for the Nazi Party. The two men talked together for some time. "We spoke at once about the things which were close to our hearts—the defeat of our Fatherland, the inequities of the Versailles Treaty," Göring said later. "I told him that I myself to the fullest extent, and all that I . . . possessed, were completely at his disposal."[96]

Hitler was overjoyed with his new recruit. Göring was a great war hero and that would bring considerable prestige to the Party. He was also from an aristocratic background and was a personal friend of high-ranking officers, counts, and even princes. When one Party official asked about the new recruit, Hitler replied, "Göring!" laughing and slapping his knee with satisfaction. "Splendid, a war ace with the Pour le Mérite—imagine it! Excellent propaganda! Moreover he has money and doesn't cost me a cent."[97]

Göring came from a wealthy family, but Germany's defeat and the inflation had left him virtually penniless. He was, however, living comfortably on the money of his wife, formerly Swedish Countess Carin von Kantzow, who turned out to be of great prestige value to the Party. The presence of this beautiful, aristocratic lady at Nazi rallies and Storm Troop parades made a good number of wealthy people reexamine their first impression of the Nazi Party. "If such a dignified, noble woman is a supporter of Hitler, perhaps he isn't a danger to respectable people after all," they said to themselves.

The Görings's villa in Obermenzing, a suburb of Munich, became a gathering place for the leaders of the National Socialist Party. Hitler, who liked pretty women, was charmed by Carin Göring. She in return embraced the Nazi cause with all the fervor of her emotional temperament.

There is no evidence, in her letters to her relatives in Sweden, that she had any objections about Hitler or the other Nazi guests in her home.[98] When her sister the Countess von Wilamowitz-Moellendorff came for a visit, she too became entranced in the atmosphere of the villa: "On the ground floor was a large attractive smoking room, with an alcove lit from outside by a bull's-eye window," she wrote. "A few steps down from it was a wine cellar with an open fire, wooden stools and a great sofa. Here came together all those who had dedicated themselves to Hitler and his freedom movement. Late in the evening Hitler would arrive and you would see around him all the early devotees of the Party, Dietrich Eckart, Hermann Esser, Hanfstaengl, etc. After the earnest conferring would come the warm, cheerful hours which filled Carin with so much joy. Hitler's sense of humor showed itself in gay stories, observations, and witticisms and Carin's spontaneous and wholehearted reaction to them made her a delightful audience."[99]

Among the other visitors to the Göring villa was a man of the greatest importance, General Erich Ludendorff. Göring and his charming wife played a key role in getting the General to back

Hitler. It is impossible to overestimate the prestige of Luden-dorff's name in nationalist circles at the time. During the war he had been the Quartermaster General of the German Army with the virtual power of dictatorship over the country. Although he no longer held any official military post, Free Corps leaders and representatives of many rightist groups came to him for advice and guidance. Initially, Count Reventlow, a well-known national-ist leader and editor of an anti-semitic weekly, had presented Hitler to Ludendorff and recommended that the General support this rising tribune of the masses. The political ideas of the Gen-eral and ex-corporal were alike in many respects; they were both nationalists and anti-Communists, they were against the Ver-sailles Treaty, the Jews, and the Bavarian separatists. At a "Ger-man Day" rally in Nuremberg on September 1 and 2, before almost 100,000 people, Ludendorff announced his support of Hitler's Party.

General Ludendorff himself had little money, but many promi-nent, wealthy men looked upon him as Germany's senior military officer and consequently the true leader of all nationalist forces. There were industrialists and businessmen, such as Friedrich Minoux of the Stinnes firm, who wanted to support the anti-Communist forces but knew very little about politics and still less about the strengths and weaknesses of the numerous right-wing groups; consequently, they gave their money to Ludendorff, a man whose honesty they could trust and whose judgment they relied on, telling him to divide it among the nationalist forces as he saw fit.[100] By 1923 a considerable portion of this money was finding its way to Hitler.

In the fall of 1923 Fritz Thyssen, heir of the Thyssen steel empire and chairman of the board of the United Steel Works (Vereinigte Stahlwerke), the greatest German steel combine, at-tended one of Hitler's rallies. Thyssen, a man with strong right-wing sympathies, was impressed. "I realized his oratorical gifts and his ability to lead the masses," Thyssen said. "What im-pressed me most was . . . the almost military discipline of his followers."[101] The revolutionary uprisings of 1918–1919 had thoroughly terrified Thyssen. For a few frightening days he was in the custody of the revolutionaries; and even after the "Red terror" was crushed, he had no faith in the institutions of the Weimar Republic to maintain "law and order." "The impression which those agitated days left upon me has never been blotted out," Thyssen recalled. "During an entire year, 1918–1919, I felt that Germany was going to sink into anarchy."[102]

In 1923, Germany was once again in a state of extreme political tension. Economic difficulties caused by the inflation and political strife produced problems in industry that bordered on class warfare. The result was increasing social distance between the classes that hardened to open "class hostility." Most of Germany's great industrialists, Thyssen among them, realized that if economic conditions were not improved soon and class antagonism smothered, they would find themselves engulfed by the tide of a Communist revolution. In such a turbulent atmosphere, a charismatic nationalist leader like Hitler seemed like the man of the hour. "We were at the worst time of the inflation [October 1923]," said Thyssen. "The money . . . sank in value from one day to the next. In Berlin the government was in distress. . . . Authority was crumbling. In Saxony a Communist government had been formed. . . . Thuringia had given itself a Communist government. . . . Amidst all this chaos . . . my first meeting with Hitler took place."[103]

However, Thyssen's support or even sympathy for Hitler at this time should not be overrated. Later in October, during a visit to the home of General Ludendorff, Thyssen gave one hundred thousand gold marks (about $23,800) to the General to distribute between the Nazi Party and the Free Corps Oberland. Although this sum amounted to a fortune in the inflation-torn country, the fact that the money was to be divided between the National Socialist Party and the Free Corps Oberland indicates that even Thyssen was supporting Hitler only as one among many nationalist forces.[104]

Another important industrialist, Ernst von Borsig, the great locomotive manufacturer, made Hitler's acquaintance at the Berlin National Club in 1922. He was impressed by the Nazi leader's sincerity and his idea of winning the workers back to nationalism. In his position as president of the German Employers Federation, Borsig was a strong advocate of bringing management and labor together for compromise. The idea of a patriotic workers' party intrigued him, so when the Communists began to grow stronger during the inflation he decided to make a small contribution to Hitler. Since 1918 he had been giving some money to the right-wing Free Corps units as a sort of insurance against a Communist uprising; the donation to the Nazis was made with the same intention. Like all other big German industrialists, Borsig contributed to many political parties and did not even consider himself a "supporter" of a particular group just because he gave it money. At the same time he contributed to Hitler, Borsig was giving much larger sums to the moderate and conservative parties.[105]

By November 1923 the inflation reached nightmare proportions. The mark soared to astronomical figures: a dollar was officially worth 5 trillion marks, unofficially 7 trillion. Banks could no longer afford to count million-mark notes; they were simply weighed in bundles or measured with a ruler. Yet there was no way to measure the human misery caused by the inflation. The ruined middle class went hungry, and suffered from malnutrition; some were actually starving. The political atmosphere was on the verge of exploding.

When Hitler and the Kampfbund leaders learned Kahr was planning to declare Bavaria independent, they moved to forestall the separatists with a putsch of their own. Before the putsch took place, the Nazis made few preparations concerning finance. The only serious plan was to freeze all private economic transactions. But there was also some talk of seizing Munich's art treasures to finance their ultimate goal of ousting the Weimar government in Berlin.

On the evening of November 8 von Kahr was speaking to an audience of 3,000 respectable people at the Bürgerbräu, a first-class beer hall on the outskirts of Munich. Arriving shortly after 8:00 P.M., Hitler and some of the Nazi leaders pushed their way into the tightly packed hall where Kahr was droning on and on with a boring speech. While waiting for all of the Nazi troops to arrive, Hanfstaengl bought several beers, at a price of 1 billion marks apiece, for Hitler and the other Nazis. Meanwhile 600 S.A. men surrounded the hall from the outside. At 8:30 the elite guard of the S.A. arrived. Göring with twenty-five Brownshirts burst into the hall and quickly set up a machine gun at the entrance. During the uproar Hitler jumped up on a chair and fired a shot into the ceiling. "The National Revolution has begun," he shouted. "This hall is occupied by six hundred heavily armed men. No one may leave the hall."

Hitler then invited Kahr, Lossow and Seisser to come to a side room to discuss plans for a new national government. They refused to comply with his proposals until the arrival of General Ludendorff, who was successful in pressuring them to join Hitler's coup against the Weimar Republic. Triumphantly Hitler led the group back into the hall where they all made short speeches. The audience went wild with excitement; the women especially applauded the loudest.

But the victory gained was soon to be lost. Informed of difficulties between some S.A. men and Army troops, Hitler left, putting Ludendorff in charge at the Bürgerbräu. Ludendorff accepted the "word of honor" of Kahr, Lossow and Seisser to be loyal to Hitler and told them they were free to go. Of course none of the three had any intention of supporting Hitler's coup; so they proceeded to call for reinforcements from the outlying Army garrisons.

As soon as Röhm received the news of the successful coup, he announced it to his troops who were assembled in the Löwenbräu beer hall. The police spies who were listening rushed off to report to headquarters. As Röhm's motorcycle courier zoomed away to spread the word of the putsch, the police were still waiting on the corner for a streetcar, as they had no other means of transportation. In contrast the putschists had adequate transportation for their troops. Trucks belonging to the Nazi Party were supplemented by rented trucks and even taxicabs.

During the rest of the night disorganized troop maneuvers continued, yet the leaders of the putsch failed to make any decisive actions or to further take control of the key centers of the city. Instead guns were taken out of hidden vaults to be distributed, and Jews were rounded up in their underwear as hostages. Trucks carrying Storm Troopers from the suburbs rumbled into the city all night long. Most of the Nazis stayed around the Bürgerbräu; some tried to sleep in the corridors and halls, while others stood guard outside in the cold wet snow. There were hardly any civilians on the streets, except for a few small groups of revelers out squandering their inflation money.

On the gray morning of November 9 at six o'clock a line of trucks with Gregor Strasser's unit of 150 S.A. men from Landshut came rolling through Munich. One of the men said, "What kind of a revolution do you call this? People are going to work as usual.

Something's wrong."[106]

Early that morning Hitler had ordered the confiscation of paper money from the Parcus and Mühlthaler printing firms. Hanfstaengl returned sometime after 8 o'clock to the Bürgerbräu: "The air was thick with cigar and cigarette smoke," he later recalled. "In the anteroom there was a little orchestra platform and on it, in a pile about five feet high, thousands of million and billion mark notes in neat banker's bundles, which the Brownshirts had 'requisitioned'. . . I could have done with a few of them myself, for my hospitality the night before had left me without a penny in my pocket, but evidently they were to be expended in a legal and formal fashion whatever their origin."[107] Some of this money was later passed out to pay the troops. Free beer had been provided for the men in the Bürgerbräu, but they all had to pay for their own food.[108]

By this time Hitler knew that Kahr, Lossow and Seisser had betrayed him. He and Ludendorff desperately tried to think up a plan which would save the putsch from impending failure. They decided on a public march through Munich to link up with Röhm's forces which were holding out in the War Ministry building.

Shortly after 11 o'clock the march of over 2,000 S.A. men and Free Corps members started from the Bürgerbräu, across the Isar River, through the center of the city, and finally down the narrow Residenzstrasse. In the front of the column marched Hitler, Scheubner-Richter and Ludendorff. Most all of the troops carried weapons; some even had machine guns.[109] At half past twelve the putschists encountered a cordon of police at the end of the narrow street. Almost instantly a shot rang out, which was followed by a hail of bullets from the police. Sixteen Nazis, including Scheubner-Richter, were killed. Ludendorff marched straight through the firing into the ranks of the police; Göring was badly wounded; and Hitler dislocated his shoulder when he fell to the ground. The young S.A. doctor, Walter Schulz, guided Hitler back to a side street where they hopped into a car and raced out of the city towards the mountains. Two days later Hitler was arrested and imprisoned. His treason trial turned out to be one of the most blatant cover-ups in judicial history, not for his sake, as is often assumed, but to protect the "good names" of those who financed him, supported him, and intrigued with him.

Once the putsch began, money was of little importance. Hitler's men were well enough equipped, but they were disorganized and lacked training to face the regular Army. The putsch failed because Kahr, Lossow, Seisser and the officers of the Bavarian Army were willing to oppose it. No amount of money could have bought their loyalty. They were Bavarian separatists and their primary allegiance was to the Bavarian king.

Looking back at the financing of Hitler's political activities from 1918 to 1923, one thing is particularly interesting. Many historians have contended that the National Socialist Party was financed and supported by "big business."[110] Yet, as has been seen, only two of Germany's major industrialists, Fritz Thyssen and Ernst von Borsig, gave anything to the Nazi Party during these early years. Donations came from some conservative Munich businessmen who gave at the height of the Communist danger, as well as small Bavarian factory owners like Grandel,the Berlin piano manufacturer Bechstein, and the publisher Lehmann. But none of these men, in spite of their personal wealth, could fit properly in the category of "big business." There is absolutely no evidence that the really big industrialists of Germany, such as Carl Bosch, Hermann Bücher, Carl Friedrich von Siemens, and Hugo Stinnes, or the great families such as the Krupps and the leading bankers and financiers, gave any support to the Nazis from 1918 to 1923. Indeed, few of them knew this small party from Bavaria even existed. Most of Hitler's donations came from wealthy individuals who were radical nationalists or anti-Semites and contributed because of ideological motivation. To a certain extent, the wealthy White Russians fit into this category; they could also be looked on as the one real interest group that hoped to gain a definite political-economic objective from their aid to the Nazis.

There was one other important industrialist (in fact the world's largest) who gave to Hitler during this period, but his story must be dealt with in a separate chapter, for he was not a German, but an American.

3
FORD and HITLER

In 1915 Henry Ford chartered a ship at his own expense and sailed to Europe with a group of supporters in an effort to end World War I by negotiating a compromise peace. On board the ship, Ford told the well-known pacifist Madame Rozika Schwimmer: "I know who started this war—the German Jewish bankers."[1] Ford later said to the Florence, Alabama, correspondent of the *New York Times*, "It was the Jews themselves who convinced me of the direct relationship between the international Jew and war. In fact they went out of their way to convince me. On the peace ship were two very prominent Jews. We had not been at sea 200 miles before they began telling me of the power of the Jewish race, of how they controlled the world through their control of gold, and that the Jew and no one but the Jew could end the war. I was reluctant to believe it but they went into detail to convince me of the means by which the Jews controlled the war, how they had the money, how they had cornered all the basic materials needed to fight the war and all that, and they talked so long and so well that they convinced me."[2] Slapping the pocket of his coat, Ford told Madame Schwimmer, "I have the evidence here—facts! I can't give them out yet because I haven't got them all. I'll have them soon!"[3] Needless to say, his peace mission failed, and left him somewhat bitter. Years later, Ford reflected on his fruitless efforts: "The whole world laughed at my Peace Expedition, I know,"[4] but Ford was far from discouraged, and the world and Hitler were soon to be deluged with evidence of Ford's anti-Semitic feelings.

At the end of 1918, Ford bought a typical country newspaper called the *Dearborn Independent*. When Ford announced his publishing plans, he justified his actions by saying: "I am very much interested in the future not only of my own country, but of the whole world, and I have definite ideas and ideals that I believe are practical for the good of all and I intend giving them to the public without having them garbled, distorted or misrepresented."[5] He must have had something serious in mind since he said that, if need be, he was willing to spend $10 million to finance the publication.[6]

The *Independent* was not to be a medium for publicizing the Ford company; in fact, the editors were told specifically to avoid any mention of Ford's industrial enterprise. Unlike most newspapers, it had no advertisements. Ford didn't want any commercial influence interfering with his editorial program. Initially, the basic tone of the *Independent* was antiprofiteer, anti-monopoly, and antireactionary; on the positive side, it supported Wilsonian ideals of postwar reconstruction at home.

Ford had apparently been planning an attack on the Jews for some time, but he kept his plans to himself, although a few of his assistants and close associates had picked up hints. Ford's first editor of the *Dearborn Independent*, Edwin Pipp, said that Ford "was bringing up the Jews frequently, almost continually in conversation, blaming them for almost everything. . . . At first he talked only about 'the big fellows' and said he had nothing against Jews in ordinary walks of life. Later he stated: 'They are all pretty much alike.' . . . We had not published the paper more than six months before [Ford] commenced to talk persistently about a series of articles attacking the Jewish people. He said that he believed that they were in a conspiracy to bring on war for profits."[7]

A year after Ford had purchased the *Independent*, he was questioned about his experiences on the peace ship by one of his company's executives.

"What did you get out of that trip, Mr. Ford? What did you learn?" the man asked.

"I know who makes wars," Ford responded. "The international Jewish bankers arrange them so they can make money out of it. I know it's true because a Jew on the peace ship told me."

Ford said that this Jew had told him that it was impossible to get peace his way. However good his intentions, no argosy such as the peace ship could accomplish anything unless he saw the right people, and the "right people" were certain Jews in France and England.

"That man knew what he was talking about—[and] gave me the whole story," Ford said. "We're going to tell the whole story one of these days and show them up!"[8]

Suddenly on May 22, 1920, the *Independent* lashed forth with a violent attack on the Jews. The boldface headline on the front page was a blunt and concise summation of the editorial's thesis: "The International Jew: The World's Problem." The first paragraph began: "There is a race, a part of humanity which has never yet been received as a welcome part." This people, the article continued, has ever been fouling the earth and plotting to dominate it. In order to eventually rule the Gentiles, the Jews have long been conspiring to form an "international super-capitalist government." This racial problem, the *Independent* said, was the "prime" question confronting all society.

The following ninety-one articles covered a wide field of topics related to the international Jew. Ranging from Jews in a world government to Jews in American finance, in Communism, theater, movies, baseball, bootlegging, and song writing, the articles had slanderous titles, such as "The Jewish Associates of Benedict Arnold," "The Gentle Art of Changing Jewish Names," "What Jews Attempted When They Had Power," "The All-Jewish Mark on Red Russia," and "Taft Once Tried to Resist the Jews—and Failed."

In subsequent articles, Ford frequently accused the Jews of causing a decline in American culture, values, products, entertainment, and, even worse, of being the instigators of World War I. Serious charges were leveled against several well-known Jews. Bernard M. Baruch was called the "pro-consul of Judah in America," a "Jew of Super-Power," and "the most powerful man" during World War I. When asked by news reporters to comment on these charges, Baruch replied, tongue-in-cheek, "Now boys, you wouldn't expect me to deny them would you?"[9]

But most Jews reacted without the humor of Baruch. Petty riots took place in Pittsburgh and Toledo, and in Cincinnati, vigorous protests by Jewish citizens influenced the city council to establish a press censorship. Street sales of the *Independent* were so reduced by opposition that Ford had to obtain an injunction. In some of the larger cities, members of the Jewish community and their friends threatened or assaulted the newspaper's salesmen. In 1921 the theatrical producer Morris Gest filed a $5 million libel suit against Ford, but soon dropped it. Some public libraries barred the *Independent* from their collections and a resolution of protest was introduced in Congress. Representatives of almost all national Jewish organizations and religious bodies issued a common declaration denouncing the Ford campaign. One hundred and nineteen prominent Christians, including Woodrow Wilson, called upon Ford to stop his "vicious propaganda." President Harding, after an appeal by Louis Marshall, president of the American Jewish Committee, privately asked Ford—through his friend Judson C. Welliver—to halt the attacks. William Fox, president of Fox Film Corporation, threatened to show choice footage of Model T accidents in his newsreels, if the industrialist persisted in attacking the character of Jewish film executives and their motion pictures. When the Jews of Hartford were preparing for a 400 car parade in honor of Dr. Chaim Weizmann and Albert Einstein, they drew nationwide publicity by ordering "Positively no Ford machines permitted in line."[10]

Soon most Jewish firms and individual Jews boycotted Ford products,* and Gentile firms who did business with Jewish concerns and were dependent on their good will followed suit to please their best customers. The drop in orders for cars was most severe in the eastern metropolitan centers of the country, and, within a few months Ford competitors began to gain the edge. Officials high in the company later agreed that during the run of the anti-Semitic articles the company lost business which was never regained,** but nevertheless, because of the large postwar

---

*Unfortunately the boycott made the innocent suffer along with the guilty. One man alone—Henry Ford—was responsible for the anti-Semitic campaign, not the whole Ford Company. The workers, executives of the company, and members of Ford's family were in no way involved; indeed, some even expressed their disapproval of the articles to Ford. It is only fair to mention that after the death of Henry Ford, the Ford Motor Company has maintained a good relation with the Jewish public. In fact, the company has given generous contributions to Jewish organizations and causes. Likewise, the Ford family has deservingly gained the esteem of the Jewish community.

**Between 1918 and 1930 the accumulated debts of the newspaper were almost $5 million.[11] The Jewish boycotts and damage done to Ford's reputation brought further losses. So the cause of the *Independent* must have been very close to his heart, if he was willing to continue the campaign despite these drawbacks.

market, the boycott was not strong enough to cripple the Ford industry.

In 1921, Ford and his friend (and fellow anti-Semite) Thomas Edison were on their way to inspect the Muscle Shoals power plant when an Alabama reporter got through the crowd to ask Ford how long his anti-Semitic articles would continue. Ford replied that his "course of instruction on the Jews would last five years."

Despite all of the attempts to silence Ford's campaign, his racist ideas spread quickly throughout the world. Within a year and a half Ford had turned the *Independent* into a notorious, mass-circulated, anti-Semitic propaganda sheet. From 1919 to 1927 the *Independent's* nationwide circulation exceeded a quarter of a million, and from 1923 to 1927 it reached the half-million mark. Reprints of the articles which appeared in the *Independent* were published in a four-volume set (1920–1922) that gained a considerable circulation in the United States. Entitled *The International Jew,* this compilation was distributed widely and translated into sixteen different languages, including Arabic.[12] It was published in Barcelona, Pôrto Alegre, Brazil, and Leipzig. In 1932, the Brazilians asked Ford whether they might buy the translation rights. E. G. Liebold, one of Ford's private secretaries, assured them that permission to publish was unnecessary, "since the book has not been copyrighted in this country."[13] Correctly assuming that Liebold had given them the green light, the Brazilians printed 5,000 copies of the book from the German translation and displayed Ford's name prominently on the front cover. Spanish translations appeared throughout Latin America; the 1936 and 1937 editions of this translation—*El Judio Internacional, por* Henry Ford—went a bit further than most editions by using the manufacturer's photograph as a frontispiece. From France to Russia, anti-Semitic and nationalist groups eagerly bought up the publications of the famous American. A prominent Jewish attorney, after completing a world tour in the mid-1920s, stated that he had seen the brochures in the "most remote corners of the earth." He maintained that, "but for the authority of the Ford name, they would have never seen the light of day and would have been quite harmless if they had. With that magic name they spread like wildfire and became the Bible of every anti-Semite."[14]

If *The International Jew* was the Bible, then to the Nazis Henry Ford must have seemed a god. His anti-Semitic publications led many Germans to become Nazis. Baldur von Schirach, leader of the Hitler Youth movement, stated at the postwar Nuremberg War Crimes Trials that he had become an anti-Semite at the age of seventeen after reading *The Eternal Jew* (title of *The International Jew* translated for the German editions). "You have no idea what a great influence this book had on the thinking of German youth," von Schirach said. "The younger generation looked with envy to the symbols of success and prosperity like Henry Ford, and if he said the Jews were to blame, why naturally we believed him."[15] One of Hitler's lieutenants, Christian Weber, boasted that Ford would be "received like a King" if he ever came to Munich.

Hitler's admiration for the auto magnate, the *New York Times* reported, was made obvious by the large picture of Henry Ford on the wall beside Hitler's desk in the Brown House. In an adjoining room there was a large table covered with books, most of which were copies of the German translation of *The International Jew.*

When news of the Jewish boycotts reached the Nazis, Hitler declared that "the struggle of international Jewish finance against Ford has only strengthened the sympathies of the National Socialist Party for Ford and has given the broadest circulation to his book, *The International Jew*."[16] And in 1923, when Hitler learned that Ford might run for President, he said, according to the *Chicago Tribune*, "I wish that I could send some of my shock troops to Chicago and other big American cities to help in the elections. . . . We look to Heinrich Ford as the leader of the growing Fascist movement in America. . . . We have just had his anti-Jewish articles translated and published. The book is being circulated to millions throughout Germany."[17]

Theodore Fritsch, editor of the Leipzig anti-Semitic publishing house, *Der Hammer,* printed six editions of *The International Jew* between 1920 and 1922; by late 1933 Fritsch had published twenty-nine editions, each of which carried Ford's name on the title page and lauded Ford in the preface for the "great service" that he had done America and the world by attacking the Jews.[18] After 1933, it became a stock item of Nazi propaganda; every schoolchild in Germany came into contact with it many times during his education. The manager of the Ford Company in

Germany in the mid-1930s, Edmund C. Heine (an American citizen), explained that *The International Jew* had the backing of the German government and was an important factor in educating the nation "to understand the Jewish problem as it should be understood." Heine further pointed out that Fritsch, who insisted that "it is Henry Ford's book about World Judaism which hits the Jews most severely," would not give up his "publication rights."[19]

When a *New York Times* correspondent asked Ernest Liebold, Ford's secretary, to comment on the report about the influence of Ford on the Nazi Party, Liebold refused to affirm or deny these reports but he did express "surprise" that *The International Jew* had become so popular in Nazi circles.[20]

There is no need for surprise, however. Not only did Hitler specifically praise Henry Ford in *Mein Kampf,* but many of Hitler's ideas were also a direct reflection of Ford's racist philosophy. There is a great similarity between *The International Jew* and Hitler's *Mein Kampf,*[21] and some passages are so identical that it has been said Hitler copied directly from Ford's publication.* Hitler also read Ford's autobiography, *My Life and Work,* which was published in 1922 and was a best seller in Germany, as well as Ford's book entitled *Today and Tomorrow.*[22] There can be no doubt as to the influence of Henry Ford's ideas on Hitler. Not only do Hitler's writings and practices reflect *The International Jew,* but one of his closest associates, Dietrich Eckart, specifically mentioned the *Protocols* and *The International Jew* as sources of inspiration for the Nazi leader.[23]

Unlike the traditional religious and social anti-Semitism which had flared up at various times since the Middle Ages, *Mein Kampf* presented a theory of racial anti-Semitism. The distinguished group of historians, including Sidney B. Fay, William Langer, and John Chamberlain, who edited the American edition of *Mein Kampf,* claimed that the use of racial anti-Semitism as the integral part of a political program was Hitler's "Copernican discovery."[24] However, this harsh new philosophy was first propagated to

---

The International Jew was first published by Ford in 1920. Hitler did not begin to write *Mein Kampf* until 1924.

the general public, not by Adolf Hitler, but by Henry Ford.**

In *The International Jew* it is clearly stated: "Neither directly nor by implication is it held . . . that the Jewish question is a religious question. On the contrary, supported by the highest Jewish authorities, it is firmly stated that the Jewish question is one of race and nationality."[25] Quotations from many prominent Jews are taken out of context and cited as proof of this contention. Louis D. Brandeis, justice of the Supreme Court is quoted as saying, "Let us all recognize that we Jews are a distinct nationality of which every Jew, whatever his country, his station or shade of belief is necessarily a member."[26] Others of a seemingly more sinister nature, like Moses Hess, "who gave Karl Marx many of his original ideas about socialism," are also quoted. "A Jew," wrote Hess, "belongs to his race and consequently also to Judaism, in spite of the fact that he or his ancestors have become apostates."[27]

In contrast to the Jews, who are presented in *The International Jew* as a race "that has no civilization to point to, no aspiring religion . . . no great achievement in any realm . . . ,"[28] the Anglo-Saxons are portrayed as explorers, nation builders, and thinkers. As Ford was fond of telling people, it was the Anglo-Saxons who overcame all odds to establish a great new civilization on the American continent. Their accomplishments throughout the centuries, Ford said, have proven that the Anglo-Saxon race is destined to "master the world."

While still in Vienna, a few months after he had read his first anti-Semitic pamphlets, Hitler, like Ford, came to the conclusion that the Jews "were not Germans with a special religion, but an entirely different race."[29] He wrote in *Mein Kampf* that the Jews adopted the appearances of a religious community as a disguise in order to divert attention from their race. Consequently, he felt that the traditional religious anti-Semitism was worthless. The Jews could always escape restrictions against them by converting to Christianity, but behind the sham they remained Jews. To

---

**It is not the purpose of this section to discuss the falsity and unjustness of Hitler's and Ford's accusations, but rather to compare the similarity of their thinking. Because their anti-Semitic beliefs are today known to be false, there is no need to refute them here at length. For a thorough analysis disproving the entire anti-Semitic concept of a Jewish world conspiracy, see Norman Cohn, *Warrant for Genocide: The myth of the Jewish world-conspiracy and the Protocols of the Elders of Zion.* Also see Herman Bernstein, *The History of a Lie.*

convince popular audiences that the Jews were an alien race and
not a religion, he usually called attention to their particular physical characteristics, such as the shape of their nose. With a
vicious mockery he once said: "The fact that the Jews are a racial
group should be perfectly clear to anyone from externals alone.
One can't tell if you meet a man whether he is a Catholic, a
Protestant, a Baptist or a Lutheran, but in this 'religious community' [the Jews] one can tell the faithful from afar. A marvelous
religion."[30]

Echoing Ford's concept of the superiority of the Anglo-Saxons,
Hitler described the "Aryans" as the only race capable of creating
great civilizations. Interbreeding with the lower races caused the
decline of these civilizations. North America, "the population of
which consists far the greatest part of Germanic elements," was
given as an example of Aryan conquest and civilization of a
continent once inhabited only by an inferior race. "The Jew forms
the strongest contrast to the Aryan," Hitler wrote.[31] The Jewish
people, despite their "apparent intellectual qualities," are
nevertheless without any "true culture" of their own. The "sham
culture" which the Jew possesses, Hitler said, is taken from other
people and is mostly spoiled in his hands. But the alleged lack of a
true Jewish culture was not the main thrust of either Ford or
Hitler's anti-Semitism. Ford's primary complaint is clearly stated
in *The International Jew:* "We meet the Jew everywhere in the
upper circles, literally everywhere where there is power. And that
is where the Jewish question begins—in very simple terms. How
does the Jew so habitually . . . gravitate to the highest places?
Who puts him there? . . . What does he do there? . . . in any
country, where the Jewish question has come to the forefront as a
vital issue, you will discover that the principal cause is the out-
working of the Jewish genius to achieve the *power of control.*
Here in the United States is the fact of this remarkable minority
attaining in fifty years a degree of control that would be impossible to a ten times larger group of any other race."[32]

Both Ford and Hitler believed in the existence of a Jewish
conspiracy—that the Jews had a plan to destroy the Gentile world
and then take it over through the power of an international
super-government. This sort of plan had been described in detail
in *The Protocols of the Learned Elders of Zion.* Despite evidence
against the genuineness of the *Protocols,* Ford continued to de-

fend its authenticity, saying, "The only statement I care to make about the *Protocols* is that they fit in with what is going on. . . . They have fitted the world situation up to this time. They fit it now."[33]

Hitler's attitude on the *Protocols* is quite congruous with Ford's, as can be seen in a private and revealing conversation he had with Hermann Rauschning, a high Nazi official. Hitler said he was "appalled" when he read the *Protocols:* "The stealthiness of the enemy and his ubiquity! I saw at once we must copy it—in our own way, of course." He continued on to say the fight against the Jews was "the critical battle for the fate of the world!" Rauschning objected: "Don't you think that you are attributing rather too much importance to the Jews?" "No, No, No!" Hitler shouted. "It is impossible to exaggerate the formidable quality of the Jew as an enemy." "But," Rauschning contested, "the *Protocols* are a manifest forgery. . . . it couldn't possibly be genuine." "Why not?" Hitler replied. He said he didn't care whether the story was historically true; if it wasn't, its intrinsic truth was all the more convincing to him. "We must beat the Jew with his own weapon," he said. "I saw that the moment I had read the book."[34] Echoing Ford, Hitler said, "The best criticism applied to them is reality. He who examines the historical developments of the past hundred years . . . will . . . immediately understand the clamor of the Jewish press [against the *Protocols*]. For once this book has become the common property of a people, the Jewish danger is bound to be considered as broken."[35]

The Jewish conspiracy thesis can basically be paraphrased in the following way: "The Jews are a people who have strived throughout the centuries to maintain their identity as a race. They have always been a state within a state and have never felt any obligation or loyalty to the country in which they happen to be living. This racial unity is concealed under the guise of religion, of which the essence is the belief in their superiority. They say they are God's chosen people and think it is their destiny to one day rule the world. Yet they were the killers of Christ."[36]

The conspiracy theory described the Jews as a people who lack any original creative ability; their only skills were knavery, cunning, and trickery. Lacking other alternatives, and being psychologically oriented toward getting money rather than making or producing goods, the Jews, throughout history had acted as middlemen and merchants. In other words, the theory continues, they make their living by financial manipulation. Because many Jews were financiers, bankers and stock brokers, Hitler and Ford jumped to the erroneous conclusion that the Jews had a controlling influence over the flow of international money.

"The finances of the world are in the control of Jews; their decisions and devices are themselves our economic laws," the *Dearborn Independent* stated.[37]

The paper claimed that in America most of big business, the trusts, the banks, the natural resources, and the chief agricultural products, especially tobacco, cotton, and sugar, were under the control of Jewish financiers or their agents. Denouncing the Wall Street bankers, Ford said: "Their power is not in their gold, because there is no power in gold; their power is in their control of people's ideas with regard to gold. . . . Money control does exist—not the control of mankind by money, but the control of money by a group of money-brokers."[38]

Expanding on the Ford ideas, Hitler focused his attention in *Mein Kampf* on the process by which the Jew supposedly acquired his wealth and what he did with it. The Jews, said Hitler, were really nothing but "blood suckers" who attached themselves to the body of an unfortunate people.[39] The profit the Jew made from his monopoly, Hitler said, was put to work to destroy his enemy: by urging the Gentiles to misuse their money, he placed them in difficult financial straits and then pressured them further by demanding interest payments. Despite the fact that Gentile financiers and bankers were more numerous than the Jews, Ford and Hitler's belief that the Jews had complete control over international financing could not be swayed because they based their reasoning on fallacious premises and spurious sources, notably, the *Protocols* which explained: "For the time being, until it will be safe to give reasonable government positions to our brother Jews, we shall entrust them to people whose past and whose characters are such that there is an abyss between them and the people." In other words, the Jews' puppets would be Gentiles with a shady past who could be easily corrupted or blackmailed. *The International Jew* said these "Gentile fronts" are used extensively in "the financial world today in order to cover up the evidence of Jewish control.[40] Hitler also considered the Gentiles in the international money market as mere robots of the

Jews; thus he claimed that "the directors of the international stock exchange were without exceptions Jews. I say 'without exception,' for the few non-Jews who had a share in them are in the last resort nothing but screens, shop-window Christians, whom the Jew needs in order to deceive the masses."[41]

Ford clashed with the Wall Street financiers not only in the pages of his newspaper and books, but in reality as well. Authorities say that many of his ideas about Jewish financiers came from unpleasant personal experiences with bankers; one of the most violent conflicts between Ford and the financiers occurred early in 1921. At that time, rumors circulating the nation claimed that Ford was in difficult financial straits. Reports varied but each represented some aspect of the truth. It was said that Wall Street intended to foreclose on Ford and bring him to his knees. Many bankers were eager to supply him with capital. Some people thought that General Motors would obtain financial control of the Ford Company. However, Ford was adamant in his refusal to part with one share of his stock. "Henry Ford has reached his limit," the Dow-Jones Financial Ticker Service informed its clients. "It is beyond the powers of any one man to raise money and carry forward single-handed the manifold enterprises in which he has started." Many newspapers dramatized the situation. In bright red ink, the *Denver Post* announced in its front-page headline, "FORD BATTLES WALL STREET TO KEEP CONTROL OF PROPERTY." Offers of assistance for Ford came from numerous sources; one Detroit woman wanted to loan him a few dollars, while a fellow industrialist thought several million might help. But Ford declined all offers of assistance and returned the unsolicited contributions.

Due to a lack of capital, Ford was forced to curtail production for several months; then, on February 1, the Ford Highland Park plant reopened, bringing back 15,000 men who had been out of work since Christmas. Other Ford assembly plants around the country began producing cars from stock on hand. The February output was 35,000 units; these and 30,000 other unconsigned cars produced in late 1920 were immediately shipped to dealers who had not yet sold their last consignments of vehicles. As was customary, the local agents were required to pay for the cars upon arrival. Many dealers complained about the consignments, but in the last resort each had to pay for them or forfeit his franchise.

Most of the dealers went to their bankers, borrowed the money, and gradually saw demand overtake the excess supply. Ford, instead of borrowing money himself, had forced his dealers to borrow for him. The company also saved $42,600,000 by cutting down inventory, cashing Liberty bonds, selling by-products, and collecting dividends from foreign investments. By April, Ford had paid his debts in full and had spare cash on hand. Soon the story of how Ford had "outwitted the bankers" and "paid his way out" was printed in almost every American newspaper. Following the publicity of his "victory over the bankers," Ford's cars sold at a record-breaking rate; in the eyes of the average American he had become a folk hero. The Ford-Wall Street battle even drew attention abroad; Hitler told reporters that the struggle of international Jewish finance against Ford increased the support of the Nazis for their American hero.

As Ford was the world's most prominent industrialist, it was only natural that German businessmen would pay a certain amount of attention to what he said on the topic of business, even if they disregarded his political opinions. Like many conservative middle-class people from rural origins, Ford deplored "the lack of moral standards" in modern commerce and blamed this on the Jews. Ford told one reporter: "When there's wrong in a country you'll find Jews. . . . The Jew is a huckster who doesn't want to produce but to make something of what somebody else produces."[42] Nothing irritated the industrialist more than the idea of somebody getting something for nothing.

The International Jew wasn't the only book in which the industrialist condemned the Jews. In his autobiography, *My Life and Work,* and in *Today and Tomorrow,* Ford revealed the same ideas and accusations against the Jews.[43]

In his autobiography, Ford said he believed that a man should be permitted to take away from the community an equivalent of what he contributes to it. "If he contributes nothing, he should take away nothing."[44] In America he saw a "sinister element" . . . made up of Jewish middlemen, whose only aim was to get money. The *Dearborn Independent* said a Jew "has no attachment for the things he makes, for he doesn't make any; he deals in the things which other men make and regards them solely on the side of their money-making value."[45]

One evening during a private dinner conversation with his

friends, Hitler spoke of the lack of standards in modern commerce and, like Ford, blamed such conditions on the Jews. He compared the financial probity and honesty of the merchants of the Hanseatic League (mid-1200s to the 1800s) to the knavery and cupidity of the Jewish merchants. Each tradesman who possessed the approval seal of the Hansa was obligated to maintain the standard price and to produce only high-quality goods; if he failed in his obligation, retribution followed. A baker, for example, who cheated on the quality of flour was ducked several times in a basin filled with water in such a way that he came close to drowning. But "as soon as the Jews were allowed to stick their noses out of the ghetto, the sense of honor and loyalty in trade began to melt away." Hitler went on to explain how the Jews made the fixing of prices depend on the law of supply and demand rather than on the intrinsic value. European commerce had been dragged down to such a level that a remedy was needed urgently; and the first step of the remedy, Hitler said, was "to do away with the Jews."[46]

"Quick turnover and quick profit," was the essence of Jewish business, according to *The International Jew*. It is "the old Yiddish game" of changing the styles to speed up business and make people buy. Nothing lasts any more, bemoaned Ford's *Dearborn Independent:* It is always something "new" to stimulate the flow of money to the pockets of the Jews.[47] Ford himself often grumbled about the decline in the quality of items produced by industries that had "fallen into the hands of Jews." One night an office worker at Ford's Dearborn factory bit into a candy bar and quickly thumbed through the pile of his accumulated mail. He had just returned from Washington that evening and had taxied to the office on the way home to see if anything had taken place during his absence. The train had been so crowded he had not been able to get into the diner. So on the way to the factory he had picked up a couple of candy bars to tide him over until he got home for dinner. He had been sitting there at his desk only a few minutes when he noticed a face pressed against the glass panel of the door and the knob turned.

"What's up that you're here at this hour?" asked Ford, perching on a corner of the desk.

The executive said he was cleaning up odds and ends and catching up on the work he missed while out of town. Ford reached over and helped himself to a piece of candy. He munched on it for a while and made a frown.

"This stuff isn't as good as it used to be, is it?" he remarked, putting the untouched remainder back on the tinfoil.

"Don't you think so?" the executive replied without looking up from his work.

"The Jews have taken hold of it," Ford shook his head in disgust. As he slid off the edge of the desk, he said, "They're cheapening it to make more money out of it."[48]

Ford apparently proposed milder remedies to the "Jewish question" than Hitler. Ford said the only invincible course was to return to "the principles which made our race great. Let businessmen go back to the old way when a man's word was his bond and when business was service and not exploitation. Learn to test quality in fabric and food."[49]

In the years following World War I, American jazz and Hollywood movies were all the rage in Europe. As might have been expected, Hitler denounced the "degenerate Negro music" and the immoral themes of the "Jewish dominated" cinema. But it was Henry Ford's publications, not Hitler's, that first announced to the world that the export of modern American "Jewish" culture was a part of a deliberate conspiracy.

After examining the names of the actors, screenwriters, directors, and producers, the *Dearborn Independent* came to the following conclusion: The motion picture industry of the United States and the whole world "is exclusively under the control, moral and financial, of the Jewish manipulators of the public mind."[50] The Jews used the movies and theater to poison the American people with sensuality, indecency, appalling illiteracy, and endless liberal platitudes. *The International Jew* stated that the use of vulgarisms and slang in the movies was so extensive that Shakespeare wouldn't have recognized his own language.

Jazz and "popular music" were anathema to the ears of Ford and Hitler. "Monkey talk, jungle squeals, grunts and squeaks camouflaged by a few feverish notes"—this was the way Ford described it. *The International Jew* said that this kind of music was not really "popular," rather an artificial popularity was created for it by high-pressured advertising. The Jews had supposedly created the popularity of the African style to destroy the moral fabric of the white race. In Ford's opinion, the beat of the jungle and other "Congo compositions" degenerated into more bestial sounds than the beasts themselves made.[51]

Both Ford and Hitler believed that Jewish capitalist and Jewish Communist were partners aiming to gain control over the nations of the world. Their views differed somewhat, but this was mainly a result of their contrasting positions and nationalities. Ford placed more emphasis on Jewish financiers and bankers, because as an industrialist he naturally came into close contact with them. Hitler, on the other hand, was more concerned with the Jew's use of Communism was a weapon, since it was a powerful opposition force to the Nazis in Germany at that time.

Ford was frightened by the Russian Revolution and the rapid spread of Communism through other countries. If Marxism established itself in America he would obviously be one of the first to suffer. The Communist threat was one of the first topics he discussed in his autobiography. "We learned from Russia," said Ford, "that it is the minority and not the majority who determine destructive action. We learn also that while men may decree social laws in conflict with natural laws, Nature vetoes those laws more ruthlessly than did the Czars. Nature has vetoed the whole Soviet Republic. . . .

"Russia could not get along without intelligence and experience. As soon as she began to run her factories by committees, they went to rack and ruin; there were more debates than production. . . . The fanatics talked people into starvation. The Soviets are now offering the engineers, the administrators, the foremen and superintendents, whom at first they drove out, large sums of money if only they will come back. . . .

"There is in this country a sinister element that desires to creep in between the men who work with their hands and the men who think and plan. . . . The same influence that drove the brains, experience, and ability out of Russia is busily engaged in raising prejudice here. We must not suffer the stranger, the destroyer, the hater of happy humanity, to divide our people. In unity is America's strength—and freedom."[52]

Ford told to Charles W. Wood, Collier's reporter, that radical unions "are organized by Jewish financiers, not labor." Their aim is to interrupt work. "A union is a neat thing for a Jew to have on hand when he comes around to get his clutches on an industry."[53]

The use of capitalism and Communism as weapons by the Jews

was more vividly explained by Hitler, who profited from Ford's instruction on the matter: "While Moses Cohn, stockholder, stiffened the back of his company until it became as stern and uncompromising as possible towards the demands of its workers, his brother Issac Cohn, labor-leader, would be in the courtyard of the factory rousing the workers. 'Look at them,' Isaac would cry out, 'they only seek to crush you. Throw your chains away.' Both Isaac and Moses (who would quickly sell his stock, secretly being aware of the coming strike) would eventually profit from the collapse of the Gentile company which they could then take over."[54]

In the minds of Ford and Hitler, Communism was a completely Jewish creation. Not only was its founder, Karl Marx, the grandson of a rabbi, but more importantly Jews held leading positions, as well as a high percentage of the membership, in the Communist parties throughout the world. *The International Jew* stated that since the time of the French Revolution Jews had been involved in numerous movements to overthrow ruling regimes. If the Jews were not always visible in these revolutionary activities, it was concluded that they were operating behind the scenes, planning and manipulating the forces in their hands. "Revolutions are not spontaneous uprisings, but carefully planned minority actions, and the subversive elements have been consistently Hebrews."[55] In *Mein Kampf* there is a similar discussion of the Jews sneaking in among nations, and subverting them internally by the use of lies, corruption, and liberalism. The most modern weapon in the Jewish arsenal was Communism: "In Russian bolshevism," said Hitler, "we must see Jewry's twentieth-century effort to take world domination unto itself."[56]

According to *The International Jew*, the Russian Revolution was financed in New York by Jewish bankers. No evidence is given to support this accusation. Jacob Schiff of Kuhn, Loeb and Company is the only Jewish financier mentioned in this connection.[57] It is impossible to determine if Henry Ford sincerely believed that Jewish bankers financed Communism or if the accusation was just being used to slander the Jews. It is true that a few wealthy Jews did actually give some small contributions and loans to revolutionary movements in Russia, because of a hatred of the anti-Semitic policies of the Czarist government.[58] However, the revolutionaries they gave to were generally Mensheviks rather than Bolsheviks. This important distinction could have been missed by people like Ford, who were not knowledgeable of the Russian political situation and automatically labeled all left-wing movements as "Communist."

When Hitler accused the Jews of being behind Communism he could offer as "proof" quotations from Henry Ford's own newspaper, the *Dearborn Independent*. Moreover, this charge against the Jews was believed by many middle-class Germans because it did seem to conform to the facts. Both Hitler and Ford contended that about 75 percent of the Communists were Jews.

Count Witte, the liberal Russian prime minister, said that while there were only seven million Jews among the total Russian population of 136 million, their share in the membership of the revolutionary parties was about 50 percent.[59] Police statistics showed the ratio of Jews participating in the revolutionary movement to the total Jewish population was six times that of the other nationalities in Russia. However, most Jews were not in the rank and file, but rather in the upper echelons of the Soviet bureaucracy. This fact was corroborated by a statement from Lenin who, during a lecture on the 1905 revolution delivered in Zurich, said that "the Jews provided a particularly high percentage of leaders of the revolutionary movement. . . . It should be said to their credit that today Jews provide a relatively high percentage of representatives of internationalism compared with other nations."[60]

At the second congress of the Social Democratic Party in London, where the split into the Bolsheviks and Mensheviks occurred, there were some twenty-five Jewish delegates out of a total of fifty-five. Of the 350 delegates at the 1907 congress, nearly a third were Jews. However, an important point which the anti-Semites overlooked is that of the Jewish delegates over a fifth followed the Menshevik line, as compared to 10 percent who were pro-Bolshevik.[61] Most of the Jewish Marxists in Russia were idealistic and humanitarian-minded and sided with the Mensheviks.

Hebrew-Yiddish writer Reuben Brainin, who had met Trotsky during 1917 in New York, said: "If Trotsky and his Jewish friends, who now head the Russian government, destroy Russia, then this will be the revenge taken by the Jewish people on their torturers and oppressors, their persecutors, foes and executioners of yesterday. The dog deserves the stick."[62]

The famous Jewish writer, Steinman, spoke of the trinity of "Zion, Hebrew and Communism." He believed in an amalgam of Zionism and Communism because the origins of the socialist ideals were rooted in the tradition of old: "Look into the Torah, the Prophets, and the Hagiographa, every page of which cries out for revolution! The reign of justice or eternal desolation!"[63]

But Jews were involved merely as individuals because their existence was threatened by the anti-Semitic Czar and peasants.

Even though Leon Trotsky had renounced his religion, he remained very attached to his Jewishness. It is said that his acceptance of the principles of the Marxist revolution were to a noticeable extent a disguise—though he never publicly confessed this—for a revolt against the squalor and wretchedness under which the Russian Jews lived in the ghetto. During the trial following the 1905 uprising, Trotsky came very close to admitting his true feelings as he hurled bitter accusations against the Czar: "If you tell me that the pogroms, the arson, the violence . . . represent the form of government of the Russian Empire, then yes, then I recognize . . . that in October and November we were arming ourselves against the form of government of the Russian Empire."[64]

After the revolution the Jews were gradually pushed aside by the more brutal leaders arising from the non-Jewish masses. The change that occurred in the top Soviet leadership from 1926 to 1937 is an historical example of this process: The Jewish leaders of the revolutionary period, Trotsky, Zinoviev, Kamenev, were shoved aside by Stalin and other non-Jews.

As far as its influence on the upper-middle-class Germans was concerned, what was said in *The International Jew* about the German revolution of 1918 was probably even more important than what Ford said about the Russian Revolution.[65] In the early twenties when Hitler was still an obscure agitator, his charges that the Jews were responsible for the revolution in Germany in 1918 and the subsequent loss of the war were taken seriously by many people who would have ignored them if Ford's publications had not stated the very same arguments. The Jew is the "world's Bolshevist and preeminently Germany's revolutionist," Ford's *Dearborn Independent* claimed.[66] In *The International Jew* there appeared over one entire page of names of Jews who gained high governmental positions during or after the German revolution. These Jews "would not have gained these positions had it not been for the Revolution, and the Revolution would not have come had not they brought it." The influential factors which destroyed the German people's morale and encouraged defeatism in 1918 were directed by the Jews; furthermore, *The International Jew* said, "the Jews of Germany were not German patriots during the war."[67] That exact accusation was later made by Hitler: "Almost every clerk a Jew and every Jew a clerk," he said. "I was amazed by this multitude of fighters of the Chosen People and could not help comparing them with the few representatives they had on the front."[68] Summing up the principal Jewish influences which supposedly caused the downfall of Germany, *The International Jew* listed the following three reasons: "a) the spirit of Bolshevism which masqueraded under the name of German Socialism, b) Jewish ownership and control of the Press, c) Jewish control of the food supply and the industrial machinery of the country."[69] Compared with Hitler's comments and conclusions about the revolution, Ford's ideas appear uncannily parallel.

The democratic political system in Germany began only in 1918 as a result of the revolution and was never very popular with many people of the upper classes. The fate of democracy hung by a slim balance. But even the German Right was hesitant to turn to the kind of authoritarian system advocated by Hitler. They feared foreign disapproval, which would be reflected in the international money market and could cause a collapse of the fragile Germany economy.* The fact that Henry Ford, the leading American industrialist, condemned democracy almost as strongly as Hitler must have been seen by some German businessmen as an indication that America would have no fundamental objection to Germany becoming an authoritarian state. Even later, after Hitler became Chancellor, protests by American journalists and politicians against the abridgement of the human rights of the Jews were disregarded by the Germans, to some extent because they thought the real powers in America, the industrialists like Ford,

---

*French disapproval of the proposed Austro-German Customs Union in 1931 did lead to the use of financial pressures and resulted in the collapse of the Austrian and German economy. See Chapters 6 and 7.

secretly approved of their policies.

To understand their contempt for democracy it must be pointed out that neither Ford nor Hitler believed in human equality. Ford had no qualms about expressing his disdain; he said there could be "no greater absurdity and no greater disservice to humanity in general than to insist that all men are equal."[70] If no two things in nature are alike and if each Ford automobile, which has completely identical parts, is unique in some way, then how can men be equal in any way?—this was Ford's rationale. Since men were "certainly not equal," any democratic effort to make them equal would only block progress. The crux of Ford's theory of inequality was the fact that "men cannot be of equal service." Because there are few men of great ability, it is possible for a mass of men with small ability to pull the greater ones down—"but in so doing they pull themselves down." It is the greater men who give the leadership to the community and enable the smaller men to live with less effort, asserted Ford. With equal frankness, Hitler said that "men are not of equal value or of equal importance."[71] He also spoke of the varying achievements of men and the obvious necessity to entrust the administration of economic and political affairs to the men who had proved themselves most capable.

Democracy is nothing but a "leveling down of ability" which makes for waste, complained Ford.[72] It was described by the *Dearborn Independent* as a "tool" that the Jews used to raise themselves to the ordinary level in places where they are oppressed below it, and then gain special privileges to make themselves superior.[73] But the very Jews who sponsored democracy publicly did not privately believe in the equality of men. This was revealed in the *Protocols,* which *The International Jew* quoted: "We were the first to shout the words, 'Liberty, Equality, Fraternity,' among the people. These words have been repeated many times since by unconscious poll-parrots, flocking from all sides to this bait with which they have ruined . . . true personal freedom. The presumably clever . . . Gentiles did not understand the symbolism of the uttered words . . . did not notice that in nature there is no equality."[74] It was in the *Protocols*, claimed the *Dearborn Independent,* that the Jews admitted they had won their first victory over public opinion with the weapon of democracy. Hitler's explanation was almost identical: Democracy was "the mastery of the herd over the intelligentsia, the mastery over

true energy through the dead weight of massed numbers."
Therefore it was very simple for the Jewish rulers, small in
number and completely invisible to the public eye, to
propagandize and ultimately control the masses.[75]

Both *The International Jew* and *Mein Kampf* use the term
"Gentile fronts" to describe the politicians in a democracy.[76]
These are men with a "past" who can be easily discredited and
thus must bow to the demands of the Jews or lose their position.
In fact, the *Dearborn Independent* claimed the Jewish manipulation of the American election campaigns have been so skillfully
handled that even if a good man would be elected, the Jews would
have a sufficient amount of evidence to force him under their
control. If he still refused to obey, then "scandals," "investigations," and "impeachments" would remove him easily. As to the
election campaigns, *The International Jew* said that they are
"staged as an entertainment, a diversion for the people." This
charade allows the people to think and act as if they were really
making their own government, but it is "always the Jews that
win."[77]

When *The International Jew* began to make its impact, a
prominent American Jew, Isaac Landman, of the *American Hebrew* challenged Ford to prove that a Jewish plot existed. Landman said he would guarantee to provide sufficient money to hire
the world's leading detectives and would agree to print their
findings, whatever they might be, in at least one hundred leading
newspapers. Henry Ford had always had a liking for detectives.
His plant was infested with them. They spied on the workmen,
the executives, and upon each other. This was a chance too good
to miss. But naturally they had to be his own detectives; he was
afraid the Jews would find it very easy to corrupt any outside
agency.

Ford set up an elaborate headquarters in New York and hired a
group of agents to unmask the operation of the "Secret World
Government." The agents themselves were a varied lot: two were
former senior members of the U.S. Secret Service, some were
professional detectives, and some were just fanatical anti-
Semites. They shadowed prominent Jews, investigated such improbable bodies as the War Finance Corporation, and carried on a
melodramatic correspondence with headquarters in Detroit
using code names as signatures. The detectives spent a great deal

of time trying to trace a private telephone line from the home of Justice Brandeis of the Supreme Court to the room in the White House were President Wilson lay gravely ill. Not surprisingly, they failed, since Justice Brandeis had no private phone. No story seems to have been too wild for these sleuths to investigate. In the end they declared that such prominent Americans such as President Wilson and Colonel House were "Gentile fronts" for the "Secret World Government."

Both Ford and Hitler believed that the Jews were buying up newspapers and other public communications media. News was all powerful, it could create an economic crisis, a war, or the fall of a government. The press was "almost completely dominated" by Jewry, claimed the *Dearborn Independent*. Sometimes it was difficult to detect the Jewish influence, because ownership was not always synonymous with control. *The International Jew* recommended that the reader take a glance at the names of the editors and their social connections, at the names of the journalists who wrote for the paper, and at the major firms and department stores which advertised in the paper. Hitler and the Nazis made a major issue of the Jewish control of the press in Germany. The *Frankfurter Zeitung* and the *Berliner Tageblatt,* which were both Jewish owned and the most outstanding newspapers in Germany, were their favorite targets. In *Mein Kampf* Hitler ranted about the "crowd of the simple ones and the credulous" who read the Jewish press, believe everything they read, and then go to the polls to make all the major decisions for the country.

This alleged control was thought to be of such importance that one entire chapter of *The International Jew* was devoted to it. "The primary means used by the Jews to manipulate the general public is their control of the Press," including not only newspapers, but also magazines, journals, and books.

The International Jew quoted from the *Protocols* to provide an explanation: "All our papers will support most diverse opinions: aristocratic, republican, even anarchist. . . . These fools who believe they are repeating the opinions expressed by their party newspapers will be repeating our opinions or those things which we wish them to think." By the apparent disagreement of the diverse newspapers, the Jews could deny that there was any conspiracy among them. Furthermore, said the *Dearborn Independent,* by having a voice on all sides, the Jews were able to manipulate fake arguments and replies as they chose. These contrived attacks would also convince the people of the freedom of the press.[78] Hitler likewise accused the Jews of using apparent impartiality as a cover for their deceptions. By avoiding all ideas which seemed outwardly alien, the Jews could slowly "pour the poison" into their readers after they had been lulled into having a deep and unquestioning faith in the press.[79]

Some people believed Ford did not write *The International Jew.* They contended that Ford was unaware of the anti-Semitic rampage encouraged by his own newspaper, because it was written by someone else. Their contention, like most cover-ups, contains a grain of truth; Ford did not write the book word for word.[80] Actually his editor Bill Cameron transcribed Ford's ideas onto paper, but Ford's secretary, Ernest Liebold, stated that "the *Dearborn Independent* is Henry Ford's own paper and he authorizes every statement occurring therein."[81] When the first articles from *The International Jew* were published, a public statement, marked "Authorized by Henry Ford," was released and signed by E. G. Liebold. It stated: "The Jewish question, as every businessman knows, has been festering in silence and suspicion here in the United States for a long time, and none has dared discuss it because the Jewish influence was strong enough to crush the man who attempted it. The Jews are the only race whom it is 'verboten' to discuss frankly and openly, and abusing the fear they have cast over business, the Jewish leaders have gone from one excess to the other until the time has come for a protest or a surrender."[82]

But those who were tempted to believe that Ford was not involved in writing *The International Jew,* only needed to look at the most recent edition of his autobiography for clarification. There he spoke of the "studies of the Jewish question" which he published in the *Dearborn Independent* and which were distributed in book form under the title *The International Jew.* The articles, said Ford, were "offered as a contribution to a question which deeply affects the country, a question which is racial at its source. . . . Our statements must be judged by candid readers who are intelligent enough to lay our words alongside life as they are able to observe it. If our words and their observation agree, the case is made. . . . The first item to be considered is the truth of what we have set forth. And that is precisely the item which our critics choose to evade.

"Readers of our articles will see at once that we are not actuated by any kind of prejudice, except it may be a prejudice in favor of the principles which have made our civilization. There had been observed in this country certain streams of influence which were causing a marked deterioration in our literature, amusements, and social conduct; business was departing from its old-time substantial soundness; a general letting down of standards was felt everywhere. It was not the robust coarseness of the white man, the rude indelicacy, say, of Shakespeare's characters, but a nasty Orientalism which has insidiously affected every channel of expression—and to such an extent that it was time to challenge it. The fact that these influences are all traceable to one racial source is a fact to be reckoned with. . . .

"Our work does not pretend to say the last word on the Jew in America," said Ford. "For the present, then, the question is wholly in the Jews' hands . . . there is still room to discard outworn ideas of [Jewish] racial superiority maintained by economic or intellectually subversive warfare upon Christian society. . . . If they are as wise as they claim to be, they will labor to make Jews American, instead of laboring to make America Jewish. The genius of the United States of America is Christian in the broadest sense, and its destiny is to remain Christian. . . . Our opposition is only to ideas, false ideas, which are sapping the moral stamina of the people. These ideas proceed from easily identified sources, they are promulgated by easily discoverable methods, and they are controlled by mere exposure. We have simply used the method of exposure. When people learn to identify the source and nature of the influence swirling around them, it is sufficient. Let the American people once understand that it is not natural degeneracy, but calculated subversion that afflicts us, and they are safe."[83]

Throughout the 1920s Henry Ford continued to publish anti-Semitic articles in his *Dearborn Independent*. Then in 1927 he became involved in a lawsuit with Aaron Sapiro, a prominent Chicago attorney. Sapiro charged Ford with libel for saying that he was involved in a plot with other Jewish middlemen to gain control of American agriculture. The case was settled out of court when Ford published a personal apology to Sapiro and a formal retraction of his attacks against the Jews.

Undoubtedly the motives for issuing the public apology and retraction were complex. Ford's company was in the process of a critical changeover from the Model T to Model A and many local dealers were complaining that Jewish hostility was hurting business. Many Jewish owners of automobile fleets and also a number of Gentile fleet operators, in response to the insistence of Jewish financial backers, now found the Chevrolet and other cars an alternative to the Model T. The details of Ford's retraction and apology were worked out by two of Ford's associates and two well-known Jews, Lewis Marshall and Congressman Nathan Perlman. Marshall wrote the retraction, which he hoped would serve as the basis of Ford's apology to the Jews and would also make the industrialist look ridiculous. "If I had his money," Marshall told a friend, "I would not [make] such a humiliating statement for a hundred million dollars."[84] To Marshall's great astonishment, the retraction letter which he submitted to Ford's representatives was printed without changing a word and bearing the signature of Henry Ford.

In essence, the retraction and apology letter written by Marshall said that Ford had been so busy that he had not paid any attention to the articles printed in the *Dearborn Independent*. He admitted that the charges against the Jews were malicious and false. Ford asked for the forgiveness of the Jewish people and made a humble apology for the injustices done to them through his publications.

After Ford's death it was revealed that he had not signed the apology letter after all. The retraction and apology had been delivered to Ford's assistant, Harry Bennett, who forged Ford's signature to the papers. Bennett admitted the whole story: "I phoned Mr. Ford. I told him an 'apology' had been drawn up, and added: 'It's pretty bad, Mr. Ford.' I tried to read it to him over the phone but he stopped me. So I signed Mr. Ford's signature to the document. I had always been able to sign his name as realistically as he could himself. I sent the statement to Untermeyer and Marshall. The signature was verified, and the case closed."[85]

Evidently Ford considered the matter a fait accompli and did not want to pursue it further. However, he in no way changed his attitude toward the Jews. In 1940 he told Gerald Smith, "I hope to republish *The International Jew* again sometime."[86]

But publishing his accusations against the Jews was only the first step for Ford. Shortly after he began the anti-semitic articles, Ford took stronger action by financing the global anti-Semitic campaign. He struck at the Jews where they would later prove to be the most vulnerable.

"That Henry Ford, the famous automobile manufacturer gave money to the National Socialists directly or indirectly has never been disputed," said Konrad Heiden, one of the first biographers of Hitler.[87] Novelist Upton Sinclair wrote in *The Flivver King*, a book about Ford, that the Nazis got forty thousand dollars from Ford to reprint anti-Jewish pamphlets in German translations, and that an additional $300,000 was later sent to Hitler through a grandson of the ex-Kaiser who acted as intermediary.[88] The U.S. Ambassador to Germany, William E. Dodd, said in an interview that "certain American industrialists had a great deal to do with bringing fascist regimes into being in both Germany and Italy."[89] At the time of Dodd's criticisms, the general public was aware that he was speaking of Ford because the press made a direct association between Dodd's statement and other reports of Ford's anti-Semitism. The *Manchester Guardian*, one of the outstanding liberal newspapers in Europe, reported that Hitler received "more than merely moral support" by an American who sympathized with anti-Semitism and thought that Hitler would be of assistance in the battle against bankers' capital.[90] The *New York Times* reported in 1922 that there was a widespread rumor circulating in Berlin claiming that Henry Ford was financing Adolf Hitler's nationalist and anti-Semitic movement in Munich. In fact, the rumor was so rampant that the *Berliner Tageblatt*, one of the largest newspapers in Germany, made an appeal to the American ambassador, Alanson B. Houghton, requesting an investigation of the issue and interference in order to prevent any further financial support for Hitler,[91] but the outcome of this request has never been determined. Throughout the 1920s there were numerous leaks of information about Ford's financing of Hitler, but since then they have been suppressed and forgotten.

Ford's major motivation for financing the Nazis was his desire to support an organization which would further the fight against the Jews. Since America and Germany were the two largest industrial powers, Ford thought that the control of the Jews would be greatly shaken if there were strong anti-Semitic factions in these two countries. Ford's financial support and his well-known book against the Jews would gain him recognition and respect in the ranks of the Nazi Party. And if this party did eventually become an influential political force in Germany, then Ford's philosophy would play an important role in the battle against the Jews.

There was also a point in the Nazi program which was advantageous to Ford's economic interests. Hitler's vehement protests against the injustices of the Versailles Treaty were secretly applauded by the American industrialist. Not only did the trade restrictions set up by the Versailles Treaty hurt Germany, they also hurt American businessmen who operated in foreign markets, such as Ford. America could benefit from trade with Europe only if Europe recovered from the destruction of World War I, and as the economist J. Maynard Keynes said, Europe could be made prosperous only by making Germany prosperous. But as long as the Versailles restrictions were wrapped around Germany's neck, there could be no hope for her recovery.

As a boy Ford had worked for a toolmaker from Germany who taught him many useful things. He liked Germans because "they are a talented and thrifty people." In the 1920s Ford wanted to set up a factory in Germany where he could benefit from the availability of skilled labor.

In 1921 a Ford executive was sent to tour the defeated and occupied Germany, to locate a possible site for a Ford automobile factory, but because of the financial restraints the Versailles treaty placed on the German automotive industry, the Ford plant could not possibly be built.[92] That year, Ford had sold only three Model T cars and trucks and six tractors in all of Germany during 1921. Ford thought that if Hitler and the Nazis could bring pressure to bear upon the Berlin government, and therefore on the Allied governments, perhaps the Versailles restrictions would be lifted and the automobile business would improve.

In the early 1920s there was nothing illegal about the Nazi Party, so Ford had every right to give his support openly. However, just as most political funding is secretive, it was obviously more prudent for Ford that there be no evidence linking his name with a radical rightist party. The State Department would not have appreciated his interference in the internal affairs of a foreign country. The Nazis also had a very good reason for wanting the source of funds to remain anonymous. If the German people found out that Hitler was financed by Ford, he would be accused of being the puppet of a foreign capitalist.

The best way of disguising the origin of the money was to channel it through a middleman or agent, who had contact with Ford and indirectly with Hitler. For example, some Ford employee, who was already receiving a salary, could inconspicuously receive a bonus which would then be transferred to a Hitler supporter who would be receiving the money for an ostensibly different reason. Of course there are myriad other possible ways in which funds could have been transmitted, ranging from a more complex chain of middlemen to a more direct yet equally untraceable method.

Fortunately, in the Ford-Hitler case there is enough evidence to reduce the numerous possibilities to three or four definite channels through which money flowed. Rather than taking the risk of giving one lump sum of money, Ford broke it up into several deliveries.

The primary intermediaries between Ford and Hitler were the White Russians. Shortly after Ford made himself known as an anti-Semite, a small cluster of White Russians started to work for him. One of these emigrés was Boris Brasol. Born in Russia in 1885, Brasol was a short man with sharp features, and piercing eyes who closely resembled Joseph Goebbels. He had the same aquiline nose, receding forehead, same shape of mouth, and the same cunning and ruthless look in his eyes. Trained as a lawyer, Brasol had gained investigative experience serving as the assistant of the anti-Semitic Russian Minister of Justice Shchegolitov who organized the infamous Beiliss trial against an innocent Jew accused of ritual murder. As chairman of the Association of Russian Army and Navy Officers, Brasol came to America in 1917, followed by his friend Major-General Count Cherep-Spiridovich, and together these two fanatical Czarists collaborated with all kinds of right-wing groups to further the restoration of the monarchy in Russia.* In 1918, Brasol was employed by the United

---

*According to Peter Koltipin, former assistant to Boris Brasol, Brasol's primary goal was to alert America to the danger of Communism, not to obtain U.S. support for the Russian restoration movement. Author's interview with Peter Koltipin.

States government for secret service work, a job gave which him an opportunity to introduce American intelligence officers to the *Protocols*.[93] During the next two years he worked hard to promote the publication and circulation of the *Protocols* in the United States. In 1920 he was hired onto the writing staff of Ford's *Dearborn Independent* where he provided much of the historical background and factual information to support Ford's accusations against the Jews.

Brasol's friend Count Cherep-Spiridovich also wrote a number of anti-Semitic pamphlets and books, such as *The Secret World Government*. Henry Ford and newspapers like the *Financial Times* in London took him seriously and helped him to reach a fairly wide public by publishing his stories.[94] Spiridovich also worked for Ford by soliciting subscriptions for the *Dearborn Independent*. A photographed check gives proof that Spiridovich was employed by Ford.[95]

Brasol and Spiridovich were both involved with fascist and anti-Semitic groups in America. John Roy Carlson, author of the book *Under Cover,* used an alias to disguise himself in order to interview hundreds of radical rightists in America; one of the men he spoke with was Boris Brasol. Carlson asked Brasol's opinion of numerous North American fascists, many of whom Brasol knew "very well." "Yes, I've met Adrian Arcand," Brasol said, referring to the Canadian Nazi leader. "I'm sorry to see him in jail. What we should do from now on is to train leaders secretly, keep them in the background so that when they put us in concentration camps these leaders can keep up the movement." When asked his opinion of the anti-Semite Father Coughlin, who was associated with Ford, Brasol replied firmly, "A great man." Toward the end of their conversation Brasol gave Carlson a dozen copies of his latest article in *Schribner's Commentator,* a small rightist newspaper. Carlson recalled that the most remarkable point of the one hour interview was that Brasol did not utter one anti-Semitic statement.[96] But this is not so surprising in view of Brasol's very suspicious and cautious nature. He refused to give interviews to those he did not know, said little to those he did not know well, and carried out his work in an inconspicuous manner. These traits in his character, combined with his experience as an investigator for the Czarist secret police, made him the ideal sort of man to be involved in a covert funding operation. No one seemed to notice his frequent trips to Germany, during the twenties and thirties, to confer with high Nazi authorities. He collaborated in Nazi intrigues on three continents and assisted in training an American fifth column.

During these trips, Brasol had plenty of opportunity to convey substantial sums of Ford's money to Hitler. Norman Hapgood, the well-known journalist and later U.S. ambassador to Denmark, wrote a number of articles on Henry Ford's shady political connections. In one of the articles, he stated that the former head of the Russian constitutional government at Omsk said, "I have seen the documentary proof that Boris Brasol has received money from Henry Ford."[97] With Ford's and Hitler's reputation, as well as his own, at stake, Brasol was fully aware that direct delivery of the money was highly imprudent. He had to be discreet. He had to have a plausible reason for transporting money to Germany—which he did. Boris Brasol was the U.S. representative of Grand Duke Cyril Vladimirovich, the first cousin to the last reigning Czar, Nicholas II, and one of the rightful pretenders to the Russian throne. Grand Duke Cyril had asked Brasol to collect funds for the Russian monarchist cause in America.

In 1921, Kurt Lüdecke visited Boris Brasol in the United States and was given a letter of introduction to Grand Duke Cyril, whereupon Lüdecke went to Nice, France, where Cyril and his wife Victoria were living in the Château Fabron. Lüdecke, who was received "with all due formality,"[98] quickly discovered that the Grand Duchess was "an intelligent, artful, and ambitious woman . . . [who] ruled over her husband." "So," Lüdecke said, "I cast my nets mainly toward her." He suggested that, through her kinship in the Spanish Court, she might be able to interest Primo de Rivera in supporting Hitler's plans. By stressing the advantages which would come to the White Russians if Hitler came to power, Lüdecke hoped to gain their cooperation, but due to their "stiff-necked" reaction Lüdecke did not even bother to ask for money, "as it was obvious that every rouble they had rescued from the Red Terror was desperately needed to keep up their regal charade."[99] If the Duke and Duchess were so short of money, how could they have contributed to Hitler? Nevertheless, between 1922 and 1924 Victoria gave General Ludendorff an "enormous sum" for the German right-wing extremists.

In 1939 General Biskupsky tried to get back this money for the

White Russians. He argued that the Nazis were obliged to repay to the Russian emigrés the money Cyril had provided when he was living in Munich in the early 1920s. Biskupsky wrote to Nazi official Arno Schickedanz, "Here I must note that the Grand Duke Cyril and his wife gave General Ludendorff a sum of nearly half a million gold marks in 1922–23."[100] These were not the ordinary inflated marks, but marks that were backed with gold. Actually, Biskupsky was trying to get back money which originally had come from someone other than Cyril and that is perhaps the reason why the Nazis did not return it. It seems apparent that the half million gold marks in question had been supplied by Henry Ford, with Boris Brasol acting as the intermediary. Of course, the Grand Duchess Victoria did give Hitler some of her jewels and Cyril perhaps also contributed some financial aid, but not the "enormous sum" described by Biskupsky, for the very good reason that Cyril and his wife did not have that much money to spare.

In 1924 Grand Duchess Victoria herself had made a trip to America to obtain funds for her husband's cause, and although it was never mentioned in the press, for the Nazis as well. The White Russians' most generous patroness in the United States was Mrs. Henry Loomis, an aunt of the former Secretary of State Stimson. Victoria was the guest of Mrs. Loomis at her Tuxedo Park home.* According to one source, three seats in the Coburg Regency Council were sold to Americans. Henry Ford and Mrs. Loomis were probably two of the buyers, or rather contributors, since the seats represented little significance.[101]

The second channel through which Hitler received Ford's financial support has documented evidence to verify an exchange of money. The evidence was given by the vice-president of the Bavarian Diet, Herr Erhard Auer, a very respectable Social Democratic official, in a report to President Ebert: "The Bavarian Diet has long had information that the Hitler movement was partly

---

*There is reason to believe that Mrs. Loomis may also have contributed to the Nazis. Lüdecke said this "splendid lady" invited him to dinner at her Tuxedo Park home. "Definitely nationalistic and folkic in her sympathies," Mrs. Loomis offered Lüdecke her "whole-hearted cooperation." She agreed to arrange for him a series of lectures to women's organizations. In return Lüdecke was to help prepare her trip to Germany during the summer of 1933.[102]

financed by an American anti-Semitic leader, Henry Ford. Mr. Ford's interest in the Bavarian anti-Semitic movement began a year ago when one of Mr. Ford's agents, seeking to sell tractors, came in contact with Diedrich Eichart [sic] the notorious Pan-German. Shortly after, Herr Eichart asked Mr. Ford's agent for financial aid. The agent returned to America and immediately Mr. Ford's money began coming to Munich. Herr Hitler openly boasts of Mr. Ford's support and praises Mr. Ford as a great individualist and a great anti-Semite. A photograph of Mr. Ford hangs in Herr Hitler's quarters."[103]

When Auer mentioned Henry Ford's agent, he was referring to Warren C. Anderson, better known as "Fuzzy" Anderson, one of the many bicycle racers who entered the automobile business in its early stage. He had joined the Ford Company in 1905 as a branch manager and spent several years working for the company in St. Louis, after which he was promoted and moved to Chicago. In 1919, after a survey of the entire Ford organization, Anderson was selected as the man best qualified to take charge of the Ford business in Europe. He was sent abroad with full control of production and sales and quickly established a record that automobile men and Ford officials admitted was remarkable.

However, shortly after he made contact with Eckart, Anderson was abruptly recalled from his post in Europe, and in February 1921, he and a number of other top executives were fired. Anderson wrote a letter to Edsel Ford (Henry's son and an executive in the company), which clearly indicated how he was offended by his sudden dismissal: "When I received the cable to report, at once, at the factory in Detroit I was very much surprised to note Mr. Liebold's name at the foot of the message, as this is the first time, in my many years of service, that I had ever received an order from anyone but an executive of the organization. Then, upon my arrival in Detroit, to have been shifted around from one to another, finally to receive my instructions from Mr. Ryan [Mr. William A. Ryan, a sales manager] was more than I could understand. Not one time during my stay did I see Mr. Ford . . . and I want to go on record as saying that I feel I have been treated anything but fairly in my leave-taking.

"It was no easy task for me to give up my friends and go to a strange country, but I did, and I gave the company the very best that was in me while in Europe and left no stone unturned to further its interest while there . . . and in leaving it seems to me that it would have been fitting and proper to have been accorded the same courteous consideration that I have always shown in the past. I feel that I should have been at least granted an interview with Mr. Ford personally."[104]

A cloud of uncertainty remains around the real issues due to the absence of official statements from the Ford Company, and due to Anderson's reluctance to discuss it. A close friend of Anderson claimed that Anderson had resigned because he disagreed with Ford's propagation of anti-Semitism. Supposedly, Anderson believed that the virtual boycott of Ford products in Europe resulted from the publicity about Ford's attacks on the Jews. Anderson, who was regarded as one of the most competent men in the foreign field, made repeated requests, appeals, and finally demands that the Jewish attack cease, but his efforts were in vain and the attacks became even more bitter.[105]

On the one hand, it is possible that Anderson disagreed with the anti-Semitic campaign only because it hurt the company's business; therefore, he may have had no moral objections to acting as the liaison between Ford and Eckart, Hitler's representative. But on the other hand, existing evidence shows that Anderson also complained about the inhumanity of Ford's racist propaganda. It is probable that Anderson's later complaints either angered Ford so much that he had Anderson fired, or else Ford felt that if Anderson remained with the company, it might become known that Ford had sent money to Eckart.

Ford was clever to have fired Anderson along with a group of other top executives, thereby making Anderson's dismissal less obvious. Due to the depression of 1920–1921, Ford was trying to cut back on the number of employees and any unnecessary expenses. Some of his officials, such as vice-president and treasurer Frank L. Klingensmith, who was supposedly "half-Jewish," had advised Ford to borrow money rather than trying to retrench by selling surplus material and lowering the number of workers. But Ford despised bankers and would only borrow money as a last resort. Furthermore, the depression provided him with a good opportunity to eliminate anyone who displeased him. Klingensmith was the first to go. Anderson, William S. Knudsen, Louis H. Turrell, Dean Marquis, Louis Block, and others followed soon after. However, even after he was fired, Anderson was probably afraid to publicly expose the Ford-Nazi connection, because he would have had to admit that he had been the link between them. If questioned, Ford could have pretended that Anderson had given the money to the Nazis on his own. In any case, despite the mystery surrounding the circumstances of Anderson's dismissal, the fact remains that the Nazis used him to solicit funds from Ford .

The third channel for Ford's contributions to Hitler was a shorter and more direct route. On January 28, 1924, a typical cold, gray day in New York City, Siegfried and Winifred Wagner checked into the old Waldorf Hotel. The next day they would leave New York for a tour on which Siegfried was booked to conduct the music composed by his father, Richard Wagner, in the principal cities of the United States. While Siegfried was visiting Detroit, Baltimore, St. Louis, and other towns, Winifred would give lectures at various exclusive ladies' clubs along the way. The main mission of their tour was to collect enough financial contributions, about $200,000, to be able to reopen the yearly Bayreuth festival in Germany. Bayreuth, a small, picturesque town in southern Germany, surrounded by rolling hills and deep forests, was the site chosen by Richard Wagner in 1872 for his theater, known as the Festspielhaus, and for a home for his family.

The outbreak of the war in 1914 put an end to all performances, and even after the signing of the Versailles Peace Treaty, Bayreuth remained a ghost town. The Festspielhaus remained empty; no foreigners were interested in traveling to hear German music, and the German people were still struggling to survive in the wake of destruction left by the war. At the height of the anti-German war hysteria, Wagnerian operas were either shelved in the Allied countries or at best performed in modified translations while mobs demonstrated against the treason of playing German music at all. Even the war brides had to find substitutes for the *Lohengrin* wedding march. All music needs patronage, and since Wagnerian opera was held in such disrepute, Siegfried was in serious financial difficulty. In order to restore a good image and hopefully to reawaken interest in the annual Bayreuth festival, the Wagners had come to America; even if they did not find many contributors, at least the concert fees would be of some help.

It was more than a coincidence that the Wagners were accompanied by Kurt Lüdecke, who had come to America to collect funds for Hitler.* The Wagners, Lüdecke said, "were here on a mission not very different from mine."[106] Actually, their missions were the same. In his autobiography Lüdecke mentioned his discussion with the Wagners in their hotel suite: "So here I sat, talking with the man for whose nursing the incomparable "Siegfried Idyll" had been composed—and we scarcely mentioned music!. . . We were discussing money. More particularly, we were speaking of the chance of interesting Henry Ford (to Europeans the incarnation of money in its alluring bulk) in the Nazi movement." Winifred was a very active woman who managed her husband's business affairs, and, Lüdecke said, "she now took a hand in mine."[107]

As they sat in their hotel room discussing various maneuvers, the Wagners and Lüdecke finally decided to pin their hopes on Mrs. Ford's interest and hospitality toward celebrities. The hours slipped past midnight as they continued to debate whether Mrs. Ford could be relied upon to extend an invitation. Lüdecke laughingly said that, in the case of Mr. Ford, perhaps it would have been better to present their case through some hillbilly fiddler, as his musical tastes were "intensely folksy." Before going to bed the trio concluded their planning with the hope that Ford's wife and son would be eager to meet the Wagners, if only for the change of hearing tidings of the world outside Detroit.

That a respectable, well-known composer and his wife could be conspiring with a Nazi may at first be difficult to believe. However, Siegfried Wagner had not been able to escape from inheriting the prejudices of his father. Lüdecke said that Siegfried fully subscribed to his father's written opinion that the Jew is "the plastic demon of decay."[108]

In bitter, vituperative language Richard Wagner denounced the "parasitic Jews" as a completely alien element who were responsible for the corruption of the German spirit. In 1881 he wrote a letter to his patron, King Ludwig II of Bavaria, in which he described the Jews as the congenital enemies of humanity and all that is noble in it.[109] One of Wagner's most notorious diatribes against the Jews was his essay entitled "Jewry in Music" written

---

*It is possible that during this trip in 1921 Lüdecke received money from Ford through Cameron, whom Lüdecke described as "very receptive," as Cameron was eager for outside assistance on anti-Semitic arguments which he could use in the *Independent*.

in 1850. The Jewish period in modern music, he said, must be categorized as "the period of consummate uncreativeness — stability run to seed."[110] Wagner flaunted his anti-Semitic attitude in public. At a concert in London in 1855 he wore kid gloves while conducting Mendelssohn's "Italian" Symphony in order to show his contempt for this Jewish composer, and to further emphasize his hatred he dramatically removed the gloves when he proceeded to Weber's *Euryanthe* overture. When critics rebuked Wagner for this malicious gesture, he called them "a pack of vagabond Jews."[111]

Wagner's close friend Count de Gobineau was a strong influence on his racist attitudes. Gobineau's *Essay on the Inequality of Races,* written in 1855, proclaimed the superiority of the white-Aryan race and the inferiority of all other races. Wagner helped make the book famous, and eventually it became a pillar of Nazi racial theory through its propagation by Wagner's disciples, especially his son-in-law Houston Stewart Chamberlain. Combining the racial ideas of Nietzsche, Gobineau, and Wagner, Chamberlain produced *The Foundations of the Nineteenth Century* (1899) which became one of the seminal works of the Nazi movement and a book that Kaiser Wilhelm believed had been sent to his people by God.

Wagner wrote numerous essays on art and music, among them several anti-Semitic essays. "Know Thyself," his most rabidly racist essay, declared that the German people were "exposed defenseless against the incursions of the Jews,"[112] and that only when his countrymen awakened and stopped their petty political bickerings could the power of the Jews be broken. Wagner also claimed that any interbreeding between Aryan and Jew would produce a Jewish offspring and thus lead to further racial degeneration. His last opera *Parsifal* represented the Aryan's struggle to maintain his racial purity and to prevent any sexual contact leading to amalgamation of Aryan blood with inferior races. Many of Wagner's essays were so radical that they can only be compared with the barbaric outpourings of Nazi propoganda. Unlike Nietzsche's writings, which the Nazis had to edit, trim, and take out of context, Wagner's prose was reprinted in the Third Reich without any changes.

Hitler read all of Wagner's writings and said the composer's political essays were his favorite reading. Hitler never hesitated to acknowledge his debt to Wagner: "Whoever wants to understand National Socialist Germany must know Wagner."[113]

In 1914 Siegfried met Winifred Williams, a beautiful English girl. She had been born in Hastings in 1897, the daughter of a Welsh journalist and his half-English, half-Danish actress wife; but at the age of two both her mother and father died. When she was about ten years old she was adopted by the musician Karl Klindworth, a former friend of Richard Wagner. It was Klindworth who introduced Siegfried to Winifred in Bayreuth; one year later they were married. In spite of the great difference in their ages—Siegfried was forty-six at the time of his wedding, his bride eighteen—the marriage was very successful. Four children followed in quick succession and after Winifred's maternal duties subsided somewhat she assisted in all of the business affairs of her husband's concert tours. But Winifred also had interests of her own; one of these interests was sponsoring Adolf Hitler, a young man with radical political ideas. She originally had heard of Hitler in the Munich home of her guardian, Herr Bechstein, whose wife was a close friend of Hitler's. In 1920 or 1921 Winifred joined the Nazi Party and Hitler became a frequent visitor in Bayreuth during the twenties. Siegfried had no objections to his wife's young friend. According to Winifred, his attitude to Hitler was that of a benevolent uncle: "The young man had some bright ideas—good luck to him if he could bring them off."[114]

In her memoirs, Friedelind Wagner, Siegfried and Winifred's eldest daughter, described one of Hitler's first visits to Wahnfried, the Wagner home: "For a long time we waited. Mother was talking to Father eagerly, telling him how wonderful the young man was. Presently Wolfgang [one of Friedelind's brothers] and I grew impatient and went to the front door to watch for a car coming up the drive between the borders of the chestnut trees. At last one turned in from Richard Wagner Street. We called Father and Mother and all of us went to greet the visitor at the front door. A young man jumped out of the car and came toward us." After Winifred introduced Hitler to her husband, they all went into the garden. There Hitler told them about the coup which the Nazis were planning to enact in 1923. Long after Hitler left the Wagner home, Winifred was still talking about him; at luncheon she said she felt that he was destined to be the "savior of Germany."[115]

Like Hitler, Siegfried hated the Social Democrats and Communists. "Father was disillusioned with postwar Germany," Friedelind recalled. "He could never understand or forgive the Kaiser's flight and had no sympathy with the Weimar Republic which failed." The Communist revolution and resulting bloodshed throughout Germany distressed Siegfried to no end, and when he called Weimar Germany a "pig sty," he meant it. But despite Siegfried's disdain for the "decadent" Jewish culture which pervaded Germany and the impotent political crowd in Berlin, he remained politically inactive until 1923.

On November 9, 1923, Siegfried and his wife went to Munich, where he was scheduled to conduct a concert. However, after his arrival he discovered that the concert had been cancelled because the Nazi putsch had begun the night before in the Bürgerbraükeller. The Wagners' room in the hotel overlooked the Feldherrnhalle, where the climax of the putsch took place. Hearing a commotion in the street, Siegfried and his wife peered out the window to see Hitler and General Ludendorff marching down the middle of the avenue at the head of a company of Storm Troopers in their brown uniforms. Suddenly, as the Nazis approached the side of the Feldherrnhalle, they were stopped by a burst of machine-gun fire. Those who had not been killed fled. In the confusion it was difficult to see what had happened to Hitler and Ludendorff. In a short time news reached the hotel that the general was unharmed, but Hitler had injured his shoulder and no one knew where he was hiding.

Siegfried was "horrified to think that the Bavarian government would fire on General Ludendorff, the idol of all Germany."[116] So the Wagners decided that they must help the Nazis in any way possible. Through Winifred's connections with the Party members, she was able to discover a few days later that Hermann Göring had fled across the Austrian border to Innsbruck, where he was lying in a hospital severely wounded. Immediately, the Wagners made the journey across the snow-covered mountain passes to Göring's bedside. There they found he was being cared for by his wife, Carin, who was very ill herself and without any money. Siegfried paid all their bills and arranged for them to go to Venice where they lived for a year in the Hotel Britannia whose proprietor, a German friend of Siegfried's, never charged them a cent.

Soon after a wonderful Christmas celebration at Wahnfried, Siegfried and his wife began to prepare for a fund-raising tour in America. The children watched the large trunks being carried upstairs and the beds in their mother's room being covered with dresses which were to be packed for the voyage. During the parents' absence the four children were to be taken care of by the nanny, Emma Baer, who had been an early member of the Nazi Party.

After a short stay in London, the Wagners arrived in New York on January 28, 1924. It was at this time that they formulated their plans with Lüdecke about the coming meeting with Ford. The plans depended on whether Mrs. Ford would invite the Wagners to be her guests. If fortune ceded this much, Lüdecke said, "the rest of the plot was obvious—a word in Mr. Ford's presence, a hint, a request."[117]

The trio took the train to Detroit, arriving there early on Wednesday the thirtieth. From the first moment that Lüdecke stepped out of the station and looked about at the "grimness" and "industrial grime," Detroit and its suburbs stuck in his memory as "the least delightful scene" to which his travels ever carried him. Despite the bleak appearance of Detroit and its gray, cold weather, their spirits were greatly lifted when they checked into the Statler Hotel and the Wagners found an invitation from the Fords already waiting.

Wednesday afternoon Siegfried was interviewed by R. J. McLauchlin of the *Detroit News* in Orchestra Hall. McLauchlin described Siegfried as "a pleasant person, of small stature, smiles readily, smokes cigarettes and affects bow-ties." Siegfried's short, white hair, which was conventionally arranged, his beak nose inherited from his father, and his slight plumpness created a very "unheroic" impression on the reporter. The interview was not very elucidating since Siegfried talked only a little. He said he liked America and had a smile and a good word for everything. However, there was one subject which he refused to discuss—politics. "I won't talk politics," he said; "it is a very unpleasant subject and I'd rather not think about it." This was, indeed, a perfect excuse for avoiding any embarrassing questions. That evening Siegfried seemed to be delighted to have a chance to speak over the radio as a guest of the Detroit News Radio Station WWJ. He told his listening audience that at 10 A.M. he had had an orchestral rehearsal with the "splendid" Detroit Symphony. They were such a "fine body of musicians" that the rehearsal was completed almost an hour before the time scheduled. The aim of his trip, he said, was to interest Americans in a plan to assist in the restoration of the Bayreuth festival theater, but besides seeking financial aid, he wanted "to have a chance of hearing some American artists, who would be available for future performances at Bayreuth."[118]

The next afternoon, Thursday, January 31, the Wagners went to the Fords' home for an early supper. Ten miles from Detroit, driving west on Michigan Avenue, just beyond its junction with Southfield Road, the Wagners turned into a driveway heading northwest through an area wooded with old towering oaks and elms. This was Fair Lane, the 2,000 acre estate of Henry Ford. They were stopped briefly at the iron entrance gate where a guard was always stationed to make sure that Ford could enjoy his privacy, and to keep out uninvited visitors. From the gates the driveway stretched a mile through the forest to the large, gray stone house overlooking the calm Rouge River. Although Fair Lane was only a few miles away from one of the largest Ford industrial plants, there was enough quiet and solitude that natural wildlife, such as rabbits or deer, might be seen dashing across the road. Ford's love and respect for the animals on his "farm" was manifested by the 500 birdhouses located throughout the estate. The Wagners saw wire baskets of food hanging about on the trees and later Ford said that there was even a big basin of water which was electrically heated to prevent freezing. Soon the house came within view. Fair Lane was built of Kelly Island limestone, with thick walls and large windows. Although the structure was a blend of architectural styles and had a very simple design, it was slightly reminiscent of an early Frank Lloyd Wright. The porch and rooms facing west gave a wonderful view up and down the river where tall trees were mirrored in the water.

The Wagners were greeted by their hosts and then escorted into the sitting room. At first the conversation was very light, combining comments on the weather and the beauty of Fair Lane. But soon the discussion became more serious, leading logically from one topic to another—music, Wagner, Bayreuth, Germany, and finally politics in Germany. After a simple, but good meal of salad, fresh vegetables, and a very skimpy portion of meat (of which Ford disapproved because of his basically vegetarian health program), the conversation again rolled around to politics.

In their discussion about the Jewish question and the Nazis, Frau Wagner and Ford did most of the talking while Siegfried only added an appropriate comment now and then. At first Frau Wagner was a bit surprised that Ford could express himself so well on political topics. He explained to the Wagners that the Jews had a tremendous power in America and that their influence was growing every day. He was trying through the articles in the *Dearborn Independent,* he said, to provide a "course of instruction" for the American people on the conspiracy of the Jews. Then they spoke about the threat of Communism in Europe, the Versailles Treaty, and the power of the Jews over the press. "The philosophy and ideas of Ford and Hitler were very similar," Frau Wagner later recalled.[119] Winifred and Ford began to talk about Hitler and the Nazi Party. She was amazed to find that "Ford was very well informed about everything that was going on in Germany. . . . He knew all about the National Socialist movement."[120] But before Frau Wagner had time to gently bring up the subject of Hitler's need for money and suggest the possibility of a contribution, Ford himself mentioned the matter. "Ford told me," Frau Wagner recalled, "that he had helped to finance Hitler with money from the sales of automobiles and trucks that he had sent to Germany."[121] At her charming best, Winifred then suggested that Hitler was now more in need of money than ever. Ford smiled and made a vague comment about still being willing to support someone like Hitler who was working to free Germany from the Jews. Finally, Frau Wagner asked if a special representative sent by Hitler, Kurt Lüdecke, might be given an appointment to talk with Ford and discuss the matter of further cooperation between Hitler and Ford in detail. Ford nodded his assent and said he would be very interested to talk with the fellow.

After a pleasant evening the Fords and Wagners drove back to Detroit together for the concert that night. A quick change into evening clothes in their hotel room and the Wagners were ready to go to Orchestra Hall. The concert began at 8:30. While the orchestra tuned up, Lüdecke joined Winifred in her box. Even before she told him the good news, Lüdecke recalled, "her charming smile told me she had been successful."[122] He was to see Ford the next day to explain any further details about the Nazi Party which Frau Wagner was unable to supply, and if possible get a definite commitment for more financial support.

When Siegfried entered on stage, a good-sized audience greeted him with an echoing ovation that lasted several minutes. However, one reviewer of the concert commented that the audience was not as large as it might have been, considering the predominance of German descendants in Detroit; for such a special event, the "orchestra hall should have been packed to the doors."[123] Besides this smaller-than-expected crowd, Siegfried also noticed a certain "cautious reserve" on the part of some of the Americans whom he met. Supposedly Siegfried later discovered that one of his enemies spread a rumor that the Wagners had contributed to the Hitler putsch all the money for the reopening of the festival, some of which had been contributed by Wagner enthusiasts throughout the world.[124] Although it is not true that Siegfried financed the putsch, he did give money to the Görings. Certainly Frau Wagner had always been a generous contributor to the Nazi Party, but her gifts never amounted to any great sums of money.

The evening's program was composed of four of the masterly works by Richard Wagner—"The Flying Dutchman," "Siegfried Idyll," "Tristan and Isolde," and "Tannhäuser"—and two of Siegfried's own compositions—"An allem ist Huetchen Schuld," and "Sonnenflammen." At the conclusion of the program, the audience stood as their applause brought Wagner back on stage again and again. After the concert the Wagners went to a reception held in their honor at the Harmonie Club, and Lüdecke returned to his hotel.

The next morning at nine Liebold, Ford's secretary, picked up Lüdecke at the hotel and drove him out to meet Ford. Lüdecke was rather nervous at first, for Ford rarely received visitors, but no sooner had Liebold left him in an office when Ford entered with an alert step and a cheerful greeting. Lüdecke described him as "the *Dearborn Independent* in the flesh! His clear, bright eyes and his strong face, almost free from wrinkles, did not betray his more than sixty years." After showing Lüdecke around the laboratory, Ford led him into an office, and after shutting the door, eased himself into a big armchair, put one foot up on the desk and clasped his hands over his knee. Lüdecke observed his friendly gray eyes, his firm, pleasant voice, his lean figure, and "well-shaped head" which he said showed "character and race."

Lüdecke opened the conversation with a brief outline of the aims of the Nazi movement in relation to the critical political situation in Germany. As soon as Hitler came to power, Lüdecke explained, one of his first acts would be to inaugurate the social and political program which had been advocated in the *Dearborn Independent*. But it was urgent that Hitler be successful soon or the Jews would destroy Aryan solidarity by drawing corrupt politicians into a war between the countries of the white world. Ford listened attentively, hearing things he could not learn from American newspapers, which he thought were controlled by the Jews. Money, said Lüdecke, was the only obstacle that stood between the Nazis and the fulfillment in Germany of Ford and Hitler's mutual views. He explained that the time was not ripe to unseat the Jews from their positions of power in the United States but that Germany—because of her geographic position, her historic past, and the terrific pressure of her present suffering—was the country which was to become the "torch-bearer of liberation" from the Jews.

At various points in the discussion Ford would interject curt remarks, such as "I know . . . yes, the Jews, these cunning Jews. . . ." Encouraged, Lüdecke continued to elaborate on the fact that Hitler's success or failure was a world issue, involving the future of America as much as that of any other nation. Anyone who helped the Nazis now would benefit from a business standpoint as well, Lüdecke said. Agreements could be arranged which would guarantee concessions in Germany as soon as Hitler came to power. Since a Nazi regime in Germany might lead to a change in the Russian situation, the reopening of that vast market would bring tremendous business rewards to those who had befriended Hitler.

Lüdecke's memoirs indicate that this long-winded discussion was all in vain. He says that Ford made no definite commitment of financial assistance, but considering that Lüdecke was a Nazi, one can certainly expect him to deny that Ford gave any money to Hitler. A promise from the Nazis to keep silent about the financial contribution was probably part of the bargain which Ford requested. Despite Lüdecke's denial of any transfer of money at that time, he carefully pointed out that Ford's reputation was at stake: "No man in the public eye can endow an insurgent revolutionary movement as casually as he would contribute to the Bide-A-Wee Home for Homeless Animals; there being a profound difference of opinion about what constitutes human welfare, donations in that direction may backfire."[125] Lüdecke hinted at why he could not tell the truth without hurting Ford. The Jewish boycott, Lüdecke said, "pinched him in the ledgers where even a multimillionaire is vulnerable."[126] If Ford was willing to reach in his pocket for the Nazis, they would have to be willing to keep the secret.

On their return voyage the Wagners stopped in Rome to meet Mussolini. Siegfried wrote in his diary: "He [Mussolini] is all will, strength, almost brutality. Fanatic expression in the eyes, but without the light of love as in Hitler and Ludendorff. Romans and Germans! We spoke mainly about ancient Rome. He bears some resemblance to Napoleon. Splendid race of people! A man like that rules Italy, and Bernhardchen rules us! It is really pitiful to see Germany sunk so low."[127]

Henry Ford's reward from Hitler finally came in July 1938, when on his seventy-fifth birthday he was awarded the Grand Cross of the Supreme Order of the German Eagle. Ford was the first American and the fourth person in the world to receive this medal, which was the highest decoration that could be given to any non-German citizen. Benito Mussolini, another of Hitler's financiers, had been decorated with the same honor earlier that year.[128]

The presentation was made in Ford's Dearborn office by the German Consul of Cleveland, Karl Kapp, and Consul Fritz Hailer of Detroit. Kapp placed the red silk sash over Ford's right shoulder. The sash was worn in a diagonal line from the right shoulder to the left hip where it was clasped with a gold and white cross. Kapp then pinned a large, shining star-shaped medal on Ford's white suit. The decoration was given "in recognition of [Ford's] pioneering in making motor cars available for the masses." Hitler's personal congratulatory message accompanied the award.[129] At Ford's birthday dinner on July 30, 1938, the citation was read aloud by Kapp to the 1,500 prominent Detroiters in attendance.

American Jews and the leftist press voiced strong objections to Ford's acceptance of the award from Nazi Germany. During a speech to a women's Zionist organization, the Jewish entertainer

Eddie Cantor called Ford "a damn fool for permitting the world's greatest gangster to give him a citation." He told his audience, "The more men like Ford we have, the more we must organize and fight."[130]

But the most bitter criticism came from Harold L. Ickes, Secretary of the Interior. Speaking to the Cleveland Zionist Society, he denounced Ford and other Americans "who obsequiously have accepted tokens of contemptuous distinction at a time when the bestower of them counts that day lost when he can commit no new crime against humanity."[131]

Despite all the objections, Ford was determined not to give in to their demands. He told a friend: "They [the Germans] sent me this ribbon band. They [the critics] told me to return it or else I'm not an American. I'm going to keep it."[132]

4
KIRDORF and THYSSEN

In mid-November, 1923, about a week after the fiasco of the beerhall putsch, a handful of Nazi leaders gathered clandestinely in Salzburg, which was then blanketed with a deep layer of snow. The group of exiles was composed of Hermann Esser, the young, fanatical anti-Semite; Gerhard Rossbach, the daring Free Corps leader; Lieutenant Hoffmann, the calm, sedate naval officer of the Ehrhardt Brigade; Kurt Lüdecke, the Nazis' foreign representative who had missed the putsch because he was in Italy soliciting funds; and Putzi Hanfstaengl, who had made a quick getaway when the bullets started to fly and was now slinking through the shadows with his coat collar turned up and his hat pulled down, fearing that the police were after him. They were a somber, disheartened group of souls commiserating with each other about their dire situation. Putzi moaned on and on about the thousand dollars he had lent the Party: "What good is it now to have a receipt and a mortgage on the office furniture?"[1] Since no one in the group had more than a pittance of money, they had to put their heads together to figure out how they could obtain funds to start to reorganize the Party. There could be no hope for financial support from the former members, many of whom were now unemployed, arrested, or in hiding. And it would indeed be difficult to persuade anyone else that the Nazi cause still had a future. "If we only had our hands on the money you seized in Munich!" Lüdecke lamented aloud. He was referring to the money which the others told him they had seized on the night of the putsch. A detachment of Storm Troopers had invaded the publishing plant of the Parcus brothers, who were Jewish, and "in the name of the nationalist regime," confiscated several stacks of freshly printed inflation money. The total sum was 14,605 trillion marks, for which the Parcus brothers demanded a receipt, and got it. The money was hauled to the beerhall and distributed at the rate of 2 trillion marks, which in normal times would have amounted to about eight marks, or two dollars. When the putsch collapsed, the authorities recovered the money, most of which was still tied in neat bundles.

The group of exiles then brainstormed wild schemes to solve their economic problem. Rossbach excelled with his bold and daring inspirations. He first suggested counterfeiting on a massive scale, but the others decided the plan required too much capital to enact. Rossbach then said that he and his men would be willing to carry out a series of holdups which would yield more than enough to refinance the Party. After all, early in his career, Stalin had engineered the Tiflis bank robbery and other similar "expropriations" of capitalist funds to finance the young Communist Party. But the only idea which was accepted finally was that Lüdecke would go to the United States and try to raise funds; and, as we have already seen, he would be quite successful.

Fortunately for the Nazis, Hitler had better ideas than his lieutenants on how to raise money. He had had time to do considerable thinking while he was in Landsberg prison, and he realized that if his Party were ever to come to power, he would need not only the financial backing of wealthy people but, even more important, some "friends" among the key people of the German upper class. The support of one or two powerful, prominent industrialists would be far more valuable than any amount of money acquired by counterfeiting or bank robberies. But with the sudden end of inflation in 1924, and the economy improving, and there was little reason for any industrialist to continue to support an extremist party whose leader was in jail.

Yet Hitler's original, faithful supporters remained true to him even when he was imprisoned. He received a continuous and profuse supply of gifts from women admirers: flowers, chocolates, cakes, and books. After visiting Hitler, Hanfstaengl said: "The place looked like a delicatessen. . . . You could have opened up a flower and fruit and wine shop with all the stuff stacked there. People were sending presents from all over Germany and Hitler had grown visibly fatter on the proceeds." The wealthy supporters gave something more important than food—money. "Frau Bruckmann had been one of the most generous donors. . . ."

Hitler was released from prison the day before Christmas of 1924, and he immediately set about reorganizing the Party. Several thousand followers remained loyal to him and, of course, he could count on the financial support of the Wagners, Bruckmanns, Bechsteins, and Putzi Hanfstaengl. The official refounding of the Nazi Party was a major news event and the publicity naturally drew some new supporters, among them a Munich businessman, Albert Pietsch, the director and principal owner of the Elektrochemische Werke München A.G., who contributed one thousand marks to the National Socialist Party. Pietsch later said that he was attracted by Hitler's fascinating oratory and his uncompromising attitude toward socialism and Communism. He continued to give similar contributions to Hitler from time to time, but no larger amounts of money were ever mentioned.[2]

The German economy was improving steadily. The mark was stable, the unemployment rate was dropping, the people were generally content. In fact, the years between 1924 and 1928 are now referred to by historians as the German "period of prosperity." The Nazis were able to attract few new members under such conditions. But if new recruits were scarce in 1925, money was even harder to come by. In those days the major sources of Party revenue were still the members' meager dues of a mark a month (of which only 10 percent went to Munich headquarters), collections and charges of admission for meetings, and the small profit earned from the Party newspapers and the publishing house.

How then was Hitler to win some support from the upper class and big business? During the period of prosperity following the inflation, there seemed to be little he could do at first to make the industrialists take notice of his existence. In 1926, however, a new domestic issue appeared which aroused political passions. The question concerned the expropriation of the property of the many royal dynasties that had ruled the German states up to 1918. These princely rulers, such as the King of Bavaria and the Duke of Württemberg, had not only governed local affairs but had owned vast lands, palaces, and castles.

In 1918 the revolution had failed to settle the question of the deposed dynasties' properties. They were neither confiscated nor were any other arrangements made officially. The settlement had been left to the individual state governments. A few of them took over the property of the princes but "only in order to keep it secure pending negotiations." Prussia, for example, confiscated the Hohenzollern property and "temporarily" put it under the administration of the state. Kaiser Wilhelm immediately dispatched a letter to the Prussian government in which he said: "I have renounced the throne in the manner which had been suggested to me by the government. Doing this I had expected that the government . . . would free my own and my family's property."[3]

However, once the Weimar Constitution was ratified, its Article 153 established the rights of private property and also made the property of the dynasties safe from expropriation. Then in 1926 the Communists and socialists introduced a bill in the Reichstag demanding expropriation of the princely dynasties without compensation and further demanded the issue be settled by a plebiscite. Big business was generally indifferent if not opposed to the interests of the princes. However, the crucial question of the plebiscite for them was the protection of private property. Most non-Marxist parties saw the socialist-Communist bill as an attack against the right of property. Thus, by opposing the expropriation of the princes, the nonsocialist parties were primarily acting to protect private property.

In order to have any hope of ever getting support from wealthy individuals, the aristocrats, or big business, Hitler had to oppose the expropriation of the princes. Yet, the matter was not so simple, because a considerable number of Nazis, led by Gregor Strasser, were in favor of expropriation.

Strasser was a man with a strong personality who had joined the Nazi Party in 1920 and soon became the local leader in Lower Bavaria. He was a big, powerfully built man, a reasonably good speaker, and very able organizer. After Hitler, Strasser was the second most powerful man in the Nazi Party. In many ways his background was similar to that of Hitler's. Strasser was born in Bavaria, the son of a petty official. He volunteered for the Army during World War I and was awarded the Iron Cross, First Class. Following the war, he fought under the command of General von

Epp against the Munich Soviet Republic in May 1919. The next year he got married and opened his own pharmacy in the small town of Landshut. His hatred of the Communists led him to organize the town's veterans into a military battalion. At the end of 1920, he joined the Nazis and soon became the district leader of the Party in Lower Bavaria. He was arrested for participating in the Munich putsch, but was released when he was elected to the Bavarian Landtag. Due to his organizational abilities and his skill as a writer and speaker, Strasser was appointed by Hitler as the leader of the Nazis in the north of Germany.

A large, heavy-set, jovial man, Strasser was three years younger than Hitler. His good sense of humor, friendly personality, and willingness to compromise was balanced by a ferocious determination, conviction in his beliefs, and willingness to fight. As a speaker, he could roar like a lion and intimidate those who stood in his way. He was always proud to tell how he confronted the representative of the soldiers' soviet in Landshut when returning from World War I with his troops: "There he stood, the lousy bum, and chattered and clattered on with his stupid swine grunts that he had learned by heart about the International, the victorious proletariat, the bloodthirsty generals and warmongers, the sweat-squeezing capitalists and stockbrokers. I sat up there on my nag, which I secretly nudged against the guy so that he was always having to step backward again and again, and I said nothing and slowly collected a whole mouthful of spit. Finally the guy got to the end and screamed out: 'Deliver up your weapons! Rip up your flags and insignia! Vote for the Soviet of Soldiers!' And by then I was ready: I let him have the whole mouthful of spit right in the middle of his face; I *flooded* the bum away. And then I gave the order 'Battery . . . trot!' and we marched back into Landshut the same way we had marched out in 1914."[4]

Although Strasser may have seemed rather bearlike, he also had a more sensitive, calm side to his character. Some of his friends were writers and artists. He appreciated good poetry and could even read Homer in the original Greek. Strasser was not the type who would shrink from a fight or hesitate to take a risk, but he also knew when to compromise and when to negotiate. For example, unlike many leading Nazis, he was willing to associate with other völkish parties. In 1924, he proposed the merging of the Nazis and the German Racist Party (the DVFP) into one party, called the National Socialist Freedom Party. (Upon Hitler's release from prison, Strasser and the Nazis withdrew from the Freedom Party.)[5]

Early in 1925 Strasser gave up his pharmacist's practice in Landshut and devoted himself exclusively to building up the Nazi movement in northern Germany and the industrial cities of the Rhineland. With the help of his brother Otto, who was a talented journalist, he made rapid progress. Hitler quickly recognized that the growing influence of Gregor Strasser was a threat to his control over the Party. Moreover, the Strassers were inclined to take the "socialist" part of the Party program rather seriously, advocating the nationalization of heavy industry and large landholdings. Hitler, for both strategic and ideological reasons was against this movement to the left. He did not want to spoil his chances for an alliance with the ruling elite.

On November 22, 1925, Strasser called a meeting of the Party Gauleiters of northern Germany in Hanover. Along with most of the Gauleiters, Strasser was restive under the control of Munich and was opposed to Hitler on many important questions. Feelings against Hitler were running high and crystallized around the question of whether or not the property of the former German royal houses should be expropriated. Strasser and the north German leaders wanted the Nazi Party to stand behind the Social Democratic government's move to expropriate the princes' property. This view clashed with statements Hitler had already made to the effect that the Party was against the government's plan because the possessions of the deposed royal houses were their own private property.

Hitler had called the move for expropriation a "Jewish swindle." The fact that many Jews, being property owners, favored the side of the princes meant nothing to him. Naturally, he did not mention publicly that at the time he was receiving fifteen hundred marks a month, a substantial part of his personal income, from the divorced Duchess of Sachsen-Anhalt.

All those present at the Hanover meeting voted to follow Strasser's policy in favor of expropriation, except Gottfried Feder and Dr. Robert Ley, Gauleiter of Cologne. Hitler responded to the challenge of Strasser and his followers by summoning a conference of the entire Party leadership, on February 14, 1926, in the Bavarian town of Bamberg. Otto Strasser gave an account of this

conference, asserting that February 14 was a weekday and therefore none of the north German and Rhineland leaders except
Gregor Strasser and Joseph Goebbels were able to attend.[6] But the
assertion is false; the fourteenth was a Sunday and everyone who
was anyone in the north German movement was there, including
all the rebellious Gauleiters who had met in Hanover a few
months before.[7]

Chosen especially by Hitler as the site of the meeting, Bamberg
was a picturesque little medieval town in northern Bavaria. The
population of the region was generally conservative so the Nazis
would not have to worry about disruptions from the socialists. To
impress the northern delegates Hitler transported hundreds of
Storm Troopers and Party supporters from Munich. As they arrived at the railroad station, the delegates were greeted by an S.A.
band and a Brownshirt unit. Outside the station there were
several Party automobiles decorated with swastika banners waiting to drive them to the meeting. Strasser's followers were not
used to such treatment; they normally took the streetcar or
walked where they were going. Outside the meeting hall itself
enthusiastic crowds cheered and uniformed S.A. men stood at
attention along the street. Everywhere the delegates looked there
were red swastika flags fluttering in the breeze.

The Party representatives from northern Germany were impressed, as Hitler had planned. They were rarely able to wear
their brown shirts or display the swastika flag and usually they
even had to hold their meetings in some quiet out-of-the-way
place to prevent an attack by the Communists.

Now Hitler was ready to come to grips with all his opponents
within the Party, but only Gregor Strasser spoke up against him.
The two protagonists fought out their differences in a day-long
debate on Socialism versus Nationalism, and the expropriation of
the princes' property.

In a speech that lasted several hours Hitler denounced the
advocates of expropriation as deceitful because they never mentioned expropriating the property of the Jewish lords of banking
and the stock exchange. He admitted the princes should not
receive anything they had no right to, but what justly belonged to
them should not be taken from them. The National Socialist
Party stood for the concepts of private property and justice. His
south German followers applauded these sentiments and were

hesitantly joined by a few north Germans. Then Hitler began to tear up the whole leftist program of the Strasser group point for point, by comparing it with the Party program of 1920. Could any true Nazi deviate from the founding document of the Party? Would it not be a betrayal of those comrades who died for the movement in the November putsch? Shall we create chaos, asked Hitler, or shall we "legally" worm our way to power? Will the Party rule the masses or the masses rule the Party?

Since they had given public endorsement to expropriation, Gregor Strasser and Goebbels were humiliated. After the meeting Goebbels wrote in his diary: "What kind of a Hitler is this? A reactionary? Amazingly clumsy and uncertain. Russian question: altogether beside the point. . . . Our duty is the destruction of Bolshevism. Bolshevism is a Jewish creation! . . . a question of not weakening private property (sic!). Horrible!"[8] Although the left-wing Nazis were distraught by the results of the meeting, they bowed to Hitler's will.

Hitler's success in stifling dissent and debate within the Nazi Party turned out to be more important for him than the results of the plebiscite. To pass the proposed bill, approval of a majority of all eligible voters (approximately 39½ million votes) was necessary. But when the people went to the polls on June 20, 1926, only 15,551,218 votes instead of the required majority were registered in favor of expropriation without compensation. However, the fact that the Nazis opposed expropriation was hardly noticed by big business, because the Nazis had the support of very few people compared to the established moderate parties. Of course, if Hitler had not been able to control the left-wing Nazis on the expropriation issue, he might well have lost the help of the few individuals whose support he had, like the Wagners, the Bruckmanns, and the Bechsteins.

In spite of Hitler's several wealthy friends, one of the best providers for the Party was Julius Streicher, who had a large following in Nuremberg and sometimes slightly "murky" sources of money. (Streicher was said to have privately boasted that one of his most reliable contributors was a wealthy Party comrade, whose wife was his mistress). But it was not until 1927, when the period of prosperity was drawing to a close, that Hitler won his first new supporter from among the big industrialists, and that was Emil Kirdorf.

Emil Kirdorf was born in 1847 near Düsseldorf into a family of textile manufacturers.[9] He began his business career during the hectic age of German industrial expansion and helped found Gelsenkirchener Bergwerks A.G., which became a very successful coal-mining firm. Kirdorf was an extremely hard worker; even on cold winter nights a light could be seen burning in his office long after the other executives had gone home. In 1892 he was made the managing director of the Gelsenkirchener Company. A year later he played a central role in the cartelization of the bituminous coal industry and became the director of the powerful Rhenish-Westphalian Coal Syndicate. His short stature, bald head, and round wire-rimmed glasses gave him a rather unimpressive appearance, but in spite of this handicap and in spite of his aggressive and cantankerous personality, he was recognized as one of the best speakers among Germany's leading businessmen. In the years before 1914, he spoke frequently in defense of the cartels, denounced the demands of the trade unions for collective bargaining, and criticized any plans to extend the government's role in social welfare beyond the programs adopted by Bismarck.

His views on labor matters were so reactionary that he called the policies of the Imperial government "dangerously radical." Kaiser Wilhelm himself was responsible for this, according to Kirdorf, because he had allowed Bismarck's antisocialist law to lapse. Once when discussing the Kaiser's toleration of the Social Democrats, Kirdorf became so agitated that he turned red in the face, began to shout at the top of his voice, and pounded his fist on the table, sending a wine glass crashing to the floor. His feud with the Kaiser was carried so far that he refused to appear at any social functions where the monarch was present.

During World War I Kirdorf belonged to the Vaterlandspartei, the organization of the uncompromising annexationists. He was the only important industrialist who endorsed even the most radical demands of territorial expansion put forward by the High Command. Like many others who were later drawn to Hitler, Kirdorf felt the German defeat in 1918 was caused by treason at home. When hundreds of striking workers wearing red armbands blocked access to one of his company's buildings during the revolutionary period of 1919, Kirdorf displayed considerable courage by walking straight through the crowd alone with the black-white-and red Imperial colors pinned to his lapel. He thought the Weimar Republic was merely a continuation of the "betrayal" of 1918 and referred to it as the "rule of the rabble." Becoming a member of the German Nationalist Party, he supported its extremist wing, led by Alfred Hugenberg, and was among the group of wealthy men who provided much of the capital for Hugenberg's press empire.

In 1927 the eighty-year-old Kirdorf was quite perturbed and pessimistic about the German political situation. Hindenburg, his wartime hero, was now President; but to Kirdorf's distress, the old Field Marshal gave his approval to the Locarno agreements, which guaranteed the Franco-German frontiers, and called for Germany's entry into the League of Nations. For a time the Nationalist Party remained in opposition on this question, but in 1927, anxious to gain a position in the coalition cabinet, they too agreed to support Stresemann's conciliatory foreign policy.* What was still worse, from Kirdorf's point of view, was that the Nationalist Party yielded to the other parties of the coalition and agreed not to oppose new legislation limiting the hours of the workday in industry and establishing a national program of unemployment insurance. Kirdorf did not have much understanding of the problems and sufferings of the common laborer. Although he came into contact with workers and servants daily, he always growled at them in the tone of a drill sergeant addressing recruits and avoided any personal familiarity. Believing in the survival of the fittest, Kirdorf generally thought that those who were unemployed were either lazy or stupid and deserved no help from the state.

In the spring of 1926 Hitler began a campaign to win support among the German business community. He spoke to numerous "private" gatherings of businessmen, and was thus able to elude the Prussian government's ban against his speaking in public.[10] The disillusioned Kirdorf heard Hitler speak for the first time at such an appearance in Essen in the spring of 1927. Kirdorf was already familiar with the Nazi Party, for he had attended one of their rallies in Munich in 1923 while there on a business trip, but on that occasion another speaker had been substituted for Hitler

---

*Gustav Stresemann was Chancellor from August to November, 1923; and Foreign Minister from 1923–1929.

at the last moment. Many of the important props that usually accompanied a Hitler speech were missing from the Essen gathering; there were no swastika flags; bands, or uniformed Storm Troopers. Hitler, dressed in an ordinary blue suit; looked very unimpressive as he walked through the stuffy and over-crowded lecture room to the podium, but once he began to speak a silence settled over the room. Kirdorf then heard his own fears, beliefs, and hates expressed in a new dynamic way that made a lasting impression on him. Kirdorf had long lamented the weak character of most nationalist politicians, and at the end of the meeting Kirdorf was so favorably impressed that he pushed his way forward through the crowd to shake the speaker's hand.

Although he had sympathized with almost everything Hitler had said, Kirdorf did not immediately join the National Socialist Party. There was too much class difference separating the great industrial figure from the lower-middle-class Nazi movement. It was only through a "respectable" introduction that Hitler and Kirdorf finally had a personal meeting at which the old coal tycoon was completely won over to the Nazi cause. This introduction was provided by Frau Elsa Bruckmann, who was always soliciting support for Hitler in high society. She wrote to Kirdorf in the summer of 1927 and told him that "as an enthusiastic follower of the Führer, she had made it her mission to bring him [Hitler] together with the leading men of industry."[11] She further explained that a mutual friend, Prince Karl zu Loewenstein (also a Nazi sympathizer), had said to her that Kirdorf would be interested in the Nazi Party.

The meeting between Hitler and Kirdorf took place on July 4, 1927, at the Bruckmann home in Munich. Hitler, who was a frequent guest of the Bruckmanns, found it easy to relax amidst the plush setting of antiques and fine old paintings. He and Kirdorf were soon settled in comfortable lounge chairs overlook-ing the garden. Their conversation lasted for four hours. Hitler spoke much of the time, refreshing himself only occasionally with a sip of cool lemonade. Kirdorf listened thoughtfully and asked frequent questions; every so often he would scratch his bald head and adjust his wire-rimmed glasses. Once or twice during the discussion Hitler became so involved in the point he was explaining that he jumped up from his chair and paced back and forth. On the whole, however, his manners were excellent.

There was a free flow of conversation between the two men and never once did Hitler raise his voice.

The old industrialist found himself in agreement with Hitler on most important questions and was especially interested in the Nazi leader's decisive plans for political action. Ten years later Kirdorf commented on his first meeting with Hitler in an interview for the *Preussische Zeitung:* "The inexorable logic and clear conciseness of his train of thought filled me with such enthusiasm with what he said. I asked the Führer to write a pamphlet on the topics he had discussed with me. I then distributed this pamphlet in business and industrial circles . . . . Shortly after our Munich conversation and as a result of the pamphlet written by the Führer and distributed by me, several meetings took place between the Führer and leading industrial personalities."[12]

This interview and one other in the *Berliner Lokal-Anzeiger*[13] are the only sources which mentioned the existence of this pamphlet. Yet in neither article was there any mention of its title or contents. Entitled *The Road to Resurgence (Der Weg zum Wiederaufstieg)*, the pamphlet was printed privately by the Hugo Bruckmann publishing house and was distributed quietly by Kirdorf in the summer of 1927. It was intended only for a limited and exclusive audience—the nation's leading industrialists— because the conservative parties, had they found out about it, could have warned businessmen against it. However, another reason the Nazis wanted to keep the pamphlet *top secret* was the even greater danger of the pamphlet's falling into the hands of the Marxists: Hitler's Machiavellian tone about pacifying the workers to prevent a social transformation of society would have made quite an exposé.

The fact is well known that Hitler tried to gain support from among the business community after the depression had destroyed the confidence of many industrialists in the Weimar Republic. However, this pamphlet, which remained secret until discovered by an American historian, Henry A. Turner, in 1966, makes it obvious that Hitler had prepared careful arguments with which to woo the leaders of heavy industry well before the depression. What Hitler wrote and discussed with Kirdorf during the Republic's period of prosperity was almost identical to what he later said in his famous speech to the Düsseldorf Industry Club in January 1932 during the middle of the depression.

The cause of Germany's problems was the lack of national unity, Hitler claimed. The weaknesses of liberal democracy had permitted such an alien and unnatural doctrine as Marxism to divide the German people into two hostile factions. Naturally the nation could not even begin to think of taking an aggressive position in foreign affairs when it could not count on solidarity at home. Hitler said only a new inspiring political philosophy could bridge the internal divisions which prevented Germany from regaining her place in the world market.

Germany, Hitler said, must become "a nation firmly welded into a single common community of interests," one which recognizes that the survival and future of all nations and peoples depend on three "fundamental principles":

1. The merit of their race;
2. The extent to which they accord significance to the role of the individual personality;
3. Recognition of the fact that life in this universe is synonymous with struggle.

"It is, however," said Hitler, "precisely the repudiation of these three great laws to which I attribute our present-day decline rather than to all the petty failures of our current political leadership.

"Instead of raising aloft the merits of race and nation, millions of our people pay homage to the idea of internationality.

"The strength and genius of the individual person are, in line with the absurd nature of democracy, being set aside in favor of majority rule, which amounts to nothing more than weakness and stupidity.

"And rather than recognize and affirm the necessity of struggle, people are preaching theories of pacifism, reconciliation among nations and eternal peace.

"These three outrages against mankind, which we can recognize through all history as the true signs of decadence in races and states, and whose most zealous propagandist is the international Jew, are the characteristic symptoms of Marxism which is progressively gaining a hold on our people."[14]

Hitler's remark about the "international Jew" was the only blatantly anti-Semitic comment in the pamphlet. By connecting the Jew with Marxism he led the reader to believe that any non-communist German Jew would be treated like everyone else. There were none of Hitler's usual kind of comments about the "hooked nose kikes with smelly black caftans and greasy hair." Hitler was obviously making every effort to appear reasonable and respectable, and he undoubtedly knew that Kirdorf like most German industrialists was not an anti-Semite.

Attempting to seem as moderate as possible, Hitler was in a difficult position: He did not want his proposals to seem too "revolutionary," yet he could not water his ideas down too much lest they lose their uniqueness and logical dynamic, making it seem as if he were nothing more than another conservative nationalist. In 1927, when the pamphlet was written, the German economy was enjoying a period of relative prosperity. It is not an easy matter to interest businessmen in the criticisms of a healthy economy; however, Hitler pointed out that the "so-called prosperity" was only temporary, warning that unless Germany's basic political problems were solved there could be no long-term economic stability. Unlike the usual speeches or *Mein Kampf,* where he dealt with economic problems only in general terms, here he spoke of the questions of unemployment, unfavorable balance of trade, and other concrete economic issues.

In one of the most important passages of *The Road to Resurgence* Hitler gave a surprisingly accurate critique of Germany's overall economic position in relation to other world powers: "Since our own soil cannot possibly sustain the sum total of our population, we are forced to leave the domestic sphere of our economy and adjust our production to the export market. The most difficult problem for the future, however, will by no means be in increasing production, but rather in the organization of marketing and sales. In addition to Germany, there are three other countries in Europe which in nourishing their citizens depend on a set of preconditions similar to those of Germany. England, France, and Italy are dependent on exports. Indeed, even America is leaving the purely domestic economic circuit and is emerging as an industrial competitor on a worldwide scale, helped, to be sure, by sources of raw materials that are . . . just as cheap as they are inexhaustible. Especially in the sphere of the motorization of the world, America appears to be cornering the whole world market. Not to be overlooked is the fact that in many importing countries industry is also slowly beginning to develop.

... In addition, the outside world has succeeded in breaking down a number of German monopolies on the world market ... thanks to the coercive restraints of wartime and as a result of the peace treaties. ... Finally, however, the economies of the world's great industrial states are backed up by their political power. And the decisive factor in economic conflict in this world has never yet rested in the skill and know-how of the various competitors, but rather in the might of the sword they could wield to tip the scales for their businesses and hence their lives."[15]

In other words, Germany was encircled by the empires or trading monopolies of Britain, France, and their allies and was slowly being economically strangled. Access to world markets was even more restricted than before World War I.[16] The decisive factor in Germany's struggle for economic survival would be the military might she could put behind her demands for a fairer share of world markets. Before it be thought that Hitler's ideas on international policy were too extremist or radical to appeal to the industrialists, a comparison should be made with what Hitler said in his pamphlet and the speech Gustav Stresemann delivered on December 14, 1925, at the Arbeitsgemeinschaft der Landsmannschaften (a worker's organization). In the statements to both Stresemann and Hitler there is the same determination not to accept the Versailles system, to regain great-power status, and to change the eastern borders at the first possible opportunity, by means of war if necessary.[17]

Absent from the pamphlet are the radical semisocialist economic proposals outlined in the twenty-five points of the original Nazi Party program (such as the demand for "profit sharing in large industries"), or the sharp castigation of bourgeois society found in *Mein Kampf*. Instead, Hitler tried to reassure his readers that he was opposed to any real transformation of the German economic or social structure. By praising the "strength and genius of individual personality," he hoped the industrialists would make a favorable association in their minds between the idea of private enterprise and the authoritarian principle of the Nazi Party. As clearly as possible Hitler tried to indicate that there was no reason to fear revolutionary socialism from the Nazis. Hitler knew that for many businessmen even the word socialism was enough to bring to mind the revolution of 1918, the mobs waving red flags, and looting by Communist requisitioning detachments, and upper-class hostages being lined up against walls and shot down by Marxist executioners. Revolutionary Marxism had nothing to do with "true" socialism. His Party, he wrote, had succeeded in uniting the concepts of nationalism and socialism which had previously been thought incompatible. They were the first to recognize that the ideas of nationalism and "true" socialism were in their "highest form the same thing: love of the Fatherland and the German people.

"The National Socialist movement," said Hitler, "furthermore recognizes that complete incorporation of the so-called Fourth Estate [the proletariat] into the national community is the most essential precondition to . . . the establishment of a cohesive national body." It was his goal, he explained, to win the workers away from the control of their "international and mainly un-German seducers and leaders." To do so, a nationalist program would have to be balanced with a few welfare-state measures. Such measures, he warned, were the price that would have to be paid to lead the masses back to the nationalist camp. This, however, was a small cost, he claimed, in comparison with the "immense gain" to be derived from an "all-embracing national community."

Because he was attracted by Hitler's promise to win the working class away from the Marxist trade-union leaders, Kirdorf finally decided to join the Nazi Party.[18] On a warm summer day, August 1, 1927, Kirdorf drove to the Party headquarters; there he took an oath of allegiance and received his membership card, which was numbered 71032.[19]

As a new Party member he immediately began campaigning among his industrial colleagues. His knowledge of the views and political sympathies of most every important German industrial figure enabled him to distribute Hitler's pamphlet most effectively. He sent it to some of his friends through the mail, accompanied by a short note and followed up by a telephone call; he gave it quietly to others while chatting after a business meeting or social occasion. Because they were personally given the pamphlet by a respected member of the business community, many of the recipients probably felt obliged to read it; this certainly would not have been the case if Hitler had distributed it himself.

Within a month or two Kirdorf's work began to yield results. On October 26, 1927, he was able to bring together fourteen leading industrialists in his home, the Villa Streithof, for a meeting with Hitler. Considering the skepticism, if not hostility, with which most businessmen then viewed the Nazi Party, the arrangement of this gathering was no small feat. Hitler, who had arrived slightly before the other guests, was somewhat apprehensive as he watched one long, black limousine after another glide up to the front entrance. He was even more uncomfortable during the introductions, handshaking, and small talk. Once everyone was quietly seated in the overstuffed armchairs in Kirdorf's living room, Hitler hesitantly began to explain his ideas. He spoke slowly and carefully at first, but then he began to relax and his delivery acquired the kind of spellbinding quality for which he was famous. Although he used his hands to gesture occasionally, he retained the style of an intimate discussion between colleagues and never became overdramatic or theatrical. According to Kirdorf's memoirs, the meeting was a success: "All the participants were without question deeply moved by his [Hitler's] stirring statements and not even objections regarding the socialistic and tactically erroneous anti-Semitic aspects of his position could detract from the impression that here had spoken a man with firm patriotic beliefs and a fully conscious conviction of his calling to rescue the Fatherland."[20] From Hitler's point of view, however, the meeting was probably only a "qualified success." It is highly doubtful if he won any new converts to his Party, but as Kirdorf's statement indicated, his guests left the meeting considering the Nazi leader as an intelligent and very articulate political figure rather than just another fanatic of the extreme Right.

Although Hitler's secret pamphlet was received with interest by many conservative business leaders, few of them considered his proposals seriously. Germany's economic position was not yet desperate enough. Even heavy industry, which was in more difficult circumstances than the rest of the economy, was not about to support such radical political changes unless no other alternatives were available. For the time being the industrialists were willing to continue to work through the democratic system of the Weimar Republic. The various interest groups within big business—heavy industry, light industry, finance, commerce, etc.—had their own methods of exerting influence on politics. Even though these methods were not as absolute as those suggested by Hitler, as long as the economic situation was not too serious they would suffice.

Kirdorf's involvement with the Nazi Party was not completely one-sided. In addition to his efforts to propagate Hitler's cause, he was also interested in influencing the Party in a more pro-capitalist direction. The problem here was not so much with Hitler as with the local Party organization in the Ruhr that had a strong socialist streak in it.

One night at a dinner party old Kirdorf was seated alongside the attractive widow of a wealthy coal-mine owner. During their conversation the widow told him she had an intelligent young "protégé" whom she was trying to help. The young man, she explained, was an avid follower of Hitler. Perhaps Kirdorf could get him a position in the Nazi Party? The old industrialist thought for a moment and then told the lady that he just might be able to help. The job he had in mind, he said, would be of great service not only to the Fatherland but to German industry as well.

The lady agreed to send her young "friend" to talk with Kirdorf, and the next morning he presented himself punctually at the coal tycoon's estate. He was a tall, slim man about twenty-five years old who wore his straight, dark-brown hair slicked back in an effort to look like Rudolf Valentino. His name was Josef Terboven. He was fairly well educated and for a while had worked as a bank clerk but was now unemployed. All of his expenses, however, were taken care of by the attractive widow in return for his services as her lover.

Kirdorf was a fairly good judge of character. After a few questions, he recognized the young man's usefulness. Kirdorf's proposition was simple: He would help Terboven to secure a high post in the Nazi Party if the latter would agree to use his position in the best interest of heavy industry. Terboven consented. Otto Strasser, who worked with Terboven from the time he joined the Party, later wrote: "I remember him as a rather hard-working Party member who seemed to have a good deal of spending money on his person at all times. Since most of our members were poor, his frequent small gifts to them were not without effect—and at the first election he was voted leader of the Essen district. From this new position as one of the leaders in the Nazi Party, Terboven did much to bring Hitler and the industrialists together."[21] Kirdorf now had his own representative within the Party itself.

Although Kirdorf had begun campaigning for Hitler with enthusiasm in the summer of 1927, he remained in the Party for only a little over a year.[22] On August 12, 1928, he wrote an angry letter to Munich headquarters submitting his resignation from the Party. His alienation from the Nazi movement had been building for several months. He was so irritated by the Nazis' attacks on other patriotic groups, such as the Nationalist Party and the Stahlhelm, that he voted for the Nationalist Party in the Reichstag elections of May 1928. In addition, he was disturbed about the "leftist elements" within the Nazi movement. Hitler had made it clear in their personal conversations and in his pamphlet, *The Road to Resurgence,* that there was no reason to fear revolutionary socialism from the Nazis. However, there were many other spokesmen of the Party, such as Gregor Strasser and Gottfried Feder, who still believed that one of the aims of National Socialism was to destroy the bourgeois system.

Die Neue Front, a small, leftist Nazi newspaper published in the Ruhr, printed a bitter attack on the Rhenish-Westphalian Coal Syndicate in August 1928. Although Kirdorf was annoyed by the anticapitalist statements of Gottfried Feder and other leftist Nazis, he usually managed to ignore them; but this attack on the bituminous coal cartel was the last straw. The old industrialist considered his role as a founder and head of the board of overseers of the coal cartel as one of his proudest accomplishments. In his letter of resignation to the Munich headquarters, Kirdorf complained that the article in *Die Neue Front,* by inciting the workers against the capitalists, was using the same methods as the Marxist trade unions.[23]

After his resignation from the Nazi movement, Kirdorf rejoined the Nationalist Party, which had elected his old friend Hugenberg as its chairman only a few months earlier. Although Kirdorf was no longer a Nazi, his personal friendship with Hitler remained unchanged. In August of 1929 Kirdorf was invited to the annual Party rally in Nuremberg as Hitler's guest of honor. He and his wife stood in the reviewing stand next to Hitler, watching thousands of Brownshirts marching through the medieval streets of Nuremberg with their black-white-and-red swastika flags fluttering in the breeze. Tones of martial music filled the air from the numerous Nazi bands taking part in the parade, but perhaps the most awesome moments came when the bands would occasion-

ally fall silent and the pounding thunder of thousands of marching feet would roar up out of the narrow cobblestone streets. It
was a spectacle not easily forgotten. Afterward Kirdorf wrote a
letter of appreciation to Hitler which was immediately printed in
the *Völkischer Beobachter*.

"Dear Herr Hitler: On our return home, my wife and I are eager
to express our thanks to you for asking us to attend the convention of your party held between August 2 and 4, and for the
elevating impressions we obtained there. Our intention was to
express this thanks to you at the end of the session and for that
reason we were in the Deutscher Hof [hotel] where, unfortunately, we awaited you in vain, since without doubt your time was
taken up with the brutal attacks of the Communists on your
faithful party members and with concern for the protection of the
latter. . . . We shall never forget how overwhelmed we were in
attending the memorial celebration for the World War dead and
the dedication of the banners in the Luitpold Grove, at the sight of
your troops marching by on the Hauptmarkt, of thousands and
thousands of your supporters, their eyes bright with enthusiasm,
who hung on your lips and cheered you. The sight of the endless
crowd, cheering you and stretching out their hands to you at the
end of the parade, was positively overwhelming. At this moment
I, who am filled with despair by the degeneration of our masses
and the failure of our bourgeois circles toward the future of
Germany, suddenly realized why you believe and trust unflinch-
ingly in the fulfillment of the task you have set yourself, and,
conscious of your goal, continue on your way, regardless how
many sacrifices it may demand of you and your supporters. Any
man who in these days, dominated by a brutal destruction of the
patriotic qualities, could gather together and chain to himself
such a troop of nationally-minded racial comrades, ready for every
sacrifice, is entitled to nourish this confidence. You may be proud
of the honors and homages done you; there is hardly a crowned
head who receives their equal. My wife and I are happy to have
been able to witness them. . . .

"Anyone who was privileged to attend this session will, even
though he may doubt or decisively reject particular points in your
party program, nevertheless recognize the importance of your
movement for the rehabilitation of our German fatherland and
wish it success. With this wish, which we utter from a full heart,

there rises in me even a small hope that it may be realized. Even if my doubts in the future of the German people cannot be entirely dispelled, since my observation, extending years back into the Bismarckian golden age of Germany and further, has shown that the German bourgeoisie are nationally speaking at a low level such as can be found in no other country, yet I have taken with me from the Nuremberg Congress the consoling certainty that numerous circles will sacrifice themselves to prevent the doom of Germanism from being accomplished in the dishonorable, un- dignified way I previously feared. With true German greetings from my wife and self; in friendship, Your Kirdorf."[24]

Public praise for Hitler was only one side of the coin: Behind the scenes Kirdorf was still trying to exercise an influence over the Nazis. When it looked as if the socialist-minded followers of the Strassers were getting out of hand, Kirdorf sent for Josef Terboven, now the Nazi Party leader in Essen. Terboven was given 5,000 marks and was told to take the money and go to Munich at once, and tell Hitler that Kirdorf wanted to see him urgently.

Late the next night Terboven returned, accompanied by Hitler and Rudolf Hess. Only the butler of Villa Streithof was awake to greet them; he showed them to their rooms and told them that his master would see them at breakfast. In the morning the three men had breakfast with old Kirdorf; it was obvious that he was not in a good mood. They all remained seated while the table was cleared.

The large dining room of the Kirdorf villa looked beautiful that morning. The rich oak paneling extending from floor to ceiling gently reflected the warm rays of the morning sun. Along the one wall on a massive sideboard the brightly polished silver service picked up and reflected the glowing reds and blues of the deep- piled Persian carpet. The air in the room smelled fresh from the newly cut flowers in a crystal bowl that stood in the center of the long dining table.

The four men grouped at one end of the table had no time to notice the beauty of their surroundings, however. They were deeply engrossed in conversation. Kirdorf, who never wasted words any more than he wasted money, came quickly to the point. He wanted to know whether or not Hitler could control the entire National Socialist Party. If he thought he could, just how did he propose to do it? If he could not, then no more need be said. Hitler responded in a tone of thoughtful sincerity. He said he needed only three things to fully enforce his authority of the Party.

"What are those three things?" asked Kirdorf bluntly.

"I want a little time, a lot of money, and the ban against my political activities in Prussia lifted."

"And if I give you all those," Kirdorf asked quietly, "what would the Party line be then?"

"You and the other industrialists," Hitler said slowly, as if he were weighing the impact of every word, "could dictate the Party line in so far as it affected you and the properties you own."[25]

From that day forth Hitler basically lived up to this agreement, not out of a sense of honesty, of course, but because he still needed the support of Kirdorf and his friends.

Hitler continued to be invited to the Kirdorf home where he had a chance to explain his ideas to many more prominent industrialists.[26] In 1930, rumors that he was still a Nazi forced Kirdorf to issue a press statement in which he clarified his position. He explained that he had broken with the Nazi movement because of the views of the Party's spokesmen in the Ruhr. He went on to emphasize, however, that his friendship and admiration for Hitler was not at all affected by his disagreement with the "socialistic elements" of the Nazi Party.[27] Kirdorf continued his contacts with Hitler because he hoped for the formation of a "national" bloc that would unite all the political forces of the Right. In his opinion, the Nazis, being representative of the lower and middle classes, would be an indispensable component of such a new rightist alliance. Moreover, if Hitler brought his views in line with those of the more orthodox nationalists, it would mean the end of the "leftist elements" within the National Socialist Party.

Surprisingly, the resignation of one of his most notable supporters caused Hitler little difficulty. Most people continued to consider Kirdorf as a supporter of Hitler, if not of the Nazi Party, so there was no loss of prestige as would have occurred under other circumstances.

Contrary to popular opinion, Kirdorf's personal fortune was small, at least in comparison with the fortunes of other industrial tycoons. Being a self-made man who was one of the first great managers in German industrial history, most of his money was earned from his salary as a managing director of the Gelsenkirchener Bergwerks A.G. For a man in his position, his style of living was modest, and although he was a fanatical supporter of various right-wing causes, his donations to them were never overly generous. His personal contributions to the Pan-German League usually amounted to RM 1,000 every two or three months and it is assumed that his donations to Hitler were of a similar sum.[28]

Even if Kirdorf did not contribute a tremendous sum of his own money to Hitler, there remains the question of whether or not he channeled funds of the coal industry to the Nazis. According to some historians he persuaded the powerful Rhenish-Westphalian Coal Syndicate, Germany's most important mine-owners association, to set aside fifty pfennigs (thirteen cents) per ton of coal sold as a subsidy to the National Socialists. If true, this would have meant a steady annual donation of about RM 60,000,000 (approximately $14,500,000). Rumors of these contributions began circulating in the thirties.[29]

It was only in July of 1947, however, that the Rhenish-Westphalian Coal Syndicate was again given serious attention, when Hugo Stinnes's son, Hugo Stinnes, Jr., was tried by a denazification court. Stinnes, Jr., stated that the Rhenish-Westphalian Coal Syndicate had definitely not contributed one mark to Hitler before he came to power in 1933. Albert Janus, who had formerly been on the board and director general of the Rhenish-Westphalian Coal Syndicate, testified in Stinnes, Jr.'s, defense that from his intimate knowledge of the syndicate's operation the charge about the fifty pfennigs donation was "completely untrue."

Of course, critics said it was only natural that Stinnes, Jr., and Janus would issue denials. However, Stinnes, Jr., and Janus received support from an unexpected source, the Works Council of the Rhenish-Westphalian Coal Syndicate. The Works Council was made up of the representatives of the miners. Since these representatives had access to the books of the syndicate, they would have been negligent in their duties if they had either failed to detect that 60 million marks a year were going to Hitler, or, having discovered this huge diversion of funds, had not objected. A press release was given on August 5, 1947: "The Works Council feels impelled to issue the following declaration: affidavits were taken from those workers and employees who served the Rhenish-Westphalian Coal Syndicate from the period before National Socialism to the present and who had unhampered access to the books. . . . It has been established that the rumors . . . in the press about a special assessment by the Rhenish-Westphalian Coal Syndicate in favor of the Nazi Party are without any foundation whatsoever."[30]

It might have been thought that this testimony by the representatives of the workers themselves would have silenced the rumor once and for all. However, a Berlin Communist newspaper, *Neues Deutschland,* on August 8, 1947, claimed that the assessment for Hitler was five and not fifty pfennigs and that it was raised at a secret directors' meeting. It became a matter of public knowledge, they said, because the state of Prussia owned some of the coal mines and was therefore compelled to meet its quota of the assessment.

Again Dr. Janus categorically denied that any coal syndicate money had been given to Hitler before he came to power. Two other former chairmen of the board of the Rhenish-Westphalian Coal Syndicate, Herbert Kauert and Hermann Kellermann, also testified that all stories of the alleged subsidies to Hitler before 1933 were completely unfounded. Dr. Janus challenged *Neues Deutschland* to produce evidence of its allegation. The newspaper did not reply.

The charge itself seems rather strange. The state of Prussia throughout almost the entire period of the Weimar Republic was governed by the Social Democrats. The Social Democrats in the Prussian government would have been delighted to uncover an attempt by the "capitalist" directorate of the Rhenish-Westphalian Coal Syndicate to divert money earned by various mine owners, including the state of Prussia, to Hitler. For the sake of a political scandal, it would have made little difference whether the donation to the Nazis was fifty or five pfennigs per ton of coal. It is almost unbelievable that only in 1947, fifteen years later, the Communists would discover this swindle of Prussian state funds.

Although the specific charges against the Rhenish-Westphalian Coal Syndicate were false, there was some truth behind all these stories. Individual mining companies and mine owners did contribute to Hitler, but the money came out of their own funds, not the general treasury of the Rhenish-Westphalian Coal Syndicate. Certainly in some of these cases Kirdorf's advice and prestige influenced the decision to contribute. After 1931 the mining industry was to give a monthly subsidy to the Nazi Party. Yet strangely enough, most of the money would not go to Hitler but to his rival Gregor Strasser, whom Kirdorf feared.[31]

The combined heavy industry of the Ruhr (steel and coal) *did* have a secret political fund, for which all were assessed a certain amount. Donations were then made, by the twelve directors of the funds, to various political parties, occasionally including the Nazis. Ironically, Emil Kirdorf was not one of the directors of this secret Ruhr treasury, properly called the Ruhrlade.[32]

Throughout the period of prosperity Hitler received relatively few donations from important businessmen. The Nazis themselves spoke of their progress in business circles a bit more optimistically, but even their own figures are revealing. On March 30, 1927, Rudolf Hess wrote a letter to a Nazi sympathizer living abroad, in which he described Hitler's campaign to win support among the industrialists: "Last year he [Hitler] spoke three times before invited [audiences of] industrialists from Rhineland, Westphalia, etc.; twice in Essen; and once in Königswinter. Each time it was as successful as that time in the Atlantic Hotel in Hamburg. Because he could attune his speech to a fairly uniform audience, he was able to stick to a consistent line. As in Hamburg, so in this [first] instance the attitude [of the audience] was at first rather cool and negative, and some sat smiling condescendingly at the people's tribune. It was a great pleasure for me to be able to observe how the men slowly changed their outlook, not without visible signs of their inner resistance. At the end they clapped in a way *these* men probably clap rarely.

"The result was that at the second meeting of industrialists in Essen about five hundred gentlemen accepted the invitation.* Hitler will probably speak to industrialists in Essen for the third time on April 27. It is planned to have the ladies invited this time also, because once they have been won, they are often more important than the men and exert an influence on their husbands that should not be underestimated."[33]

From Hess's letter it seems the meetings were rather successful, but the fact that such occasions occurred only four times a year indicates that there was little serious support for Hitler

---

*Kirdorf was probably in the audience on one of these occasions.

among the industrialists.* At such gatherings, the audiences were usually composed of those of nationalist sympathies; during the speech itself, Hitler was able to stir their enthusiasm. However, his efforts were soon compromised, as in Kirdorf's case, by the radical stance of the left-wing members of the Party. In 1929, three years after Hitler's speech before the Hamburg National-klub at the Atlantic Hotel, a Nazi Party representative in Hamburg reported that the speech was still remembered favorably in business circles, but that there was general alienation from the Nazi movement because of the leftist views of the Party's local leadership.[34]

All evidence seems to indicate that Hitler's campaign to win support among the industrialists from 1926 to 1928 was not very successful. During these years the National Socialist Party was, for the most part, financed by membership dues, collections at speeches, and the sales of Party newspapers. In other words, Hitler's hard core of fanatical followers kept the movement going by contributing generously from what little they had. So the financial position of the Party remained desperate throughout this period. Even by the end of August 1928 there were debts amounting to over RM 14,000 and most of the *GAU* organizations* suffered from similar monetary problems.[35] Schwarz, the Party treasurer, was able to balance the books only by such questionable methods as listing dues of expected membership increase on the credit side of the ledger and subtracting RM 40 per month from the salary of each Nazi legislator.

Despite the Party's financial difficulties, it should not be thought that Hitler himself was living in poverty. His personal income after 1925 was said to have come primarily from the royalties he received on his book and the fees from articles he wrote for the Party press. The first volume of *Mein Kampf* was published in June 1925. It cost twelve marks, double the price of the average German book, but despite the high price Max Amann

---

*Hitler had also spoken before smaller groups of businessmen during this period; for example, Hess made no mention in his letter of three speeches Hitler delivered to business audiences in Hattingen.

*A *GAU* was a Party district. These districts basically corresponded with the thirty-four Reichstag electoral districts. The Nazi Party leader in each district was called a Gauleiter.

sufferings and the hopes of all the soldiers at the front. When he came home on leave he saw that the civilian population was growing weary of the hardships of the war economy. In the Rhenish-Westphalian industrial region where his father's factories were located, the fires of revolution had been smoldering for a long time. In 1917 there had been strikes and serious disorders. A great number of demonstrators had been arrested in the various industrial centers of the Rhine. The strikers were principally motivated by a lack of food and other material hardships, but political agitators took advantage of these causes to fan the flames of class hatred.

In the fall of 1918 came the Kiel mutiny. In the Rhineland cities the moderate socialist leaders were at first able to prevent any disorders, but the arrival of the Kiel mutineers accompanied by professional Communist agitators tipped the balance. In the big industrial cities of Essen, Mühlheim, and Hamborn, workers' and soldiers' soviets were formed and quickly seized power. To prevent disorder and sabotage in the Rhenish-Westphalian industrial region, Hugo Stinnes, one of the area's most prominent industrialists, opened negotiations with the trade unions. He agreed to recognize the rights of the unions to collective bargaining, an eight-hour day, and various social benefits. In return he secured from the workers' representatives promises to guarantee order and social peace in the region. Fritz Thyssen strongly supported Stinnes's agreements with the workers. Yet even before the negotiations were completed some of the workers, influenced by revolutionary propaganda, turned away from the leadership of the Social Democratic Party. The workers' and soldiers' councils marched to the prisons and freed the political prisoners who had been arrested for revolutionary activity during the war. Along with them many common criminals were turned loose on the public.[40]

At Mühlheim the situation was tense for the next few weeks. Although the workers' and soldiers' councils which now held power had posted notices that excesses and looting would be punished, the streets were no longer safe. Gradually the moderate elements which had at first held a majority in the councils were pushed aside by radical agitators.

At this time Hitler was still a common soldier in Munich, watching the revolution develop there. Being an unknown man without property, he was essentially in no danger from the revolution and so could study its developments from the sidelines. His studies of anti-Communist political parties in Vienna had prepared Hitler intellectually for the 1918 revolution. Although a fervent nationalist, he had no strong loyalty to monarchy as a political system and so was already thinking of alternative systems of government. Thyssen and the men of his class, on the other hand, found themselves completely lost. They had been loyal monarchists up to 1918, and unlike Hitler had never thought of any alternative method of government. They and their property were under direct attack from the revolution, but none of them had any ideas of how to meet it. They attempted compromise, but Hitler was already certain the Communists would have to be confronted by something stronger than compromise.

On the evening of December 7 a group of men armed with rifles pounded on the door of the Thyssen villa. They had come to arrest Fritz Thyssen, but they also decided to take away his father, despite his advanced age. Along with four other industrialists the Thyssens were thrown into the prison at Mühlheim. In the middle of the night they were awakened by a dozen rough-looking men carrying rifles and wearing red armbands. They pushed the six prisoners down a narrow corridor and into a dark courtyard illuminated by the glare of a single spotlight. The industrialists were ordered to line up against the wall. "I thought they were going to execute us," said Thyssen. There they waited. The moments seemed like hours.

Then finally the silence was broken. One of the guards shouted something; the prisoners would be taken to the railway station to catch the train for Berlin. The industrialists were placed in a third-class car and their guards took up posts near the doors in order to prevent any attempted escape. There was no heat in the train and it was very cold. Fortunately the elder Thyssen had been able to take a blanket with him. The train arrived at the Potsdam station in Berlin the following evening. On the platform a Red guard detachment was waiting. The Mühlheim Communists handed their prisoners over to them and jeered at the "capitalist pigs," who they said would soon meet their fate. Old August Thyssen, who had left his blanket in the train, politely asked one of the guards wearing a red armband if he could go and get it for him. "What are you talking to me for?" the man responded indignantly. "I am the chief of police of Berlin."

They later learned that this was Emil Eichhorn, whom Fritz Thyssen described as "a dangerous Communist agitator in the service of Soviet Russia." During the early days of the revolution the radical socialists had nominated Eichhorn chief of the Berlin police. He had transformed the central police station into a fortress known as the "Red House" and had picked his personal bodyguard from the most radical elements of the Berlin proletariat. Many of them were fugitives who had been released from prison only a few weeks earlier. At the time, it was rumored that Eichhorn had ordered the arrest of many political enemies and officials of the old regime, and that he had had them executed in the courtyard of the police headquarters without trial. Naturally the Thyssens and their companions again feared for their lives.

Eichhorn's men took the prisoners from the Potsdam station to police headquarters for "interrogation." The prisoners were assembled before Eichhorn. "You are accused," he said, "of treason and antirevolutionary activities. You are enemies of the people and have asked for the intervention of French troops in order to prevent the socialist revolution." The industrialists all protested that they had had no contact with the French Army of occupation.

Eichhorn interrupted insolently: "Don't try to deny it. I am well informed. The day before yesterday you had a conference at Dortmund with other industrialists and you have decided to send a delegation to the French general asking him to occupy the Ruhr. This is treason. What have you to say, gentlemen?"

The prisoners looked at each other in astonishment. None of them had gone to Dortmund. Thyssen and his father said they knew nothing of such a conference. Moreover, they had an alibi. Neither of them had left Mühlheim for a week; numerous witnesses could affirm this.

"Those witnesses! All bourgeois! Their statements have no value whatever," Eichhorn shouted brutally. "Take 'em away."[41]

As they were led out of Eichhorn's office the industrialists again trembled for their fate. Had they escaped death at Mühlheim only to be shot in Berlin? After a short time their guards were told that there was no more room for prisoners at police headquarters. "Take them to Moabit," a Communist leader growled. Moabit was the main prison of Berlin. At the gate of the

Red House a prison van was waiting for the industrialists. Through the bars of the van they could see the agitation in the Berlin streets as they drove along. Near the Alexanderplatz machine guns were set up and an armored car was on patrol. After about twenty minutes, the van entered the prison yard. An official came out to meet the industrialists and said: "I don't know anything about this affair. At any rate, it is perhaps much better for you to be here. With me at least you are safe."

This seemed to confirm the sinister rumors they had heard about the executions at the Red House. The director of the Moabit prison was an old official who was responsible to the Prussian state administration and not to Eichhorn. Thyssen's father was placed in the infirmary because of his age. He endured everything with the utmost calm. "Never mind," he said, "at my age no great accident can befall me."[42] The other industrialists and Fritz Thyssen were placed in regular prison cells.

The next morning the prison chaplain arrived. He thought Thyssen had been condemned to death. He had never met an industrial tycoon before and hardly knew what to say. "He made a little speech," said Thyssen, "that I shall remember all my life."

"It's always the same story," said the chaplain, "the first day you pretend to be full of courage, and you don't believe anything will happen to you. But wait for the third day—you'll see what will happen when you know what is awaiting you. Then you will be crushed."[43] It was the same speech that the chaplain gave to regular criminal prisoners awaiting execution, in order to persuade them to repent. Somehow he sensed that this little formula did not apply in Thyssen's case, but he didn't know anything else to say. On the fourth day Thyssen and his father were freed along with the four other industrialists. Eichhorn had had their statements verified and had no evidence against them. His position in Berlin was precarious at the time and so he decided it was better to release them.

It is easy to see how a close call with execution would have a traumatic effect on anyone. To a great extent Thyssen's later association with and financing of Hitler was motivated by his dread of the "Red Terror." Although none of Hitler's other financial supporters were actually put through the agonizing mental torture of being stood up against a wall in the middle of the night, to a certain extent they all feared for their lives during the revolutionary days of 1918–1919. In the newspapers they read daily of the brutal murders of the Russian upper class by the Bolsheviks. Then in Germany itself twelve upper-class hostages were shot down in the courtyard of school in Munich. The friends of those killed became some of Adolf Hitler's first supporters.

After their harrowing experience, the Thyssens returned home only to face another crisis. At the nearby town of Hamborn, where the Thyssens also owned a factory, the radicals had gained power.[44] Thyssen believed the man behind this trouble was Karl Radek, a Russian Communist agitator.[45] On Christmas Eve a strike was proclaimed at Hamborn. Alarmed, the mayor of Hamborn called Thyssen on the telephone and asked him to come over and attempt to settle the dispute. However, Thyssen replied that Hugo Stinnes had already negotiated an agreement with the trade unions in the name of all the industrialists of the Rhineland. He told the mayor he would not conclude any separate arrangements beyond what Stinnes had agreed upon.[46]

Early the following morning five armed Communist workers arrived at the Thyssen villa in Mühlheim. They had come to take Thyssen to Hamborn by force. "I did not fancy the prospect of repeating my recent Berlin experience," Thyssen recalled. He told the butler to let the men know that he was dressing and ask them to come in and take some coffee while he was getting ready. While they were drinking coffee, Thyssen warned his wife and told her to take their daughter and go to Duisburg, which was occupied by Belgian troops. In the meantime, Thyssen himself was to go and warn his father, who was living about eight miles from Mühlheim in the Castle of Landsberg on the Ruhr. Leaving by a secret passage and a hidden door, Thyssen proceeded to Landsberg. He told his father what had happened and they left immediately on foot along the road. Fortunately they were soon given a ride in a passing car which saved the elder Thyssen a painful walk of about seven miles. "We had good reason to fear that we would be arrested once more," recalled Fritz Thyssen. "Already the rumor was spreading that well-known personalities had been shot by Communist bands. . . . the impression which those agitated days have left upon me have never been blotted out," said Thyssen. "I have spent my life among workers. My father had worked with them at the beginning of his career. Never have the workers of our factories shown us any kind of hostility, still less of hatred . . . all disorders and excesses have almost always been due to foreigners."[47]

Thyssen believed that the organizers of the strikes and riots were professional political agitators and agents of Moscow. "Radek . . . Leviné . . . Axelrod . . . these were the men responsible for the riots and murders," Thyssen said. All the revolutionary leaders Thyssen came in contact with or mentioned were Jewish. Although he later denied being an anti-Semite, he certainly felt the Jews were one of the principal forces behind Communism. Without doubt, Thyssen's experiences in 1918-1919 made him ripe for Hitler's anti-Semitism.

Despite their completely different backgrounds, the thinking of Hitler and Thyssen were shaped by the events of 1918 in a very similar way. Although Hitler was already an anti-Semite, the major role Jewish leaders played in the November revolution was probably more important than any other factor in confirming his anti-Semitic beliefs. Certainly blaming the Jews for the revolution was completely unfair, for only a small percentage of the total Jewish population were Communists; but one would hardly expect someone like Hitler to view the matter fairly. However, Thyssen, of all people, should have known better because he was personally acquainted with prominent Jewish leaders, such as Rathenau, Silverberg, and others.

In contrast to Thyssen's suspicions about the Jews, he thought the Social Democratic Party consisted of "reasonable and moderate" people. When the miners went on strike in January of 1919 he took part in the negotiations with the strikers. "They understood the difficult position of the industrialists," he said. The owners in return tried their best to ease the food shortages of the workers' families which resulted from the continuation of the Allied blockade. The agreement made between the Ruhr industrialists and their workers broke down only because of the intervention of radical outside agitators.

"During the entire year, 1918-1919, I felt that Germany was going to sink into anarchy," said Thyssen. "Strikes followed one another without either motive or results." During that chaotic period it seemed impossible to reorganize industrial production. The mining of coal had come almost to a standstill. There was even fear that saboteurs might destroy the machinery of the mines. "No one was any longer assured of his individual freedom," recalled Thyssen. "Or even of the safety of his life. A man could be arrested and shot without any reason.

"It was then," said Thyssen, "that I realized the necessity—if Germany was not to sink into anarchy—of fighting all this radical agitation which, far from giving happiness to the workers, only created disorder. The Social Democratic Party endeavored to maintain order, but it was too weak. The memory of those days did much to dispose me, later on, to offer my help to National Socialism, which I believed to be capable of solving in a new manner the pressing and industrial social problems of . . . Germany."[48]

In the late spring and summer of 1919 Fritz Thyssen served as an economic advisor to the German delegates at the Versailles Peace Conference. He stayed nearly three months at Versailles and left in mid-June to accompany the German delegates back to Weimar where the government and the National Assembly were in session. He tried to convince the deputies of the Catholic Center Party whom he knew that it would be an error to accept the conditions of the Allies. Most of the deputies realized that the terms of the treaty could not be fulfilled, but they felt there was no choice but to sign. Thyssen thought this was a mistake. By signing, the Germans pledged themselves to the treaty. Yet they knew fulfillment was impossible.[49] The dilemma the German leaders found themselves in was a tragic one. Rejection of the treaty would mean surrendering the country to immediate foreign occupation and revolutionary upheaval. President Ebert and the Social Democratic Party decided in favor of signing. They were supported by the Catholic Center Party and its leader, Matthias Erzberger, whose political style was one of compromise and subtle maneuvering. Thyssen and his father, who were Catholics and probably the wealthiest members of the Catholic Center Party, dropped out of the party when Erzberger agreed to sign the Versailles Treaty. The signature of this humiliating treaty, said Thyssen, "condemned a whole nation to a sort of economic slavery." The conditions of the treaty were made even more insulting by forcing the Germans into an admission of "war guilt." The revolutionary upheavals and the humiliation of the Versailles Treaty which followed gave rise to a violent nationalist reaction which gathered momentum throughout the country.[50]

The fight against the Versailles Treaty was a key issue of Hitler's program. In time Thyssen would be in complete agreement with Hitler on this point, for both political and economic reasons. Again, he was personally involved in the issue. He saw for himself the intransigence of the French and how the articles of the treaty were designed to rob Germany and put her in an economic straitjacket. Although he was completely unaware of it then, one by one Fritz Thyssen's personal experiences were bringing him closer and closer to Hitler. First there was his fear of Communism, then his suspicions of the Jews being behind Marxism, then his determination not to accept the Versailles Treaty.

In March of 1920 the extreme reactionaries attempted to seize power in the Kapp putsch. In the Rhineland the consequence of this clumsy counterrevolution was a new Communist insurrection. In Essen, Duisburg, Düsseldorf, and Mühlheim, Communist revolutionary committees seized political power under the pretext of the general strike proclaimed by the Ebert government. The radicals immediately organized a well-armed workers' militia.

As soon as the trouble began, Thyssen left Mühlheim with his family and proceeded to Krefeld on the left bank of the Rhine where the occupation troops were preventing any disorders. The bridge over the Rhine was guarded by Belgians, who allowed Thyssen and his family to pass. The German industrialists were very apprehensive about the new revolutionary movement, which again disorganized the whole economic life of the region. The insurrection lasted about two weeks. Finally the Army was obliged to intervene to reestablish order. Bloody battles took place at Duisburg and Wesel between the Army and the revolutionary militia. The abortive Kapp putsch and the wave of revolution that followed it had lasting repercussions in the Ruhr. There was a feeling of antagonism that could no longer be calmed. During the following year more strikes and street battles occurred in many industrial cities.

The recurrence of revolutionary uprisings resulted in a strong yearning for political stability on the part of the upper class. Thyssen told some of his friends that he wanted law and order "at any price." That was just what Hitler was offering. Thyssen never completely endorsed Hitler's authoritarian ideas, but he wanted a "strong state" enough that he was willing to sacrifice a few freedoms to get it.

When the French occupied the Ruhr in 1923, Thyssen, unlike some other industrialists, remained at his factory and helped organize the passive resistance.[51] The German coal syndicate called a meeting in Hamburg. Thyssen attended along with other prominent industrialists, such as Stinnes, Krupp, Kirdorf, and Klöckner. He was of the opinion that the coal owners should resist the delivery of goods demanded by the French.

A second meeting of the syndicate was held several days later in Essen. The other industrialists supported Thyssen's view and asked him to act as their spokesman. The meeting passed a resolution declaring that the syndicate would deliver coal to the Allies if they received the consent of the German government. At the same time they sent a representative to Berlin to ask the government to give them protective cover by forbidding the deliveries. However, not all industrialists supported the intransigent attitude of Thyssen and his associates. Two days after the occupation, French officials arrived and contacted the mine owners; a few of these owners agreed to a deal with the French. In order to enforce the resolution they had made in Essen, the coal syndicate decided to institute a secret tribunal which would punish businessmen cooperating with the French. It was a very critical moment for Germany," said Thyssen. "If France had succeeded in getting possession of the Ruhr industry, the country would never have been able to recover."[52] A few days after the entry of the French troops into the Ruhr, Thyssen was summoned to French headquarters. He was received by a general who asked: "Have the industrialists decided to effect the deliveries which Germany has agreed to make under the treaty?" Thyssen replied that the occupation of the Ruhr was considered by the German government to be a violation of the treaty and that the industrialists had received orders not to make any deliveries to the French. In that case, the general told him, the industrialists themselves would have to suffer the consequences of their refusal.

On January 20 Thyssen and several other mine owners were arrested and transferred to the military prison at Mainz. He was charged with inducing organized labor to resist, and with disobeying French military orders under martial law. When they heard the news of his imprisonment, the workers of the Thyssen factories became agitated. At his trial Thyssen's defense culminated in the fearless sentence: "I am a German and I refuse to obey French orders on German soil." Several clashes between the people and the French Army of occupation had already occurred. In the face of this unrest among the workers, the French government decided it was best to be lenient. Instead of condemning Thyssen to five years' imprisonment as had been expected, the court-martial imposed a fine of 300,000 gold marks.

The humiliating treatment he received from the French left a permanent scar on Thyssen's character. Up to that time he had been relatively international-minded, but now he was intellectually and emotionally ready for Hitler's sort of extreme nationalism. When Hitler argued that Germany had to rearm to protect itself against the aggressive French Army camped on the Rhine, many men like Thyssen reluctantly agreed that he was right.

As he left the court, the population of Mainz and the delegations of workers who had come from the Ruhr staged a great demonstration in Thyssen's honor. He was carried to the railway station in triumph. When he returned to Mühlheim, Thyssen began in earnest to organize the passive resistance which was Germany's only defense against the occupation. The German government had forbidden coal deliveries to the Allies and had instructed all the workers to refuse to obey the orders of the French authorities. The railroad employees went on strike. Navigation on the Rhine came to a standstill. As a result, the French themselves had to provide means of transporting all passengers and freight. The coal accumulated in great mountains at the mouths of the mine pits, because no train or boat would transport any of it to Belgium or France.

In order to break the passive resistance, the French established a customs cordon between the occupied territories and the rest of Germany. No goods or raw materials were allowed to leave the Rhineland for Germany. Nevertheless, Thyssen and his men succeeded in several instances in shipping whole trainloads of coal and steel. The Thyssen foundries at Mühlheim had their own freight stations, which were guarded by Belgian troops. In order to distract the soldiers' attention, Thyssen sent attractive young women to them, who, he commented, "performed their mission very well." During such "a period of distraction" perhaps four trains could be loaded and dispatched for Germany. Unfortunately one of the loads was too heavy and the couplings of the cars broke loose. Thyssen's men were caught in the act. Although the passive resistance in the Mühlheim region was organized entirely by Thyssen, he had the absolute cooperation of the whole population including the trade-union leaders. His experiences during the passive resistance campaign led Thyssen to believe that Germany could still have a bright future if only the class hostility between the workers and employers could be put aside in the name of nationalism.

Thus Thyssen began to think, as Hitler had already, of the possibility of a patriotic, nationalist workers' party that would win the lower classes away from Marxism. When this idea was combined with the beliefs that Thyssen drew from his unpleasant personal experiences since 1918, the result was amazingly similar to Hitler's basic political program.

In October 1923, just a month before Hitler's putsch, it looked as if there was about to be another Communist revolution in Germany. Thyssen decided to visit General Ludendorff in Munich and ended up giving him 100,000 gold marks to distribute between the Nazi Party and the Free Corps Oberland.[53] On November 9, 1923, Hitler's attempted putsch was brought to an abrupt halt.

For the next five years the Nazis heard nothing from Thyssen. Then in the fall of 1928 Hitler became desperate for money to finance the purchase of his new palatial Party headquarters, the Brown House. Rudolf Hess approached Emil Kirdorf for the money, but Kirdorf said he was unable to raise such a large sum on short notice. The old coal tycoon suggested that Hess try Fritz Thyssen. With Kirdorf's assistance a meeting was arranged. Hess, who was well educated and from a good background, presented Hitler's case with considerable skill. Thyssen decided it was once again time to help the Nazis. He arranged for a loan of the required sum (which he later claimed was only RM 250,000, but was probably five times that amount) through a Dutch bank in Rotterdam, the Bank Voor Handel en Scheepvaart N.V. The exact terms of the deal are not known, but it is clear that Thyssen expected Hitler to repay at least some of the money. There are also strong indications that by obtaining the money for Hitler, Thyssen hoped to be able to exercise an influence over Nazi policy. He later said, "I chose a Dutch bank because I did not want to be ınixed up with German banks in my position, and because . . . I thought I would have the Nazis a little more in my hands."[54]

According to Thyssen's account, the Nazis repaid only "a small part" of the money. [55] He then had no alternative but to quietly pay the balance due the Dutch bank. This supposedly amounted to RM 150,000 (or about $36,000). However, the modest sum of RM 150,000 would not even have covered the downpayment on the Barlow Palace (Brown House). One leading Nazi estimated that just the remodeling of the palace, which Hitler directed himself, cost over RM 800,000 (or about $200,000).[56] Naturally Thyssen later tried to give the impression that he gave less to the Nazis than he actually did. But when the Barlow Palace was transformed into the splendid new Nazi Party headquarters, the Brown House, there could be no doubt that Hitler now had considerable funds at his disposal.

The Brown House was located on the Briennerstrasse in the most aristocratic neighborhood of Munich. The building itself was three stories high, set back from the street between narrow, fenced gardens. When one Nazi saw the Brown House for the first time, he said: "Only the swastika flag floating over the roof convinced me that this was not a cardinal's palace or a Jewish banker's luxurious residence."[57] The former palace was elegantly remodeled according to Hitler's own plans. He transformed great halls into moderate-sized rooms by constructing new walls and intermediary floors.

The result was impressive. The visitor entered through two huge bronze doors where two S.A. men were always on guard. He would then pass into a large hall decorated with swastika flags. A grand staircase led to the second floor where the offices of Hitler and his staff were located. The interior of these rooms were decorated with dark wood paneling and rich red-leather armchairs. "Everything had that air of richness which comes only from expensive materials," said a visitor. One of the distinctive features of the building was a cozy beer-cellar restaurant in the basement. Here a fat, jolly chef and his wife prepared meals to suit every taste from Hitler's vegetarian dishes to Göring's gourmet feasts.

After Thyssen financed the purchase of the Brown House for the Nazis, his relationship with Hitler became much closer. This would hardly have been the case if the Nazis had defaulted on the payment of the loan. Hitler and Hess were invited to spend the weekend at one of Thyssen's Rhineland castles.[58] And whenever Thyssen was in Munich he tried to arrange to have lunch or dinner with Hitler, during which they discussed current political events. It was also during this period that Thyssen developed a close personal friendship with Hermann Göring.

One day Wilhelm Tengelmann, whose father was the director of a coal-mining company affiliated with the United Steel Works, told Thyssen about a certain Herr Göring. Göring, he said, "is trying very hard to do some good for the German people, but he is finding very little encouragement on the part of German industrialists. Wouldn't you like to make his acquaintance?" Thyssen soon met Göring. "He lived in a very small apartment in those days, and he was anxious to enlarge it in order to cut a better figure. I paid the cost of this improvement," said Thyssen. "At that time Göring seemed a most agreeable person. In political matters he was very sensible. I also came to know his first wife, Carin, who was a Swedish Countess [sic] by birth. She was an exceedingly charming woman."[59]

Thyssen frequently visited Göring in Berlin. Before long he gave him money not only for political expenses but for his personal financial needs as well. According to Thyssen's own statements, he made three donations to Göring at this time of RM 50,000 each (totaling about $36,000). Whenever Göring was in the Rhineland he was invited to stay with Thyssen. The two men shared a common passion for gourmet food and works of art. Göring walked through Thyssen's palatial home admiring the Rembrandts, El Grecos, and Canalettos, dreaming of the day when he too would have fine paintings like his industrialist friend.

"I saw something of Fritz Thyssen in 1929 and 1930," wrote the well-known journalist R. G. Waldeck, "when we both used to take the cure at a spa in the Black Forest." According to Waldeck, Thyssen had already "staked everything on Hitler." It was widely rumored that the United Steel Works would soon be facing bankruptcy. Economic motives were to become increasingly important for Fritz Thyssen as the depression began, but they were not enough to account for his support of National Socialism. During their long walks through the cool pine woods, it became obvious to Waldeck that Thyssen "believed in Hitler and liked Göring." He spoke of them "with warmth" and explained that they were a kind of "new men" who would make Germany united and strong again and put an end to the threat of Communism. To his more apprehensive fellow industrialists, Thyssen would say, slightly irritated: "None of *us* can get the country out of the mess!" And he would shrug off that part of Hitler's program that advocated discrimination against the Jews. Hitler himself did not mean it, he assured Jewish friends. As for Hitler's socialism: "Good God, a leader of the masses on the make has to say many things." The revolution was to be a strictly national revolution, not a social one. He had Hitler's word for it.[60]

Did Emil Kirdorf and Fritz Thyssen support Hitler for the same or similar reasons?[61] Although the answer to this question is not clear cut, a comparison of their motivation is enlightening. The personalities of the two men were very different. Old Emil Kirdorf was a belligerent character who would have been a maverick from society under almost any circumstances. Fritz Thyssen, on the other hand, had an affable manner, enjoyed his pleasures, and was, for an industrialist, unusually preoccupied with moral obligations.

On matters of labor policy Kirdorf was an unrealistic reactionary opposed to the idea of trade unions altogether. His advanced age probably had something to do with this attitude for, when he began his career in business, unions themselves were thought of as being very radical. Thyssen, a devout Catholic, had been deeply impressed with the encyclicals of Popes Leo XIII and Pius XI in which these pontiffs pleaded for better social relations. He thought the trade unions played a useful role as the rightful representatives of the workers.

Thyssen's personal encounter with the revolution was a traumatic experience for him. At the time of his arrest in December of 1918 when he, his father, and some other industrialists were herded into a courtyard and stood up against a wall in the middle of the night, he was sure he was about to die. He never forgot the brutal interrogation by Emil Eichhorn, the Red Chief of the Berlin police. Never in his life had anyone addressed him in that tone of voice before. He viewed Communism not just as a threat to his wealth and property but as a moral evil, a vicious brutality determined to conquer the world.

In Thyssen's mind the Communist uprising and the Jews were

closely associated. He felt "foreigners" like Eichhorn and Radek were responsible for the agitation among the workers. Yet, unlike Henry Ford, Thyssen never became an ideological anti-Semite. He continued to be on good terms with Jewish business associates, separating in his mind "good Jews" (patriotic and pro-capitalist) from "bad Jews" (Communists and socialists).

Although Emil Kirdorf had many biases and prejudices, anti-Semitism was not among them. In fact, Kirdorf had business connections and several personal friends among Jewish banking circles in Berlin. Regardless of how extreme his other views were, he never exhibited any hostility against the Jews. Not so easily deceived as might have been assumed, Kirdorf recognized from the beginning that anti-Semitism was a central part of Hitler's program. This he regretted; but, as he wrote to a Jewish friend, the prominent Berlin banker Dr. Arthur Salomonsohn, the anti-Semitism of the National Socialist Party was only a pragmatic means used to win popular support. Once the masses had turned away from Marxism and become nationalist-minded again, Kirdorf assured his friend, such unsavory methods would be dispensed with.[62]

Certainly Kirdorf was strongly opposed to Communism, but it never frightened him as much as it did Thyssen. Like many other members of the pre-1914 generation, he never fully understood Marxism. Kirdorf's political philosophy could best be described by the phrase "Bismarckian nationalism." He believed Germany was surrounded by enemies determined to deprive her of her rightful place as a world power. As he grew older, Kirdorf became very pessimistic about Germany's fate. After the loss of World War I he felt all was hopeless and consequently was susceptible to radical proposals like Hitler's as a last alternative. Being businessmen, both Kirdorf and Thyssen realized the desperate economic position Germany was in. The empires of Britain and France gave them a virtual monopoly over one-quarter of the earth's surface. The restrictions of the Versailles Treaty were designed so that German industry would be uncompetitive even in those few markets that were left open to it.

Both Thyssen and Kirdorf were magnates of heavy industry (steel, iron, coal, etc.). Up to 1918 a considerable portion of their business had involved war materials; now all that was forbidden by the Versailles Treaty. German heavy industry was also closed out of many of its old markets, such as eastern Europe. More than a few of the big coal and steel firms were about to go bankrupt. In order to remain competitive they had to cut wages, which naturally caused discontent among the workers and a conflict with the Weimar government. Although Thyssen believed in improving the social conditions of the laborers, his firm was in such a tenuous economic position by 1928 that even he was forced to ask the government to permit wage cuts. This is one of the primary distinguishing characteristics of the sectors of the German economy that supported Hitler; they were on the verge of collapse and saw his extremist measures as a last alternative.

5
WHAT DID
BIG BUSINESS WANT?

In 1902 young Bertha Krupp, the daughter of Friedrich Krupp, became the sole owner of one of Germany's largest steel firms. Her father had been at the head of the third-generation of Krupps to rule over the family's industrial empire, but he died leaving no sons, meaning that the Krupp name would die out with the fourth generation proprietress. Then a young Prussian aristocrat named Gustav von Bohlen und Halbach,* who was engaged to Bertha Krupp, was permitted after the marriage to precede his family name by his wife's, and in 1906 the young bridegroom became Gustav Krupp von Bohlen und Halbach. He was a man of medium height and build and was no doubt always somewhat embarrassed that his wife was taller than he was. His face rarely displayed emotion of any sort; the small tight mouth, domed forehead, and spartan nose were always frozen in the same stern look. His brisk almost mechanical movements revealed that he was a graduate of Prussian diplomatic training, which even Bismarck contemptuously called the school for dullards. He always wore the right clothes for every occasion, but there was a rigid, overdone neatness in his dress. Without any experience in business, he was suddenly placed at the head of the huge firm in a very competitive industry. His business colleagues were either men whose fathers or who themselves had created their com-

---

*Gustav von Bohlen, incidentally, was the great-grandson of General William Bohlen, who was killed in the Battle of the Rappahannock in 1862 while fighting on the Union side in the American Civil War.[1]

panies or men of great managerial skill who after years of work had been appointed president of their firms.

Gustav Krupp saw himself not as an entrepreneur but as an administrator of his wife's fortune. He learned to manage the Krupp firm the hard way, by familiarizing himself with a business that was new to him and by regulating his life in such time-clock fashion that he sometimes gave the impression of being an automaton rather than a human being. The fact that he considered himself merely the trustee of the Krupp family fortune and not an industrial tycoon in his own right, led him to be extremely cautious. He shied away from anything that might in the long run damage the Krupp interests.

As a product of the rigid German civil service, he had a very strong respect for authority and duty. His first and foremost duty as he saw it was to his country, but his patriotism was not of the narrow ideological type. Once in the early 1920s, during a reception at the palatial Krupp home, the Villa Hügel, the name of President Ebert, a Social Democrat, was mentioned in a discussion. In an effort to ridicule the President, a gentleman of rightist sympathies commented on Ebert's humble origins with a disparaging remark about "that saddle-maker Ebert." (As a young man Ebert had worked as a saddle-maker.) Krupp, who usually exhibited perfect self-control, immediately flared up and declared he would not stand for an insult to the chief of state.[2] Next to his duty to his Fatherland was his obligation to the Krupp family, the Krupp tradition, and the Krupp workers and employees. He carried on and even expanded the famed Krupp social projects, such as workers' insurance, pensions, medical care, and housing. This patriotic philosophy of duty also turned out to be excellent for business. From 1906 to 1914 Germany was arming rapidly and the Krupp firm prospered. During World War I they were the leading German manufacturer of big guns and armaments. Then in 1918 came disaster.

The Kaiser abdicated and fled to Holland; a Social Democratic government was formed in Berlin under President Ebert. When the German people heard the news, some responded differently than others. In a military hospital, Corporal Adolf Hitler cursed these Social Democrats as traitors to the Fatherland. In Essen, Gustav Krupp immediately sent a telegram to Berlin to find out what the new government wanted him to do. Krupp did not believe in democracy and he had always respected Kaiser Wilhelm, but he felt his first duty was to the German state, whoever might be governing at the time.

On November 10, 1918, there was trouble at the Krupp factory in Essen. Crowds gathered in the streets. There were demonstrations and speeches by socialist agitators. Over 100,000 families in Essen directly depended on the Krupp firm for their livelihood. If there were no more armaments orders, everyone would be unemployed; so the workers were in an ugly mood. Gustav was so frightened that he armed all the servants in the Krupp home, the massive Villa Hügel, which sat high on a hill above Essen. But no angry mobs came storming up the hill.

Before sunrise on May 7, 1919, messengers scurried throughout Paris to deliver copies of the Versailles Treaty to the Allied officials. Because no one had yet seen it in its finished form, it came as a shock to many of them. Herbert Hoover, at that time chief of the Allied Food-relief Services and a senior American economic advisor, was awakened from a sound sleep at 4 A.M. to receive his copy. Still blear-eyed, Hoover read the document and was horrified by its severity. Too upset to go back to sleep, he dressed at daybreak and walked the deserted Paris streets. After walking only a few blocks, he met General Smuts of South Africa, and then John Maynard Keynes of the British delegation. "It all flashed into our minds," Hoover said, "why each was walking about at that time of the morning." Even Woodrow Wilson thought the Versailles Treaty was too harsh; he said: "If I were a German, I think I should never sign it."[3]

Not surprisingly, the one political issue which was considered by German business to be more important than any other was to free Germany from the Versailles Treaty. This was a question of economic survival for German business, not of ideological passion. They had to have access to foreign markets and they could no longer afford to pay the high taxes caused by reparations. The leaders of the German business community decided it best to deal with the problem of Versailles in two ways: They would give full support to Chancellor Stresemann's attempts to negotiate with the Allies for reasonable reform, but at the same time, in case the Allies refused to see reason, they would carry out a secret program of rearmament. To understand why the industrialists felt clandestine rearmament to be an absolute necessity, we must look back at the Versailles Treaty.

The Treaty of Versailles was finally signed by the Germans on June 28, 1919, after the resignation of several German officials who refused to sign their names to such an "unjust" treaty. The terms of the treaty made it impossible for Germany to regain economic stability. Territorially, Germany lost 25,000 square miles in Europe inhabited by over six million people, and all her colonies totaling more than a million square miles. In raw materials, she lost 65 percent of her iron ore reserves, 45 percent of her coal, 72 percent of her zinc, 12 percent of her principal agricultural areas and 10 percent of her industrial establishments. The German Army was limited to 100,000 men with no reserves, the Navy was reduced to insignificance, and the Air Force was totally abolished. In the atmosphere of economic chaos and depression that followed the treaty's enactment, radicalism of both the Left and Right flourished in a way that would have been impossible in a stable society.

Despite the antagonisms that divided Germany on most political questions, the Versailles Treaty was one issue on which general agreement could be reached. It was almost universally condemned. Newspapers, irrespective of party affiliation, attacked its terms and called for its rejection. The democratic *Frankfurter Zeitung* wrote in bold headlines: "UNACCEPTABLE!" It then commented that the terms "are so nonsensical that no government that signs the treaty will last a fortnight. . . . Germany is crushed." The socialist *Vorwärts* demanded rejection. The *Berliner Tageblatt* predicted that if the treaty was accepted "a military furor for revenge will sound in Germany within a few years, and a militant Nationalism will engulf all."[4] Protest meetings made up from people of all classes were held throughout Germany. In the industrial section of Berlin, workers dressed in grimy overalls assembled outside their factories to protest. At the University of Berlin the student fraternities, dressed in their colorful Renaissance uniforms, some covered with gold braid and others with great white plumes in their caps, marched carrying shiny sabers and signs calling for an honorable peace.

The Versailles Treaty was an example of the disastrous economic rivalry between sovereign nation-states. Britain and France designed the treaty as a weapon to forever weaken Germany, their number-one industrial competitor. The objectives of most of the provisions of the treaty were economic in nature rather than outbursts of a desire for revenge or heavy-handed stupidity, as was popularly believed. In addition to losing some of her richest provinces, much of her natural resources, and her colonies, Germany had to forfeit all rights, trade concessions, and property in foreign countries. The treaty provided that in these areas the Allies reserved "the right to retain and liquidate all property and interests of German private nationals or companies." Naturally, the Allies did not fail to take advantage of Germany's departure.

In addition to limiting Germany's potential to move into ex panding overseas markets, the Allies obtained a virtual blank check from Germany in terms of reparations. The Allies claimed that since Germany was responsible for the war she was liable for the costs and damages incurred by the victors. The total indemnity was to be set at $32 billion, plus interest. The schedule of payments would be a fixed annuity of $500 million, plus a 26 percent tax on exports (another technique to make Germany less competitive in world markets). Upon threat of invasion, the German government accepted the terms. But the annuities would not even cover the interest charges, so the indebtedness would increase every year no matter how faithfully the payments were made.[5]

In retrospect it is clear that the Versailles Treaty was one of the primary causes of the failure of German democracy. It completely discredited the moderate leaders who for months had insisted that only a new, democratic German government could count upon a just peace from the Allied democracies. It made little difference that President Ebert denounced the treaty along with the patriots, or that Philipp Scheidemann, one of the most important moderate Social Democrats, resigned from the cabinet because he refused to sign this "death warrant." The clearest indication of popular dissatisfaction would come with the elections of June 6, 1920. The Social Democrats and the Catholic Center Party, who led the drive to sign the treaty, would lose a total of eleven million votes, with three million going to the Nationalists. These parties would never recover sufficiently from this blow to gain the majority needed to rule effectively.

Was the Versailles Treaty designed simple to protect the world from the threat of German militarism, or was the treaty deliberately planned to strangle Germany's economy and make her uncompetitive in world markets? To answer this question it is only necessary to look at the treatment of nonmilitary German shipping. Understandably the Allies would have wanted to restrict the size of the German Navy in the interest of their own defense, but what was the military significance of the German merchant marine? Certainly the military importance of unarmed vessels was very slight, yet their economic significance was very great.

By 1900 Germany was rapidly becoming the world's greatest industrial power. In order to gain new export markets and obtain vital raw materials, Germany built up a large merchant marine to develop trade in all parts of the world. In fact, Germany's bid for industrial and commercial supremacy was based in large part on her great merchant fleet. "It was that particular form of German rivalry," said American economic reporter Ludwell Denny, "that perhaps threatened British supremacy most and for which, had there been no other reason, Britain went to war. Therefore, it was not surprising that Britain in dictating the peace terms took away from Germany virtually all her merchant marine."[6] The treaty called for the confiscation of Germany's entire ocean-going fleet, with the exception of some small craft under 1,600 tons (fishing boats). All German freighters and great passenger liners were handed over to the Allies. "That," said Denny, "was one of Britain's major war gains."[7]

Britain and France claimed that Germany was being forced to forfeit her nonmilitary fleet simply to pay for war reparations, but everyone knew that without a merchant fleet Germany would only have a more difficult time paying reparations.

The commercial value of a merchant marine is often underestimated. British shipping in 1928 contributed $650 million net to that country's "invisible exports." Cargo liners under the national flag of the exporter are one of the chief tools in the extension of foreign trade. This accounts in part for Britain's success as a world commercial power. Establishment of American shipping lines was a major factor in the increase of American trade with South America by 277 percent, and with Asia by 380 percent, during the period from 1914 to 1928. "It is true that when it is convenient and profitable for our competitors to carry our products for us they will place their ships at our disposal, but our competitors will not build up and develop our foreign market; this we must do with ships of our own." This statement was made by Commissioner Sandberg of the U.S. Shipping Board, but the principle applied to Germany as well as to the United States. Thus, in terms of shipping alone, the Versailles Treaty gave Britain and France a stranglehold over German export trade.

Yet in spite of the Versailles Treaty, with hard work and ingenuity German business gradually began to recover, so other ways were found to restrict Germany from foreign markets. High tariff barriers became one of the principal weapons used against Germany. No foreign-made goods could successfully compete with English goods in the British Empire. France put outright quotas (in addition to high tariffs) on the importation of German iron and steel products, textiles, and electrical equipment.[8]

The tariff barriers themselves were often given a more severe effect by the method of their enforcement. This administrative attack was directed in particular against certain kinds of German goods. For example, there was the practice of inspecting German imports by customs officers. To discourage import they would open a crate of one hundred radios and instead of examining ten examine each of the one hundred separately. The goods were thus tied up for weeks and the importer was unable to make his scheduled deliveries.

The process of tariff classifications by customs officials was also used as a weapon of commercial warfare against German exports. For example, under the McKenna Tariff, Britain had a duty of 33 1/3 percent on all foreign automobiles. A German toy manufacturer sent a shipment of toy dogs and dolls to England which moved by a clockwork mechanism. These toys were taxed as automobiles on the implausible argument that they moved under their own power. This made it impossible for the German exporter to maintain his contract price and the shipment was sent back.

The British McKenna Tariff also levied a duty of 33 1/3 percent on automobile parts and accessories. A shipment of plate glass from Germany was held up and classified, not as plate glass, but as automobile parts and accessories, with the argument that it might all be cut up and used for automobile windows and windshields. Even though the German people accepted a lower standard of living in order to build up an export surplus and sell over tariff walls, they were prevented from being successful.[9]

If the Versailles Treaty had been based on President Wilson's Fourteen Points as the Allies had originally promised, the Germans might have accepted it as a just peace and complied with its regulations. However, it was so obvious to the leading German businessmen that the treaty was simply designed to enslave them economically that their first thought was of clandestine evasion.

"In those days," wrote Gustav Krupp, "the situation seemed hopeless. It appeared even more desperate if one remained as firmly convinced as I was that 'Versailles' could not represent the end. If ever there should be a resurrection for Germany, if ever she were to shake off the chains of Versailles, then Krupps would have to be prepared. The machines were demolished; the tools were destroyed; but one thing remained—the men, the men at the drawing boards and in the workshops, who, in happy cooperation had brought the manufacture of guns to perfection. Their skill would have to be saved, their immense resources of knowledge and experience. Even though camouflaged I had to maintain Krupps as an armament factory for the distant future, in spite of all obstacles."[10]

After the Kapp putsch on March 13, 1920, when President Ebert and his cabinet fled from Berlin and ordered the labor unions to proclaim a general strike, the radical leftists in the Ruhr were given an excuse for an uprising.[11] The radical socialist Rote Soldatenbund (Red Soldiers League) seized an arsenal of weapons in Bochum. Seventy thousand men were armed and began marching toward Essen. On March 19 the Red soldiers fought a hard battle with the Essen police and a Free Corps unit. Over three hundred men were killed; the Red soldiers won, and the Krupp factories were occupied.

Just before dark on the evening of March 20, an armored car manned by socialist workers and appropriately painted bright red turned off the Alfredstrasse and headed up the hill toward the dark fortresslike Villa Hügel. The domestic staff inside nervously fingered the triggers of their rifles. Something like this had been expected. There had been stories in the German press of the murder of Czar Nicholas and his family by the Russian Communists. It was feared that the German revolutionaries might try to butcher the first family of German industry, the Krupps, in the same ghastly manner. The armored car stopped in the center of the driveway; several Red soliders came toward the main door of the Villa. They pounded and shouted "Open up." One of the footmen, Karl Dohrmann, went to the door. Of all the male servants he had had the most military experience and it was thought that he could best deal with other ex-soldiers. The armed men announced that they were a requisitioning unit with orders to collect food for the Red Army. Dohrmann led them down to the kitchens and gave them all they could carry. Loaded with food they departed, without even asking about the Krupps.

If the Red soldiers had tried to arrest the Krupps they would have failed. None of the family were in Villa Hügel that evening. When he had received the first reports of trouble, Gustav had put his wife and children in cars and set out for Sayneck, the family hunting lodge on the Rhine. But the Red soldiers didn't even try to arrest Gustav Krupp. Perhaps he was just lucky, or perhaps the Ebert government had made a special request through socialist channels that Germany's number-one arms maker be left alone.

Finally the German Army intervened and marched into the Ruhr on April 2, 1920. (This was technically a violation of the Versailles Treaty which forbade German troops from entering the Ruhr.) There was bloody fighting, but by April 10 the insurgents had been crushed and the Army withdrew. The Krupp factories immediately resumed production. Forbidden by the Versailles Treaty to make arms, the Krupp firm and other arms factories heavily advertised their new peacetime products—agricultural and textile machines, dredgers, motor scooters, cash registers, and locomotives, but all the while, means were devised whereby these agricultural and domestic implements could be useful for the "war of liberation."

In the winter of 1920–1921 Gustav Krupp bought five hundred acres for a new plant in Merseburg near some of the best lignite mines in Germany, and at the same time acquired a number of new coal mines which gave his company a coal reserve of over ten million tons. Where was the money for this expansion coming from? Not from sales, for the peacetime line of products was hardly breaking even. "The Allied spying commission was fooled," boasted Krupp. was involved in secret projects for the government of the Weimar Republic and in return was receiving government subsidies. The study and development of heavy tractors laid the groundwork for the construction of tanks, and in 1928, little more than a year after the departure of the Allied Control Commission, the first tanks were produced at the Krupp firm's Grusonwerk factory.[12]

The many foreign journalists who toured the Krupp plant in the twenties were, in Gustav's own words, "hoodwinked." A reporter of the *Christian Science Monitor* remarked at the ease with which the manufacturers of arms were adjusting to peacetime production. *The Manchester Guardian* commented: "One can have no hesitation in affirming, after a visit at Krupps, that everything connected with war industry has been scrapped." The newspapermen, however, should have noticed an odd coincidence. Those who brought cameras to the Krupp factory all found that their film could not be developed. Surprisingly, every roll had been overexposed. Gustav Krupp knew the answer to the mystery. Before leaving the plant the reporters had been invited to have a snack in the company lunchroom, courtesy of the firm. Their cameras were put in a checkroom and, while they ate, an infrared ray was aimed at their lenses. It was later said that this had been done because the barrels of giant artillery pieces had been set upright in the factory and surrounded by bricks to camouflage them as chimneys. Krupp was more subtle than that. Forbidden work was in progress, but at that stage it was not yet being manufactured. Everything was still on the drawing boards, but there was some fear that an innocent photograph might later be examined by the trained eye of an ordnance engineer and reveal something.

Gustav Krupp's reactions to the revolutionary upheaval, the Versailles Treaty and rearmament are significant not only because they are the personal experiences of a prominent industrialist, but because they reflect the political attitude of German business leaders as a whole. In the meantime, top industrialists like Krupp acknowledged the authority of the new government of the Weimar Republic and cooperated in every possible way with the moderate Social Democrats. This attitude of restraint and open-mindedness did not emerge by chance, but was the result of the liberal political philosophy held by the most advanced sectors of German business for the past fifty years.

Up to the last days of World War I Germany was an absolute

monarchy. Most big businessmen, such as Gustav Krupp, were completely loyal to their sovereign, yet they hoped for liberal reforms that would gradually bring about a true parliamentary government and a constitutional monarchy.[13] In Imperial Germany big business, although influential and indispensable, was subordinate in actual power to the traditional political elite which was made up of a complex power structure of monarchy, officer corps, nobility, and high bureaucracy. In the great, glittering reception salons of the Kaiser's court, people were always received in order of their rank. First came the higher nobility, princes and dukes, in regal uniforms covered with gold. Next came the Army officers in blue and white uniforms that were only slightly less splendid, with military medals and decorations of every conceivable sort sparkling on their chests. They were followed by the diplomats and civil servants who were also entitled to wear a uniform, though it was not nearly as chic as that of the Army. Last came the civilians dressed in black. Industrialists and businessmen, regardless of their wealth, were placed in this category. Socially, they ranked lower than the most humble young lieutenant. The military collapse in 1918 distressed business leaders as much as anyone else, but to a certain extent they blamed the collapse on the incompetence of the old political rulers and their mismanagement of the war economy. Many of Germany's most important businessmen regarded the passing of the old regime with ambivalent feelings and a sense of opportunity.

Carl Duisberg, the founder of I.G. Farben, the great chemical trust, and the president of the National Association of German Industry (Reichsverband) from 1925 to 1930, expressed this viewpoint in a letter he wrote to a colleague in October 1918, three turbulent weeks before the Republic officially came into existence: "From the day when I saw that the [Imperial] cabinet system was bankrupt, I greeted the change to a parliamentary system with joy, and I stand today, when what is at stake is what I consider to be of the highest value, namely the Fatherland, behind the democratic government and, where possible, I work hand in hand with the unions and seek in this way to save what can be saved. You see I am an opportunist and adjust to things as they are."[14]

By November, Duisberg was of the opinion that in the "Red

republic" a "more commercial-technical spirit would replace the largely formalistic way of thinking and doing things brought into our administration by the jurists." Like most other influential men of industry, commerce, and finance, Duisberg shed no tears over the passing of the "holy bureaucratism" of the past.[15]

Duisberg's remarks are an excellent example of the basic conflicts between the industrialists and the old political elite. German business leaders, like their colleagues everywhere, believed in the primacy of economics over politics. The "opportunism" of which Duisberg spoke was one of the keys to the survival of big business during the early days of the Republic. By rapidly concluding an alliance with the trade-union leaders before it was too late, the industrialists established a base from which they could unobtrusively exercise a decisive role in regulating the economic affairs of the Weimar government.

Fritz Ebert, a moderate Social Democrat who had been chosen President of the Republic, had worked constructively with the Army and government throughout the war. A short man with a double chin and a large stomach, Ebert was the perfect image of a cautious bureaucrat. Like the rest of his colleagues, he had neither wanted nor planned a revolution. Indeed, he would have been willing to accept Prince Max of Baden as Regent of the Empire and even Prince August-Wilhelm, the Kaiser's youngest son, as Regent in Prussia. The maximum demand made by the Social Democrats in their ultimatum of November 8 to the Chancellor was for the abdication of the Kaiser and the Crown Prince.

On the dark night of November 9, 1918 as revolutionary mobs roamed Berlin, Ebert sat alone in the Chancellor's office afraid the Communists were about to overthrow his moderate socialist government. Although the windows were closed and the thick velvet curtains drawn, the noises of the demonstrators in the streets still could be heard. Ebert had no military unit on which he could depend to enforce his authority. Suddenly the ringing of the telephone on his desk drowned out all other sounds. It was General Gröner calling on the secret line from the military headquarters at the front. The General and Ebert were in complete agreement as to the necessary action to be taken.[16] They agreed on the desirability of getting rid of the radical socialists from the government, eliminating the soldiers' and workers' councils from any position of influence, and getting the Army out of the revolutionary atmosphere as soon as possible.

Although most businessmen would have preferred a government oriented more toward laissez-faire economic principles than Ebert and the moderate Social Democrats, they realized that it was necessary to make some concessions to the working class in order to avoid a real social revolution. The strategy of big business leaders who cooperated with the moderate Social Democrats was effectively summed up by a Social Democratic official of the Prussian government: "The Social Democrats," he said, "are the most effective defenders of capitalism. For they, better than anybody else, have learned the technique of explaining convincingly to the workers how it is not yet possible to take steps toward setting up a socialist state and why it is necessary to wait . . . a while longer."[17] The General Staff of the Army went along with this strategy because they realized that only by this means could Germany comply with President Wilson's prerequisites for peace; furthermore, they secretly welcomed the existence of a moderately "revolutionary" government in Berlin that would take the odious responsibility of negotiating and signing the peace treaty.

Certainly it should be mentioned that under the Republic the workers and peasants won vital economic and political advantages: the extension of universal suffrage to both sexes, the eight-hour day, general recognition of union agreements, unemployment insurance, and the right to elect shop committees. However, the gains of the farm laborers employed on the great estates of East Prussia were much more limited than those of the industrial workers. Although they won the right to organize unions, in order to elect a shop committee they had to have at least twenty workers in the same establishment as compared with only ten in industry. The agricultural workday was fixed at ten, not eight hours, and farm servants were excepted from union agreements.

In spite of the limited nature of the reforms for agricultural workers, the new labor laws threatened the interests and prestige of the Junker landowners far more than they harmed big business. True, some of the more conservative businessmen resented having to make concessions to the workers, but key leaders of big business, such as Duisberg, Krupp, and Stinnes, stood squarely behind the Republic.

Among that segment of society generally classified as "big business" there were many different political points of view. For example; although Krupp and Duisberg both supported the Weimar Republic, they and their firms, Krupp and I.G. Farben, backed different political parties. For the most part the political differences between big business were based on economic interests rather than personal preferences.[18] In order to understand more clearly the political goals of "big business," it is necessary to identify its limits as a group and its component parts, each of which had different political objectives. Actually the term "big business" does not imply a homogeneous entity. Various groupings within it—industry (heavy and light), commerce, and finance—have different economic interests. Such groupings are closely interrelated and the lines of demarcation between them are not always very sharp; but this by no means prevents the existence of antagonisms.[19] One must be aware of these groupings to pinpoint where and how Hitler was able to utilize the divisions within big business to his own advantage.

To the average person all factories must have looked alike. From the Ruhr to Hamburg their tall smokestacks all belched the same sooty clouds. Whether they were producers of steel or chemicals, the air in their vicinity was always polluted with foul odors. The large, gray factory buildings sat in rows, some low and flat, some high and windowless, but all with the same half-deserted look. Yet the noise of these buildings never seemed to cease: the clanging of metals, the pounding of hammers, and the shrill sound of the factory whistle. At night the illumination cast by the furnaces gave the scene the look of a kind of inferno. It might also have been said that, like the factories, German big businessmen all looked alike. From appearance alone it would have been difficult to tell the difference between a mine owner or a banker. They all were middle-aged, portly gentlemen wearing dark-blue or gray pinstripe suits and riding in long, black Mercedes limousines. But just as their wealth was dependent on different goods, so they needed different political conditions, taxes, tariffs, and wage laws to give them advantages over their competitors. The need for these advantages, of course, would become more acute if business were not good.

In a time of general economic difficulties, such as Germany experienced after World War I, the antagonisms inherent in the capitalist system swell up and often lead to unrestrained conflict and possibly even to a revision of the political structure. From 1918 on, the conflicts within German big business centered primarily around two groups, heavy industry (iron, steel, and mining, etc.) versus light industry (electrical, chemical, textiles, etc.) The magnates of heavy industry and their bankers were struggling to regain their former markets and economic position: consequently, they wanted to take back many of the concessions made to the workers in 1918-1919. Light industry, producing consumer goods for the most part, adopted a policy of collaboration with organized labor. This difference in political strategy can be traced to the economic structure of the two contending groups. The capital invested in heavy industry was of a "higher composition" than that in light industry—i.e., more was invested in large, expensive plants and less in wages. This imposed on heavy industry a crushing load of fixed expenses from interest, depreciation, and maintenance of plant, which could not be reduced simply because production fell off. The only alternative was that wages, the chief flexible item in heavy industry's costs, had to be reduced drastically in periods of depression. Light industry, which had comparatively few expenses, did not need such rigid control over labor and so could follow a more conciliatory policy.

Light industry and commerce (department stores, retail merchants), whose revenues derive primarily from direct trade with the retail market, wanted an economic policy that would restore prosperity by restoring the purchasing power of the people. Heavy industry, of course, did not want to see the purchasing power of the lower classes wiped out completely; they simply wanted to revive purchasing power on a lower price level, one that would give them an advantage in world markets and control over all domestic industry.

Light industry, which was gaining an increasingly significant role in the economy, rebelled against the dominant position of heavy industry which forced it to pay monopoly prices for the raw materials and machines it needed. Walther Rathenau, president of the powerful A.E.G. (The General Electric Association) publicly denounced the dictatorship of the great metal and mining industries. Just as medieval nobles had scoffed at the German Emperor and divided Germany into Grand Duchies, said

Rathenau, leaders of heavy industry were dividing Germany into economic duchies "where they think only of coal, iron, and steel and *neglect, or rather absorb, the other industries.*"

The aftermath of the war and the obligations of the Versailles Treaty impelled heavy industry to favor a foreign policy that would recapture its lost markets and sources of raw material, particularly in eastern Europe, and shake off reparations which added greatly to their production costs. The dominant groups in heavy industry were strong advocates of the Reichsbank's inflationary policy because, among other reasons, it created an excellent opportunity for them to regain some of their foreign markets. At a private meeting of steel producers in Düsseldorf, Hugo Stinnes, who was the moving spirit behind one of the most powerful business organizations, the National Association of German Industries, said: "If we have the coal we need, our country will be the natural land of quality production, on the one hand because of our exchange situation (inflated currency), and on the other hand because of our wages, which, in view of our exchange situation, are the lowest in the world."[20] Although this so-called inflation boom was profitable for heavy industry, it was not conducive to harmony even within the business community. Light industry suffered from the scarcity and high prices of raw materials. Frequently light industry combined with labor in the struggle against the pricing policies of heavy industry, but to no avail.

Under the Hohenzollerns, heavy industry, which earned a significant portion of its profits from the munitions orders of the German government as well as "friendly powers," favored an imperialistic foreign policy. An immediate return to such a policy was impossible after the defeat in 1918, and from 1924 to 1929 a strategy of international collaboration was needed because the reorganization of German industry was carried out largely on foreign capital. However, with the onset of the depression, foreign loans ceased and there was no longer any motive for collaboration. Heavy industry then saw no other alternative than to return to its old expansionist program in order to obtain the raw materials it needed, while at the same time it sought to defend its home market by protectionist tendencies.

Light industry on the other hand was oriented chiefly toward export trade and therefore favored a policy of international cooperation and free trade. Companies such as A.E.G. (The General Electric Association) and I.G. Farben were closely connected with international finance and their counterparts abroad, such as General Electric of America and Dupont Chemical. Carl Duisberg, the president of I.G. Farben, often said: "The world is the chemist's field of activity." Most of the products of light industry were nonmilitary and hence it had little to gain from the secret rearmament plans of heavy industry and the General Staff. Thus, even before the beginning of the depression, big business was seriously divided as to what strategy the government should pursue in both domestic and foreign policy.

Faced with such harsh determination on the part of the victors to restrict Germany from world markets, it is not surprising that most German business leaders had only limited faith in the possibility of peaceful revision of the Versailles Treaty and turned to rearmament as the only alternative. To the unbiased observer it was becoming obvious that the antagonisms between the European states had merely been suspended for a while and would sooner or later break out again with a still more violent intensity. The Versailles Treaty had placed the German economy in an even tighter straitjacket than it had been in before World War I.

The causes of Germany's expansion, however, had not been abolished. It was not a matter of choice that had driven German industry toward imperialist expansion, but rather it was the result of irresistible economic forces. The dynamic strength of German imperialism rested upon the nation's basic economic drives for survival; therefore, it could not be swept away merely by the defeat and limitation of the Army.

Before World War I, Germany had become the number-one industrial power in Europe, yet she had been cut off from foreign markets by the empires of Britain, France, and the Allies. By 1929, German industry had been modernized and rebuilt and was under considerable pressure to open up new markets for itself abroad; however, because of the restrictions of the Versailles Treaty, it was not even able to obtain prewar foreign trade levels. Economic rivalry between the industrialized nations of Europe, the ultimate source of the dangerous tensions which had led to World War I, was not liquidated but continued to exist and was even intensified.

Big business was committed to a policy of "national liberation" and expansion by a matter of economic necessity. However, if Germany were to overcome "the Versailles system" and regain equality with the other powers, the rearmament program would ultimately have to be directed by the Army; the industrialists could not do it alone.

The task of "neutralizing the poison contained in the disarmament clauses of the Versailles Treaty,"[21] as he put it, was carried out primarily by General Hans von Seeckt, the Commander-in-Chief of the Reichswehr from 1920 to 1926. At first glance General von Seeckt seemed to be a typical Prussian officer, but despite his neat, precise, military appearance, Hans von Seeckt was well traveled, well read, and had a very keen intellect. When he wanted to be, he was a warm and fascinating conversationalist, but when the occasion demanded he could also present a very cold exterior that led people to call him "the sphinx with the monocle." During his period as Commander-in-Chief of the Army, von Seeckt concentrated all his energies on two primary objectives: (1) reorganization of the Army within the restrictions imposed by the treaty, but with such a high level of technical efficiency that in due course it could be expanded into a mass national Army, and (2) preservation of the Prussian military traditions despite the same treaty restrictions. In other words, he wanted to evade the treaty without openly violating it. Unlike most of his military colleagues, von Seeckt had a clear understanding of politics; it was said that he was one of few German generals with an appreciation of the political and economic aspects of war. The real secret of von Seeckt's political and military genius was his ability to take the long view. Like Lenin, von Seeckt recognized the value of strategic retreat in politics; he was willing to abandon an immediate objective in order to obtain a greater goal.

Von Seeckt understood, above all, the vital fact that the intellectual demilitarization of Germany was more important for the Allies and consequently more dangerous for the Germans than the mere limitation of the Army. Hence, in the early twenties he believed it was best to support the Weimar Republic and operate behind a facade of democracy for the next few years at least. On this matter his opinion agreed with that of a rising nationalist politician in Munich, one Adolf Hitler, who told his audiences that it was spiritual and intellectual rearmament that counted; if only Germany had the *will* to defend herself, all else would follow naturally.

When Hitler denounced the Versailles Treaty in the dark, cavernous back rooms of Munich's beerhalls, his speeches were based on emotional rather than logical appeal. The smoke-filled air and the noisy clatter of beer mugs hardly provided the ideal atmosphere for a political meeting, but once Hitler began to speak a hushed silence settled over the room. The men and women in the audience were desperate, their clothes were threadbare, and their faces gaunt from hunger. They knew nothing about economics or industry; they only knew they couldn't face unemployment, hunger, and poverty much longer. Standing on a solid wooden table, Hitler spoke with fiery determination that gave the people faith. He said the Versailles Treaty was responsible for their misery; if they only had the will to resist, the treaty could not be forced upon them. Businessmen would not have been swayed by such arguments, but then again they were not among the listeners. The rise and fall in the volume of Hitler's voice and the increasing tempo of his speech held the audience spellbound. Men sat and listened with their mouths hanging open; women began to sob. The speech thundered to a climax and with a dramatic, sweeping gesture of his right arm Hitler seemed to be, as he said, "pushing the Versailles *Diktat* into the dustbin of history."

General von Seeckt admired Hitler's ability to win the masses for the cause of nationalism, for he envisaged the day when such a surge of patriotism would be necessary for "national liberation." The two men met for the first time on March 11, 1923, in Munich; von Seeckt was favorably impressed but did not show it at the time. Later he made the very revealing comment: "We were one in our aim; only our paths were different."[22]

The Nazi Party certainly played a part in the rearmament program. Until the Army could openly increase its size, Hitler's S.A. was a kind of military reserve. When the Storm Troopers would first begin to assemble in some remote field to drill, they did not look very impressive in their ski caps and baggy brown shirts; but when the sergeant-major barked out the command to "fall in," the rowdy group of street fighters suddenly became a disciplined body of men. True, their arms were haphazard and they had no heavy weapons, but these could always be provided by the Army in time of national emergency.

Almost a year before the Treaty of Rapallo officially reestablished diplomatic relations between Germany and Soviet Russia,* General von Seeckt was instrumental in formulating a secret agreement of Russo-German military collaboration. Germany would help train the young Red Army and build up the Russian arms industry; in return, the agreement provided Germany with a place to train its officers and build its own arms industry beyond the watchful eyes of the Allied disarmament commission. On the vast, empty plains of Russia, where the eye could see to the horizon, there was no one to hear the whistle and whine of the bullets or the dull thud of artillery shells as the Reichswehr tested its new weapons. This accord with Soviet Russia would also be of considerable benefit to German big business. Large orders were received by German industrial firms, like Krupps, which would not only bring them financial profit, but would permit them to expand their plants, to progress scientifically and technically in arms building, and to maintain the thousands of specialized workers necessary for the secret rearmament program soon to be carried out within Germany itself.

The little Army which von Seeckt was in the process of perfecting for future expansion had to be matched by an economic organization, equally capable of expansion, that could equip and maintain the military might of Germany once it had been restored. A highly secret office was set up in November 1924 under the direction of General Wurzbacher to act as a kind of economic general staff. Von Seeckt believed the outcome of the "war of liberation" would ultimately depend upon the work of this office. In the meantime, its task was to prepare plans for the economic mobilization of Germany, to equip and maintain an Army of sixty-three divisions. In addition, this office was to obtain the cooperation of industry in establishing "spear-head organizations" which would concentrate on the development of economic and industrial rearmament not only within the Reich but also in Austria, Italy, the Netherlands, Spain, Sweden, and Switzerland. A study was made of foreign raw materials and industries that

---

*At Rapallo, Italy, in 1922 Russia and Germany made a treaty by which they renounced all claims of war damages against each other and agreed to resume all normal relations.

would be particularly useful to Germany, and special emphasis was placed in training military officers in economic affairs.

The activities of this secret economic planning office were received with enthusiasm in the leading circles of German industry. One of the goals was to replace the machines and property demolished by orders of the Allied disarmament commission. Property of the Krupp firm, for example, worth over 104 million gold marks was destroyed. Nine thousand three hundred machines weighing over 60,000 tons were demolished; 801,420 gauges, moulds, and other tools with a total weight of almost one thousand tons, along with 379 installations such as hardening ovens, cranes, oil and water tanks, and cooling plants were smashed.

This so-called "dismantling" demanded by the Versailles Treaty was a very bitter experience for many German industrialists and undoubtedly played a part in their later willingness to accept Hitler. Thyssen, Krupp, Kirdorf, and other executives stood helpless as they watched the work of generations senselessly destroyed. The forges were shut down and the dismantling began. It was a grim business. Toiling in the summer heat of 1920, the workers were forced to destroy their own source of livelihood and were bitter and sullen. They scarcely spoke a word to one another. The Allied engineers paced the shop floors, marking with colored chalk the machine tools, lathes, and other equipment to be shipped abroad. Once the cranes had hoisted them away, the dynamiting began. Each morning shortly after dawn explosions rocked Essen, Düsseldorf, and other rural industrial cities.

The Krupp factories were to be cut down to one-half their former size.[23] Building after building was demolished; bricks and steel were crushed. The gutting and razing of their factories was a degrading experience for the industrialists and the workers. Gustav Krupp became so enraged that he refused to watch any more of it. He got in his car and drove away to the Black Forest. Even years later Krupp was incensed by the memory of the "uncouth, irreconcilable attitude of the Allied Control Commission."

Immediately after the Treaty of Rapallo was signed, Walther Rathenau, who was then Foreign Minister, urged Gustav Krupp to take over a large trading concession in Russia to prove that German business was prepared to collaborate in a practical way in furthering the aims of the treaty. Krupp consented at once. In explaining his new Russian project to his firms board of directors, Krupp stated that a German Army officer had told him that Lenin had said, "The steppe must be turned into a bread factory, and Krupp must help us." Shortly thereafter Krupp agricultural machines were sent to plow up 65,000 acres between Rostov and Astrakahn.

Von Seeckt and Krupp had more important things in mind than agricultural machinery, but they could not be done in haste. Karl Radek, Trotsky's chief lieutenant, had to come to Berlin to work out the arrangements for the munitions industry. The details were negotiated with him in the apartment of Kurt von Schleicher, who would eventually become Minister of Defense and Chancellor. Von Seeckt and Schleicher represented the Army and Friedrich von Büllow represented Krupps. The results benefited all three parties. Gustav Krupp was very pleased with the new Soviet deal and had no ideological qualms about doing business with the Communists. In this respect he was very different from Fritz Thyssen, who put political beliefs above pragmatic business policy.

While secretly rearming in Russia, Germany was pursuing a policy of good will or "fulfillment" with the western Allies. The chief architect of this policy was Gustav Stresemann, a politician with a strong probusiness background.[24] Stresemann had come a long way since the war when he had acted as the mouthpiece of the High Command in the Reichstag and the arch-apostle of annexationist claims. He had even progressed since the days of the Kapp putsch when he had tried to find a face-saving formula for the fallen "dictator." Like General von Seeckt, he was a monarchist and conservative at heart, but he too realized that if Germany was to be restored to her former position as a world power she must have a period of peace and recuperation. The restrictions of the Versailles Treaty would not be relaxed until the fears and suspicions of the Allies had been, at least to some extent, allayed.

Stresemann's bald head, puffy cheeks, and narrow slanting eyes made him the butt of vicious Nazi caricatures depicting him as an evil, leering Mongolian. Undoubtedly, the fact that he had a Jewish wife did not help to endear him to Hitler's followers. In the spring of 1928, Stresemann came to Munich to deliver an election speech. Five hundred Storm Troopers in brown shirts led by

Hermann Esser, an experienced rabble-rouser, pushed their way into the meeting and took seats in the front of the room. During the dark days of the occupation of the Ruhr, Stresemann had once spoken of seeing "a small silver stripe on the horizon." The five hundred S.A. men had fastened glittering stripes of tinfoil and silver paper to their hair, their buttonholes, and some even to the seat of their pants. In unison they chanted: "Where is the silver stripe, Herr Stresemann?" For a while Stresemann managed to speak over the roar. At their wit's end, the Nazis suddenly stood up and began to sing the national anthem *Deutschland über Alles*. The audience rose to their feet and also began singing. The gentlemen on the speaker's platform stood up too. Stresemann's political associates—an industrialist, a banker, a lawyer, and a retired general—obediently joined in the singing, for it was the national anthem and they were all patriots. Thus the meeting was broken up and the German Foreign Minister looked ridiculous in the eyes of the world.

Such incidents, which illustrate the great difference in the political tactics of Hitler and Stresemann, have led many historians to overlook the fact that the ideas of Stresemann and Hitler did not differ on the most important long-range foreign policy goal—Germany's reemergence as a world power. Up to 1930 moderation was what was needed in foreign policy; Hitler's tactics were simply too hard-line. In contrast, both Stresemann and von Seeckt turned their backs on what they considered the "glamorous but unattainable" dreams of monarchist restoration and conservative dictatorship. They decided to use a facade of democracy, which was provided by the Weimar Republic, as a convincing weapon in their campaign to reassure the Allies. Though neither of them was sincerely democratic-minded, both were sincere in their efforts to strengthen and protect the Weimar Republic; both worked for the future greatness and power of Germany. Although he denied it, Stresemann "unofficially" knew of Germany's illegal rearmament in Russia while he was negotiating with the western powers.

Germany's secret activities for the circumvention of the military clauses of the Versailles Treaty were by no means confined to Russia. By using anonymous companies and foreign subsidiaries, the Krupp firm was able to carry out experimental arms construction outside Germany in neutral countries. Through

Siderius A.G., the Krupp-controlled shipbuilding yards of Rotterdam, a special center for the manufacture of naval weapons was established, and staffed by the engineers and skilled workers transferred from the Germania shipyard at Kiel. Similar holding companies operated in Barcelona, Cadiz, Turkey, and Finland, where U-boats were built under the direction of the best German naval architects.[25] The blueprints and experts were always provided by the research department in Essen.

Because the government of the Weimar Republic was secretly committed to a policy of rearmament, it gave every possible covert assistance to business engaged in the productions of munitions. Heavy financial support from the Reich government enabled Krupps to gain a controlling interest in the Bofors Arms industry of Sweden in 1925, where they immediately began to manufacture tanks, antiaircraft guns, and heavy artillery.[26] Yet in spite of such close cooperation between the government of the Republic and big business, most of the tycoons of heavy industry were still distressed. As Fritz Thyssen said, they recognized that "Germany after 1918 was overindustrialized." The tremendous productive capacity of German industry simply did not correspond to the severely limited markets available to them, though the leaders of light industry *might* hope for relief if the international economic situation improved a bit and favorable trade agreements were worked out with the Allies through a policy of compromise.

The Krupp firm was Germany's principal armaments manufacturer and for that reason alone received government subsidies. Such government help, however, was given to very few other firms of heavy industry. Thyssen's United Steel Works, for example, was a much bigger corporation than Krupps, but it received virtually no government assistance and was slowly going bankrupt. Thus heavy industry as a whole could see no solution to their problems other than *total* rearmament.

The plans for economic and industrial mobilization proposed by the Army's secret economic staff received the approval of big business and almost all political forces, with the exception of the Communists, and these plans were pushed forward as part of the general industrial development of the country. From 1924 to 1927 the emphasis was placed on planning and designing prototypes. With the departure of the Allied Control Commission on January

31, 1927, the second phase of German rearmament began and factories were adapted for the mass production of the prototypes built abroad. The budget of the Army increased rapidly from 490 million marks in 1924 to 827 million marks in 1928. For the next few years it decreased slightly due to the depression, but in 1930 it was still comparatively high at a figure of 787 million marks.

The size of the Army's budget and its key role in directing rearmament should not, however, lead to the conclusion that it was all powerful. Von Seeckt had opposed any security pact with the western powers, preferring instead to maintain his secret accord with Moscow; but by the mid-twenties big business viewed his continued hostility to the West as a hindrance to the economic advantages offered in the Dawes Plan. Stresemann turned against von Seeckt and carried his policy to a successful conclusion in the Locarno Agreement in spite of the General's resistance.* By the fall of 1926 von Seeckt was forced to resign his post as Commander-in-Chief of the Reichswehr.

Although they opposed big business on many fundamental questions, the Social Democrats were in general agreement with the rearmament program.[27] In 1928, when some of the members of their party opposed the construction of "pocket-battleships" as an extravagant expenditure, General Gröner, the Minister of Defense, pointed out that, on the contrary, the new naval building program would actually benefit the national economy and the workers in particular because it would ensure the employment of over 3,000 laborers in the Kiel shipyards. Gröner also went on to say that approximately 70 percent of the expenditure for this program, or 56 million marks, would be returned to the people in the form of wages.

The secret rearmament program does not necessarily prove that Germany was planning aggressive warfare or that the German character was instinctively militaristic. Too often it goes unnoticed that the Germans were not the only ones to violate the spirit of the Versailles Treaty. The preamble of Part V of the Treaty of Versailles, introducing the limitations on Germany's military and naval powers, read: "In order to render possible the initiation

---

*By the Locarno treaties of 1925 the Franco-German border and the Belgian-German border were guaranteed. England and Italy promised to fight whoever violated the frontier. France and Germany agreed to seek arbitration to settle their disputes. In return Germany was accepted as a member of the League of Nations.

of a general limitation of the armaments of all nations, Germany undertakes strictly to observe the military, naval, and air clauses which follow." The disarmament of Germany, however, did not ease the nerves of the world, because it was a method of political and economic oppression rather than a sincere step toward universal disarmament.

While the Germans were secretly drawing plans for new tanks and making one or two prototypes, France was producing thousands of them. The German Army was limited to 100,000 men with no reserves, while France maintained a standing Army of 612,000 men with an active reserve of 3,488,000. Germany was forbidden to have any tanks while France had 3,500. All the planes of the German Air Force were destroyed in 1919 and building any new ones was strictly outlawed, while France, who was not alone in steadily increasing the size of her military forces, had 2,800 planes. Even Poland, for example, had a standing Army of 266,000 men, over twice the size of Germany's, and an active reserve of 3,200,000 men, and an Air Force of 1,000 planes.

One of the best justifications of Germany's rearmament was stated in an article written by Gustav Krupp entitled "Objectives of German Policy." He protested that the Germans were being treated as second-class members of the world community: "The vital rights of national defense enjoyed by all other peoples are withheld from them. Not *increase* in armaments but *equality* of armaments must therefore be the aim of every German government. In Germany we have no interest in any increase in armament throughout the world . . . as a businessman I am of the opinion that international disarmament must be the general aim."[28]

Regardless of their particular party loyalties, the gaining of national independence was the real aim of all the Weimar governments. Political and economic as well as military equality were to be reestablished relative to the other great powers. Thus, the ultimate goal was the restoration of Germany as an imperial state. The only disagreement among the German power elite was on the question of how national resurgence would be accomplished. Light industry favored a policy of international cooperation; heavy industry wanted complete rearmament; agricultural interests, commerce, and labor all had their pet programs; but for all, the objective was basically the same. Germany was just beginning to make some headway toward recovery when the depression began. With the coming of economic collapse rivalries and hostilities intensified. As the possiblity of sinking into ruin became very real, everyone began to think only in terms of saving himself. Germany's options narrowed: national recovery would have to come quickly, before internal collapse.

The advocate of drastic measures, the one politician who had predicted the economic collapse and prepared himself for it, was waiting in the wings. Stirring up the nationalistic passions of the people and motivating them with the concepts of duty, honor, and self-sacrifice, was Hitler's specialty. A police report of one of Hitler's meetings in 1927 illustrates the patriotic, militaristic atmosphere of the Nazi Party and the copying of symbols from Mussolini's "movement of national revival" in Italy: "From the entrance come roars of 'Heil.' . . . Then a trumpet blast." Amid cheers from the spectators, disciplined columns of Brownshirts march into the hall, led by two rows of drummers and the bright red swastika flag. "The men salute in the Fascist manner, with outstretched arms. The audience cheers them. On the stage Hitler has also stretched out his arm in salute." Then two brass bands begin to play a military march. "The flags move past, glittering standards with swastika inside a wreath, and others with eagles modeled on the ancient Roman military standards. About two hundred men march past . . . the flagbearers and standard bearers occupy the stage."[29] This was the right mood for Hitler to begin his speech.

Although Hitler's methods and tactics were more blatant and extreme than those of the industrialists, generals, or politicians of the established parties, his primary goal, at least in the matter of foreign policy, was the same. *"The aim of German foreign policy today,"* he said in *Mein Kampf, "must be the preparation for the reconquest of freedom for tomorrow."*[30] From the beginning Hitler had a unique grasp of the harsh realities of international power politics. On April 10, 1923, shortly after the occupation of the Ruhr by the French, he delivered a speech in Munich which was a strange combination of insight into the decisive elements of the relations between states and the most vicious kind of rabble-rousing: "No economic policy is possible without a sword, no industrialization without power. Today we no longer have a sword grasped in our fist—how can we have a successful economic policy? England has fully recognized this primary maxim in the healthy life of states; for centuries England has acted on the principle of converting economic strength into political power, while conversely political power in its turn must protect economic life. . . . Three years ago I decided in this same room that the collapse of German national consciousness must carry with it into the abyss the economic life of Germany as well. For liberation something more is necessary than an economic policy, something more than industry: If a people is to become free it needs pride and willpower, defiance, hate and once again hate."[31]

In *Mein Kampf* Hitler often discussed questions of foreign policy with crude slogans and oversimplifications; there are, nevertheless, some passages in which he revealed an understanding for the real nature (as contrasted with the idealized popular conception) of international politics. In rebutting the optimistic ideas of some German nationalists, he clearly stated that policies of alliance between world powers are never based on mutual respect or affection but only on *"expediency."* "No consideration of foreign policy can proceed from any other criterion than this: *Does it benefit our nationality now or in the future, or will it be injurious to it?* This is the sole preconceived opinion permissible in dealing with this question. Partisan, religious, humanitarian, and all other criteria . . . are completely irrelevant."[32]

Hitler understood the basic strategy of both British and French foreign policy. The primary objective of British policy, he said, was to prevent the rise of any continental power that could challenge her position of dominance; this goal was accomplished by maintaining a "balance of power" among the European states, thus guaranteeing British world hegemony. The primary goal of French policy, on the other hand, was to prevent the formation of a unified German power, to maintain a "balance of power" between petty states in central Europe and to occupy the left bank of the Rhine in order to safeguard her position of hegemony in Europe. "The ultimate aim of French diplomacy," concluded Hitler, "will always stand in conflict with the ultimate tradition of British statesmanship. . . . Just as England's traditional political aims desire and necessitate a certain Balkanization of Europe, those of France necessitate a Balkanization of Germany."[33] Thus Hitler believed that the inexorable mortal enemy of the German people is and remains France.[34]

An alliance with Italy or England, said Hitler, would give Germany the possibility of peacefully making reparations for a "reckoning with France."[35] There could hardly be doubt as to what kind of sanguinary plans were included in the proposed "reckoning" with France. Yet the"reckoning with France" mentioned in *Mein Kampf* was the same project that the generals, businessmen, and German statesmen were already making preparations for and secretly referring to as "the coming war of liberation." For the leading industrialists, generals, and politicians, the successful outcome of the future "war of liberation" was the ultimate goal; however, this was not the case with Hitler. In *Mein Kampf* he said: "Much as all of us today recognize the necessity of a reckoning with France, it would remain ineffectual in the long run if it represented the whole aim of our foreign policy. It can and will achieve meaning only if it offers the rear cover for an enlargement of our people's living space in Europe. . . . If we speak of soil in Europe today, we can primarily have in mind only Russia and her vassal border states."[36] Here Hitler's ideas on foreign policy diverged from those of the German power elite. His highest objective, once Germany had retained great power status, was realization of the concept of *Lebensraum* (living space).

Hitler had nothing but contempt and ridicule for those German conservatives who demanded the restoration of the pre-1914 borders. He considered such demands "a political absurdity." The pre-1914 frontiers, he said, "were neither complete in the sense of embracing the people of German nationality, nor sensible with regard to geo-military expediency. They were not the result of a considered political action, but momentary frontiers in a political struggle that was by no means concluded."[37] It was conceivable that a few industrialists were also thinking in terms of Germany expanding beyond her pre-1914 borders and would be sympathetic with Hitler's idea of *Lebensraum*. However, Hitler went on in *Mein Kampf* to call for a break with the strategy that had governed German foreign policy before 1914. He declared the time had come to "break off the colonial and commercial policy of the prewar period and shift to the soil policy of the future.[38] Any industrialist reading these lines would have had a difficult time reconciling themselves with such ideas, so Hitler was perhaps fortunate in that few industrialists read *Mein Kampf*.

In the realm of domestic politics Hitler charged that Weimar democracy was a morass of corruption ruled not by the people but by special interest groups and money power. In 1928 there was a sensational scandal in Berlin involving the three Sklarek brothers, clothing manufacturers who had bribed government officials to buy civil service and police uniforms at exorbitant prices. The investigation of the matter uncovered many lurid details and resulted in five suicides. The fact that the Sklareks were Jewish was a godsend to Dr. Goebbels, Hitler's number-one propagandist. In the Nazi newspaper *Der Angriff*, Goebbels ranted about the "carrion stink of political party putrefaction." He stereotyped politicians as "the grossly fat party functionaries who gobbled caviar by the spoonful and swilled champagne by the bucket at their wild carousals." When the trial of the Sklarek brothers revealed that the wives of Social Democratic civil servants had been given mink coats in exchange for their husbands' cooperation, Goebbels said mockingly: "It pays to latch on."[39]

Despite the ravings of Nazi propaganda, the German politicians were not any more corrupt than those in most other democratic societies, such as the United States, which was plagued at the time with big-city political machines and party bosses. There were, however, factors inherent in the Weimar system of government that encouraged corruption. For example, the Sklarek scandal was caused only by the fact that civil servants had accepted bribes; it was not illegal in Germany for politicians to take bribes.[40] In actuality, the political system was based on the buying of Reichstag deputies. The rule of special interest groups and the power of money played an important part in destroying the moral fabric of the Weimar Republic.

The Center Party deputy Adam Stegerwald, who served as Prussian premier and later Reich Minister of Labor, characterized the Reichstag as an *Interessentenhaufen,* meaning a herd representing not principles, but special interests. Stegerwald's accusation was true for all but two political parties: the Communists and the National Socialists. Within the other parties power lay in the hands of the party committee, or machine, whose first loyalty was to "the party interests" or rather the interests of the party's financial backers. Most deputies were little more than puppets in the hands of the party bosses. The party committees became all powerful and decided most issues by their tactical maneuverings.

Just as the Social Democratic Party was an instrument of the trade unions and the bureaucracy of organized labor, the nonsocialist parties were simply the mirrors of various capitalist interest groups. These "bourgeois" or nonsocialist parties had a majority in the Reichstag throughout most of the Weimar period; hence it is crucial to see how big business influenced them and what objectives it intended to accomplish by doing so. Without an understanding of the role of the different big business groups in German politics, it is impossible to comprehend the shifting, complex interplay of the political parties in the period which preceded Hitler's assumption of power.

There were four courses of action commonly used by big business to manipulate political parties or government administrations. Being well organized, corporations or business associations could (1) provide financial backing for particular campaigns or elections, (2) enter into an alliance with a political party by having representatives of business elected to office, (3) arrange for a definite but not publicized partnership with a government by naming the ministers of economics and finance, or (4) influence the policies of a government or the popular attitude toward certain politicians through its ownership of newspapers and other communications media.

Of these four methods, financial contributions were used most frequently and indeed became standard practice in the days of the Weimar Republic. The idea of subsidizing political parties began with the inception of the Republic. Walther Rathenau, the head of the powerful A.E.G., set an example for his industrialist colleagues to follow and he urged each, according to his own predilection, to support political parties of every philosophy and description as far left as the Social Democrats.

The exact size of these political subsidies is difficult to determine. Nowhere in the world are statements of campaign contributions paragons of honesty. For example, financial assistance might take the form of advertising space in a political party newspaper for which an excessive price would be paid. Or it might be a large contribution to a party building project, such that after the structure was completed a considerable sum would be left over to fill the campaign chest. On the books of the donors the actual recipients of these sums never appeared; they appeared merely as tax-free gifts to a worthy cause.

The tycoons of industry took little interest themselves in seeing how the money they gave to the political parties was spent. For this purpose they relied on their political advisors. True, most of the industrialists nominally belonged to one of the nonsocialist parties; but their only real political concern was limited to matters of economic policy and, of course, to see that the "system" remained relatively stable. They took no part in the day-to-day squabbles of the Reichstag, and in fact considered themselves above what the average citizen termed "political activity." When, after returning home from the university, one of the sons of Gustav Krupp began to argue about a particular political party, his father interrupted him, saying: "Politics is taboo here."

Most business associations and even the large companies contributed to several political parties at the same time. In March 1924, for example, the mine owners were assessed 2 marks 50 pfennig per worker to pay for the support given by the Bergbauverein of Essen (an association of the mining industry) to forty candidates considered "friendly" to the mining industry from various parties. This voluntary assessment, however, amounted to only 38,120 marks out of a total of 140,384 marks contributed by the firm Gutehoffnungshütte, a large steel combine, to the 1924 Reichstag and Landtag campaigns. The company was also assessed 2.50 marks per worker by the organization of the smelting industry; that added another 36,500 marks to its donations. In addition, the firm on its own contributed 20,000 marks to the German Nationalist Party, 20,000 marks to the German People's Party, and 10,000 marks to the Center Party, to be distributed to candidates in those parties who were "friendly" to heavy industry. The Gutehoffnungshütte also gave 15,764 marks to various local party organizations in the Ruhr.[41]

Simply because many of the contributions of heavy industry were going to the conservative and right-wing parties did not necessarily mean that big business as a whole, or even heavy industry, supported the more reactionary elements in these parties. It must be remembered that during the Kapp putsch, in March 1920, when the reactionary Right attempted to overthrow President Ebert's Weimar Republic, the powerful National Association of German Industries, which was strongly influenced, if not dominated by heavy industry, came out with a formal denunciation of the Kapp regime.[42] Even the Social Democratic

Party received a certain amount of money from business interests, mostly commercial and retail. It is easy to understand, for example, why some breweries helped finance the Social Democratic Party. Beer was the inexpensive drink of the "common man." It would probably have been suicidal for the brewers to have the word passed around among the workers that they refused to help the party of labor. Actually, the Social Democrats had little need of the large contributions big business made to the "bourgeois" parties, because their affiliation with the trade unions provided them with a more than adequate source of funds from union dues. In 1923, after several years of depression, with millions of unemployed on the streets, the Social Democratic unions still possessed well over one hundred million marks in assets.

On the night of January 9, 1928, one long black limousine after another drove up to the main entrance of the palatial Krupp villa in Essen. The guests were, with one exception, middle-aged men. All were attired in formal evening dress. From their bearing and mannerisms it was obvious that they were individuals of considerable importance. A servant greeted each of the guests at the door, took his hat and coat, and led him through an enormous entrance hall with huge chandeliers, past a heavily carved oak staircase, down a vast long corridor hung with portraits of generals and kaisers and fine tapestries, to a quiet study where his host Gustav Krupp awaited him. This was the first meeting of the Ruhrlade, the most powerful secret organization of big business that existed during the Weimar period.

The idea of founding such an organization was initially put forward by the industrialist Paul Reusch in 1927. He believed that the leading heavy industrialists of the Ruhr should meet informally from time to time, as circumstances demanded, to agree on joint economic and political policy.[43] There were many other big business organizations already in existence in Germany, but the Ruhrlade was to be unique in at least three important respects: (1) it was an organization only of heavy industry, (2) the very existence of the organization was to remain a secret, (3) the membership would be limited to twelve men who controlled some of Germany's greatest corporations.

Among the twelve who gathered for the first meeting on the evening of January 9 were Gustav Krupp, chairman of the board of overseers of the Krupp firm; Fritz Thyssen, chairman of the board of overseers of Germany's largest steel concern, the United Steel Works; Paul Reusch, managing director of the Good Hope Steel Company; Erich Fickler, managing director of the mining firm Harpener Mining A. G., and chairman of the board of directors of the bituminous coal cartel; Paul Silverberg, chairman of the board of directors of Germany's largest lignite mining company, Rheinisch A. G., as well as chairman of the Rhenish lignite cartel; Fritz Springorum, managing director of Hoesch Iron and Steel Works; and Albert Vögler, chairman of the board of directors of the United Steel Works.[44] The members, with the exception of Fritz Springorum, who was forty-one years old, were portly gentlemen in their fifties and sixties. They were all either directors or owners of the largest companies of the Ruhr, and they represented only the traditional and most powerful segment of heavy industry: steel and coal. Most of the members had the authority to speak for their firms and moreover to draw on the financial resources of their companies for any projects of the Ruhrlade.

On ordinary economic and political matters the members of the Ruhrlade usually worked through well-known business groups. This was easy for them by virtue of the prominent positions most of them held in important industrial organizations. Gustav Krupp, for example, was elected chairman of the National Association of German Industries in 1931. Albert Vögler was chairman of the National Organization of Iron Smelters. Paul Reusch was chairman from 1924 to 1930 of two of the most powerful regional business groups, the so-called Long Name Society and the Association of Northwest German Iron and Steel Industrialists. He was succeeded in 1930 by Fritz Springorum who became the new head of both organizations. The other members of the Ruhrlade all held important, if not the top, posts in the upper councils of German business associations.

The members of the Ruhrlade took turns playing host to meetings of the group at their residences or on their country estates. A lavish hunting party was sometimes used as an excuse to cover the real purpose of the meeting of the twelve tycoons. Occasionally they would assemble in places as far away from the Ruhr as Berlin or Vienna and to throw off suspicions take their wives along on the trip.[45]

In the summer of 1928 the Ruhrlade wanted to hold a lengthy

discussion on important economic problems arising from the discontent of agricultural interests, but they could meet for only a few hours in the Ruhr without running the risk of attracting suspicion. Gustav Krupp suggested that the group meet at his castle in the Austrian Alps, Blühnbach. The sparsely populated Alpine region in which the castle was located was almost inaccessible and an ideal place for a secret meeting. The Krupps owned miles and miles of thick pine forests and snow-capped mountains further than the eye could see. Even after the vistor reached the main gate of Blühnbach, he still had a long journey to the castle. There was little danger here from government spies or snoopy reporters. The members conducted their business in complete tranquility and found ample time to enjoy themselves. The four-storied ivy-covered castle was an artistic masterpiece both on the interior and exterior. There were tiger skins on the floors and antique portraits and mounted chamois horns on the walls. These tycoons from the smoke-polluted industrial cities of the Ruhr found the mountain air most invigorating. When their business was done and they were ready to leave, however, they again took care not to attract any undue notice. Gustav Krupp arranged different departure times for his guests so the small local railway stations would not suddenly be full of Germany's most prominent industrialists.[46]

Considering the financial power of its members, it is hardly surprising that the new organization was an immediate success. It proved useful in dealing with problems within the iron and coal industries and in deciding questions of wages. The Ruhrlade also concerned itself with conflicts between heavy industry and other sectors of the economy, the most significant being agriculture. Agrarian interests wanted protection against agricultural imports by heavy duties which, if enacted, would have caused other nations to retaliate against German industrial exports. In order to obstruct the passage of such protectionist legislation the Ruhrlade gave a number of minor concessions and some financial contributions to key agricultural groups like the Landbund. In March of 1928, for example, in order to pacify powerful Prussian agrarian interests, the Ruhrlade agreed to purchase 400,000 marks worth of stock in a meat packing factory in East Prussia.[47]

The Ruhrlade also acted as a secret pressure group exerting influence on the government in Berlin. If important matters were involved, the members, after conferring with each other, met directly with the authorities—even the Chancellor and the President, to whom they readily had access—but on such occasions they spoke as individuals, preferring to keep the existence of the Ruhrlade secret, but this new organization whose members had such wealth and power could not be concealed forever. Before long, rumors of a Ruhr treasury that controlled a large political slush fund began to circulate among journalists and socialist intellectuals.[48] They had no precise information about this mysterious, all-powerful group, but it was assumed, from the way other political fund raising by big business was operated, that this Ruhr treasury raised millions annually by a levy collected from the big firms of heavy industry. Since most heavy industrialists were known to be anti-Communist, some writers went on to charge that a large amount of the money collected went to finance Hitler.[49] In time, those in the higher circles of government also became aware of the organization and by 1932 Chancellor Brüning not only knew about its existence, but also when its meetings took place. Still, Brüning's information was not very extensive because he did not even know the identity of all the members.[50]

Although the gentlemen of the Ruhrlade frequently influenced the political decisions of government officials, they always did so in a low-key manner. Sitting in a comfortable leather armchair in a quiet office, they would calmly "suggest" or "urge" a particular course of action. More was seldom needed,· but if it became necessary then by one means or another the Ruhrlade brought pressure to bear on the government in favor of "sound" economic policy. They strongly opposed additional welfare legislation and the regulation of the length of the workday. They protested against any expansion of the state's role in the economy, especially in regard to compulsory government arbitration in wage disputes. Lest these views make the men of the Ruhrlade seem like "greedy capitalists" trying to exploit the workers by every means possible, it must be remembered that German heavy industry was at that time in a very difficult economic position. The members of the Ruhrlade continually complained that production was hardly profitable anymore because of the economic burdens imposed by the Versailles Treaty. They personally urged various politicians including the Chancellor and the Foreign

Minister to make every effort to reduce the amount of reparations payments. Their views on foreign policy were conservative but realistic. They were fully aware that Germany's wisest course of action, for the time being at least, would have to be based on compromise with the Allies. The overall political views of the Ruhrlade were far more in line with the policies of the traditional conservative parties than they were with the radical ideas of Hitler and the Nazis.

At a meeting on March 5, 1928, the members of the Ruhrlade decided to take over the role of managing the political funds of heavy industry.[51] This task had been performed by the National Association of German Industries for a short while, but the results were disappointing because of continual conflict within the organization between the representatives of light and heavy industry.[52] The political funds of heavy industry were, as usual, raised by a levy which assessed a certain contribution to each company depending on how many workers it employed. The Ruhrlade then decided how and where the money was to be spent. The amount of the levy varied from year to year but averaged about 1,500,000 marks annually. Naturally, the disbursement of this money was handled with the greatest secretiveness. Even within the Ruhrlade itself, the levy was referred to by the code name *Konto Wirtschaftshilfe*. Negotiations with the political parties were carried out through an intermediary, Martin Blank, who was Paul Reusch's representative in Berlin.

The political funds raised by the Ruhrlade subsidized many activities including newspapers and pressure groups. Most of the money, however, was given to political parties and politicians, who were "friendly" to heavy industry. The major donations were made to finance election campaigns, but smaller sums were given out in the form of monthly subsidies.

Although the members of the Ruhrlade belonged to various conservative and moderate parties, there was usually general agreement on political questions: all had the good of heavy industry as their primary concern. Three members, Krupp, Silverberg, and Vögler, belonged to the German People's Party (DVP); two, Springorum and Thyssen, supported the Nationalist Party (DNVP); and one, Klöckner, was a member of the Catholic Center Party; the rest were politically unaffiliated. But even for those who did belong to political parties, their allegiance to them was in most instances not very strong. Thyssen, for example, had formerly been a member of the Catholic Center Party until he broke with them over their acquiescence to the Versailles Treaty. Paul Reusch had belonged to the German People's Party, but he resigned in protest over Stresemann's termination of the passive resistance in the Ruhr. Although Albert Vögler was aligned with the German People's Party in 1928, he was soon to switch over to the Nationalists.

What did the men of the Ruhrlade think of the National Socialist Party? As we have seen, Thyssen gave to the Nazis before the putsch in 1923, but after that had no further contact with them until 1929. As far as the other members of the Ruhrlade are concerned, with the exception of Krupp, very few records of their attitudes about the Nazi Party have survived. Most of them regarded it with interest, but still thought of it as being a splinter party of the extreme Right.

Gustav Krupp encountered Hitler in the late twenties, just before the beginning of the depression, when the Nazi leader was making a propaganda tour of the Rhineland. While in Essen, Hitler decided it might be both interesting and of propaganda value to visit the famous Krupp factory.

At the main gate a huge sign blocked the path of Hitler and his staff:

IT IS REQUESTED THAT, TO PREVENT MISUNDERSTANDING, NO APPLICATION BE MADE TO VISIT THE WORKS, SINCE SUCH APPLICATION CANNOT BE GRANTED UNDER ANY CIRCUMSTANCES WHATSOEVER.

Nevertheless, Hitler demanded a tour of the factory. He was, however, restricted from entering the workshops, "because he was too unknown to be trusted." Gustav Krupp was afraid that he might see rearmament work and later boast about it. Instead, the company tried to pacify him with a visit to the firm's historical exhibit. "Even there he displayed a sense of theater," wrote William Manchester. "Recognizing the political value of any association with Krupp, he had signed the exhibit register with a flourish and underscored his signature as though he knew that soon the Krupp destiny would be inextricably entangled with his own. The name was still there, slashed across the guest book like a jagged prophecy: *Adolf Hitler*."[53]

From the viewpoint of the Ruhrlade, differences among the nonsocialist parties were merely necessary but irritating obstacles based on the support of lesser interest groups. Before the 1928 Reichstag election campaign, the Ruhrlade decided to give its money primarily to the more important conservative and moderate parties: the German People's Party, the Nationalist Party, the Catholic Center Party, and the Bavarian People's Party. The only records available that mention precise sums are for the Nationalist Party. They show that the party's headquarters received 200,000 marks from the Ruhrlade.[54] From all indications it is likely that the German People's Party would have received a slightly larger sum, and the Center Party about half as much as the Nationalist Party. After the election, monthly contributions of 5,000 marks each were given to the German People's Party and the Nationalist Party, and 3,000 marks were given on the same basis to the Bavarian People's Party[55]

To be sure, the moderate or even conservative parties were not simply tools in the hands of heavy industry but rather were based on a coalition of many forces, some of them economic and some of them social. The Catholic Center Party, for example, was primarily based on religious loyalties, with the authorities of the Church playing a very influential role in molding its policies. Compromises were worked out with other interest groups that gave the party financial support, such as commerce, light industry, and heavy industry, but these compromises could never be so extensive as to endanger the party's appeal to its lower and middle-class Catholic voters on whom it was ultimately dependent for its existence. The Ruhrlade, on the other hand, made certain demands on the parties in return for its contributions. The primary objective of the organization was to improve the positions of those candidates who were thought to be particularly "valuable" to the interests of heavy industry.

In the 1928 election campaign the Ruhrlade's 200,000 marks was the largest donation by a single organization to the Nationalist Party. However, contrary to popular belief, the ultraconservative Nationalist Party was not controlled by heavy industry or big business but by Junker-agricultural interests. In return for its money, the Ruhrlade demanded that certain Nationalist candidates it favored be given high places on the party's electoral lists, which in the system of the Weimar Republic almost guaranteed their election. In negotiations with Count Westarp, the party's chairman, Fritz Springorum emphasized that continued financial support would be dependent on the party's responsiveness to the views of the donors. But in spite of the party's need of money, the dominant Junker-agricultural forces were not willing to yield completely. Finally a compromise was reached by which two of the four candidates favored by the Ruhrlade were given high positions on the election list.

The Ruhrlade was certainly not the only secret business organization that attempted to influence the economic and political policies of the Weimar Republic. There were also many undisclosed political funds set up by regional business groups, such as the carefully concealed Board of Trustees for the Reconstruction of German Economic Life, which was organized by the industrial firms and banks of Berlin.[56] However, of the known political funds of big business groups in the Weimar Republic, the Ruhrlade's seem to have been the largest. Yet even its tremendous financial resources did not give it complete control over any political party; the German People's Party, for example, was known as the party of the industrialists, but even here heavy industry had to compromise with the interests of light industry and the small businessman. Compromises continually had to be made with other forces and, as long as the economy remained relatively stable, this provided a system of checks and balances.

By the late 1920s the Ruhrlade was having considerable difficulty maintaining its influence over the right-wing German Nationalist Party, in spite of its large contributions to the party coffers. The dissident Nationalist forces crystallized around the leadership of Alfred Hugenberg, who had been on the board of directors of the Krupp firm from 1909 to 1918. Although he was not a follower of Hitler like Thyssen, Hugenberg was to do more than any other individual in helping to bring Hitler to power.

Throughout World War I Hugenberg had been involved in the propagation of Pan-German plans for an expansionist peace.[57] He had heated disagreements with Gustav Krupp on the question of war aims. This fact, coupled with the charge by some business leaders that Hugenberg's aggressive demands for an expansionist peace had tarnished the image of heavy industry, led Krupp to gradually ease Hugenberg out of the firm. After the war Hugenberg was not on friendly terms with Gustav Krupp but maintained a close friendship with the more reactionary industrialists such as Emil Kirdorf, Fritz Thyssen, and Albert Vögler.

Germany's loss of World War I filled Hugenberg with bitterness and reinforced his hatred of the socialists and democrats. He felt that their temporizing had frustrated the plans for Germany's victorious territorial expansion. Convinced that only ardent nationalism could save Germany from the "cancerous infiltration" of Communism and socialism, Hugenberg put aside his business career to become more directly involved in politics. He was first elected to the National Assembly as a representative from Posen, in East Prussia, with the support of the powerful Junker landlords. Some historians have mistakenly considered Hugenberg as an agent of heavy industry. Actually his primary support was from right-wing Prussian agricultural interests. His supporters among heavy industry were limited to the extremists like Kirdorf and Thyssen.

Along with his new political career, Hugenberg began buying up one newspaper after another. The necessity of arousing popular support for the war effort had given him the idea of using the media as an instrument for influencing national policy. For his venture of building up a nationalist-minded newspaper chain he secured the financial support of right-wing industrialists such as Thyssen and reactionary Junker aristocrats. During the inflation, when many newspapers were going bankrupt, Hugenberg bought up everything in sight. By 1927 he controlled a vast media syndicate of newspapers, wire services, publishing houses, film companies, and movie houses.

The power base of Hugenberg's new syndicate was the Scherl Verlag. With its headquarters in Berlin, this company published three major newspapers for the capital city: *Der Tag*, which was a daily for the upper class; the *Berliner Lokal-Anzeiger*, which had a daily circulation of over a quarter of a million, and was a family-type newspaper which appealed to the middle class; and the *Berliner Illustrierte Nachtausgabe*, which had over three hundred thousand readers, and was a cheap, evening scandal sheet aimed at the masses of the city. In addition to these Berlin newspapers, Scherl Verlag published several weekly papers including *Der Montag* and *Die Woche*, both of which had a circulation of about a quarter of a million. The firm also produced several other well-known publications, such as *Die Gartenlaube*, a popu-

lar women's magazine, along with other periodicals on such topics as trade and industry. The Scherl Verlag was, however, only a
part of Hugenberg's vast empire.[58]

The German reading public generally preferred the local press
of their own provincial cities to the big newspapers of the capital,
so Hugenberg expanded his business in this direction. Through a
company called "Ala" he centralized newspaper advertising for
the provincial press and consequently could exert financial influence on local papers which used the facilities of this company. As
early as 1921, "Ala" had 315 branches throughout the country. To
gain absolute control over many local newspapers, Hugenberg
formed two credit institutions, the Mutuum Darlehns A.G. and
the Alterum Kredit A.G., to assist newspapers that had incurred
financial problems. Through these credit firms, Hugenberg was
able to dictate policy to fourteen major newspapers in cities like
Munich, Stuttgart, and Darmstadt.

Realizing that limited financial resources prevented local papers from covering national news events, Hugenberg sought to
turn this weakness to his own advantage. He developed a syndicated news service, the Wirtschaftsstelle für die Provinzpresse, to
provide set copy for 300 newspapers every day. Hugenberg also
formed his own wire service, the Telegraph Union, which broke
the semiofficial monopoly of the Wolff Telegraph Bureau. Almost
half the German press, about 16,000 newspapers, subscribed to
this news service.

However, newspapers were not the only medium which influenced public opinion. The government controlled the radio, but
Hugenberg recognized that he could have considerable influence
through the newest media, the cinema. When the "Ufa," Germany's largest movie concern, ran into financial difficulty in
1927, he used the opportunity to gain control of the company. By
purchasing the controlling shares in "Ufa," Hugenberg gained
control not only of a major film studio but also of a chain of movie
houses throughout Germany. Most importantly, he could see that
only his version of the news was given in the very popular
newsreels presented in a majority of German theaters. The
newspapers, the wire services, the films, and the newsreels of
this extensive media empire were all tightly controlled by Hugenberg through his Ostdeutsche Privatbank. Hugenberg's own financial backers or their representatives sat on the board of this

East Prussian Bank and acted as the administrators of a secret "trust fund" which supported the Hugenberg media empire. These men, who were the ultimate source of most of Hugenberg's capital, were Junker landlords and a few reactionary industrialists.[59]

Although he was not a popular man, the Pan-Germans and ultrareactionary elements within the Nationalist Party looked to Hugenberg for leadership because he was an ideologue, a man dedicated to the principles of nationalism, agricultural self-sufficiency, and free enterprise industry. Ambitious, domineering, and unscrupulous, Hugenberg was a very able administrator. His organizational talents seemed to qualify him for the leadership of the diverse elements that made up the Nationalist Party. The control he exercised over a significant portion of the German press and his success in the business world made him the kind of man conservatives could respect as their leader.

In 1924 the Nationalists won over six million votes, 20 percent of the total, and were the third largest party in the country. Although the party was led and financed by the Junkers and always acted to protect their interests, its primary support at the polls came from the peasants and the Prussian middle class. Being traditionally conservative, millions of peasants were initially attracted to the patriotic appeal of the Nationalist Party. However, considering the difficult economic conditions, the party's leaders soon recognized that they would have to appeal in some way to the mood of discontent that was so strong in the lower classes or else lose three-fourths of their voters. How could the party controlled by the Junkers be revolutionary without hurting their own interest? The answer came from their own meetings; the party's most popular speakers were the ones who attacked the "alien Jews" or made similar anti-Semitic comments in their speeches.[60]

The Pan-Germans and radicals in the party began to circulate blatantly anti-Semitic propaganda. The most popular of this sort of literature was a novel by Wilhelm von Polenz entitled *Der Büttnerbauer (The Peasant from Büttner)* that sold into the millions. Hitler read the book and admitted that it somewhat influenced his thinking. The plot was very direct. A peasant becomes indebted to a Jew who forecloses on his farm. The Jew then sells the property to an industrialist who builds a factory on it. In the end the peasant hero hangs himself, his eyes reverently focused on his former land: "The eyes which were leaving their sockets stared at the soil, the soil to which he had dedicated his life, to which he had sold his body and soul." The Jew was thus identified with the evils of modern industrial society which uprooted the peasant and deprived him of his land.

This image of conflict between the Jew and the peasant was not just propaganda but had some foundation, however slight, in reality. Jews functioned as middlemen in many German agricultural communities. It was usually in the capacity of a cattle trader or small merchant that the Jew came into contact with the peasants. As a money lender, he was hated most when the peasants were in financial difficulties, such as after a bad harvest, and had to rely on his loans at high interest rates to tide them over. There were probably many generous Jews engaged in such business. Nevertheless, to the debt-ridden peasant the Jew was the most easily identifiable representative of modern capitalist society.

While the respectable Nationalist leaders, like Hugenberg and Class, dressed in top hats and frock coats and moved in the best social circles playing parliamentary politics, their aides were on the street corners disseminating racist propaganda. The leaders of the party were certainly well aware of this, for even Oskar Hergt, one of the more moderate party executives said, "The wave of anti-Semitism will facilitate in an extraordinary manner the electioneering of the Nationalist Party."

Within the party itself the anti-Semitic sentiments were most pronounced in the propaganda department. Although the party's program only hinted at a mild prejudice against the Jews by calling for an end to immigration from eastern Europe and speaking of a Christian spirit of government, the drive for popular support at the polls led the Nationalists' propagandists to emphasize the Jewish question. At first anti-Semitic propaganda was merely an undercurrent, an option for local party chapters, but in time it was endorsed by the party leaders.

The fear of a Jewish conspiracy by international bankers or Communists, depending on the situation, was used extensively. Beginning in 1919, the Party circulated a poster depicting Jewish stereotypes called the "Cohn types," which warned the people that if they failed to vote for the Nationalist candidates Germany would become a slave of the Jews. As the Nationalists gained

greater electoral strength, their anti-Semitic appeal was intensified and the fear of a Jewish conspiracy was used for all it was
worth. Posters issued in 1920 asked the question: "What has
become of Berlin?" and answered: "A playground for the Jews!"

Caricatures of the Jew as the stock exchange speculator and
the corpulent banker were widely disseminated. The stock exchange was used as the symbol of a feverish, unrestrained
hunger-for-money that had been foisted upon the Germans by
the Jews. The industrialists frowned on such propaganda, but the
Junkers who dominated the Nationalist Party secretly encouraged it. Some pamphlets went so far that the party's name did not
appear on them; they fused the theme of the Jew's hunger-for-
money with his lust for Aryan women. The resulting image,
frequently shown in propaganda, pictured a fat Jewish banker
caressing a blond woman on his knee with one hand and sifting
through a bag of gold coins with the other. By 1924 the Nationalist
Party declared that its efforts had been expanded to battle "Jewish
influence on all fronts."[61]

This crude campaign of propaganda was actually more sophisticated than it appeared, for it enabled the Nationalists to appeal
visually to traditional bigotry without actually making it a part of
the party program. If a man were a member of the Nationalist
Party, he was not considered to be a radical or fanatic. The party
clothed itself in such respectable garb that the upper class dismissed its election propaganda as being designed solely for the
masses. As a result, it drew to its ranks professional people,
industrialists, and bankers who would never have dreamed of
supporting Hitler. Yet by getting the upper class to tolerate anti-
Semitic propaganda, the Nationalists prepared the way for them
to eventually support the Nazis. Most historians have ignored the
anti-Semitism of the Nationalist Party and minimized its crucial
role in cooperating with Hitler.[62]

In August of 1924 the first major strife within the Nationalist
Party occurred over the Dawes Plan.* The reactionary elements

---

*From January to April 1924 a committee of experts under the chairmanship of the
American banker Charles G. Dawes met in Paris. The plan provided that a large
international loan of 200 million dollars would be made to the German government.
Although the total amount of reparations was unchanged, it was made payable in
annual installments of 2.5 billion marks over an indefinite period of time. Also the
French agreed to remove their troops from the Ruhr within a year.

within the party were absolutely opposed to accepting such an agreement on reparations. Like Hitler and the Nazis, they used criticisms against the Dawes Plan as an excuse for a general campaign of vilification against the Republic. However, the National Association of German Industries, whose members were to be the main beneficiaries of the loans, was strongly in favor of the Dawes Plan. Since this industrial organization was one of the principal financial supporters of the Nationalist Party, its opinions could not be ignored. Differing with the overwhelming majority of his colleagues in the National Association of German Industries, Hugenberg stood firmly opposed to the Dawes Plan. Even many of Hugenberg's own friends and supporters, such as Fritz Thyssen, disagreed with him on this issue. Of Germany's prominent businessmen, only old Emil Kirdorf remained adamantly against the Dawes Plan. Hugenberg himself complained that heavy industry was exerting unusually strong pressure in favor of acceptance, but he would not surrender the economic independence of his country by ratifying such a plan. His stand against the Dawes Plan clearly indicates that Hugenberg was not an agent of big business or heavy industry, but rather the leader of the Pan-German reactionaries.

After the passage of the Dawes Plan by the Reichstag, Hugenberg devoted the next few years to further building up his media empire and strengthening his influence over the Nationalist Party. In the fall of 1927 he tried to undercut the position of the party chairman, Count Kuno von Westarp, by gaining control of the subsidies which big business gave to the party. Westarp appealed for help to Paul Reusch and Fritz Springorum of the Ruhrlade. They responded by going around Hugenberg and supplying Westarp with additional funds raised from a special new levy. Once again, in October 1928, Hugenberg and his faction tried to replace Westarp. The Ruhrlade again intervened and made it clear that its monthly subsidies to the party were being entrusted to Westarp personally and would be subject to reconsideration if the party's leadership changed.[63] Yet in spite of the fact that most of the party's industrial backers rejected him as being an inflexible, provocative agent of the Junkers and agrarian interests, Hugenberg was elected party chairman. Under Hugenberg's leadership the Nationalist Party drifted further and further to the right.

On June 7, 1929, a committee of experts appointed by the Allied powers under the chairmanship of the American banker Owen D. Young, and hence called the Young Committee, signed a report which required the Germans to pay reparations for another fifty-nine years, that is until 1988. However, the annual payments were considerably lower than on the Dawes Plan (2,050 million marks a year as compared to 2,500 million). Direct international control over Germany's economy was to be removed as well, and the total sum demanded in payment was less than the 132 billion gold marks originally claimed by the Allies.

Within Germany the new agreement encountered boisterous opposition. Nationalist crowds carrying signs and waving flags gathered to protest ouside the Reichstag in Berlin. Even those with a realistic understanding of the Reich's difficult international position were disappointed. There was an element of cruel mockery in forcing Germany to agree to payments for the next fifty-nine years when she could not afford to make even the first few annual payments. Over two hundred prominent men, including many liberals and moderates, such as the former Chancellor Hans Luther, Carl Duisberg of I.G. Farben, and Konrad Adenauer, then mayor of Cologne, issued a public statement of concern against the agreement. Eleven years after the end of the war, the Young Plan once again exposed the Allies' merciless attitude toward the defeated.

Although the terms of the Young Plan were far stiffer than Stresemann had hoped for, he decided to accept them, confident that he could then secure the evacuation of the remaining zones of the occupied Rhineland. Finally he succeeded in persuading the French to begin the withdrawal of their troops in September, five years before they would have been required to do so by the Versailles Treaty. This was to be the last of Stresemann's triumphs. Until his death on October 3, he was very ill, worn out by the exertions of public office. Before he died, he had succeeded in overcoming the opposition of the French, but the Germans still remained to be convinced. The parties of the Right, including the Nazis, were in close conference, planning a united campaign of rejection against this new reparations settlement.

Any rightist coalition against Stresemann's policy would undoubtedly be led by the powerful German Nationalist Party. Only they had the money, the press, the deputies in the Reichstag, and a large enough party to make such a campaign a success.

A national committee was formed on July 9, 1929, to organize a campaign for a plebiscite rejecting the Young Plan and the "lie" of German war guilt which was the "legal" basis of the Allies' claims. For the next nine months the press and parties of the German Right united in a vicious campaign to defeat the government's reparations policy. The leader of the campaign against the Young Plan was Alfred Hugenberg. Dr. Bang, a Nationalist political financier from Dresden, had introduced Hitler to Hugenberg in June at the Deutscher Orden, a Nationalist club in Berlin. Hugenberg had tried to persuade Hitler to join his alliance against the Young Plan. He already had the support of the Nationalist Party, the Stahlhelm (Germany's largest veterans organization), and the Pan-German League. In addition, he could count on the financial backing of many important aristocrats and industrialists and of course his own media empire; but what he needed was someone who could arouse the masses, someone who could win over the lower middle class and at least a few workers. True, Hitler's party was not of significant size in 1929; they had only twelve representatives in the Reichstag and 120,000 members. However, these members were all well-disciplined, devoted fanatics who could be used as propaganda shock troops. They could be counted on to work day and night pasting up billboards, marching, and holding rallies, things that the "respectable gentlemen" of the Nationalist Party would never dream of doing.

Hugenberg also thought the campaign against the Young Plan would give him a chance to assert his leadership over the divided forces of the Right, including the Nazis. The more conservative elements of the upper class might even be able to regain their lost initiative. With all the arrogance of an upper-class gentleman toward a man of the masses, Hugenberg was confident he could make use of Hitler. He would use the ex-corporal's gift for agitation to lead the masses back to conservatism. At least Hugenberg was intelligent enough to see that the traditional spokesmen of the conservative cause were isolated by their own class consciousness. But he foolishly believed that he would know how to put Hitler back in his place when the time came.

Hitler could not allow himself to be easily persuaded to join the alliance because he knew Strasser and the party radicals would be opposed to working with the reactionary Hugenberg and would denounce the move as a sellout to the industrialists. However, the advantages of being able to draw on the big political funds at Hugenberg's disposal and the possibilities of using his vast media network were too tempting to resist.

On July 9, 1929, when the committee was formed for the purpose of organizing the plebiscite, the membership of this committee showed clearly the delineation of the new national unity front: Hugenberg of the Nationalist Party; Seldte, the leader of the Stahlhelm; Heinrich Class, chairman of the Pan-German league; and Adolf Hitler, the leader of the National Socialist Party. This committee appealed to the German electorate with a demagogically formulated "Law against the Enslavement of the German People," which denounced the war-guilt clause of the Versailles Treaty, demanded the immediate end of all reparations payments, and stated that the Chancellor and the members of the cabinet should be liable to prosecution for treason if they accepted the Young Plan.

At a meeting of Nazi Party leaders which followed the alliance with Hugenberg, Strasser acted as the spokesman for the critics. Hugenberg's hopes for the alliance were Strasser's fears: the National Socialists would no longer be able to fight against the "respectable" elements of the Nationalist Party; they would be overwhelmed by the other's superior financial strength; they would now be nothing but a pawn of the stronger party. Hitler remained unmoved by Strasser's arguments. He was not about to lose his chance to profit from an alliance with the established order. This opportunity meant a great deal to him, for his plans still called for following Karl Lueger's example of utilizing the existing implements of power.* Moreover, Strasser had personally underestimated Hitler, who did not become anyone's "pawn." The Führer responded to his critics with a lengthy speech, much of which included the usual emotional phrases about the Versailles Treaty and the Jews. Yet in concluding he made a statement that should have been clear even to the thickest heads among his listeners: "We shall carry on our propaganda at the expense of the

---

*Dr. Karl Lueger was the leader of the anti-Semitic Christian Socialist Party and Mayor of Vienna (1897–1910). While Hitler lived in Vienna from 1908 to 1913, he greatly admired Lueger.

others . . . at least we are gaining access to the funds which up to now have been reserved for the German Nationalists."[64]

In order to submit the "Freedom law" to the Reichstag, the German Right needed to secure the support of 10 percent of the electorate. This was accomplished on October 16, when their bill received a little over four million votes (10 percent). The bill, however, received less support in the Reichstag, when even some members of the Nationalist Party refused to vote for it and broke with Hugenberg. The Nationalist Reichstag deputies who favored the ratification of the Young Plan were led by Gottfried Treviranus, who was known to have the financial backing of the liberal-minded sectors of big business.

In a last, desperate attempt, the bill was submitted to a national plebiscite. The Nazis used every propaganda trick they knew, as they ranted about those who were enslaving the nation to foreign capitalists, crippling national survival for the next two generations, and turning Germany into a "Young colony." Every speech made by Hitler and other Nazi leaders was carried by all the newspapers in Hugenberg's chain. Millions of Germans who had hardly ever heard of Hitler before, now became interested in him since he was given such good publicity in the "respectable" press. In the respectable Berlin daily, the *Nacht Ausgabe*, an important organ of the Hugenberg press, one found accounts of the latest "dirty tricks" the Berlin police played on the innocent National Socialists, while thousands of newsboys across Germany selling Hugenberg papers shouted: "Herr Hitler says, Young Plan means Germany's enslavement."[65]

An examination of the names of those on the presidium of the organizing committee against the Young Plan reveals most of the sources of the funds that financed the anti-Young Plan campaign. There was Herr Schiele, leader of the Reichslandbund, Germany's most powerful agricultural association; Herr Luninck, director of the Rheinisch Chamber of Agriculture; Herr Döbrich of the Christian National Farmers Party, an association of small farmers from western Germany; and Fritz Thyssen, representing the Union of German Industry. A considerable sum of money came from the Reichslandbund, which counted most of Prussia's aristocratic families among its members, but the largest amount of the total fund was provided by right-wing heavy industry, principally those firms controlled by Fritz Thyssen.

"The Young Plan," Fritz Thyssen later wrote, "was one of the principal causes of the upsurge of National Socialism in Germany."[66] Thyssen had not been opposed to the Dawes Plan since it called for a system of reparations payments to made primarily in material goods. But under the Young Plan the German reparations payments were to be made entirely in cash. Thyssen felt the financial debt thus created was bound to disrupt the entire German economy. He then decided to use his influence to bring together the Nazis and the traditional Nationalists in opposing the Young Plan. "I turned to the National Socialist Party," Thyssen said, "only after I became convinced that the fight against the Young Plan was unavoidable if a complete collapse of Germany was to be prevented."[67]

One of the German representatives on the committee of experts which conducted the preliminary negotiations on the Young Plan in Paris was Albert Vögler, the director of the Gelsenkirchen steel firm, a subsidiary of Thyssen's United Steel. Both Vögler and Dr. Hjalmar Schacht, the president of the Reichsbank, returned to Germany because they had misgivings about the proposed Young Plan. In the end, Vögler refused to sign the Young Plan; and Thyssen proudly stated, "I must admit that I had done all that I could to convince him of the correctness of his misgivings."[68]

Thyssen later told the somewhat curious story that his opposition to the Young Plan was confirmed by the advice of an American banker, Clarence Dillon of the firm Dillon, Read & Company, described by Thyssen as "a Jew with whom we [Thyssen and Vögler] were in very friendly relations. Mr. Dillon expressedly said, 'If I may give you a piece of advice, don't sign.' "[69] Why Dillon would have given such advice, Thyssen neglected to mention.

The Young Plan, according to Thyssen, would have the effect of pledging Germany's entire wealth as security for the reparations obligation. American capital was bound to flood into Germany. Thyssen was angered that some industrialists who supported the Young Plan were attempting in advance to free their property from this huge mortgage. He complained in particular about the A.E.G. (the leading German electrical company), which transferred its stock to a Franco-Belgian holding company. Thyssen felt this meant the beginning of the financial liquidation of Germany.

The Ruhrlade was divided over the Young Plan. Most of the members including Gustav Krupp saw that Germany had no choice but to accept the plan. Only Thyssen and Vögler were in active opposition. But since the opinions of the members differed, the organization itself could take no stand without risking its own destruction.

Most of the members of the Ruhrlade could understand Thyssen's reasons for opposing the Young Plan, but they regarded his collaboration with Hitler as a foolish gesture. A considerable portion of the money Thyssen gave to the anti-Young Plan camapign went directly to the National Socialists. He knew of this and approved. "I financed the National Socialist Party," said Thyssen, "for a single definite reason: I financed it because I believed that the Young Plan spelled catastrophe for Germany. I was convinced of the necessity of uniting all parties of the Right."[70]

The money that respectable businessmen like Thyssen placed at the disposal of the Nazis was used to pay for an unparalleled campaign of propaganda and demagoguery. In addition to the coverage given them in Hugenberg's newspapers and newsreels, the Nazis staged continuous rallies and protest demonstrations throughout the country. Noting that under the Young Plan Germany would have to continue reparations payments until 1988, Nazi speakers ranted about "fifty-eight years of bondage" for a generation of Germans not yet born.[71] In order to strike fear into the masses, Goebbels designed a poster showing a powerful clenched fist throwing its menacing shadow over a child. In despair, the child, representing Germany's next generation, raises its tiny arms as a shield, a cry of fear distorting its mouth. By its side is its father, a German worker with bowed head, worn out. But a Storm Trooper, upright and virile, shakes him with an outstretched arm, points to the threat, and shouts at him: "Father, rescue your child! Become a National Socialist!"

Hugenberg and Hitler needed twenty-one million votes to win; they received less than six million. With the defeat of the plebiscite, Hugenberg's last hope was that President von Hindenburg would refuse to sign the legislation embodying the Young Plan. Some Nationalist friends tried to influence Hindenburg, but he refused to be pressured by the extremists even though they were personal friends and members of his own party. On March 13,

1930, the President signed the laws to carry out the Young Plan. Hugenberg's campaign had been a dismal failure, an obvious defeat for the powerful Nationalist Party. But a defeat for Hugenberg did not mean a defeat for Hitler. Hitler did not consider his part in the campaign a failure because in the past nine months he had succeeded in breaking into national politics for the first time and demonstrating his skill as a propagandist.

Most people felt that whatever success had been won in the campaign against the Young Plan was due to Hitler. He had criticized the conservative parties of the Right for years for their "respectable" inhibitions. Now he had demonstrated, on a larger scale than ever before, what he meant by propaganda aimed at the masses. Once the Young Plan became law, Hitler broke with the Nationalist Party and blamed them for the failure of the campaign. He said their support for the campaign had been halfhearted; after all, some of their own members had split and refused to go along with Hugenberg. Such arguments carried weight with many of the more extreme Nationalists.

This alliance with Hugenberg was the first success in an extraordinary series of political maneuvers, tactical compromises, and manipulative alliances that brought Hitler to his goal. The campaign against the Young Plan also provided him with connections among many industrialists who had supported Stresemann's foreign policy over the years but who now felt the Young Plan went too far. As the economic situation worsened, some of the men who controlled the political funds for big business and heavy industry began to look around for political alternatives. Of course, Hitler had not yet succeeded in winning them over to his side, but for the first time they became fully aware of his remarkable gifts as a propagandist.

The campaign against the Young Plan brought the Nazi Party an increase in general revenues in addition to the funds they received from Hugenberg. The income of the Party unit in the Schwabing district of Munich, for example, was RM 388.89 for the first ten months of 1929; in the last two months of the year, the same unit collected RM 803.90.[72] For the first time since 1923 the National Socialists began to receive some contributions from the well-to-do middle class. At Party headquarters names were collected for a special "S" (sympathizer) file of wealthy persons and firms who could be counted on to contribute to the support of the Party.[73] By mid-1930, several months before their great election victory, the Party was operating on a reasonably firm financial basis.

6
DEPRESSION

In the spring of 1929 the prices of German agricultural products fell drastically, impoverishing peasant and landlord alike. Misery began to spread among the farmers; many went bankrupt and were driven from their homes when they could no longer pay on their mortgages. This was one of the first symptoms of the approaching world depression. As economic disaster began to cast its shadow over the land once again, Hitler, the prophet of doom, prepared to receive his due.

In America the prices on the New York Stock Exchange crashed in October 1929. This was the beginning of the great depression which, in a few months, would spread to all continents. The Wall Street crash marked the end of American loans to Germany, thus cutting off the flow of foreign exchange which had enabled her to pay her debts. By the end of the year the economic crisis was starting to affect all segments of German society.

As early as the fall of 1928 there was cause for a certain uneasiness about the German economy. Though conditions steadily worsened throughout 1929, it was not until the approach of 1930 that people came to realize that the country was teetering once more on the edge of an abyss. One of the best indexes for the social consequences of the depression is the rate of unemployment. The number of registered unemployed in Germany rose from 1,320,000 in September 1929 to 3,000,000 in September 1930; it was up to 4,350,000 in September 1931 and 5,102,000 by September 1932. In the first two months of 1932 and again in

1933 the figures climbed over the 6 million mark. (The actual number of unemployed was much higher than the "registered" figures which did not take into account those who could find only part-time jobs and those who failed to register for one reason or another.) "Translate these figures," said Alan Bullock, "into terms of men standing hopelessly on the street corners of every industrial town in Germany; of houses without food and warmth; of boys and girls leaving school without any chance of a job, and one may begin to guess something of the incalculable human anxiety and embitterment burned into the minds of millions of ordinary German working men and women."[1]

Although Hitler was no economist, he was acutely aware of the social and political consequences of economic events which, like the inflation of 1923, affected every man, woman, and child in Germany. As the economic crisis became more serious, the population grew restive.

During the period of prosperity German farmers had been encouraged by the government to increase their production. By 1929 their crops could no longer compete with the world market. In order to maintain themselves and their families, the peasants borrowed money from the banks and mortgaged their farms. Within a short time the rate of interest doubled. In spite of the agricultural crisis, the high taxes on German farms were not reduced.

Unable to pay the interest on their loans or the taxes on their farms, many peasants went bankrupt. Foreclosures began. Families were driven from their homes and their property put up for auction. The desperate farmers responded with open rebellion; they refused to pay interest and taxes and in some areas gathered into armed mobs throwing stones at the tax offices. In several towns there were clashes between the police and crowds of club-wielding peasants. The Communists, rigidly following Marxist principles of class struggle, tried to incite the small peasants against the large landholders. In this they followed Lenin's Russian example, which, like so many of the Communist International's methods, was totally unsuited for export. In Germany their propaganda met with no success because the big landowners and the peasants had the same interests: higher prices on produce and lower interest rates on loans. Unlike Russia, the only "land hunger" among the German peasants was a hunger to keep the land they already had.

The National Socialists had a far better understanding of the agrarian struggle. Convinced that the most fertile field for agitation was now in rural rather than urban areas, Hitler proclaimed a new agrarian policy for the Party. "The country people were the chief bearers of hereditary and racial wealth," he said, "the people's fountain of youth, and the backbone of our military power. . . . the preservation of an efficient peasant class in numerical proportion to the total population constitutes a pillar of National Socialist policy. . . . German agriculture must be protected by tariffs and state regulation of imports. . . . The fixing of prices for agricultural produce must be withdrawn from the influence of stock exchange speculation, and a stop must be put to exploitation of farmers by large middlemen. . . . The high taxation cannot be met out of the poor returns for labor on the land. The farmer is forced to run into debt and pay usurious interest on loans. He sinks deeper and deeper under this tyranny, and in the end forfeits his house and farm to the money-lender, who is usually a Jew."[2]

But the Nazis did more than just talk about the problems of the peasants. When a farmer would be forced to declare bankruptcy and his home and property would be put up for auction, Nazi Party members would turn up in large numbers for the sale. They would interrupt the auctioneer with ridiculous questions and ask if the poor farmer's family was to have their home taken away from them just so some Jew could make a fat profit. They would outbid serious buyers only to say later they misunderstood the price and could not pay. If all else failed, the Storm Troopers present would start a fight and in the process break up everything in sight. Thus by one means or another the foreclosure sales on many farms were interrupted by the Nazis, and they gained the reputation of being the protectors of the impoverished farmers.

The increasing success of the Nazis at the polls was a direct reflection of the economic conditions which had impoverished the peasants and were beginning to spread to other sectors of the economy. In the 1928 Reichstag elections Hitler's party had won a mere 2.8 percent of the votes. In May 1929 the National Socialist Party won 4.95 percent of the vote in the state elections in Saxony, and five out of ninety-six seats in the Landtag. On October 17, 1929, the Nazis received 6.98 percent of the votes in the Landtag elections in Baden. Less than a month later Hitler's party won 8.1 percent of the vote in the municipal elections in Lübeck. The citizens of Thuringia went to the polls on December 8, 1929, to elect their state Landtag and 11.3 percent of them cast their ballots for the Nazis.

As a result of their success in the Thuringian elections in December, the Nazis held the balance of power in the state legislature. Hitler accordingly demanded that a National Socialist become a member of the right-wing coalition cabinet that was to take office. For the post he proposed Wilhelm Frick, one of the few Nazi leaders with governmental administrative experience. However, the other right-wing parties in the coalition, particularly the German People's Party (DVP), objected to taking a Nazi into their government. Hitler then showed his skill in political manipulation by pressuring the leaders of the German People's Party from behind the scenes with a direct appeal to their financial backers.[3]

The industrialists decided that the National Socialists should be given a chance. The politicians quickly yielded to the power of money and Wilhelm Frick became the first Nazi minister of a state government.

Many people were puzzled as to why so many respectable middle-class farmers who had the reputation for being rather sober, traditional men would vote for a radical party like the Nazis. But it must be remembered that many of them were desperate and when neither the government nor any of the established parties seemed able to solve their problems they turned to Hitler. "He was our last hope," they said, "we thought we might at least try it with him."[4]

Although the farmers who voted for Hitler were now impoverished, many of them came from middle-class backgrounds and hence, unlike the workers or very poor, they had relatives and friends who still had money and who were converted to National Socialism by their example.

In explaining why he joined the National Socialist Party, a young business executive recounted his attempt to save his family's farm from a Jewish money-lender: "One day my brother visited me and told me that despite all diligence and frugality could do, my parents' homestead became more heavily indebted each year. It was then, when our plot of native soil seemed in danger, that I roused myself from my middle-class complacency. I had to forestall the catastrophe that threatened our homestead. My sisters wanted to marry, but they had no dowries. Consequently my father proceeded to mortgage the farm. At first he found the money-lenders willing and ready to help him out at the rate of 10 percent or more interest. The instant he was unable to pay all the interest and amortisation debts, however, it would be all over for him. The Jew threatened to drive him from the soil his ancestors had tilled for over 300 years. I was struck by the terrible realization that the government sought to seize all farms through the granting of credit. The Jew at the bottom of it all had to tame the farmer in order to achieve his plans. After this shocking realization, it occurred to me that these facts had long been exposed by the preachers of National Socialism without my having paid any attention to them. I went to ask the advice of my party [Nationalist] leaders. But their shrugs and discouraging attitude taught me that no rescue could be expected from that quarter. . . . I then tried to contribute as much as I could out of my modest income, in order to avert the worst. In 1930 I turned my back on the Deutschnationale Volkspartei [German Nationalist Party] and after attending National Socialist party meetings regularly, I was won over to National Socialism."[5]

Within a year the depression that had ruined German agriculture began to affect industry. In the inflation of 1923, money had lost its value. Now in 1930, work began to lose its value; three million men could no longer sell their labor, and millions more could expect to lose their jobs in the near future. However, the economic effects of the depression were not limited to the working class but also struck the middle class and small businessmen almost as sharply. The small shareholders in Thyssen's Steel Trust saw their stock fall to a third of its original value; landlords were unable to collect their rents; and mortgage holders received no interest payments.

Everyone got some idea of just how serious the world economic crisis had become when news arrived from South America that the fire boxes of the locomotives were adapted to burn coffee beans instead of coal. The Germans could no longer afford to buy South American coffee, so naturally the South Americans had no foreign exchange with which to buy German coal or locomotives;

the vicious downward cycle of the depression was just beginning.

Germany suffered far more heavily from the world economic crisis than the other advanced industrialized nations. Her industrial production dropped by approximately half.[6] Neither the United States, Britain, nor France were affected so severely. It was a matter of decisive importance whether the crisis struck an economically strong and socially stable country or whether it struck one which was already badly shaken, and therefore highly vulnerable. Unlike Britain and France, which possessed large foreign investments, Germany was a debtor country. When the crash came and the creditors began to demand repayment of their loans, Germany had nothing to fall back on and thus quickly found the situation becoming catastrophic.

The German government decreased wages by decree and also lowered prices, but not enough to compensate for the wage cuts. Despite the shrinking salaries and all the sacrifices of those who were still employed, more and more workers were discharged every day. The official unemployment figure was over 3 million in the spring of 1930; but the actual number was more than that, as German industry had a tendency to give its workers partial employment in hard times. So this unemployment figure reflected graver economic distress than it would have in other countries. The huge smelting furnaces of Fritz Thyssen and the German Steel Trusts, which were capable of producing twice as much steel as England, now stood useless, cold, and still. Kirdorf's coal found no buyers, so it lay in great piles around the mines; meanwhile, the unemployed miners spent the winter with their families in unheated rooms.

In the woods around Berlin tent colonies sprang up; here lived those unemployed who could no longer pay their rent in city tenements. There were community soup kitchens in the tent camps and the residents shared such tasks as the removal of garbage. Despite the poverty, discipline and order prevailed. Yet in the potato fields around Berlin the peasants had to post guards with loaded rifles, because large groups of starving men came from the city and carried away all their sacks would hold, even in broad daylight while traffic went by on the roads. Young men who had seen the last of their families' property dwindle away and had never learned the meaning of work now wandered through the countryside in famished bands of desperate marauders often literally singing with hunger. Residential sections resounded with the terrible songs of poor people, who had never dreamed they would some day be singing for bread.

It was still "good times" for those unemployed who could stand in the long, shabby lines along the sidewalk outside the employment office. Slowly they moved forward and finally presented a little booklet at a window, where a clerk pasted in a stamp certifying that they had presented themselves in vain to ask for work. This entitled them to unemployment benefits which amounted to as much as seventy marks a month. Soon the gray, disheveled mob had swollen beyond measure and they were allowed to come only twice a week. After thirteen weeks of unemployment a person was transferred to another category where the benefits were much smaller and actually based on a kind of state charity. Originally what the unemployed worker received had been an insurance benefit that he had paid for in good times by a compulsory deduction from his wages, but after a time it became a gift from the state. According to a popular joke, the optimist predicted: Next winter we will all go begging. The pessimist asked: From whom?

The mass discontent caused by the depression frightened many industrialists. With poverty and unemployment stalking the land, Communism was on the rise again. Fritz Thyssen and a considerable number of his colleagues wanted the paramilitary organizations of the Right to unite in case they were needed to suppress a Red uprising. With this end in view Thyssen proposed to Hitler that the Nazi S.A. unite with the powerful rightist veterans group, the Stahlhelm. The negotiations for an alliance between the two organizations were directed by Thyssen himself.[7] The union would open up almost unlimited money and other resources to the Nazis.

Although the Stahlhelm was closely affiliated with the German Nationalist Party, it was an independent organization of considerable strength and prestige. Reactionary monarchism and nationalism were the political creeds of the Stahlhelm. On the matter of foreign policy it was almost as extreme as the Nazi Party, as its proclamation of September 1928 revealed: "We hate the present form of government with all our hearts because it bars the prospect of liberating our enslaved Fatherland, of cleansing the German people of the war-guilt lie, and of winning the necessary living space in the East."[8]

This did not prevent President Hindenburg from being an honorary member of the Stahlhelm nor the Army from patronizing this organization which it regarded as a vast reserve and school for military training. Financing was never a problem for the Stahlhelm; they had abundant funds from both the aristocratic landlords and the industrialists. Nevertheless the dominant voice in the organization belonged to retired Junker Army officers. The commanders of the Stahlhelm were two former officers of the Imperial Army, Lieutenant Seldte and Lieutenant Colonel Duesterberg.

Founded in Magdeburg in 1918, the Stahlhelm developed very rapidly. It had 23,000 members at the end of 1919, 60,000 in 1920, 175,000 in 1923, and 425,000 by the end of 1929. It was composed of two basic sections; one was for ex-servicemen and the other was the Jungstahlhelm (Young Steel Helmet) for recruits under twenty-three years of age. The organization was structured along military lines and divided into battalions, regiments, and brigades. Its members wore a field gray uniform and a cap with a steel-helmet emblem. They were obliged to drill regularly and attend frequent exercises, consisting of day and night marches, map reading, marksmanship practice, and reconnaissance work. Their flag was the old Imperial standard, white with a black Iron Cross and the Hohenzollern eagle in the center.

On the surface it seemed that the Nazi S.A., which had only 60,000 members, would be swallowed up by the larger and wealthier Stahlhelm. Yet Thyssen wrote that: "Hermann Göring declared his willingness to place the National Socialist Storm Troops . . . under the leadership of the Steel Helmet [Stahlhelm]."[9] Hitler also approved of Thyssen's efforts to unite the two organizations, but he and Göring had further plans of which their industrial benefactor was not aware.

The imposing outward strength of the Stahlhelm concealed an inner flaw which Hitler was quick to recognize. The officers of the organization were mostly reactionary monarchists of the old school, but its younger members were radical nationalists whose views differed little from those of the Nazis. This division of political views within the Stahlhelm would provide Hitler with an opportunity to take it over from within. Once the S.A. and the Stahlhelm were united, Hitler felt his superior skill as a propagandist would quickly win for him the allegiance of the younger men, and for a paramilitary group these were the ones who counted most.

Unaware of Hitler's secret ambitions, Thyssen tried to persuade the leaders of the Stahlhelm to accept an alliance with the S.A. He conferred with Lieutenant Colonel Duesterberg for a whole night, promising larger financial subsidies from industry if the two groups united. But all efforts were in vain. The leaders of the Stahlhelm sensed that their old-fashioned monarchist principles would not be able to compete with Hitler's skill as a demagogue. Furthermore, the aristocratic-agricultural interests, which provided a major portion of the funding for the Stahlhelm and controlled it through the Junker officer corps, were afraid that industrialists like Thyssen, who ultimately had much more money than they, would come to exercise a decisive financial influence over the organization. In spite of the fact that the proposed alliance came to nought, Hitler profited from the incident because Thyssen believed that Hitler had been ready to compromise and subordinate his own goals to those of a united nationalist movement.[10] A few years later when the question would arise whether or not Hitler should be taken into the government, Thyssen would cite the case of the negotiations with the Stahlhelm as proof that Hitler was a reasonable individual willing to compromise.

Hermann Müller, the last Social Democratic Chancellor of Germany, resigned in March 1930 because his government, based on a coalition of democratic parties, could not hold together on the dispute over the unemployment insurance fund. He was replaced by Heinrich Brüning, the parliamentary leader of the Catholic Center Party, who as a captain had won the Iron Cross during the war and was known for his conservative political views.

The three political parties that had been responsible for the adoption of the Weimar Constitution—the Social Democrats, the Catholic Center, and the Democrats—had never again obtained a majority after 1919. In order to govern they had had to take other parties into the coalition, thus making any firm policy almost impossible. The party leaders were absorbed in bargaining and maneuvering for party advantages, "cattle trading" as the German politicians called it. Many were not at all displeased with the situation. Weak governments suited them because it made those in power more accessible to party pressure and economic interests. In the economic crisis which intensified after March of 1930, it became impossible to assemble a coalition government which could be sure of a majority vote in the Reichstag. Instead of coming together, facing the depression, and forming a government of unity, each economic interest group—the labor unions, the farmers, the small shopkeepers, the Junkers, and the industrialists—demanded sacrifices from the others while seeking state aid for itself.

As soon as he took office Chancellor Brüning was confronted with the same problem as his predecessor: He had to rely on precarious Reichstag majorities laboriously reassembled for each piece of legislation. There were continual disputes over where the economic burdens were to be placed, whether wages and unemployment insurance were to be cut, or taxes raised or tariffs increased. The debating became so turbulent that the government was unable to accomplish anything by parliamentary methods. When Brüning failed to get a majority in the Reichstag to support his financial program, he asked Hindenburg to invoke Article 48 of the Weimar Constitution and under its emergency powers approve his financial bill by presidential decree. The Reichstag claimed that such action was unconstitutional and voted for the withdrawal of the decree. Parliamentary government was breaking down in the very moment of economic crisis when decisive governmental action was more necessary than ever. By July Brüning could see no way out of the deadlock, so he asked President von Hindenburg to dissolve the Reichstag. Hindenburg agreed and new elections were called for September 14, 1930.

Although Heinrich Brüning was an able man, he was not appointed Chancellor and granted such sweeping powers by President Hindenburg on his merits alone. Behind Brüning stood a very powerful sponsor, General von Schleicher, who was to play a major role in the downfall of the Weimar Republic. Brüning had been made Chancellor simply because Schleicher "suggested" his name to Hindenburg as a man who could solve the economic crisis.

Brüning's sponsor was a man of mystery; only a very few Germans had ever even heard of him. Actually, General Kurt von

Schleicher had a high post behind the scenes in the elaborate hierarchy of the German Army.[11] The remarkable success of his military career was due to two factors: an unusual talent for organization and intrigue; and the good will of highly placed patrons. Schleicher came from a noble Brandenburg family and, like most young men of his class, was sent to a military academy. His excellent record at the academy attracted the attention of General Gröner, who was so impressed with young Schleicher's ability that he made him his protégé. When Schleicher received his officer's commission he entered President Hindenburg's old regiment, the Third Foot Guards, and had the good fortune of becoming the close friend and mess-mate of Hindenburg's son Oskar. Schleicher was a frequent guest at the Hindenburg home. He was very clever, a good conversationalist, and could be charming whenever it suited his purpose.

During World War I Schleicher served on the General Staff. When General Gröner succeeded Ludendorff as the First Quartermaster General of the German Army, he appointed Schleicher, who was then only thirty-six years old, as his personal aide-de-camp. In 1919 Gröner had his protégé transferred to the Ministry of War. In his new capacity Schleicher helped to plan the foundations for the new Reichswehr. During the next few years he made the most of his social contacts to push himself forward. With his smoothness and his capacity for patient, meticulous work his progress continued. His goal was the highest: to make himself the behind-the-scenes director of the Reichswehr.

What Schleicher wanted was power without responsibility. Hindenburg's election to the presidency brought him closer to his goal. Through Oskar, who now served as his father's personal adjutant, Schleicher was able to gain admittance to the presidential palace whenever he wished. The old President was tremendously impressed by the intelligence of his son's friend. Schleicher got to know all the members of Hindenburg's entourage. Before long Oskar von Hindenburg, Schleicher, and State Secretary Meissner formed the so-called "palace camarilla" which exerted a tremendous influence over Hindenburg and eventually controlled him completely.

In 1928 the man who was appointed the new minister of war was none other than Schleicher's favorite patron, General Gröner. A few months later Schleicher was made a major general and a special post was created for him in the War Ministry. His official title was "Chief of the Ministerial Office" and his functions were similar to those carried out by the secretaries of state in other ministries. The new post carried with it broad authority and enormous power. It put Schleicher in control of the military intelligence services and of all relations between the Reichstag and the armed forces. As time went on, the scope of the post expanded and Schleicher's influence behind the scenes grew with it. He established contact with the leaders of many political parties, including the Social Democrats, but was careful never to publicly identify himself with any particular group.

Although he continued to shun the political spotlight, Schleicher aspired to a more important role in governing the Reich. The traditional parties, according to his thinking, had demonstrated their incapacity to serve the country and therefore new political movements were needed. He envisioned a new party embracing younger elements of all the nonsocialist parties, to be led by officers who had fought in the trenches and who, by virtue of this experience, would be able to provide the leadership so lacking in the old parties.[12] With this in mind, Schleicher did everything he could to encourage some of the younger deputies of the Nationalist Party to break with Hugenberg's leadership. In this enterprise he cooperated closely with some powerful industrialist friends, a few of whom were members of the Ruhrlade.

Although certain big business interests were willing to make a few unimportant concessions to the Nazis, most industrialists strongly objected to Hugenberg's efforts to drive the Nationalist Party further to the right or into an alliance with the Nazis. The Nationalists became more clearly divided into two factions: conservatives, supported by heavy industry; and Hugenberg's reactionaries, supported primarily by agricultural interests. At a fateful meeting of the party leadership on June 30, 1930, the decision not to support the Brüning cabinet was carried by only two votes, because some of Hugenberg's opponents were absent from the meeting. Within a short time the more moderate Nationalists were in open revolt against Hugenberg's intransigent leadership. The Ruhrlade was encouraged by this development and General von Schleicher actively used his influence in an attempt to destroy Hugenberg's grip on the party. The bulk of the party's industrial wing seceded and formed their own Conservative group in the Reichstag. Hugenberg remained chairman of the Nationalist Party but his following was now limited to agrarian interests and a few extreme reactionaries in heavy industry like Emil Kirdorf.

Like Hugenberg, Hitler was also having trouble keeping his followers in line. Even though he still had relatively few supporters among the industrialists, socialist elements in the Party became increasingly alarmed by Hitler's contacts with what they called "the reactionary forces of big business." This simmering dispute broke into the open in April 1930 when the trade unions in Saxony went out on strike. Otto Strasser, Gregor's brother, who controlled several Nazi newspapers in northern Germany, came out in full support of the strike. Strasser's newspapers had for some time maintained a radical socialist line which irritated and embarrassed Hitler. Even those industrialists who were sympathetic to the Nazis had always been afraid of the Party's socialism; now they made it clear that unless Hitler immediately repudiated the stand taken by Strasser there would be no more subsidies.

Being able to count on the loyalty of the Gauleiter of Saxony, Hitler ordered that no Party member could take part in the strike. However, he was unable to silence Strasser's papers; the time for a showdown with this rebellious individual was clearly at hand. On May 21, 1930, Hitler, acting with his characteristic suddenness, arrived unannounced in Berlin with his staff. Shortly after their arrival, Hess telephoned Otto Strasser and invited him to come to the San Souci Hotel to discuss his disputes with Hitler. The only account of this discussion, which was held before a very small group of Party leaders, is Otto Strasser's; nevertheless, it is probably basically accurate because it was published by Strasser shortly afterward and Hitler never challenged it.

Hitler reprimanded Strasser for deviating from the Party line; his purpose, however, was persuasion rather than coercion. He tried to bribe Strasser by offering to put him in charge of all Nazi newspapers throughout Germany. Only after such appeals failed did he threaten to run Strasser and his supporters out of the Party if they refused to submit. A long debate followed, extending over into the next day. Strasser insisted vehemently on five points: a thorough revolution, opposition to bourgeois capitalism, real socialism, no coalitions with the reactionary parties, and no attacks against Soviet Russia. Hitler countered by accusing Strasser of advocating democracy and Bolshevism.

Strasser said it was the "Idea" of the movement which is eternal and the Leader only its servant. "This is all bombastic nonsense," Hitler responded. "It boils down to this, that you would give every Party member the right to decide on the Idea—even to decide whether the Leader is true to the so-called Idea or not. This is democracy at its worst, and there is no place for such a view with us. With us the Leader and the Idea are one, and every Party member has to do what the Leader orders. The Leader incorporates the Idea and alone knows its ultimate goal. Our organization is built upon discipline. I have no wish to see this organization broken up by a few swollen-headed litterateurs. You were a soldier yourself. . . . I ask you, are you prepared to submit to this discipline or not?"

The debate continued; then Strasser came to the heart of the matter. He accused Hitler: "You want to strangle the social revolution for the sake of legality and your new collaboration with the bourgeois parties of the Right." Strasser was voicing the opinion of many radicals in the Party who opposed Hitler's policy of legality from the start; they wanted a violent social revolution that would overthrow the old order, not make compromises with it. Angered by this attack, Hitler retorted: "I am a Socialist, and a very different kind of Socialist from your rich friend [Count] Reventlow. I was once an ordinary working man. I would not allow my chauffeur to eat worse than I eat myself. What you understand by Socialism is nothing but Marxism. Now look: the great mass of working men want only bread and circuses. They have no understanding for ideas of any sort whatever, and we can never hope to win the workers to any large extent by an appeal to ideas. We want to make a revolution for the new dominating caste which is not moved as you are, by the ethic of pity, but is quite clear in its own mind that it has the right to dominate others because it represents a better race: this caste ruthlessly maintains and assures its dominance over the masses. What you preach is liberalism, nothing but liberalism."

The next day the debate was taken up again. Hess, Max Amann, and Otto's brother Gregor were present. Having had time to recover his courage, Strasser began by demanding the nationalization of industry. "Democracy has laid the world to ruins," commented Hitler with scorn, "and nevertheless you want to extend it to the economic sphere. It would be the end of the German economy. . . . The capitalists have worked their way to the top through their capacity, and on the basis of this selection, which again only proves their higher race, they have a right to lead. Now you want an incapable Government Council or Workers' Council, which has no notion of anything, to have a say: no leader in economic life would tolerate it." Lowering his voice a bit, Hitler said that the economy of Germany depended upon the cooperation between the industrialists and the workers. A factory owner is dependent on his workmen. If they went on strike, then his so-called property would become utterly worthless.

At this point he turned to Amann (the Party business manager) and said: "What right have these people to demand a share in the property or even in the administration? Herr Amann, would you permit your typist to have any voice in your affairs? The employer who accepts the responsibility for production also gives the working people their means of livelihood. Our greatest industrialists are not concerned with just the acquisition of wealth or with good living, but above all else, with responsibility and power." Hitler then mellowed a bit. "But Socialism," he explained, "does not mean that factories must be socialized, only that they may be when they act contrary to the interest of the nation. So long as they do not, it would simply be a crime to disturb business. . . . Just as the Fascists have already done, so in our National Socialist State we will have employers and workers standing side by side with equal rights."

Not satisfied, Strasser asked: "What would you do with the Krupp industries if you came to power?"

"Why nothing," Hitler replied. "Do you think I am so senseless as to destroy Germany's economy? Only if people should fail to act in the interests of the nation then—and only then—would the State intervene. But for that . . . you do not need to give the workers the right to have a voice in the conduct of the business: you need only a strong State."[13]

Hitler was forced to tread a narrow path because he needed both the support of big business interests, who had the money to finance the Party, and the support of the masses, who had the votes. In origin the National Socialist Party had been to a certain extent truly "socialist." This anticapitalist part of the Nazi program was not only taken seriously by many loyal members but was becoming increasingly important as the depression spread unemployment and poverty across the land.

Neither Hitler's threats nor pleadings had succeeded in convincing his rebellious lieutenant. Strasser was more certain than ever that the Führer was only the pawn of "reactionary" interests, working hand-in-hand with the "Jewish stock exchange" to uphold capitalism. For over a month the issue was left unfinished. Then, in the provincial elections of Saxony held in June 1930, the Nazi representation rose from five to fourteen deputies, making them the second largest party in Saxony, in spite of Hitler's repudiation of the strike a few months earlier. Much of the Nazi election victory was due to support from the small and medium-size firms of Saxony. Now Hitler felt safe to run Otto Strasser out of the Party. In a General Assembly on June 30, Strasser was bitterly attacked by Dr. Goebbels and ejected from the meeting. On July 1, Strasser telegraphed Hitler in Munich, demanding an explanation within twenty-four hours. None came. Strasser then seceded from the Party and established "the Union of Revolutionary National Socialists," better known as the "Black Front." But the response among Party members was very small; even his own brother Gregor remained loyal to Hitler.[14]

As the fall Reichstag elections of 1930 approached, the dominant sectors of heavy industry and the Ruhrlade in particular were using their influence in an effort to strengthen the moderate parties of the center. They tried to force Hugenberg and the Nationalist Party to be amenable to compromise and cooperate with the moderates rather than retreat into a negative opposition. Although the Ruhrlade approved of Brüning's use of the presidential emergency powers to impose fiscal measures by decree, their actions in 1930 seemed to indicate that they regarded such use of emergency powers as a temporary expedient and expected the Reichstag to resume full legislative powers as soon as possible. Thus, when the election campaign began, the leading heavy industrialists were still willing to work with the democratic, parliamentary system.[15]

It was a very short-sighted action on the part of Chancellor Brüning to call for a Reichstag election in September 1930 in the middle of an economic crisis. Although he had the support of Hindenburg and faced no danger of a vote of "no confidence" from the Reichstag, he insisted on dissolving the legislature in order to increase his majority. The existing Reichstag, which had served for less than two years, would normally have continued until 1932, but the industrialists wanted Brüning to weaken the strength of the Social Democrats, who, although out of office, were still by far the largest single party. Much of the election campaign consisted of the moderate bourgeois parties attacking the "Marxism" of the Social Democrats, which they saw as the main issue. As it turned out, Hitler and the Nazis tapped a deeper vein of public opinion, a basic distrust of the whole democratic system.

The Nazi Party organization, which Hitler had long been preparing for just such an occasion, moved quickly to saturate the cities and rural areas with propaganda. Anxiety and resentment were the mood of the time. The people wanted some explanation for their misfortunes. It was the Allies, especially the French, who were to blame, Hitler said. The Versailles Treaty had enslaved the German people and destroyed their economy. The Republic, with its corrupt self-seeking politicians, money barons, monopolists, and speculators, was no better. There were the Marxists, who fostered class hatred and kept the nation divided, and above all the Jews, who grew rich on Germany's poverty. There was only one hope, insisted Hitler. Germany must turn to new men and find a new movement that would restore security, prosperity, and dignity to her people. The old gang politicians and their parties could offer no solutions because they were part of the system that had brought about the collapse in the first place.

There was little need for Hitler to attack the Social Democrats; that was already being done for him by the moderate bourgeois parties. This left him free to concentrate his attack on the moderate parties themselves. He accused Brüning and bourgeois politicians generally of being out of touch with ordinary people and there was just enough truth in this accusation to make it stick. The Social Democrats were also under attack from the Communists, who accused them of betraying Marxism. Almost no one bothered to reply to Hitler's campaign; the professional politicians refused to believe the Nazi Party was of any significance.

The hard-pressed middle class saw the Nazis as something new and different. One white collar worker later recalled his participation in the 1930 elections: "I had been unwilling to join any of the old parties. I usually voted for the moderate candidates but I never had any real faith in 'politicians.' Before the elections the people were always right but after the balloting the voter was just a nuisance. The so-called representatives of the middle class would then proceed to make every sort of shady deal with the stock exchange barons and the representatives of the Marxist parties.

"A few weeks before the 1930 elections I attended my first National Socialist meeting at the urging of a friend. The speaker said the old parties had betrayed the German people. He talked about the November criminals, the Versailles Treaty, the inflation, and finally the mass unemployment. Hitler, he said, provided the only hope. Then he mentioned the Jewish question and their conspiracy. I had never thought about the Jews or the racial issue before, but that night I couldn't get to sleep. Thinking back, I remembered that the Jews I met at work never seemed concerned about Germany's problem, but if the Jews were involved in any issue, whether it be in Russia or Palestine, they got very excited . . . also many of them were Marxists. The next day I went to the [Nazi] Party office in my neighborhood and offered my services. . . . A few days before the election I became so involved in the campaign that I even offered to give one-fourth of my meager week's salary to help buy extra propaganda literature."[16]

To audiences overwhelmed with a sense of helplessness, facing poverty and the bread line, Hitler cried: "If economic experts say this or that is impossible, then to hell with economics. What counts is the will and if our will is strong enough we can do anything. We must renew the old German virtues of discipline, industry, and self-reliance. Not so long ago Germany was prosperous, strong, and respected by all." Hitler would then pause for a second as if to look each member of the audience in the eye. With a tone of sincerity he assured them: "It is not your fault that Germany was defeated in the war and has suffered so much since. You were betrayed in 1918 by Marxists, international Jewish bankers, and corrupt politicians; and these same forces have exploited you ever since, prospering on Germany's misery. All we need to do is clear out the old gang in Berlin."

Only the Communists could rival the Nazis in methods of agitation, but they deliberately limited their appeal to the working class. They were also hampered by the rigid beliefs of Marxist doctrine. Unlike the Communists, the Nazis could appeal to the powerful sentiment of nationalism which provided an almost unlimited audience. Hitler intended to unite the discontented of all classes.

In the last days of the campaign Hitler made almost impossible demands on his Party members, most of whom came from the traditionally unpolitical classes of the population. They threw themselves into the contest with winner-take-all spirit. The vigor and zeal of the National Socialists was in sharp contrast with the dull routine way in which the established parties went through the motions of an election campaign. Being, on an average, much younger than the members or leaders of rival parties, the Nazis had a purely physical energy and militancy that the middle-aged bureaucrats of the bourgeois and socialist parties could not match. Two days before the election the National Socialists held twenty-four mass rallies in Berlin alone. Almost every wall and fence in the city was covered with their shrieking red posters.

Where did all the money for this huge Nazi election campaign come from? True, unlike the bourgeois parties, most of the Nazi campaign workers received no salaries and paid their own expenses; nevertheless the costs were tremendous. Big business gave very little, aside from the usual contributions from Thyssen, Kirdorf, and a few other wealthy Nazi sympathizers. Some small firms that were being ruined by the depression looked favorably on Hitler, but the Nazis' chances of winning any sizeable number of votes were still too unsure to lead such financially overburdened companies to contribute.

A considerable portion of the campaign funds were produced by the Party treasurer, Franz Xavier Schwarz. A skilled accountant, Schwarz juggled the Party books to produce money that literally wasn't there. He delayed the payment of Party salaries, and the bills for regular day-to-day expenses. He mortgaged some of the Party automobiles and whatever other items of value he could find, those which were not already mortgaged, that is. Due to his reputation for thoroughness, he was also able to obtain extensive credit for campaign literature, posters, rent of meeting halls, and other expenses.[17] Schwarz's methods had only one flaw; if the Party did not gain a substantial victory they would be bankrupt.

On Spetember 14, 1930, almost five million new German voters went to the polls; most of them were young people representing an entirely new force in politics. The majority of them did not want to be counted as belonging to any definite social class and many of them had never really had a class. This was the generation born in the early 1900s, which grew up in an age when employment was rare, when the economic crisis had thrown millions out on the streets; the youngest in particular could find virtually no jobs at all. A very young man beginning his adult life in Germany in 1930 faced a dismal future. Between the ages of fifteen and seventeen he might have learned a trade, or if his parents had the money he might have stayed in school until he was twenty-two; but in both cases there was a strong possibility that he would then sit idle without work. Those lucky ones who were able to find a job received no more than a subsistance wage.

Many young people openly admitted that they were for Hitler—at least he represented something "new and different." Yet only a few days before the elections no one foresaw the extent of the coming Nazi success. It was obvious that the Party had made quite a bit of progress since 1928, but even the most optimistic Nazis themselves were discussing the possibility that with luck they might win as many as fifty seats in the new Reichstag. In spite of his understanding of mass psychology, Hitler himself had little expectation of the breakthrough on the horizon.

On the evening of September 14, 1930, all Germany waited with anticipation as the election results began to trickle in. By about three o'clock in the morning the historic significance of the occasion was becoming apparent. Everyone, including Hitler, listened in amazement as the news of the Nazi landslide was announced. This was the turning of the tide. Adolf Hitler, who only a few days ago had still been considered an extremist political crank, was now one of the nation's key political figures. His triumph signaled the Republic's doom. It would not collapse immediately, but its death agony had begun.

The National Socialists polled 19 percent of the electorate, which meant 6,409,600 votes compared to 810,000 in 1928. They won 107 seats in the Reichstag compared with twelve in 1928, and had suddenly become Germany's second largest political party, with only the Social Democrats still ahead of them. Although the Communists' gains were not quite as spectacular, they received 4,592,000 votes and increased their seats in the Reichstag from 54 to 57. This was actually convenient to Hitler because a strong Communist Party terrified the upper class and Hitler presented himself as the only man capable of saving·Germany from Bolshevism.

The two parties which had openly campaigned for the overthrow of the existing regime, the National Socialists and Communists, had together won almost a third of the votes and seats in the new Reichstag. The Communists primarily took votes away from the Social Democrats, whose representation fell from 152 to 143. Hitler, on the other hand, increased his strength by eroding the moderate and the conservative parties. The three moderate bourgeois parties—the People's Party, the German State Party (Democrats), and the Economic Party—lost well over a million of their 1928 votes. The biggest losers in the election were Hitler's right-wing rivals, the Nationalists, whose vote fell from 4,381,600 in 1928 to 2,458,300 in 1930. It was clear to all that Hugenberg's party was in decline; their lost voters had gone over to the National Socialists. Hitler, who commanded 107 deputies compared to 41 for the Nationalists, was now the undisputed leader of German nationalism. A future indication of the radicalization of German politics was seen in the fact that an overwhelming number of the new voters supported either the Nazis or the Communists; thus the youth of Germany was drifting into the hands of the extremists.

Literally overnight Hitler had become the force to be reckoned with in German politics. The Nazis registered spectacular gains in all electoral districts and increases of 90 percent over the 1928 vote were not uncommon. However, the best showings were among the farmers and lower-middle-class voters in the rural and Protestant areas of northern Germany. Relatively less impressive, though still formidable, were the returns from Catholic areas and the working-class districts of the large industrial centers. The National Socialist vote in Berlin was typical of the percentages they received throughout the country; in Wedding, a working-class neighborhood, the Nazis received 8.9 percent of the vote; in Steglitz, a middle-class area, 25.8 percent of the vote; and in Zehlendorf, a middle to upper-class neighborhood, 17.7 percent of the vote.[18]

Until now the majority of Hitler's supporters were individuals who were totally opposed to the democratic values of the Weimar government. But in the 1930 election many middle-class people with otherwise moderate political views cast their ballots for Hitler, not because they agreed with everything he said, but because they hoped he could save them from the miseries of the depression. To be sure, it was not the *haute bourgeoisie* or the new rich who supported Hitler, but those whom the economic crisis had squeezed to the wall: the clerks, office workers, small shop-keepers, and farmers.

The notion of a genuine social revolution as proposed by the Communists was anathema to these "respectable," though impoverished, members of the middle class, yet they were profoundly dissatisfied with the existing political and economic system. The tension between their desire to preserve their status and their equally fervent desire to radically alter the established system was resolved by Hitler's appeal for patriotic revolution which would revitalize the nation without revolutionizing its structure. Ultimately the Nazi revolution was the ideal nationalist revolution; it was a "revolution of the will" which actually threatened none of the vested economic interests of the middle class. However, Hitler's struggle against the Jews, stereotyped as the speculator, internationalist, and big banker, provided a truly revolutionary outlet to the more radical among his followers.

After the great Nazi victory no one knew exactly what to expect from Hitler. Would he use the Nazi deputies in the Reichstag to discredit democracy and bring the government to a standstill? Would he then seize power by force? Or did he think that his popularity would continue to grow in landslide proportions, enabling him to come to power legally as a result of election victories and to postpone any revolutionary action until after he had gained control of the machinery of the state? In public, at least, he was still expounding the same policy he had before the election: "It is not parliamentary majorities that mold the fate of the nations. We know, however, that . . . democracy must be defeated with the weapons of democracy."[19]

Like most important businessmen, the members of the Ruhrlade regarded the Nazis as an untrustworthy and insignificant splinter group. They gave no financial assistance to Hitler or his party during the election campaign and, in fact, one of the conditions they placed on their aid to the Nationalist Party was that Hugenberg sever all ties with the National Socialists. But after the votes were counted and the Nazis emerged as the second largest party in the Reichstag, the Ruhrlade was forced to take them into account.

When the divided moderate parties, which they had financed heavily, suffered severe setbacks at the polls, the leaders of heavy industry became disillusioned with politicians and parliamentary democracy in general. Undoubtedly the election of 1930 marked the turning point in heavy industry's attitude toward the Weimar system. The Ruhrlade, for example, was still willing to work within the existing political structure before the elections, but when the nonsocialist parties refused to cooperate with each other and the campaign ended in a Nazi victory they began to look for other alternatives.

At first the Ruhrlade thought they had found an answer to Germany's political problems in the Brüning government. Since the elections had failed to provide a parliamentary majority, they approved of Brüning's circumvention of the Reichstag and his use of presidential emergency powers. In the first months of 1931 the Ruhrlade used its power to stop reactionary forces in the coal industry from discrediting Brüning by resigning from the National Association of German Industry in protest against the organization's acquiescence to the government's adherence to the Young Plan. Even heavy industry was now divided and fighting among itself. The larger, more successful firms like Krupps maintained a conservative position, while those firms which were being ruined by the economic crisis and could no longer compete were becoming more reactionary and were beginning to consider cooperation with the Nazis who were now a firmly based party.

Hitler considered the various alternative strategies. He certainly planned to have his revolution, but it would have to wait until after he came to power. Why risk defeat in the streets, as he had in November 1923, when the Party was making more progress than ever before? The sudden entrance into the ranks of the major parties was immediately reflected in the movement's membership and financial status. The very fact that other political parties took the National Socialists seriously for the first time since 1923 led to a bandwagon effect and rapid increases in the membership rolls. Special clerks in Munich had to work a 6 to 11 P.M. shift to process the applications that poured in to Party headquarters. The flow of application fees and the simultaneous influx of business advertising revenue for the *Völkischer Beobachter* and other Party newspapers put the National Socialist Party on a reasonably firm financial footing and wiped out most of its staggering debts.

One of the biggest sources of day-to-day income for the Nazi Party now came from the subscriptions sold for the *Völkischer Beobachter*. The printing of this paper and other propaganda literature also constituted a large expenditure from the Party budget. This was all carried out under the financial management of Max Amann, the former Party business manager. The occasional donations from wealthy sympathizers, and the big collections from rallies where Hitler spoke, were a welcome but irregular source of income. The circulation of the Party newspaper was a more consistent gauge of success, for it provided a significant sum that the Party administration could count on.

The *Völkischer Beobachter* had been operating on a sound financial footing since 1926, but from September 1930 on it began to produce a substantial profit. Quite rightly Hitler credited this accomplishment to the "exemplary industry" of Max Amann. "Thanks to a quite military discipline, he has succeeded in getting the very best out of his colleagues, suppressing particularly all contact between the editorial and administrative staffs. I don't know how often Amann, when telling me of the great financial development of the newspaper, begged me to make no mention of the fact in front of Rosenberg, the editor-in-chief, or of the other members of the editorial staff. Otherwise, he used to say, they would plague him for higher salaries."[20]

After the September elections of 1930 the Party newspaper also earned a large revenue from advertising. Once in anger Hitler wrote an open letter to an innkeeper reproaching him for the commercial demagoguery of the big brewers, who pretended to be the benefactors of the little man, struggling to ensure him his daily glass of beer. The next day Amann came to Hitler's office "completely overwhelmed," to tell him that the big beerhalls were cancelling their advertising contracts with the newspaper. This meant an immediate loss of 7,000 marks, and of 27,000 over a longer period. "I promised myself solemnly," said Hitler, "that I would never again write an article under the domination of rage."[21]

The one businessman on whom the Nazi Party was most dependent was not a great industrialist who contributed money to the movement, but the Munich printer, Adolf Müller. Müller was not a Nazi, but a member of the Bavarian People's Party, and he printed most of the political newspapers in Munich. In appearance, Müller looked more like a tavern keeper than a press magnate. He was a short, stout man and almost completely deaf. He had done business with the Nazis since before the putsch. When Hitler wanted to start publishing the *Völkischer Beobachter* again after his release from prison in 1924, Müller advanced the editor's wages and supplied the paper on credit. According to Hitler, Müller was a man of "infinite flexibility" in his political views. Several Communists worked for his firm and he was in the habit of saying to them that if anything displeased them with the activities of the company he would make the changes they wished provided that in return he could pay them their week's wages in orthodox opinions instead of money. Müller, who was a self-made man, had a great admiration for Hitler and the two became close personal friends.

In spite of their long association, Hitler continually haggled with Müller over his prices: "The best trick I played on him," said Hitler, "was the adoption of the large format for the *Völkischer Beobachter*. Müller had thought himself the cunning one, for he supposed that, by being the only man who possessed a machine corresponding to our new format, he was binding us to him. In reality, it was he who was binding himself to our newspaper, and he was very glad to continue to print for us, for no other newspaper used our format. Müller had become the slave of the machine."[22] After the beginning of the depression, however, Müller was glad to have the Nazis as customers because their newspaper was the only one that did not have a drop in circulation.

The exact details of all the Nazi Party's business and financial affairs were worked out under the direction of Party treasurer Schwarz. "It's unbelievable what the Party owes to Schwarz," said Hitler. "It was thanks to the good order which he kept in our finances that we were able to develop so rapidly."[23] Schwarz had started to work for the Nazis in 1924; before that he had been employed in the Munich City Hall and had been the treasurer for the right-wing "Popular Block." Coming to see Hitler in Landsberg prison, the fat, bald, bespectacled Schwarz said that he was fed up with working for the petty individuals who controlled the "Popular Block" and would be pleased to work for the Nazis for a change. "I was not slow to perceive his qualities," said Hitler. "As usual, the man had been stifled by the mediocrities for whom he worked."

"Schwarz organized, in a model fashion," said Hitler, "everything that gradually became the Party's gigantic [financial] administration. . . . He had the fault—and what luck that was!—of not being a lawyer and nobody had more practical good sense than he had. He knew admirably how to economize on small things—with the result that we always had what we needed for important matters. It was Schwarz who enabled me to administer the Party without our having to rely on petty cash. In this way, unexpected assets are like manna. Schwarz centralized the [financial] administration of the Party. All subscriptions [monthly membership dues] are sent directly to the central office, which returns to the local and regional branches the percentage that's due to them."[24] Schwarz's centralization of the Party's financial affairs was an important instrument of control in Hitler's hands and useful in controlling rivals such as Strasser.

All the data concerning the sources of the Nazis' Party income was assembled in Schwarz's office. Every pfennig was booked as to its origin with meticulous care. Treasurer Schwarz's accounts have never been found. This is one of the greatest mysteries surrounding the last days of the Nazi regime. Hitler trusted Schwarz completely and consequently told him the source of even "anonymous" contributions, so the name of the donor could be recorded and he could be approached again in the future. Which industrialists contributed to Hitler before 1933? Precisely how much did they give? These questions would undoubtedly have been answered in detail by the books of the Party treasurer, just as the Party membership records which were also kept in the Brown House revealed every individual who belonged to the Party.

It is not unlikely that all of Schwarz's records were purposely destroyed as the Allied Armies neared Munich. We do know that as far as the Party membership files were concerned, they were taken to a Munich paper plant with orders to tear them to shreds to be recycled for new paper. But the owner of the paper factory had them dumped on a huge, empty floor in one of his warehouses; and to hide them from discovery by Gestapo agents, he had them covered with mis-cut pages, smudgy cast-offs from pages of books in the process of printing, and other waste paper. When the American Army entered Munich the paper manufacturer reported to the U.S. security offices the important records hidden in his warehouse.

It is probable, therefore, that some other firm was given orders to destroy the records of the Party treasurer and that this company obeyed. Although the financial records had vanished, Schwarz himself was taken prisoner. He was continuously and brutally interrogated by overzealous American investigators trying to discover information that would incriminate German big business. The use of such heavy-handed methods was a stupid mistake, for the Nazi treasurer was in poor health and could not withstand the strain. He died in 1946 carrying his secret with him to the grave.

Naturally Chancellor Brüning was appalled by the September election results. Rather than getting a more manageable Reichstag he was now faced with one in which it was almost impossible to form a working majority. One possibility would have been for him to attempt to "tame" the Nazis by giving them posts in a coalition government. Some tentative moves were made in this direction, probably through Fritz Thyssen who had close connections with the Catholic Center Party. According to the official version, Hitler insisted that his Party, which would be the largest in the coalition, should have the key post of Minister of Interior (which controlled the police) and Minister of Defense. Brüning considered such a proposal out of the question. However, Thyssen later wrote that an "accomodating offer had been made by the National Socialists to the cabinet of Chancellor Brüning. They [the Nazis] were willing to tolerate Brüning, without being represented in his cabinet, if the Chancellor would be prepared to say that he would part company with the socialists."[25] Thyssen makes it clear that he thought Brüning should have accepted the offer, but it was refused.[26]

When the attempted compromise with Brüning failed, the 107

National Socialist deputies in the Reichstag became anxious to test their strength. On October 14, 1930, at the behest of Strasser, Feder, and Frick, the Nazi faction introduced a bill to limit the interest rate to 4 percent; furthermore, "the entire property of the bank and stock exchange princes . . . must be expropriated without indemnification for the welfare of the German people as a whole"; the same would be done with the property of all eastern Jews; and "the large banks must be taken over by the state without delay."[27] This was actually nothing new; Strasser and Feder had submitted this same proposal to the Reichstag before and no one had paid any attention to the radical little group. But this time 107 deputies, a sixth of the Reichstag, were demanding the expropriation of the banks. The upper class and Hitler's financial backers were shocked: This was Communism!

Hitler was furious. He tried to put his financial backers at ease by ordering the Nazi deputies to withdraw their bill for the expropriation of the banks and "stock exchange princes." They obeyed with silent rage. Then the Communists indulged in a clever trick by reintroducing the bill exactly as it was worded by the Nazis. Hitler commanded his followers to vote against their own bill and reluctantly they did so, to the great amusement of all their enemies. However, what looked like an embarrassing situation to the general public was actually a triumph for Hitler. Big business leaders, even those who had no sympathy for the Nazis, remarked with amazement at the absolute control Hitler had over his followers. The wealthy supporters of the Party who feared its left-wing elements were now reassured.

Not only did Hitler have to contend with his financial backers, but he also had to worry about assuring the Army of his good intentions. As early as 1927 the Army had forbidden the recruitment of National Socialists in its 100,000 man force and even banned their employment as civilian workers in arsenals and supply depots. In spite of this, it had become obvious by 1930 that Hitler's propaganda was making headway in the Army, especially among the young officers who were attracted by his promises to restore the size and glory of Germany's fighting forces. The Nazi infiltration into the Army became so serious that the Minister of Defense, General Gröner, issued an order on January 22, 1930, warning the soldiers that the Nazis were only trying to woo the Army because they were greedy for power. He said that the

National Socialists were trying to convince the Army that they alone represented the national interests, and he requested all troops to refrain from politics and "serve the state" aloof from political strife.

A few months later three young lieutenants from the garrison of Ulm were arrested for spreading Nazi propaganda in the Army. They had also committed the more serious offense of trying to persuade their fellow officers to agree that in case of a Nazi putsch they would not fire on the insurgents. This offense would ordinarily have been considered high treason, but General Gröner did not wish to publicize the fact that treason existed among the officer corps, so he attempted to hush up the matter by trying the three lieutenants on the charge of a simple breach of discipline. When one of the defendants smuggled out an inflammatory article to the *Völkischer Beobachter,* General Gröner's plan became impossible. Shortly after Hitler's victory in the September elections of 1930, the three officers were brought before the Supreme Court at Leipzig on charges of high treason.

Hans Frank, the Nazi defense lawyer, arranged to call Hitler as a witness. This was a calculated risk. It would be embarrassing to disown the three young officers whose activities were proof of the growth of pro-Nazi feelings in the Army. And yet the prosecution had charged that the National Socialist Party was a revolutionary organization intent on overthrowing the government by force. Hitler had to deny this charge if anyone was to believe his policy of legality. However, he also had a more important objective to accomplish. As the leader of the second largest political party, which had just scored a stunning popular victory at the polls, he wanted to assure the commanders of the Army that they had nothing to fear from National Socialism.

It was not the accused who occupied the limelight at the trial, but Adolf Hitler. He made good use of this opportunity. Every statement was designed to have a particular effect, not on the Court, but on the Army. He went out of his way to reassure the generals that he did not intend to set up the S.A. as a rival to the Army. "They [the S.A.] were set up exclusively for the purpose of protecting the Party in its propaganda activities, not to fight against the State. I have been a soldier long enough to know that it is impossible for a political party to fight against the disciplined forces of the Army. . . . I did everything I could to prevent the S.A.

from assuming any kind of military character. I have always expressed the opinion that any attempt to replace the Army would be senseless . . . my only wish is that the German State and the German people should be imbued with a new spirit. . . . We will see to it that, when we come to power, out of the present Reichswehr a great German People's Army shall arise. There are thousands of young men in the Army of the same opinion."

Full of self-assurance, Hitler spoke the truth. It is amazing how exactly his plan, as he described it before the Court, was to be realized in the years to come.

The president of the Court asked: "How do you picture the establishment of the Third Reich?" Hitler: "The Constitution prescribes the theater of war but not its goal. We shall gain control of the Reichstag and in this way make our Party the decisive factor. Then, when we control the constitutional bodies, we shall pour the State in the mould we consider correct."

The president of the Court then referred to a Nazi handbill which declared: "Reform is only half. Revolution is all."

Hitler: "The German people are being intellectually revolutionized by our propaganda. . . . Our movement does not require violence. The time will come when the German nation will get to know our ideas. Then thirty-five million Germans will stand behind us. It makes no difference to us whether we join a government today or remain in opposition. The next election will turn the hundred and seven National Socialists in the Reichstag into two hundred. . . . It is our opponents'· interest to represent our movement as inimical to the State, because they know that our goal is to be attained by legal means. Of course, they also see that our movement must lead to the complete reshaping of the State."

The president of the Court asked: "Only by constitutional means, then?"

Hitler answered loudly: "Certainly!"

The president of the Court: "How do you interpret the expression 'German National Revolution'?"

Hitler: "The concept of a 'National Revolution' is always taken in a purely political sense. . . . When we have had two or three more elections, the National Socialist movement will have a majority in the Reichstag, and then we shall pave the way for the National Socialist Revolution. . . . Germany is muzzled by the peace treaties. The whole of German legislation today is nothing but an attempt to anchor the peace treaties on the German people. The National Socialists look on these treaties not as law, but as something forced on us. We will not have future generations which are completely guiltless burdened with them. If we defend ourselves against them with every means, then we shall be on the way to revolution."

The president of the Court asked timidly: "Also with illegal means?"

Hitler: "I am assuming now that we shall have triumphed, and then we shall fight against the treaties by every means, even though the world looks on these means as illegal."

All of this was intended for the generals, but there was also the Party to be considered, so Hitler added with sinister ambiguity: "I can assure you that, when the National Socialist movement's struggle is successful, then there will be a National Socialist Court of Justice too; the November 1918 revolution will be avenged, and heads will roll."[28] With this closing comment the public gallery broke into cheers.

No one could say that Hitler did not give fair warning of what he would do if he came to power; however, the audience in the courtroom apparently welcomed it, for they applauded the threat loud and long. It made a sensational headline in the newspapers throughout Germany.[29] Lost in the excitement of Hitler's testimony was the actual case at hand. The three young lieutenants, Ludin, Scheringer, and Wendt, were found guilty of conspiracy to commit high treason but were given the mild sentence of eighteen months fortress detention. This was of little importance to Hitler; his primary concern was the effect of his comments on the Army. As he had hoped, the generals now felt reassured. The opinion of many of the Army's leaders was expressed by General Jodl, when he later stated that it was the Leipzig trial which changed his mind in favor of Hitler. After all, the Army probably suffered more from the Versailles Treaty than anyone else, so the Officer Corps could hardly object to a revolution which intended to destroy the treaty, as long as it did not threaten their power or plunge the nation into civil war.

The Officer Corps of the Army was one of the most important groups of the German ruling class. The German Army was nonpolitical only in the sense that it usually did not interfere in the disputes within the establishment. If the establishment were threatened by an outside force, such as the Communists or Nazis, the Army probably would have become "political." The German Army like any other modern army had close connections with the industrialists and munitions makers, but it was an independent force to a far greater degree than the British or American Armies. Naturally the Officer Corps was nationalistic and adamantly opposed to the Versailles Treaty which limited the size of their force to 100,000 men. Thus they favored the same sort of foreign policy that big business did, which would eventually free Germany from the restrictions of the Versailles Treaty. On this point they agreed with Hitler. Most members of the Officer Corps were also Junkers, so there was a considerable community of interests between this group and the Army. The political views of the Junkers were primarily represented by the Nationalist Party, which had already demonstrated its willingness to cooperate with the Nazis.

Henceforth, Hitler's struggle for power was waged on two levels. Outwardly, there was his propaganda effort to increase the size of the Party and his popular support among the masses. At the same time, behind the scenes he would try to convince the key individuals of the German power elite that he did not threaten their economic interests and thus should be appointed Chancellor, a position to which his mass following entitled him. In this quiet but highly important campaign he employed a strategy of ambivalence. First he swore his loyalty to the Constitution, then he promised that heads would roll. In one breath he would give some encouragement to Strasser's socialist wing of the Party, and in the next he would severely rebuke them. All this ambiguousness was primarily intended for those who controlled the levers of power, especially Hindenburg and those around him. On the one hand Hitler was making an offer of alliance, and on the other warning them what might happen if they weren't willing to compromise with him.

From 1928 on Hermann Göring was living in Berlin with his aristocratic Swedish wife. Although he complained of always being short of money, he lived well, dining in the city's most exclusive restaurants almost every night. He still considered himself a Nazi, but he had not been active in the leadership of the Party for some time. From time to time he tried to win over a few of his upper-class friends to the Nazi cause. Göring was a man comfortable in both the world of the drawing room and the company of beerhall fighters. Once while dining at Horcher's, Berlin's most exclusive restaurant, he gestured toward the room full of well-fed faces surrounding him and said: "One day we will sweep all this away, and bring justice back to Germany. It is time we cleared out these bloodsuckers and fed the German people instead."[30]

Göring's first real chance to regain a leadership position in the Nazi Party came when Hitler asked him to stand for the Party in the 1928 Reichstag elections. In spite of the fact that Göring was ultimately intended to be a contact man with the upper class, he waged a rough and rowdy election campaign aimed at the masses. Having modeled his style of speaking closely after Hitler's, Göring was an effective rabble-rouser. He had a talent for exchanging insults and challenges with the Communist hecklers who followed him from meeting to meeting. Considering his background and upbringing, he had a surprisingly good ear for vulgar slang and popular humor. When his mood was at its most sarcastic he seemed to have the best rapport with his audience.

"All Berlin has election fever," Carin Göring wrote home to her mother, Baroness von Fock, on May 18, "and it will be settled on Sunday. They have already begun to shoot each other dead. Each day Communists with red flags with hammer-and-sickle on them drag their way through the city, and always there are clashes with Hitler-men carrying their red banners with swastikas on them, so then there is strife, killings and woundings. We have to wait to see how the election goes on Sunday."[31]

As one of the twelve Nazis elected to the Reichstag in 1928, Göring received a letter from the Kaiser's eldest son, Crown Prince Wilhelm, congratulating him on his victory: "Your extraordinary talent, your skill with words, and your bodily strength are just what are needed for your new profession of people's representative."[32] What did the Prince mean? Carin Göring asked her husband. He laughed and said that Wilhelm was anticipating the fights between the young Communist agitators in the Reichstag and the Nazis. "Hermann is now so terribly busy," Carin Göring wrote in June of 1928, "that I only see him when he pops in and out. But he gives me all his free time and at least we can eat together. But I don't think there is a single meal we have had alone, there are always people there."[33] The "people" were businessmen, politicians, aristocrats, and bankers. Some had come to talk about the Nazi Party and some simply to do business with Göring. Eventually, however, all of them were given a sales pitch about Hitler.

Even after Göring became a Nazi representative in the Reichstag he continued to pursue his own personal business activities as an agent for several aircraft manufacturers. In fact, the two occupations blended well and complimented each other. He was also representing a Swedish parachute manufacturer and traveling frequently to Zurich and Bern to give "lectures" and demonstrations of the Tornblad parachute. After one such visit to Switzerland, Göring's wife acted as hostess at a luncheon in Berlin for a group of Swiss generals and colonels who had come for further conversations with Göring on the development of an air force.

The most important of Göring's personal business affairs began when he met an ex-Army officer, named Erhard Milch, who was now head of the German Civil Airline, Lufthansa.[34] A few days after their first meeting it was agreed that Hermann Göring would lobby for the airline in the Reichstag. Milch was very pleased with the man he had found to represent his growing firm. He said of Göring: "His record as a hero of the air war was well known, and his postwar experience in flying planes, in selling engines, in acting as an agent, had given him assured understanding of aircraft and air transport problems. We knew him to be enthusiastically behind our aims as well."[35] In return for a monthly retainer of 1,000 marks Göring's voice in the Reichstag now spoke on behalf of both Lufthansa and the National Socialist Party.

Hitler assigned Hermann Göring the task of making the Nazi Party look more respectable and "civilized" to the upper class and the aristocracy, whose power had been only slightly diminished by the fall of the monarchy. The most important individual to succumb to Göring's persuasion was Prince August Wilhelm, the second son of the Kaiser. Within a short time Göring was even calling the Prince by his nickname, Auwi. Carin Göring's closest friends in Berlin were now the Prince and Princess Victor zu Wied, both of whom were captivated by her beauty and charm. The Prince and Princess also admired the energy and enthusiasm of her husband and were sympathetic to the aims of the Nazi Party. Through these royal connections the social world of the Görings widened and soon the names of those on the guest list for their dinners were to be found in either the *Who's Who in Germany* or the *Almanac de Gotha*.

The fact that he often had some of the wealthiest people in Germany as guests did not stop Göring from making his home a kind of headquarters for any member of the Party, no matter how humble his origins, who happened to be in Berlin looking for a place to stay and a free meal. It became the talk of Berlin society that at the Görings a princess might find herself with a farm laborer as a dinner partner. This demonstration of social equality emphasized to Göring's guests and their friends the democratic policy of the Nazis; and, of course, it did no harm to Göring's reputation among the rank-and-file Party members.

An excellent description of the success of the Görings' proselytizing among the German royalty and aristocracy was given by his wife Carin in the letters she wrote home to her mother. "The [Prince and Princess] Wieds want everyone they know to become interested in the Hitler movement, and Hermann is bombarded with questions—they are the same old ones, only from different people. It is an attempt to find chinks in Hitler's armor, criticisms of his program, etc. And so Hermann must explain, answer, elaborate to an exhausting degree. . . . But I can see that it is all for the best, and that the circle around is constantly growing and that we have already won many for Hitler and his cause. [Prince] August Wilhelm now follows us, as do the Wieds, together with a large group of interesting people. Yesterday we had breakfast with Prince Henckel-Donnersmarck, he is forty years old and is confined to a wheelchair, paralyzed, it is so sad. He goes to every meeting where Hermann is speaking. We like him very much and he is so good and intelligent. . . . A few days ago Baron Koskull was here for lunch, he is at the Swedish Legation here, and at the same time were the von Bahrs, August Wilhelm, and two National Socialist workers, who had come up from Munich and were staying with us. Later Count Colms arrived with his wife and the Duchess von K. with daughter. You can imagine what big eyes the Swedes made of this mixture!!!"

"Yesterday we had the Wieds for lunch together with Doctor Goebbels, the leader of the movement in Berlin," she wrote on

March 22, 1930. "The princess had made a wonderful drawing of a Hitler company on the march, with swastikas held high, and between the soldiers one could see the shining shapes of those who had been murdered by the Communists. The whole effect was so beautiful, so inspiring. I will bring it with me when I come to see you."[36]

Lest one get the impression that Göring's campaign among the upper class was the only activity of the Nazis in Berlin it must be remembered that when Dr. Goebbels was first appointed as the Party leader in the capital most all the members were from the lower and lower middle classes. The Berlin Party headquarters was in a filthy basement and was better known by the Nazis as "the opium den." "The rays of the sun never penetrated down there," said Goebbels, "and the electric light was left burning day and night. As soon as you opened the door the smell of stale cigarette smoke overwhelmed your nostrils . . . all corners of the place were stuffed with heaps of old newspapers. . . . there was complete confusion. The finances were in a mess. The Berlin Gau then possessed nothing but debts."[37] The Nazi Party in Berlin was almost totally unknown at that time. There were only about 600 members and they confined their activities to the middle-class suburbs. Dr. Goebbels immediately ordered a change in strategy; a determined effort would be made to obtain a foothold in the proletarian neighborhoods in the north and east of the city. He realized the Nazis needed more members from the ranks of the workers and thought he might be able to win some of them over by boldly marching into the lion's den, the Communist-controlled district of north Berlin.

In the first week of February 1927 glaring red posters which screamed the Marxistlike slogan "The Bourgeois State is approaching the end" appeared in Berlin. The posters announced an invitation to a mass meeting at the Pharus Hall, located in Wedding, one of the most solidly Communist neighborhoods in Berlin. As a deliberate act of provocation, Goebbels ordered every member of the Party in Berlin to parade in uniform, with flags, through Wedding before the meeting began. The parade and the meeting itself were "an open challenge," wrote Goebbels. "It was meant that way by us. It was understood that way by the opponent."[38]

The Communists turned out in force. The meeting erupted

into a terrible brawl but in the end the Storm Troopers threw their opponents out of the hall and Dr. Goebbels was able to finish his speech. The next morning the Nazis made the headlines of almost every newspaper in Berlin. Within a few days 2,600 applications for membership were received by the Berlin Party headquarters and 300 of the applicants wanted to join the S.A.

Goebbels recognized that the Communist Party provided the workers with an outlet for their resentments against the "system." Yet he thought the average laborer was not attracted by the theories of Marx but by the slogans, banners, and marches of the Communist Party. If he could manipulate the symbols that appealed to the workers, Goebbels felt he could win them over to the Nazi cause. By using slogans such as "Down with the Bourgeois State," he portrayed the Nazis as the defenders of the workers and the Marxist parties as the defenders of the "system." The Nazis offered the German masses a "third way" between Communism and capitalism, against the Jewish leaders of international Marxism and the Jewish bankers of international capitalism.

Goebbels's anticapitalist propaganda posed no threat to the Party's prospective financiers, for the resentment of the masses was not directed against German big business "but against the Jewish stock exchange speculators." "Who once made Germany the proudest and happiest country in the world?" asked Goebbels. "Who sacrificed two million of our best men far away on the battlefields? Who fought and starved and suffered during the war? It was us Germans." He paused for a moment, then went on: "Who has besmirched [our] honor and made it a laughing stock of our enemies? Who has taken our free soil from us and stolen our money? Who owns our mines and railways today? Who has made a profit out of our misery while we starved and suffered? It was our enemies the Jews and the serfs of the Jews."[39]

The strength of the Nazi Party in Berlin was certainly not based on the few upper-class supporters won over by Göring or the infrequent donations they gave. Tremendous sacrifices for "the cause" were made by thousands of ordinary Party members of the poorest backgrounds.

Nazis who were unemployed usually devoted their entire time to Party work. They could get their meals from the S.A. soup kitchen, but the burden of supporting their families fell upon their wives. "My wife," said a Nazi with a large family, "underwent untold hardships throughout these years. To enable me to pay my Party dues, and spend an occasional penny, she worked hard at sewing, constantly harassed to provide a meager living for me and the family. Frequently, if I returned late at night from a meeting or a propaganda trip, I still found her bent over her work, happy to see me come home unharmed. This went on for weeks, months, and years. But she willingly endured it, for she too could not be robbed of her faith in the ultimate victory of National Socialism."[40]

The only activity of thousands of young Nazis without jobs was to sit day after day in the "S.A. centers" found throughout Berlin and in most every other major German city. The "centers" were usually back rooms of beerhalls where both the proprietor and customers were loyal National Socialists. There in their "headquarters" sat the unemployed S.A. men in their coarse khaki uniforms. They would sit for hours over half-empty beer mugs and at mealtimes would be fed for a few pfennigs on soup from a large iron kettle. Often their uniform was their only suit of clothes, and even it had been sold to them on credit from the S.A. field ordnance department. Twice a week they would spend a few hours in line at their "employment office," and with the dole they received from the state they paid for their uniforms and meals.

But when the shrill sound of a whistle was heard in the back room of the beerhall and the squad leader shouted "Attention!" then these men rotting in inactivity sprang up, formed ranks, and stood at attention. The squad leader would then announce: "In the name of the Führer it has been ordered that . . ." and then they would march off.

One night a Berlin S.A. unit was given orders by Dr. Goebbels to undertake an unusual mission. Free theater tickets were distributed among the men. This had never happened before; being short of funds, the Party was not in the habit of providing the S.A. with free entertainment. But when small boxes in which something seemed to be moving were also distributed, the S.A. hooligans began to grin, having some idea as to what their mission might be. Dr. Goebbels explained that their assignment was to secure a ban against the "pacifist" film, "All Quiet on the Western Front," which had been adapted from the German novel by Erich Maria Remarque. The group leaders then explained what each unit was to do. In an optimistic mood the Storm Troopers set out. The Nazis entered the theater and waited until the film began. Then in the darkness the signal was given; white mice and snakes were released and a few stink-bombs were set off for good measure. With hundreds of mice running through the theater women jumped up on the seats and railings, while a snake slithered its way down the center aisle. The police were called, but by the time they arrived no trace of the culprits could be found. Everyone present merely stated that he wanted to see the film. The following day the government banned the film as being likely to cause more disturbance.

The activities of the Berlin S.A. were usually not so harmless. The traditional domination of the capital city by the Marxist parties provided an excellent reason why it had to be taken. Gauleiter Dr. Goebbels was determined to "smash the Reds" in the very center of their strength. Berlin's East End had been in a virtual state of seige since May 1, 1929, when open hostilities broke out between the Storm Troopers and the Red Front Fighters. The basement taverns and corner cafes served as bases for the rival armies and were described by S.A. men as "fortified positions in the battle zone." For days at a time whole rows of streets were in the grip of a new kind of urban guerilla warfare that raged through the tenement districts and the grim terrain in the networks of alleys between the tall old buildings. Only massive intervention by the police was able to temporarily quell the fighting in which nineteen were killed and forty were seriously injured.

In spite of his proletarian background and his familiarity with the workers of Berlin, Dr. Goebbels also made his coup in high society. This triumph did not come through influential friends or from having persuaded an industrialist to contribute, but by way of a romance. One evening a beautiful and elegant lady, attracted by the sound of military music and the excited faces of the large crowd pushing their way to the box office, decided to attend a Nazi meeting at the Sportpalast, just out of curiosity. Ten thousand people cheered Dr. Goebbels as he walked across the platform past an honor guard of burly young Storm Troopers wearing brown shirts. The front of the stage was lined with red swastika flags. Goebbels began to speak; there was perfect silence in the hall. A torrent of words poured down on the enemies of the people, the bosses and the November criminals; the eyes of the speaker flashed. He then spoke of Adolf Hitler, the savior of the German people who would lead them out of their misery. The people jumped up, shouted, and were beyond themselves with ecstasy. The beautiful young lady, who at first had felt out of place among these rough, fanatical people who smelled of sweat, sat fascinated by what she had heard and the man on the platform. The next day she joined the local Nazi group in west Berlin. Her name was Magda Quandt. She was twenty-nine years old, divorced, and bored with a life that seemed to her monotonous and senseless.

Born in Berlin on November 11, 1901, Magda Quandt was the daughter of Oskar Ritschel, a well-to-do engineer, who had married her mother, Augusta Behrend, after Magda's birth. Three years later the Ritschels were divorced and Magda's mother married a Jewish businessman named Friedlander. Thus Magda acquired a Jewish stepfather whose name she used until she was nineteen. The family moved to Belgium and the six-year-old girl was put in the school of Sacré Coeur run by the Ursuline nuns. Before the outbreak of World War I the Friedlanders returned to Germany, where Magda entered the *gymnasium*, graduating in 1919. In the meantime her mother had divorced again and Magda was sent to a very exclusive finishing school, Holzhausen in Goslar. One day on the train from Berlin to Goslar she made the acquaintance of a wealthy manufacturer, Gunther Quandt, who fell in love with the pretty eighteen-year-old girl. He was thirty-eight and a widower with two sons.

Quandt and Magda were married in January of 1921 in Bad Godesberg. In November of 1921 Magda gave birth to a son. However, the marriage soon proved a failure and was kept up only as a facade. Magda's qualities as a society hostess were exploited by her industrialist husband, particularly during their journeys to North and South America. But in 1929 the marriage was dissolved when Quandt discovered Magda's love affair with a medical student. Quandt agreed to give his divorced wife 50,000 marks for the purchase and furnishing of an apartment, plus a monthly allowance of 4,000 marks for as long as she remained unmarried.

Magda rented an elegant seven-room apartment in the west end of Berlin which she furnished with excellent taste. Her love for the young student did not last long and he soon began to bore her. Her life was without a care, but empty. She had been looking for something worthwhile to do when she discovered the Nazi Party.

Magda Quandt offered her services to the local Party group in west Berlin, which was overjoyed to enlist such a refined lady. She was asked to take charge of the local Party's women's group. This was hardly a fitting job for Frau Quandt, since the members of the group even in this fashionable neighborhood belonged mostly to the lower classes. Among them were servants, concierges, and small grocer's wives. Magda didn't go for that very long, and soon went to the Berlin headquarters of the Party to offer her services as a volunteer. By now the main Party office in Berlin was anything but the "opium den" where Goebbels had begun a few years ago. The beautiful, elegant new member, from a class all too sparsely represented in the Party, and who needed no pay, was naturally greeted with open arms. Magda soon generously offered to contribute one-tenth of her monthly income (400 marks) to the Party. It was not long before she was noticed by Dr. Goebbels himself. When Goebbels got to know her better, he put her in charge of his private files. Both met daily and got to know each other more and more intimately. He was fascinated by her beauty and her elegant manners. It took some time for the two to become lovers, but by the summer of 1930 they had become engaged.

Hitler met Magda Quandt for the first time in the fall of 1930 at a small party. Despite Göring's warning that Magda was "Goebbels's lover," Hitler took an immediate liking to her. He was charmed by her refined appearance and her beauty. "There was no doubt," wrote Otto Wagener, "that a bond of deep friendship had begun to form between Hitler and Frau Quandt."[41] For a time it almost looked as if Magda would have her choice between Hitler and Goebbels. But in the end Hitler encouraged her to marry Goebbels, for Hitler was already deeply involved with Eva Braun.

Magda's family was horrified with the prospect of her marriage to Dr. Goebbels. Her mother, her father, and also her ex-husband, with whom she now enjoyed a much better relationship than she had had during their marriage, tried to discourage her. But their opposition simply strengthened her determination. On December 19, 1931, she and Goebbels were married at the country estate of her ex-husband in Mecklenburg. There was an elaborate party after the ceremony. Hitler attended both the religious services and the party that followed.

The next day Goebbels gave up his small bachelor's quarters in the lower-middle-class Steglitz district and moved into Magda's splendid apartment. Magda, however, lost her 4,000 marks monthly allowance. By marrying, they had no doubt worsened their financial condition. Goebbels earned only 1,000 marks from his two jobs as member of the Reichstag and Berlin Gauleiter. But Hitler immediately raised his income to 2,000 marks. In the long run the marriage was financially advantageous to the Party. Although the Party leader in Berlin was not acceptable in high society, his wife was. She was invited even to the most exclusive parties given by the Crown Princess, where she had the opportunity to find more than a few wealthy supporters for Hitler.[42]

On March 23, 1930, Hermann Göring began a speaking tour of East Prussia and the Rhineland with Prince August Wilhelm as his companion. Carin Göring wrote that the Prince was now "a real and true Hitler-man . . . so modest, helpful, obedient, and hard-working."[43] The fact that Prince August Wilhelm had joined the Nazi Party and was openly campaigning for Hitler was indeed a triumph for Göring. The monarchists were still a very powerful force in Germany, enjoying tremendous social prestige and popularity among the upper class. The two largest conservative political parties, the German People's Party and the Nationalist Party, were promonarchist. Moreover, the monarchists controlled tremendous financial resources: the fortunes of the various royal and princely families, the money of the aristocracy, and the support of a considerable number of conservative industrialists who still considered themselves loyal subjects of the Kaiser. The fact that Fritz Thyssen counted himself among the latter category may have had a great deal to do with the association of the Hohenzollerns and the Nazis.

Kaiser Wilhelm and his sons were actively plotting for a restoration of the monarchy. They had the support of a majority of the Officer Corps but what they lacked was a following among the masses. Now that the Nazis had become the largest non-Marxist party in the Reichstag, it became imperative to seek their cooperation. Prince August Wilhelm's signing up with the National Socialist Party was the first tentative step toward an alliance between Hitler and the Hohenzollerns. The one would supply the popular support and the other the money and contacts among the power elite.

In light of his achievements, Göring was appointed by Hitler as the chief political spokesman for the Nazis in the Reichstag. There were, however, those within the Nazi Party who objected to Göring's "courting" of the aristocracy. Soon Göring was complaining to Hitler that each time he was about to bring another industrialist or count into the Party ranks, the left-wing elements of the Party around Strasser would spoil everything with a prosocialist newspaper article or a demonstration against some factory.

In the fall of 1930 Hitler was looking for a new commander for the S.A. after the dismissal of Captain Franz Pfeffer von Salomon. It was a job that Göring had once held and wanted again. He realized that it was the most powerful post in the Party. But instead of appointing Göring, Hitler wrote a letter to Bolivia to Ernst Röhm, asking him to return to Germany at once and take over the command of the S.A. Dismissed from the Army after the 1923 putsch, Röhm had become disenchanted with conditions in Germany and in 1928 had gone to South America to be an instructor for the Bolivian Army.

As Hitler and Göring both knew, Röhm was a homosexual. Actually he had never made any particular secret of his sexual preferences, but the moment he replied to Hitler's letter, saying that he was leaving for Germany, a series of scandal stories about this "pervert" began appearing in the German press. Some letters which he had sent from South America to his friends complaining of the Bolivian ignorance of "my kind of love" were printed. Someone had learned that Hitler intended to appoint Röhm chief of the S.A. and had leaked the letters to the press. This someone could only have been an individual inside the Party, and no one could have been more interested in sabotaging Röhm's chances than Hermann Göring, who wanted the S.A. commander's post for himself. Hitler, however, refused to be swayed in his judgment. Göring had no choice but to swallow his dissatisfaction and accept Röhm's appointment with good grace.

On Christmas day 1930 the Görings gave a party for their intimate friends, all of whom were loyal Nazis. The atmosphere was very festive, with a Christmas tree, candles, and presents for everyone. The Prince and Princess zu Wied brought their two daughters, Prince August Wilhelm arrived with his son, and Dr.

Goebbels came. Many of the other guests were prominent people in Berlin society. "In the dining room sat 14 guests!!!" wrote Carin Göring. "[Prince] August Wilhelm arrived bringing some lovely gifts, a great bucket of white lillies and a huge camel-hair rug, light as a feather, for me, as well as many other little things, a silk shawl, a Dürer madonna, writing blocks, etc. I had stitched or painted things for everyone, and I think they were pleased with them, and Hermann had gathered together his own presents for the guests."[44]

By 1931 Göring was receiving money from Fritz Thyssen, who found the ex-air ace "a sensible [and] most agreeable person." With the financial backing of this new sponsor, Göring was now able to entertain on a more lavish scale, and Thyssen himself became a frequent guest at the home of Hitler's Reichstag spokesman. With his aristocratic charm and ebullient manner, Göring began to exercise a strong influence on Thyssen. Just how significant this influence was is illustrated by an incident that took place shortly after Hitler became Chancellor. After every important reception given for Hitler a list entitled "Contributions for the Party" was placed at the door of the reception room. One evening the industrialists decided on a plan together. No one was to sign for more than 20,000 marks. Thyssen was the first to leave. He wrote down 20,000 marks. Then Göring suddenly appeared and slapped him on the back with a laugh. "What's all this, Herr Thyssen? You know everybody expects you to write down 100,000 marks tonight."[45] Thyssen gave a weak smile and corrected the figure.

Yet in spite of the fact that Göring was suddenly receiving substantial sums of money from Thyssen, it must be admitted that he did not abandon his friends who were stricken by the depression, or neglect his duty as a Nazi leader. Some idea of the desperation of the times is conveyed in the letters of Carin Göring. "Yesteday we had a small tea party here," she wrote to her mother, "and while we were sitting there a certain Count X arrived with his wife for a visit, quite unannounced. She is Swedish by birth. He is a young man, really pleasant, two children, he without employment, the whole family living dispersed among relatives, and he looking for work and here to ask Hermann's help. All poor Hermann could do was show him a list of applicants with over a hundred names on it. On Christmas Eve twenty-eight people shot themselves because of want and hunger and despair. Among them was a young officer, a flier, well known during the war. On Christmas morning Hermann received a letter which began by saying: 'My true comrade and friend, by the time this letter is in your hands I shall be no more.' He went on to write about his fight to keep himself, his son, and the small estate where his family had lived for over 600 years. Now he was completely penniless, and the only way for his wife and son to save the house was for him to shoot himself and allow them to collect on his small life insurance. Hermann telegraphed at once by express telegram: 'Don't be too hasty, I'm hoping to help you,' but his wife telegraphed back that he was already dead."[46]

While Göring was soliciting the support of industrialists and aristocrats, his rival Captain Ernst Röhm, who was now chief of the S.A., was trying to work out an accord with the Army. This project was facilitated by Röhm's friendship with General Kurt von Schleicher. After having several talks with Schleicher, who was playing an increasingly important role in German politics, Röhm was able to convince him that the Nazis were eager to cooperate with the Army. In the meantime Schleicher had been doing some thinking of his own. Impressed by the Nazi success in the September elections and their nationalist program, he began to play with the idea of somehow winning Hitler's support for the Brüning government and changing the National Socialist movement with its mass following into a prop of the existing regime, instead of a legion marching against it. Schleicher began to woo the Nazis by removing the ban on the Army's employment of National Socialists in arsenals and the prohibition against their enlistment in the Army.

Observing the increasing sentiment of discontent among the masses, Schleicher wanted to establish a strong government as soon as possible. He recognized the weakness of the Weimar system in which political coalitions bargained for special advantages for the groups which elected them, and the national interests be damned. If a stable government did not appear soon to master the political and economic crisis, Schleicher was afraid that the Army would be forced to intervene to suppress the discontented population. He thought he had found a possible way out of the crisis when he persuaded Hindenburg to appoint

Brüning as Chancellor and allow him to govern by the President's emergency powers. But in the September elections of 1930 it became obvious that Brüning had failed to win the confidence of the German people. It was the two extremist parties, the Nazis and the Communists, who had won the most spectacular successes at the polls. This worried Schleicher; he was afraid that, as in 1923, Nazi and Communist uprisings might break out simultaneously. If such a situation did occur, foreign powers, especially Poland, would have an opportunity to extend their borders even further at Germany's expense, while the German Army would be fully occupied dealing with uprisings. With few other alternatives, Schleicher approached the Nazis with whom he thought he might be able to compromise because of their nationalist views.

When Brüning had first taken office as Chancellor, President Hindenburg consulted many of the country's leading industrialists to ascertain their views and opinions of the new government. Although representatives from all sectors of big business (heavy industry, light industry, finance, commerce) were consulted, they all agreed on the most important point. All saw Brüning's main task to be the stabilizing of conditions. To some this meant simply political quiet, and to others a political and economic climate in which they could pursue, undisturbed, their own interests. However, there was little stability after the Reichstag elections of 1930, for the depression became worse and worse.

In desperation the trade-union leaders and representatives for the country's largest employers' organizations met to discuss the economic crisis. They explored the possibility of reviving the economy by means of a general reduction of prices and wages. Both sides exhibited an unusual amount of good-will, and the conversations went further than any previous attempts by capital and labor to achieve a working agreement. The employers wanted a revision of existing wage scales. They contended that there was no other way to cut the costs of production. The union leaders, for their part, demanded lower prices. The immediate objective, it was agreed, was a decrease in unemployment, which had reached the three-million mark.

Shortly after the negotiations were over, the Rhenish and Westphalian producers of iron and steel instituted reductions in prices ranging from four to seven marks a ton. They did, however, remind the Brüning government that such a move would be successful in combating unemployment and restoring prosperity only if the government refrained from increasing those taxes that weighed most heavily on industry. Simultaneous with the price cut of their employers, about 200,000 workers in the Westphalian heavy industry took a 7½ percent cut in wages. This gesture evoked high hopes throughout the nation, but the feeling that better times might be ahead was short-lived. A few weeks later the United States passed the Hawley-Smoot tariff which instituted the highest rates in American history, increasing the duty on a number of products more than 20 percent. This was a hard blow to the German export trade, which already was in a bad slump. And the prosperity of the country depended in large measure on what happened to its foreign trade.

In April of 1931 Germany announced the formation of a customs union with Austria. Despite German assurances that this was not a step toward political union (which was clearly forbidden in the Versailles Treaty), Paris, Rome, and Prague protested that Austrian independence would be jeopardized by the move. Austria, a country without appreciable natural resources, where the peasants barely made a living on their stony mountainsides, was even more deeply shaken by the economic crisis than Germany. The customs union was an emergency move to allow exhausted Austria to enter into an economic partnership with impoverished Germany. In this way an enlarged economic market was to be created and an even larger one was planned for all the Danubian countries southeast of Austria—Hungary, Yugoslavia, and Romania—all of which lived on the sale of their agricultural products to Germany. Germany and Austria offered to take them into their new economic union. This was to be Brüning's first step in his peaceful policy of "liberation."

France wanted to keep Germany economically weak and thus argued that such a union was illegal under the terms of the treaties of Versailles and Saint Germain, by which Austria had promised to maintain its independence from Germany. The dispute was referred to the World Court, but in the meantime, in order to discourage the union, France recalled all short-term loans from Austria and Germany. Both countries were vulnerable to the French economic pressure. Austria was quickly brought to her knees; the slow economic decline turned into a crash. On

May 8, 1931, the largest Austrian bank, the Credit-Anstalt (a Rothschild institution), which had extensive interests amounting to control over almost 70 percent of Austria's industry, announced that it had lost over 140 million schillings (about 20 million dollars). The real loss totaled well over a billion schillings, but the bank had actually been insolvent for years. The Rothschilds and the Austrian government gave the Credit-Anstalt 160 million schillings to cover the loss, but it was too late; public confidence had already been destroyed. A run on the bank began. To meet the run, the Austrian banks called in all the funds they had in German banks. Then the German banks began to collapse and called in all their funds in London. Even the London banks began to fall as the gold flowed outward.

In this new crisis the Reichsbank lost almost 200 million marks of its gold reserves and foreign exchange in the first week of June and about 1,000 million by the end of the next week. The discount rate (interest rate) was raised as high as 15 percent without stopping the loss of reserves; however, this did "succeed" in bringing the activities of German industry to a standstill.[47] The German banking crisis rapidly became more acute. The Reichsbank was faced with its worst run on July 7. The following day the Northern Wool Company in Bremen collapsed with debts of over 200 million marks; this pulled down the Darmstadter Bank (one of Germany's "Big Four Banks"), which had lost over 20 million marks in the failure of the Northern Wool Company. The Schroder Bank of Bremen went under and other collapses were imminent. The Brüning government could find no means of preventing bank crashes other than proclaiming a bank holiday. Several banks were placed under state control and the flow of money halted; salaries and wages were paid in dribbles or not at all.

The worse the economic disaster, the better for the National Socialists. Or as Gregor Strasser had written: "Everything that is detrimental to the existing order has our support. . . . The collapse of the liberal system will clear the way for the New Order. . . . All that serves to precipitate the catastrophy of the ruling system—every strike, every governmental crisis, every disturbance of the State power, every weakening of the system—is good, very good for us and our German revolution."[48]

As long as capitalism was expanding and profits continued, the basic antagonisms between the different economic groups, such as industry and labor, were not threatening to the system itself. The depression, however, dramatized the weakness of the pluralistic form of government when the antagonisms of the various interest groups prevented continual, harmonious compromise. Confronted with economic stagnation, and unable to rally the lower and middle classes behind the drab, middle-of-the-road political parties, the German upper class in desperation began to look to authoritarianism. Only a strong leadership could hold the society together and revive the economy. Firm controls would be needed to keep the class struggle from erupting, while limiting the power of the unions would keep wages at a level comparable with prices.

The industrialists probably exercised greater direct influence on the German People's Party than on any other major political group. It is significant that this party turned against the Weimar Republic at the same time that the United Steel Works demanded that the government help to weaken the system of union contracts. In April 1931, the German People's Party demanded a revision of the Constitution: Parliamentary rule should be terminated, and President von Hindenburg should be granted the power to appoint a federal government. In effect, the party was demanding an end to democracy and the establishment of a dictatorship.

By the summer of 1931 heavy industry was becoming dissatisfied with the Brüning government. A few months later, in the fall, the Ruhrlade was so bitterly opposed to the economic policies of the cabinet that they began an all-out editorial campaign against them through the *Deutsche Allgemeine Zeitung*, a Berlin newspaper that they controlled.[49] But the government remained unresponsive to the demands of heavy industry. Chancellor Brüning, who was now becoming more closely associated with the interests of light industry, was still recommending "collaboration" with organized labor.

Curiously enough, the *Deutsche Allgemeine Zeitung*, which was financed by the Ruhrlade, was looked upon in informed circles as a "conservative but pro-Nazi" newspaper.[50] Its director, Joachim von Stuelpnagel, was known to be a Nazi sympathizer. As early as Christmas of 1930 the *Deutsche Allgemeine Zeitung* published a circular inquiry which read: "How do you feel about

Hitler's possible inclusion in the government?" The answers to the inquiry were illuminating. President Hindenburg's best friend, Count Oldenburg-Januschau, laconically and eloquently replied: "Rather Frick [a Nazi leader] than Wirth [a leading Social Democrat]. Reichsbank President Schacht answered: "It is impossible to govern against the extreme right wing." The most decisive response came from General von Seeckt: "Not only do I deem Hitler's inclusion in the government desirable, I think it is a necessity!"[51]

In the summer of 1931, on Thyssen's recommendation, the Ruhrlade made its first contribution to a Nazi cause. A small sum of money was given to Walther Funk, who had become one of Hitler's advisors earlier in the year and who began publishing a newsletter on economics for the Nazis. Most members of the Ruhrlade, like Thyssen himself, expected Funk to encourage "sound" economic thinking within the National Socialist Party and act as a counterweight to the semi-socialistic radicalism of Gottfried Feder. The money given to Funk was not intended merely to help the Nazis, but rather to exercise an influence on them.

Born in Königsberg on August 18, 1890, Walther Funk was the third child of a Prussian family of businessmen and artisans. He grew up to be a young man interested in a wide variety of subjects, including music, literature, philosophy, law, and political economy, all of which he studied at one time or another. He played the piano extremely well and for a time it looked as if he would be a professional musician. Before World War I, he started to take courses in philosophy at the University of Berlin, then shifted to law, and finally to political economy. In his spare time, he began to write financial articles for newspapers in Berlin and Leipzig. When the war began in 1914, he was drafted into the Army but discharged two years later because of a defective bladder.

After his release from the military he became a journalist for the conservative *Berliner Börsenzeitung*, one of the leading financial newspapers in Germany, and by 1920 was appointed chief editor of its business section. Funk's ideas appealed to the businessmen who read his columns. He was passionately anti-Communist and well informed on the latest financial developments. In 1922 he became the editor of the paper, a post he kept until he resigned to devote his full time to working for the Nazi Party. Most of his articles were based on the theories of the pragmatic postwar economists who argued that the workers' demands for higher wages were inflationary, but acknowledged the basic justice of taxing away any war profits that remained after the German collapse.

Funk was an outspoken nationalist; he attacked the French invasion of the Ruhr and opposed the "ineffective" Weimar parliamentary system. He stressed the need for a "nationally integrated economic system responsible to the needs of the general public." Funk knew Gregor Strasser well and approved of most of his theories. Strasser, he said, was a man who favored the basic principles of free enterprise, in spite of the fact that Strasser was actually one of the best-known socialists among the Nazis. It was through Strasser that Funk met Hitler for the first time in 1931 and became a member of the National Socialist Party. Hitler recognized that he could make good use of Funk's "conservative" connections and economic principles, and he soon made the economist his personal advisor and chief of the Party Office of Private Economy.

Walther Funk was a "soft" looking man. He was partially bald and had a large potbelly. His bulging eyes were always bloodshot and his face frequently looked flushed from having too much to drink. When his Nazi sympathies became known, his enemies accused him of being a homosexual and an alcoholic and said Hitler was using him only for his connections. On one occasion it was reported that Funk was so drunk at one of his own parties that he could not say good-bye to his guests. It seems, however, that his drinking did not become excessive until after the Nazis came to power.

Seeing that the father of every third German family was unemployed in the late twenties and thirties, Funk proposed solutions for reviving the economy that were to be adopted by most of the industrialized world. He stressed the need for public works, a vast road-building program, the increased manufacture of automobiles, and the mechanization of German agriculture. He believed that these programs, with easier credit to be obtained through the Reichsbank, would bring Germany out of the depression. Funk discussed Germany's economic problems with all the leading Nazis, most of whom told him they held the same views. Göring, of course, stressed the importance of the role that the creative, that is, entrepreneurial, personality must play in the economy. For his part, Funk accepted Hitler's authoritarian leadership; for how else was a strong, nationalistic, solvent Germany to emerge from the depression? Hitler soon appointed him chief of the Party Committee on Economic Policy, with its strange collection of advisors, including the businessman Wilhelm Keppler, the radical Gottfried Feder, and the socialist Gregor Strasser, for whom Funk occasionally wrote speeches.

Funk's principal job, however, was to act as liaison between the Nazi Party and big business. He was admirably suited for this role since he spoke the language and held the views of both groups at the same time.

The importance of Funk's general contribution to Hitler's accession to power was described in a book published by the Central Publishing House of the Nazi Party: "No less important than Funk's accomplishments in the programmatic field in the years 1931 and 1932 was his activity of that time as the Führer's liaison man to the leading men of the German economy in industry, trade, commerce, and finance. On the basis of his past work, his personal relations with the German economic leaders were broad and extensive. He was now able to enlist them in the service of Adolf Hitler, and not only to answer their questions authoritatively, but to convince them and win their backing for the Party. [At that time, that was terribly important work.] Every success achieved meant a moral, political, and economic strengthening of the fighting force of the Party."[52]

Later, when he was tried as a war criminal at Nuremberg by the Allies, Funk admitted that he became a contact man between Hitler and a number of important men in big business. Several of his friends who were officials in the big Rhineland mining concerns had urged him to join the National Socialist movement, said Funk, "in order to persuade the Party to follow the course of private enterprise. . . . my industrial friends and I were convinced that the Nazi Party would come to power in the not-too-distant future." Explaining his work with the Nazis in greater detail, Funk said: "At that time the leadership of the Party held completely contradictory and confused views on economic policy. I tried to accomplish my mission by personally impressing on the Führer and the Party that private initiative, self-reliance of the

businessmen, the creative power of free enterprise . . . [should] be recognized as the basic economic policy of the Party. The Führer personally stressed time and again during talks with me and industrial leaders to whom I had introduced him that he was an enemy of state economy and so-called 'planned economy' and that he considered free enterprise and competition as absolutely necessary in order to gain the highest possible production."[53] After the Nazis came to power, Funk was rewarded for his services on his birthday when he was given an estate in Bavaria by a group of industrialists.

Funk and his industrialist sponsors wanted what they called "organized capitalism." In fact, the German economy was ready to be taken over by a strong man. Under the Weimar Republic, prices of raw materials were controlled; government loans were made to the owners of the great Prussian estates; key public utilities, the railroads, telephone, telegraph, gas, and water supplies were government owned; agriculture was supported by subsidies and tariffs; and government funds were made available to private banks that had no capital left after the 1923 inflation. The big banks controlled much of German private industry through the great vertical trusts and 2,500 cartels. Most all businessmen looked to the state to revive the economy during the depression.

Although Funk had originally joined the Nazis as an agent of big business, he gradually began to use his influence and close personal friendships with some of the greatest industrialists in Germany on behalf of Hitler. In the classic pattern of German conservatives, Funk saw Hitler as the only alternative to a Communist takeover of the collapsing Weimar regime. Funk became a front man for the National Socialist Party. Included in the list of his influential friends was the president of the Republic. During his frequent visits to Hindenburg, he was one of the conservatives who assured the old Field Marshal that Hitler was not as bad as everyone said.

Funk's testimony at the Nuremberg trials threw some light on the relationship between heavy industry and the Nazi Party. He stated that the big German firms, like big business in other countries, gave contributions to competing parties whether or not they approved of all of their principles, and the amount given to the National Socialists was less than the sums given to "some" of the other parties, in particular the German People's Party and the Nationalist Party. According to Funk, even the Social Democrats were heavily supported by big business. "Some" of the directors of Germany's largest firms were pro-Nazi, said Funk. In this category he mentioned the directors of Siemens, I.G. Farben, Krupp, and several Hamburg shipping companies.

The contributions of industry were rarely given to the Nazi Party as such, but to various groups within it. Naturally Funk could only speak with authority for the contributions given directly to himself or one of his agents, which he then passed on to Hitler. But he said he knew that big business was also contributing money through, or "perhaps" directly to Göring, Röhm, and Strasser. By making various Nazi leaders vie for their favor, the contributors felt they could exercise a more decisive influence over the Nazis.

On July 9, 1931, Hitler himself went to Berlin to meet Alfred Hugenberg, the Nationalist Party leader. Their meeting was a success and afterward they issued a statement saying that they would henceforth cooperate to bring about the downfall of the existing "system." This new alliance did not bear fruit until August when Hitler and Hugenberg jointly demanded a plebiscite for the dissolution of the Prussian Diet. The Nazis and Nationalists united in an effort to throw out the coalition of Social Democrats and Catholic Center Party which dominated Prussia, by far the most powerful of the German states. The Communists continued to denounce their more moderate "Marxist" rivals, the Social Democrats, and ordered their supporters to vote along with the Nazis and reactionary Nationalists. During the plebiscite the police dispersed a crowd of Nazis in the city of Königsberg, using their clubs; it so happened that Prince August Wilhelm, the son of the former Kaiser, was in the crowd. A member of the National Socialist Party and an S.A. man, the Prince wrote to his father about his new experience. Kaiser Wilhelm answered from his place of exile in Holland: "You may be proud that you were permitted to become a martyr for this great people's movement."[54] However, even with the aid of the Hohenzollerns and the Communists, Hitler and Hugenberg were unable to arouse enough people against the Prussian government. They won 9,800,000 votes (35 percent), far short of the majority they needed.

As might have been expected, the Nazis and the Nationalists blamed each other for the failure in the Prussian plebiscite. So the alliance cooled off for a while.

In the fall of 1931 General von Schleicher arranged an interview between Hitler and President von Hindenburg in an attempt to persuade the Nazis to support the Brüning government. The Field Marshal and former corporal met for the first time on October 10. Hitler was nervous and unsure of himself in his first encounter with this tradition-bound old Junker. Unable to face the Field Marshal alone, he wired Göring, who was in Sweden at the deathbed of his wife, whose long illness was reaching its termination. Like Hitler, Göring thought the meeting might be a turning point in German history; even his dying wife agreed and urged him to go. Leaving Sweden, Göring met Hitler in Berlin and together they went to see President Hindenburg.

Hindenburg was not at all anxious to meet Hitler, whose followers had repeatedly insulted and vilified him. They said that he was not true to his duty, did not love his Fatherland, and had no sense of honor. But his advisors, his son, and his Secretary of State insisted that he speak with the leader of the second largest political party; so he yielded. There was a fundamental difference of character that stood between the two men. Hindenburg had a rigid and fixed formula for conversation with people he met for the first time. "Where were you born? What was your father?" This rigid pattern of conversation was useless in this case; Hitler's flood of words tore down every fixed traditional barrier.

There are no complete accounts of what was actually said at the meeting. However, Secretary of State Meissner said afterwards that the meeting lasted an hour and a quarter and Hitler had spoken for an hour. A cataract of words bore down on the old man of eighty-two without hindrance and without interruption. It is probable that Hitler spent much of the time on the theme that only the National Socialists could save the country from Communism. He certainly complained of how his "patriotic" followers were being persecuted by the government, and threatened that under such circumstances no spirited resistance by his men could be expected if the Poles were to overrun the eastern border.

The meeting ended in failure. Schleicher claimed Hindenburg grumbled afterward that such a strange fellow would never make a Chancellor, but at most a Minister of Posts. Obviously Hitler had made the mistake of talking too much in an effort to impress the old man; instead he had bored him.

The day after his interview with President von Hindenburg, Hitler hastened off to Bad Harzburg, a Thuringian resort town nestled in the Harz Mountains. The Spa of Harzburg was famous for its chloride and ferrous waters. The mountains directly above the town were covered with a heavy evergreen forest and the skyline to the south was dominated by the eery summit of the highest peak in the Harz range, called the Brocken, where in years past witches were said to have held their sabbaths. On October 11, 1931, this picturesque setting was the scene of a great patriotic rally. Represented were the National Socialists, the Nationalists, the Stahlhelm, the Junker Landbund, the Bismarck Youth, and the Pan-Germans. On hand too were members of the royal families, representatives of industry and big business, and generals and admirals. It was the largest right-wing political gathering that had ever taken place in Germany. Among the notables present were Fritz Thyssen, Alfred Hugenberg, Franz Seldte, Hjalmar Schacht, and two sons of the Kaiser—Prince August Wilhelm and Prince Eitel Friedrich. The purpose of the meeting was to unite all rightist elements in a common effort to oust the Brüning cabinet and set up a "national government."[55]

The reasons which led the Nazis to join the other opposition groups were stated by Wilhelm Frick shortly before the proceedings of Harzburg got underway. Union of the country's national elements, he explained, was necessary in order to facilitate the assumption of power by those who were really entitled to govern. True, some members of the Party disliked the idea of making common cause with other groups. But they had forgotten that in the beginning Mussolini too acquiesced in the establishment of a coalition government. The National Socialists were prepared to follow this example, and within the resulting alliance they, and they alone, would play the leading role.

Hitler arrived just in time for the beginning of the demonstration of the forces of "national opposition." The meeting was opened by Alfred Hugenberg. With the tone of a schoolmaster lecturing his pupils, the Nationalist leader warmed up to his theme: Germany must be saved from the Red peril. He described Braun and Severing, the leading Social Democrats in the Prussian cabinet, as the "German Kerenskys." Germany, he went on, faced a crucial decision. The time had come to choose either the Russian or the German road. For years the national opposition had protested the refusal of successive governments to suppress "the bloody terror of Marxism." It had protested against the spread of "cultural Bolshevism" and the disintegration caused by the class struggle. In order to save the country from Bolshevism and economic bankruptcy, the national opposition was ready to take political office in Prussia and the Reich as a whole. In this great task the cooperation of anyone who honestly wished to help would be welcome.

Hitler spoke on a similar topic. He predicted that either Communism or nationalism would soon triumph in Germany. He dwelt at considerable length on the duties of a statesman. He declared that the leaders of the national opposition did not want war because they were most all former soldiers who knew what war really meant. But no nation could surrender the right to fight to the last man should the necessity arise. Some critics said Hitler did not put the usual fire into his speech because he felt oppressed by a lack of self-confidence in the midst of all these officers' uniforms, noble titles, and top hats. If anything was lacking in Hitler's speech it was quickly forgotten when the S.A. paraded past in review with hundreds of swastika banners. The thousands of jackboots pounding the paving stones and the rhythmic chanting of Heil, Heil, Heil, in what was normally a peaceful resort setting, was an ominous warning of what was to come in Germany.

But the speech which most disturbed the government and received all the headlines in the press was neither Hugenberg's nor Hitler's. Shortly before the end of the rally, Dr. Hjalmar Schacht, the former Reichsbank president, delivered a speech which he considered "brief but sharply formulated." Stressing that he spoke only as an economist and not as a member of any particular party, he quickly outlined the general economic situation: production was off one-third, unemployment was rising steadily, and foreign indebtedness was growing. Then he charged that the currency was not being properly protected but was being used to cover the bankruptcy of the banks and the state treasury. Schacht said that the public reports of the Reichsbank did not show its real status because most of its security was borrowed. He concluded his speech by charging the Reichsbank of lending money to the government without proper coverage, something which he termed "a dangerous practice."[56]

Naturally Schacht's speech brought the full wrath of the government down on his head. In a country which had already suffered a disastrous inflation and in which the people remained suspicious of government finances, the man who had formerly held the most important position in the nation's economy had, in effect, charged that the currency was unstable and the banks and government treasury insolvent. Even though Schacht's career as a banker would certainly place him among the German power elite and financial establishment, he had always been thought of as being somewhat of an "adventurer." No one would deny that he was intelligent, but perhaps he was too intelligent, for he had now broken the unwritten rules of the game.

The government attempted to refute his accusations but had little success. Its position was weakened by having to admit the truth of much of what Schacht said. Thus, when government officials assured the public that he had lied in other portions of the speech, their assurances were not accepted. This "adventurer" had dared challenge the nation's financial system, yet he was astute enough to realize that he would survive because with the economy in such desperate shape the government would not want to pursue the matter further. At first, the Minister of Finance, Hermann Dietrich, told a press conference that Schacht had lied at Harzburg and that the government was not trying to conceal the facts from the people. A few days later, the government changed its argument: "It did not object to Schacht's facts, but deplored the form of the presentation."[57]

Before the rally was over Hitler deliberately created a scene when he refused to eat at the same table with Hugenberg and the conservative leaders on the grounds that he could not enjoy a five-course meal while knowing some of his Storm Troopers were going hungry. Then he rushed off before the parade of the Stahlhelm, which to his irritation had attended in larger numbers than the S.A. Yet the Harzburg rally had not turned out so badly for Hitler after all, because the blow that Hjalmar Schacht had dealt the government was worth its weight in gold, even if the Nazis didn't realize it at the time. Schacht's speech at Harzburg was an indication of the growing feeling of dissatisfaction with the

Republic on the part of many members of the German power elite themselves. After all, former Reichsbank President Schacht and General von Seeckt, the former Commander-in-Chief of the Army, had once been the strongest defenders of the Republic. Now they were attending a rally against the government along with Hitler.

The power behind the Harzburg Front was a force to be reckoned with. Listed among its financial backers were:

(1) Numerous leaders of big business and industry: Dr. Hjalmar Schacht, Dr. Ing. Brandi, Dr. Schlenker, Managing Director Moeller, Privy Counsellor Kreth, Managing Director Gottstein, Director Grosse, Director Meydenbauer, Wharf Director Gok, Dr. Blank, Dr. Grauert, Privy Counsellor Poensgen, Managing Directors Louis Ravene and Paul Rohde, Privy Counsellor Boehringer, Herr Reinecke of Chemnitz, Dr. Regendanz, Director Cubier, Dr. Sogemeier, Dr. Meesmann of Mainz, Herr Delius of Bielefeld, and of course Fritz Thyssen.

(2) The leaders of all the powerful agricultural associations: Freiherr von Gayl, Dr. Wendhausen, Herr von Sybel, Sieber, Presidents Bethge and Lind, Director von Kriegsheim, Director Baron von Wangenheim, Herr von Muenchhausen, Herr von Helmholt-Hessen.

(3) Four princes: Prince Eitel Friedrich, Prince August Wilhelm, Prince zu Schaumburg Lippe, Prince zu Salmhorstmar, as well as dukes, counts, and barons too numerous to mention.

(4) Generals: Col. General von Einem, General von Gallwitz, Herr von Hutier, Herr Kuehne, Lieut. General Waechter, General von der Goltz, General Faupel, Major General Bock von Wuelfingen, Admiral von Levetzow, General von Dommes, Herr von Behrendt, Herr von Luettwitz, Herr von Moehl, Lieut. General von Ziethen, Col. General von Seeckt.[58]

As impressive as this list might seem, it must be pointed out that there were still many more business leaders, industrialists, and even aristocrats supporting the Republic than there were opposing it. Unfortunately, however, those who were against Hitler were not nearly as well united as those of the Harzburg Front who were willing to cooperate with him. Moreover, the formation of the Harzburg Front indicated three significant developments:

(1) The economic crisis was forcing many formerly "respecta-

ble" businessmen, such as Hjalmar Schacht, into the extremist camp.

(2) With the threat of financial ruin, right-wing interests like the powerful agricultural associations were beginning to take ever more desperate measures.

(3) Hitler's mass following had increased to such an extent that the reactionaries were openly courting his cooperation.

In December of 1931 Hitler stepped up efforts to win support among the industrialists by forming a circle of business advisors for the Party. This project was part of a deliberate campaign to make inroads into the worlds of industry and finance that he had been working on since the summer of 1931.[59] He asked Wilhelm Keppler, a depression-stricken small industrialist who had been advising him on economic matters, to take charge of this effort. "During a conversation which I had with the Führer in December 1931," Keppler related, "the Führer said: Try to get a few economic leaders—they need not to be Party members—who will be at our disposal when we come to power."[60] Hitler's general plan was for Keppler to ask about twelve prominent businessmen to form a "Circle of Friends from the Economy" for the purpose of discussing economic affairs informally, with no minutes taken. The Circle was to discuss and advise Keppler primarily on two things: how to solve the problem of unemployment and how to revive German industry. Keppler, in turn, would communicate what he had heard to Hitler. At this time, according to Keppler, Hitler had no ideas on perspective members other than Dr. Schacht and Albert Vögler, the director general of the United Steel Works. The choice of the rest of the members was left to Keppler.[61]

Hitler now had several representatives working for him in business circles. On December 11, 1931, Walther Funk met with Baron Kurt von Schröder, a partner of the banking firm J. S. Stein of Cologne, who had many connections with reactionary industrialists. Schröder was interested in finding out the real views of Hitler on certain questions affecting the international banking business. Later events seemed to indicate that Funk was able to satisfy Schröder. Meanwhile, Hitler's early admirer, old Emil Kirdorf, although no longer a member of the Party, was still arranging for Hitler to meet important industrialists at his home. The fact that such meetings were arranged by a prominent industrialist like Kirdorf increased the receptivity of many of the guests to Hitler's appeals and a few like Wilhelm Tengelmann, an official of Essen Bituminous Coal A.G., joined the Party.[62]

The fact that the High Command of the Reichswehr and General von Schleicher himself still represented a force of moderation in German society was proven in the fall of 1931 when President von Hindenburg suffered a complete mental breakdown for a period of about ten days—knowledge of which had to be kept completely secret from the press and the public.[63] During his illness Hindenburg developed a violent antipathy for Chancellor Brüning, with whom he had formerly been most friendly, and suddenly decided that the Chancellor should be dismissed from office. Brüning was saved from this fate only by the direct intervention of the commanders of the Reichswehr. Generals Gröner, von Schleicher, and von Hammerstein, acting together, finally were able to make it clear to the old President that if he insisted on a change in the government, he would have to find a Chancellor who would either include the Nazis in his cabinet or else suppress them by force, which might well cause a civil war. Not willing to face either of these alternatives, Hindenburg submitted to his generals and agreed to continue to support Brüning and his policies, on the condition that the two ministers particularly obnoxious to him, Wirth and Curtis, were dismissed from the government. Brüning quickly accepted this agreement.

By the end of 1931 the results of Hitler's propaganda activity in business circles gradually became visible. In a New Year's article for 1932, Friedrich Reinhardt, director of the Commerz und Privatbank, and one of the first nine members of the Keppler Circle, launched a campaign for German economic autocracy, a policy which would mean difficulty for German exporters, merchants, and consumers, but which was welcome to some of the almost bankrupt producers of coal and steel. Reinhardt called for a rearmament program to make up for the sacrifices involved, but again only heavy industry would directly benefit from rearmament.

7
HITLER'S
FOREIGN FINANCIERS

Contact between the Italian Fascists and the Nazis began in September of 1922 when Kurt Lüdecke met Mussolini for the first time. Mussolini did not make his march on Rome until October 29, 1922, but the Nazis were able to foresee that a showdown was coming. It was Lüdecke's assignment to size up the Italian Fascists, estimate their chances for success, get Mussolini's opinions on certain issues, and find out how the Nazis and Blackshirts might cooperate.

Upon arriving in Milan, Lüdecke telephoned Fascist headquarters. He said he wanted to speak with Signor Mussolini because he had traveled from Munich to bring him an important message from important people. Within a few moments Mussolini was on the phone and expressed his agreement to set up an interview with Lüdecke at three that very afternoon.

When Lüdecke arrived at the "office" of the *Popolo d'Italia*, the Fascist newspaper, he found that it occupied an entire building of immense size, quite a contrast to the miniature headquarters of the Nazis. A Blackshirt showed him the way to Mussolini's room on the second floor. As Lüdecke walked up the steps, he tried to visualize what Mussolini would look like, as he had never even seen a picture of him. Would he have the countenance of a typical Italian, or would he resemble Verrocchio's statue of Colleoni, whose face is full of force and brutality? These preconceived images vanished from his mind as soon as Lüdecke crossed the threshold. At a desk in the farthest corner of the room sat a square-cut man, in a dark shabby suit and rumpled shirt, with a high dome of bald forehead, and piercing, almost frightening, eyes. Mussolini welcomed him in a pleasant, resonant voice. After Lüdecke conveyed the greetings of General Ludendorff and Adolf Hitler, they sat down to talk. Since Mussolini spoke only a few words of German, and Lüdecke only a smattering of Italian, they conducted the discussion in French. Although the Italian Fascist leader had an unhealthy appearance due to a sallow complexion, a tired sagging mouth, and fingernails bitten to the moons, his strong gaze and his powerful, eloquent manner of speaking made a favorable impression on the young Nazi.[1]

Lüdecke recalled that he had to explain the German political situation from the beginning, as Mussolini had never even heard of Hitler. While Lüdecke gave a brief, but thorough explanation of the goals of the Nazi movement, Mussolini listened with obvious sympathy and understanding, asking many astute questions. He agreed that the Versailles system was impossible for Germany and for all concerned; he therefore thought it would not last much longer. The two men then talked about Bolshevism, Fascism, and liberalism. When Mussolini described the internal chaos in Italy and the advance of his Blackshirts, his eyes sparkled with pride.

Judging from the confidence with which Mussolini was able to answer all questions, and from his eagerness to assume the reins of government, Lüdecke was certain that the Fascists would soon make their bid for power. "Signor Mussolini," Lüdecke asked, "in case the government does not yield, are you prepared to resort to force?" Without hesitation, he answered: *"Nous serons l'état, parce que nous le voulons!"* ("We shall be the state because we will it.")[2] On this note their discussion concluded; it was after seven in the evening. Mussolini was not a man to spend four hours discussing something he did not think was important.

Returning from Italy, Lüdecke telephoned Nazi headquarters; Hitler said that he would like to hear a detailed report of the interview with Mussolini as soon as possible. Within a few minutes they were sitting together at a table analyzing the Italian situation. Lüdecke pointed out the numerous similarities between Nazism and Fascism: both were extremely nationalist and anti-Communist; both were dedicated to a radical new order; both had leaders who were men of the people, veterans, self-made, and outstanding political speakers. These likenesses would help to build the foundation for a solid relationship between Hitler and Mussolini in the future. The discussion then moved to the important role of Italy in Nazi foreign policy. Hitler asserted that the natural future ally of Germany should be England and thus when the Nazis came to power they would try to alienate England from France. But at the present time the Nazis were not in a position to manipulate or bargain with England, or with any of the major foreign powers. If there were any hope of an ally in Europe, it would be Italy—that is, if Mussolini came to power. Both Hitler and Lüdecke considered the repercussions the Italian struggle might have on the Nazis. They felt that, if only for the psychological effect, it would be a great advantage to have a fascist group in another country defeat Communism and parliamentary liberalism. The more they talked about Mussolini's imminent role in European affairs, the more evident it became that the Nazis' struggle for political supremacy was not merely within Germany itself, but also in foreign spheres from which any support would greatly facilitate the progress of the Nazis in their own country.

As Lüdecke had predicted, Mussolini became the Prime Minister of Italy on October 29, 1922. Most Nazi leaders believed that Mussolini would give them his sympathetic, although silent, support. But not until the Nazis initiated some action could he be expected to commit himself. As a Prime Minister and statesman, he first had to consider if such a commitment would be useful to Italy. In another meeting with Hitler, Lüdecke said that if the Nazis could prove their strength, Mussolini probably "would go a long way with us." Hitler agreed enthusiastically: "Good, good! I believe you are right and that your most valuable work lies ahead of you in Italy. . . . Will you go to Rome at once?" It was decided that Lüdecke's mission would have four goals:

(1) Obtain the sympathy of the Italian press and their consent to use the Nazis as their source of German news rather than the Berlin news agencies.

(2) Weaken the influence of the Berlin government and use every opportunity to further the prestige of the Nazi Party.

(3) Assure Mussolini that Nazi Germany would not claim any interest in the area of the South Tyrol.

(4) *"And finally, if possible, to get money."*[3]

That evening Hitler, Lüdecke, and some other Nazi officials had a little party in the old Austrian town of Linz, where Hitler had lived as a child, to celebrate the Italian venture in advance. The next day Hitler and Lüdecke climbed to the top of the Poestlingberg, a towering peak which rises abruptly out of the fields and woods. From the mountaintop there was a magnificent panorama of the Danube stretching into the distance and the farms and villages scattered across the plain. As they gazed over the vast landscape, Hitler spoke with brilliance and intensity about the future of the Nazi Party. He seemed certain of the National Socialists' ultimate victory. But one of the main prerequisites for victory was money. Lüdecke later wrote of Hitler: "He wanted money, because money paves the road to power."[4]

When it was time for farewells, Lüdecke was still feeling inspired from Hitler's talk on the mountain. Just after the small group of Nazis had wished him good luck and he was turning away, Hitler shouted to him a final command so brutal that it made even the unscrupulous Lüdecke shudder: *"Fetzen Sie aus Mussolini heraus, was Sie können!"* ("Rip out of Mussolini whatever you can!)[5]

Following a short business trip to Budapest,[6] Lüdecke traveled to Milan at the end of August 1923. Mussolini was scheduled to arrive there the next day; it would be his first visit to the city since he had become prime minister. Mussolini's brother Arnaldo, who had taken over the position of editor of the *Popolo d'Italia*, told Lüdecke that Mussolini would stop by the office at three that afternoon.

The moment that Lüdecke stepped forward to greet the dictator, Mussolini recognized him instantly. He chatted with Lüdecke in a very friendly tone, but slightly more aloof than at their first encounter. The improvement in his appearance was quite noticeable; with a healthy bronze tan, normal-looking fingernails, and an energetic spring to his step, he now looked like a dictator. Mussolini examined the credentials stating that Lüdecke was a representative of the National Socialists, and then suggested, this time speaking in fairly good German, that they continue their conversation on his train to Rome that evening.

At each station on the route, the dictator's train was cheered enthusiastically by large crowds. Not until 4 A.M. was Lüdecke informed that Mussolini would be able to see him, and then only for a short time. So Lüdecke tried to make his message brief and impressive: The political crisis in Germany was on the verge of explosion; the Nazis would take action very soon. Thus the aim of his trip was not to admire the Italian countryside, nor the artwork; rather it was to increase Italy's knowledge of Hitler and its sympathy with his goals. Courteous, but very tired, Mussolini seemed to miss the urgency of the Nazi's plea. Lüdecke asked for another meeting in Rome and Mussolini nodded his approval.

The moment Lüdecke had finished unpacking his luggage, he began to draw up a schedule of all the interviews and public relations meetings to be arranged to advance the acceptance of the Nazi Party. His first aim was to gain the support of the Italian newspapers. This would be no easy task. There were many well-known German journalists in Italy representing great newspapers of international reputation, such as the *Frankfurter Zeitung* and the *Berliner Tageblatt*. In contrast, Lüdecke had no experience in journalism and represented only the *Völkischer Beobachter*, the small, radical Nazi paper. Although the Italian newspapers had some reporters in Germany, they usually took their interpretation of German news items from the most important German newspapers like the *Frankfurter Zeitung*. The idea that one lone foreigner could oppose the entire German press and news media and succeed in having major Italian papers accept his view of German news seemed almost too incredible to be true. Nevertheless, this is exactly what happened.

At this time many large Italian newspapers were beginning to fall under the increasing influence of the Fascist Party. Using this to his advantage, Lüdecke began his work by talking with editors and journalists about the similarity of the Nazis and Fascists. The change to Lüdecke's rightist interpretation of the news would be additional propaganda for the new Fascist Italian government.

As soon as Lüdecke had formed good relations with the large newspapers, the tone of the news changed to the Nazis' favor. Compared with a few months earlier, Hitler's name began to be much better known and carry greater authority.[7] Special interest was focused on the German political scene. Interviews and articles appeared which transformed the Italian people's ideas about the strength of the Nazis and their opposition against the Berlin government.

Lüdecke's relations with the *Idea Nazionale* and other pro-

Fascist newspapers were excellent. The editors of the *Corriere d'Italia,* which at that time was the semiofficial organ of the government, granted special privileges to him, and at his suggestion they sent one of their correspondents, Leo Negrelli, to Munich. Using Lüdecke's letters of introduction, Negrelli made front-page interviews with Hitler and Ludendorff. The Nazis gave him royal treatment, which later brought good results.

Due to the growing coverage of the Nazis in the Italian media, the reporters of other countries wrote articles about Lüdecke's activities for their home press. Everyone seemed to have some comment on Lüdecke and the Nazis, even the enemy socialist press. The *Avanti,* the socialist paper in Milan, was so perturbed by the attention Lüdecke was drawing that it devoted a front-page article to "*Il Signore Lüdecke—L'Anima Damnata di Hitler.*" It strongly criticized the Italian government for permitting such "propaganda" to be printed against the German government. If a socialist German had the gall to speak as Lüdecke had, the article claimed, he would have been thrown out of Italy by the seat of his pants. Lüdecke said he "basked in this back-handed compliment."[8] It was true that he was lashing out vehemently against Hitler's political enemies. In the pro-Fascist journal *L'Epoca,* for example, the whole front page of the October 25, 1923, issue covered one of Lüdecke's interviews under the headline "The Government of Berlin Is Accused of Treason by Hitler's Representative." News of these denunciations reached Berlin where the press replied with bitter recriminations.

Lüdecke was busy from morning to night writing slanderous articles, meeting with Italian journalists, and preparing reports and clippings of his work to send back to headquarters in Munich. His activities were often splashed across the front page of the *Völkischer Beobachter* and his accomplishments were acclaimed by Rosenberg, the Nazi editor.

Lüdecke requested another appointment with Mussolini, but the Duce was too busy with political problems at home and instead arranged for Lüdecke to meet with Baron Russo, the secretary of foreign affairs, who promised to relay Lüdecke's message to the Duce. Baron Russo was very attentive while Lüdecke told of the Nazis' difficulties, but "no help or special commitment was offered at this time." Of course, Lüdecke explained, since Mussolini was legally prime minister of Italy and in friendly relations with the Berlin government, he could not "officially" recognize the representative of a party opposing the government.

Having no reason to reveal the Nazis' financial supporters, Lüdecke claimed that the Italian government gave no "official" aid to the Nazis. Yet his use of the word "official" makes his statement ambiguous enough to be interpreted to mean that there were "unofficial" ties between them. Lüdecke wrote this denial of receiving any money in 1938, when Mussolini was still somewhat concerned about the world's opinion of him. Therefore, not wanting to hurt Mussolini's reputation, Lüdecke hedged by making the clever and partially true excuse that Mussolini did not "officially" give any money.

His denial that any Italian aid was given to the Nazis seems even more dubious when considering the treatment which Lüdecke was accorded by the government. When a limited number of invitations were sent out for Mussolini's first reception with the King at the Palazzo Venezia, many important foreign representatives were excluded. Yet one of these sought-after invitations was sent to Lüdecke—the representative of a radical party which did not hold even one seat in the Reichstag. If the Nazi ambassador was acceptable enough to be part of a formal government occasion, then why would his party not be worthy of "unofficial" support?

Covert funding to sponsor international fascism was an essential policy of Mussolini's government. Adrian Lyttelton, a renowned Oxford historian, wrote that "Mussolini's secret, personal policy gives . . . concrete proof of his desire to disrupt the European order."[9] Thus, contributions were made not only for ideological motives, such as the brotherhood of fascists, but also in order to cause unrest in the countries whose governments opposed Mussolini's plans for the territorial aggrandizement of Italy. Mussolini realized that discretion and covert methods were necessary to weaken his enemies from within. The "fondness for tactics of internal subversion and intrigue with foreign political movements was a marked feature of Fascist policy from the beginning," Lyttelton said.[10] Mussolini provided military supplies for the Hungarian nationalists and the German Army.[11] Italian aid was also sent to the rightist revolutionaries in Corsica, Malta, Macedonia, and Croatia. In 1928 the Duce agreed to back the

Austrian conservative paramilitary organization, the Heimwehr, with weapons and money.[12] During the Spanish Civil War, Mussolini sent 50,000 troops, 700 planes, plus supplies to help Franco. It is also rumored that Mussolini financed fascist organizations in Britain.[13]

Mussolini's feelings toward France were those of resentment and antipathy. He was contemptuous of the French leftist politicians and their antifascist attitudes. "In France we have no friends," he said in 1923. "All of them are against us. In the eyes of every Frenchman we are only *sales macaronis*."[14] The major reason for the Franco-Italian discord stemmed from their rivalry for power in the Mediterranean and their conflicting colonial ambitions in Africa, especially in Tunisia.

Mussolini was also concerned about blocking French hegemony in Europe. In the early 1920s the French were courting the Bavarian separatists, encouraging them to break from Germany. Rather than let Bavaria fall under French influence, Mussolini decided to examine the possibility of forming an alliance with the Bavarian nationalists. Five days after taking office as prime minister, Mussolini requested a report "on the possibility of action by elements of the extreme right" in Bavaria.[15]

According to the report made by Adolfo Tedaldi, the Bavarian right wing was more than willing to accept aid from Italy. However, the report warned that nearly all the rightist groups were in strong opposition to Italy's possession of the Alto Adige (also known as the South Tyrol), which was the area in the northeastern part of Italy, ceded by Austria in 1919 by the Treaty of St. Germain. This region, with a population of approximately 250,000 Germans, was the crucial issue of Italy's relation with the German nationalists. Tedaldi pointed out in his report "the dangers that would accrue to Italy were Bavarian secession to take place, not under our control but under that of another power," such as France. Mussolini's problem was how to make an alliance with the Bavarian nationalists and yet be able to keep the South Tyrol under his control.

Fortunately for the Italians, Tedaldi had discovered one Bavarian rightist organization which was willing to exchange the South Tyrol for Italian support. This was the Nazi Party. Even before Mussolini came to power, Hitler expressed a willingness to make such a bargain. This attitude about the South Tyrol was made clear in the *Völkischer Beobachter.*

If the Nazis were successful in a coup against the Berlin government, then they would have great influence over the Germans of the South Tyrol and Italy's control of the area. Mussolini realized that the Weimar Republic was based on a weak foundation under which latent nationalism was growing. Thus he believed that the Nazis had a good chance of coming to power. In September 1923 he wrote in the preface of *La Germania repubblicana:* "The fall of the Empire has left a void in the German mind. The Republic has not filled it. . . . perhaps in consequences of the Republic, the whole of Germany is moving uniformly and progressively toward the right. . . . It is important to seek out and know what is the state of mind of the new generation of Germans."[16]

Although Tedaldi made his report in November 1922, some claimed that Mussolini himself had already made contact with the Nazis in March 1922 after a trip to Berlin where he met Stresemann and Rathenau.[17] However, it seems unlikely that Mussolini met with the Nazis, considering his preference for secrecy in his contacts with rightist organizations. Rather than using the Italian embassy in Berlin, he used unofficial agents to communicate with German nationalists. The Italian ambassador to Germany, Alessandro De Bosdari, complained about Mussolini's bypassing the Italian embassy and sending secret cover agents to south Germany. In March 1924, the ambassador said that he had "positive information" of frequent secret meetings of Italian agents with German nationalists "to prepare for future developments." According to the ambassador, these Italian agents who visited Munich in late 1923 were carrying identification which verified them to be Fascist Party representatives.[18]

The Italian ambassador wasn't the only one to notice Mussolini's clandestine contacts with the Nazis. Baron Konstantin von Neurath, the German ambassador to Italy, reported that an anonymous Nazi agent was conferring with Mussolini in Rome during March 1923. This agent could not have been Lüdecke, because he was in a German prison at the time.[19] Filippo Anfuso, Mussolini's last ambassador in Berlin, mentioned in his memoirs "emissaries bearing verbal messages" between Hitler and Mussolini in 1923 and listed several names besides that of Lüdecke.[20]

In 1929 Hitler was accused by a German journalist, Werner

Abel, of accepting Italian Fascist money six years earlier. In turn Hitler sued him for libel. During the trial Abel testified that he introduced Hitler in 1923 to Captain Migliorati, who worked with the Italian embassy in Berlin. Abel said that Migliorati admitted to him that he personally transmitted Italian Fascist funds to Hitler for the putsch.[21]

Abel was sentenced to three years' hard labor on the count of perjury. However, the verdict was no indication of the truth, nor of justice, because by 1932, when the case was decided, the Nazis had many friends in the Munich courts who clearly acted in favor of Hitler throughout the trial.[22]

More evidence showing the relation between the Italian Fascists and the Nazis came from the trial in Rome of an Italian official accused of embezzlement. After it was obvious that the missing funds had been intended for Hitler, the trial was finished in secret.[23]

Three other top level sources, men who had access to highly classified secret intelligence information, also confirmed that Mussolini gave financial aid to Hitler. André Francois-Poncet, who was the French ambassador to Germany in the 1930s, an expert on German foreign policy, and a master of diplomatic intrigue, wrote in his account of prewar diplomacy that the Nazis received financial backing from the Italian Fascists.[24] S.S. General Karl Wolff, an intelligence mastermind, who was Himmler's personal chief of staff and who served as one of the top commanders of the German Army in Italy during World War II, said that he was certain that Mussolini had given money to the Nazis before they came to power. The fact that Francois-Poncet, a French diplomat, and Wolff, an S.S. general, who represented the opposite poles of the political spectrum, both confirmed the donor-recipient relationship between Mussolini and Hitler greatly adds to its credibility. There was also confirmation from a high official of the government of the Weimar Republic, Otto Braun, minister president of Prussia, who indicated he had evidence that the Nazis received funds from the Fascists even after the 1923 putsch. Braun told Hermann Ullstein of the famous publishing company that Mussolini contributed money which helped Hitler to win his early electoral successes.[25]

Some say Hitler received more than just money. For instance, Raffaele Guariglia, a young Italian diplomat in the 1920s, claimed that secret shipments of Italian weapons were sent to the Nazis of Austria and Bavaria.[26] This seems to be accurate, considering that Mussolini was also sending military supplies to the Reichswehr to help Germany rearm against France.[27]

The numerous reliable sources which have cited that the Nazis received financial support from Mussolini are more than enough evidence for a sound conclusion. Alan Cassels, a well-known historian of Italian Fascism and an astute scholar who has made a thorough study of the relation between Mussolini and the Nazis, stated: "Certainly Hitler was the recipient of Italian money."[28]

As has been seen, there is overwhelming evidence that Mussolini gave financial aid to the Nazis before the 1923 putsch and that he may have done so again in the early 1930s. However, just because it is known that he gave to the Nazis on these occasions does not mean that he was ready to contribute whenever they asked for money. Mussolini gave only when it suited his purposes and the interests of Italian foreign policy.

During the spring of 1924, while living in Venice with his wife, Hermann Göring was trying to wheedle a loan of 2 million lire from the Italian Fascists. His first attempt involved corresponding with Leo Negrelli, the Italian Fascist whom Lüdecke had sent to meet Hitler. Göring promised in writing that the Nazis would back Italy's claim to the South Tyrol, if in return Mussolini would grant the 2 million lire loan (to be paid back within five years) and promise to see Hitler as soon as he was released from prison.

Göring fluctuated between humble entreaties and pressured persuasion; he pulled on every cord of sympathy that might bring money. "The Fascists were at one time small and laughed at," just as the Nazis are now, he pointed out. But "one should not believe that National Socialists have no future."[29] He tried to pretend that Mussolini would get the best of the bargain because the South Tyrol was worth far more than 2 million lire; furthermore, the loan would be paid back in full. Appealing to a sense of comradeship, Göring explained that "it would really be good if the greatest national movements would have more understanding of each other. . . . Anti-Semitism must in a certain sense be international. The Jew must be fought in all countries."[30]

Despite all of his arguments, no results were forthcoming. So Göring decided that he would have to go to Rome to see Mussolini in person. Still suffering from the severe thigh wound which had been inflicted in the putsch, Göring was barely able to scrape together the train fare for himself and his wife Carin.

Due to their impoverished condition, they had to settle for lodgings in a small pension and live on a diet of cheap pasta and bread while they were in Rome. Göring spent several days trying to set up a meeting with Mussolini; something was finally arranged with the help of his friend Prince Philipp von Hessen, who was in Rome courting Princess Mafalda, the King of Italy's daughter. The day of the appointment, Göring took a heavy dose of painkillers so that he wouldn't be bothered by his wound.

As soon as the two men met they got along splendidly; both were jovial and good natured. Göring told Mussolini the story of the unsuccessful putsch in Munich, and Mussolini expressed some interest in meeting Hitler after he was out of prison. But the only thing Mussolini gave was a friendly handshake—no money! Too proud to admit his straitened circumstances, Göring left the government palace completely disheartened and depressed. Years later he told his stepson how he had thought of committing suicide: "I remember once standing before the Trevi fountains at three o'clock in the morning, and wondering what everyone would say if they found me lying at the bottom of it instead of those coins that people throw in for luck. Then I decided that the water was too shallow to drown in, and I did not throw myself in."[31]

The Görings escaped from near starvation in Rome only after Carin went to see Hitler in Munich in April 1925 to plead for help. Hitler, who by this time was out of prison, was touched by her story of misadventures. He immediately went to the cupboard in his office, pulled out a stack of money, comprising lire, marks, and Austrian schillings, and placed them in her hand. She was forever grateful. Traveling on Hitler's money, the Görings were finally able to return to Sweden, Carin's home. One wonders where Hitler got the Italian lire he gave to Carin Göring, whether it was money left over from Mussolini's last contribution before the putsch.

In November 1932, Göring was again sitting beside Mussolini at a banquet in Rome, this one being given in honor of the guests attending the European Congress of the Academy of Science. During the middle of the evening Göring received the news of von Papen's resignation and, bubbling with excitement, he told Mussolini that the Nazis were about to take power in Germany. Mussolini was anxious to help, and he immediately ordered an Italian military plane to fly Göring to Venice where an aircraft rented by Hitler would be waiting to take him to Berlin. Providing Göring with the use of a military aircraft for political purposes was an open show of Mussolini's support. The Italian leader had reason to be excited too, for only a month earlier he had boasted that "within ten years all Europe will be fascist or fascistized."[32] If Hitler came to power it would be a victory for the Duce as well.

While Göring was trying to get something out of Mussolini during 1924, Kurt Lüdecke was in America visiting Henry Ford* and campaigning in the large cities for more funds from German-Americans. Before leaving for the United States, Lüdecke received credentials verifying him as a representative of the National Socialist Party in the United States, and authorizing him to collect money for the Party. Hitler, still in prison, wrote a letter thanking Lüdecke for his work in Italy and approving of his plans for a trip to America:

Much Esteemed Herr Lüdecke: Dated 4, Jan. 1924

First expressing my heartiest thanks for your representation of the movement in Italy, I ask you to solicit in the interests of the German Liberty movement in North America and especially to assemble financial means for it. I ask you to receive these means personally and, if possible, to bring them over in person. Thanking you in advance for your efforts, I greet you most heartily.

(signed) Adolf Hitler[33]

This letter was typed on the stationery of Hitler's lawyer, Lorenz Roder, who brought it in person to Lüdecke before his departure. There is special significance to this document because Hitler always refused to admit that he ever solicited—let alone accepted—money from abroad.

After meeting with Ford in Detroit, Lüdecke took the train to Washington where a German society had invited him to address a meeting. His heartrending speech described how desperately the Nazis needed money. Most of the people in the audience had

*For Henry Ford's financial support to Hitler see Chapter III.

never heard of Hitler; so they listened with wide-eyed amazement to the story of the beerhall uprising. Judging from the look on their faces, Lüdecke thought he would collect a good size sum. But suddenly someone started to shout out in opposition; a fat, blond man, who was the perfect image of the typical cartoon "Dutchman," stood up to denounce the Nazis' racial, political, and economic program. He concluded with an insulting attack on Lüdecke. As he spoke, the change in the crowd's attitude was obvious. The "Dutchman" was one of the respected leaders of the community and easily turned the people against the Nazis. After he sat down, Lüdecke tried to win back the ground he lost, but to no avail. In fact, the crowd became so hostile they almost threw him out of the hall.

In Pittsburgh, Cleveland, Chicago, Milwaukee, St. Louis, and other cities Lüdecke met with similar disappointments. The minority of German-Americans who sympathized with the Nazi viewpoint were outnumbered by the majority who condemned it. But Lüdecke didn't blame himself for his lack of success: "Had the Sirens themselves sung my cause, results would have been just as negative. The eloquence I wasted might easily have raised a fund to rescue moths from the sun; but Hitler and the Nazis rated nothing better than a perpetually empty collection plate. I was howled down in derision each time I spoke of him as a coming world power."[34]

Actually, the German-Americans were not as unresponsive as Lüdecke would have us imagine. The Teutonia organization in Chicago was very generous in giving contributions to Hitler. By 1930 they had only sixty members; so evidently the dues from this small group were supplemented by other financial sources. Much of the organization's funds came from the members who were employed by the large industrial corporations in Detroit, one of which was the Ford Company. Even as early as April 1925, Teutonia was sending money to the National Socialists in Germany. Hitler wrote a postcard thanking Fritz Gissibl, leader of Teutonia, for a generous birthday gift: "If the affluent ones among the Germans and Germans in foreign countries would sacrifice in equal proportion for the movement, Germany's situation would soon be different."[35] Although most of the members had little money to spare, they gave enthusiastically over the next eight years. One donation of five hundred Reichsmarks was to pay for the travel expenses of S.A. men to the 1929 Party Day. Never negligent in expressing their thanks, the German Nazis must have been grateful. For example, Goebbels sent a long letter to Teutonia in 1932 thanking the members for their frequent contributions to the Party.[36]

After leaving Washington in the spring of 1924, Lüdecke stopped off in England before returning to Germany. Although he claimed that he didn't receive any financial contributions, he admitted the "real profit" was the personal contacts he had made with wealthy, influential men whose power with the media and the government might be of much greater importance to the Nazis than a contribution.

One of the British elite who went down in Lüdecke's book of achievements was the Rt. Hon. Lord Sydenham of Combe, a former governor of Bombay, and the author of the radical pamphlet, *The Jewish World Problem*. He was known in the House of Lords for his attacks against the British mandate over Palestine, which he described as the "mad policy of protecting the Jews against the Arabs in Palestine with the help of English bayonets, which cost the British taxpayer five hundred thousand pounds a month." If Sydenham was not generous to Lüdecke with his money (although it seems likely that he might have been), he was overflowing with advice and recommendations for a fellow anti-Semite. Sydenham urged him to read the novels by Disraeli in order to "grasp the Jewish problem." Of more importance to Lüdecke were the introductions into British high society arranged by Lord Sydenham. For example, it was through Sydenham that Lüdecke had the fortune of meeting the Duke of Northumberland, the leading shareholder in the most distinguished right-wing Tory paper, the *Morning Post*. One of the oldest London papers, it was known for its strong anti-Communist stance.

Lüdecke was invited to spend the weekend with the Duke and his wife at their lovely home in Albury Park. Between pleasant walks in the gardens and the excellent meals, Lüdecke told of the difficulties enveloping Germany. The Duke listened politely to the Nazi viewpoint but seemed to be too "aloof and faraway" from the current political realities to respond in any way to Lüdecke's arguments.

After Lüdecke's attempts, there was not much Nazi activity in Britain until the 1930s, when Dr. H. S. Thost was sent to London as a correspondent for the *Völkischer Beobachter*. Besides reporting on parliamentary news and the growing anti-Semitism in the East End, Thost was busy trying to find people who might be sympathetic to the Nazi cause. He participated in the founding of the Anglo-German Club at Oxford; the chairman of the club was a Baltic German prince whose father had been murdered by the Bolsheviks. Thost always kept tab on any Englishmen who happened to write an article or a letter to the editor which was favorable to Germany. Then he would try to contact them and arouse their interest in the Nazi Party; if they were going to Germany on a trip, he would see that they were well received.

Although Hitler was still not very well known in Britain, there was a growing interest in the Nazis, as was manifested by the number of visitors to the *Völkischer Beobachter* office in Berlin. A few of the British visitors on record were Rennie Smith, who was the parliamentary private secretary of the Foreign Secretary Henderson, and Thomas Jones, the former assistant to Lloyd George. They were both given a copy of Alfred Rosenberg's book *The Future Course of German Foreign Policy*, which should have opened their eyes to Germany's intentions.

One of the best English contacts was made through Arno Schickendanz, who worked for the *Völkischer Beobachter*. Being from the Baltic Provinces, he was a close friend of Alfred Rosenberg, the editor of the Nazi paper, who was also a Balt. Although cool and reserved, Schickendanz was very skillful in gathering information and discovering useful contacts, one of whom was Baron Wilhelm de Ropp of an aristocratic Baltic family. Ropp had lived in Britain since 1910. During World War I he became naturalized, joined the Wiltshire Regiment, and later flew with the R.A.F. After the war, the property of the Ropp family in Lithuania was seized by the Bolsheviks. The Baron then took a job in Berlin as a freelance journalist and contributed political articles to *The Times*. Baron de Ropp was of a robust build, nearly six feet tall with sandy hair and mustache, and pale-blue eyes. His dress and appearance was that of a typical Englishman, but due to his skill with languages, he could easily pass as a German or a Russian. He and his slim, brunette English wife lived in a very comfortable apartment on the Kurfurstendamm, one of the gayest and liveliest streets in Berlin.

Having their origin in common, Schickendanz and Ropp established a close relation. At first Ropp was just curious about the Nazi movement, but after Schickendanz gave him an introduction to Rosenberg, one of the highest Nazi officials, Ropp recognized the growing importance of the new party.

One connection quickly led to another, like the links of a chain. Ropp told the news about the Nazis to his friend Major F. W. Winterbotham, who was the chief of Air Intelligence of the British Secret Intelligence Service.* Winterbotham had served in the R.A.F. with Ropp and since then they had been close friends. After discussing some of the aims, methods, and followers of the Nazis, the two Englishmen, supposedly on their own, decided that it would be a good idea to find out more about this grass-roots movement which was sweeping Germany. According to Winterbotham, Ropp suggested to him that he invite Rosenberg to London. Since Rosenberg was almost completely unknown in Britain, the visit would arouse no comment. Furthermore, Rosenberg would be an excellent entree into Nazi higher circles.

On a chilly, late autumn day in 1931, Winterbotham met Ropp and Rosenberg as they got off the Harwich boat train at Liverpool Street, London. The British Major recalled: "My first impressions of Alfred Rosenberg . . . were of a keen, intelligent and cheerful type, rather heavily built, in his late thirties, like myself, height about five-feet-ten, rather coarse features, anxious to make a good impression and, above all, to talk of his beloved movement."[37]

They drove Rosenberg to a luxury hotel where a room was reserved for him. For the next few days they gave him a whirlwind tour around London, including a visit to the exclusive Carlton Club, whose members were noted for their rightist political opinions. They also took him sightseeing on an excursion of the Surrey countryside. The Nazi seemed to like what he saw and was especially impressed with the friendly and charming manners of the English people. But of more significance were the appointments with leading figures of Britain arranged by Ropp

---

*F. W. Winterbotham is also the author of The Ultra Secret (New York, 1974). During World War II he was in charge of the security and dissemination of "Ultra" intelligence which Winston Churchill described as "my most secret source."

and Winterbotham.

As a well-known correspondent, Ropp easily set up a luncheon appointment for Rosenberg to meet Geoffrey Dawson, who was the editor and controlling influence of *The Times*. The Baron acted as their interpreter, since Rosenberg did not speak English.

Rosenberg and Dawson agreed on many issues. Both men favored good relations between Britain and Germany. Dawson considered the Versailles Treaty to be very pernicious and weakening to the European economy; thus he accepted the Nazis' grievances on this issue.

Wearing a gray pinstripe suit, with his round shell-rimmed spectacles perched on his long bony nose, Dawson was the image of conservative respectability and his ideas matched his apparel. The pivotal point of his political philosophy was the preservation of the British Empire. Seeing how Germany's colonial empire was taken away from her after World War I, he was sympathetic to her loss. Although *The Times* did not suggest a complete restoration of the colonies to Germany, it advised that any rectification of the Versailles Treaty should definitely reconsider the expropriation of the colonies. Dawson's attitude about the Versailles Treaty was strengthened by his talk with Rosenberg; but to what extent Rosenberg might have changed or formed Dawson's opinion of the Nazis is unknown.

Was there a real possibility of cooperation between the most reputable English newspaper and a radical movement like the Nazis? The possibility of such cooperation was not so remote as it might seem today. Although it is conveniently ignored by most historians, *The Times* printed an article on May 8, 1920, which aimed to raise suspicion that the Jews were the authors of *The Protocols of the Learned Elders of Zion*. The article made no blatant indictments, but its subtle implications planted the seeds of anti-Semitism in the minds of the readers: "What are these 'Protocols'? Are they authentic? If so, what malevolent assembly concocted these plans, and gloated over their exposition? Are they a forgery? If so, whence comes the uncanny note of prophecy, prophecy in parts fulfilled, in parts far gone in the way of fulfillment? Have we been struggling these tragic years to blow up and extirpate the secret organization of German world dominion only to find beneath it another, more dangerous because more secret? Have we, by straining every fibre of our national body, escaped a

'Pax Germanica' only to fall into a 'Pax Judaeica'?"[38] When the
evidence against the *Protocols* began to pile up and the British
Jewish community raised a storm of protest, *The Times* finally
issued a retraction of the article more than a year later. Nevertheless, the fact that they were willing to print such vicious anti-
Semitic propaganda in the first place indicated that they would
have no moral objection to Hitler.

Despite this flirtation with anti-Semitism, *The Times* was
never pro-Nazi; however, it was far from hostile in its reporting on
Hitler and National Socialism prior to the war. Any positive
achievements of the Nazis were acknowledged and recognized for
their merit—more than many papers were willing to do. On
February 3, 1933, for instance, *The Times* wrote of Hitler: "No one
doubts Herr Hitler's sincerity. That nearly 12 million Germans
follow him blindly says much for his personal magnetism." Favorable comments like this were of priceless value to the Nazis; no
amount of money could buy space in the news section of *The
Times*. After Hitler came to power, Dawson was accused of being
soft on the Nazis. Francis Williams, one-time editor of the *Daily
Herald,* said that Dawson always watered down news dispatches
for *The Times*'s correspondent in Berlin in order to keep any
stories about Nazi atrocities out of the paper.

Winterbotham introduced Rosenberg to Oliver Locker-
Lampson, who was then the leader of a fascistlike organization
called the Blueshirts. After fighting against the Communists
during the Civil War in Russia, he became the leading advocate of
those who wanted Britain to break relations with Russia.
Locker-Lampson invited Rosenberg and his English companions
to a superb lunch at the Savoy. Rosenberg was quite impressed
with the elegance of it all and later sent a large gold cigarette case
to Locker-Lampson as a sign of his appreciation.

Some have said that Rosenberg also met Lord Hailsham, at that
time Secretary for War; Lord Lloyd of Dolobran; and the conservative M.P. Walter Elliot. But the apex of the visit to England was
Rosenberg's meeting with Montagu Norman, the governor of the
Bank of England.[39]

Norman was the Gibraltar of the British financial community.
A revered symbol of the establishment, he was beyond reproach;
he was seen as being incorruptible and infallible. In March 1920,
when he was selected as the governor of the Bank, the position

was already one of vast autocratic power. During his twenty-four-year reign he exercised this power ruthlessly and fastidiously. No governor had held office for such a long period in the two and a half centuries since the founding of the Bank.

All who met Norman were impressed by his appearance. Émile Moreau, head of the Bank of France, said: "He seems to have walked out of a Van Dyck canvas; the long face, the pointed beard, and the big hat lend him the look of a companion of the Stuarts."[40] According to his biographer, Norman's princely Mephistophelean image, dramatized by his black silk hat and cloak, was carefully contrived in order to give an air of aloofness and omniscience.

But why did Norman want to meet Rosenberg? Well, for one reason, the governor was "instinctively pro-German."[41] Ever since his stay in Dresden, as a young student, he had a special liking for Germany. Thus when he became head of the Bank of England he was determined to do everything within his power to relieve Germany from the oppressive burden of the Versailles Treaty. The sooner the guilt and punishment in form of the reparations was removed, the better Germany and Europe would be. Norman argued that there could be no advantage to France nor any of the Allied countries in forcibly demanding repayment on the belief that blood could somehow be extracted from stone. Although this policy of "economic lunacy" drove Norman to despair, he never openly opposed the decisions of the government and the politicians. Perhaps time would show them the folly of expecting more than bitterness from their economic strangulation of Germany. If anyone was guilty, he thought, it was Germany's political rulers, not her industrious merchants, bankers, and workers. The Bank of England and the unstable British economy were affected both directly and indirectly by the financial chaos in Germany. If Germany was restored to normal economic conditions, then, Norman said, the Allies would also benefit. When the French invaded the Ruhr in January 1923, Norman called it a typical act of "French madness." This move confirmed his disdain for France and his favoritism for Germany.

But just because he was pro-German one cannot jump to the conclusion that there was a connection between Norman and the Nazis; however, the fact that he also hated Jews arouses suspicion even more.

Ernest Skinner, the governor's devoted private secretary for

thirteen years, said that Norman "had some fundamental dis-
likes. . . . the French, Roman Catholics, Jews."[42] His disdain for
Jews was also noticed by Émile Moreau: "M. Norman . . . appears
to be full of contempt for the Jews. He speaks of them in very bad
terms."[43]

Moreau soon became aware of Norman's hatred of the French
during a conversation in which Norman said, "I want very much
to help the Bank of France but I detest your government and your
treasury. For them I shall do nothing."[44] In contrast, Moreau
noticed, Norman had a strong sympathy for the Germans. In fact,
one of his best friends was the well-known German banker, Dr.
Schacht. Moreau seemed suspicious of their closeness: "He
[Norman] sees him [Schacht] often and together they hatch up
their secret plots."[45]

This brings us to one of the connections tying Norman to the
Nazis—Dr. Hjalmar Schacht, the president of the Reichsbank.
From their first meeting in 1924 until Norman's death in 1945,
they maintained a close personal and business relationship. On
the eve of World War II Norman went to Berlin to attend the
christening of Schacht's grandchild, named Norman in his
honor.[46] This was seven years after Schacht had started to give
support to the Nazis; so Norman was on friendly terms with a
Nazi representative from 1932 onward. After Hitler came to
power, Norman and Schacht conferred on arrangements for loans
to Germany. In May 1934, a private meeting took place between
the two bank presidents. Then on June 11 a "secret conclave" took
place at Badenweiler, in the Black Forest, where Norman again
saw Schacht for an "unofficial discussion." Early in October, they
met once more at the same Black Forest rendezvous and again
undertook the secret negotiations for loans to Nazi Germany.

On September 30, 1933, the financial editor of the British
newspaper the *Daily Herald* wrote an article exposing "Mr. Montagu Norman's decision to give the Nazis the backing of the
Bank." According to the article, Norman had continued to rely on
Schacht for advice even though he had expressed his opposition
to the Weimar government. "In these circumstances," the article
concluded, "Mr. Montagu Norman's financial support for the
Nazi regime raises questions of the utmost political importance,
particularly as this is the first time on record that the Bank of
England has ever used its influence in this way to support any

foreign bonds or has actually advised a purchase."[47] Here the author was referring to a rush of speculation in German bonds that occurred after an announcement that the Bank of England had agreed to take part in a financial plan aiming to stabilize the Nazi government.

That Norman made loans to the Hitler regime shortly after it took office in January 1933 is a fact. But did Norman finance the Nazis *before* they were in power? His biographer John Hargrave thought so: "It is quite certain that Norman did all he could to assist Hitlerism to gain and maintain political power, operating on the financial plane from his stronghold in Threadneedle Street."[48]

Naturally Norman did not supply Hitler with money from the Bank of England; but there is evidence that he played a significant role in arranging the financing of the Nazis.

After talking with Norman, Rosenberg met with the representatives of the Schroder Bank of London which was affiliated with the financier Baron Kurt von Schröder of Cologne.[49] Kurt von Schröder's cousin Baron Bruno von Schröder moved to London in his youth and became a British citizen in 1914. Until his death in 1940 Baron Bruno was the head of the banking firms J. Henry Schroder & Company of London, and the J. Henry Schroder Banking Corporation of New York, both of which had been founded by an earlier member of the Schröder family. Baron Kurt von Schröder was a partner in the private Cologne banking house of J. H. Stein & Company. The Stein Bank of Cologne and the Schroder Banks of London and New York acted as correspondent banks for one another and were often involved in the same transactions. The managing director of the British Schroder Bank, F. C. Tiarks, was also a director of the Bank of England and an associate of Norman.[50] Thus there was a direct line of communication between the Stein Bank (Kurt von Schröder), the Schroder Bank (Bruno von Schröder), and the Bank of England (F. C. Tiarks and M. Norman).

When the directors of the Stein Bank were considering whether or not to arrange financing for Hitler, they decided it was first necessary to find out Hitler's prospective standing in the international financial community, of which London was the center and Norman was the head.

Acting for the Stein Bank, the directors of the London Schroder

Bank were interested primarily in one thing: Did Norman find the Nazis acceptable? In other words, did Norman think that a Nazi government would be harmful to British interests? And would Norman be willing to advance a substantial loan to Germany if Hitler were Chancellor? If Norman thought the Nazis were no threat to British interests, and if he would be willing to grant a loan to Nazi Germany, then the German financier Baron Kurt von Schröder would arrange to finance the Nazi Party.

German big business and finance, represented by Baron Schröder, were so extremely cautious because they were afraid that if a radical like Hitler became Chancellor there would be repercussions against Germany in the international financial community. If England did not find Hitler acceptable, they could have applied various types of financial pressure on Germany, such as cutbacks in trade and withdrawals of loans and investments. For this same reason the German industrialists had hesitated to nominate Hindenburg for the presidency in 1925. They feared the election of a field marshal would antagonize foreign opinion.[51] Later, in 1931, when Brüning attempted to form the Austro-German Customs Union, France expressed her disapproval by putting financial pressure on Austria and Germany, which resulted in the collapse of the German economy.[52] German big business did not want this repeated.

When von Papen finally decided the time had come to finance the Nazi Party prior to forming a coalition government with Hitler, he went to the financier who was most aware of international opinion toward the Nazis—Baron Kurt von Schröder. The arrangement to cover the debt of the Nazi Party and finance their expenses until they were in power was made among Hitler, von Papen, and von Schröder in the financier's own home in Cologne on January 4, 1932.[53]

Before Rosenberg left England he saw Lord Beaverbrook, the owner of the *Daily Express,* the *Sunday Express,* and the *Evening Standard.* The British press would play a very important role in helping the Nazis to obtain money. As has been seen, the German industrialists, aristocrats, and bankers were all very sensitive to how foreign opinion would regard the Nazis. When even moderate Germans were debating about the merits of joining the Hitler bandwagon, a favorable comment or two in the respectable, neutral British press could be very influential.

Like Dawson and Norman, Lord Beaverbrook was opposed to the Versailles Treaty and was a staunch advocate of the British Empire. On December 6, 1931, he wrote to his friend Arthur Brisbane (who was also a close friend of Henry Ford) about his recent meeting with a Nazi: "I had a call from Hitler's man, who came here to find out if the success of the Conservative-Liberal and petty-Labour Coalition should be attempted in Germany.

"I advised him that a strong policy is damaged by coalition. Plainly, he had already come to that conclusion; and got the advice he was seeking. He went off to telegraph to his master.

"He is a strong anti-Semite, is Hitler's representative, and like many another man who is opposed to the Jews, he has their racial marks upon him."[54]

Even though Rosenberg did not have the countenance of a Jewish person, it seems probable that it was he who saw Beaverbrook because of the date of their meeting. Beaverbrook's comment about Rosenberg's appearance may not have been very flattering to a Nazi but it betrayed a certain racist bias. Moreover, the whole tone of Beaverbrook's letter is very strange. He expressed no disapproval of Hitler's policies, including anti-Semitism, yet it is obvious he was aware of them. Also, he advised the Nazis not to enter a coalition government, because "a strong policy" is damaged by it. There is no information as to whether or not Brisbane conveyed this message to his friend Ford.

Why did Winterbotham and Ropp provide Rosenberg with introductions to conservative leaders and some of the most important men in Britain? Where Baron Ropp's real loyalties lay it is impossible to say. He was one of those journalists who was closely involved with foreign intelligence activities. Despite his British citizenship, he remained closely attached to Germany and found much in the Nazi movement that was worthwhile. Winterbotham, on the other hand, was obviously acting as an agent of British Intelligence; but what was his mission? Did British Intelligence just want more information on the Nazis—or were they considering collaborating with them? If information was all they wanted, wouldn't it have been better to send agents to Germany to meet the leaders of the Nazi Party rather than assisting a Nazi official to meet the key people in Britain?

Why would British Intelligence have been laying the groundwork for possible cooperation with the Nazis? Here one must remember the basic aim of British foreign policy—to prevent any one power from becoming dominant on the Continent and consequently stronger than herself. Communist Russia was already looming as a considerable threat. By 1931 the British could see that the depression was already very severe in Germany, and would get worse. The starving German masses might well turn to Communism. If Germany fell to the Communists, a Russian-German Marxist state stretching from the Rhine to Vladivostok would certainly be the dominant power in Europe and a grave threat to British security. This had to be prevented at all costs. Naturally, the most obvious way to forestall this was to support the democratic government of the Weimar Republic and the German Army. If this failed, the Nazi Party and its paramilitary organization would be an excellent second-line defense. It was ultimately thought that a Nazi regime in Germany would bring stability to central Europe, something Britain wanted. The Munich agreement in 1938 was a culmination of this policy.

Although no record exists to show that Rosenberg met with him, there was one powerful press lord who was much more favorable to the Nazis than Beaverbrook. In fact, he was so pro-Hitler that there was really little need for Rosenberg to see him. The wealthy newspaper magnate, Viscount Rothermere, gave the Nazis pages of praise and accolades in his paper the *Daily Mail*. There is also some indication that Rothermere gave actual financial support to Hitler through Putzi Hanfstaengl, the Nazis' foreign press chief,[55] but the publicity he gave Hitler was worth more than money.

Shortly after the Nazis' sweeping victory in the election of September 14, 1930, Rothermere went to Munich to have a long talk with Hitler, and ten days after the election wrote an article discussing the significance of the National Socialists' triumph. The article drew attention throughout England and the Continent because it urged acceptance of the Nazis as a bulwark against Communism: "These young Germans have discovered, as I am glad to note the young men and women of England are discovering, that it is no good trusting to the old politicians. Accordingly they have formed, as I should like to see our British youth form, a Parliamentary party of their own. . . . We can do nothing to check this Movement [the Nazis] and I believe it would be a blunder for the British people to take up an attitude of hostility towards it. . . . We must change our conception of Germany. . . . The older generation of Germans were our enemies. Must we make enemies of this younger generation too? If we do, sooner or later another and more terrible awakening is in store for Europe.

"Let us consider well before we lay our course toward that peril. If we examine this transfer of political influence in Germany to the National Socialists we shall find that it has many advantages for the rest of Europe. It sets up an additional rampart against Bolshevism. It eliminates the grave danger that the Soviet campaign against civilization might penetrate to Germany, thus winning an impregnable position in the strategical center of Europe."[56]

Rothermere continued to say that if it were not for the Nazis, the Communists might have gained the majority in the Reichstag. The tremendous success of the Nazi "German Party of Youth and Nationalism" should receive the closest possible attention from the statesmen of Britain, Rothermere advised.

Lord Rothermere was a man of large stature, with a high forehead and such an extreme conservative political attitude that some people said he was "very near to being unbalanced on the issue of Communism"[57] Although he was not the only one with an obsession about the dangers of Communism, he was one of the few who devoted so much money to the anti-Communist cause. In England he was a well-known backer of the British Union of Fascists (B.U.F.), whose members wore black shirts. On January 8, 1934, when Rothermere decided to help the B.U.F., the headlines of the *Daily Mail* shouted "Hurrah for the Blackshirts." The front-page article following claimed that Italy and Germany were "beyond all doubt the best governed nations in Europe today." The leader of the B.U.F., Sir Oswald Mosley, could do the same for Britain, replacing the "inertia and indecision" of the present government. Generous space, plus pictures, were given to cover the fascist activities. Leading articles and editorials were devoted to commending the efforts of the B.U.F.

Suddenly in July of that year Rothermere withdrew his support. The rumor on Fleet Street was that the *Daily Mail*'s Jewish advertisers had threatened to place their adds in a different paper if Rothermere continued the profascist campaign. Sometime after this, Rothermere met with Hitler at the Berghof and told how the "Jews cut off his complete revenue from advertising" and compelled him to "toe the line." Hitler later recalled Rothermere telling him that it was "quite impossible at short notice to take any effective countermeasures."[58]

As for the Nazis, it has already been shown that Rothermere started to give them favorable press coverage in 1930. The *Daily Mail* criticized "the old women of both sexes" who filled British newspapers with rabid reports of Nazi "excesses." Instead, the newspaper claimed, Hitler had saved Germany from "Israelites of international attachments" and the "minor misdeeds of individual Nazis will be submerged by the immense benefits that the new regime is already bestowing upon Germany."[59] Rothermere encouraged his journalists to write articles favoring the Nazis. For example, on September 21, 1936, Ward Price, the most outstanding correspondent for the *Daily Mail*, wrote that Bolshevism was a greater threat to the British Empire than the Nazis, and said that if Hitler did not exist, "all Western Europe might soon be clamouring for such a champion."[60] In 1938, one British newspaper told its readers that it was the *Daily Mail* which had spent the last five years assuring the people that " 'Dolfie' Hitler is a wonderfully good fellow and is very fond of Britain."[61]

A reviewer for the *Sunday Times* once tried to explain Rothermere's political viewpoint: "He saw Hitler as a sincere man who had defeated Communism in his own country and whose programme was now to reverse the *Diktat* of Versailles. He did not see him as a conqueror whose ambitions for world power inevitably mean, if not conflict with, then hostility to, the British Empire."[62] In fact, Rothermere hoped that England and Germany would be allies. Hitler said that the "Beaverbrook-Rothermere circle" came and told him: "In the last war we were on the wrong side." In one of his conversations with Hitler, Rothermere explained that he and Beaverbrook were "in complete agreement that never again should there be war between Britain and Germany."[63]

Before Rothermere's visit to Germany, he and Hitler exchanged a series of letters.* Rothermere wrote saying that he would gladly

---

*Princess Hohenlohe later sought permission of the court to have these letters published, but the judge refused.

use his press "to further a rapprochement between Britain and Germany." His offer was of course eagerly accepted. Later Hitler expressed his gratitude for the *Daily Mail*'s "great assistance" to the Nazis at the time of their reoccupation of the Rhineland, as well as its favorable attitude to Germany over the question of her naval program.[64] Perhaps Hitler should have said that he was grateful for the *Daily Mail*'s pro-Nazi stance in general over the past decade.

Each morning almost two million people, mostly of the upper and middle class, were exposed to Rothermere's pro-Nazi ideas in the *Daily Mail*. The value of this publicity campaign for Hitler is inestimable. The favoritism shown toward Hitler in one of Britain's most popular daily papers assured the German ruling elite that there would be no complaints in Britain if Hitler were selected as the German Chancellor.

Hitler was known to have many sympathizers in British high society, but there was one individual whose importance stood far above the others. This was the Prince of Wales, who later became King Edward VIII, and finally after his abdication was known as the Duke of Windsor. The Prince's affinity for Germany had been strong since he was a youth. Many of his relatives were German (his mother was a German princess before she married King George V), and he often spoke German in private. As soon as all the courtiers had left the room, closing the heavy, carved oak doors behind them, then the Prince would relax and start to converse in German with his mother.

In June 1935, the Prince gave a speech at the Annual Conference of the British Legion. He said he felt that the Legion was the most appropriate organization of men to "stretch forth the hand of friendship to the Germans," whom they fought in World War I. This speech was regarded by many in England and Germany as "the seal of the friendship agreement between the two countries."[65] He was reprimanded by his father, King George V, for speaking about political matters without prior approval of the Foreign Office. Indeed the speech did bring wide repercussions. Sir Henry Channon wrote in his diary shortly after the speech: "Much gossip about the Prince of Wales' alleged Nazi leanings."[66] When the Prince became Edward VIII, Channon wrote of the new king: "He, too, is going the dictator way, and is pro-German, against Russia and against too much slip-shod democracy. I shouldn't be surprised if he aimed at making himself a mild dictator."[67]

Legend has it that Edward was compelled to abdicate due to his refusal to give up "the woman he loved." However, this issue was used as a facade to conceal the more critical objection which the government had with the King—namely, his pro-Nazi attitudes. Evidence is found in both English and German sources. A memorandum from Ribbentrop to Hitler dated January 2, 1938, stated the following: "National Socialism, however, is thought capable of anything. Baldwin already apprehended this and Edward VIII had to abdicate, since it was not certain whether, because of his views, he would cooperate in an anti-German policy."[68]

Hermann Göring was certain that Edward VIII had lost his throne because he wanted an Anglo-German agreement and did not share his government's disdain for the Nazis. The so-called unsuitable selection of Mrs. Simpson for his wife was only a pretext to get rid of him, according to Göring.[69] Hitler thought the "real reason for the destruction of the Duke of Windsor was . . . his speech at the old veterans' rally in Berlin, at which he declared that it would be the task of his life to effect a reconciliation between Britain and Germany."[70] Anthony Eden, the Foreign Secretary, was reported to have said that if King Edward continued to speak independently on foreign affairs, there were "ways and means of compelling him to abdicate."[71] Hugh Dalton, a Labor M.P., mentioned the "widespread rumors that he [the King] was unduly sympathetic to the German Nazis, and a general feeling that, for a constitutional monarch, he was inclined to hold and express some dangerously personal views."[72] The Duke affirmed the suspicions that he looked with admiration upon the Nazis when he spoke at a meeting in Leipzig, Germany, in the fall of 1937. The former king told his audiences: "I have traveled the world and my upbringing has made me familiar with the great achievements of mankind, but that which I have seen in Germany, I had hitherto believed to be impossible. It cannot be grasped, and is a miracle; one can only begin to understand it when one realizes that behind it all is one man and one will, Adolf Hitler."[73]

Considering the abundant amount of evidence, from various sources, it can hardly be denied that the King was pro-Nazi.

Certainly this does not mean he financed Hitler; however, his opinions did encourage many important Englishmen and Germans to back the Nazi leader. In the early thirties the influence of the monarch on the British upper class was still very great. Members of the British ruling class tried consciously or subconsciously to please the sovereign. Although Edward was not yet king at the time of Rosenberg's 1931 visit, men like Norman, Dawson, and Rothermere were undoubtedly aware of Edward's pro-German feelings and this gave them a certain amount of moral support for their own beliefs. Likewise, German industrialists and businessmen were impressed by Edward's favorable view of Hitler. In fact, most Germans believed that the British royal family held the reins of political power in their hands.[74] Thus, when they heard that the heir to the throne was pro-Nazi, the Germans mistakenly thought that the English government would accept his viewpoint as soon as he became king. This was one more reason why the Germans thought that a Nazi government would be welcomed by Britain.

In May 1933, Rosenberg made his second and last trip to England. Although his mission was not an outstanding success due to his tactless anti-Semitic remarks which were reported in the press, there was one noteworthy event during this trip. One weekend Rosenberg stayed at Sir Henri Deterding's palatial country home at Buckhurst Park, Ascot, only about a mile from Windsor Castle. Two newspapers reported that they had reliable information which verified the Rosenberg-Deterding meeting. *Reynold's Illustrated News* stated: "In the light of the present European situation, this private talk between Hitler's foreign advisor and the dominant figure in European 'oil politics' is of profound interest. It supports the suggestion current in well-informed political circles that the big oil interests have kept closely in touch with the Nazi Party in Germany."[75] This was not Rosenberg's first meeting with Deterding; they had met as early as 1931.[76]

Who was Sir Henri Deterding and why did he invite a Nazi to his estate? Deterding was one of the wealthiest men in the world. His clandestine meetings with Hitler's representative gave little indication of the plots, intrigues, and secret transfers of money that were taking place between Deterding and Hitler.

The son of a seaman, Hendrik August Wilhelm Deterding was

born in Amsterdam in 1866. Fascinated by the swaying ships in the busy harbor, the young Hendrik dreamed of becoming a sailor. But due to his father's death when Hendrik was only six years old, the boy's career had to be something more practical and profitable to help the family's failing finances. After finishing his schooling, he got a job for six years as a bank clerk. Bending over ledgers filled with columns and columns of figures was grueling, monotonous work; nevertheless, he was quick to learn how business transactions were made and the importance of good investments. Soon he found a better job with the Netherlands Trading Society, and finally in 1896 Deterding joined the Royal Dutch Petroleum Company. Within four years he was Managing Director of Royal Dutch-Shell, an international combine created as a result of his successful efforts to merge the British Shell Oil Company with Royal Dutch.

Whether Deterding should be considered Dutch or English is a debatable question. The New York *Wall Street Journal* printed a statement by Richard Airey, president of Asiatic Petroleum Co., a Royal Dutch subsidiary, claiming that even though Deterding was made a Knight of the British Empire in 1920, "he was born a native Dutch subject. . . . and will remain so until his death."[77] However, the British Embassy of Washington said that "to the best of its knowledge" Deterding was a naturalized British citizen. Despite his national origin, he lived in England, he wore finely tailored English clothes, he rode in English hunts, and he spoke English perfectly, though with a slight accent.

Judging from his appearance, one could not determine his nationality; he just looked like a wealthy European industrialist. Sir Henri was a short, stocky man with an ambitious, energetic, and effervescent personality. His rather large head seemed closely set on his body. Despite a headful of white hair and a bristly, trimmed white mustache, he seemed younger due to his ruddy complexion and black flashing eyes.

Each day he sat behind his large, carved wooden desk with the row of telephones at one end. These were Sir Henri's link with his worldwide business and political informants. Each ring of a phone would bring reports from important outposts, news of production, movements of oil tankers, fluctuations in the stock market, activities of his competitors, or the latest information about political tremors which might affect his investments.

By 1913, Deterding possessed the controlling interest in the oil fields of Romania, Russia, California, Trinidad, the Dutch Indies, and Mexico. He was also pumping oil out of Mesopotamia and Persia. Deterding was acknowledged as a man who had the sole executive rule over a large portion of the world's "black gold." One English admiral described him as "Napoleonic in his audacity and Cromwellian in his thoroughness."[78]

Before the Communist Revolution in 1917, Dutch-Shell had large investments in the Russian Baku oil fields, as well as holdings in the Grosni and Miakop oil fields. When the British Army withdrew from Baku in the spring of 1920, the Red Army moved in and Moscow nationalized the oil fields. To add insult to injury, the Communists started to export oil in 1922 and their competition became a serious threat to the markets of Dutch-Shell.

From this point onward, Deterding aimed to destroy Bolshevism. His hatred drove him to support every anti-Communist or White Russian organization that he heard of. In 1924 he married a lady who was the daughter of a White Russian general. As a tireless enemy of the Soviet regime, he would always give his financial backing to anyone who proposed a plan that might have a chance of overthrowing the Communist rulers. Likewise, his wife was known to give large contributions to the exiled White Russian community; the money she distributed was of course her husband's, since she had little of her own.

Deterding was often accused of encouraging armed uprisings in Soviet Russia, such as the Georgian-Caucasian rebellion in 1924. This was the location of many of Russia's oil fields and if the rebellion had succeeded it would have greatly weakened the stability of the Moscow government. A *New York Times* correspondent wrote an article appearing on September 13, 1924, which stated: "It is understood, according to well-informed persons, that the Revolution is being financed [by] ... former proprietors of Baku oil wells." Essad Bey, a member of the White Russian community, claimed that it was Deterding who supplied the money for the rebellion.

On January 5, 1926, there appeared in the *Morning Post* a vituperative letter by Deterding denouncing the Soviets as thieves: "What else is it [Communism] but lawlessness and an attempt to go back to the prehistoric world of right by force and brutal force only." Besides his own anti-Communist writings,

Deterding financed the quarterly English publication of the Society of Ukrainian Patriots—an organization whose aim was to break the Ukraine away from Soviet Russia.

Then, early in 1930, the trial for the chervonetz-forgery attempt was held in Berlin. Chervonetz were Russian [Georgian] banknotes, a tremendous number of which had been forged in order to create political turmoil and disorder in the Georgian Soviet Republic in the Caucasus. During the period of resulting chaos and economic instability, the White Russians were to have made a lightning attack on the Bolsheviks. Karumidze, the leader of the Georgians; General Max Hoffmann, a famous German Army general who died shortly before the trial; Georg Bell; a Bavarian businessman named Willi Schmidt; and Sir Henri Deterding were cited as accomplices in this scheme of forgery and plotted uprising. Schmidt said he had paid £250 for General Hoffmann's travel expenses to go to London, where certain financial and industrial leaders were anxious to see the plan succeed. Under cross-examination Schmidt said he trusted General Hoffmann not only because of his personal character but also because of his association with "big oil interests in England."[79] It was recorded that Karumidze mentioned Deterding as one of those who was in favor of the plan. General Hoffmann's widow testified that her husband had been invited by Deterding to London where the General explained his plan in exact military terms. Deterding admitted that he was connected with Hoffmann: "It is true that I knew General Hoffmann. I admired him as a man. I admired him as a soldier and leader of men."[80] However, Deterding denied that he was involved in the forgery scandal.

Since the forged notes had not yet been circulated, all of the accused were acquitted. After the trial the *New York Times* reported: "Although the [German] Foreign Office and the British Embassy declare that nothing will be kept from the public, it is an open secret that the police have orders to hush up the whole matter."[81]

Georg Bell, a mysterious German of Scottish origin who had many useful business and political connections, was said to be an agent of Deterding. He had attended a number of the "Ukrainian Patriots" meetings in Paris as a representative of both Hitler and Deterding. Because he knew Rosenberg and was a close friend of

Röhm, Bell was an excellent contact for Sir Henri to have with the Nazis. In 1931, the same year as Rosenberg's first visit, Bell came to London with orders signed by Röhm. His mission was to further the existing ties between England and Germany for a future alliance against Russia. The *Morning Post* somehow found out that Bell's instructions were "the same in substance as those carried by Herr Rosenberg on his recent visit to London."

Johannes Steel, a German writer and former agent of the German Economic Intelligence Service, gave evidence at the Inquiry into the Reichstag Fire that Sir Henri Deterding was giving money to the Nazis. In his book *Escape to the Present*, Steel wrote: "A private meeting of the Inquiry Board was called and I pointed out to the meeting that there were certain well-understood connections between Hitler and an international oil trust. I went into detail, citing the specific facts behind my allegations and telling the Inquiry Board where and how they might obtain documents to substantiate my points."[82] Almost as soon as Steel had finished his indictment, the former editor of an important German newspaper jumped up quickly to remind the members of the board that these facts linking English business with Hitler could not be mentioned publicly since it might embarrass the British Foreign Secretary. A vote was then taken confirming the decision to keep the "facts" secret.

A *Daily Telegraph* reporter believed that Bell and Rosenberg met an international magnate in London and "big credits for the Nazis followed."[83] The Dutch press stated that Deterding sent to Hitler, through Georg Bell, about four million guilders.[84] Some said Sir Henri gave the Nazis money in exchange for their agreement to give him preferred standing in the German oil market when they came to power.[85] In 1931, it was reported that Deterding made a loan of £30 million to Hitler in return for a promise of a petroleum monopoly. Some claimed the loan was as much as £55 million.[86] Louis Lochner, former foreign correspondent and authority on the relation between Hitler and big business, mentioned an alleged "ten million marks" contribution by the Dutch oil lord to the Nazis.[87] With so many sources agreeing on the matter, there can be little doubt that Deterding financed Hitler. All that remains uncertain is the exact sum of money; nevertheless, one would not be injudicious to say it was substantial. Deterding had much to gain by financing the Nazis. They were a strong anti-Communist party that was planning to eventually attack Russia and throw out the Bolsheviks.[88] But even if the Nazis did not come to power, Deterding had much to gain; as the largest party in the German Reichstag, the Nazis could use their influence to push the German government in an anti-Soviet direction.

In the middle of 1936, Sir Henri divorced his wife and married a thirty-year-old buxom German woman, who was his former secretary and a devoted Nazi. For a while they lived on the outskirts of Berlin near the Wannsee, but they soon moved to his estate in Mecklenburg. His German estate was presumably tax exempt, according to a report written by Rosenberg. The report said "the misunderstanding over the tax situation connected with Deterding's German property" was straightened out and resulted in "a closer link" between the Nazis and the Deterding circle. This bargain prevented any change in Dutch-Shell's arrangements with Germany, which included some "important commissions."[89]

Deterding's biographer, Glyn Roberts, said that after Sir Henri's new marriage he "thought like a true Nazi."[90] His new scheme to help the Nazis was to send all of Holland's agricultural surplus to Germany, which was in need of more food for her people. The Nazis, of course, were always pleased with a helping hand even after they were in power.

Bavaria had always been one of the most powerful German duchies; however, in 1806 Napoleon made it a kingdom as a reward for being his ally against Austria. Maximilian, head of the Bavarian royal house of Wittelsbach, was crowned king. To further strengthen the tie between Bavaria and France, Napoleon arranged a political marriage between his stepson Eugené and Princess Augusta, a daughter of Maximilian. At first Eugené was not too pleased with the idea of an arranged marriage, but when he saw his bride he was completely enchanted, for she was a very beautiful woman.[91]

This historical account might facilitate an understanding of the financial contribution made by France to the Bavarian monarchist and anti-Weimar political parties in the 1920s. For several centuries one of France's major aims in foreign policy was the containment of her continental rival, Germany. After World War

I, when America and Britain had refused to join in a pact against any future German aggression, France was forced to make her own defense. Besides agreements with Belgium and Poland, France formed an alliance with Czechoslovakia, Romania, and Yugoslavia in 1921 known as the "Little Entente." These states were given financial assistance and promises of French military support against the Germans. France was searching madly for any other possible way to emasculate Germany. One plan was to promote and finance separatist groups in the German states, especially in the Palatinate, Württemberg, and Bavaria.

This plot was no secret to the Germans. In August 1920, King Ludwig III of Bavaria was informed that France was favoring a federated Reich and in it a Bavarian monarchy.[92] If Germany had refused to sign the Versailles Treaty, the French military was prepared with plans for an attack on Berlin. However, Marshal Foch said the Allies would have to make separate and *lenient* treaties with certain German states, such as Bavaria and Württemberg, in order to break them away from the main German government.[93] Toward the end of the war there was a faction in Bavaria which wanted to make a separate treaty with the Allies in order to get better terms than the rest of Germany.[94]

Proud of their historic traditions and Catholicism, Bavarians regarded themselves as being distinctly different from the Protestant Prussians. Most of the enmity between them resulted from the Bavarians' resentment of being ruled by the Berlin government. Due to the basically agrarian economic structure of Bavaria, the people were also more conservative politically than the industrial workers of north Germany. When the Republic was formed in 1919, the new constitution took away Bavaria's authority on all issues dealing with the military, the state treasury, the postal system, and railroads. This aggravated the Bavarians even more.

As a result of these factors there were several monarchist and anti-Weimar political parties in Bavaria. The Bavarian People's Party (Bayerische Volkspartei, or B.V.P.), which was the largest party in the Diet, had a very pro-Wittelsbach, federalist program. Some of its members broke away to form the more radical Bavarian Royalist Party (Bayerische Koenigspartei, or B.K.P.). The separatist faction within the Royalist Party was led by Count von Bothmer. He accepted separatism as the best means by which the

Bavarian monarchy could be reinstated. Because of Bothmer's prominence in the party, the B.K.P. was marked thereafter as not only promonarchist, but also proseparatist. Documentary evidence was published to show that Bothmer had received financial support from the French.[95]

The B.K.P. wasn't the only party to which the French gave assistance. Some of the other small monarchist, anti-Weimar parties, such as the Bavarian Home and Royalist League, were recipients of covert French financial backing. Even the ruling Bavarian People's Party (B.V.P.) was accused by the Social Democrats of having received French money.[96] Gustav von Kahr, leader of the B.V.P. and Bavarian state commissioner in 1923, was planning to use Hitler and the Nazis in a Bavarian separatist putsch of his own.[97] The French money given to the B.V.P. went to Kahr, who in turn may have passed some of it on to Hitler in an attempt to gain control over the Nazis.

Did the Nazis accept French funds? Throughout 1923, French Intelligence was stirring up revolution in Bavaria against the Berlin government.[98] In 1921 the Nazi *Völkischer Beobachter* wrote of the French people, "whose essential nobility we ungrudgingly recognize and honestly esteem." In 1922, Hitler said that the French had been incited against Germany by the Jews, who aimed "to stir up and exploit the conflict."[99] Therefore, he concluded, the Germans should hate the "November Criminals," not the French.

Then in early 1923 the former editor of the *Völkischer Beobachter*, Hugo Machhaus, conspired with two friends, Professor Georg Fuchs and a Munich city official, Kuhles, with French assistance, to separate Bavaria from Germany. An "energetic but bumbling" French Intelligence agent, Lieutenant Colonel Richert, was the liaison between France and Munich. But the plot was uncovered by the government and the intriguers were arrested. Before the trial took place, Machhaus was found in his cell, hanged by his own belt. It was questionable if suicide was the cause of his death, because most prisoners are not allowed to keep their belts for this very reason. Hitler and the Left accused the Bavarian government of being responsible for Machhaus's death. They claimed he had been killed by government agents.[100]

It must be pointed out that there is no concrete evidence to show that Hitler knew of Machhaus's dealings with the French.

Hitler, of course, denied ever having received any foreign funds. As one Nazi official remarked, "The legend that Hitler was in French pay . . . kept cropping up for years and gave him grounds for a number of lawsuits against various newspapers and individuals."[101]

But there is further warrant for suspecting the Nazi–French connection. In October 1923, a socialist member of the English parliament, E. D. Morel, came to Munich to see Dr. Gustav von Kahr. Morel revealed some startling news: "I should like to tell you that some highly-placed Paris friends of mine have definitely assured me that a large part of the money received by Hitler is derived from a French source." Kahr refused to believe it; he knew that Hitler was a German nationalist, not a separatist nor a monarchist. So Morel continued: "One of my informants is a member of the French cabinet. The money passes through eight or nine places across the occupied area."[102] Morel's testimony is a strong indictment against the Nazis. It is possible, though, that Hitler was unaware of the source of the money coming into the Nazi treasury. If he had known, he probably would not have accepted the money for fear of being labeled a French puppet and traitor.

It is forgotten that Germany was not the only defeated nation after World War I which suffered under the restrictions of a harsh treaty drawn up by the Allies. The Treaty of Trianon with Hungary was even more severe than the Versailles Treaty. Hungary's losses dealt her a staggering blow. Two-thirds of her former territory were given to the surrounding "Succession States," Yugoslavia, Czechoslovakia, and Romania. This meant that 60 percent of Hungary's population suddenly became the inhabitants of other countries. Many of Hungary's natural resources were taken away: almost all of her ore deposits, about 90 percent of her water power, and 90 percent of her pine forest. Important industries and markets were also handed over to the new nations created from the treaty.[103] Not surprisingly, the Hungarian people refused to bow to the judgment of Trianon; from the Right to the Left, from conservatives to liberals, the Hungarians were united in their response to the treaty—NO! NEVER! Even the leaders of the Succession States were skeptical about the justice of the treaty. Eduard Beneš, president of Czechoslovakia from 1935 to

1938, remarked: "I am alarmed when they give me everything I ask for—it is too much."[104]

Trianon completely discredited democracy in the eyes of the Hungarians, for the promises of Wilson's Fourteen Points had not been fulfilled; instead they had been replaced by blatant injustices. Hungarian historian Nagy-Talavera remarked that the treaty "contributed incomparably more to the rise of fascism (in Hungary) than Versailles undermined the Weimar Republic and aided the rise of Hitler."[105]

Hungary had already tried Communism under the three-month "Red Terror" of Bela Kun in 1919. With the help of a group of fellow revolutionaries, Kun tried to forcibly transfer all landed property into the hands of the proletariat. The peasants were the predominant victims; several hundred were butchered for refusing to give up their homes. Famine in the cities and economic chaos were the main results of Kun's program. These three months were enough to give the Hungarians very bitter feelings about Communism and Jews. The latent anti-Semitic prejudices of the Hungarians were stirred into a fire of hatred because Kun's government was composed of a high percentage of Jews. The stage seemed set for fascism.

One of the first symptoms of Hungarian fascism was the growth of secret societies. Basically they appealed to the lower middle class and *petite bourgeoisie* and their struggle against "the International of Gold and the International of Moscow," by which they meant Jewish finance and Communism.[106] Two of the largest of these societies were the Association of Awakening Hungarians (Ébredö Magyarok Egyesülete, or E.M.E.) and the Association of Hungarian National Defense (Magyar Országos Véderö Egyesület, or M.O.V.E.). The leader of M.O.V.E. was Gyula (Julius) Gömbös. Although an ardent Hungarian patriot, he was of Swabian [German] origin. After serving in the Hungarian Army as a captain, he became a member of parliament in 1920. Describing his political stand as "Hungarian National Socialist," Gömbös was anti-Semitic, anti-Habsburg, anticapitalist, and anti-Trianon. In his speeches to the working classes, he denounced the idle aristocracy and the Jewish financiers who took advantage of the poor industrious peasant.

The anti-Semitic newspaper which he edited became known in National/Socialist and right-wing circles in Germany. Gömbös first came into contact with monarchist Bavarians, such as Gustav von Kahr and Otto Pittinger, who wanted a Wittelsbach restoration.[107] If the Bavarian Right succeeded in a coup to overthrow the Weimar Republic and the Versailles Treaty, Gömbös thought Bavaria would help Hungary in her fight to regain what Trianon had taken away.

One of the earliest contacts between the Hungarians and the Nazis was through András Mecsér. An ex-officer of the Hussars, Mecsér was known to have participated in the anti-Communist and anti-Semitic campaigns of terror carried out by the secret societies. When he wasn't out "Jew-baiting," he worked on his estate to produce an improved type of corn. Supposedly on a trip to Germany in 1921 or 1922 to market his new produce, he happened to attend one of the Nazi meetings and heard Hitler speak. He was overwhelmed by Hitler's fiery eloquence. When the collection basket was passed around at the end of the meeting, Mecsér dropped in a large sum of cash, saying: "This is how Hungarians behave!"[108] Mecsér's donation was worth more than its face value. Because of the inflation, Hungarian money, like all foreign currency, had a high purchasing power in Germany.

Due to his close relationship with the Nazis, it was probably Mecsér who invited Kurt Lüdecke to Budapest in August 1923. When Lüdecke arrived in Budapest, the Hungarian aristocracy gave him a warm welcome, and quickly set up meetings for him with some important people. As Lüdecke expected, not many were familiar with the name Hitler; so he painted as rosy a picture as possible, hoping to gain friends and supporters.

In Budapest Lüdecke met Julius Gömbös and Tibor von Eckhardt, both of whom he described as leaders of the Hungarian racists. A minor refugee official from Transylvania, von Eckhardt was the president of Awakening Hungarians. Thus, much of the responsibility for that organization's terror raids, bombings, and killings belonged to von Eckhardt.[109]

Gömbös was friendly to Lüdecke as well as frank about his political views. He gave his promise that the secret societies of which he was the leader would never tolerate a Habsburg restoration. This was good news to Lüdecke, because the Habsburgs were a Catholic dynasty and might exert a strong influence in urging the Catholic Bavarian monarchists to break from Germany, which the Nazis did not want.

Gömbös invited Lüdecke to a fashionable resort on Lake Balaton, two hours away from Budapest. There Gömbös and von Eckhardt introduced their young Nazi friend to everyone worth meeting. It was a field day for Lüdecke; the place was full of wealthy Hungarians who had nothing better to do than listen to stories about Hitler and the great potential of the Nazi Party. "They listened with sympathy and understanding," Lüdecke said, "and their interest was increased."[110] By the end of his visit, he felt that Hitler was no longer unknown to the Hungarians who might be of some assistance.

This trip was the beginning of a close collaboration between the Nazis and Hungarians. Gömbös sent financial aid to the Nazis in 1923, before the putsch. Sometimes this "aid" consisted of fine horses and cattle from Hungary sold to the Nazis at only a fraction of their real value.[111] The worth of this aid must not be underestimated. At the height of the inflation in 1923, when people were starving for a lack of meat and the country had gone over to the barter system, a horse or cow could often be traded for an automobile.

Gömbös participated in the preparations for the beerhall putsch.[112] The plan was for a simultaneous uprising in Munich and in Budapest, where Gömbös would establish a fascist regime. With his control of M.O.V.E. and other secret militaristic societies, and his influence over the profascist student group, the Turúl, Gömbös believed that he had a sufficient military force. However, the scheme went awry when someone leaked the plan to the Hungarian police. Gömbös claimed he was innocent and, with a good word from Admiral Horthy, he was released from any charges. The other Hungarian fascists involved received light sentences due to their "patriotic motives," and the general leniency of the courts toward any political rightists.[113]

Behind the scenes there was another participant in the plot—the young Archduke Albrecht. He was the son of Archduke Frederick, who had been the Commander-in-Chief of the Austro-Hungarian Armies and before World War I had been one of the wealthiest men in the Habsburg realm. Some of Frederick's most valuable estates and properties had been expropriated by Czechoslovakia, Yugoslavia, and Austria after the war. Nevertheless, in the early 1930s he still had about forty thousand acres of land.[114]

Albrecht's parents, Archduke Frederick and especially his mother, Archduchess Isabella, were pushing him as a candidate for the Hungarian throne. Historian C. A. Macartney discovered that "it was the Archduke Frederick's money which largely financed the M.O.V.E., the Awakening Hungarians, and also the Munich circles with which the Hungarian Right was connected and in which the seeds of the German National Socialist Party germinated."[115] Frederick probably contributed his funds to an intermediary like Ludendorff, who then gave the money to the Nazis.

If the Nazi putsch had succeeded, Archduke Albrecht was supposedly to have been made King of Hungary. This seems a bit incomprehensible when one considers that Gömbös, who was much more closely tied with the Nazis, was anti-Habsburg, as were the Nazis. However, despite the fact that Albrecht was of the Habsburg family, it had been declared that he was "no longer a member of the House of Habsburg," because of his marriage to a divorcée, Madame Rudnay.[116] This made him a popular candidate for the Free Elector Party in Hungary, composed of those who wanted a king but did not recognize the claim of the senior Habsburg. Actually, Gömbös had a very sensible reason for linking himself with Albrecht. In exchange for Gömbös's agreement to see that her son Albrecht was made the Hungarian king, a "national king," Archduchess Isabella contributed generous sums of money to Gömbös's political activities.[117]

The United States minister to Hungary from 1933 to 1941, John Montgomery, said he and his wife entertained Albrecht four or five times a year, because he was always very popular with their American dinner guests. Montgomery described the young Archduke as "brilliant and as nice a person as you would want to meet socially, but absolutely eccentric and undisciplined." After several unsuccessful attempts to be made king, "he sold himself to National Socialist Germany—probably with ideas of getting back some of his father's estates," Montgomery said.[118]

After his father's death* Albrecht continued to deal with the Nazis. In Hungarian politics he was known as an extreme pro-Nazi and anti-Semite.

---

*Personal representatives of Hitler attended Archduke Frederick's funeral, perhaps as a sign of gratitude for his earlier support to the Nazis.

When the Nazis fell to their nadir after the failure of the putsch, Lüdecke made another trip to Hungary in December 1924, seeking succor, especially in a monetary form. The ostensible reason for the trip was an invitation asking him to represent Hitler and Ludendorff at the convention of Awakening Hungarians in Budapest.

Before Lüdecke gave his speech to the twelve hundred delegates gathered in the town hall, he was given a warm introduction by von Eckhardt. Speaking to a sympathetic yet skeptical audience, Lüdecke spent most of the time allotted to him trying to assure them that the Nazis would make a quick comeback, and that they were not ruined. He blamed the failure on the overwhelming size of the government forces and the treason and trickery of certain individuals who had promised to help Hitler. But defeat was in the past; in the future there would be nothing but victory, he claimed. And the fruits of the Nazis' success would be shared with their Hungarian allies and fellow fascists. The audience evidently liked what they heard, because they gave Lüdecke a thunderous applause when he finished the speech.

But Lüdecke found it much more difficult to persuade Gömbös that the Nazis were not a worthless investment. Their several-hour discussion took place in Gömbös's impressive headquarters, where Lüdecke said he felt like "a poor relation of the rich Hungarian racialists."[119] Gömbös acted as if Lüdecke were a false prophet, because he had come to Budapest three times predicting the approaching victory of the Nazis, and then, after Gömbös had finally convinced his party to support Hitler, the putsch failed. Gömbös frankly admitted that he was disillusioned and doubtful about the potential of the Nazis. He was giving Lüdecke a hard time. Using every possible argument, Lüdecke was able at last to make Gömbös consent that there was still hope for the Nazis in the future.

At the end of their discussion, Gömbös invited Lüdecke to speak that evening at a small private meeting of the leading minds of the right wing. Eager to make as many converts as possible, Lüdecke accepted willingly.

Following his speech, there was an animated question-answer period. Gömbös kept Lüdecke on his toes with a series of difficult questions. But by the end of the evening, Lüdecke felt "the satisfaction of knowing that the rehabilitation of Hitler was well begun in Hungary."[120] Gömbös teased Lüdecke jokingly afterward: "I made it pretty hard for you, didn't I? But you came through all right. Now why not come down into the country with me over Christmas, to get your breath back? I'll have a little surprise there for you."

The next day, they drove to Gömbös's country home. The surprise turned out to be Lieutenant Heinrich Schulz, formerly an officer in the Imperial German Army and one of the two assassins of Matthias Erzberger, who had been the main signer of the Versailles Treaty. Schulz's appearance was such that one would never have suspected him to be an assassin: he was a handsome, soft-spoken, and mild-mannered man. Nevertheless, he was on the top of the "most-wanted list" throughout Europe and the Hungarian police were trying to track him down.

Gömbös told Lüdecke that the police weren't certain if Schulz were there in hiding. "But they dare not enter to find out," the Hungarian said confidently. "My immunity as a deputy [of parliament] bars them; my guest is safe." Still, Gömbös was taking a great risk by giving asylum to an assassin.

Lüdecke recalled that after dinner on Christmas Eve the three of them sat in front of the crackling fire drinking hot punch. There he heard "as macabre a tale as was ever unfolded by the light of a Christmas tree." The shadows flickered across the face of the lieutenant as he told the story of the murder. Both Gömbös and Lüdecke admired this man who had given up his home, his friends, and family in order to do what he thought was his duty— to kill the enemy of the Fatherland, the man who stabbed Germany in the back by signing the surrender. "Remember all this, Lüdecke," Gömbös said. "When you get back to Munich, tell them how quickly your revolutionaries forget their own people."[121]

In October 1932 Admiral Horthy appointed Gömbös Prime Minister. This meant that Gömbös's party would have more money available for covert purposes such as financing Hitler. Certainly if they had contributed in 1923 when the future of National Socialism was doubtful, they had all the more reason to do so in 1932 when the Nazis were the largest party in Germany. If Hitler came to power, there would be definite advantages for Hungary. Hitler's determination to revise the Versailles Treaty would also lead to a revision of the Treaty of Trianon. A rearmed

Germany would be a useful ally to Hungary against both Soviet Russia and their enemies of the Little Entente. And a Nazi government in power in Germany would be another ideological ally to the Hungarian fascist regime against Communism. Now that Gömbös headed the Hungarian government, it was easier for him to cover up the exchange of funds between his friends and Hitler.

Gömbös's appointment as Prime Minister also encouraged the German upper class to accept Hitler as Chancellor. With fascist regimes coming to power in other countries, there would be fewer objections from Britain and international opinion.

As soon as Hitler was made Chancellor in 1933, Gömbös sent the Hungarian ambassador in Berlin "to pay a courtesy call on Chancellor Hitler to transmit his felicitations and greetings." The ambassador was also to remind Hitler of the friendly assistance which Gömbös had given the Nazis over the past years. Gömbös wanted Hitler to know that they should discuss "with sincerity what two race-protectors [racists] owe to each other."[122]

Two of Hitler's top money-seekers—Lüdecke and Rosenberg—were sitting in the office of the *Völkischer Beobachter* in 1932 talking about the accusations of Hitler being in foreign pay. Rosenberg thought it was a "very delicate affair." Speaking in a "voice of veiled irony accompanied by a suggestive smile," he said, "You know, of course, that Hitler has declared in court that we never received foreign pay from any source and never even asked for it."[123]

What was the total sum that Rosenberg's smile was suggesting? Perhaps it is inestimable, because Italy, America, England, France, and Hungary were not the only countries from which money was given to the Nazi Party. As seen earlier, contributions also flowed in from Austria, Switzerland, Finland, and Czechoslovakia, and this does not complete the list.[124] Hitler had many other wealthy admirers who probably favored his party, but as of now no definite proof of their contributions has been found. Two notable people in this category were Queen Marie of Romania and King Ferdinand of Bulgaria. Queen Marie is known to have "rather admired" some of Hitler's policies, and King Ferdinand was often seen wearing a swastika pin encircled with diamonds in his lapel.[125]

In time, more evidence will undoubtedly turn up and the contributors and the sums they gave can be cited more precisely, but the basic picture of the Nazi Party's primary sources of foreign money given here will remain much the same.

8

BIG BUSINESS ATTEMPTS TO STOP HITLER

In the early autumn of 1931 a young man named Doctor Otto Dietrich was appointed "Chief of the Press Bureau of the National Socialist Party." Newspapers throughout Germany reported that Dr. Dietrich was the "Liaison man of Rhineland heavy industry."[1] It was also stated that he had previously negotiated the support and financing of the Nazis by the "coal barons" and had now been called to Munich by Hitler in order to establish closer links between himself and the industrialists.

After the war, Otto Dietrich flatly denied this account and stated in his memoirs that he "had nothing whatsoever to do with heavy industry."[2] The truth, however, was not so easily concealed. In 1928 Dietrich had been a business and commercial editor on the staff of the *München-Augsburger Abendzeitung,* a well-known conservative newspaper. He had previously been a business agent for the Rheinisch Steel-Goods Syndicate, then commercial editor of the *Essener Allgemeine Zeitung.* But Dietrich's most important connection was that he happened to be the son-in-law of Dr. Reismann-Grone of Essen, the owner of the *Rheinisch-Westfälische Zeitung,* a newspaper considered to be the mouthpiece of heavy industry. Reismann-Grone was also the political advisor of the Mining Association (Bergbaulicher Verein), one of the wealthiest employers' associations in Germany and one of the chief financiers of the Pan-German Party. Although Dietrich was only thirty-one years old at the time, through his father-in-law he had gotten to know most of the important Ruhr industrialists and was on especially friendly terms with old Emil Kirdorf.

Dietrich's postwar denial of having had anything to do with heavy industry even contradicts what he himself wrote in 1934 about the part he played in helping win over the tycoons of heavy industry for Hitler. According to Dietrich, in 1931 most big businessmen were still opposed to the Nazis except for "some praiseworthy exceptions."[3] Unfortunately, he does not elaborate on who these "praiseworthy exceptions" were. In his account, entitled *With Hitler on the Road to Power,* Dietrich does, however, describe in detail Hitler's efforts to gain contributions and support from big business.

Hitler, said Dietrich, "realized that, besides striving to gain the support of the broad masses, he must make every possible appeal to the economic magnates, the firmest adherents to the old system." In the summer of 1931 in Munich, he suddenly decided to concentrate systematically upon convincing the influential economic magnates "who, through their financial power controlled the moderate non-Marxian parties." "These prominent men," wrote Dietrich, "formed the main resistance [against the Nazis] and Hitler thus hoped, step by step, to break them away from the existing system of government."[4] In the next few months Hitler and Dietrich traveled from one end of Germany to the other in a big black Mercedes "holding private interviews with prominent personalities." Some of these meetings were so secret that they had to be held in "some lonely forest glade." "Privacy was absolutely imperative," said Dietrich; "the press must have no chance of doing mischief. Success was the consequence. The pillars of the government began to crumble. This seemed alarming [to the democratic politicians] yet indiscernible—incomprehensible. The 'Deutsche Volkspartei' [German People's Party] was alienated from the government, the support of the 'Wirtschaftspartei' [Economics Party] could only be purchased by heavy sums of money. Adolf Hitler was satisfied."[5]

At first there were some Nazi leaders, such as Gauleiter Albert Krebs of Hamburg, who complained of Dietrich's appointment to an important Party post as a sign of the growing influence of big business within the Party. In fact, Otto Dietrich was an openly acknowledged double agent. This is not to say that he was betraying anyone: he simply had a double mission: to help Hitler gain business support and to report to big business on Hitler's real strength and economic program.

From the first Dietrich was impressed with the devotion of Hitler's followers. Young and old, men and women, all with faces full of enthusiasm, they were always crowding around their "Führer" wherever he went, trying to shake his hand and speak with him. It soon became obvious to Dietrich that Hitler could claim the allegiance of the masses of people in a way that the leaders of the traditional parties never could.

Even the sophisticated Dietrich was impressed by an incident which took place while he was accompanying Hitler on one of his campaign tours. On his way to a rally at Stralsund, Hitler's plane was forced down in the night by a storm and had to make an emergency landing far from its original destination. His usual caravan of cars was not at the landing place, so different automobiles had to be secured. It was already late, so this took some time. Hitler realized that at best he would be several hours late for the rally which had been scheduled for eight o'clock, but he decided to proceed nevertheless in the hope that the crowd would wait for him. Shortly after the caravan of rented cars departed, the powerful headlights of Hitler's Mercedes flashed upon it from the opposite direction; the wireless message sent ahead from the emergency landing place had reached the drivers. On the dark highway Hitler and his staff quickly changed cars and drove off at top speed. But there was another delay before they reached Stralsund. "Anxious adherents stopped us in a small village," said Dietrich, "and warned us that danger lay ahead. A forest close by, through which we had to pass, was occupied by armed Communists in ambush, and ready to way-lay us." Hitler ordered his caravan to proceed with caution. "As we came to the forest," recounted Dietrich, "we saw police scouring the countryside, with loaded rifles. They had already pounced upon the Communists." A light rain was falling as they finally drove through the deserted suburbs of Stralsund at 2:30 A.M. They had almost abandoned hope of even the most devoted followers waiting so long in the rain and cold. But an imposing sight met their eyes. Said Dietrich: "In the open air, and in the pouring rain, we met the crowd drenched to the skin, weary and hungry, just as they had gathered over the night, and patiently waited. . . . We stood amidst the mighty assembly, as the red streaks of morning appeared in the sky. . . . The night had been long and the way to Stralsund far, but now we had forgotten all inconveniences." Hitler spoke to the audience as the day slowly dawned. "Was there ever such a spectacle—a gathering of 40,000 people at four o'clock in the morning?" Dietrich asked himself. "Was there ever a finer proof of devotion and boundless faith?"[6]

Dietrich's industrialist friends regarded the tremendous popularity of Hitler with interest. But what did Dietrich think of Hitler's plans and ideas? Was he responsible? What kind of economic programs did he have? These were some of the questions German business leaders wanted answered.

Being a young man, Dietrich was more aware of the economic misery caused by the depression than the older industrialists of his father-in-law's generation. He recognized that some social welfare measures like those proposed by Hitler were absolutely necessary if the lower classes were to be kept from turning to Communism.[7] Dietrich himself was undoubtedly attracted to Hitler's policy that national recovery would be achieved only along with social measures, and that socialist aims could be attained only on a nationalist basis. Hitler proposed the creation of a classless state by establishing a racial people's community, by eliminating the evils of class warfare and the party system. The guiding principle of this national folk community was to be "common good before the good of the individual."

"The socialistic concept developed by Hitler," said Dietrich, "started from the question: by what principle can social justice and harmony of economic interest best be achieved, given the natural differences among men?" Hitler's answer was similar to Napoleon's "careers open to talent." Equal opportunity was to be created for all, privileges of birth and class abolished, and the educational monopoly of the upper class ended.

"Hitler also presented the solution of the Jewish question on a humanitarian basis," said Dietrich naively. "There was no talk at all of extermination of the Jewish race. Although he demanded the curbing of their 'excessive' influence upon the government and the economy, the Jews were still to be allowed to lead their own lives."[8]

Big businessmen were undoubtedly interested in Hitler's social welfare policy and his views on the Jews, but what concerned them most was the question of capitalism and free enterprise. At first Dietrich himself was disturbed by Nazi slogans about "eliminating unearned income" and "smashing the bondage of interest." After discussing economic matters with Hitler at some length, Dietrich was reassured. He later wrote: "Hitler accepted private property and the role of capital in modern economic life because he recognized these as the economic foundations of our culture." He opposed only the abuse of capitalism, but not capitalism in principle. Although "smashing interest slavery" was one of the points of the Nazi program, Hitler recognized that he could not eliminate the system of interest from the economy, "without undermining his own political existence."[9]

Hitler's political offensive for 1932 began at midnight on New Year's Eve. While others partied and celebrated, Hitler was addressing his followers in Munich: "After twelve months more, the road to German freedom will be open! . . . Let us march into this new year as fighters, in order that we may leave it as victors."[10]

Brüning hoped to be able to hold out until economic conditions improved. Whether or not he would be able to do so depended on the reelection of Hindenburg as president at the end of his term in office. Hindenburg was eighty-four years old and in failing health, so no one could tell how long he would last. Only with great difficulty had Brüning prevailed on the old man to agree to serve on if parliament prolonged his term, thus making it unnecessary for him to have to shoulder the burden of a bitter election campaign. Brüning realized that an election campaign for the presidency during a time of such economic hardships could only benefit the radical parties. He made every effort to avoid this alternative, and so he invited Hitler to come to Berlin for new negotiations.

The Chancellor's telegram arrived while Hitler was conferring with Rosenberg and Hess in the *Völkischer Beobachter* offices in Munich. He read it with satisfaction and then slammed down his fist, saying: "Now I have them in my pocket! They have recognized me as a partner in their negotiations."[11]

Hitler conferred with General Gröner on January 6, and on the seventh, he met with Brüning and Schleicher. Essentially, the Chancellor repeated the proposal he had made in the fall; Hitler was asked to agree to an extension of Hindenburg's term as president for a year or two until economic conditions began to improve and the problems of reparations and armaments had been settled. In return, Brüning agreed to resign as soon as the Allies had cancelled the reparations. Hitler listened politely and then asked for time to consider his reply. He then went back to the Kaiserhof, the big hotel in the Wilhelmstrasse opposite the Reich Chancellery where the suite which served as his Berlin headquarters was located.

The most important Nazi leaders were waiting for Hitler when he arrived at the Kaiserhof. Strasser was in favor of accepting Brüning's proposal, arguing that if the Nazis insisted on an election, Hindenburg would undoubtedly win it. Goebbels and Röhm argued that it would be a fatal mistake for the Party to appear to avoid this chance of letting the people decide, especially after the recent Nazi successes in the provincial elections. A long debate followed. Goebbels wrote in his diary for January 7: "The presidency is not really in question. Brüning only wants to stabilize his own position indefinitely. . . . The contest for power, the game of chess, has begun. It may last throughout the year. . . . The main point is that we hold fast, and waive all compromise." The night before he had written: "We discuss the state of affairs within the Party. There is one man . . . whom nobody trusts . . . Gregor Strasser."[12]

Hitler knew that an election campaign against Hindenburg would be a considerable risk, but he was not about to strengthen Brüning's hand by giving the Republic a breathing spell. He rejected Brüning's proposal but was subtle enough to do so in such a way as might drive a wedge between the Chancellor and the President. He addressed his reply to Hindenburg over Brüning's head, warning him that the Chancellor's plan was unconstitutional. He offered, however, to support Hindenburg as the presidential candidate if he would dismiss Brüning, form a "National" government of Nazis and Nationalists, and call new elections for the Reichstag and the Prussian Diet.

Hindenburg refused to agree to Hitler's conditions. The Nazis and the Nationalists responded by refusing to support the prolongation of his term in office. Feeling that he had been betrayed by his friends and supposed supporters, the Nationalists, Hindenburg finally agreed to stand for reelection. In addition to his resentment against the right-wing parties for refusing to spare him the strain of another political campaign, the old president was now displeased with Brüning who he felt had fumbled the whole affair and was forcing him into conflict with the same nationalist forces that had elected him president in 1925. Poor Hindenburg could be reelected only with the support of the socialists and the trade unions, for whom he had always had a certain contempt.

Hitler, however, was faced with a difficult decision. Was he himself to risk running against Hindenburg for the presidency? Hindenburg seemed unbeatable. He was the ideal candidate, the legendary hero of the World War, whom many people on the Right would probably support for sentiment's sake alone. His position as the defender of the Republic against extremists would win the support of the moderate parties and even the Social Democrats, who had been against him in 1925. By running against the old Field Marshal, the Nazis would risk their reputation of invincibility which had been built up in one provincial election after another since their great triumph in September 1930. But if Hitler wished to continue convincing people that National Socialism was on the threshold of power, could he risk evading such a contest?

Fortunately for Hitler, he had several weeks to make up his mind. There were many questions to be considered; for one, how were the Nazis to finance such a massive campaign? By now Hitler had several agents working for him in big business circles, soliciting contributions and trying to win the support of wealthy individuals. Göring, Funk, Keppler, and Dietrich all reported limited success. Later, when questioned after the war, each could honestly say that they knew of only a few industrialists who supported the Nazis. However, this was only because Hitler never let any one of his agents know what the others were doing. "Hitler knew how to keep silent," said Dietrich. "With rigid strictness he carried out the principle 'Nobody need know more about important matters than is absolutely necessary for the performance of his duties. If only two persons need know about something, no third person is to hear of it.' "[13] Yet in spite of the efforts of all his upper-class contact men, the Party was deep in debt.

On January 5, Dr. Goebbels wrote in his diary: "Money is wanting everywhere. It is very difficult to obtain. Nobody will give us credit. Once you get the power you can get the cash galore, but then you need it no longer. Without the power you need the money, but then you can't get it."[14] However, a little over a month later, on February 8, he was much more optimistic: "Money affairs improve daily. The financing of the electoral campaign is practically assured."[15] Perhaps one of the reasons for Goebbels's more encouraging reference to money matters was a speech which Hitler delivered to the Industry Club in Düsseldorf on January 27.

The Industry Club of Düsseldorf was chiefly composed of the heavy industry magnates of the Ruhr region, the lords of coal, iron, and steel, but the membership also included bankers, corporation lawyers, editors, and publishers. Speakers were invited regularly and their addresses covered a wide range of topics usually dealing with economic matters or cultural affairs. The members insisted, however, that the club was not to become a political debating society, so party politics was taboo.

In the fall of 1931 the officers of the Industry Club invited Max Cohen-Reuss, a Social Democratic Reichstag deputy, as a guest speaker. Cohen-Reuss was then a member of the Reich Economic Council, a government advisory body. He was expected to speak on the work of the Council, in which all political parties were represented. Instead, he launched into a typical Marxist propaganda speech. As a result, a number of the members, with Fritz Thyssen as their spokesman, protested. In order to restore the equilibrium, Thyssen argued, some representative of the Right must be invited to address the club. He had one such representative of the Right in mind: Gregor Strasser, the Nazi organizer who was very popular in the Ruhr.

A few days later Thyssen was in Berlin, where he claimed he met Hitler by accident. He mentioned the upcoming speech at the Industry Club and Hitler replied: "I think it would be better if I came myself."[16] Thus an announcement was sent to all the members that Herr Adolf Hitler was to be the guest speaker of the Düsseldorf Industry Club.

At seven o'clock on the evening of January 27, over 600 members of the Industry Club assembled in a large ballroom at the Park Hotel in Düsseldorf to hear Hitler's speech. The attendance was much larger than usual; it was the first opportunity many of the industrialists had had for getting a close view, in their own familiar surroundings, of a man about whom they had heard so much. These busy businessmen were not the type to run around

to turbulent mass meetings. However, to attend an address organized by the club might prove to be both stimulating and interesting. The majority of those present were supporters of Gustav
Stresemann's German People's Party, which was known for its
probusiness attitude, or one of the other moderate "bourgeois"
parties. There were some with more reactionary opinions who
were members of the German Nationalist Party, but with the
exception of Fritz Thyssen and possibly a few others there were
no avowed National Socialists among the group.

"The room was overcrowded," said Otto Dietrich in his description of the scene. "Huddled together, sat the chief West German
magnates. . . . Men in the public eye, and those quiet, but no less
influential powers, who, moving behind the scenes, control the
fate of the ecomony by the soft sounds issuing from their private
offices—men said to bear a ledger rather than a heart.

"Joyful expectation brightened the faces of those already converted. But the vast majority bore an air of superiority and cool
reserve—probably flattered that Hitler had approached them.
Mere curiosity, and general interest lured them to the meeting.
They wanted to hear Hitler speak. They had no intention of being
converted; they came to criticize, seeking confirmation of their
own infallible opinion."[17]

The audience was surprised and even a bit affronted when at
Hitler's approach they heard bullying voices in the entrance hall
shouting "Alles aufstehen" [Everybody up]. Some, flabbergasted,
actually rose. Others made a gesture of rising in unwilling con-
formity, and some remained seated. Hitler strode to the rostrum
amidst strong silence, followed by Fritz Thyssen, the chairman of
the evening, and a score of S.A. men in their brown-shirt uniforms, who took a position behind their Führer as a sort of stage
backdrop. Hitler was wearing a rather ill-fitting cutaway coat and
striped trousers, an attire in which he never looked quite comfortable. After a brief introduction by Fritz Thyssen, he received
"chilly" applause from the tightly packed audience. He was
scheduled to speak for an hour and had requested that there be
no smoking.[18] Standing on a slightly raised platform, Hitler looked
out at his audience and rested his hands lightly on an ornamental
railing.

The audience feared Communism more than anything else.
Realizing this, Hitler made the danger of Marxism the central

theme of his speech. He discussed the topic with rational logic and made some startlingly accurate predictions about its future development. He said it was no use dismissing Communism as a mere delusion of misguided manual workers.

"Bolshevism today is not merely a mob storming about in some of our streets in Germany, but it is a conception of the world which is in the act of subjecting to itself the entire Asiatic continent, and which today in the form of a State (Russia) stretches almost from our eastern frontier to Vladivostok.

"The situation is represented as if here it was merely a question of purely theoretical problems, of views held by a few visionaries or evil-disposed individuals. No! A philosophy of life has won over to itself a State, and starting from this State it will gradually shatter the whole world and bring it down in ruins. Bolshevism, if its advance is not interrupted, will transform the world as completely as in times past did Christianity. . . . It is not as if this gigantic phenomenon could simply be thought away from the modern world."

Hitler argued that liberal democracy and the idea of human equality would inevitably lead to Communism. "You maintain, gentlemen, that German business life must be constructed on a basis of private property. Now such a conception as that of private property can only be defended if in some way or another it appears to have a logical foundation. This conception must deduce its ethical justification from an insight into the necessity which Nature dictates. It cannot simply be upheld by saying: 'It has always been so and therefore it must continue to be so.' For in periods of great upheaval . . . institutions and systems cannot remain untouched just because they have previously been preserved without change. It is the characteristic feature of all really great revolutionary epochs in the history of mankind that they pay astonishingly little regard for forms which are hallowed only by age. . . . It is thus necessary to give sound foundations to traditional forms which are to be preserved so that they can be regarded as absolutely essential, as logical and right. Then I am bound to say that private property can be morally and ethically justified only if I admit that men's achievements are different. Only on that basis can I assert: since men's achievements are different, the results of those achievements are also different. And if the results of those achievements are different, then it is reasonable to leave to men the administration of those results to a corresponding degree. It would not be logical to entrust the administration of the result of an achievement which was bound up with a personality either to the next best but less capable person or to a community which, through the mere fact that it had not performed the achievement, has proved that it is not capable of administering the result of that achievement.

"Thus it must be admitted that in the economic sphere men are not of equal value or of equal importance. And once this is admitted it is madness to say: in the economic sphere there are undoubtedly differences in value, but that is not true in the political sphere. It is absurd to build up economic life on the conceptions of achievement, of the value of personality, and therefore in practice on the authority of personality, but in the political sphere to deny the authority of personality and to thrust into its place the law of the greater number—democracy."

This statement illustrates one of Hitler's most effective arguments. It relates directly to the personal interest of the audience. By a strong logical development based on fallacious premises, Hitler was leading to the inescapable conclusion that the concept of private property would gradually be destroyed by democracy because democracy has as its ethical justification, its inner logic, the idea of human equality. If democracy continued to develop, it would gradually submerge the idea of private property, which was founded on a very different moral and ethical basis: the idea of individual differences and rewards allotted to talent.

The whole edifice of civilization, Hitler continued, is "the result of the creative capacity, the achievement, the intelligence, and the industry of individual God-favored geniuses." The men of average capacity are only a "human labor-force" which carry through the creations of genius and talent. "So it is only natural that when the capable intelligences of a nation, which are always in a minority, are regarded only as of the same value as all the rest, then genius, capacity, and the value of personality are slowly subjected to the majority and this process is then falsely named the rule of the people. For this is not rule of the people, but in reality the rule of stupidity, of mediocrity, of halfheartedness, of cowardice, of weakness, and of inadequacy. Rule of the people means rather that a people should allow itself to be governed and led by its most capable individuals, those who are born to the task, and not 'a chance majority which of necessity is alien to these tasks.'

"In periods of national decline," he said, "we always find that in place of the value of personality there is substituted a leveling idea of the supremacy of mere numbers—democracy." But now "the concept of human equality itself has been developed into a political and economic 'system' and this system . . . is Communism.

"In the last resort political decisions are decisive" and determine the conduct in every sphere of national life. "For fifty years you can build up the best economic system on the basis of the principle of achievement, for fifty years you may go on building factories, for fifty years you may amass wealth, and then in three years of mistaken political decisions you can destroy all the results of the work of these fifty years."

There were murmurs of "Very true!" and many members of the audience were nodding their heads in consent. Hitler had finally succeeded in breaking through the icy reserve of his audience. "To sum up the argument," he said: "I see two diametrically opposed principles: the principle of democracy which . . . is the principle of destruction; and the principle of the authority of personality which I would call the principle of achievement, because whatever man has achieved in the past—all human civilizations—is conceivable only if the supremacy of this principle is admitted." By associating his racist and elitist philosophy with the ideas of private property and individual initiative, Hitler had established a common interest with his audience.

At this point in the speech Hitler began a detailed discussion of economic history and colonialism. He said that there are a number of nations in the world which through their outstanding inborn worth have built up a standard of living which has no relation to the territory they inhabit. "But I am quite unable to understand this privileged position, this economic supremacy, of the white race over the rest of the world if I do not bring it into close connection with a political conception of supremacy which has been peculiar to the white race for many centuries."

He then supported his contention with several illustrations: "Take any single area you like, take for example India. England did not conquer India by the way of justice and law: she conquered India without regard for the wishes and views of the natives, or their formulations of justice; and when necessary, she has upheld this supremacy with the most brutal ruthlessness. Just in the same way Cortez or Pizarro annexed Central America and the northern States of South America, not on the basis of any claim or right, but from the absolute inborn feeling of the superiority of the white race. The settlement of the North American continent is just as little the consequence of any claim of . . . right in the democratic or international sense; it was the consequence of a consciousness . . . of the superiority and therefore of the right of the white race. . . . It matters not what superficial disguises in individual cases this right may have assumed, in practice it was the exercise of an extraordinarily brutal right to dominate others and from this political conception was developed the basis for the economic annexation of that world which was not inhabited by the white race."

Hitler then began a brief analysis of the world economic crisis. The populations of Germany, England, and France, he stated, have increased to such an extent that their survival can be guaranteed only if the continued export of goods to world markets is maintained. Competition has driven the European peoples to ever increasing inprovements in the methods of production; this in turn has led to a continuous economizing of the number of men employed. As long as the opening of new export markets kept pace with the reduction of the number of workers, those who were withdrawn from work in agriculture and later the handicrafts could easily be transferred to new productive activity. "But," said Hitler, "we see that since the World War there was no further important extension of export markets: on the contrary, we see that relatively those export markets contracted, that the number of exporting nations gradually increased and that a great many former export markets became themselves industrialized, while finally a new wholesale exporter, America—which perhaps today is not yet all-powerful in all spheres, but certainly in individual cases—can reckon on advantages in production which we in Europe assuredly do not and cannot possess."

In this discussion of the world economic crisis it is obvious that Hitler's grasp of economics went beyond simply attributing all economic difficulties to a conspiracy of international Jewish finance. Some of the ideas expressed in this part of the speech were understood and shared by only the more progressive economists of the day. He had accurately identified many of the major problems facing European capitalism: an increase in the number of industrial nations; an end of imperial expansion, resulting in a lack of new export markets; and the sudden rise of America as an exporting nation.

"The essential thing," Hitler went on to point out, "is to realize that at the present moment we find ourselves in a condition which has occurred several times before in the history of the world: there have been other times when the volume of certain products in the world exceeded the demand." For example, there were times "when the tonnage of sea-going ships was far greater than the amount of goods to be carried as freight. . . . If you read history and study the ways by which men sought relief . . . then you will always find the same thing: the freight was not increased to match tonnage but the tonnage was reduced to match the freight." And of course that did not come about "through the voluntary economic decisions of the shippers, but through decisions enforced by political power." That was the case between Rome and Carthage, England and Holland, and between England and France.

"I know . . . that the view is held that one can conquer the world by purely economic means, but that is one of the greatest and most terrible illusions . . . there was no Carthaginian economic life without the fleet of Carthage, and no Carthaginian trade without the Army of Carthage . . . there can be no flourishing economic life which has not before it and behind it a flourishing powerful State as its protection.

"Gentlemen," said Hitler, ". . . the crisis is very serious. It forces us to cut down expenses in every sphere. The most natural way of economizing is always to save in human labor-power. Industries will continuously be forced to ever greater rationalization, that means increased achievement and reduction in the number of men employed."

Most people "see only six or seven million men who take no part in the process of production: they regard these men only from the economic standpoint and regret the decline in production which this unemployment causes. But, gentlemen, people fail to see the mental, moral, and psychological results of this fact. Do they really believe that such a percentage of the nation's strength can be idle . . . without exercising any mental effect; must it not have as its consequence a complete change of spirit?" How could the unemployed see Communism as anything but their salvation? Hitler asked.

The subject of unemployment was traditionally a topic discussed at Social Democratic or Communist meetings. Many industrialists even believed that a certain amount of unemployment was healthy for the economy, because it kept wages down. But Hitler built his argument against unemployment so that the audience could see how the problem directly threatened them. By associating the appeal of Communism, the number-one fear of his listeners, with unemployment, Hitler threw an entirely different light onto the question.

Hitler then went on to his next major point. "In the life of peoples the strength which can be turned outward depends upon the strength of a nation's internal organization, and that in its turn is dependent upon the stability of views held in common on certain fundamental questions. What use is it for a government to publish a decree with the aim of saving the people's economic life, when the nation . . . itself has two completely different attitudes toward economics? One section says the precondition for economics is private property; the other section maintains that private property is theft; 50 percent declare for one principle and 50 percent for the other."

By now the eyes of every man in the audience were fixed on Hitler with intense interest. They knew what he was saying was true; Marxist doctrine considered private property as "theft."

"Gentlemen, these conflicts strike at the power and strength of the nation as a whole. How is a people still to count for anything abroad when in the last resort 50 percent are inclined to Bolshevism and 50 percent are nationalist or anti-Bolshevist? It is quite conceivable to turn Germany into a Bolshevist State—it would be a catastrophe, but it is conceivable. It is also conceivable to build up Germany as a nationalist State. But it is inconceivable that one should create a strong and sound Germany if 50 percent of its citizens are Bolshevist and 50 percent nationally minded."

There were murmurs of "Yes! Yes! Very true!" Then loud applause from most of the audience.

Hitler had them now. He pressed his advantage: "Unless Germany can master this internal division . . . no measures of the legislature can stop the decline of the German nation."

His listeners nodded in consent, "Very true!"

If Germany were to recover, a "new idea" that would reunite the people of all classes was required. This new idea, said Hitler, already existed and had millions of converts. The industrialists only need look at many of their own workers who as members of the Nazi Party were fighting against Communism. "Remember that it means a tremendous sacrifice when hundreds of thousands of S.A. and S.S. men . . . every day have to climb on their trucks and go to protest meetings, undertake marches, sacrifice themselves night after night and then come back in the gray dawn either to the workshop and factory or as unemployed to take a pittance of the dole: it means a sacrifice when from the little which they possess they have to buy their uniforms, their badges, yes and even to pay for their own fares. Believe me, there is already in this the force of . . . a great ideal."

There were those among the German bourgeoisie who thought the National Socialists were too radical. But, said Hitler, "if it were not for us then there would be no more bourgeoisie alive in Germany today: the question of Bolshevism . . . would long ago have been decided. Take the weight of our gigantic organization—by far the greatest organization of the new Germany—out of the scale of the nationalist fortunes and you will see that without us [the Nazis] Bolshevism would already tip the balance—a fact of which the best proof is the attitude adopted toward us by Bolshevism. Personally I regard it as a great honor when Mr. Trotsky calls upon German Communism at any price to act together with the Social Democrats, since National Socialism must be regarded as the one real danger for Bolshevism . . . and when people complain of our intolerance, we proudly acknowledge it—yes, we have formed the inexorable decision to destroy Marxism in Germany down to its very last root."

There was an outbreak of loud applause among the audience. Hitler had to wait a moment for the clapping to die away before he could continue.

"The bourgeois parties have had seventy years to work in; where, I ask you, is the organization which could be compared with ours? Where is the organization which could boast, as ours can, that, at need, it can summon 400,000 men into the street, men who are schooled to blind obedience and are ready to execute any order—provided that it does not violate the law?"

Hitler obviously realized that the industrialists were not about to condemn an intolerance toward Communism. If it were not for Hitler, who had won over millions of impoverished and unemployed Germans to his brand of nationalism, these desperate people would have most logically turned to the Communists, who were the only other radical party which promised quick solutions to Germany's problems.

Without shouting or losing the impression of reasonableness, Hitler's voice now thundered with volume as he began his conclusion. "Today we stand at the turning point of Germany's destiny. If the present course continues, Germany will one day land in Bolshevist chaos, but if this development is to be broken, then our people must be enrolled in a school of iron discipline. . . . Either we shall succeed in forging from this conglomerate of parties, associations, unions, ideologies, upper-class conceit, and lower-class madness, an iron-hard body politic, or else, lacking this internal consolidation, Germany will fall in final ruin.

"I hear it said so often by our opponents, 'You, too, will be unable to master the present crisis.' Supposing, gentlemen, that they are right, what would that mean? It would mean that we should be facing a ghastly period and that we should have to meet it with no other defenses than a purely materialistic outlook on every side. And then the distress would, simply in its material aspect, be a thousandfold harder to bear, if one had failed to restore to the people any ideal whatsoever.

"People say to me so often: 'You are only the drummer of national Germany.' And supposing that I were only the drummer? It would today be a far more statesmanlike achievement to drum once more into the German people a new faith than gradually to squander the only faith they have. Take the case of a fortress, imagine that it is reduced to extreme privations: as long as the garrison sees a possible salvation, believes in it, and hopes for it, they can bear the reduced ration. But take from the hearts of men their last belief in the possibility of salvation, in a better future—take that completely from them, and you will see how these men suddenly regard their reduced rations as the most important thing in life. The more you bring it home to their consciousness that they are only objects to bargain with, that they are only prisoners of world-politics, the more will they, like all prisoners, concentrate their thoughts on purely material interests. On the other hand, the more you bring back a people into the sphere of faith, of ideals, the more they will cease to regard material distress as the one and only thing which counts."[19]

Hitler had hardly uttered his last word when the audience broke into "long and tumultuous applause." Fritz Thyssen, the chairman of the evening, then delivered the thanks of the audience and the Industry Club: "Only National Socialism," he said, "and its Leader's spirit could save Germany from her doom."[20]

The effect of the speech had indeed been "astounding." From now on, no one could simply dismiss Hitler as a "beerhall demagogue" or "rabble-rouser of the masses." His versatility as an orator and his ability to persuade any audience could no longer be questioned. He had succeeded in winning over this group of listeners composed entirely of members of Germany's economic elite: a group which differed vastly from the type of mass gathering he usually addressed.

He was careful to put aside his agitator's methods and sell himself to this powerful and important assemblage as a man with reasonable economic and patriotic ideas. By associating his ideas of racism with their ideal of private property, he convinced this conservative audience that he was not a radical. He merely alluded to racial regeneration without making any of his usual attacks against the Jews; in fact, he did not even mention the word "Jew" once throughout the entire speech. But beneath his cover of logic and reasonableness was an attack on almost every Judeo-Christian moral principle, a ruthless sort of social Darwinism glorying in struggle, the survival of the fittest, and the will to power.

When Hitler spoke to well-educated, intelligent people, the rational and logical basis of his arguments often made a lasting impression on them. After the first time Houston Stewart Chamberlain heard Hitler speak (on September 30, 1923) he wrote Hitler, "You are not in the least like the descriptions I have had of you as a fanatic. In fact, I should describe you as the exact contrary to a fanatic. A fanatic wants to talk over people—you want to convince them." Of course, Chamberlain was a racist and extreme nationalist, but his opinion that Hitler's arguments were convincing was also shared by the German historian Konrad Heiden, a staunch anti-Nazi.

After personally observing Hitler's skill as a speaker, Heiden said: "His utterly logical way of thought is Hitler's strength. There seems to be no other German politician of the present day who has the moral courage that he possesses to draw the inevitable conclusions from any given situation, to announce them despite the mockery of those who think they know better, and above all, to act on them. It is this gift of logic which makes Hitler's speeches so convincing."[21]

After the speech was over the members of the club went into the dining room. In the relaxed atmosphere of a quiet dinner they discussed and analyzed the address that they had just listened to. Most of them felt that Hitler's ideas contained many good points. Some thought his ideas on economics were too vague and did not offer any practical immediate solutions to the crisis. Almost all of them, however, found him an unusually interesting personality, with extraordinary oratorical talent.

There are those, however, who believe that Hitler's speech had only a temporary effect on the industrialists which rapidly diminished once they were out of range of the magic voice. Not denying the initial impact of the speech, but feeling that it could not hold up under sober analysis, the American journalist Louis Lochner wrote: "Hitler was a spellbinder of rare ability. His oratorical gifts were unusual. I have often seen people carried off by Hitler's eloquence—people who later asked themselves, 'What did he actually say?' and then discover that there were many contradictions, inaccuracies, and evidences of confused thinking which they had not noticed while under the ban of an almost hypnotic influence which he exerted as he spoke."[22]

The question remains: Did the speech have any lasting effect? Did it bring any large contributions from industry into the Nazi treasury? First of all, the mere fact of Hitler's appearance before so distinguished and important a group as the Industry Club added to his prestige. Thyssen's statement of support for Hitler and National Socialism must have made an impression on some of his business associates. Gustav Krupp did not attend Hitler's Industry Club speech. Instead, he sent a high-ranking member of his board of directors, who was also a member of the club, with instructions to bring back a complete report. The emissary returned with more; he himself had been converted and his report was full of passages of National Socialist propaganda. Krupp, who had always been against Hitler, now began to waver: "The man must have something," he said.[23] Fritz Thyssen later wrote: "As a result of the address, which created a deep impression, a number of larger contributions from heavy-industry sources flowed into the treasury of the Nazi Party."[24] Although the Nazis may have received enough contributions to help them finance their coming election campaign, there was no "flow" of money from industry. The industrialists continued to give most of their contributions to the moderate parties as they had always done. In fact, the Nazi Party was nearly bankrupt again at the end of the year. But the speech was certainly a great victory for Hitler because many of the industrialists no longer saw him as a radical but as a reasonable politician with whom they could work and who might be needed to save them from the Communists. As things turned out, Hitler's speech to the Düsseldorf Industry Club was probably the most important he ever delivered.

Throughout the most of January and February of 1932 Hitler tried to make up his mind whether or not he should run for the presidency. Hindenburg still seemed unbeatable. Should he risk a defeat, just when the Party seemed to be doing so well? Dr. Goebbels tried to persuade him to announce his candidacy. They traveled to Munich together on January 19 and that night Goebbels wrote in his diary: "Talked over the presidency question with the Führer. . . . No decision has as yet been reached. I strongly urge him to come forward as a candidate himself."

Goebbels went over his estimates of the votes with Hitler on February 12. He admitted it was "a risk," but one had to be taken. At almost the last moment a cavalry captain who represented the Crown Prince made contact through Gregor Strasser. The Crown Prince wished to offer himself as the Nazi candidate for the presidency.[25] Naturally this produced a sensation in the Party. Negotiations began at once. There would be three definite advantages to having the Crown Prince as the Nazi candidate: (1) The Party would have access to the vast wealth of the Hohenzollerns; (2) Hugenberg's Nationalist Party would undoubtedly also support the Crown Prince; (3) contributions to the campaign would flow in from the aristocracy. But the disadvantages might outweigh the advantages. The revolutionary Nazi Party could hardly afford to be too closely associated with the reactionary forces of monarchism. Would not the Crown Prince with his extreme arrogance try to take over the leadership of the Party himself? And furthermore, what guarantee was there that he would be able to win the vote of the common people in the election?

Hindenburg formally announced his candidacy for the presidency on February 15. Goebbels was jubilant: "Now we have a free hand." But by February 21 Hitler still had not made up his mind. Goebbels wrote: "This everlasting waiting is almost demoralizing." Then the next day, February 22, negotiations with the Crown Prince were broken off: "At the Kaiserhof with the Führer . . . we once more go into the question of the presidential candidate. The chief thing now is to break silence. The Führer gives me permission to do so at the Sportpalast tonight. Thank God!"

That night Goebbels recorded: "Sportpalast packed. . . . Immense ovations at the very outset. When after about an hour's preparation I publicly proclaim that the Führer will come forward as a candidate for the presidency, a storm of deafening applause rages for nearly ten minutes. Wild ovations for the Führer. The audience rises with shouts of joy. They nearly raise the roof. An overwhelming spectacle!"[26]

It was Goebbels who set the tone of one of the most bitter election campaigns Germany had ever known, when in the Reichstag he branded Hindenburg as "the candidate for the party of deserters." He was expelled from the chamber for insulting the President. Nevertheless, the Nazis knew they were fighting against heavy odds, so spared neither the President nor anyone else in their attacks against the "system." Traditional party and class loyalties were upset in the confusion of the compaign. Hindenburg, a conservative Prussian monarchist and Protestant, was supported by the Social Democrats, trade unions, the Catholic Center Party (Brüning's party), and the other moderate parties. The conservative middle and upper classes of the Protestant north voted either for Düsterberg, the candidate of the Nationalist Party (to which Hindenburg formally belonged), or for Hitler, the hero of the lower-middle-class masses. The Communists denounced the Social Democrats for "betraying the worker" by supporting the "reactionary" Hindenburg and ran a candidate of their own, Ernst Thälmann, the party's leader.

A few weeks before the election campaign began, the

Frankfurter Zeitung reported that Hitler had gained the support of Ludwig Grauert, the executive director of the Northwest German Employers' Federation.[27] On the surface this seemed to be a notable triumph for the National Socialists. However, Grauert's "support" of Hitler was a far more involved matter than was stated in the press. One day in early January, Walther Funk called on Fritz Thyssen in Düsseldorf requesting a donation of RM 100,000 (about $24,000) for his newspaper, the *National Socialist Economic News*. Hoping that Funk's relatively conservative ideas might have an influence upon Party economic policy and counteract the unorthodox thinking of men like Gottfried Feder, Thyssen agreed to the request. However, the steel tycoon was momentarily short of cash, so he asked Ludwig Grauert to make this sum available to Funk. Because of Thyssen's powerful position within the Federation, Grauert complied with his request. But when this contribution was reported to the full board of the Federation, it was sharply disavowed. Grauert was reprimanded and threatened with dismissal, which was only averted when Thyssen agreed to repay the sum in question. A resolution was then passed that no further political contributions would be made from the funds of the Federation.[28] The Grauert incident was a clear indication that Hitler would receive support from only a very few heavy industrialists during the presidential campaign.

Although most of the leaders of the German business community supported Hindenburg for the presidency, they did so reluctantly.[29] The old Field Marshal was not popular with the industrialists because they saw him as being too closely associated with reactionary Junker interests. The old President had little understanding or appreciation for the problems of big business. In October 1931, former Chancellor Wilhelm Cuno, then head of the Hamburg-American shipping line, met secretly with Hindenburg to suggest that some of Germany's most prominent businessmen be brought together in a special economic council on the depression. It quickly became obvious to Cuno that Hindenburg did not even recognize the names of most of the industrialists on the list.

From the beginning businessmen had disliked Hindenburg. In 1925 the industrial spokesmen of both the Nationalist Party and the German People's Party had opposed his nomination for the presidency, but the power of the old Field Marshal to attract the vote of the average citizen was something that could not be ignored. Now, in the middle of the depression, the ability of Hindenburg to inspire the confidence of the people was more important than ever before. Millions were desperate and longing for a strong leader, but other than the members of the Nazi Party, who would vote for Hitler rather than Hindenburg? To answer this question it is necessary to examine closely the existing social and economic conditions in Germany in February of 1932.

In Germany the winter of 1931–1932 was generally acknowledged as "the hardest winter in one hundred years." But it wasn't just the record low temperature and heavy snowfall that made the situation so severe. The frigid weather struck Germany in the depths of the depression when only a few people could afford warm clothes or coal for their furnaces. Including the families of the unemployed, the total number of Germans living on the dole in February 1932 was approximately 17,500,000, almost one-third of the population.

The average unemployed German received fifty-one marks a month for himself and his family on the government dole. After paying the usual tenement rent, the money left for food rations was just about enough for one poor meal a day. It was enough to live on—in the sense that it might take ten years to die on it. When asked what kind of food she could buy for her family on the few marks her unemployed husband received from the state, one German woman replied: "Bread and potatoes; mostly bread. On the day we get the money we buy sausage—can't resist the temptation to have a little meat. But the last two days of the week we go hungry."[30]

An iron screen guarded the buffet of a Berlin restaurant; behind it lay a platter of fried horsemeat and a pair of horsemeat sausages. The guests were hungry. They sat at their tables gazing through the screen at the horsemeat. Even though it was dinner time they ordered nothing. Their hunger had nothing to do with dinner time; it had been with them for months. There were about forty guests in the restaurant but only two had anything on their table. Between one old man and woman stood a mug of malt beer. First he would take a sip, sit the mug down, and stare at the horsemeat. Then she would take a sip, sit the mug down, and stare at the horsemeat. They were the liveliest guests in the room, until a tall young man came in. His skinny neck was sticking awkwardly out of a tattered overcoat that flapped about his ankles. He wandered through the room holding out a once-white dress shirt. He was willing to trade the shirt for the price of á horsemeat sausage but found no takers.

The restaurant was the Zum Ollen Fritz [At the Sign of Old Fritz] and the seal of Frederick the Great was on its door, even though it was located in the almost solidly Communist neighborhood of Wedding. Here in the densely populated north of Berlin, one could see German poverty in its most acute form. In the Zum Ollen Fritz there were plenty of witnesses who could explain why the capital city of Germany had more Communists than any city outside Russia.

There was a sign on the wall at the Zum Ollen Fritz that read, "Men's Home—Bed 50 pfennigs." Beneath the sign sat a half dozen men with their heads resting on the table, sleeping. "Why don't they go to the men's home and get a decent sleep?" a stranger asked. "Because they haven't got 50 pfennigs," answered the waiter. In another Berlin restaurant, the Medow Spring, twenty or thirty men and a few women sat and watched as several young couples danced the snaggled tune of an old phonograph. It was still dinner time and signs on the wall advertised, "If you want to whip Max Schmeling, eat our goulash—35 pfennigs," but few had anything on their tables. "How do these proprietors get along?" asked an American journalist. "They don't," was the reply. "They're not much better off than their customers."

Since the September elections of 1930, there had been a political landslide in Germany toward the two extremist parties, the National Socialists and the Communists. Throughout the country the extremist vote went hand in hand with unemployment. Two-thirds of the Communist vote and one-half of the National Socialist vote in the 1930 elections came from regions containing much less than half the population of Germany but where the percentage of unemployment was considerably above that of the whole country. The centers of unemployment and the strongholds of Communism were the same: Berlin and its industrial environs, the giant chemical works of Merseburg, the mill towns of Thuringia and Saxony, the steel and coal regions of the Ruhr, and the mines of Silesia.

Which region was the most impoverished in Germany? That

was difficult to say. "We drove through the Forest of Thuringia on a winter afternoon," wrote an American journalist touring Germany. "The smokeless stacks of abandoned glass works threw occasional shadows across the snowdecked roads, and the gaping windows of deserted factories eyed us coldly. All the 75 miles from Jena we passed not a half dozen automobiles, although the towns and villages crowded one upon the other. We were not the only travelers, but the others were on foot."[31] This was the Thuringian Forest, the traditional home of Europe's most famous glassblowers. Here, in a series of communities whose average population numbered about 6,000 men, at least 5,500 of them were unemployed. This degree of poverty, which existed in the most highly industrialized country in Europe, was unparalleled in history.

Thuringia may have been the most impoverished region in Germany, but things were almost as bad everywhere else. In 1932, it was said that the population of Saxony had a bible in one hand and a dole ticket in the other. Half of the textile mills and half of the lace factories in the Saxon town of Falkenstein were closed. The other half only ran three days a week. In one of the textile factories, open prayers could be heard in a back room at noon. There, most of the workers were gathered praying for help. Of the 15,000 inhabitants of Falkenstein, 7,500 were unemployed or dependents of the unemployed. Of the other half of the population, 2,500 were workers still employed but whose wages had been cut to the point where they were barely more than the unemployed received from the dole.

The owners of the factories, however, were not much better off. Half of the villas outside the town were for sale and some of the former owners were now on public charity along with their former workers. Small factories and businesses like those which were so numerous in Saxony were even more vulnerable to the depression than large industry. Facing bankruptcy, the owners of such enterprises were easily tempted by the promises of Hitler. Angry and frustrated with the traditional parties in which they had once placed their confidence, they now contributed to the National Socialists in the vague hope that Hitler could somehow make Germany strong again and bring back the good old days. Individually their contributions were small, but when taken together the sum of such donations was substantial.

Saxony and Thuringia were poverty stricken, but what of the industrial heartland of Germany, the Ruhr? Through town after town, through endless rows of factories and squalid homes, the road led across the country, but "country" in the Ruhr did not mean open fields. For there were no unused spaces in the Ruhr. Here the chief natural scenery was the mountains—mountains of coal waiting for market. Ten million tons, nearly a year's normal production, were heaped outside the pitheads in the Ruhr. In the winter of 1932, millions of German families huddled together shivering from the cold, unable to afford to heat their homes and apartments, yet the coal just sat, unable to find any buyers.

In Essen there were smokestacks on the horizon as far as one could see—smokestacks in rows, smokestacks in clusters, a whole forest of smokestacks. But less than half of the smokestacks were belching the sooty brown smoke they were noted for; the others were idle. This was the most highly concentrated industrial area in the world: the home of German heavy industry, the land of Krupp. The Krupp firm had employed 180,000 men in 1918; now there were 50,000 workers on their rolls, many of them part-time.

A long, broad industrial building in Essen belonging to the Krupp firm was dark except at one end where three white, blazing maws opened periodically and men shoveled manganese into bubbling vats of boiling steel. Human eyes cannot look uninjured at boiling steel, so it was necessary to peer at these pots of incandescence through blue glasses. But as bright as the light was, it was not strong enough to illuminate all of the huge building where five other 100-ton furnaces lay empty. Economists estimate that stell factories can exist for only a very short time producing at less than 40 percent of capacity, but nevertheless Krupp kept going.[32]

An American journalist, H. R. Knockerbocker, toured the Krupp firm in the winter of 1932. He saw "the battery of massive presses: one of 3,000 tons, one of 4,000, and one of 5,000, all still in a huge deserted hall. And the monstrous grandfather of all presses, larger than any in America, larger than any in the world. . . . It loomed there in the dusk of a housing fifty yards high, in a hangar-like building full of shadows but not of men. . . . Its 15,000 tons of power were enough to crush a mass of steel like butter. Its chain, forged to carry burdens heavier than locomotives, hung like a necklace unsubstantial in the twilight. Not a sound in that vast building. Not a movement. The cool air felt like a cathedral. Someone said we ought to take off our hats. We passed a steel cylinder fifteen yards long, two yards in diameter, sticking out of the cold mouth of a furnace like a half-chewed match. We passed the press. Heavy with idleness, it was Germany today. Potent, it was Germany tomorrow."[33]

The Communist Party was strong in the Ruhr and among the unemployed workers in Essen. Communist agitators denounced the lords of heavy industry who oppressed their workers. But what was the winter of 1932 really like for Germany's big capitalists? Germany's wealthiest family, the Krupps, who lived in Essen were losing so much money during the economic crisis that they were forced to close down over half the rooms of their home, the palatial Villa Hügel, and confine themselves to the sixty rooms of its "small wing." The big capitalists were still able to afford caviar and champagne, but many of them lived in fear— fear of Communists, of the economic crisis, and that the economic crisis would create more Communists.

With Germany still in the depth of the worst depression in history, Hitler began his first campaign for the presidency in late February 1932. The weather was still bitter cold; the impoverished masses would not easily forget the miseries they had gone through for the past three months when it came time to cast their votes on March 13. Hitler realized this and launched the Nazi Party on a campaign which was a masterpiece of organized agitation, attempting to take the country by storm. Every constituency down to the remotest rural hamlet was canvassed. The Nazis sent some of their best speakers to the little Bavarian village of Dietramszell, where the old President spent his summer holidays, to win 228 votes against Hindenburg's 157, a clever propaganda stunt. They plastered the walls of the cities and towns with over a million screeching colored posters, distributed eight million pamphlets and twelve million extra copies of their Party newspapers. Introducing two innovations into German politics, the Nazis sent trucks with loudspeakers through the streets spouting forth from gramophone records which had been distributed in mass numbers, and films of Hitler and Goebbels were shown everywhere.

However, the major Nazi effort was based on propaganda of the spoken word. The leading Party speakers, Hitler, Goebbels, Gregor Strasser, and others, crisscrossed the country, addressing several mass meetings a day, working their audiences into a state of hysterical enthusiasm by the most unrestrained mob oratory.

Hitler threw himself into the campaign with furious energy. By car and train he conducted a speaking tour which rocked the rival parties and exhausted companions and opponents alike. From one town to another, from one mass meeting to another, Hitler covered the entire country as no politician had ever done before. He usually traveled in a convoy of cars, and was accompanied by his staff. With Hitler's big black Mercedes in the lead, the cars were usually met on the outskirts of a town by a guide sent from local Party headquarters to take them through the back streets to the meeting hall. Sitting in the front next to his chauffeur, Hitler left nothing to chance and always had a map on his knee ready for use. The precaution was probably not superflous, since the Communists were always anxious for a chance to attack the hated Nazi leader.

On two different occasions, in Breslau and Cologne, wrong turns took the convoy into "Red" controlled neighborhoods which they got through only after a foray and general uproar. The Communists were a strong and violent force in the winter of 1932. In "Red cities" like Chemnitz, people did not even dare display Christmas trees in working-class neighborhoods for fear of being attacked by fanatics. Driving through Bamberg late one night, two of the cars in Hitler's convoy had their windshields shattered by revolver shots. In Nuremberg, a bomb was thrown from the roof of a house onto Julius Streicher's car which, forunately for him, had only his chauffeur in it at the time. Several times during the campaign Hitler's convoy was attacked by "Red mobs" throwing everything from rotten eggs to rocks. On such occasions, Hitler would berate the local Gauleiter at the top of his voice for not having anticipated the action of the Communists.

In spite of the fact that the Communists were Hitler's most vocal and violent opponents, the only other serious contender for the presidency was Hindenburg. Chancellor Brüning worked tirelessly to win the election for the old Field Marshal. For once he was ruthless enough to reserve all radio time for his own side, and although this tactic infuriated Hitler, it later gave him an excuse to do the same thing. Hindenburg spoke only once, in a recorded broadcast on March 10: "Election of a party man, representing one-sided extremist views, who would consequently have a majority of the people against him, would expose the Fatherland to serious disturbances whose outcome would be incalculable."

The organization that bore the burden of Hindenburg's election campaign was the Social Democratic "Iron Front," the recognized version of "Reichsbanner," the old paramilitary unit of the Social Democratic Party. Naturally, Hindenburg also had the support of the moderate bourgeois parties which were more to his liking. German big business financed the old Field Marshal's campaign and three important industrialists, von Siemens, Duisberg, and Bosch, belonged to "The Hindenburg Reelection Committee." Almost all of the prominent industrialists and bankers came out in support of the old President. However, the moderate nonsocialist parties that big business had financed so heavily were rapidly losing contact with their following among the masses, so the number of votes they could deliver was doubtful. The presidential election campaign clearly illustrated that Hugenberg's Nationalist Party was not the party of big business. Düsterberg, the Nationalist candidate, was supported by the aristocrats, the big landowners, and the agricultural associations. With the agrarian forces for Düsterberg and both capital and organized labor for Hindenburg, who would be left to vote for Hitler? His following was estimated in the millions, but every major newspaper in the country was against him.

Late on the evening of the elections, many of the Nazi Party leaders sat in the living room of Goebbels's Berlin home, "confident of victory." Goebbels himself was skeptical. He wrote in his diary: "We listened to the results of the election on the wireless. News comes slowly trickling through. Things look queer for us. At about ten o'clock the situation receives a summing up. We are beaten; awful outlook for the future! We have not so much miscalculated our own votes as underrated those of our opponents. . . . We have gained 86 percent since September 1930; but that is no consolation. The Party is deeply depressed and discouraged. Only a bold stroke can retrieve matters.

"Phone the Führer late at night. He is entirely composed and is not at all upset."[34]

The results of the elections were astounding:

Hindenburg	18,651,497	49.6%
Hitler	11,339,446	30.1%
Thälmann (Communist)	4,983,341	13.2%
Düsterberg (Nationalist)	2,557,729	6,8%

The Nazi vote had risen from slightly less than six and a half million in September 1930 to almost eleven and a half million, an increase of 86 percent, giving Hitler approximately one-third of the total votes in Germany. But all the Nazi efforts still left them more than seven million votes behind Hindenburg. The Nazis were disappointed; they had gotten used to landslides since September 1930 and had actually expected Hitler to win. However, Hindenburg's supporters were also disappointed for they had fallen just .4 percent short of the absolute majority needed to win, and so had to face a runoff election. The Communists did not do as well as might have been expected in the middle of a depression, but they did receive two and a half times as many votes as they had seven years before. The only notable Communist success was in Berlin, where they received 28.7 percent of the vote against Hitler's 23 percent.

At midnight on March 13 Hitler was sitting in the Brown House in Munich with other Party leaders and officials. Dr. Otto Dietrich, one of Hitler's contact men with big business and his press advisor, was present. He recorded the reactions of the gathering as the election results came in: "After the publication of the first figures declaring the final results, deep despondency seized those whose hopes were naturally fixed far too much upon their own desires during the heat of battle. Already, there were loud cries of abandoning the Reich presidential election campaign as hopeless, and instead of bleeding to death in a second [runoff] election campaign cries of husbanding all strength for the later Prussian election . . . Our Führer . . . never worried, but stated with satisfaction the immense advance of the National Socialist Party fighting a lone battle against the foe's eleven united parties. . . . At this moment, when the will of his followers threatened to waver beneath the prodigious burden of the struggle, Adolf Hitler proved an absolute leader.

"It was midnight, and no time was to be lost. The extra editions [of the *Völkischer Beobachter*] lay there before going to press. At this very moment, with the publication of the figures of election result,the public and our movement must be told that Adolf Hitler was not beaten. . . .

"Our Führer rapidly dictated: 'We must resume attack immediately and most ruthlessly. The National Socialist, recognizing his foe, does not relent till his victory is complete. I command you to begin this instant the fight for the second election! I know that you, my comrades, have accomplished superhuman tasks during the past weeks. Only today, there can be no pause for reflection. Previous sacrifices only serve to prove further necessity for battle. The work shall and must be increased, if necessary redoubled. Already this evening, orders are being issued to our organizations for the continuation and reinforcement of the stuggle. The first election campaign is over, the second has begun today. I shall lead it!' "[35]

The runoff election would be an uphill fight for the Nazis. It was now obvious that Hitler couldn't beat Hindenburg, so there was a danger that some of his supporters would not bother to vote. On March 19, Goebbels wrote in his diary: "We shall only be able to reenlist the interest of the masses by some striking efforts."[36] Hitler would make his campaign tour by plane and the theme would be "Hitler Over Germany."

On April 3, the new campaign began with four mass meetings in Saxony. In a rented plane Hitler flew from Dresden to Leipzig to Chemnitz to Plauen, speaking to a total of over a quarter of a million people. The airplane was just the tool Hitler needed. It made possible a new kind of campaign that corresponded to his own indefatigable energy, and offered the possibility of utilizing his supreme power of personality in a way never previously anticipated. His campaign flights captured the imagination of Germany and the world. Never before had a politician conducted a speaking tour by plane. "It was," said Otto Dietrich, "political propaganda which eclipsed even American methods."[37]

The pace of campaign by air imposed extreme hardships on Hitler and his staff. Their day began in the early morning when the Führer's adjutant Schaub awakened the group. Hitler was usually the first out of bed and ready. The others had difficulty getting dressed and shaved as quickly, but if they were late it was at the expense of their breakfast. Coffee was strictly forbidden in the morning, because of its bad effects during flight. Their usual diet consisted of milk, porridge, and toast. During breakfast

Hitler discussed the program of the day with his adjutant Bruckner who had already made up a preliminary schedule. After Hitler approved the map and timetables, last-minute coordinating arrangements were made by phone with the Party headquarters in the cities where the mass meetings were to be held.

Everything was timed to the last minute. The cars were waiting at the hotel to race the group to the airport where the plane had already warmed up its engine and was prepared for takeoff. On landing at their first destination, the group would hurriedly get into waiting cars that would speed them to the meeting. As soon as Hitler was finished speaking to the multitudes, it was back to the plane and the routine began again. The furious speed of the campaign tour allowed no time for relaxation and no one got to bed before midnight. Hitler made up for lost sleep by napping during flight, but even this was not easy, as flying in the early passenger planes was anything but comfortable.

Who paid the bills for Hitler's presidential campaign? The expenses were enormous. Not everything used in the campaign was as expensive as Hitler's rented airplane, but the rented plane was a good illustration of the fact that no cost was too great if the Nazis thought it would bring them victory. The price of the paper and printing for the pamphlets, posters, and newspapers alone was a staggering sum. The rented cars, trucks, meeting halls, the travel expenses for party propagandists, all had to be paid for by someone.

Although a vast majority of industrialists and big businessmen supported Hindenberg, there were a few exceptions who contributed to Hitler. Of those who gave to the Nazis, most tried to keep the fact of their donations secret. Publicly, they only admitted a "sympathy" for some of Hitler's ideas. For business and social reasons they remained members of their conservative parties. A typical example was Fritz Thyssen who was still a member of Hugenberg's Nationalist Party long after he had been contributing heavily to the National Socialists. In truth, many of these men did not agree with everything Hitler said and by their donations they were seeking some kind of leverage over Hitler. Nevertheless, they supplied a significant portion of the money for the Nazi election campaigns.

A few weeks after the first presidential election, wealthy men who were members of the Keppler Circle, which was ostensibly formed to give Hitler advice on economic matters, came to the Kaiserhof in Berlin to meet Hitler. The meeting lasted several hours, but unfortunately there is not a complete record of everything that was said. Yet it is known that Hitler spoke at length, giving an account of the Party's performance in the election and of the expenditures incurred. Simply a list of the names of those present and their business affiliations explains the importance of the occasion: there was Hjalmar Schacht, former president of the Reichsbank; Baron Kurt von Schröder, a Cologne banker; Emil Meyer, of the Dresdener Bank; Friedrich Reinhardt, of the Commerz and Privatbank,[38] Count Gottfried von Bismarck, grandson of the Iron Chancellor and landowner; Rudolf Bingel, of Siemens & Halske; Ewald Hecker of Ilsede Hütte (a steel firm); Emil Helfferich of the Hamburg-America Line; August Rosterg, potash magnate; attorney Heinrich Schmidt, representing several industrial firms of Hanover; Otto Steinbrinck of the Flick Steel and Mining concerns; and Albert Vögler of United Steel.[39] Knowing he had the support of such men, Hitler was able to state with confidence that he would commit the Party to the runoff election, rather than conserve the Party's resources for the Prussian election as the other leaders were afraid they might have to do.

The 1932 presidential elections found the Ruhrlade divided over the question of National Socialism. Fritz Thyssen now actually belonged to the Nazi Party. He had kept the matter of his membership secret until the beginning of the runoff campaign, then he openly acknowledged his support for Hitler and even distributed a Nazi propaganda pamphlet to his fellow members of the Ruhrlade. Of the other eleven members, most were opposed to the Nazis, and a few were ambivalent toward them. Paul Reusch of the Gutehoffnungshütte, for example, felt that National Socialism might be of some use to Germany on matters of foreign policy but he was opposed to its domestic program.

For many years Reusch had been involved in Bavarian politics. In 1932 he decided that the Bavarian People's Party (Bayerische Völkspartei), the conservative Catholic party that had dominated Bavarian politics since 1919, was in a position to exercise a moderating influence on the National Socialists. Reusch's firm owned two large factories in Bavaria and had controlling interests in two of the state's major newspapers, the *Münchener Neueste Nach-*

richtung and the *Fränkischer Kurier* of Nuremberg. Consequently, Reusch had close ties with the leaders of the Bavarian People's Party. On March 19, 1932, he met Hitler in Munich and tried to convince him of the desirability of a coalition between the Nazis and the Bavarian People's Party.[40] But like most others who tried to influence Hitler, Reusch instead was manipulated by him. Hitler deceptively encouraged the industrialist's hopes for a coalition and thus led him to accept, as an interim agreement, that the two Bavarian newspapers controlled by the Gutehoffnungshütte would discontinue personal attacks on the leaders of the National Socialist Party, including Hitler himself, while the Nazi press would also refrain from personal attacks against the leaders of the Bavarian People's Party. Since the agreement was made just before the presidential elections, it enabled Hitler to silence criticism of his candidacy by a significant part of the press during a campaign in which the leaders of the Bavarian People's Party were not directly involved and therefore Nazi attacks on them would have been of no importance. As soon as the presidential election was over, Hitler made no attempt to keep his side of the agreement and the Nazi press resumed its attacks against the leadership of the Bavarian People's Party.

From the first presidential election to the second there was a fundamental change in Hitler's campaign strategy. In the first campaign, Hitler had attacked his enemies, in the second he spoke of himself. In the first, he had spoken of the miseries in Germany—"the people in debt; the children going hungry; the unemployed young men; literally millions of them standing in line for the dole without any possible hope of a job." Now he described the brilliant future awaiting Germany when he was in power. Sometimes at his fourth mass meeting of the day he was so hoarse that he could hardly speak, but he continued to depict a future of boundless happiness for Germany. On one occasion he went as far as to say: "In the Third Reich, every German girl will find a husband."

The climax of Hitler's second campaign for the presidency came on April 8 when a violent storm raged over Germany and all air traffic was grounded. Undoubtedly, Hitler guessed the propaganda value of keeping his engagement under such conditions. He ordered the plane to be prepared for takeoff as planned; "the masses were waiting for him in Düsseldorf." As Hitler and his staff flew through the tempest, thousands waited patiently at the race track in Düsseldorf. A local Party speaker kept the crowd from leaving by giving them progress reports from time to time, saying that the Führer's plane had just been reported passing over such and such a place and was still struggling on its way. The Führer was risking life and limb, flying through a terrible storm just to speak to them. When Hitler finally arrived, the thousands were still waiting and Nazi propaganda blared away that here at last was the man with the courage needed to save Germany.

The German people went to the polls to cast their votes in the second presidential election on April 10, 1932. The day was dark, cold, and rainy. A million fewer citizens took the trouble to vote in this runoff election. Late that night the final results were announced:

Hindenburg	19,359,983	53%
Hitler	13,418,547	36.8%
Thälmann	3,706,759	10.2%

By his brilliant campaign performance Hitler had increased his total vote by more than two million and Hindenburg had gained less than one million, but the old President was in by a clear majority. Hitler was able to capture most of the former Nationalist voters since Düsterburg was no longer in the running. The Kaiser's eldest son, Crown Prince Friedrich Wilhelm, who had quietly voted for Düsterburg in the first election, then broke with Hindenburg publicly by making a statement to the press: "Since I regard it as absolutely necessary for the national front to close its ranks, I shall vote for Adolf Hitler." However, it was not only the Nationalists who were going over to the Nazi camp, for Thälmann's vote fell by over a million since the first election. Those who had voted Communist in the first election out of desperation were perfectly willing to shift their support to anyone who might provide a change. In his diary Goebbels wrote: "To our great satisfaction, we can affirm that our numbers have everywhere increased. We come far short of defeating the enemy, but have managed to rope in nearly all the votes of the conservative parties. Thälmann has failed miserably. His defeat is our greatest success." Then, thinking of the Prussian state elections which were little more than a week away, he said: "The Prussian campaign is prepared. We go on without breathing space."[41]

While the Party was once again launching itself on a furious election campaign, Hitler and the other leaders of the movement had much to ponder. In spite of its impressiveness, how was Hitler's electoral success to be turned to political advantage when a majority still eluded him? Strasser thought that the Party should make a deal with the government. He argued that Hitler's refusal to compromise was destroying the very success of the "policy of legality." Although Hitler distrusted Strasser and was not yet ready to enter a coalition government, he did not dismiss the idea completely. Still, there were others who felt that the whole policy of legality should be scrapped. After talking with the commanders of the S.A. and S.S., Goebbels noted in his diary: "Deep uneasiness is rife everywhere. The notion of an uprising haunts the air." Again on April 2, he wrote: "The S.A. getting impatient. It is understandable enough that the soldiers begin to lose morale through these long-drawn-out political contests. It has to be stopped, though, at all costs. A premature putsch . . . would nullify the whole of our future."[42] But before Hitler could make up his mind how to respond to Strasser's criticisms or the impatience of the S.A., the government struck.

When the government of Prussia declared that police raids on the homes of various important Nazis furnished evidence that they were preparing for a putsch, Chancellor Brüning thought that his moment for a decisive move against Hitler had come. Three days after the second election, under pressure from the Social Democrats and trade unions, General Gröner, as Minister of Interior, declared that the S.A., S.S., and Hitler Youth were banned throughout Germany. There was some difficulty in getting Hindenburg to sign the decree because Schleicher, who had approved of it at first, began to whisper objections to the old man. But President von Hindenburg yielded and signed the decree, which officially dissolved the uniformed Nazi units because they "formed a private army whose very existence constitutes a state within the State."[43]

At last the government had taken a decisive measure against the Nazis. This was a stunning blow for Röhm and the S.A. leaders. They urged resistance to the order; after all, the S.A. had 400,000 men under its command, four times the size of the German Army which the Versailles Treaty had limited to 100,000 soldiers. But Hitler, sensing that this was no time for a rebellion, demanded the ban be obeyed. Overnight the Brownshirts disappeared from the streets, but the organization of the S.A. remained intact. The S.A. went underground; its men now appeared as ordinary Party members. Röhm had little to fear, for only weak organizations are destroyed by attempted suppression. Fully confident, Hitler declared Brüning and Gröner would get their answer in the coming Prussian elections. He had received information that there was a growing division within the government itself. On April 14, the day the ban was enacted, Goebbels noted in his diary: "We are informed that Schleicher does not agree with his [Gröner's] action." And a few hours later that day: "Phone call from a well-known lady, a friend of General Schleicher's. [She says] the General wants to resign."[44]

In addition to winning elections, Hitler would have to concentrate on intrigues with other parties and be willing to make compromises and alliances, for his principal objective was now to bring about the dismissal of Brüning and Gröner at any cost before they took further action against him.

It took the German government a long time to take any decisive measures against the Nazis. In the meantime, however, a few of the more courageous industrialists had taken steps on their own to break the strength of the Nazi Party. Since their weapon was money, their strategy would necessarily have to be covert.

Once a large segment of the people begin to look upon a revolutionary political movement as the source of their deliverance, it is very difficult to stop that movement by direct suppression; its momentum is simply too great. However, this does not mean that the established order is simply to give up. Any rapidly growing revolutionary party is subject to schism. In the case of the Nazis with the monolithic leadership of Hitler, they were less vulnerable to this weakness, but not completely immune.

Between 1930 and 1932, there was a certain amount of internal friction within the Nazi Party. The dissatisfaction emanated mainly from the S.A., who felt that their position in the Party was not what they deserved. They particularly objected to Hitler's policy which aimed at coming to power by legal means; they saw this as a betrayal of the revolutionary spirit of the movement. The S.A. leaders also had serious misgivings about the right of the Gauleiters to influence the appointment of high S.A. officers.

In late August of 1930 just before the Reichstag elections, the
S.A. leader of Berlin and northeast Germany, Captain Walter
Stennes, asked Dr. Goebbels, the Gauleiter of Berlin, for more
financial support for the S.A. Goebbels refused and the
Brownshirts went on strike; in other words, they refused to protect the Party's rallies. This paralyzed the Nazi election campaign
in Berlin, so Hitler rushed to the capital to use his personal
persuasion on the S.A. His arrival at some of the beerhalls where
the S.A. gathered was greeted with enthusiasm and a loud volume of applause. Hitler easily won the men over with his speech,
but he actually said little about the S.A.'s grievances except for
promising to pay them more money. Hitler's appearance and voice
was all that was needed to quickly bring the mutineers back into
the Party fold. Nevertheless, real dissatisfaction within the S.A.
remained and was soon again to break out in a more violent
form.[45]

On March 28, 1931, the Brüning government issued an
emergency decree to curb acts of political violence. It stipulated
that all political rallies had to be approved by the police twenty-
four hours before they were held. Immediately, Hitler sent instructions to all Party officials to comply with the new law. Captain Stennes, however, refused. He denounced both the Brüning
decree and Hitler's decision to obey it. He and his staff of S.A.
officers met at midnight on March 29 to plan their next move.

Actually, Brüning's emergency decree only served as an excuse
for an S.A. revolt that had been brewing for a long time. Many
causes of the old discontent remained. Stennes's men were overburdened with work and exhaustion from the strenuous election
campaign. Dr. Goebbels's battle with the Communists in Berlin
had led to a succession of street fights and beerhall brawls that
had put the main burden on the S.A. They had incurred many
casualties and demanded a greater participation in the Party
policy. Many of the S.A. men were very poor or unemployed and
some did not even have enough to eat. Stennes had again asked
Munich headquarters for more money for his troops but he was
refused.

Political differences also played a part in the S.A. rebellion.
Stennes originally had disapproved of the cooperation between
the Nazis and the reactionary Hugenberg at the time of the
Young Plan plebiscite. His political advisor was Otto Strasser, who

had been expelled from the Party because he wanted to build a "true socialist" movement. Furthermore, many members of the Berlin S.A. were former Communists who did not want to see the Nazis abandon the fight against the "reactionary capitalists."

As soon as Dr. Goebbels received information of the coming rebellion, he left Berlin to report to Hitler. At noon on April 1, Hitler expelled Stennes from the Party for insubordination. Stennes promptly retaliated by dismissing the Party leaders in Berlin and placing both the Party and the S.A. under his control. That night the fighting began.

The principal objective of the mutineers was to gain control of the meeting places of the S.A. men still loyal to Hitler. These were generally beerhalls where the Brownshirts spent their time while waiting for marching orders. Before any large-scale series of attacks could be launched against the beerhalls, a command post for the rebellion had to be established from which orders could be issued and to which reports could be made. For this purpose, Stennes decided to seize the Berlin headquarters of the Nazi Party which was in a five-story building that also included the district S.A. headquarters and the publishing plant of *Der Angriff,* Dr. Goebbels's newspaper. The headquarters building was a rich prize, for it would put into Stennes's hands not only a newspaper to turn out propaganda, but also a fully equipped short-wave broadcasting station to maintain contact with the S.A. troop trucks, all of which had receivers.

As the chief of the S.A. for the entire northeast region of Germany, Stennes potentially had a force of 80,000 men under his command. This northern S.A. army was a highly mobile, splendidly equipped armed force upon which wealthy industrialists had recently "showered money."[46] Stennes ordered the main body of his forces to hold themselves in readiness. Then, with a force of about one hundred men, he raced by truck to the Berlin Party headquarters and stormed it boldly. The regular Nazi guards stationed there were taken by surprise.[47]

The fight in the Party headquarters was short but bloody. All of the guards loyal to Hitler were either beaten up or wounded within a half hour. The fight was actually more like a barroom brawl than a battle. Stennes's men rushed the front of the building and the guards retreated, firing a few shots as they went. Other groups of Stennes's men then forced their way into the

building from side and rear exits. Surrounded, the guards retreated to the second floor and offered stiff resistance as Stennes's
men forced their way upward. The struggle proceeded to the
third floor and finally the fourth. By now the fighting was mostly
man to man, with some of the guards barricading themselves
behind desks and overturned tables.

An oppressive silence settled over the building after about
thirty minutes, disturbed only by the groans of the wounded that
littered the halls and stairways. In the broadcasting room on the
fourth floor the commander of the attacking force snapped out
his orders to the main body of his men who were waiting in trucks
on nearby side streets: "Advance and occupy." Within a few
second huge troop trucks were converging on the building from
all sides. Within an hour a force of about 5,000 Brownshirts were
barricaded behind the thick, yellow-brick walls of the Party
headquarters. The first "battle" of the S.A. rebellion had succeeded.

Arriving at his newly acquired headquarters, Stennes gave
orders over the short-wave system to his troops throughout the
city. His commands sent hundreds of trucks roaring onto the
streets, each filled with fifty heavily armed S.A. men. These units
were the roving shock troops of Stennes's army whose job it was to
smash any of Hitler's loyal followers they might come across. Each
truck was equipped with a short-wave set for immediate contact
with headquarters.

As he sat in the wrecked Berlin Party headquarters, Captain
Walter Stennes didn't look much like a revolutionary leader. He
was a small, almost elegant man about thirty-five years old with
blond hair and blue eyes who wore a neatly pressed S.A. uniform.
The typical son of a Junker family, he had won many citations for
bravery during the war. In 1919, he joined the Free Corps Pfeffer
and became the second in command. When Pfeffer later became
the head of the S.A., he appointed Stennes to a high post in that
organization. Amazingly, Stennes was allowed to accept the position without being required to join the Nazi Party.

Trucks full of S.A. men went thundering down the night-
shrouded streets of Berlin howling the Brownshirt song at the top
of their lungs. People hearing the martial tune of "Clear the
streets for the Brown battalions" discreetly ducked out of sight
into the nearest doorway. There were many sporadic clashes that

night between Stennes's men and those loyal to Hitler.

Then, in a quick change of strategy, Stennes ordered his men to take over the beerhalls frequented by the S.A. A gang of burly Storm Troopers would burst through the doorway of a beerhall, with clubs and guns held ready, and order the frightened customers to line up against the wall. The men were searched and those who carried membership cards of the Nazi Party were forced to swear allegiance to Stennes or receive a severe beating. Although brutal, such tactics were a bit childish since a man could easily say that he favored Stennes and still remain loyal to Hitler. Indeed, many verbally changed allegiance whenever threatened. The effect on morale, however, was very strong. If Hitler couldn't protect them, why should they remain loyal to him? As a result, more than a few went over to the mutineers.

The next morning the citizens of Berlin went to work oblivious to what was taking place around them, unless of course the fighting broke out in their immediate neighborhood. Even the S.A. men themselves, if they were employed, went to their jobs during the day and then rushed home in the evening to change into their uniforms, grab up their weapons, and join their troop for the night's fighting. In that respect the private Nazi war hardly seemed serious. Yet blood was shed, and more than a few men were to die. From the beginning the police and the Army were instructed not to intervene as the Nazis exhausted themselves in this private war, unless the fighting got out of hand.

On the second night of the fighting, the forces loyal to Hitler began to counterattack to reestablish their control over the beerhalls. They would leave a lookout in front of the beerhall they were taking over, and if he spotted opponents approaching, the alarm was given. Tables were overturned for barricades, and when the enemy forces rushed into the hall, they were met with a blast of gunfire that sent them reeling back. The rivals then counterattacked by taking cover in the darkness outside and firing through the windows into the lighted interior. Walls were chipped as bullets tore into them and blasted out chunks of plaster; windows shattered and sprayed glass all over the room. The hysterical screeching of innocent customers and the moaning of the wounded could be heard between the staccato gunshots. Then one by one the lights would be shot out, either intentionally by the losing side or accidentally. In the dark, groups of running figures would be heard. A few men would come to blows with clubs and blackjacks. Seconds later a truck's motor would start up and the battle would be over. Scores of such conflicts raged in Berlin, but miraculously few people were killed.

Actually, most of the shooting was over after the first few minutes of an encounter. In the crowded beerhalls a friend might receive a bullet as well as a foe, especially since everyone wore the same brown uniform. Most injuries came from swinging clubs and punching fists. After the fight was over, the hall would be a confused mass of broken chairs, overturned tables, shattered beer mugs, and the still forms of unconscious men.

Realizing that the Party might be on the verge of ruin, Hitler took decisive action. With his newly appointed S.A. Commander-in-Chief Ernst Röhm and several S.A. battalions from Munich, Hitler himself came to Berlin to suppress the revolt. Backed by a storm detachment of 500 of the roughest and biggest Brownshirts, Hitler and Röhm went from beerhall to beerhall. Taking over at these various halls, the S.A. would maintain order and keep the customers seated while Hitler would climb onto a table and speak to the crowd. He pleaded with the Nazis present to remain loyal to him in his hour of need. He begged, cajoled, and promised with tears in his eyes and emotion in his voice. Each of his listeners felt as though he were speaking to him directly. Hitler assured them he intended no reprisals but would increase the pay for all those who returned to his ranks.

His words played on the strings of the Storm Troopers' inner-most emotions. Men who only a short time before were his bitter enemies felt ashamed that they had deserted him. By the fourth day, Hitler's voice had turned the tide. However, one major obstacle remained: Stennes and his men still occupied the Berlin Party headquarters. Hitler was wise enough to see that from the military standpoint his position would be dangerous. An open attack against the headquarters would cause such bloodshed that even if it were successful it would alienate many people from the Nazi cause. On the morning that the courts reopened after the Easter holidays, Hitler went to the Berlin high court and secured a legal statement of ownership of the Party headquarters and the Party newspaper *Der Angriff*. His claim rested on the grounds that as the duly elected and legal head of the Party, his faction held the title to all Party property. Stennes was a trespasser and Hitler received a "dispossessed" notice to file against him.

Barricaded in the headquarters building, Stennes's men were well armed and prepared to withstand a long siege. Then a lone Berlin policeman in uniform knocked on the door of the Party headquarters and was admitted. He handed the court's notice to Stennes. The captain's face became white. His entire plan to defend the building would now be useless. While Stennes was ready to fight against Hitler he had no desire to antagonize the government, since this might result in the Army being called out against him. After the loss of the Party headquarters, the morale of Stennes's men collapsed. Within a day or two the mutiny was over.

The importance of the Stennes rebellion has often been overlooked, yet it not only threatened to divide the Party at a crucial time, but the evidence indicates that Stennes was financed by several important industrialists who were intent on destroying the Nazis. Hitler's statement that Stennes was a "paid agent" has been dismissed as a sign of his exaggerated imagination.[48] However, Otto Strasser later wrote that he was with Stennes when Captain Ehrhardt arrived at their headquarters during the rebellion and said: "I have come to offer you money."[49] Ehrhardt then went on to explain that he was acting as the intermediary for Otto Wolff, the owner of a multimillion dollar steel and coal concern. Wolff, who was from a Jewish background and had converted to Christianity, saw Hitler as a "grave threat" to the peace and security of Germany. Captain Stennes accepted the offer of financial assistance. With the money "lavishly bestowed by Wolff," said Strasser, Stennes was able to offer the S.A. men more money than Hitler was offering.[50]

New documents have recently come to light which indicate that the great industrialist Hermann Bücher, who was head of the German General Electric Company (A.E.G.), also gave considerable money to finance the Stennes mutiny.[51] Bücher was well known for his liberal political opinions and his willingness to compromise with organized labor. The German General Electric Company which he headed was a very progressive firm that had been founded by Walther Rathenau's father, so it is probable that Bücher had his company's support in his actions. The failure of the Stennes mutiny did not dim Bücher's opposition to the Nazis, but thereafter he limited his actions to those political measures taken by light industrial groups as a whole.[52]

There was another prominent industrialist, Paul Silverberg, who also tried to disrupt the Nazi party by financing Hitler's rival, Gregor Strasser.

Son of Adolf Silverberg and Dorothea (née Schönbrunn), Paul Silverberg was born on May 6, 1876, in Bedburg, a small town in the Rhineland. On both sides of his family, Silverberg's ancestors were Jewish businessmen. His father, Adolf, founded a wool factory and a linoleum industry in Bedburg. Later, he also became head of the Fortuna lignite mining and briquet manufacturing company.

Paul and his two sisters were raised as Protestants. He attended school in Bedburg and Koblenz, after which he went to the University of Munich and Bonn to study law. In a short time he graduated with a doctorate of law and in 1903 set up a law practice in Cologne. In September of that year his father died. Following the previously expressed wishes of Adolf Silverberg, the board of directors of the Fortuna Company selected his twenty-seven-year-old son as the new president of the company. Within a few years he became head of the Rheinish Coal Mining and Briquet Manufacturing Company (R.A.G.), which grew to be one of the largest coal companies in the world.[53]

Because Paul Silverberg was concerned about the prosperity of the German industrial community, he naturally took a great interest in the nation's political activities and problems. During the inflation, he came to the realization that the multiparty system of the Weimar Republic was not working in the difficult conditions that existed in Germany after World War I. He decided that other ways would have to be found to overcome the economic problems, the class hostility, and the restrictions of the Versailles Treaty. One possible approach to strengthen the government would be a Chancellor ruling by presidential decree. But Silverberg saw no easy solutions to the problems facing German industry and Germany as a whole, although he thought that Dr. Heinrich Brüning, the former secretary of the German Catholic Trade Unions who had taken office as Chancellor in March of 1930, was the one man with the intelligence and the character to save Germany.[54]

More a scholar than a politician, Brüning was very well read and highly cultured, but he was too austere to be popular, too upright and too high principled to have many friends. However, Paul Silverberg was one of them. Silverberg recognized Brüning's intellectual abilities and was attracted to his rational approach to politics. They both agreed on the urgent necessity of making the parliamentary system work in Germany.

Shortly after Brüning took office as Chancellor, he accused the Reichstag of not living up to its task, and told the representatives that they would have to find a way to make the Reichstag work or else the parliamentary system would dig its own grave. Brüning was certainly not the first one to accuse the political parties of disrupting national unity. In this decisive hour it was he who clearly put the question before the nation: Was democracy able to work in German?

Behind Chancellor Brüning stood his own party, the Center, as well as the Democratic Party and the German People's Party. He had the financial backing of light industry and some of the more liberal-minded heavy industrialists, particularly Silverberg. In order to save German industry and keep it competitive on world markets he was compelled to pass very unpopular antisocial measures, but he somehow managed to maintain a comparatively good relation with the Social Democrats. Because of the party schisms Brüning was forced to act by means of emergency decrees which were only subsequently confirmed in the Reichstag. Silverberg was somewhat disillusioned when he saw that Brüning's programs were consistently blocked by opposition from the bickering political parties.

To bring about an end of reparations payments, Brüning was first obliged to produce evidence that Germany was not in a position to bear the burdens laid upon her. That Germany was incapable of paying was doubted abroad, so Brüning placed almost intolerable burdens on the people to prove his point. Expenditures were cut down to a minimum in order to balance the budget. The economies and privations which he placed on the nation caused considerable hardship.

Silverberg was apprehensive about Brüning's policy, both from the economic and political point of view. He urged Brüning to take a "common sense" approach to the political situation. Realizing that the people were almost at the limit of their endurance, he suggested an increase in expenditures, thus putting more money into the economy. Brüning, however, was stricken with panic by the specter of a new inflation, and was prepared to accept any other equally catastrophic destruction of the economy provided only that the mark remain a mark. He simply lacked Silverberg's grasp of economic issues. The Chancellor was conducting a business which ran counter to his own nature. The solemn, bitter man, who let no one, not even his friend Silverberg, see the thoughts hidden behind his wire-rimmed glasses, was not at all sure of his own attempts to preserve the economy.

When the Center Party reactionaries led by Franz von Papen began to turn against Brüning in the spring of 1932, Silverberg was the staunchest supporter of the Chancellor among the heavy industrialists. In fact, for a heavy industrialist, Silverberg held exceptionally liberal political opinions. He certainly knew that although he was a Protestant, a racist movement like the Nazis would consider him "non-Aryan." Logically, this would have led him to favor a political system based on individual rights rather than national rights. Only a society based on human equality would guarantee the rights of the individual regardless of his religious or ethnic background.

As a member of the Ruhrlade, however, Silverberg was in no way discriminated against because of his Jewish origins.[55] His fellow members highly respected his opinions and ideas. He had some objections to the way the Ruhrlade was organized; he felt the whole structure was too loose and too much on an informal basis. He toyed with the idea of a more broad-based business organization that would have a firmer foundation by representing more companies. While a member of the Ruhrlade, Silverberg was also the president of the Cologne Chamber of Commerce where he introduced the various progressive ideas into that organization's functioning.[56]

The ousting of Chancellor Brüning angered Silverberg. He was strongly opposed to von Papen, because of his cooperation with Hitler and his reactionary policies. Silverberg soon switched his support to General von Schleicher and together they began to study the possibilities of ousting the Papen cabinet.

After the sweeping victory of the Nazis in the July 1932 Reichstag elections, Silverberg began an attempt of his own to influence the Nazi Party. Because of his "non-Aryan" background, he thought it wise to make his approach through an intermediary, Werner von Alvensleben, the secretary of the Berlin

Herrenklub. Alvensleben wrote several letters to Hitler in which he stated Silverberg's opinion that the business community would be willing to make peace with the National Socialists *if* they would be more responsive to the needs of businessmen. In a letter written in mid-September, Alvensleben asked Hitler to meet with Silverberg's private secretary Otto Meynen and one of his business associates, Franz Reuter. The meeting finally took place in November at Hitler's suite in the Kaiserhof in Berlin, but the economic situation was discussed only in general terms and nothing specific was accomplished.

At the same time, however, Silverberg was succeeding with a far more important project to influence the Nazis. Through Alvensleben he had established contact with Gregor Strasser, who was then known to be Hitler's principal rival for leadership within the Party. During the fall of 1932, Silverberg secretly gave financial assistance to Strasser through several intermediaries.[57]

Whether Strasser was actually cooperating with Silverberg or simply taking the industrialist's money and deceiving him, it is difficult to say.[58] It is probable that Silverberg's overtures to Hitler were simply designed to cover up the arrangement he had with Strasser, in case it became known that he was negotiating with a high-ranking Nazi.

Did Silverberg hope to split the Nazi Party by financing Gregor Strasser, or did he actually think Strasser was a reasonable man with whom it would be possible to compromise?

More of an idealist and socialist than Hitler, Strasser was regarded as the leader of the Nazi left wing. To the Nazis in northern Germany, he was almost more popular than Hitler between 1925 and 1929. Strasser wanted to attract the industrial workers with policies advocating the eight-hour day, nationalization of corporate property, and the breaking-up of the large agricultural estates. Without this sort of socialist program, he was afraid that the workers would turn to Communism instead of Nazism. At the Bamberg Conference on February 14, 1926, Hitler had severely reprimanded the Nazi left-wingers for their pro-Russian attitude and their advocacy of the expropriation of the German princes. Even though they were disappointed, Strasser and the "socialist" Nazis acquiesced to Hitler's corrections.

By the spring of 1926, the ideological split in the Party had healed over and the Nazis seemed strongly united. After recovering from injuries incurred in a serious automobile accident, Strasser was given a more powerful position in the Party to bring about organizational reform. In 1928, Hitler made him the head of the Party's administration with the title of *Reichsorganisationsleiter.* Utilizing his organizational abilities, Strasser set to work tightening the administrative structure of the Party through centralization, standardization, and bureaucratic efficiency. Despite the discomfort caused by his broken vertebrae and diabetes, he was successful in achieving improvements in the Party. At the end of 1932 Strasser headed a staff of ninety-five managerial and clerical employees, spread over fifty-four separate rooms in the Brown House. The Reich Organizational Office was the nerve center of the NSDAP.[59]

Strasser hoped that with his administrative reforms, the Nazis would be able to enter into a governmental coalition and gradually neutralize any opposition groups by taking them over from within. This strategy of sneaking to power through the back door had good chances of succeeding. But its main disadvantage was the length of time which it required. The S.A. were restless and would be difficult to keep under control if Hitler did not come to power soon. By the time Strasser's plan would have been achieved, Hitler was afraid the S.A. would be disillusioned and lose their morale.

Of course, Silverberg did not want to see Strasser realize his plan, but he thought there would be more opportunity to compromise with someone willing to enter a coalition government than with someone like Hitler who was demanding the Chancellorship for himself. This opinion was shared by other business interests who subsidized the National Socialists in order to exercise an influence over the Party and strengthen the "sensible" and "moderate" elements within its leadership. According to August Heinrichsbauer, a well-known public relations man for German heavy industry and an intermediary between the National Socialists and the coal industry, a monthly subsidy of 10,000 marks (about $2,400) was entrusted to Gregor Strasser in the spring of 1931 for the use of the Nazi Party. This money was collected from the directors of one of the principal organizations of the coal industry, the Bergbau-Verein, and from individual mining firms and mine owners. "In making these payments," Heinrichsbauer explained, "the mining industry reasoned that contact must be established and maintained continuously with the [Nazi] Party and that steady subsidies seemed to be the best way to accomplish this. . . . After it became evident that there was little possibility of limiting the influence of National Socialism from the outside, there remained no other course than continuing the effort to contain the movement within proper bounds by influencing it from within."[60]

The mining industry also contributed about 3,000 marks monthly to Walther Funk for his National Socialist economic news service. For the 1931 Reichstag election Hitler was given 100,000 marks (about $24,000) by the coal companies, but this amount, Heinrichsbauer insisted, was considerably lower than what was contributed to the other nonsocialist parties. Some money went to the local Nazi headquarters in Essen. But such donations were made only by local mine operators and probably did not exceed 5,000 marks for the two years 1931 and 1932. "The money given by the coal industry about which I have knowledge," Heinrichsbauer concluded, "for the years 1930 to 1932 was not in excess of—I estimate—a total of 600,000 marks (about $144,000). This included the payments made to Strasser and Funk."

The mine owners saw the National Socialist movement as a powerful counterbalance to Communism which they considered to be "an acute danger" during the depression. In Gregor Strasser they believed they had found a man who would be willing to work in cooperation with other parties, and if necessary able to split the Nazi Party itself. The coal industry, Heinrichsbauer insisted, never wanted a one-party dictatorship. Like the coal companies, said Heinrichsbauer, the industrialist Otto Wolff also subsidized Strasser in 1932 at the request of Wolff's friend, General Kurt von Schleicher, who hoped to make Strasser more independent of Hitler.

Considering the backing Strasser was receiving from moderate industrialists like Silverberg, would he be able to oust Hitler from his position as Party leader? The amounts stated in the existing evidence of contributions to Strasser are not that substantial, but only a fraction of the donations may have been uncovered so far. Yet even if Strasser was receiving ten times the amount now known and bringing in as much from big business as Hitler, the Party treasury would still not have been dependent on him, because the primary source of Party revenue was not big business.

The increasing indebtedness of the National Socialist Party, which must have risen to around 90 million marks by 1933, could not posibly have been met by the contributions from big business alone. Even the highest figures mentioned for donation and subsidies from major German industrial interests remain far behind the Party's expenditures. However, it should be emphaiszed again that the term "big business" does not descirbe the German business community as a whole. In the early thirties there were thousands of small industrial concerns operating in Germany. Their importance can quickly be seen from the fact that they employed over half of the nation's industrial workers. There is evidence that Hitler received considerable support from small and medium-sized companies.[61] Many of these smaller firms were in serious financial difficulties as a result of the depression. Unlike the big companies and cartels, such as the steel interests, that repeatedly received financial assistance from the Reich government, the owners of small factories and businesses knew they could hope for no such government aid when they faced bankruptcy. Feeling that the Weimar government was insensitive to their plight, and that they were being squeezed by giant competitors from above and organized Marxist labor from below, many desperate small industrialists and businessmen, such as Wilhelm Keppler, turned to Hitler as their savior.[62]

Although small businessmen and industrialists undoubtedly contributed considerable money to the Nazi cause, they could hardly have supplied a major portion of the Party's income. There was not even a definite Party office set up to solicit their donations.[63] Are we then to believe the postwar testimony of an executive of the Party Reich treasury office who stated, "The [Nazi] Party during the period before 1933 was financed first and foremost by means of membership dues and collections within their own ranks"?[64]

One talent of Hitler's which has rarely been discussed was his unusual ability to raise money in small amounts from the general public, much like discount stores that profit from a large volume of small sales. Although he paid little attention to his personal income, for the Party Hitler was a clever money-maker who lost no opportunity to convert the enthusiasm he had whipped up into a flow of cash. Hitler believed that the true test of his followers' political convictions was their willingness to pay their own way.[65] In the Nazi Party there was a price tag on everything—admission fees to meetings, membership dues, pamphlets, books, newspapers, flags, uniforms, and insignias of rank. By the early thirties, the quartermaster department of the S.A. had itself become a big business, selling clothing, equipment, and even insurance to thousands of men.[66]

The Nazi Gauleiter of Hamburg, Dr. Albert Krebs, said the financial affairs of the National Socialist Party were conducted on a completely different basis than those of the other nonsocialist parties, which were absolutely dependent on large subsidies from big business. "One must not use the experiences of the middle-class parties," said Krebs, "as a standard of comparison for a Party with regularly collected dues and systematically gathered contributions, not to mention several sound businesses [The publishing houses, insurance firms, quartermaster's stores]. All this provided a financial understructure that would assure continued freedom of movement even if individual contributions from industrial and financial circles became more meager."[67]

Whatever money Hitler may have received from big business, none of it reached the local Party groups (Ortsgruppen) which formed the basis of the Nazi movement. Money from industry, business, and the aristocrats was used entirely for the support of the headquarters, the maintenance of certain elite Storm Troop units, and to help pay for the costly election campaigns. The local groups were financed principally by dues and contributions of Party members and collections at meetings. Considering that the Party local units did most of the propaganda work, it is not surprising that they were perpetually short of funds. Frequently the local group leader had to pay many expenses out of his own pocket. "I took care of finances myself," said a typical local leader. "I paid debts out of my meager resources, and gave free room and board to every speaker who came to town. This was quite a burden."[68]

The necessity of financing their own work meant a real sacrifice for many Nazi Party members. The workers of the established bourgeois parties in contrast were always well paid and were really active only during elections. On the individual level, there was a tremendous amount of dedication and fervor as many ordinary Nazis sacrificed both their time and money day after day. One Nazi industrial worker later wrote: "Both as an S.A. man and a cell leader, I was constantly on the go. We all had several jobs to take care of. And everything cost money—books, newspapers, uniforms, propaganda trips, and propaganda material. So it happened that many of us frequently went hungry."[69] The more sincere one's National Socialist beliefs, the more one was required to spend for Party activities. The S.S., for example, were required to buy a much more expensive uniform than the S.A. In addition to all this, there were continual collections for every conceivable Party cause from election contributions to aid for unemployed S.A. men.

Lest one get the impression that all Nazis were sacrificing their last pfennig for the movement, it must be pointed out that the Party frequently had difficulty collecting monthly dues. For example, the Nazi Party branch in Kraiburg, a village on the river Inn, consisted of fifty members, most of whom were unable or refused to pay their dues. The branch leader, Rudolf Kraut, a dentist, was forced to pay for the Party's activities largely out of his own pocket. His wife served as press agent and another of his relatives was the branch secretary. There was one S.A. man whose enthusiasm Kraut could rely on and who together with his dental assistant would put up posters in their own and neighboring villages. But there was no money to pay for the newspaper advertisements or printed handouts. The rest of the branch members seemed to have been perfectly content to let one man and his family carry the burden for them.

Such conditions exited not just in poor villages or during the depression. In the beginning of 1926, the Hanover Gau owed Munich Party headquarters 54,790 marks in unpaid dues. Each Party member was required to pay dues of 80 pfennigs per month, 30 pfennigs of which was to go to the local branch, 30 pfennigs to the Gau, and 20 pfennigs to the Munich headquarters. Because so many members were behind in their monthly dues, the local leaders in Hanover made an attempt to tap new sources of income. Party units were instructed to set up branches of a front organization called the Völkisch Freedom Federation to solicit financial contributions from wealthy sympathizers who for various reasons, such as the fear of repercussions against their businesses, were reluctant to join the Party. In addition, three leading conservatives in the province of Hanover, Graf Hardenberg, Baron von Rheden, a landowner and the leader of the Hanover Stahlhelm, and Werner Willikens, an important landowner, were approached for money. Hardenberg agreed to contribute fifty marks a month and Rheden and Willikens probably gave a similar sum.[70] But these measures failed to make any appreciable difference in the financial standing of the Hanover Gau. By the end of 1926, Munich was forced to write off over 2,500 marks which the Hanover Party group owed them.

This financial weakness, however, did not have much of an adverse effect on the political activities of the Party in Hanover. One of the local Party officials, Herr Dincklage, rejected the advice that they should curtail activities when there was no money to finance them: "From the point of view of good economics that is correct and would spare our nerves. But for Hanover-Brunswick it would at the moment be the wrong thing to do. The K.D.P. (Communist Party), which is badly split, offers an opportunity where the soil is prepared. . . . In Brunswick we have just held five mass meetings leading to a climax and we are doing the same in Hanover. In eight weeks we have distributed eighty thousand leaflets in six different series, not indiscriminately, but carefully aimed at suitable factories and streets."[71] This propaganda was financed out of the dues which should have gone to Munich headquarters.

The total sum of dues received by the Party treasury office in Munich in 1927 from local branches all over Germany should have been at least 210,000 marks but the Party headquarters received only 84,000 marks.[72] The Party treasury was so desperate for money that no device which might yield some cash was left untried. Picture postcards of Hitler, with his own signature on them, were for a time sold at two marks each.

For the Nazi Party, money management became a very important basis for evaluating the success of particular Gaus and local groups. Each Gau was to adopt businesslike accounting procedures and the finances of the Gau were put into the hands of a full-time salaried business manager who was accountable less to the Gauleiter than to Party treasurer Schwarz's offices in Munich. The fact that an admission fee was charged for all Nazi public meetings was an incentive to local leaders to insure that their meetings were organized efficiently and with adequate advance propaganda. Thus, by keeping strict watch on money matters, the financial situation of the Party gradually improved as its strength increased.

Yet with the numerous election campaigns in the early 1930s, the Nazi Party treasury remained continuously short of funds. In 1932 many new members of the Party received the following sort of notice from their local branch: "Dear Comrade, you now belong to the NSDAP [National Socialist Party] and realize that this membership brings with it duties. Since we wish to save the German people, we must demand from every individual member that he take on some job. You can choose one and send your declaration of agreement by return. You can be: 1) an S.A. man, or S.A. reserve man; 2) an S.S. man; 3) in the women's department; 4) a political functionary; or 5) take on special duties." One of the special duties was "to donate ten marks a month to Party funds."[73] In other words ten marks a month was the cost of maintaining one S.A. man.

Occasionally a local Nazi unit was lucky enough to have one or two generous benefactors in their area. "I was the big financier of the movement in our town," recalled a shop owner from central Germany. "Of course, during the depression my business wasn't doing very good either, but I had received a tidy little inheritance from an uncle who had gone to America.

"When the Party was first founded here we had only sixteen members. I paid to have some leaflets printed about the Jewish stock exchange swindle and our men handed them out at the meetings of the conservative parties; we weren't yet strong enough to hold our own meetings. For the next few years I personally paid for most of the expenses of our unit. Later on the burden became too great, but I continued to pay for more than my share.

"Things were really bad for our local Party group in the 1930s. We were always short of money. Almost half of the S.A. men were unemployed or working only part-time. Whenever our S.A. troop needed transportation to meetings in nearby towns or to the Party rally in Nuremberg each year, the group leader always came to me for help. . . .

"I kept my membership in the Party secret until about 1931 because some of the men I had to do business with were Jews. The local Marxists always carried on with a lot of silly drivel about the Nazi being financed by Krupp and the big industrialists; little did they know that it was my money that paid the bills."[74]

Since Party members with money to spare were usually few and far between and the majority of Nazis were either poor or unemployed, it is amazing that frequent collections yielded substantial sums. Nevertheless, passing the hat in the dingy back rooms of beerhalls was the main source of income for the local group. The two key factors in producing donations seem to have been the ability of Nazi speakers to stir up a "revivalist" atmosphere and the patriotic dedication of the audience.

These two factors are well illustrated by the account a young man gave after attending his first Party meeting: "At the end of his speech the leader made an appeal for contributions, since this movement, unlike the rest, did not have the support of Jewish money leaders. To this end two tables were placed near the exit, where all who wished could leave their contributions. As I stepped up to the table to give my modest bit, I saw to my amazement that there were only bills on the plate. Somewhat taken aback, I lit a cigarette and stood aside, as I had no more than three marks in my possession. Thereupon a white-haired lady came up to me, saying, 'Young man, if you smoked one cigarette less each day and gave five pfennig to the cause, you would be doing a good deed.' I never knew the exact amount of my contribution, I only know that I left the place with a sense of humility, and the knowledge that that woman was a true National Socialist."[75]

Aware that Hitler's ability to seduce the masses earned not only millions of votes for him but also, when every pfennig was counted, great sums of money, the economist Peter Drucker observed as early as 1939: "The really decisive backing came from sections of the lower middle classes, the farmers, and working class, who were hardest hit. . . . As far as the Nazi Party is concerned there is good reason to believe that at least three-quarters of its funds, even after 1930, came from the weekly dues . . . and from the entrance fees to the mass meetings from which members of the upper classes were always conspicuously absent."[76]

Once the presidential elections were over, the Nazi propaganda machine immediately switched its focus to the state elections. On April 24, 1932, almost four-fifths of the total German population would go to the polls in Prussia, Bavaria, Hamburg, Württemberg, and Anhalt. Hitler began a second series of highly publicized flights over Germany. Altogether he spoke in twenty-six cities between April 15 and 23, but the main effort of his campaign was concentrated in Prussia. By far the largest of the German states, Prussia embraced almost two-thirds of the territory of the Reich and had a population of forty million, which was more than half the total German population of sixty-five million. Since 1918 the Prussian Diet and state government had been ruled by a coalition of Social Democrats and the Center Party. Thus, for the National Socialists a victory in the Prussian elections would be almost as important as winning a majority in the Reichstag.

Hitler's campaign throughout Prussia was well received but nowhere were the masses so enthusiastic as in East Prussia. Cut off from the rest of Germany by the "Polish Corridor," patriotism ran especially high in this region. The threat of a Russian or Polish invasion had been a daily fear here for hundreds of years. The soil of East Prussia was poor and the depression was particularly harsh in this already impoverished land. On his campaign tour Hitler flew to Königsberg, the largest city of East Prussia, and from there went by car to the land of the Masurian Lakes where the famous battle of Tannenberg had been fought in World War I. Even Dr. Otto Dietrich was somewhat amazed at the overwhelming reception they received from the people.

"On our journeys through the Reich," said Dietrich, "despite all the sympathy and devotion to our cause, we had always been conscious of the inner opposition of compatriots incited against us, we had seen clenched fists and scowling faces amongst the many cheering hands. But here, in the Masurian border-districts, Adolf Hitler had the vast majority behind him, already at the time of the first Reich presidential election. But on this journey it seemed as if the whole land of Masuria was faithful to the Hooked Cross [swastika].

"Here the nation's poorest children were the most true of all. Hitler flags lined all the roads, pictures of Hitler decorated all the houses, and garlands draped the entrance to every village; hope and loyalty were prevalent everywhere!

"Wherever our Führer approached, every man and woman came out. Crowds lined all the streets. Aged grandmothers, on whose distressed faces the direst poverty was written, raised their arms in greeting. Wherever we stopped, the women stretched out their children toward our Führer. There were tears of joy and emotion."[77]

In summing up his comment on Hitler's East Prussian election tour, Dietrich admitted a fact of the utmost importance: "In Germany wherever economic and moral distress was greatest, wherever things seemed most intolerable, there, confidence in our Führer was the strongest and gripped all the people."[78]

At the time of the Prussian elections, Fritz Springorum, the treasurer and youngest member of the Ruhrlade, became concerned about the rapidly increasing strength of the National Socialists. He decided an effort should be made to strengthen what he regarded as the "sound elements" of the Party against its radical factions. This plan was to be carried out by saddling the Nazis with a share of responsibility by including them in coalition governments, at first on the local level and later in the national government. Springorum also wanted to encourage moderation within Nazi leadership by making the Party dependent on contributions from industry. It is not likely that Springorum abused his position as treasurer of the Ruhrlade to make contributions to the Nazis from the organization's funds since the other members paid close attention to the accounting.

The Ruhrlade itself was almost totally immobilized by internal divisions during the Prussian elections. In addition to the Nazi problem, the organization was divided by controversy over Hugenberg. Krupp and Reusch felt that the Nationalist leader, who was working closely with the Nazis, was the primary obstacle to cooperation among the nonsocialist parties. They suggested that the Ruhrlade stop giving financial assistance to the Nationalist Party until Hugenberg was replaced by someone more moderate. This proposal was rejected by Springorum and Vögler, neither of whom were followers of Hugenberg, but who believed that such drastic action would set off a struggle within the party that would seriously handicap it at the polls. Remaining adamant, however, Krupp and Reusch refused to contribute to the Nationalist Party during the Prussian election. Now even the leading heavy industrialists representing the most powerful firms were bitterly divided and fighting among themselves.

Election day in Prussia witnessed another Nazi landslide. The

National Socialists became by far the strongest single party in the Prussian Diet, where their representatives leaped from 6 to 162 deputies. The long-dominating coalition of Social Democrats and Center Party lost its majority and governing the state without Nazi cooperation became an impossibility. Yet once again the Nazis themselves were not able to make up a majority. They were furious, however, when Brüning allowed the socialist ministers Braun and Severing to remain in office without a majority. As one Nazi said: "Brüning's Center Party thus cheated the Nazis of their legal reward for a legal fight. The bill would be presented to them later."[79]

April 24, the day of the National Socialist victory in Prussia, also saw their party become the largest in Württemberg, Hamburg, and Anhalt. In Bavaria, the Nazis received 32.5 percent of the vote and were now as strong as the Bavarian People's Party. But everywhere they were still short of a majority. For the moment the deadlock continued, but a careful analysis of voting trends in the past three elections revealed that Hitler and his party had shattered all traditional voting patterns and were still on the rise. The once strong German Nationalist Party had now lost over half of its supporters to the Nazis. The middle class was going over to Hitler in record numbers and of course his support from the unemployed and impoverished continued to grow as this tragic group itself increased in size. The National Socialists were even beginning to make some headway among the workers, but by and large Hitler's success in winning supporters from the ranks of the socialists and Communists remained minimal.

After the success of the Nazis in the Prussian elections was to a certain extent blunted by the party deadlock, some members of the Ruhrlade like Springorum and Vögler believed it was the opportune moment to exercise a moderating influence on Hitler. Although the men of the Ruhrlade had disagreed on the question of cooperation with Hugenberg and agrarian interests, they were still willing to work together on other issues. In June of 1932, five members of the organization, Thyssen, Vögler, Springorum, Reusch, and Krupp, agreed to contribute to a project proposed by Hjalmar Schacht, who was attempting to establish a link between big business and Hitler. The contributions would finance an effort to expose Hitler and other leading Nazis to "sound" economic advice and thus exercise a moderating influence on them.

Why was a prominent banker like Schacht interested in working with the Nazis? Schacht was known to have many Jewish friends in high banking circles and was generally thought of as an advocate of liberal democracy.[80] A study of his background, however, reveals that he was always an ambitious loner and something of a maverick.

Hjalmar Schacht came from a middle-class family of Schleswig-Holstein. His father had immigrated to America in the late 1870s and became an American citizen. Schacht's mother, who was a baroness by birth, soon followed. But Germany after the victory over France in 1871 seemed more promising for a young businessman than America, so after six years the Schachts returned to the Reich. They raised three sons, one of whom, born on January 22, 1877, was named Horace Greeley Hjalmar Schacht in honor of an American his father greatly admired.

The young Schacht had many talents and interests. After receiving his secondary education in Hamburg, he first studied medicine in Kiel, then German philology in Berlin and political science in Munich, before receiving his degree at the University of Berlin in economics. As he himself said, his interest was more practical than theoretical. With his formidable intellect and his quick grasp of the essence of monetary problems, he rose rapidly in the world of banking. At the age of thirty-nine, after a brilliant career at the Dresdener Bank, he was appointed a director of the National Bank. Although he was vain and ambitious, he had unusually broad interests for a banker. As a young man he wrote criticisms of plays and art works for newspapers and all his life composed verses which showed some literary talent.

During World War I, Schacht worked in the economic section of the German administration in Belgium. His job was to obtain as high a Belgian contribution to Germany's war production as possible. Germany's defeat in 1918 left him bewildered. The disorders in the streets, revolution and violence were an unpleasant shock to his orderly and logical mind. Schacht, however, always considered himself a "democrat" and after the war he helped found the German Democratic Party, although he continued to think of himself as a monarchist at the same time. He saw no real inconsistency in these political views, just as later he would see none in the compatibility of free enterprise and National Socialism.

Although not a fanatic, Schacht was a patriot and fervent German nationalist. He was incensed by the French attempts after World War I to divide Germany, their invasion of the Ruhr, and their demand for reparation payments that could not possibly be made. Schacht immediately pointed out that the amount demanded for reparations was twelve times the 6 billion gold francs Germany had obtained from France in 1871. With his self-confidence and intellectual vanity, Schacht did not easily tolerate the arrogance of the many Allied officials with whom he came in contact after World War I. On one occasion he abruptly left the office of the French Foreign Minister because he was kept waiting twenty minutes. He had to be brought back by a panting secretary who ran after him and promised an immediate audience.

Schacht became president of the Reichsbank in 1923 at the age of forty-six and was primarily responsible for devising the method of stopping the runaway inflation by a new currency backed with foreign loans. Schacht later became disillusioned with the Weimar government's acquiescence to the demands of the Allies and resigned his post at the Reichsbank. After the sudden success of the Nazis in the 1930 Reichstag elections, Schacht began to take an interest in Hitler.

On board a ship going to the United States for a speaking tour, Schacht read *Mein Kampf* and the Nazi Party Program.[81] In his first major speech in New York to the German American Commerce Association, Schacht said that if Germany were allowed to enter into world trade she could pay reparations, but that would demand international cooperation. It was the realization by the lower classes that they had to bear the burden of the reparations that caused the rise of fascism. He concluded by claiming that the Nazi landslide in the September election had been an indictment of the Versailles Treaty. At another speech in New York before an audience of important businessmen, he said: "I am no National Socialist but the basic ideas of National Socialism contain a good deal of truth."

Schacht's first personal contact with the Nazis came shortly after his return from the United States. At the invitation of one of his old friends, bank director von Stauss, he attended a dinner where he met Hermann Göring. During the next few months Schacht carefully studied the political situation in Germany, conferring with various men in banking and industry. Then in February of 1931, he went to see Chancellor Brüning to explain that since the National Socialists had 107 seats in the Reichstag and were the second largest party they should be taken into the coalition government. He argued that responsibility would tame the Nazis and that their mass following would be very useful if harnessed, but if they were left out of the government they would probably come to power on their own. Many other influential people agreed with Schacht's thinking. The British ambassador reported that Reichsbank president Luther said the Nazis would quit their nonsense if given real responsibility. The ambassador went on to say that this view was "shared by a number of people with whom I and my staff come into contact."[82] Brüning refused Schacht's appeal to take the National Socialists into the coalition. Schacht said it was a simple choice: either the Nazis or the Communists would ultimately enter the government.

Schacht was still formally a non-Nazi, but he was now ready to use his influence to raise money for the Party. He traveled frequently in Germany and abroad to talk, as he said, to "leading cirlces" in Copenhagen, Bern, and Stockholm to explain the need for ending reparations, and described Hitler's nationalist movement. Although Brüning still called on him for financial advice during the deepening depression, Schacht's talents were increasingly placed at Hitler's disposal. He undoubtedly hoped to influence Hitler in the direction of conservative economic policies. Like Walther Funk, Schacht wanted to save as much of a free market as was salvageable. He believed the government should take a variety of progressive but conservative economic measures: rearm within prudent economic limits but keep out of war at all costs, restore employment through useful public works, put an end to strikes, and crush the threat of Communism. Schacht's endorsement of Hitler undoubtedly helped the Party to tap sources of money that hitherto had been afraid of its economic "radicalism."[83] Schacht's most important fund-raising projects for Hitler, however, were yet to come.

As the year of 1932 progressed, the German economy showed no signs of improvement. In contrast, the financial situation of the Nazi Party was good.[84] Since the beginning of the year, many small businesses which were dependent on Nazi customers were contributing to the Party. In Hanover, for example, one of the two

largest cafes, the Herrenhausen brewery, and several other businesses were all giving regularly to the S.A.[85]

With Hitler now commanding more popular support than all
the moderate nonsocialist parties put together, Chancellor Brüning was in a desperate situation. The only possible way out for
the government seemed to be to move to the left and nationalize
the bankrupt East Prussian estates that were a continuous drain
on the budget. This course of action was undoubtedly sanctioned
by the spokesmen of light industry who, as early as the fall of
1930, had been shocked by the Hitler landslide, and had urged
Brüning to take some Social Democrats into his government.[86] If
tariff protection and subsidies continued to be given to Junker
agricultural interests, it might mean the doom of German industry as a whole. Light industry in particular was suffering from the
protection the government was extending to nonprofitable agrarian enterprises. It was now a life-and-death struggle between
various sectors of the economy. Heavy industry, light industry,
agriculture, banking, commerce, and labor were each thinking
only of defending their own position and forcing the burden of the
depression onto the others. But one thing was certain: all could
not survive; someone would have to be sacrificed.

Brüning and his allies underestimated the strength of the
agrarian reactionaries. Greatly perturbed by the government land
reform program, the landowners struck back at once. They overwhelmed Hindenburg with furious protests. The old President
had been briefly informed of the plan but had not grasped its
significance until the complaints aroused his attention. On his
visit to East Prussia he was shocked to hear it denounced as an
attempt to socialize German agriculture and confiscate from
some of Prussia's oldest families land that had been theirs for
centuries. His old friend Baron von Gayl warned him that such
expropriations might undermine the will of the East Prussian
upper class to defend their country against foreign attack, and
this, he added, was a serious worry to the High Command of the
Reichswehr.

These warnings were part of a renewed reactionary effort to
convince Hindenburg that Brüning's dismissal must be delayed
no longer. "The whole thing will lead to a dictatorship which we
shall claim of course for a man of the Right," Hindenburg's
ultrareactionary friend, Oldenburg-Januschau, predicted confi-

dently. The protests also worried Oskar von Hindenburg, who had accompanied his father to the family estate of Neudeck in East Prussia. Oskar was especially disturbed by the accusation that the Brüning government was promoting socialism, because he feared that the charge might reflect on him and his father. In addition, General Schleicher was in constant communication with him and kept him informed on the Army's growing uneasiness and the insistence of the eastern front commanders that for purely military reasons a firm understanding should be reached with Hitler and the S.A. On visits to neighboring estates and nearby garrisons, Oskar von Hindenburg encountered nothing but bitter opposition against Brüning's handling of the country's political and economic problems.

In the beginning the heavy industrialists had had no fundamental objection to Brüning insofar as his economic philosophy or program were concerned, for he was basically conservative.[87] Although heavy industry was generally opposed to any socialistic measures, they had no sympathy for Junker agricultural interests, which they had always seen as an expensive liability and an obstruction to sound tariff policies; so they were not about to oppose the Chancellor over his plan to nationalize the bankrupt Prussian estates. However, being essentially a representative of light industry, Brüning refused to enact the harsh antiunion legislation and wage cuts heavy industry demanded. Chancellor Brüning was concerned with breaking the strength of the agrarian forces, primarily in order to minimize import quotas and tariff restrictions and thus increase international trade, which would benefit light industry. In some circles Brüning was popularily known as the "I.G. Chancellor," because he was receiving such heavy subsidies from the I.G. Farben chemical trust.[88] Although Brüning was not heavy industry's champion, the leading heavy industrialists did not think it worth the risk to demand a change in government, considering the chaotic political and economic situation. They were willing simply to pressure Brüning to be more responsive to their interests.[89]

Meanwhile, the economic and political situation was becoming ever more critical, and other than the proposed nationalization of the bankrupt East Prussian estates, Brüning's policy was simply to wait until an improved international situation would bring with it a general economic upturn. The heavy industrialists themselves had no real policy other than this, with the exception of wage reductions in an attempt to minimize their losses. During this waiting period it was absolutely necessary that the government should be in the hands of someone who could count upon the unquestioned support of the Reichswehr to maintain public order. When the government's plan to nationalize the bankrupt Junker estates became known, Brüning incurred the hostility of a large percentage of the Junker-dominated Officer Corps. Von Schleicher informed the leading industrialists that the Reichswehr could not be counted upon to obey Brüning in case it was necessary to use armed force against the National Socialists. It was highly uncertain if the loyalty of the Army officers to the civil government was still strong enough for them to oppose a putsch by a fanatically nationalist movement like the Nazis.

General von Schleicher, who was eyeing a better position for himself, decided that the time had come to move against Gröner and Brüning. Originally, Schleicher had been the one who had maneuvered to put Brüning in power, thinking that he would be able to gain the support of the people and unite the nation. But it was now clear that this had failed. Only Hitler had the popular support of the masses, so General Schleicher began to lay his plans for cooperating with the Nazis.

Sometime before the presidential elections, Schleicher had renewed his contacts with Röhm and Count Helldorf, the chief of the Berlin S.A. At this stage of the game, Schleicher was conspiring with Röhm behind Hitler's back to incorporate the S.A. into the Army as a militia. Undoubtedly Schleicher wanted the S.A. attached to the Army where he could control it. However, after Hitler's show of strength in the presidential and state elections, he was also attracted by the idea of bringing Hitler, the only nationalist politician with any mass following, into the government where he could control him as well.

Even before the ban against the S.A. had been enacted, General Schleicher had voiced several objections to it. Next, he went behind the back of his commander, General Gröner, to the President. He persuaded Hindenburg to write a sharp letter to Gröner asking why the Reichsbanner, the paramilitary organization of the Social Democratic Party, had not been suppressed along with the S.A. Schleicher stirred up more opposition in Army circles against his commander by circulating rumors that General

Gröner was too ill to remain in office and even that he had become
a convert to Marxism. Gossip ran that after only five months of his
recent marriage, the sixty-two-year-old Gröner had produced a
son. Jokes were heard among the Officer Corps about naming the
Defense Minister's son "Little Nurmi" in honor of the speedy
Finnish runner. One can picture Schleicher rousing the old President from one of his daytime slumbers to tell him of this "shocking disgrace to the Army."

By the first week in May, Schleicher's intrigues were developing as planned. On May 4, Goebbels wrote in his diary: "Hitler's
mines are beginning to explode. . . . The first to be blown up must
be Gröner and after him Brüning." Four days later Goebbels
reported: "The Führer has an important interview with
Schleicher in the presence of a few gentlemen of the President's
immediate cirlce. All goes well. . . . Brüning's fall is expected
shortly. The President of the Reich will withdraw his confidence
in him." He then outlines the scenario which Schleicher and the
men around Hindenburg had planned with Hitler. "The
Reichstag will be dissolved [and] a Presidential Cabinet constituted." The ban against the S.A. would be lifted and elections held
in the near future. Brüning's suspicions must not be aroused to
the plan; so late that night Goebbels drove Hitler away to
Mecklenburg. "The Führer quits Berlin as secretly as he came."[90]

The Nazis now knew that Brüning was on his way out. On May
18 Goebbels noted in his diary: "Brüning is being severely attacked by our Press and Propaganda. Fall he must. . . . His position is becoming untenable. And the amusing part of it is that he
does not seem to notice the fact. . . . His cabinet shrinks visibly
and he can find no substitutes for his losses. . . . The rats flee
from the sinking ship."[91]

General Schleicher finally approached Hindenburg, and claiming to speak with the authority of the Army, announced that the
Army no longer had confidence in Chancellor Brüning. A
stronger man was needed, he said, to deal with the situation in
Germany, and he already had a suitable candidate in mind, Franz
von Papen. Hindenburg was not sure. Schleicher then added his
winning argument: The Nazis had agreed to support the new
government. Also, with von Papen the President would be assured of a ministry which would be acceptable to his friends of
the Right and the Army. At the same time, the Papen government

would command popular support from Hitler's following. That was the elusive combination which Brüning had never been able to provide. Hindenburg was convinced. On May 29, the President summoned Brüning and abruptly asked for his resignation. The following day the Chancellor resigned.

On May 29, 1932, Hitler was in Oldenburg just wrapping up his campaign in the state elections there, which provided the National Socialists with a timely success, 48 percent of the votes and a clear majority of seats in the Diet. He had just left for Mecklenburg to begin another campaign there when the news came through that Brüning was out. Goebbels came from Berlin to meet the Führer and discuss the political situation with him as they drove back. There wasn't much time, for President von Hindenburg had requested to see Hitler at four o'clock. Once in Berlin, they met Göring who then accompanied Hitler to see the President. Hindenburg confirmed the basic points of the agreement that the Nazis had worked out with General Schleicher on May 8: a presidential cabinet of Hindenburg's choosing, the lifting of the ban against the S.A., and the dissolution of the Reichstag. The President then said that he understood that Hitler had agreed to support the new government. Was this correct? Hitler replied that it was.

On hearing that the Reichstag was to be dissolved and new elections held, Goebbels wrote in his diary: "The poll! The Poll! It's the people we want. We are entirely satisfied."[92] However, in reality political power no longer resided in the Reichstag, the voice of the people, but was now placed in the hands of the eighty-five-year-old President Hindenburg and those "friends" who were able to influence him. Hitler realized this and was clever enough to adjust his methods accordingly. Schleicher, von Papen, and the men around Hindenburg were all intriguing for power, but Hitler could play at this game too. After all, alliances and compromises could always be repudiated; besides, he had the one thing that they needed—the support of the masses.

The new Chancellor chosen by President von Hindenburg, at Schleicher's suggestion, was Franz von Papen. Everyone was amazed, because von Papen had no political backing whatsoever. He was not even a member of the Reichstag. He had strong political ambitions, but so far had achieved nothing more than a seat in the Prussian Diet. However, the fifty-three-year-old von

Papen came from a family of the Westphalian nobility and had important friends in the right places. He was a former General Staff officer, a skillful horseman, and a man of great charm. After a successful marriage to the daughter of a wealthy Saar industrialist, he bought a large block of shares in the Center Party's newspaper *Germania*. Yet he was hardly known by the public except as the former military attaché at the German Embassy in Washington who had been expelled during the war for "complicity" in planning "sabotage" while the United States was still neutral.

Although von Papen belonged to the Center Party, he had continually opposed the left-wing coalition government of Social Democrats and Center Party which had ruled Prussia up to the April elections of that year. Politically, von Papen was an ultraconservative, believing "that the man of good race and inner qualities is more highly suited to bear responsibility than the average man. We must recover the habit of looking up to men who amount to something by their mind and character; who are masters because they can serve. . . ." Papen's ideas on foreign policy were very progressive for his day. He belonged to a committee for French-German understanding and had friends among French as well as German industrialists. Feeling that democracy was a pretentious sham, he thought a lasting peace in Europe could only be brought about through an international leader class. This was one of the unspoken objectives of the exclusive Herrenklub which von Papen had helped to found. It is easy to see why such ideas did not make him a very popular politician.

With his appointment as Chancellor, the Center Party expelled von Papen, accusing him of treachery against Brüning, the party's leader. But this made little difference since President von Hindenburg had asked him to form a government of "National Concentration" which would be above parties. He was able to do so immediately because Schleicher had a list of ministers for the new government ready and waiting. Of the ten ministers, seven belonged to the nobility, two were corporation directors, and the Minister of Justice Franz Gürtner had been Hitler's protector in Bavaria during the twenties. At Hindenburg's insistence, General von Schleicher was forced to give up his position behind the scenes and become Minister of Defense.

Enjoying little support in the Reichstag, the power of Papen's

"Barons' cabinet" was openly based on the backing of the President and the Army. Some said that Papen was a man taken seriously by neither his friends nor his enemies, and everyone knew that Schleicher had chosen him because he thought he would be a willing and easy tool. This proved to be a serious underestimation of the crafty new Chancellor's ambition, tenacity, and unscrupulousness. One of the first people to take Papen seriously turned out to be President von Hindenburg, who was delighted with the background and charm of this aristocratic officer. Papen soon established a close relationship with the old Field Marshal, such as no other Chancellor ever had.

In an editorial attack against Papen's government, the Social Democratic newspaper *Vorwärts* wrote: "This little clique of feudal monarchists, come to power by backstairs methods with Hitler's support . . . now announces the class war from above."[93] Papen's first act as Chancellor was to honor Schleicher's pact with Hitler. On June 4 he dissolved the Reichstag and called for new elections on July 31. All was not well, however, between the Nazis and their conservative "allies." When the lifting of the ban on the S.A. was postponed, the Nazis became suspicious and relations between Hitler and the new government were quickly strained. Goebbels wrote in his diary on June 5: "We must disassociate ourselves at the earliest possible moment from the temporary bourgeois Cabinet."[94]

The small group of individuals who engineered the overthrow of Brüning and the formation of the Papen government could assure the industrialists that the Reichswehr lay in their hands. When confronted by the possibility of a completely National Socialist government as an alternative to the Brüning cabinet, the Papen-Schleicher coup seemed to the industrialists as a heaven-sent means of escaping such a hard alternative. The industrialists were aware that von Papen was backed by reactionary agrarian forces, but his two redeeming assets, the loyalty of the Reichswehr and apparently the ability to gain some cooperation from the Nazis, more than made up for this. Still, the heavy industrialists had not been so enthusiastic about getting rid of Brüning that they became involved in the project. At the most they remained neutral; their spokesmen in the political parties and the press were silent as reactionary pressures agains Brüning mounted. The Ruhrlade itself played no active part in the removal of Brüning or the appointment of von Papen as Chancellor.[95]

It is almost impossible to describe the tremendous momentum the National Socialist movement had at the time the Brüning government was toppled. Everyone seemed to be going over to the Nazis. Hitler was the most popular politician in the country and leader of the largest political party. By all tradition, if not by law, President von Hindenburg should have appointed Hitler Chancellor. Instead, the German ruling class staked their hopes on von Papen, a man supported only by the agrarian reactionaries and the Army. The industrialists fully sanctioned this move to block Hitler's path to power, which would probably either materially weaken the Nazi movement or push it to the left. Up to this time the conservatives had avoided a decision that would definitely align themselves against the National Socialists, and which would mean that the use of Hitler's movement as a counterbalance against the growth of Communism would become uncertain.

Did the decision of the conservative elements to prevent Hitler from coming to power mean the industrialists believed that capitalism was safe from any threat of Communism? Or did it mean that the industrialists, simply because of their dislike for Hitler, had given carte blanche to the dangerous coup of the agrarian reactionaries, and cut themselves off from the island of retreat which National Socialism offered the capitalist system?

If the downward movement in world economic conditions had continued at an uninterrupted pace, it is doubtful if the heavy industrialists would have agreed to the decisive measures which were taken in the summer of 1932 against Hitler's march to power. Instead, they probably would have tried to work out an agreement with the Nazis for some sort of coalition government. By June 1932, however, there could be seen the first faint signs of the temporary economic upturn in the United States. The economic situation in England was also showing some indications of improvement. The German industrialists came to the conclusion that this was a sign of the turn of the cycle for Germany as well. If economic conditions improved sufficiently, the Communist danger would pass and big business would no longer have any use for the National Socialist Party. In fact, if Hitler was allowed a significant share of control in the state, it might not only prevent

Germany from sharing in the hoped-for economic upswing, it might even nip in the bud the developing feeling of international confidence in the Weimar Republic, and thus destroy all hope of economic recovery. Hence, the opportunity which von Papen offered seemed worth the risk.

The dangers which the new Papen government faced were very real. When it refused to lift the ban against the S.A., it had to prepare itself to fight on two fronts, against Hitler and against the Marxist parties. But von Papen felt certain that neither of his mutually antagonistic enemies would dare to attempt a putsch against him as long as he had the machine guns of the Reichswehr and the prestige of President von Hindenburg behind him.

Political moderates rallied in surprisingly large numbers to the Papen cabinet when they perceived that the government did not intend to turn the power over to Hitler. They concluded that the real mission of the Papen government all along had been simply to bridge over a difficult period and prevent Hitler from seizing power. Actually, this was just what the industrialists had in mind when they agreed to Brüning's dismissal.

The Papen cabinet, however, did not see itself as simply a temporary government and began to consolidate its power. Papen's refusal to lift the ban against the S.A. indicated that he had planned to double-cross Hitler all along and had simply used the Nazis to get himself into power. Whether or not the "Barons' cabinet" would be able to stay in power remained to be seen, but for the moment once again Hitler was stopped.

Afraid that the Nazis might become more belligerent, von Papen lifted the ban against the S.A. on June 15. The Communist leader, Thälmann, denounced the lifting of the ban as "an open provocation to murder." A state of virtual anarchy now prevailed in the streets of Germany. With the ban lifted, the Brownshirts were everywhere in evidence again and four private armies confronted each other. There were the Nazi S.A., the Communist Red Front, the Social Democratic Reichsbanner, and the Nationalist Stahlhelm. Their weapons were clubs, brass knuckles, knives, and revolvers. They ran shouting in the squares and rampaging through the towns.

The wave of political violence continued to mount. There were 461 political riots in Prussia alone between June 1 and July 20, in which eighty-two people were killed and over four hundred wounded. The worst fighting was between the Nazis and the Communists; of the eighty-six people killed in July 1932, thirty-eight were Nazis and thirty were Communists. The Communist Red Front was more aggressive than ever before. Dr. Goebbels's election camapign in the industrial cities of the Ruhr was given a rough reception and Nazi speakers were frequently in need of S.A. protection. On Sunday, July 10, eighteen people were killed in street battles. The worst riot of the summer took place one week later on Sunday, July 17, at Altona, an industrial suburb of "Red" Hamburg. Under police escort the Nazis marched through the working-class neighborhoods of the town and were greeted by shots from rooftops and windows. They immediately returned fire. Nineteen people were killed and 285 wounded on that day alone.

All parties except the Nazis and the Communists demanded that the government take action to restore order. There was a good reason for this, even though the Nazis and Communists were suffering the greatest losses in men. Everywhere the people were swinging toward extremism and the two most radical parties were reaping the political rewards. Thousands of Social Democrats flocked to the Communists and thousands of Nationalists joined the Nazis.

Papen responded to the popular demand for order by two measures. He banned all political parades until after the July 31 elections. And he took a step which was intended not only to conciliate the Nazis but to greatly increase his own power. On July 20 he deposed the unconstitutional Prussian government and appointed himself Reich Commissioner of Prussia. As an excuse, von Papen claimed that the Altona riot proved the Prussian government could not maintain law and order and could not be relied on to deal firmly with the Communists. Besides, the Social Democratic and Center Party coalition government had remained in office without legal majority in the Diet. But the socialist Prussian ministers refused to give up without a fight, so von Papen obligingly made a show of force. Martial law was proclaimed in Berlin and the Army moved in with a few armored cars and a handful of men to make the necessary arrests.

Once again the Nazis mounted a major campaign, in preparation for the July 31 Reichstag elections, but far from being weary, the fourth election contest in Germany within five months found their propaganda machine in top form. Hitler concentrated his propaganda on the bourgeois masses suffering from the economic crisis, on working men stricken by unemployment, farmers ruined by debt and unfavorable markets, countless intellectuals who could see no way out of their distress, and the old soldiers and adventurers whom the dissolution of the Army had thrown into the streets. They had everything to gain, and nothing to lose. The promise that if the National Socialists came to power, things would change, was a powerful attraction in the summer of 1932. The German masses were driven almost to the limit of their endurance by two years of the worst economic depression in history. The unemployed, now numbering well over six million, almost a third of Germany's total labor force, swarmed the streets. And yet the government had continually failed to make the slightest progress to relieve the nation's ills. All across the country the young were rising up in defiant protest against the wretchedness of a life that their fathers' generation seemed to have spoiled for them. Whether National Socialists or Communists, they were resolved for a change, for a new order.

The Nazis were having considerable success winning over young people of all classes and social backgrounds. Even the younger generation of the upper and upper middle class was far more favorable to National Socialism than their parents. The leader of the Hitler Youth, Baldur von Schirach, was himself from a wealthy upper-class background. Years later, when Hitler was discussing his rise to power with some associates, he said that the Party had found it a very successful technique to approach industrialists through their children, who could easily be converted.[96]

The account of a conservative industrial executive seems to confirm Hitler's opinion: "One day I discovered that my seventeen-year-old son was a Nazi. Being myself a member of the conservative Deutschnationale Volkspartei [Nationalist Party], I promptly forbade my son to associate with these revolutionaries. The boy, however, paid no attention to this prohibition, and even had the nerve—or the courage—to come home in his brown uniform. Thereupon I gave him such a beating that my wife thought I would kill him. The boy, however, reassured his mother with the words, 'Even if father kills me, I shall remain true to Hitler.' That was a crucial hour for me. For a long time I pondered how it was possible that my only son would be willing to let himself be killed for an idea. It struck me that there must be something about that idea, other than what I had heard about it. In all secrecy I bought myself a copy of *Mein Kampf.* Then I went to some National Socialist meetings, and I began to see the light."[97]

Completely ignoring the sentiments and demands of the youth and the lower classes, von Papen behaved as if he were living in the past. The members of his cabinet believed that the only way to restore prosperity was to lower still further the costs of production. As a result, one of the basic points in the cabinet's program of "economic reconstruction" was to lower wages. Collective bargaining was abolished and employers were permitted to reduce wages unilaterally. The regular unions only protested against von Papen's policy of lower wages, but the Communist and sometimes the Nazi union cells fought the wage reductions with a series of "wildcat" strikes. The leaders of the moderate Social Democratic trade unions, who had tolerated Papen's decrees, had reached the extreme limit of possible concessions. If they yielded more, they risked losing their following to the Communists and being overwhelmed by the masses.

This new controversial economic program of the Papen government was, in part, designed to win the support of heavy industry. Even its policy of "reemployment" was to be accomplished through a system of subsidies for business firms. Tax rebates were granted to industries but denied to consumers. The sectors of heavy industry which were in great financial difficulty received von Papen's economic program with enthusiasm, while the leading firms of heavy industry, such as those represented in the Ruhrlade, supported the new policies of the government but remained somewhat skeptical about the cabinet itself. Light industry, in contrast, was opposed to the reactionary Papen government from the beginning and saw only danger in its policy of lower wages.

From the Right and from the Left came the cry, "Things must be different!" In the air was a swelling spirit of revolt against the capitalist system. The Nazis were able to give expression to this spirit, yet remain unhampered by the rigid doctrines and class exclusiveness of Communism. In a great speech before the Reichstag in May, Gregor Strasser voiced the demands of rebellious Germany seeking the right to work: "The anticapitalist yearnings which animate our people do not signify a repudiation of property acquired by personal labor and thrift. They have nothing in common with the senseless and destructive tendencies of the International. But they are a protest against a degenerate economic system, and they demand from the State that it shall break with the demon GOLD, with the habit of thinking in export statistics and in bank discounts and shall, instead, restore a system that gives an honest reward for honest work. . . . If today the economic system of the world is no longer capable of properly distributing the wealth of nature, then the system is false and must be changed. These anticapitalist yearnings indicate the dawn of a new age: the conquering of Liberalism, the rise of new thoughts for economic life, and a new concept of the State."[98]

The Reichstag elections were set for July 31, 1932. That summer the people saw little hope of economic recovery and increasingly turned to revolutionary solutions; the Communists might have been victorious in such a situation if they had had any strong leaders. Nevertheless, the Nazi election campaign encountered vicious hostility from the combined forces of the Communists and socialists in the industrial regions of Germany.

In his diary, Dr. Goebbels described his campaign trip through the Ruhr in mid-July 1932, just two weeks before the nation went to the polls:

"July 12. We fight our way through the seething mob at Düsseldorf and Elberfeld. A wild trip! We had no idea that the situation would turn out to be so serious. Innocuous, we drive into Hagen quite openly, uniformed, and in an open car. The streets are swarming. Full of the mob and Communist rabble.

"July 13. Now we drive through the country in plain clothes only. We are continually passing groups of Communists lying in ambush. It is hardly possible to get into Dortmund. We have to travel by secondary roads so as not to fall into the hands of the "Reds" who have blocked all principal thoroughfares.

"July 14. A drive through the Ruhr involves mortal peril. . . . We take a strange car, as our Berlin number is already known and noted everywhere.

"July 15. In front of the hotel the "Red" mob is howling. The police refuse to intervene as they do not consider it their duty to protect politicians in opposition to the government. . . . I have to clear out of my native town like a criminal. Sworn at and insulted, spat at and showered with stones."[99]

Hitler again took to the skies for a third "Flight Over Germany," during which he spoke in nearly fifty different cities and towns in the last two weeks of July. Typical of Hitler's many mass meetings during the election campaign was one that took place at a small village in Brandenburg. Several hours before the Führer arrived all the roads within miles of the village became crowded with cars, wagons, and thousands of people on foot, all headed in the same direction. A large meadow outside the village had been marked off with banners, and a high platform at one end was draped with a huge, flaming swastika flag. Below the platform, in the bright summer sun, stood hundreds of uniformed Storm Troopers ranked in solid squares. Two bands played while the audience, with many women and children among them, filed into the rough wooden benches. Those who could not find seats stood up, row after row around the field.

The first speaker, a Nazi Reichstag deputy, addressed the crowd. While he was speaking an airplane zoomed over the field; every head turned to follow its descent. As soon as it landed, Hitler emerged and hurried to the platform. He was greeted by what one witness called "the loudest cheer I had ever heard in my life." Sixty thousand arms were lifted in the Nazi salute and sixty thousand peasant faces bright with expectation looked toward the man in a simple brown shirt now standing alone on the platform. Though hoarse already, Hitler spoke "with furious power." The crowd roared its approval whenever he paused. At last, at the psychological moment, he concluded and stepped down, leaving the entire audience suspended on the oratorical heights to which he had lifted them. He had no time to wait for the applause to die away, for that same afternoon he was scheduled to speak in Potsdam, and that night in Berlin. As he walked quickly toward the plane, he stopped only long enough to pat the head of a small child who handed him flowers, and shake hands with an old Party comrade he recognized. The cheers and applause did not cease until the plane had taken off and was out of sight.

Without even counting the spectacular mass meetings, the Nazi campaign was being conducted on an impressive scale. In the streets of Berlin swastika flags were in evidence everywhere.

Huge posters and Nazi slogans screamed from windows and kiosks, blazoning forth messages about duty and honor, national solidarity and social justice, bread, liberty, and the virtue of sacrifice. Passers-by wore little swastika lapel pins and uniformed S.A. men elbowed their way through the crowds. On every newsstand copies of the *Völkischer Beobachter* and *Der Angriff* were piled high. Munich remained the organizational center of the Party, as it had been from the beginning, but the heavy political barrage was now being directed from under the shadow of the Reichstag itself. In Berlin, Hitler was waging a hand-to-hand battle with the leaders of the "system." Everything was keyed to the highest pitch. The whole city bore evidence of the intensity of the struggle, and showed how close Hitler was to victory.

A great evening rally at Grunewald Stadium in Berlin was to wind up the entire election campaign. Detailed preparations had been made by Dr. Goebbels, for unlike the Brandenburg rally this was no rural fair for peasants and villagers, but an event which had to make sophisticated Berlin open its eyes in amazement. Several hours before the meeting began, the approaches to the stadium were jammed with throngs of people. As those inside took their seats, the light of the long July day still lingered above the open amphitheater. By the time night began to steal over the field, more than a hundred thousand people had paid to squeeze inside, while another hundred thousand packed a nearby race-track where loudspeakers had been set up to carry Hitler's words. Meanwhile, at home, millions were waiting at the radio, open to the Nazis for the first time in this campaign. The stage setting inside the stadium was flawless. Around the entire perimeter of the vast stone arena, flags and giant banners were silhouetted against the darkening sky.

Here in this vast bowl, so carefully arranged for the occasion, the intensity of the long election campaign was brought to a focus. Yet not everyone in the audience was friendly to the Nazis. In the boxes one could see tight little groups of men, obviously political observers or industrialists and business leaders who had come here only to watch and corroborate the deep mistrust and fear which Hitler still inspired in many men of their class. It was interesting to observe, said a Nazi member of the audience, how the facial expressions of these hard-boiled individuals became softer as the rally progressed; some even showed undisguised emotion.

Suddenly a wave surged over the crowd; everyone leaned forward, the word was passed from man to man: "Hitler is coming! Hitler is here!" A blare of trumpets sounded through the air, and a hundred thousand people leaped to their feet in tense expectancy. All eyes were turned toward the platform, awaiting the approach of the Führer. There was a low rumble of excitement and then, releasing its pent-up emotion, the audience burst into a tremendous ovation, the "Heils" swelling up until they were like the roar of a mighty cataract.

Hitler stepped through a passageway and walked to the speaker's stand. He stood there alone, bathed in light, in his brown shirt, briskly saluting. When the tumult, like a thunderstorm receding, had finally subsided, the firm sound of his voice came over the loudspeakers and microphones into the falling darkness of night. In this vibrant atmosphere, the crowd of a hundred thousand had but one mind. "I felt," said one witness, ". . . the invisible lines of force which radiated from Hitler. To be within the sound of his voice, as I was clearly aware . . . watching the response from the masses, was like being within the field of a powerful magnet. Whether one was repelled or attracted, one was electrified."[100]

When Hitler finished speaking there was a roar of cheers that continued and even grew louder until the dozen S.A. bands struck up "Deutschland über Alles."

During the July Reichstag election campaign the Ruhrlade gave 360,000 marks to General von Schleicher (now Minister of Defense and, to those in the know, the power behind the government), to disperse among those parties backing the Papen cabinet. Apparently, little money from heavy industry went to the Nazis. Ludwig Grauert, executive director of the Northwest German Employers' Federation, later testified that heavy industry led by the Ruhrlade had decided that no funds were to be given to the National Socialist Party during the campaign but only to the parties supporting von Papen.[101] Not all industrialists necessarily abided by this decision. Fritz Thyssen was again one of the notable exceptions. He continued to contribute to the Nazi campaign because he felt the depression and high unemployment rate created the kind of conditions in which a sudden

Communist upsurge was possible. Another prominent businessman commented that Thyssen "talks of nothing nowadays
but the 'Red danger.' "[102]

Despite the successive election campaigns the Party had been
engaged in since the beginning of the year, the Nazis were not
terribly short of funds at the time of the July Reichstag elections.
Hitler credited this accomplishment principally to Party treasurer Schwarz, who, he said, was "so skilled in the management
of the revenues of the Party derived from subscriptions, collections, and the like, that our movement was able to launch the
decisive campaign of 1932 from its own financial resources."[103]

The Nazis may have been able to "launch" the campaign from
their own resources, but the enormous expenses soon far exceeded the Party funds. Even the special election contributions
did little to help meet campaign expenses.

The Party's creditors, printers, suppliers of paper, agencies that
rented cars and trucks, etc., were all threatening to discontinue
their services in the middle of the election unless they were paid
immediately. Various wealthy bankers and industrialists who
were sympathetic to National Socialism and some of whom belonged to the Keppler Circle were willing to help underwrite the
election costs, but they demanded some guarantee for the repayment of their money. Hitler met with the Party's outstanding
creditors, such as the printer Müller, and the prospective financiers. Agreements were reached. Later Hitler said: "My most
tragic moment was in 1932, when I had to sign all sorts of
contracts in order to finance our electoral campaign. I signed
these contracts in the name of the Party, but all the time with the
feeling that, if we did not win, all would be forever lost."[104]

Late on the night of July 31 the results of the elections were
announced. It was a resounding victory for the National Socialist
Party, winning 13,745,000 votes and 230 seats in the Reichstag,
more than double the support they had won in the September
elections of 1930. They were now by far the largest party in
Germany. Their nearest rivals, the Social Democrats, received
slightly less than eight million votes. The working class was
obviously swinging over to the Communists, who won five and a
quarter million votes and became the third largest party. The
Catholic Center Party increased its strength slightly, polling four
and a half million votes. However, the other moderate bourgeois

parties and even the Nationalist Party were completely over-whelmed. There were 608 deputies elected to the Reichstag:

National Socialists	230
Social Democrats	133
Communists	89
Catholic Center	76
Nationalists	37
Bavarian People's Party	21
All Other Parties	22

In the four years since 1928, Hitler had gained about thirteen million votes, an impressive victory by any standards. He had won about six million votes from the moderate middle-class parties and gained the support of most of the six million new voters. The vast increase in the Nazi poll came primarily from the impoverished middle class. About half of those who voted National Socialist in 1932 had voted for the middle-class parties in 1928. The People's Party, the Democrats, and the Economic Party received a combined vote of over five and a half million in 1928; in 1932 they polled less than one million. Of the six million new voters who backed the Nazis, about half were young people, most of whom were unemployed and saw the future as hopeless; the other half were people who had never bothered to vote before because they had little faith in party politics.

Hitler was the victor, but an absolute majority had eluded him. In a dispatch to the Foreign Secretary, the British ambassador in Germany summed up the situation: "Hitler seems now to have exhausted his reserves. He has swallowed up the small bourgeois parties of the Middle and Right, and there is no indication that he will be able to effect a breach in the Center, Communist, and Socialist parties. . . . All other parties are naturally gratified by Hitler's failure to reach anything like a majority on this occasion, especially as they are convinced that he has now reached his zenith."[105]

9
BRIBES and BLACKMAIL

The National Socialist Party was now the largest in the Reichstag. Hitler had won his greatest election triumph, but the question remained: Would he be able to translate his votes into actual power? After the July Reichstag elections, intrigue dominated the political scene in Germany. All the major political groups—the Nazis, the Social Democrats, the moderate parties, and the Communists—had so paralyzed each other that a few men representing powerful economic interest groups would be able to make history. The only official power that remained for Hitler to reckon with was President von Hindenburg. Since his reelection, Hindenburg seemed more willing than ever to govern by emergency decree. Behind the old President stood a small group of important advisors. There were Hindenburg's son Oskar, State Secretary Meissner, General von Schleicher, Chancellor von Papen, and his "Barons' cabinet."

It is a mistake to view the political intrigues of this period as the personal rivalries between "unscrupulous, ambitious" men, to place undue emphasis on the flaws in the character of these individuals: the vain ex-cavalry officer von Papen, with his aristocratic manners, striped trousers, and finely tailored jackets, supposedly wanting to make himself a reactionary dictator simply because of his inordinate ambition; the smooth General von Schleicher, who cut a dashing figure in Berlin high society and whose specialty was betraying his friends, carrying out his behind-the-scenes wire-pulling simply out of a love of Machiavellian manipulation and the sense of power it gave him. Recent evidence reveals that von Papen and Schleicher opposed each other because they were acting as the representatives for different economic and social interest groups. They intrigued with Hitler only because they found it impossible to maintain a stable government on their own.

Although it has never been properly emphasized, the major political question in Germany during this period was "Can Hitler be bought?" The upper-class economic interest groups such as heavy industry, light industry, and the Junkers were now competing against each other for their economic survival. But none of these groups was strong enough to maintain itself in power without the help of the Nazis.

Meanwhile, Hitler had problems of his own. In spite of the fact that the National Socialists had recently been victorious in the elections, they were in desperate shape financially. Hitler was faced with the tremendous day-to-day expense of maintaining the largest party in the country, with thousands of employees in addition to the gigantic S.A. army. Debts exceeded contributions and the Party faced bankruptcy. Hitler had to get to power quickly or see his Party collapse for a lack of funds.

Many of Hitler's old benefactors like Thyssen were having financial difficulties of their own and could no longer afford to contribute. But if the industrialists would not give willingly, there might be a way to compel them: blackmail. This was one of Hitler's trump cards. The Reichstag had called for an investigation of some of the corrupt deals of big business and the Junkers through which billions in public funds had been swindled. As the largest party in the Reichstag, the Nazis could vote to silence such investigations—if certain contributions were forthcoming.

But before the conflict between Hitler and the upper class could be resolved, events took a startling turn. In the fall of 1932, economic conditions began to improve slightly. As a direct consequence, those factors which caused Hitler's rise started to lose their impact. For one last moment, as in classical drama, everything seemed to reverse itself. The size of the Nazi Party began to decline immediately and some disenchanted members changed their allegiance to the Communist Party whose membership thus multiplied almost overnight. The "Red threat" was suddenly as dangerous as the Nazi one. Now the industrialists and the Junkers were faced with a crucial decision: Would they let the Nazi movement collapse and risk facing the impoverished half-starving masses alone or would they come to Hitler's aid with financial assistance and form a coalition government with him?

With the overwhelming but inconclusive National Socialist victory in the July Reichstag elections, the last series of tactical maneuvers in the struggle for power began. Certainly by tradition, if not by law, the cabinet resigned after an election if its supporters had not attained a majority and the President asked the leader of the strongest party in the new Reichstag to form a cabinet. The people's mandate had been given decisively to Hitler's party. With not even 10 percent of the new Reichstag in support of his government, von Papen should have presented the resignation of his cabinet. The men behind Hindenburg, however, saw that by observing this tradition they would be forced to work with Hitler, whom they still held in suspicion and contempt. Moreover, another cabinet seemed impossible, since no party had a clear majority in the Reichstag and a parliamentary alliance between the Nazis and the Center Party was most improbable. This provided the Hindenburg faction with a nominal excuse for continuing to govern by emergency decree under Article 48 of the Weimar Constitution. The fact that this measure required the approval of a two-third's majority in the Reichstag and that no such majority existed did not trouble the gentlemen of the Papen cabinet, but they must have realized that they could not continue for long against the constitution, against the Reichstag, and against an overwhelming majority of the people.

By the fall of 1932, an increasing number of wealthy aristocrats were supporting Hitler. The royal family, the princes of the small states, and the high nobility had lost more in the revolution of 1918 than anyone else. The precapitalist feudal order on which their power was based was largely destroyed. Nevertheless, by compromising and maintaining a low profile during the first years of the Republic, they were able to retain some of their wealth. With the coming of the depression and the obvious failure of the Weimar Republic on which big business had staked its hopes, the reactionary monarchists became more aggressive. In order to recover their lost privileges and smash the Left once and for all, many members of the nobility began to contemplate an alliance with Hitler.

The first reigning German prince to join the Nazi ranks was

Friedrich Christian Fürst zu Schaumburg-Lippe.* He was born in 1906, the sixth son of the ruling prince of a small state in central Germany. Friedrich Christian's father was one of the few princes who was really popular with the common people. He traveled through his lands without bodyguards, often stopping to visit the cottages of peasants where he was a welcome guest. It was from his father's example that Friedrich Christian got the idea that it was the duty of the nobility to care for the social welfare of their people.

By 1918 Friedrich Christian's father had died and his eldest brother was ruling the state. Like all the other small princes of Germany, the Fürst zu Schaumburg-Lippe abdicated for fear of his life during the revolution and his four brothers did likewise. However, Friedrich Christian, who was only twelve years old, was too young to officially renounce his right to the throne without a very formal procedure of a regent being appointed to speak for him. But in the hectic days of November 1918, all this was forgotten. Actually Friedrich Christian had never abdicated and thus had held the title Fürst zu Schaumburg-Lippe since November 12, 1918.

From boyhood onward the Fürst was a fervent admirer of Napoleon. With enthusiasm he studied the military career of the great general and emperor. But he was also attracted to Napoleon for another reason. Napoleon had been a popular monarch, loved by his people and soldiers. This was far different from the class hostility the young prince saw all around him in Germany. He felt the nobility themselves were to a great extent responsible for this condition, because they had neglected their responsibilities as rulers in favor of their petty pleasures and their obsession with protecting their personal wealth.

When he was twenty-three years old in 1929 the young Prince joined the Nazi Party and became an officer in the S.A. There were four principal reasons that led him to take this decision. Like many other young men, he felt a great resentment against the humiliation of the Versailles Treaty and the crippling restrictions it placed on Germany. He was disturbed by the poverty he saw all around him and the apparent helplessness of the

---

*The title "Fürst" means reigning Prince and indicates that the holder is head of his House.

government to do something for the common people. The class hostility and the hold that Marxism seemed to have on the masses frightened him, but he had to admit to himself that the traditional nationalist forces with their exclusive attitude offered the lower classes little alternative. From his first contact with Hitler, he immediately saw similarity between the Nazi leader and his hero figure Napoleon.

The Nazis gained considerable prestige from having a reigning prince within their ranks. The young Schaumburg-Lippe turned out to be an aggressive orator and able writer. He spoke frequently in his brown S.A. uniform, lashing out at his fellow aristocrats for not doing their duty for the nationalist cause. In October of 1931 the Fürst played a prominent part in the Harzburg rally. A rather handsome man of medium height and build with fine aristocratic features, the young Prince looked somewhat out of place standing next to the beefy beerhall brawlers of the S.A. Yet his presence and appearance in Nazi ranks helped emphasize that Hitler's Party was open to people of all classes and backgrounds.

Like many other upper-class followers of Hitler, the Fürst saw the Nazi Führer as the man who would free Germany from the Versailles Treaty, win the lower classes back to the nationalist camp, and smash Communism. Still young, Schaumburg-Lippe was not such a superficial thinker as some of Hitler's other wealthy admirers, for he recognized that the Nazis represented a real revolutionary force and were not just militant conservatives. The Prince himself believed a political revolution was necessary in order to, as he expressed it, "put modern politics in harmony with the natural order." Although a confirmed monarchist, the Prince wanted to build a new social and political order based on talent and ability rather than on the power and influence of money. This concept was similar to Napoleon's idea of "careers open to talent," which Hitler heartily endorsed. Like Hitler, Schaumburg-Lippe saw nationalism and socialism as complimentary not contradictory forces and looked upon Marxism as the corruption of the true socialist idea. The Prince actually thought of himself as "a revolutionary in the same sense as Napoleon."[1] That is, he was a revolutionary advocating a new order rather than disorder.

Like many other members of the old nobility, Prince Schaumburg-Lippe was somewhat suspicious of big business.

Consequently, he had mixed feelings about soliciting contributions from industry. "We were very afraid," he later recalled, "that if ever big business got an influence over the Party they would ruin the spirit of Nazi idealism with the materialistic, self-interested power of money."[2] Yet the Prince was by no means opposed to letting all industrialists support the Party. He felt Fritz Thyssen, with whom he was acquainted, was "an idealist, but a bit confused in his thinking."[3] Prince Schaumburg-Lippe himself was a "regular donor" to the Party treasury, but his personal fortune was not nearly as great as Thyssen's or Krupp's.

Hitler and the young Prince soon became close personal friends. They spoke together as equals and were completely frank with each other.[4] On one occasion, Hitler and Schaumburg-Lippe had a long talk at the old Hotel Elephant in Weimar. The Prince explained to Hitler how the aristocracy viewed the Nazis and what their hopes and apprehensions were. "It is very interesting for me to talk with you," said Hitler, "for it enables me to understand how the aristocracy think."[5] Whenever there was an opportunity, Hitler took time out for a conversation with Schaumburg-Lippe. During one of their private discussions in the early thirties, Hitler told the Prince that one day, after the Nazi movement was victorious, he hoped to retire to Ober Salzburg and appoint a constitutional monarch to rule, with the supervision of the Nazi Party.

There were several other princes and members of the high nobility who supported Hitler. The Duke of Mecklenburg, former governor of German Togoland in Africa and brother-in-law to the Queen of Holland, saw the Nazi as the only salvation against Communism. He voted for Hitler in the presidential election and used his international connections to travel abroad, propagating Hitler's ideas. The Duke was a special friend of Hjalmar Schacht and exercised a certain influence in economic affairs. Although he was not thought of as a political radical, even some of Hitler's more extreme ideas like anti-Semitism found favor with the Duke. The chamberlain of his court, Baron von Brandenstein, boasted that Hitler would abolish intermarriage and that he would put all aristocrats in jail who were married to non-Aryans or had Jewish blood. In spite of his racism, the Duke always had a cool, polite manner even when in the presence of Jews. This unnerved many people, but fooled no one. "His sleek courtesy always gives me the creeps," said the Jewish society columnist Bella Fromm.[6]

Prince Ratibor Corvey, one of the wealthiest nobles of Silesia, was an early supporter of Hitler. The income from the Prince's many estates and farms could easily match that of most industrialists. In well-informed circles it was said that he was "one of the best-paying members of the Party."[7] The Silesian aristocrats, who were known for their fanatical nationalism and support of Hugenberg, had several other pro-Nazis in their ranks. One of the biggest landowners of the region, Count Rex-Gieshubel, told his friends: "Times will improve for the landowners if Hitler comes to power. And besides, Hitler will restore the monarchy."[8]

Prince Waldeck-Pyrmont, an heir to the throne of one of the small German states, had been a Free Corps member after the war; then, in the early thirties he became an S.S. officer. The thin, quiet Prince was a friend of Heinrich Himmler and considered by the latter to be an expert on foreign affairs.[9] The Grand Duke of Hesse was a regular contributor to the National Socialists and his two sons, each the owners of thousands of acres of land, were enthusiastic Party members.[10] One of Hitler's earliest supporters among the ruling nobility was the Duke of Coburg, who was the owner of over 25,000 acres of land. Although the Duke was part English, he gave generously to the Nazis and was not shy about wearing his brown S.A. uniform in public.[11]

So many nobles and aristocratic landowners would probably not have supported Hitler if he had not found favor among the German royal family, the Hohenzollerns. The Kaiser had given his own son Prince August Wilhelm permission to join the National Socialist Party and the S.A. The son-in-law of the Kaiser, the Duke of Brunswick, was a "regular donor" to Hitler.[12] The Duke's son, the Prince of Hanover, was a member of the S.S. Why did the Hohenzollerns support Hitler? They hoped to be able to use his patriotic movement as a force to restore the monarchy.

The most unprincipled opportunist among the royal family was Crown Prince Wilhelm. Personally, he had nothing but utter contempt for most of the Nazi leaders. He had many Jewish friends and his political opinions were either moderate or nonexistent. Nevertheless, the Crown Prince supported the Harzburg Front and openly endorsed Hitler in the second presidential election. Like the other members of his family, Crown

Prince Wilhelm hoped for a restoration of the monarchy. But it was himself rather than his father, the Kaiser, that he was plotting to put on the throne.

The Crown Prince had a foot in every political camp. For a time he had been a strong supporter of Chancellor Brüning in the hope that he would sponsor his candidacy for the throne. By the early thirties, however, the moderate parties were losing their strength. It was during this time that Crown Prince Wilhelm became a regular guest in the Berlin salon of the ambitious Frau Viktoria von Dirksen. Frau von Dirksen had become infatuated with Hitler in the late twenties, and as an enthusiastic Nazi wore a large diamond swastika pin on her bosom which earned for her the nickname "the Mother of the Movement." It was widely known that Frau von Dirksen was a heavy financial contributor to the National Socialist Party. The dream of this gossip-loving society lady was the restoration of the monarchy by Hitler, who—if things went the way she wished—would designate the Crown Prince as the new Kaiser.

The Crown Prince also kept in contact with the Nazis through Hermann Göring. On May 6, 1932, the Prince celebrated his fiftieth birthday with a lavish party at his palace. The guest list was very selective; only the higher nobility, the very wealthy, and Hitler's representative Hermann Göring were invited. One of the guests said: "Göring appeared after the dinner in civilian clothes . . . and retired into a corner with the noble host and hostess, where I saw hopes arise in the Crown Princess at the explanations which he was obviously making to her."[13]

Actually, Hitler had a very low opinion of the Crown Prince, whom he regarded as a lightweight, interested only in horses and women. Yet this did not stop him from making promises to get what he wanted. On one occasion Crown Prince Wilhelm optimistically pointed to the chairs in his library where, a short time before, Hitler, Göring, Goebbels, and Röhm had sat, and credulously told his guests, "Hitler told me here: 'My goal is the restoration of the Empire under a Hohenzollern.'"[14]

Klaus Jonas, the biographer of the Crown Prince, said: "He had helped the Nazis to come to power, had himself publicly taken Hitler's side, and had published enthusiastic articles about him in the foreign press."[15] Yet the contributions Crown Prince Wilhelm gave to the Nazi Party were probably rather small. His main political hope always lay with the moderate parties. He cooperated with the Nazis only because he might be able to use them and undoubtedly he would have betrayed them as soon as he had the opportunity. His disdain for Hitler, however, did not prevent the Crown Prince from accepting the reward of a substantial annual allowance from the Prussian state for his cooperation with Hitler after the Nazis came to power.[16]

While the Crown Prince was plotting to get the throne for himself, behind his father's back, the ex-Kaiser was not sitting idle. Although in exile himself, the Kaiser had many representatives in Germany arguing the case for the restoration of the monarchy. One of the most effective of his agents was his young, attractive second wife, the "Empress" Hermine.

In 1922, while living in exile in Holland, Kaiser Wilhelm received in his mail a letter of respect and sympathy from a young boy. He answered by inviting his youthful admirer to visit Doorn. In escort came the mother, Princess Hermine, a widow of thirty-five who had been married to Prince Schönaich-Carolath. She and the Kaiser became very fond of each other and on November 3, 1922, they were married. By this time his youngest child, the Duchess of Brunswick, was herself thirty and the arrival of younger stepchildren added interest and gaiety to his life. The Empress Hermine, however, was a capable and clever woman who was determined that her husband would once again sit on the German throne.

Even before her marriage to the Kaiser, Princess Hermine had owned vast estates in Silesia and consequently was very rightist in her political sympathies. Sometime after 1930, she became a "passionate follower" of Hitler. A representative of the Crown Prince said: "The Princess [Empress] Hermine saw Germany's future in Hitler and trusted him completely. She seemed firmly convinced that when he held the power of Germany in his hands, it would be only a question of a short time until she would see her husband return to his hereditary place. In any event it was clear to me that in the Princess I had a convinced disciple of National Socialism before me."[17]

The Empress Hermine frequently came to Berlin to socialize and advance her husband's cause. When attending an afternoon reception given by Countess von der Groeben, she was greeted by her eighty-five-year-old hostess who said in an impeccably courteous and grand manner: "Your Majesty, I have been told that your sympathies are with the National Socialists. Is it true that His Majesty has made a donation to the National Socialists?"[18] The Empress stood in embarrassed silence, then turned and walked away.

By 1932 the political stalemate seemed to hold more promise for the monarchists, who had been relegated to a role of political insignificance for so long. An article appeared in the monarchist's paper *Sueddeutsche Monatshefte*. Only monarchism, it stated, could solve the present political crisis. Germany had experienced first the unlimited rule of political parties, then the terror of political armies, and now was sliding into the abyss of civil war. The article concluded that the people would again call for "the protective power which stands above all parties: the monarchy."

At Doorn the ex-Kaiser and his wife testingly began to probe the German political climate. In the summer of 1932 Baron von Senarclens-Grancy made a secret trip through Germany, revealing an ambitious plot to various rightist leaders and influential Army and Navy officers. The Baron had formerly been a captain in the Imperial Guards, and after the Kaiser's abdication, he had become Wilhelm's confidential agent. Arguing that the reestablishment of the monarchy had become a question of life or death for Germany, he presented a provisional plan which centered around the reliably monarchistic naval officers. Units of the Navy would sail into the North Sea and at a prearranged rendezvous pick up the Emperor and bring him to the naval base of Wilhelmshaven. Once in Germany, the Kaiser would issue a proclamation declaring that responsible men of all political parties had summoned him to save the nation. Chancellor von Papen would resign, Hindenburg would hand over all his powers to the Kaiser, and a new government with a general as Chancellor would be set up.

The cooperation of the Navy was promised by Rear Admiral von Eschenburg. Then Baron Senarclens-Grancy tried to get the help of the Army, and of Hitler as the leader of the largest political party. The Baron contacted several top officers in Berlin and told them that he had talked to Hitler and that Hitler had expressed his willingness to support the coup d'etat provided that the Army would also cooperate. However, Hitler demanded an important concession. He wanted to become Chancellor; a general would be acceptable to him as Vice-Chancellor, and von Papen would become Foreign Minister. Oskar von Hindenburg halfheartedly gave his approval to the plan but he warned the Baron not to inform his father prematurely. He believed that the President could easily be "persuaded" if he were presented with a fait accompli. Everything seemed to be going well, but Oskar von Hindenburg did not have the authority to speak for the Army. General von Schleicher, who at that time was the power behind the Reichswehr, would hear nothing of this monarchist's plot. In fact, he even refused to receive Baron Senarclens-Grancy. Henceforth, the monarchists considered Schleicher as their enemy.

Who supported the idea of the restoration of the monarchy besides the ex-Kaiser and his ambitious wife? Surprisingly, a very large number of influential and wealthy people: a majority of the nobility and Officers Corps and even many industrialists. Aware of the financial power wielded by the monarchists, Hitler was very careful not to irritate them. In two pamphlets published in 1929 and in 1932 respectively, it stated that Hitler intended to establish a National Socialist dictatorship for "a transitory period" only. The Nazi Party wanted to take over the state only until the German people had been freed from the threat of Marxism and could then reach a decision as to whether the final form of government would be a republic or a monarchy.

Fritz Thyssen was among those industrialists still loyal to the Kaiser. "I thought at that time," related Thyssen, "that Hitler's taking office as Chancellor was merely a transitional stage leading to the reintroduction of the German monarchy. In September 1932, I invited a number of gentlemen to my house in order to put their questions to Hitler. Hitler answered all questions put to him to the utmost satisfaction of all present. On that occasion he said in distinct and unambiguous tones that he was merely the pacemaker of the monarchy." Among the industrialists assembled at Thyssen's home were Hitler's old conservative sympathizer Emil Kirdorf and Albert Vögler, the director of United Steel. "In the fall of 1932," Thyssen further notes, "Göring paid a whole week's visit to ex-Kaiser Wilhelm II at Doorn."[19] Even the simple fact that Hitler and Göring were invited to dine with the Crown Prince did much to confirm the wishful thinking of many ultraconservatives about the Nazis' ultimate aims. The contact between Hitler and certain monarchist circles appeared to be so close that it alarmed some of the more socialist-minded Party leaders. Ernst Röhm repeatedly voiced his concern that Hitler might become, or perhaps already was, the captive of the monarchist clique.

Despite the many aristocrats who supported the Nazis, the leading political representative of the upper class, von Papen, was no more willing to cooperate with them than ever. When Hitler failed to receive a summons from von Papen to discuss the possibilities of a compromise after the Nazi election triumph in July, he became worried. He hurried to Berlin, not to see the Chancellor, but for an interview with the man behind the government, General von Schleicher. On August 5 at Fürstenberg barracks, north of Berlin, Hitler saw Schleicher and made his demands: the Chancellorship for himself, and other Nazis appointed head of the state government of Prussia, the Reich and Prussian Ministries of Interior (which controlled the police), the Ministry of Justice and two new Ministries, Aviation and Popular Enlightenment and Propaganda. Naturally Schleicher himself would remain as Defense Minister and have control of the powerful Ministries of Foreign Affairs and Economy. Hitler said that this was a true compromise on his part, and in turn demanded that the government allow him to seek an enabling act from the Reichstag authorizing him to rule by decree for a specified period. And if the enabling act was refused, the Reichstag would be "sent home."

Whatever Schleicher said, Hitler came away from the meeting with high hopes, under the impression that the General would cooperate with his plan. But Goebbels remained cynical, even after listening to Hitler's optimistic report of the meeting with Schleicher. "It is well to watch developments with reserve," he wrote in his diary. He was, however, certain of one thing: "Once we attain power we shall never relinquish it unless we are carried off dead."[20]

On August 9, Wilhelm Frick and Gregor Strasser came to see Hitler in Bavaria with discouraging news. The violent behavior of the S.A. after the election was making conservative people ask if the Nazis were really fit for power. There were also rumors General Schleicher had changed his mind and was now saying that if Hitler became Chancellor he would have to rule with the consent of the Reichstag. Then Funk arrived with the report that his friends in big business were worried about a Nazi government taking power. He also carried a message from Schacht saying established business interests were afraid the Nazis might begin "radical economic experiments."

On August 11, Hitler decided to bring matters to a climax one way or another. He arranged for appointments with the Chancellor and the President before beginning the drive north to Berlin. On the way he stopped for a conference with other Nazi leaders by the shore of Lake Chiemsee. Summing up the results of the conference, Goebbels said: "If they do not afford us an opportunity to square accounts with Marxism, our taking over power is absolutely useless."[21] After reaching Berlin late on the evening of the twelfth, Hitler had his interview with von Papen and Schleicher the next day at noon. The discussion quickly became stormy. Schleicher backed out of the agreement he had made the week before. He supported von Papen in maintaining that the most Hitler could possibly have was the Vice-Chancellorship for himself and the Prussian Ministry of Interior for one of his lieutenants. They politely set aside Hitler's claim that the leader of the largest party in the Reichstag was entitled to be Chancellor. Papen said Hindenburg was insistent that an extremist party leader like Hitler could not head a presidential cabinet. Hitler was outraged. Losing his temper and beginning to shout, he said that he must be Chancellor, nothing less. He talked wildly of mowing down the Marxists and of a coming St. Bartholomew night. Schleicher and von Papen were both shocked by the raging figure who now confronted them. He assured them that he had no designs on the Ministries of Defense, Foreign Affairs, or Economics, but was only asking for as much power as Mussolini had claimed in 1922. Stunned, von Papen terminated the interview by saying the final decision would have to be left up to Hindenburg.

Hitler left in a rage of disappointment and went back to Goebbels's apartment. At about 3 P.M. a phone call came through from the President's office. Frick answered and said there was no point in Hitler's coming to see Hindenburg if a decision had already been reached. "The President will talk to Hitler first," was the reply. This revived a vague hope. Perhaps the "Old Bull" would bow to the voters' mandate and allow Hitler to become Chancellor after all.

It is difficult to say just how involved the old President actually was in the decision-making process. He was eighty-six years old and his mental powers were not what they had been. He did have periods of lucidity, especially in the mornings, but he liked to get business over quickly and then fall into reminiscences about his earlier military career. He frequently had difficulty recalling the details of World War I, but his memory was clear about the wars of 1860 and 1870. Often he would sit for hours, talking about the officers and men who had served under him more than fifty years ago. Sometimes his conscience troubled him. "How is history going to judge me?" he would say. "I lost the greatest war. I was unable to help my country which honored me with its highest post."

Hindenburg might have been capable of acting as a purely ceremonial head of state, for he still made an imposing appearance on the parade grounds. But with no majority existing in the Reichstag, a role of almost unlimited power fell on his office. Being a monarchist, he felt uncomfortable as President of the Republic. He was further perplexed when he found it impossible to govern by the constitution he had sworn to uphold. Yet this tired old man was the only real power the German state had left, so he continued to govern by emergency decree, heavily dependent on his small circle of "advisors."

Accompanied by Röhm and Frick, Hitler went to the President's palace. Hindenburg waived all formalities and courtesies. He did not even ask Hitler to sit down. Standing up, leaning on his cane, flanked by his son and his secretary Meissner, he asked the Nazi leader point blank whether he would accept the Vice-Chancellorship and support a "national" government as he had promised. In this way, the fiction of a "promise" was to be maintained. Once again Hitler refused; cooperation in a position subordinate to Papen was out of the question, he must be Chancellor or nothing. Hindenburg wasted few words. He said that he could not in good conscience risk transferring power to a new party such as the National Socialists who were intolerant, noisy, and undisciplined. Then the three Nazi leaders were dismissed. The interview had lasted barely ten minutes.

Hitler hardly had time to return to Goebbels's apartment when the newsboys in the streets begam screaming the headlines: "Hitler Demands Entire Power"—"Hitler's Breach of Faith"— "Hitler Reprimanded by the Reichspresident." These accounts were based on an official bulletin, issued with such amazing speed that evidently it had been in the hands of the government press office before Hitler had left the presidential palace. The whole thing had been a clever propaganda move. It worked so well that within an hour the world press was shouting Hitler's disgrace. "And the world believed it," wrote Otto Dietrich. "In vain we tried to set things straight but our press could get no hearing."[22]

The superlative Nazi propaganda machine had been caught off guard and beat at its own game. The incident did considerable harm to Hitler's cause, not only among the general public but also among the National Socialists themselves. It did Hitler little good to respond that he had not asked for "complete power" but only for the Chancellorship and a few ministries. Gregor Strasser was not the only one in the Party who, for a long time, had felt that Hitler's uncompromising demand would win the Nazis nothing.

What Hitler could not obtain from the government by compromise, he now tried to win through a war of nerves. In the hands of a clever strategist like Hitler, a mass of fanatical followers such as the S.A. could become a weapon of flexibility and finesse. The Storm Troopers were the uprooted and disinherited who had absolutely nothing to lose and everything to gain by a civil war. Many of them even felt that if worse came to worst and they were defeated, they at least would have the satisfaction of taking their hated enemies down with them. Hitler could mobilize these belligerent legions and bring them to a halt just short of catastrophe, but the willingness of the Brownshirts was so obviously genuine that the Hindenburg clique could not know where they would stop—or even be sure that they would stop.

In spite of the temporary victory of Schleicher and von Papen, Hitler realized that intrigue was a game that two could play. In late August, the Nazis approached the Center Party. Together they could command a majority in the Reichstag, so Hitler proposed they pass a joint motion to depose the current president of the Reichstag, a Social Democrat, and elect a National Socialist in his place. In his diary Goebbels wrote: "We have got into touch with the Center Party if merely by way of bringing pressure to bear upon our adversaries." He saw three possible courses of action: 1) a presidential cabinet; 2) coalition with the Center Party; or 3) remain in opposition. But he also noted: "It is quite impossible to see through all this intrigue. So many are pulling in different ways that one cannot tell who on the other side is the betrayer or who is the betrayed." Late that night he returned to Berlin and discovered "Schleicher already knows of our feelers in the direction of the Center Party." He added: "That is a way of bringing pressure to bear upon him. I endorse and further it."[23]

The contacts between the National Socialists and the Center Party, though never intended to be more than a means of pressuring the Papen government, paid off on August 30 at the reconvening of the Reichstag when the Nazis and the Center Party joined in electing Göring as the president of the Reichstag. Paul Loebe, the bespectacled, shy little Social Democrat who had clung to the Reichstag presidency for twelve years, had to step down for the Brownshirt Nazi colossus—Captain Hermann Göring. Göring was well suited to the job, at least from the Nazi point of view. Through practice and sincere effort he had developed into an able speaker, and although he aped Hitler's style and phrases, he had the necessary volume and imposing physical bulk to make himself noticed. Göring was also a war hero with an upper-class social background that would serve him well in his dealings with the aristocrats around Hindenburg. After the election of its first National Socialist president, the Reichstag adjourned until September 12 when it would reconvene for its first working session.

Anticipating trouble, Chancellor von Papen had obtained in advance from President von Hindenburg a decree for the dissolution of the chamber. This was the first time that the death warrant of the Reichstag had been signed before it had even met to discuss business. Papen was confident he was in complete command of the situation. However, the actual course of events on September 12 took everyone by surprise. When the session opened before a crowded audience in the public galleries, Ernst Torgler, a Communist deputy, introduced a motion for a vote of censure against the government.

Papen had neglected to bring his dissolution order along for this first working session. He had with him instead a speech outlining his government's program, having been assured that one of the Nationalist deputies would object to a vote on the expected Communist motion for censure of the government. The objection of any one of the 600-odd deputies would have been sufficient to postpone a vote. But when the moment came, neither a Nationalist deputy nor any one else rose to object, so the chamber sat in a puzzled and embarrassed silence. "The situation was now serious," said von Papen, "and I had been caught unawares."[24] He sent a messenger back to the Chancellery to bring the dissolution order as quickly as possible. Finally, Frick rose to his feet and asked for a half hour's adjournment on behalf of the National Socialist members.

An excited crowd filled the lobbies and corridors. Meanwhile, the Nazis held a hurried meeting at the palace of the Reichstag president across the street. It was an embarrassing situation. In order to bring down the Papen government, the Nazis would have to vote for a Communist motion. They felt the Nationalists had double-crossed them by not requesting that the vote be postponed. Hitler, Göring, Strasser, and Frick all decided in favor of trying to outsmart von Papen and defeat the government before the Reichstag could be dissolved. Since Göring would be the presiding official, everything would depend on his ability to pull some swift and daring tricks in parliamentary procedure.

As soon as the deputies had taken their seats again, Göring as president announced that a vote would be taken at once on the motion of "no-confidence" proposed by the Communists. By this time von Papen had the familiar, red dispatch case which traditionally carried the dissolution order. But when he rose to request the floor to read it, Göring managed not to see him, so the voting began. Papen was red-faced and on his feet waving the order in the air for all to see. All but the president of the Reichstag, that is, for he was turned the other way counting votes. Papen then strode up to the president's rostrum and slammed down the decree of dissolution. Still, Göring had eyes only for the voting. According to eye witnesses, von Papen's face had now turned white with anger. Finally he and the other members of the government walked out of the chamber in disgust. The Communist motion of no-confidence was carried by 513 votes to 32, and Göring promptly declared the government deposed. At last he noticed the piece of paper which had been thrust on his desk. After reading it to the Assembly, he ruled that since it had been countersigned by a Chancellor who had already been voted out of office it had no validity.

Whether or not Göring's clever charade did much more than make a joke of von Papen was not clear. Yet it was obvious that the overwhelming majority of the Reichstag was opposed to Hindenburg's "presidential cabinet." For the moment, von Papen had the advantage which counted, Hindenburg's support. The Chancellor insisted the order of dissolution had already been signed and placed on the rostrum before the vote took place, and thus the result was invalid. After sitting for less than a day, the deputies yielded and went home when President von Hindenburg declared the Reichstag dissolved; however, the constitutionality of this action was clearly arguable. The Chancellor set new elections for November 6 and the Nazis now faced their fifth major political campaign in less than a year.

It was the intention of Schleicher and von Papen to wear Hitler down and bankrupt the Nazi Party so that it would be ready for collapse at the decisive moment. Hitler was racing against time; but he had one trump card in his hand. Many industrialists and Junkers were reluctant to see the Nazis pushed to desperation at a time when a Reichstag investigation into certain deals that had taken place during the regimes of Brüning and von Papen would prove dangerous. Thus the Gelsenkirchen case was highly significant in influencing Hitler's relationship with heavy industry during the period of von Papen's chancellorship.

The Gelsenkirchen matter was the direct outcome of the desperate efforts of Friedrich Flick to save his bankrupt industry from disaster. Flick was one of Germany's greatest steel tycoons. In a sense, he was the counterpart of Hugo Stinnes—full of energy and initiative, forever acquiring and selling industrial properties and stocks, getting in and out of combines. About 1915, Flick emerged as a power in the world of iron and steel and soon became the director of Charlottenhütte, Ltd. With large credits borrowed in the name of Charlottenhütte he managed to gain control over the Rhein-Elbe Union, another large steel firm which in 1926 consolidated with one of its subcompanies, the old and respected Gelsenkirchen Mining Company, and assumed the latter's name. In order to expand his control, he repeated this technique again several years later, this time using Gelsenkirchen Company to buy up the stock of the United Steel Works, of which Gelsenkirchen had been a cofounder and minority stockholder.

If the depression had not interrupted his speculative grab for power, Flick might have consolidated his position and replaced

Fritz Thyssen as the dominant figure in United Steel. But by early 1932 Flick's position was precarious. He was overextended as a result of his massive debts. Gelsenkirchen stock was selling on the market at 22 percent of its former value and even United Steel was in difficulty. Flick decided to retrench and sell his Gelsenkirchen stock. Shortly after the beginning of the year, Flick and Albert Vögler, the director-general of United Steel and the chairman of the board of both Gelsenkirchen and Charlottenhütte, notified the Reich that Charlottenhütte was facing bankruptcy unless saved by government intervention. Flick's whole financial empire was threatening to collapse. Then Fritz Thyssen entered the matter by offering to buy up Gelsenkirchen stock for a group of investors he headed. The discovery that the great French armament firm Schneider-Creusot was part of Thyssen's group was used by Flick and Vögler to increase pressure on the German government to buy the shares. As soon as he learned the government was willing to purchase, Flick sent a letter (which he later published) to Thyssen, rejecting the offer of his group, ostensibly for patriotic reasons. A few days later the price of Gelsenkirchen stock started to rise; this was an indication Flick had reached a preliminary agreement with the government. With the approval of Chancellor Brüning, Reich Finance Minister Dietrich, who concluded the transaction, agreed to pay Flick 90 percent of the par value for the Gelsenkirchen stock, though their market value was 22 percent at the time.[25] The deal provided Flick with enough money to meet his obligations and reestablish himself on a sound basis.

Why did the Brüning cabinet support the activities of an industrial speculator by buying stock from him at over 300 percent of its market value? Was it, as Flick later claimed, to prevent him from selling to the French? There was more to the Gelsenkirchen scandal than was visible on the surface; in fact, the matter had a deeply hidden background that much resembled the famous "Putilov case." In 1926, Flick had acted as a secret trustee for the Reich in a very sensitive matter. Upon the government's request he acquired control of the Bismarck Mining Company and other important firms in Upper Silesia, which had been lost to Poland in 1918 but which Germany tried to keep under its influence. The fact that the German government practically owned these companies was not allowed to become known in Poland, since it violated the Versailles Treaty and would have given the Poles an excellent reason to seize the property. If Flick had sold his steel interests to a group including the French, they would have had access to this information and naturally would have reported it to their Polish allies. Thus, he was virtually committing an act of political blackmail when he informed the German government that the Thyssen group included the French firm of Schneider-Creusot. The public, however, never found out about the real background of the transaction; this information remained secret until it was revealed in Flick's Nuremberg trial.

Still, the news of a deal in which the government paid three times the market value for stock created considerable uproar even if some of the vital facts remained hidden. In the Reichstag, deputies from various parties demanded a clarification of the matter. Flick and his associates now faced another crisis which was almost as serious as the one from which they had escaped. While critics from the press spoke of corruption and called for a public investigation, most industrialists, with the exception of those who were in on the deal, were bewildered and feared government plans for a general socialization of industry. Many nonsocialist newspapers immediately demanded that the stock be turned back to private ownership.[26] Both Paul Reusch and Fritz Springorum spoke out publicly against attempts to replace a free economy with a kind of state capitalism. In early July, the Ruhrlade attempted to repurchase the Gelsenkirchen stock from the government but could not raise sufficient funds.[27]

In an effort to silence criticism and prevent a Reichstag investigation of his transactions, Flick spent liberally from the ample funds he had just received from the government. During the critical year of 1932, he contributed to every political party, perhaps with the exception of the Communists. He admittedly gave the following amounts:

> RM 450,000—to the Hindenburg election campaign (March)
> RM 500,000—to the Hindenburg election campaign (April)
> RM 100,000—to Chancellor Brüning
> RM 120,000—to Schleicher (July)
> RM 30,000—to Hugenberg (July)
> RM 100,000—to von Papen (October)

RM 100,000—to the Democratic and Social Democratic
        Parties
RM   50,000—to the moderate parties of the Center
RM   50,000—to the National Socialist Party
RM 1,500,000—Total contributions[28]

Flick, like Vögler, who was a member of the Keppler Circle, supported the Nazis. He did so in the apparent hope of saving his companies from disaster by a policy of lowering wages, getting government orders, and sponsoring general rearmament. As early as February 1932, he had had his first interview with Hitler, through the initiative of Walther Funk. The meeting, however, was not an immediate success. Hitler overwhelmed his visitor in a torrent of words which prevented Flick from saying what he wanted. Moreover, at the time Hitler was hardly able to make definite promises on a policy that would save the steel industry from ruin. Flick naturally preferred to deal with the established government, but when the public found out about his transactions, he again needed Nazi help. In consideration of the fact that von Papen controlled only a small minority in the Reichstag, Flick and his associates involved in the Gelsenkirchen scandal could not hope to survive the wave of popular criticism unless they could work out some sort of understanding with the National Socialists. At his Nuremberg trial Flick vigorously denied that his donations to the Nazis indicated he was in any way sympathetic to their cause.[29] He contended that the figures alone explained his political sympathies:

The moderate parties received 81.8 percent of his money:

RM 950,000—to the presidential election campaign
RM 150,000—to Brüning and other moderate parties
RM 120,000—to Schleicher
RM 1,220,000 = 81.8%

The parties of the Right received 8.7 percent:

RM   30,000—to Hugenberg
RM 100,000—to von Papen
RM 130,000 = 8.7%

The Democrats and Social Democrats (Flick considered them

"parties of the Left") received 6.7 percent:

RM 100,000 = 6.7%

The National Socialist Party received 2.8 percent:

RM   50,000 = 2.8%[30]

The fact that the Brüning cabinet which concluded the Gelsenkirchen deal received over RM 1,000,000 in contributions from Flick, most of it for the Hindenburg reelection fund, shows how far things had gone in the Weimar Republic. Unable to hold their own in the depression, heavy industry and the moderate political parties saved their economic and political existence by helping themselves to the taxpayers' money. Hitler's attacks against the "corrupt system of political democracy" and "monopoly capitalism" found a receptive audience in such an environment.

Using a weapon from the political arsenal of democracy, the Nazis sent Hermann Göring to see Flick. As a member of the Reichstag, Göring was ostensibly performing his duty in investigating the Gelsenkirchen case. Hitler's choice of an emissary could not have been better. Göring, with his good background, aristocratic manners, jovial humor, and keen intellect was the right man to work with the industrialists. Although Flick had not liked Hitler, he and Göring agreed with each other from the start. After several days of discussions, Göring and Hitler both gave their approval to the Gelsenkirchen deal. According to Flick, one of Hitler's main reasons for going along with the transaction was because Emil Kirdorf, the founder of the Gelsenkirchen, was still one of the two chairmen of its board of trustees, the other being Albert Vögler. Of course, Hitler's interests in Kirdorf and Vögler was not just sentimental. By protecting the country's largest steel cartel, he could count on a certain amount of political and financial cooperation from them. After Gelsenkirchen was taken over by the government, Thyssen, Vögler, Flick, and the other leading men of United Steel were more determined than ever to see that the cabinet remained in the hands of nonsocialist forces so the Reich's control of this stock could not be used for socialist purposes.

On a sunny October afternoon just before the opening of the November election campaign, Hitler's caravan of three big Mercedes convertibles left Munich for Potsdam where a Nazi Youth rally was to take place. Hitler rode in the first car, wearing a long leather coat, leather aviator's helmet, and motoring goggles. Even though he never took the wheel himself, Hitler had a passion for speed and always sat in front next to his chauffeur. The second car was filled with the Führer's eight S.S. bodyguards who, with their black uniforms, leather aviator's helmets, goggles, revolvers, and sjamboks-whips, were described by one witness as looking like men from Mars.

After spending the night in a small Bavarian inn, they were on the road early the next morning and by 4:00 P.M. entered Brandenburg and began passing trucks full of Hitler Youth who were overjoyed at the sight of their Führer. About eight o'clock they reached the outskirts of Potsdam where they were met by Baldur von Schirach, the Nazi Youth leader, and his staff in two big cars. The procession of five cars then continued into the city, which looked as though an Army had occupied it. Tents and trucks were everywhere. Children from fourteen to eighteen wearing the Hitler Youth uniform were seen on all sides. Near the Potsdam stadium the human mass became so dense that both the police and the S.S. had all they could do just to get Hitler's convoy of cars through.

The stadium was lit with thousands of torches. Massed units of boys and girls stood in formation on the field surrounded by a vast ring of humanity. Hitler mounted the platform and was saluted by Schirach who made his official report to the Führer—some 64,000 boys and 15,000 girls present and accounted for. Hitler stood alone on the platform now, still wiping the road dust from his eyes and a fantastic roar of jubilant cheers rose up into the night. Then he raised his arms and dead silence fell over the stadium. He burst into a flaming speech which lasted only about fifteen minutes, but for that short time his oratory was "fiery, spontaneous, and full of appeal." Then, again, the roar of applause and cheers.

Immediately after the speech, Hitler and his staff went on into Berlin where they were to have dinner with Prince August Wilhelm, the son of the Kaiser. The Prince, who had joined the Nazis several years before, had become a Reichstag deputy and a brigadier general in the S.A. Considering that Hitler used to be uneasy in the company of the upper class, it was interesting to observe his manner with the Prince. He was courteous, addressed him as "Royal Highness," but was absolutely poised. The Prince, who was wearing his S.A. uniform, was exceptionally respectful but equally at ease, even when his elbow knocked a wine glass to the floor.

Hitler was distressed when the Prince, who had a villa in Potsdam, told him of the difficulties the rally had created. The two had been prepared to take care of 40,000 children at the most, but twice that number had arrived and thousands of them had been on the road for days.

"What are we going to do?" asked Hitler, in a worried tone. "Those thousands of children mustn't sleep under the open sky."

"I've taken fifty-five into my house—impossible to take more," replied the Prince equally troubled. "Perhaps we could make a house-to-house canvass."[31]

Hitler was so concerned that after dinner he drove out to Potsdam again at midnight and did not return until he was sure that everything possible was being done for the comfort of the children. However, in spite of this, thousands of them had to sleep in the open, which was no joke in October. The Führer didn't get to bed until well after four, but by seven he was back again in Potsdam, walking around trying to inspire the cold and weary children.

Some consider it to be a revelation of the human side of Hitler's character, that he "fussed with anxiety" about the sleeping arrangements of the Nazi Youth, and that "his face glowed like that of a proud parent and tears came to his eyes as he looked at them."[32] However, every great leader is genuinely concerned about the fate of his followers, just as the good mechanic takes care of his tools. This is not to say that Hitler had no human feeling for his men, because he certainly did consider them as his comrades, partners in his struggle. But this is a part of the function of any charismatic leader: he must have a true understanding and sympathy for his adherents.

By eleven o'clock the next day, the morning mist with its chill was gone and a warm breeze was blowing at Potsdam. The great review, the climactic moment for which thousands of children had endured days of hardships, finally began. From out of the forest behind the stadium there came marching a steady column of brown-shirted Hitler Youth. For several hours they marched on, children from every part of Germany, even from Austria, Bohemia, Memel, and Danzig, with their thousands of banners fluttering in the light breeze.

When one strong teen-ager came marching at the head of his section, carrying his five-year-old brother on his shoulders, a storm of applause rang through the air. Hitler signaled the two brothers to approach the reviewing stand and shook hands with them. Finally, in the fading sunset, six thousand black-uniformed S.S. men drilled past in a parade march that the old Imperial Guard would have envied, and the rally was over. "Its propaganda value," said one Nazi, "would be incalculable. No spectator could escape its pull. There was no longer the slightest doubt in my mind that, whatever the political setbacks ahead, the Führer would triumph."

The great enthusiasm shown at the Potsdam rally was an indication that in spite of setbacks the Party members would remain loyal to Hitler. But what about the masses of uncommitted voters who had cast their ballots for the Nazis in July? Would they do the same in the coming election on November 6? It was not likely, for the average German was tired of elections and the unending political disputes. Realizing that this campaign would be the most difficult of all, Dr. Goebbels wrote on September 16: "Now we are in for elections again! One sometimes feels this sort of thing is going on for ever. . . . Our adversaries count on our losing morale, and getting fagged out."[33]

Underlying all the difficulties the Nazis were encountering was the fact that economic conditions were beginning to improve. The bottom of the depression had been hit in the summer and early fall of 1932; by late fall the recovery had begun. There were a growing number of optimistic predictions which were seen to have some basis in reality, because industries were reporting more orders and more work to do. The number of unemployed, which had been well over 6 million during the winter of 1931–1932 had declined to 5,100,000 in the autumn. Meanwhile, the burden of international political debts had practically vanished. It was now clear that France would not resort to force or other restrictive measures in an attempt to collect reparation payments. It was no coincidence that the first signs of confidence and recovery appeared just at the same time as the first signs of Hitler's decline.

In addition to the problem of maintaining its hold on the electorate, the Party itself was in deep financial difficulties. Big business and banking interests were now backing von Papen, who had given them certain concessions. As Schacht had warned, the upper classes were becoming increasingly distrustful of Hitler because of his refusal to cooperate with Hindenburg and his voting with the Communists to embarrass Papen. Instead of moderating their position, the Nazis replied to the conservatives' criticism by ever more violent attacks on the "Government of Reaction." The results could have been expected. In the middle of October, Goebbels complained in the privacy of his diary: "Money is extraordinarily difficult to obtain. All gentlemen of 'Property and Education' are standing by the Government."[34]

Chancellor von Papen, however, had problems of his own. Throughout the summer and fall of 1932, difficulties for the Papen government had continually mounted. As long as no one had been quite sure what the government intended to do, the success of this small group of aristocratic conspirators had been phenomenal. Even the Social Democrats had felt a certain relief when the Papen cabinet had shown that it intended to oppose Hitler's advance to power. Consequently, for a time the opposition of the Social Democrats against von Papen had been more formal than real. But after the takeover of the Prussian government, the Social Democrats became seriously alarmed and began a series of bitter attacks against the cabinet in their press. Their anger increased as more and more government officials who were Social Democrats were dismissed and their places filled with conservative Nationalists. Added to the popular opposition against the Papen cabinet that was now developing on every side, the industrialists withdrew their support of von Papen and began to exert their influence against him.

Why did the industrialists choose this time to oppose the head of a conservative government? The fact that the small band of von Papen's conspirators could halt Hitler's sweep to power had been considered almost impossible prior to the event. But after it had actually been done without the Nazis offering any armed resistance, German businessmen breathed easily again and soon began to think that it had only been a nightmare after all. Consequently they felt that it was no longer necessary to support the Papen government unless it demonstrated its willingness to give proper consideration to the interests of industry.

The Papen cabinet, on the other hand, primarily had the interests of agriculture at heart. To a certain extent this was because the principal party support for the government came from the Nationalists, who by now were largely a Junker, agrarian party. In addition, the von Papen cabinet thought of itself as the government which would be controlling Germany's destiny for a long time, and in view of the desperate conditions of the depression, it was determined that a policy which would have some permanent effect upon the economy should be taken. The Papen government decided that a fundamental step in this direction would be to secure the home market almost exclusively for the produce of German agriculture. Therefore, a policy of quotas was introduced in order to restrict the importation of agricultural products. Almost immediately other countries began to retaliate against German manufactured goods. The industrialists reacted at once and began a strong opposition against the government's quota policy.

Not only did the industrialists oppose the government's foreign trade policy but they also began to view von Papen's plans for constitutional "reform" with suspicion. Unlike light industry which was opposed to the reactionary nature of the "reforms," heavy industry had no objection to the "reforms" as such and might even have favored them, if they had appeared to be attainable. However, the heavy industrialists realized that the Papen government was not strong enough to push through such comprehensive changes without arousing determined resistance from the masses and perhaps even civil war. German businessmen, like businessmen of every nationality, feared internal disorder, because it would interrupt commerce and trade. Accordingly, they viewed the plans of the Papen government as dangerous and impractical.

A few days before the election, the streetcars and subways in Berlin came to a stop when the transportation workers went out on strike. For once, the Nazis were forced to demonstrate the sincerity of their campaign against "reaction." The strike was caused by the Papen government cutting the workers' wages as an "emergency measure" necessitated by the depression. The trade unions and the Social Democrats disavowed the strike because they had agreed to go along with the government's measures of "economizing." However, the strike was supported by the Communists, and to everyone's surprise the Nazis joined them in backing the workers. This caused a further drying up of financial contributions from business interests, just when the Nazis needed funds most in order to bring the campaign to a whirlwind finish.

It looked as if many of the Party's most reliable financial supporters were about to drop away. Some of them had gone back to the Nationalists and others like Fritz Thyssen were having money problems of their own. In early November, Thyssen told Hitler that his ability to contribute to the Party was almost at an end. He would buy one more carload of political pamphlets for the *Völkischer Beobachter*, but after that they could no longer count on him. Even Adolf Müller, the printer of the *Völkischer Beobachter*, threatened to stop his presses unless he was paid at least some of the money the Nazis owed him. Hitler tried to pacify Müller and considered his good favor almost as important as Hindenburg's. Once in a while he would lose his temper and shout, but the printer was partially deaf, so it made no difference. In his calm, good-natured way, Müller would explain to Hitler that the *Völkischer Beobachter* was ruining him; he was able to make ends meet only because he was doing a good business printing literature for the Catholic Church. Even though Müller himself was not a Nazi but a member of the Catholic Bavarian People's Party, he always reluctantly agreed to go along with Hitler "until next month," because the Nazi orders were too big to lose, even if they weren't paid on time.

On November 2, Goebbels wrote: "Scarcity of money has become chronic in this campaign. We lack the amount necessary for carrying it through efficiently. The strike is grist for the mill of the bourgeois press. They are exploiting it against us freely. Many of our staunch partisans, even, are beginning to have their doubts. But in spite of that we must hold firm. . . . Middle-class people are being scared away from us on account of our participating in it. But this is only temporary. They are easily to be regained; but once the worker is lost, he is lost for ever."[35]

Further explaining the reasons for the Party's course of action, Goebbels wrote: "The entire press is furious with us and calls it

Bolshevism; but as a matter of fact we had no option. If we had held ourselves aloof from this strike . . . our position among the working classes would have been shaken. Here a great occasion offers once again for demonstrating to the public . . . that the line of action we have taken up in politics is dictated by a true sympathy with the people, and for this reason the National Socialist Party purposely eschews the old bourgeois methods."[36]

In an effort to publicize the Nazis' support of the strike, Goebbels pulled some tricks which certainly went beyond "the old bourgeois methods." He ordered some of his Brownshirts to dress as workers and put them to "work" on the streetcar tracks. Other Nazis also disguised as workers stood along the sidewalk threatening them and cursing them as "scabs." Soon the police appeared and drove the hecklers away. Order then prevailed as the "scabs" ripped up the rails under the protection of the police, who were convinced that the work was done under the direction of the transit company.

In contrast to the conservative, procapitalist stance Hitler had taken in his speech to the Industry Club at the beginning of the year, this election campaign conducted against "the clique of nobles" and "the corrupt Junker regime" seemed to indicate that the National Socialists were drifting to the left. Once again Gregor Strasser and his followers had a short period of encouragement. "Against reaction" was the official election slogan given out by Hitler. S.A. bullies began breaking up Nationalist meetings and brawling in the streets with the Stahlhelm. The Party propaganda office secretly issued slogans to be spread by word of mouth to create a mood of panic against von Papen and his cabinet. At mass rallies staged throughout the country, National Socialist speakers denounced the economic policies of the Papen government for favoring the interests of "monopoly capital" against the people.

Although the conservatives accused the Nazis of "Bolshevism," Hitler's economic proposals remained ambiguous as usual. The people must begin to think in terms of "German labor" rather than "the working class," said the Nazi speakers. As they described it, the true idea of socialism was represented by the principle of achievement of the self-sacrificing German civil servant. Slogans such as "an honest living for honest work" had a more persuasive ring than all of Marx's theories put together. In fact, it was the vagueness of the Nazi language that made it so popular and enabled it to find supporters among all classes of the population.

Despite all disadvantages, the heavy industrialists supported the Papen government during the fall Reichstag election campaign, first of all because they could find no better alternative, and second, because they thought they might be able to obtain the changes in policy they wanted by various pressures after the elections. Before the beginning of the campaign, Fritz Springorum, the treasurer of the Ruhrlade, approached the members of the organization individually to raise a fund to back the Papen government. An important change, however, was made with the handling of the money, for it was no longer entrusted to General von Schleicher as in the July campaign. The Ruhrlade had received information from several sources accusing the general of misappropriating some of their contributions in order to purchase for himself a Berlin newspaper, the *Tägliche Rundschau*. When confronted with these accusations after the election, Schleicher vigorously denied them, but the members of the Ruhrlade remained suspicious.[37]

The Nazi leaders were not overly optimistic about the outcome of the election. In this fifth campaign of the year, their propaganda encountered a mood of stubborn apathy and indifference on the part of the people. Hitler campaigned hard, waging an uphill fight. Once again he used an airplane and spoke in forty-nine cities in a period of less than four weeks. November 5 was the last day of the election campaign; that evening Goebbels wrote in his diary: "Last attack. Desperate drive of the Party against defeat. . . . We succeed in obtaining ten thousand marks at the very last moment. These are to be thrown into the campaign on Saturday afternoon. We have done all possible. Now let fate decide!"[38]

The German people went to the polls on November 6; that night the results were announced. It was a severe setback for the Nazis, who lost two million of the 13,745,000 votes they had received in July. Their deputies in the Reichstag were reduced from 230 out of 608, to 196 out of 584, though they remained the largest party in the country. The Communists gained almost a million votes and the Social Democrats lost about the same number; thus the Communists increased their seats from 89 to 100, while the

Social Democrats fell from 133 to 121. The only party in the election which supported the Papen government, the Nationalists, had their first success in years and increased their seats from 37 to 52.

The reasons for the Nazis' defeat were twofold and seemingly contradictory. On the one hand, those who recognized the signs of economic improvement left the National Socialists and went back to the Nationalist Party. These individuals, mostly members of the middle and upper classes, saw von Papen as the first Chancellor who was unafraid to come to grips with the depression by cutting wages and instituting a voluntary labor service. But on the other hand, there were the unemployed and impoverished who had not yet noticed even the slightest improvement in the living conditions. What did it matter to them if factories were reporting a *few* more orders? True, industries were beginning to hire a few more workers but this was little consolation to those who were still unemployed. Many of the most desperate felt they had gotten nowhere by supporting the Nazis, so they were willing to give the Communists a try.

It was the corresponding success of the Communists that made the defeat of the Nazis particularly significant. It indicated that Hitler was beginning to lose his hold on the wave of discontent and revolt which had so far carried him forward. Looking for a truly revolutionary party, the disillusioned supporters of the Nazis and Social Democrats were turning to the Communists in large numbers. Although von Papen was jubilant with what he considered to be "his" victory over the National Socialists, many other upper-class Germans were asking themselves, How long can Hitler hold the allegiance of the masses? How long would it be before more of the unemployed and destitute turned to the Communists?

For the first time the legend of Nazi invincibility had been shattered; its spell was broken. Papen was convinced that their fall would be as rapid as their rise. He thought Hitler was in a much weaker position to bargain for power than he had been in July. In fact, if the Nazis wanted any consideration from his government at all, they had better come to terms before their votes dwindled still further. Feeling that he could at last force Hitler to accept his conditions, von Papen put aside his "personal distaste" for the Nazi leader and on November 13 wrote him a letter inviting him to bury their differences and renew negotiations. However, the Chancellor was a bit shocked when on November 16 he received a reply from Hitler that could only be considered an open rebuff. This time the Nazis were sitting tight. Hitler demanded several conditions for the renewal of negotiations, the first of which was that all agreements would be put down in writing, so that there could be no "misunderstanding" this time about what was said. With this, von Papen rashly abandoned all further efforts of reaching a compromise with "the Nazi upstart."

Papen, who was perfectly willing to plunge Germany into another election in order to bring the Nazis to their knees, encountered unexpected opposition in his own cabinet, from his friend and sponsor General von Schleicher. The clever General was irritated by von Papen's attitude of increasing independence and the close relationship he had established with the old President. In addition, he was alarmed by the Chancellor's personal quarrel with Hitler, especially since he seemed determined to force it to the limit. This was becoming an obstacle to obtaining a coalition of "patriotic" forces which, in Schleicher's view, had been the only reason for making von Papen Chancellor in the first place. Meanwhile, von Papen had some new ideas of his own and was beginning to talk about governing by authoritarian methods, if Hitler refused to come to his senses.

Reflecting on the ominous increase in the Communist vote and the willingness of most Nazis to support such a radical cause as the Berlin transportation workers' strike, General von Schleicher was worried. He was more afraid than ever of the possibility of a simultaneous uprising of the Nazis and the Communists. Papen, like Brüning before him, was becoming more of a hindrance than an asset to the General's plan of bringing the Nazis into the government.

The industrialists were not at all impressed by the small degree of support which the Papen cabinet had attracted among the voters. Heavy industry consequently withdrew its backing from von Papen and once again began to oppose the government's foreign trade policies. Light industry, on the other hand, which had never supported the Papen government in the first place, changed from merely attacking the cabinet's tariff and quota policy to mounting a full scale campaign to force von Papen out of office.[39]

Soon after von Papen's failure to bring Hitler into the cabinet, it became obvious that light industry, led by the big chemical, electrical, and exporting firms, was supporting the candidacy of Schleicher for the Chancellorship, while the Junker agrarian interests continued to back von Papen. The heavy industrialists were in a predicament; liking neither Schleicher nor von Papen and having no alternative candidate of their own, they, for the most part, remained neutral.

Why had Schleicher suddenly emerged as a candidate? Certainly the General had had his own ideas for a long time about solving Germany's political and economic problems, but in the past he had preferred to remain as the *éminence gris* manipulating from the background. Now, however, he saw in the weakened position of the Nazis an opportunity to destroy them by a strategy of divide and conquer. It seemed to him that the effect of the election setback upon the Nazi leaders would be to strengthen the position of those who supported Gregor Strasser and would be willing to enter a coalition cabinet.

The light industrialists were so adamantly against von Papen's policy of quotas which were destroying the German export business that they began to look for a possible candidate for Chancellor. General von Schleicher seemed to be the right man; he was in a powerful position and his plans for coping with the political and economic crisis seemed to be compatible. As the intrigue behind the scenes developed, it became apparent that the backers of Schleicher desired a compromise cabinet which would rule with dictatorial powers, but which would attempt to work out an accord with the trade unions and even the Social Democrats. It was hoped that Schleicher's military background would guarantee him the unquestioned loyalty of the Reichswehr, and rally to his support all who were interested in protecting public order. Schleicher let it be known that he favored a foreign trade policy which was very similar to that desired by the light industrialists, and that as soon as he was in office the policy of import quotas would be abandoned. In contrast, those who favored a cabinet led by von Papen wanted an authoritarian government which would not compromise with the trade unions, Social Democrats, or export industries. A Papen cabinet would mean an agrarian, Junker, no-compromise cabinet.

Papen was urged to resign, in order to break the political

deadlock. Confident that Hindenburg could not reach a compromise with Hitler, von Papen cleverly swallowed his anger and resigned on November 17, feeling sure that his friend the old President would soon reappoint him. President von Hindenburg immediately sent for Hitler, who had not expected to be called to Berlin so quickly. He wanted Göring to accompany him when he saw the President, but Göring and Rosenberg had gone to Italy to attend a European congress of the Roman Academy of Sciences. As soon as Göring received the news, he rushed back to Berlin by plane in less than six hours.

On the morning of the nineteenth, Göring went to see State Secretary Meissner to negotiate a proper reception for his Führer. When Hitler arrived for his appointment with President Hindenburg, he found the old Field Marshal much more cordial than he had been on August 13.

The President received Hitler in his study. The room, which reflected a somber Prussian atmosphere, usually awed most visitors. War pictures hung along the walls: "Schwering's Death at Prague," a portrait of the Iron Chancellor, and one of Frederick the Great. There were heavy dark tapestries, and heavy dark furniture. By the window was a bulky, carved writing desk. Across the room in a corner were deep leather armchairs and a low round table. In his deep voice Hindenburg told Hitler to sit down, and motioned to a chair. The two men sat down and talked for over an hour. This time Hitler succeeded in arousing the President's interest.

Later Hitler described the meeting to some of his close associates: "Hindenburg said to me: 'Herr Hitler, I wish to hear from your own mouth a summary of your ideas.' It is almost impossible, across such a gap, to communicate to others one's own conception of the world. I tried to establish contact with the Field Marshal by having recourse to comparisons of a military nature. Connection was fairly rapidly made with the soldier, but the difficulty began the instant there was a question of extending our drawing comprehension to politics. When I'd finished my summary, I felt that I'd moved Hindenburg and that he was yielding. At once he made this a pretext for reproaching me with an incident that had occurred in East Prussia: 'But your young people have no right to behave as they do. Not long ago, at Tannenberg, they shouted out, so that I could hear: Wake up, wake up! And yet I'm not asleep!' Certain uncharitable souls had given the old gentleman to suppose that the shout was meant for him personally, whereas in reality our supporters were shouting 'Wake up, Germany!'"[40]

After a long general conversation, Hindenburg got down to business and offered Hitler the Chancellorship if he could obtain a working majority in the Reichstag. On the surface this seemed like a fair offer but it was impossible for Hitler to accomplish. The Center Party had agreed to support him, on the condition that he not attempt to establish a dictatorship, but Hitler still could not obtain a workable majority because the Nationalists refused to cooperate. Besides, Hitler really did not want to be a parliamentary Chancellor anyway, limited by shifting coalitions; so he renewed his demands for the same powers Hindenburg had given to von Papen. The old President, however, refused to appoint the leader of a "radical" party as a presidential Chancellor. If Germany had to be governed by decree, there would be no point in replacing his friend von Papen. Once again Hitler's policy of legality had led him to a cul-de-sac.

Hitler's interview with the President went exactly as von Papen thought it would. He fully expected to be reappointed Chancellor when he and Schleicher would officially call on Hindenburg on December 1. Meanwhile Schleicher was maneuvering behind von Papen's back. The General had been in contact with Strasser, proposing that the Nazis join a coalition cabinet. In this cabinet, Schleicher rather than von Papen would be the Chancellor.

Some historians have thought that von Papen was unaware of Schleicher's "betrayal."[41] If the intrigues had been based merely on personal rivalry, this might have been so, but actually von Papen was well aware that he and Schleicher represented different social and economic interest groups and was expecting competition from the General. However, he was still not able to determine exactly what Schleicher was planning.

Although von Papen officially resigned on November 17 in order to facilitate President von Hindenburg's negotiations with Hitler, in fact he continued as acting Chancellor. During this interim period of "cabinet crisis" which lasted from November 18 to December 2, the wildest rumors circulated in the press. The morning newspapers would report that a Schleicher cabinet had been decided upon, while the midday papers would state that von

Papen was certain to resume office, only to be followed by a report in the evening papers that Schleicher was bound to be the next Chancellor. Naturally the newspapers owned or controlled by interests affiliated with light industry were instrumental in circulating notorious reports which undermined von Papen and pointed to Schleicher as the better alternative. Of course, von Papen was not without his advocates too, especially among the conservative and reactionary sections of the press.

In Berlin, on the evening of December 1, von Papen and Schleicher went together to make their official call on President von Hindenburg. Papen confidently proposed his program for the future: He would resume office as Chancellor, adjourn the Reichstag indefinitely, and "amend" the constitution to reestablish the rule of the conservative classes, as in the days of the empire. While his "reforms" were being carried out he would declare a state of emergency, govern by decree, and if necessary use force to suppress any opposition. He assured Hindenburg, in the most solemn tone, that he was justified in considering the welfare of the nation before his oath to the constitution, as Bismarck had once done, "for the sake of the Fatherland."

Schleicher then interrupted with objections. The General, who was well aware of Hindenburg's reluctance to violate his oath to the constitution, stressed that the actions proposed by von Papen were unconstitutional. And since von Papen was unpopular with the vast majority of the people, as had been seen in the past two elections, such "reforms" would place the government in a difficult position in case of civil war. There was no excuse for such drastic action, Schleicher argued, if it could be avoided— and he was sure it could be. He was convinced that if he himself were to head a cabinet it could secure a majority in the Reichstag. Briefly, the General outlined his plan: He would win over Strasser and at least fifty Nazi deputies from Hitler, he could count on the moderate bourgeois parties and, with a little persuasion, on the Social Democrats.

Schleicher thought the old President would have no choice but to accept his plan, because in the last few days many prominent industrialists and important trade-union leaders had called on Hindenburg urging him not to reappoint von Papen. But the influence of big business meant nothing to the old Field Marshal. This was one of the crucial imbalances in the Weimar government. Hindenburg, who now had the only real power left in the state, had absolutely no realization of the importance of economic issues.[42]

The aged President sat in silent amazement for a few seconds and then, as if nothing the General said had registered with him, he turned to von Papen asking him to go ahead and form a new government. Schleicher was dumbfounded; for the first time the old man had disregarded his "advice." A heated argument developed between Schleicher and von Papen and continued after they had left the President. On parting, the General looked at von Papen, then in the famous words addressed to Luther as he left for the Diet of Worms, said: "Little Monk, you have chosen a difficult path."[43]

Papen thought he had been victorious until the cabinet met the next morning. Then General von Schleicher in his capacity as Defense Minister declared that the Army no longer had confidence in von Papen. The Army, he said, was not prepared to take the risk of a civil war, against both the Nazis and the Communists at the same time, which von Papen's policy might cause. To support his case, the General called in Colonel Ott, who had made a strategic study for the General Staff on the possible outcome of a civil war. Ott assured the cabinet that the Army and the police were not strong enough to suppress a simultaneous Nazi and Communist uprising, and at the same time protect the nation from a foreign invader. Therefore, it was the "recommendation" of the Army that the government not declare a state of emergency.

Papen was finished; there was nothing he could say. As a last chance he hurried to Hindenburg with the news, hoping that he might convince him to dismiss Schleicher. The old President was deeply stirred by von Papen's report. He asked "his" Chancellor not to think ill of him, but went on: "I am an old man, and I cannot face a civil war. . . . If General von Schleicher is of this opinion, then I must—much as I regret it—withdraw the task with which I charged you last night."[44]

On December 3, 1932, the press and stock exchange received the news of the formation of the Schleicher government with great satisfaction. In his maiden speech, delivered over the radio, the new Chancellor said that he was neither a capitalist nor a socialist and repudiated the rumors that he intended to set up a dictatorship. The General made it clear that he had no intention of carrying out any plan of constitutional reform, but instead intended to devote all his energies to the pressing problem of unemployment. The speech had a most favorable reception after the severe lectures from von Papen.[45] For a moment Germany breathed easier. The long awaited "strong man" had stepped from behind the scenes to take up the reins of power.

Schleicher's intrigues and maneuvers, which had brought about the dismissal of Müller, Gröner, Brüning, and most recently von Papen, had finally brought him to the Chancellorship. Although he preferred to conceal his manipulations, he was now forced to come out in the open and assume personal responsibility for his plans, even if they failed. The "General Chancellor" was immediately confronted with two problems: He could not get von Papen out of the way completely and he had lost the trust of the President. Schleicher offered to make the ex-Chancellor ambassador in Paris, but von Papen declined. President Hindenburg, said Papen, had asked that he stay in Berlin "within reach." Berlin was the best place to plot intrigues against the new Chancellor whose influence over the President, which he had used heavily in the past, was destroyed. The old Field Marshal had tolerated the maneuvers which led to the dismissal of Gröner and Brüning, but he could neither forget nor forgive the "shameful" way Schleicher got rid of von Papen.

All his intrigues notwithstanding, Schleicher was a very intelligent man. Of the men around the President, he was the only one who had any idea of the real seriousness of the economic and social crisis which had plagued Germany since 1929. Unlike von Papen, he did not allow class prejudices to cloud his thinking and was not foolish enough to believe that a "strong" government in itself would remedy the crisis. From 1930 on, Schleicher had correctly estimated the strength of the extremist appeals made by the Nazis and Communists. His objective, which he consistently pursued for three years, was to harness the dynamic energy of the National Socialists by bringing them into the service of the state.

Two factors were in the Chancellor's favor: the series of reverses from which the Nazis had been suffering, and the strong desire of all political parties to avoid another repetition of the general elections which had already convulsed the country five times in less than a year and from which, it was generally realized, the Communists alone stood to gain. In his political armory Schleicher had but one weapon, that of attempting to divide the parties from within by intrigue. He now employed this weapon on the Nazis and concentrated his energies more than ever on the negotiations with Gregor Strasser.

The situation, however, was not really as difficult for Schleicher as it might have seemed, for the forces of light industry were backing him.[46] Even heavy industry had not committed itself to opposing the cabinet. In fact, Schleicher succeeded to the last in keeping the support of the eleven Reichstag deputies of the German People's Party, the party of the heavy industrialists. True, they supported the Schleicher government more because it had abandoned von Papen's policy of import quotas on agricultural products than out of any loyalty to the Chancellor, but they supported it nevertheless.

For some time General von Schleicher had been working on an agreement with Gregor Strasser, the most popular Nazi leader next to Hitler. In these years of poverty and economic uncertainty, it was Strasser's anticapitalist radicalism that won millions of working-class votes for the Nazis. As head of the Party organization, he was in direct contact with the local branches and thus realized more than anyone else the feeling of disillusionment spreading through the movement. He was particularly worried because the more radical Nazis were going over to the Communists. In addition, the Party was practically bankrupt.[47] There simply was no money to pay the salaries of thousands of party officials or to maintain the S.A. Even Goebbels had admitted as much in his diary on November 11: "Received a report on the financial situation of the Berlin organization. It is hopeless. Nothing but debts and obligations, together with the complete impossibility of obtaining any reasonable sum of money after this defeat [November 6 elections]."[48] Strasser was convinced that the only way to save the Party from immediate collapse was to make a compromise and get into power, even if as part of a coalition. He believed Hitler's "all or nothing" demand for the Chancellorship was destroying any possible benefits of the policy of legality.

The day after he was appointed Chancellor, Schleicher met with Strasser, asking him to enter his cabinet as Vice-Chancellor and president of Prussia. If Strasser wished, he could administer Schleicher's great reemployment project, the "voluntary labor service." He could put the S.A. in charge of the labor service and burden the government treasury with its debts and expenses. To be sure, he would have to cooperate with the Social Democratic unions, but Strasser was already respected by many socialist leaders so an understanding was not inconceivable.

Offering the Vice-Chancellorship to an important National Socialist was a clever move on Schleicher's part. Not only was the idea attractive to Strasser as a way out of the Party's difficulties, but it would almost certainly cause a split between the Nazi leaders. If Hitler persisted in his refusal to cooperate with the government, Strasser might enter the cabinet bringing about one-third of the Party with him. On the evening of December 3, several hours after Schleicher's conference with Strasser, the results of the Thuringian state elections came in, showing nearly a 40 percent decline in the Nazi vote since July. This added a new sense of urgency to Schleicher's offer, in order to avoid more elections at all costs.

Although there is no existing record of Paul Silverberg having played any direct part in Schleicher's negotiations with Strasser, it looked as if his plan of splitting the Nazi Party from within was about to be accomplished. The liberal-minded industrialist Otto Wolff of Cologne, who was a friend and business associate of Silverberg, was known to be in almost daily contact with Schleicher at this time. Like Silverberg, Wolff had contributed heavily to Strasser because he too saw him as the one Nazi leader with whom it might be possible to compromise. Just how much Strasser's great power in the Nazi Party was due to the subsidies of the moderate industrialists is difficult to say. Certainly Strasser was an able leader in his own right and it was only natural that his socialistic economic philosophy would have great appeal during the depression, but extra money could only have helped, not hurt.

On December 5, the Party leaders and Nazi Reichstag deputies met at the Kaiserhof in Berlin. Strasser demanded that the Nazis at least "tolerate" the Schleicher government and he was supported by Frick, the head of the Nazi block in the Reichstag. More and more of the unexpressed sentiment in the Party was gathering behind Strasser. Göring and Goebbels argued against compromise and Hitler stated that their point of view was correct. He would not "tolerate" the Schleicher cabinet; however, he was ready to "negotiate" with it. But for this task he appointed Göring, not Strasser whom he felt had already gone behind his back. Then, in an attempt to inspire his Reichstag deputies with courage, Hitler delivered a short speech in which he tried to minimize the defeat in the Thuringian elections. But everyone realized how serious the situation really was. Continuing, Hitler insisted that no great movement had ever achieved victory by taking the road of compromise. As the showdown drew near, the sacrifices must become greater. "Only one thing is decisive," he said: "Who in this struggle is capable of the last effort, who can put the last battalion in the field." However, for Reichstag deputies afraid that they themselves would be the first sacrificed in the next election, this was little consolation.

Did the thousands of Party officials possess the moral courage to struggle on in desperate opposition if Strasser's plan offered them the opportunity of becoming ministers, mayors, provincial officials, police sergeants, or even civilian employees in Army arsenals? Many Nazi leaders thought it would be better to have a share of government posts, some access to the state treasury, and some relief from the tremendous debts the Party had accumulated rather than nothing at all. Would it not be more reasonable to accept Schleicher's bribe, they asked?

Hitler and Strasser had another discussion on December 7 at the Kaiserhof, but without the restraints of a large audience this time. In the course of the conversation Hitler bitterly accused Strasser of betrayal, of going behind his back, and of trying to oust him from the leadership of the Party. Strasser angrily replied that he had been loyal and was only trying to save the Party from almost certain collapse. The argument ended with mutual threats, reproaches, and accusations of betrayal.

Overflowing with rage, Strasser returned to his room at the Hotel Excelsior and wrote Hitler a long letter in which he gave vent to the anger and resentment that had been swelling within him since 1925. He accused Hitler of betraying the ideals of the movement, of irresponsibility, personal ambition, and inconsistency in tactics. He ended the letter with his resignation from his position in the Party.

The letter reached Hitler at noon on December 8, with the impact of a bombshell. This was the most serious threat to the

Party's survival since the putsch in 1923. Strasser's revolt threatened to undercut the very base of Hitler's own authority within the Party and left him more deeply shaken than any election setback ever had. That evening Goebbels invited the Führer to his apartment where several of the Nazi leaders sat around brooding. In his diary, Goebbels described the mood that night: "It is difficult to be cheerful. We are all rather downcast, especially in view of the danger of the whole Party's falling to pieces, and of all our work being in vain. We are confronted with the great test. Every movement which desires power must prove itself, and this proving generally comes shortly before the victory, which decides everything. . . . Phone call from Dr. Ley: The situation in the Party is getting worse from hour to hour. The Führer must immediately return to the Kaiserhof."[49]

At two o'clock in the morning Goebbels was called to join Hitler at the Kaiserhof. It seemed that Strasser had given his story to the morning newspapers, which were just beginning to appear on the streets. Röhm and Himmler were also summoned to join the group at the Kaiserhof where everyone was "dumbfounded" that Strasser had actually given his story to the papers, although they had been aware that the split was brewing for some time. "Treachery! Treachery!" noted Goebbels. "For hours the Führer paces up and down the room in the hotel. It is obvious that he is thinking very hard. He is embittered and deeply wounded by this unfaithfulness. Suddenly he stops and says: 'If the Party once falls to pieces, I shall shoot myself without more ado.' "[50]

However, Strasser lacked the necessary determination to carry through with the challenge to Hitler's leadership. He was never thorough or Machiavellian enough to plan a mutiny such as Hitler suspected. Just when he might have rallied the prosocialist wing of the Party against Hitler, and perhaps changed the course of history, Strasser gave up. In vain, Frick was driving around Berlin searching for him, in the hope that he might be able to convince him to patch up the dispute with Hitler to save the Party from disaster. But Strasser was nowhere to be found; fed up with it all, he had taken the train south for a vacation in sunny Italy.

With the news of Strasser's disappearance, Hitler recovered his confidence and acted decisively, striking the opposition swift and hard. The powerful office of Party organization which Strasser had formed was broken up, part of the duties being taken over by

Dr. Ley, under the Führer's supervision, the rest being transferred to Goebbels and Hess. Several of Strasser's friends were purged from their positions of authority in the Party, while all the Gauleiters, deputies, and Party leaders were summoned to Berlin to sign a new declaration of loyalty to Adolf Hitler. When Gottfried Feder, one of the coauthors of the original Party program, who sympathized with Strasser's socialist ideas, questioned the purpose of a "declaration of loyalty," he was told to sign or get out. He quickly signed. Using his usual combination of threats and persuasion, Hitler then made a short speech in which he appealed to the loyalty of his old comrades, bringing tears to their eyes. With a sob in his voice, he said that he never could have believed Strasser guilty of such treachery. Julius Streicher stood up and stammered: "Maddening that Strasser could do this to our Führer!" At the end of the meeting, said Goebbels, "the District Leaders and deputies burst into spontaneous ovations for the Führer. All shake hands with him, promising to carry on until the very end. . . . Strasser now is completely isolated, a dead man."[51]

Meanwhile, Chancellor Schleicher continued his efforts to establish a stable government. Even though his plan to attract Strasser had failed for the time being, he was optimistic; the Reichstag had given him a free hand and at last the economy seemed to be improving. On December 15, Schleicher made a "fireside" broadcast to the nation outlining the policy of his government. Asking his listeners to forget that he was a general, he said: "My heretical view is that I am a supporter neither of capitalism nor socialism. For me concepts like private economy or planned economy have lost their terrors." His principal objective, he told them, was to provide work for the unemployed and get the economy going again. There would be no tax increases or further wage cuts. In addition, he would end the agricultural quotas which von Papen had established for the benefit of the large landowners; instead, he was beginning a program to take over 800,000 acres from the bankrupt Junker estates in the east and give them to 25,000 peasant families. The Chancellor concluded with the promise that the government would keep down the prices of such essentials as coal and meat by rigid controls if necessary.

This attempt of Schleicher's to win the support of the masses was unsuccessful. Even after his promises, the Social Democrats and trade-union leaders still mistrusted him and declined to cooperate. The broadcast not only failed to convince the Left, but worse, it stirred up violent opposition among reactionary circles of the Right. Many industrialists were frightened by Schleicher's overtures to the trade unions; however, the Chancellor was to find his most dangerous foe in the East Prussian landowners who denounced his program of land settlement as "agrarian Bolshevism." Though many of their estates were bankrupt, the Junkers were still a powerful force in the German power elite. Their opposition had brought down Brüning; how they would deal with Schleicher remained to be seen.

The leading figures in the German chemical and electrical industry seemed to be standing firm behind Schleicher and opposing the Nazis. Ernst von Borsig of the Borsig machine and locomotive works, Hermann Bücher of the German General Electric Company (A.E.G.), and Robert Bosch, the famous producer of the sparkplug and other electrical goods, were all opponents of Hitler. Even earlier, Carl Friedrich von Siemens, head of the Siemens electrical firm, became aware of the Nazi danger. In 1931, speaking to a group of General Electric executives in New York, he pointed out that Hitler was a threat because he appealed to the patriotism and unselfishness of the Germans. "Too few people realize that Hitler is drawing idealists from all sections of the population to his banner." He left no doubt that industrialists like himself were opposed to Hitler, but that this circumstance should not blind one to the fact of his popularity among the masses.

The chemical industry had a strong liberal tradition. Carl Duisberg, the founder of the giant I.G. Farben chemical trust, and his successor Carl Bosch were both determined anti-Nazis. But even under these two men there were a few directors on the board of I.G. Farben who believed the company should establish some contact with the Nazis. The political activities of the chemical trust were much like those of Flick. From its formation in 1925, the firm gave financial assistance to all political parties with the exception of the Communists and the Nazis.[52] In the late twenties and early thirties, some of the political contributions of the company were made through an intermediary, W. F. Kalle, director of Kalle and Company of Wiesbaden, a subsidiary of I.G. Farben.[53] The annual subsidies given through Kalle were:

RM   200,000—to the German People's Party
RM   30,000—to the German Democratic Party
RM   50,000—to the Center Party
RM   200,000—to local organizations of the German People's
                  Party
RM   50,000—to local organizations of the German Democratic
                  Party
RM   70,000—to the local organizations of the Center Party
RM 1,000,000—to the Hindenburg election (1932)[54]

I.G. Farben always prided itself on the fact that none of its executives attended Hitler's famous speech at the Düsseldorf Industry Club. During the critical years of the depression, 1931–1933, I.G. Farben enabled the liberal *Frankfurter Zeitung* to continue operating by covering its large deficit.[55] The directors of the company considered it essential that a newspaper with such importance in the business world and with such outspoken democratic views continue publishing.

However, according to the postwar testimony of one of the executives of I.G. Farben, the National Socialist Party was added to its list of recipients of political subsidies sometime in 1932. Because it was then the depth of the depression, the firm's total contributions to one of the Reichstag election campaigns was only about RM 300,000, of which 10 to 15 percent went to the Nazis.[56] Like Flick, I.G. Farben had a vested interest in keeping on good terms with all political parties. The company had invested heavily in a process to manufacture high-grade synthetic gasoline. The initial production costs were so high that I.G. Farben could hope to enter the domestic market only if there were a protective tariff against imported oil. The Brüning government, which Farben had heavily subsidized, had passed such a tariff and it was later approved by the Papen cabinet, but because of the country's continued political instability the directors of the firm remained anxious about the tariff question. When attacks against I.G. Farben began to appear in the Nazi press in 1932, the company suddenly became concerned about the attitude of the nation's largest political party. Two representatives of the firm were sent to Munich in the fall of 1932 to see Hitler and "to clarify the position of the National Socialist Party regarding the question of German synthetic gasoline production."[57] In return for vague assurances of financial assistance from the company's representatives, Hitler gave an equally vague promise to stop attacks against I.G. Farben in the Party press. However, Hitler did tell his visitors that when a Nazi government came to power he would actively support the production of synthetic gasoline.

Did I.G. Farben thus acquire an economic interest in the installation of a Hitler government? Hardly, for the Papen and Schleicher governments were also willing to maintain a protective tariff on oil imports. I.G. Farben evidently got just what it wanted, an end of attacks against the firm in the Nazi press. In return, the Nazis received a small share of the money given by I.G. Farben to political parties in the November Reichstag elections. Certainly there is no evidence that the chemical trust wanted Hitler to become Chancellor or that it gave a decisive portion of its financial support to the National Socialist Party. There was a diversity of conflicting interests within a huge combine like I.G. Farben, and in spite of the fact that the company wanted a tariff on oil imports, it, like light industry as a whole, was basically dependent on exports. Hence, the directors were very apprehensive at the prospect of the government falling into the hands of a party that preached economic autarky.[58]

In spite of his difficulties, Chancellor Schleicher continued to be confident. In mid-December, one of the nation's leading industrialists made a statement which led investors to think the depression was almost over. "The world economic situation," said Gustav Krupp von Bohlen, "in the money market, shows signs of an improvement; the low point seems definitely past." The improvement of the economy was sufficient reason for optimism, but Schleicher's confidence was also based on a fatal underestimation of his opponents' strength. When Kurt von Schuschnigg, the Austrian Minister of Justice, visited him a few weeks after his broadcast, he assured his guest that "Herr Hitler was no longer a problem, his movement had ceased to be a political danger, and the whole problem had been solved, it was a thing of the past."[59]

Undoubtedly there were some indications that the strength of the Nazis was declining. The Party was seriously short of the funds needed to keep the "state within a State" running. On December 10, Goebbels noted in his diary: "The financial situation of the Berlin district is hopeless. We must institute strict measures of economy, and make it contrive to become self-supporting." And again on December 22: "We must cut down the salaries of our District Leaders, as otherwise we cannot manage to make shift with our finances."[60] The biggest expense on the budget was maintaining the S.A., whose hard core was made up of unemployed men living free in S.A. barracks. The costs were immense. As a last desperate measure to keep the Party going, Hitler sent his Storm Troopers into the streets to beg for money. The S.A. men, many of whom were clad only in their thin brown shirts, stood on street corners shivering in the December wind, rattling their metal cups as an appeal for a few pfennigs from patriotic passers-by. Hitler, Goebbels, Ley, and Göring were speaking several times a day to Party members throughout Germany in a desperate effort to keep up morale, but the future looked dim. At the end of 1932, Goebbels brooded in the privacy of his diary: "The year 1932 has brought us eternal ill luck. . . . the future looks dark and gloomy; all chances and hopes have quite disappeared."[61]

Hitler and Goebbels were not the only ones disturbed by the declining fortunes of the National Socialist Party. Many members of Germany's established power elite, including ex-Chancellor von Papen, were worried to see Hitler's followers deserting to the Communists. Although no longer Chancellor, von Papen remained as Hindenburg's unofficial advisor. The old President had requested that he stay near him; so even though von Papen was now only a private citizen he still retained his apartment in the Chancellery. By coincidence, the adjacent presidential palace was being remodeled that winter and as a result Hindenburg had to move into the Chancellery for a while. Thus, during the crucial months of December and January 1932–1933, Hindenburg and von Papen lived down the hall from each other, and together with the President's son Oskar and State Secretary Meissner they made up a kind of family. It is easy to imagine what the main topic of their conversation on those cold winter evenings must have been: What will we do about the National Socialists? After all, we wanted to use them, not destroy them. Aren't we missing our chance?

However, during the month of December von Papen kept in contact with the Nazis through men like his old Army friend Joachim von Ribbentrop and Wilhelm Keppler, who was known as the Nazi "contact man" in industry. The reason why von Papen sought an understanding with Hitler is not what some sensationalists have tried to make it out to be. His primary motives were not envy of Schleicher, or a desire for revenge against the man who ousted him. With each passing day, Communism was becoming more appealing to the unemployed and impoverished; von Papen wanted to make use of Hitler, soon, while he could still bring the masses into the nationalist camp.

Both Schleicher and von Papen were reasonably intelligent men trying to accomplish definite programs for the best interests of Germany, as they saw them. By the dark winter of 1932 few German politicians sought high office for reasons of personal glory. In fact, everyone shunned responsibility; no one wanted to be held accountable by the hungry masses in the streets. That is why the leaders of the Social Democratic administration in Prussia, weary with failure, had allowed themselves to be ousted from power with an indifference which would have been unthinkable five years before. That was also why Gröner and Brüning abandoned their posts in disgust almost without a word.

After a speech at the exclusive Herrenklub on the evening of December 10, von Papen had a private chat with a fellow member, Baron Kurt von Schröder, the Cologne banker, who was known to be sympathetic to the Nazis. Papen hinted that the financier might try to arrange a secret meeting for him with Hitler.[62] A few days later, Wilhelm Keppler got in touch with Schröder with a similar proposal from Hitler. The date of the meeting was set for January 4, when von Papen would be staying in the Saarland and Hitler would be opening an election campaign in nearby Lippe. Every possible precaution was taken to keep the meeting secret. Accompanied by his staff, Hitler took the night train to Bonn, where he was met by his car the next morning, and proceeded on to Godesberg. After a short stop for breakfast, Hitler, Keppler, Himmler, and Hess changed into an inconspicuous car in which they departed for an unknown destination. The rest of the staff were instructed to drive on to Cologne in Hitler's Mercedes, where they were to wait for him three kilometers the other side of the city on the road to Düsseldorf.

When von Papen arrived at the meeting place, the home of Baron Schröder in Cologne, he was surprised to see a photographer as he went in the gate, but gave it little thought until the next day. After a light lunch, Hitler and von Papen left their aides in the parlor and retired to Schröder's study, where they continued their discussion behind closed doors, witnessed only by their host, the Baron. Papen came quickly to the point: He was interested in the prospects of replacing Schleicher's government with a Nationalist and Nazi coalition in which he and Hitler would be joint Chancellors. But Hitler replied that "if he were made Chancellor it would be necessary for him to be head of the government, but that supporters of Papen could go into his government as ministers when they were willing to go along with him in his policy of changing many things. These changes included elimination of Social Democrats, Communists, and Jews from leading positions in Germany and the restoration of order in public life."[63] Hitler and von Papen reached an agreement in principle, but decided that further details would have to be worked out later.

To the great embarrassment of both participants, their "secret" meeting was reported in the headlines of the Berlin newspapers the next morning. Chancellor Schleicher's agents had followed von Papen; one of them was the photographer who had snapped his picture as he entered Schröder's home. Harsh editorials accused von Papen of trying to undermine the Schleicher government, but the ex-Chancellor denied that the meeting was in any way directed against Schleicher; his main purpose, he claimed, had been to persuade Hitler to enter the Schleicher cabinet. General von Schleicher, of course, was well aware of what was afoot, for as Bismarck would have said: "No story is worth believing until it has been officially denied."

It would be wrong to suppose that a Hitler-Papen government was agreed upon at the Cologne meeting; further negotiations would certainly be needed before von Papen would submit to serving as Hitler's subordinate. However, the first contact had been made; both parties were now desperate and willing to deal with each other. Moreover, Hitler got one thing of the greatest value from the Cologne meeting. Papen, who had been intervening in business circles to cut off financial support from the Nazis, made it clear that he no longer disapproved of large contributions to the National Socialists. But this was not enough for Hitler; the Nazi Party was overburdened with debts and creditors were threatening to foreclose.

Now it was Schröder's turn to enter the discussion. The meeting had not been held at his house simply by chance, as if a wayside cafe would have done just as well. Schröder was an internationally known financier well connected with industry, and known to be a supporter of Hitler.[64] According to Otto Strasser, Schröder then agreed to "foot the bill" for the National Socialist Party.[65]

However, it is not likely the deal was so simple, for that is not the way bankers operate. The evidence seems to indicate that instead of paying the Nazi Party's bills himself, Schröder formed a syndicate of investors who agreed to underwrite the Party's debts.[66] Schröder later said: "When on November 6 the National Socialist Party suffered its first setback and appeared to have passed its peak, the support of German heavy industry became a matter of particular urgency."[67] Most of those whom Schröder got to "invest" their money to cover the debts of the Nazi Party came from heavy industry and big banking circles. The exact identity of all those involved is not known, but a good indication of the kind of people and firms sponsoring the Schröder deal was later revealed by Walther Funk at Nuremberg. He mentioned: Springorum, Tengelmann, Thyssen, Vögler, Kirdorf, Ernest Buskühl and H. G. Knepper of the Gelsenkirchen Mine Company, Heinrich von Stein of the Stein Bank of Cologne, to which Baron Schröder was affiliated, Emil Georg von Stauss of the Deutsche Bank, Otto Christian Fischer of the Reichskredit-Gesellschaft Bank, Friedrich Reinhardt of the Commerz und Privat Bank, Dr. Hilgard of the Allianz Insurance Corporation, August Rosterg and August Diehn of the potash industry, the Hamburg-America Shipping Line, Deutsches Erdöl—Germany's largest petroleum company, the Brabag Coal Company, the Anhaltische Kohlenwerke of the brown coal industry of central Germany, and Dr. Erich Lubbert of the A.G. fur Verkehrswesen and the Baugesellschaft Lenz.[68]

As far as their participation in the Schröder deal to cover the Nazi Party's debt was concerned, the "investors" could later claim that technically they had not contributed to the Nazi Party. Once it was known that Baron Schröder and his syndicate of investors were standing behind the Party's debts, none of the creditors tried to foreclose on Hitler but on the contrary were willing to extend further credit. And once Hitler became Chancellor, the Party had no difficulty paying off its debts from the government treasury. So Schröder and his associates were never actually required to give any of their money to the Nazis; instead they ended up collecting a generous amount of interest on their original capital.[69]

The involvement of major German banks, such as the Deutsche Bank, the Commerz und Privat Bank, and the Reichskredit-Gesellschaft Bank, is of the greatest significance. The Deutsche Bank, for example, was more than an ordinary bank; it possessed extensive influence and control throughout the entire Germany economy. If Hitler could get the Deutsche Bank to use its widespread financial influence on his behalf, his money problems would be over.

There were over four hundred branches of the Deutsche Bank in Germany. The bank directly owned assets valued at three billion dollars, but even this figure gives little indication of its real influence over the nation's finance and industry. Even more significant than the amount of money were the directorships and offices held by the bank's executives and directors in other companies, and the power to represent stockholders at stockholders' meetings that came from having large blocks of shares on deposit from individual investors. Less than fifty executives and directors of the Deutsche Bank held over five hundred positions as directors and officers of other firms; about two hundred of these were chairmanships or vice-chairmanships of boards of directors of other companies.

The strength of the Deutsche Bank came from its combination of deposit banking with investment and management functions, a practice not permitted in the United States. In Germany, where securities of corporations were payable to "the bearer," most stockholders deposited their shares with banks for safekeeping and the banks voted the shares entrusted to them.

The Deutsche Bank had an influential voice in the management of some of Germany's principal firms, including I.G. Farben, Siemens and Halske, Mannesmann Steel, Reemtsma Cigarettes, V.G.F. Rayon, B.M.W., Daimler-Benz, DEMAG—the machinery combine, and Philip Holzmann A.G., the world's largest building firm. Considering the influence of the Deutsche Bank over the latter companies, the political involvement of Mannesmann Steel is particularly interesting.

Two of the key directors of Mannesmann, Wilhelm Zangen and Dr. Niemanns, were supporters of Hitler.[70] Zangen had been a member of the Nazi Party since 1930. He had joined Mannesmann as a representative of the Deutsche Bank, which had controlled the steel firm since 1908. The bank controlled between 50 and 80 percent of the stock and saw to it that executives of the bank were appointed to the board of directors and supervisory positions of Mannesmann subsidiary firms.

Why did the Deutsche Bank have a pro-Nazi like Zangen appointed as its representative in a powerful steel firm like Mannesmann? It was certainly not done by accident. Professor James Martin, an American government investigator who traced Nazi influence in German industry in preparation for the Nuremberg trials, stated: "A member of the board of the Deutsche Bank . . . never joined the board of directors or the management of an industrial concern on a personal whim, as if he were joining a club. The bank directors had to give unanimous consent. Once he took the job, the director was personally responsible for seeing that the policies of the company meshed with the general plans of the bank."[71] Was it then the policy of the Deutsche Bank and firms over which it had a controlling interest, such as Mannesmann, to give their full support to Hitler? No, a certain measure of support perhaps, but full support definitely not.

It was the policy of the giant firms like the Deutsche Bank, Mannesmann, and the Commerz und Privat Bank to be involved in the financial affairs of *all* nonsocialist parties. Up to 1932, the National Socialist Party was generally excluded from these contributions. Since those firms which participated in the Schröder deal were probably never even required to part with any of their capital, their support to the Nazis was insignificant compared to what they gave to the traditional parties. Moreover, it must be remembered that von Papen and Schröder arranged to underwrite the debts of the Nazi Party, not to put them in power, but to save them from bankruptcy so they could be used later. The financial arrangement Baron Schröder worked out for Hitler's Party soon accomplished its primary purpose. Eleven days later, on January 17, Goebbels noted in his diary that "the financial situation has improved all of a sudden."[72]

By meeting with Hitler, von Papen was also thwarting Schleicher's renewed attempts to break up the Nazi Party. The Chancellor's efforts were just then entering a critical phase. Although Hitler had dismissed him from his party posts, Strasser had reentered the political arena. He returned to Berlin on January 3 and Schleicher once again offered him the Vice-Chancellorship. On January 4, the day when von Papen and

Hitler met in Cologne, Strasser had been taken to see the President. Hindenburg was impressed with Strasser's disciplined calm, so different from the tense awkwardness of Hitler. President von Hindenburg indicated that he would welcome Strasser as a Vice-Chancellor in Schleicher's cabinet. In fact, he now thought he had a choice of National Socialist Vice-Chancellors: Strasser under Schleicher or Hitler under von Papen. Papen, in reporting his meeting with Hitler, gave the aged President the impression that he, von Papen, would head a Papen-Hitler cabinet.[73] But even after the news of the Hitler-Papen meeting broke, Schleicher remained greatly encouraged. The old Field Marshal seemed to be coming over to his side again.

Heavy industry generally remained opposed to Schleicher. They feared his apparent indifference to orthodox economic principles and traditional class alignments. In accordance with the conciliatory labor policies of light industry, he also courted the trade unions and this caused fears of an alliance between the military and the working class. The members of the Ruhrlade, however, had an additional reason for hostility toward Schleicher, for they still suspected him of using some of their political funds to buy a newspaper for himself.

On January 7 in Dortmund, von Papen met with some of the most important members of the Ruhrlade—Krupp, Reusch, Springorum, and Vögler. The former Chancellor requested the backing of heavy industry in his efforts to set up a Papen-Hitler coalition government.[74] As an initial commitment, von Papen asked the industrialists for funds to finance an office and staff of aides for his use. This request was rejected by the men of the Ruhrlade.[75] Even though some members of the organization had been willing to participate in Schröder's effort to save the Nazi Party from bankruptcy, apparently they were not yet willing to contribute money directly for the purpose of making Hitler Chancellor. It was subtle, but nevertheless there was a difference between the two projects. It is also possible, of course, that von Papen's request was rejected only because a few of the more liberal members such as Paul Silverberg refused to go along with it and unanimous approval was required on such a measure.

Walther Funk's trip through the Ruhr late in 1932 to collect money for the Nazi Party from heavy industry was a dismal failure, the only significant contribution being 30,000 marks given to him by Otto Steinbrinck for the Flick interests. A few months earlier after the November elections, Wilhelm Keppler, Baron von Schröder, and Dr. Hjalmar Schacht decided, with the approval of Hitler, to approach the leading heavy industrialists with the request to sign a petition in which President von Hindenburg was urged to make Hitler Chancellor. Hitler's appointment, the letter asserted, would help stabilize conditions, for "we recognize in the National movement . . . the promise of a new era. By ending the class struggle it will create the indispensable foundation for a new rise of the German economy." The response outside the circle of the United Steel group was not encouraging. The only major heavy industrialists who signed the petition were Thyssen and Vögler. Other signers were either politically minded small industrialists like Keppler or right-wing bankers like Schacht, Schröder, and Reinhardt, plus a few aristocrats and wealthy extremists.[76] Dr. Schacht's report to Hitler on the progress of the campaign was worded very carefully: "I have no doubt that the present development of things can only lead to your becoming Chancellor. It seems as if our attempt to collect a number of signatures from business for this purpose was not altogether in vain, although I believe that heavy industry will hardly participate, for it rightfully bears its name 'heavy industry' on account of its indecisiveness."[77]

With heavy industry unwilling to openly oppose his government, Schleicher felt safe for the time being. In addition, there was another factor that boosted the Chancellor's confidence; for the moment Hitler did not want a showdown with him. The National Socialists did not want an immediate vote in the Reichstag nor were they willing to have the Reichstag adjourned for a considerable period. A vote of no-confidence against the Schleicher cabinet would have meant another national election. For this, the Nazis had neither the desire nor the financial resources. On the other hand, Hitler was not willing to wait quietly and allow Schleicher to benefit from an improvement in the economic situation. He did not believe that an improvement was going to occur, but he did not want to take any chances. What Hitler needed was a period of a few weeks in which to maneuver.

To counter Schleicher's threat to dissolve the Reichstag, Hitler began making the initial moves in a clever project he had been planning ever since his cold rejection by Hindenburg on August

13. The objective of the plan was no less than the impeachment and removal from office of President von Hindenburg himself on a charge of unconstitutional use of Article 48 of the Weimar Constitution. In launching this project, Hitler showed himself to be a master of parliamentary maneuvering; again he was using the weapons of democracy to destroy democracy itself. A motion of impeachment of the President of the Reich under Article 59 of the constitution required the support of at least 100 deputies of the Reichstag, and the National Socialists held 196 seats. To remove the President from office, however, the approval of a two-thirds majority was needed. Yet Hitler was confident of obtaining the required 290 votes, for in addition to the 196 Nazi deputies he could safely count on the cooperation of the 100 Communists on an issue such as this that would be a disaster for the established order. It was even possible that the motion would receive the support of a few left-wing Social Democrats who were anxious to avenge von Papen's humiliating takeover of the Prussian government.[78]

Before Hitler's plan would become operational, however, there was one important obstacle to be remembered. In the event of the President's death or a vacancy of his office for "other causes," under Article 51 of the constitution the functions of the head of state were to be temporarily exercised by the Chancellor until a successor had been elected. Naturally, Hitler was not about to see Hindenburg replaced by Schleicher, so to rule out such an eventuality he ordered his men in the Reichstag to introduce legislation substituting the president of the Supreme Court for the Chancellor. On December 9 the bill was passed by 404 votes to 127 and became law. By finding one "revolutionary" issue which the Nazis and Communists could support in common, Hitler had shrewdly taken advantage of the principal weakness of the current situation—the two "revolutionary" parties held the majority in the Reichstag. It was after the legislation necessary to activate his plan was passed, however, that he showed the real subtlety of his intellect. Instead of immediately using his advantage to embarrass the old order and bring about a chaotic situation in which anything might have happened, he restrained himself, setting aside his personal dislike of Hindenburg. He kept the threat of impeachment to be used as a weapon of blackmail in the crucial moment for "negotiation" with the President or government.

As the days of early January 1933 passed, Hitler experienced a growing feeling of desperation. The economic situation might improve drastically overnight. The Nazis had to get power before that happened. Time was running out. Hitler knew he would have to make his bid for power before the end of February, while the impoverished masses were still in the gloom and misery of a harsh winter. Impatiently, the Nazis looked for a sign of weakness in their adversaries. The forces of the old order would have to be divided before they could be conquered. Clever maneuvering had given Hitler several trump cards, but the crucial thing was to play them at the right time before it was too late. The most agonizing thing for Hitler was that he had to sit and wait for his opponents to act; he could not take the initiative until they moved first.

There were about six million "officially registered" unemployed in mid-January 1933, which was approximately the same number as that date the previous year. The number of unregistered unemployed was undoubtedly higher than the preceding year, but at least the rate of increase in unemployment had greatly slowed up. Industrial production had increased from about half the 1929 level in August 1932, to over 60 percent of the 1929 level in December 1932. The price of both stocks and bonds had advanced considerably above their low points of the previous year. But there was no real improvement in the living conditions of the lower or middle classes. With the price of dairy and poultry products sinking lower, the peasants were more dissatisfied than ever. The masses of the population were not interested in statistics about the "rate of increase in industrial production" or stock prices. They only knew that things had not improved for them. In fact, among the masses there was little hope of improvement; the people had waited too long and been disappointed too often.

Chancellor von Schleicher hoped to persuade the Reichstag to adjourn for a few months and that in the meantime his "program" for creating employment through public works would begin to produce results. At least, this was the "official position" of the cabinet. Actually, less confidence was placed in the public works program than in a gradual economic upturn resulting from "natural causes." This was the real economic program of all German capitalists, liberals, and even Social Democrats—to wait until the world economic situation somehow began to improve. It was assumed that since past economic crises had been succeeded by periods of prosperity, the same cycle was bound to occur eventually in the present situation. Consequently, the political game was to be in power at the moment when the economic upturn began.

At the present, the economic conditions favored Chancellor von Schleicher's chances of imposing a dictatorship. By the end of 1932, a consensus was developing among the German upper class that an authoritarian government was needed, at least until the economic 'situation improved. Up to the middle of 1931, big business and the Junkers had differing opinions on how to handle the economic crisis. The industrialists thought to overcome the depression by reducing the economic functions of government, while the Junkers wanted to see these functions—particularly in the form of subsidies to agriculture—increased. With the deepening of the depression, however, the credit and currency crisis, the leaders of industry lost hope of overcoming the depression by weakening organized labor, cutting wages, and imposing a "sound" (deflationary) economic policy through the democratic mechanism of the Weimar Republic.

The heavy industrialists had completely abandoned their advocacy of a weak government by the fall of 1932. Some desperate manufacturers such as Friedrich Flick wanted more government intervention than others, but most agreed that if drastic wage cuts were enacted a strong government would be needed to keep the masses in check. At this time, however, a strong government could not possibly be realized through the existing democratic parties because their majority had steadily shrunk. Thus, the idea of a fundamental change in the political system gradually became acceptable to all segments of the upper class; they ceased to be conservatives and lost interest in trying to maintain the status quo.

Some of the same factors that offered Chancellor von Schleicher an opportunity to extend his authority also weakened the resistance against Hitler. After all, Hitler had been one of the first politicians to call for a strong government and he could deliver one thing that Schleicher could not—the support of a considerable section of the masses. In addition, Hitler's prescription for overcoming the depression was becoming increasingly popular. The Treaty of Versailles had to be eliminated, the reparations cancelled, and the power of union labor broken. An aggressive foreign policy, said Hitler, was necessary to achieve "military equality" with other powers. First, Germany would have to be strong again; prosperity would automatically follow. It was obvious that the other major industrialized nations, Britain, the United States, and France, which were not saddled with the restrictions of the Versailles Treaty, were not suffering as much from the depression as Germany. An increasing number of heavy industrialists were sympathetic to such demands because rearmament would mean a revival of business. "Military equality" was also popular with another important segment of the upper class, the Officer Corps. As the chances for rearming Germany became better, an increasing number of high-ranking military officers ideologically deserted the Weimar Republic and accepted the idea of a national dictatorship.

The economic historian Arthur Schweitzer has pointed out that "for the majority of the German upper and middle classes democracy was merely one political credo, one mode of government among many, to be chosen according to its practical usefulness in a specific situation."[79] But had democracy really done anything to inspire the confidence of the German people? As far as combatting the depression is concerned, the answer is definitely no.

What measures were Germany's political leaders planning to take in this emergency? Late in 1932 President von Hindenburg met with the leaders of the four principal nonsocialist parties (with the exception of the Nazis) to ask their advice on solving the crsis. The talks, however, produced no solutions. Hugenberg (Nationalist Party), Kaas (Catholic Center Party), Dingeldey (German People's Party), and Schäffer (Bavarian People's Party) all agreed on the need for a "strong government" and that the Nazis should be taken into the cabinet if possible, but with the exception of Kaas they had reservations about Hitler's appointment as Chancellor. Although he had once been Hitler's ally, Hugenberg had the strongest misgivings, perhaps because of the several difficult experiences he had had with him. "I have not found much willingness on Hitler's part to honor commitments," he warned; "his way of handling political matters would make it very difficult to entrust him with the Chancellorship. I would have the most serious objections."

Monsignor Kaas's reluctant willingness to accept Hitler as Chancellor stemmed from his fear that a dictatorship without popular backing might plunge the country into civil war. "We are facing a terrible winter," he warned the President; "twelve million Germans oppose the government on the Right and thirteen-and-a-half million on the Left. The goal of a 'national concentration' including the National Socialist is thus a necessity." He urged the opening of thorough, serious negotiations. "The need for a positive result is so great that I would consider it a disaster if these negotiations were carried on merely as a formality or if they were broken off the moment the Nazis rejected them. . . . We shall support the President whenever demands are being made which he feels he cannot accept; but we also ask the President to make whatever concessions he can without sacrificing basic convictions."[80]

Behind Kaas's urgency lay the haunting fear that the decline of the Nazis would benefit the Communists. If Hitler's desperate lower-class followers became dissatisfied, where would they turn for an even more radical alternative? Millions of hungry, unemployed workers might also desert their traditional moderate Social Democratic leaders and suddenly bolt into the Communist camp. With one hundred seats in the Reichstag the Communists presented less of a threat than the Nazis, but their sweeping challenge to the existing order aroused apprehensions that made the Nazis seem the lesser evil. Moreover, Hitler and his propagandists skillfully nursed such fears and warned that their electoral setbacks were not a victory for their bourgeois opponents. In *Der Angriff* Dr. Goebbels wrote: "We are entering a winter which lets us expect the worst. . . . Overnight the one hundred Bolsheviks in the Reichstag may double in number as a result of the economic depression and the limitless misery in which the majority of the German people finds itself. The hopeless desperation in which the masses are vegetating allows for even the most absurd possibility to come true. As a rule, the 'responsible circles' do not take our warnings very seriously; but if words carry no conviction, the facts are speaking an unmistakable language."[81] A few industrialists thought these warnings were well founded. "Should we let the Nazis break their back," one businessman asked, "and have the whole tide of the masses come flowing back upon us?" Here the words of Baron von Schröder are to be remembered: "When on November 6, the National Socialist Party suffered its first setback and appeared to have passed its peak, the support of German heavy industry became a matter of particular urgency."[82]

The majority opinion in big business circles, however, was not ready to support a movement like Hitler's. The *Deutscher Volkswirt,* a journal widely read by bankers and industrialists, warned that any attempt to channel the Nazi movement into the normal governmental process was bound to end in disaster, "not because of its program, which is nonexistent, but because of its spiritual and moral structure." What sort of a Chancellor would a man be, who staked his personal honor on the Potempa murderers* and who recently saved two bomb throwers from prison by appointing them to the Reichstag? (Two Nazi deputies had been asked to resign to make room for these convicts.) There could be no understanding, the journal concluded, with someone who defied the most basic standards of morality, whatever his pledges to act legally.[83]

If Hitler hoped to get the best possible terms in his deal with von Papen, it was necessary to remove the impression that the strength of National Socialism was declining. In order to do so, he decided to concentrate the total resources of the Party on winning the election in the little state of Lippe. The best Nazi orators were thrown into this campaign, even though the total vote at stake was only 90,000. Hitler himself, who for years had been addressing thousands, traveled around the small state for ten days speaking in villages to audiences of a few hundred peasants at the most. The idea that a famous national figure would make the effort to come and talk to them greatly flattered the peasants of Lippe. People of all political persuasions came in record numbers to the Nazi meetings, which were usually held in big tents since there were no meeting halls large enough in the villages, and even the most devoted listeners could not be expected to stand outdoors in January.

Each night Hitler and his staff would go back to their secret campaign headquarters at the beautiful medieval castle, Schloss Vinsebeck, well isolated in the midst of a lake. Here in the romantic surroundings of ancestral paintings, and an old

---

*The Potempa murderers were five Nazis who had been convicted for the murder of a Communist in the Silesian village of Potempa.

executioner's sword hanging over the fireplace, the Führer and his men enjoyed relaxing evening conversations with their host and hostess, Baron and Baroness von Öynhausen, both supporters of the movement. The reporters covering the Lippe election were troubled to no end that they could never discover where the Nazi campaign team disappeared to at night.

On January 15, the National Socialists were rewarded for their efforts in Lippe by a victory at the polls in which they obtained 40 percent of the votes, an increase of almost 17 percent over the last election. Immediately the Party propaganda machine began to beat the drums of success: "The tide is turning"; "The Party is on the march again." "Signal Lippe" became the slogan of a postelection propaganda campaign by Goebbels to impress the nation with the scale of the victory. The Nazis succeeded in making so much noise over their "renewed offensive" that even the Hindenburg clique was impressed.

A strenuous propaganda campaign helped to swell the number of Nazi votes in the Lippe election but there was another factor, with broader national implications, that gave the peasants reason to take a renewed interest in Hitler. In the winter of 1932–1933, German agriculture was "cursed" with a record harvest. There was a surplus of grain, potatoes, and even meat, that unemployed people without money could not buy. The result was insufficient demand and crashing prices. Germany's military leaders had always insisted that the country should be able to feed itself "like a beseiged fortress," without imports. Now that the German peasants and landowners had finally achieved this historic feat, it was destroying them. In a country with more than its share of starvation, the Minister of Food Supply, Baron von Braun, said that emergency measures had to be taken to limit grain production in order to obtain "healthy prices."

In December of 1932, British tariffs destroyed the market for Danish butter in England. The desperate Danish producers responded by dumping their butter on the German market at prices that undercut the already overproduced German butter. The small dairy farmers in western and northern Germany loudly demanded that Chancellor von Schleicher bar Danish butter from Germany as von Papen had planned to do. When Schleicher refused, the leading German farm organization, the Landbund, declared the Chancellor was "hostile" to the interests of German agriculture. The Junker landowners could now become more aggressive since the enraged peasants and small farmers had joined them in demanding Schleicher's dismissal.

The industrialists regretted the necessity of allowing high tariffs on grain, since it interfered with foreign trade and increased their difficulties in selling the products of industry abroad. Nevertheless, they were willing to compromise on this matter in order to avoid antagonizing the Junkers. But the demands of the peasants, who produced secondary argricultural products (meat, poultry, butter, eggs, milk, cheese, vegetables, etc.), to share in this protection was more than the industrialists could bear. Heavy industry was automatically opposed to any increases in food prices, which would directly raise the living costs of the workers and consequently result in increased wage demands. But more importantly, dairy and poultry products which were imported into Germany came from the very countries with which Germany had an active balance of trade. There had been little danger in placing a tariff on grain coming from countries like the United States, because the United States exported more to Germany than she imported. With the Scandinavian countries and the Netherlands, which depended upon their exports of food products to Germany to pay for their purchases from German industry, the case was quite different. To cut off these imports would mean instant retaliation against German exports. Both heavy and light industrialists were consequently determined to oppose any increase in tariffs on secondary agricultural products.

This issue of proposed tariff increases on food products brought the Junkers into direct conflict with the interests of the industrialists, for they feared if the demands of the peasants were not met a wedge would be driven between themselves and the peasants and their influential positions in the powerful agricultural associations would be undermined. In their desperation, the small farmers turned to Hitler as their savior. As early as the fall of 1932, the Nazi takeover of agricultural interest groups was so obvious that the Papen government had attempted countermeasures "to drive the peasants away from the National Socialists."[84] The Junkers, however, were forced to take increasingly extreme measures in order to maintain their alliance with the small farmers. Thus peasants and landlords, although their interests were by no means identical, became united in their opposition to the Weimar system.

When the leaders of the Social Democratic Party refused to back him, General von Schleicher turned elsewhere for support. He thought he could build up a popular following among the landless farm laborers, who made up about 28 percent of the rural population,[85] and the unemployed by beginning to enact his land settlement program for the impoverished. This program was very similar to Brüning's, which promised the impoverished 800,000 acres from the bankrupt estates of East Prussia. On January 12 the Landbund, the most powerful agricultural association, launched its counterattack against the Chancellor. Its president, Count von Kalkreuth, called in person upon Hindenburg to protest against the planned confiscation of the bankrupt estates. Taking agrarian matters most seriously, President von Hindenburg immediately summoned Schleicher and several key cabinet ministers for a meeting with the spokesman of the Landbund. The old President chaired the meeting himself, as the representatives of agrarians told grim stories of the plight of farmers in all parts of the country. There were warnings that the farmers were turning to Communism because their problems were being neglected. One of the Landbund officials looked in the President's direction and hinted that the latter's wishes were being ignored. Schleicher's resettlement plan was sharply attacked; if the Junkers as well as the small farmers were being abandoned, the defense of the nation would be seriously endangered. The argument fell on receptive ground; as a military man, Hindenburg was familiar with the theory that the grain-producing estates of the east would be needed to make the country self-sufficient in food in wartime. The representatives of the Landbund concluded by asking for a suspension of all foreclosures for three to six months as an emergency measure to save German agriculture.

Chancellor von Schleicher replied by pointing out that the farmers did not exist in a vacuum. He cautioned that other sectors of the economy (i.e., industry and commerce) also had rights that he could not ignore. A suspension of all foreclosures would ruin tradesmen, rural businesses, and even some banks—therefore it was out of the question.[86]

A few days later the Chancellor counterattacked against the Junkers with a threat to publish the report of the Reichstag investigation into the government-sponsored Osthilfe loans. These loans had been given to the East Prussian agricultural districts to modernize the farms so they would be more efficient. As it turned out, most of the money went to the great estates rather than the smaller farms. The Reichstag investigation turned up more than a few unsavory scandals. There was, for example, a landowner, bankrupt through his own ineptitude, whose estates had been given subsidies three times; after a fourth financial breakdown, his estates had been ceded under the Osthilfe to a daughter who was still a minor. There were absentee landlords who splurged the government-loaned money on automobiles, women, and trips to the Riviera, leaving banks and tradesmen who had given them credit to sing for their money. Implicated in the scandals were the aristocratic leaders of the Landbund itself and some of the oldest families of Prussia, including the highest lady of the land, the ex-Kaiser's wife and Hitler's financial patron, the "Empress" Hermine.

The Osthilfe matter even touched—though indirectly— President von Hindenburg himself. In 1927, when the family estate of Neudeck had been presented to the old Field Marshal on his eightieth birthday, the deeds had been made out in the name of his son Oskar in order to evade the payment of inheritance taxes. This illegality was customary among Junker families at the time, and though it had no direct connection with the Osthilfe scandal, the President's friend Oldenburg-Januschau immediately warned Oskar that Schleicher would certainly publish the story of the tax evasion along with the Osthilfe Report.

With the threatened disclosure of the Osthilfe Report, Schleicher hoped to cower the Junkers into submission. Once again he was using his favorite weapon of "divide and conquer"; he planned to pit the Nazis against the Nationalists, since he was certain of National Socialist support on an issue which would be popular with the masses. However, the Chancellor failed to recognize that he was cutting himself off from his base of support. For over two hundred years the Junkers and the Officer Corps had been inseparably bound by common interests. Although a member of the exalted caste himself, Schleicher was threatening to divide these interests. In embarking upon his struggle against the Landbund, he underestimated the strength of the political and economic interests he was attacking.

The role of the Junker class in the German political struggle in 1933 is an interesting case of differentiation and interaction between political and economic power. Big business had increased its economic status as a result of the depression, which provided it with an opportunity to consolidate its position against the trade unions. In contrast, the Junkers experienced a decline in their economic status during the depression which brought many estates to the brink of bankruptcy. The Junkers, however, maintained their hold on the principal institution of the state's power, the Army, whereas big business had seen their political influence, which rested on the democratic and moderate parties, steadily eroded.

So great was the military and social prestige of the Prussian Junkers that they were able to resist almost all attempts by democratic forces after 1918 to weaken their privileged position. In the mist-laden region east of the Elbe, a feudal atmosphere lingered into the twentieth century. On the great East Prussian estates, the Junker landlords, preserving a medieval idea of their authority, were accustomed to treating their farm laborers like serfs. Most of these agricultural laborers were deprived of basic political rights. They had to vote alongside their master for the conservative candidate or else "pack their bundles."

The coming of the depression, however, undercut the economic basis of the Junker aristocracy. Because of poor soil, great efforts were needed to make the Prussian estates profitable even in prosperous times. During the economic crisis, state subsidies became an absolute necessity. But Junker agricultural undertakings were not the only sector of the economy that was in difficulty. By the winter of 1932–1933, every interest group was clamoring for state assistance and there was no longer enough money to go around. Big business came to the conclusion that all unprofitable sectors of the economy would have to be cut if the German economy as a whole was to survive. It was obvious that the country could no longer afford the luxury of a subsidized aristocracy. The battle lines were drawn between the progressive big business interests and the Junkers, with the latter fighting for their very survival.

On January 20, the Nationalist Party, in an open declaration of war, withdrew its support from the government. Two days later Hitler, who fully realized the implications of the Nationalist move, asked Oskar von Hindenburg to meet with him. Aware of some of the pressures that might be used on him, the President's son asked State Secretary Meissner to accompany him and remain present during any conversation he might have with Hitler. On the evening of January 22, young Hindenburg and Meissner left the presidential palace on foot to avoid being noticed. They walked a few blocks, hailed a taxi, then proceeded directly to the suburban home of Joachim von Ribbentrop, von Papen's friend and a supporter of Hitler. They were met there by von Papen, Hitler, Frick, and Göring. Up to this time Oskar von Hindenburg had been opposed to any dealings with the Nazis. However, after about half an hour of general conversation, Hitler insisted on having a talk with the President's son alone; to Meissner's astonishment Hindenburg agreed and withdrew with Hitler to another room. In about an hour the two emerged.

There is no record of what was said between Hitler and Oskar while they were alone. However, it is not difficult to imagine the arguments Hitler used: If he was not appointed Chancellor soon, the National Socialists would proceed with their threat to impeach the President and would disclose Oskar's tax evasion on the Neudeck estate. On the other hand, if Oskar would use his influence with his father in Hitler's interests, the Nazis would loyally support the Field Marshal as chief of state and Oskar would receive a military promotion.* "In the taxi on the way back," said Meissner, "Oskar von Hindenburg was extremely silent, and the only remark he made was that it could not be helped—the Nazis had to be taken into the government."[87]

Sunday, January 22, had been a good day for Hitler; not only did he gain the support of Oskar von Hindenburg, who probably exercised more influence on his father than anyone else, but earlier in the day the S.A. had won a significant victory over the Communists. While Hitler spoke of order and legality to the Papen-Hindenburg group, he spoke to his Storm Troopers of violence and terror in the streets. In the last months of his struggle for power, Hitler practiced a brilliant strategy of duplicity.

---

*In August 1933, seven months after Hitler had taken office as Chancellor, 5,000 acres were added, tax free, to the Neudeck estate, and a year later, when Hitler became Supreme Commander of the Army on the death of President von Hindenburg, Oskar was promoted to the rank of Major General.

He methodically shattered what was left of the political order in Germany by fighting with the Communists in the streets and collaborating with them in the Reichstag. After their electoral victory in Lippe, the Nazis used every trick they knew to prove they were capable of smashing Communism. They sent the S.A. more boldly than ever into working-class neighborhoods, the centers of Communist power. Meanwhile, in the Reichstag, the National Socialist-Communist majority stood together in opposition to the feeble moves of the government.

In support of Hitler's strategy, Goebbels began a new propaganda effort designed to prove that a decline of the National Socialist Party would be the greatest possible misfortune for middle-class Germans. It was not difficult to convince people of the truth of this argument, especially when Chancellor von Schleicher privately admitted the National Socialist Party must not be allowed to disintegrate, for if it did, there would be ten million Communists in Germany the next day. In order to convince the people that only the Nazis could stand up to the Communist danger, it was announced that some ten thousand men of the Berlin S.A. would demonstrate on Sunday, January 22, in the Bülowplatz, facing the broad facade of the Karl Liebknecht House, Communist Party headquarters. Two days before the demonstration, Goebbels wrote in his diary: "The S.A. is to parade in front of the Karl Liebknecht House. . . . We shall stake everything on one throw to win back the streets of Berlin for the German nation."[88]

When the Communists ordered a counterdemonstration at the same hour, the most violent street battle since 1923 seemed inevitable. Attempting to appease the larger party, Schleicher's government banned only the Communist demonstration and offered the Nazis all possible police protection. This was quite a change from the days when only the socialists enjoyed the protection of the law in Berlin and the Nazis faced a new ban at every turn; this in itself was a sign of the times. Escorted by police, the S.A. marched to conquer "Red Berlin" as the Marxists so proudly called it. Goebbels, the man who organized this dress rehearsal for the coming Nazi revolution, described the scene: "Our marching in the Bülowplatz has caused great commotion. The police are patrolling the slums with machine guns and armored cars. In spite of the prohibition, the Communists have proclaimed a huge demonstration. It if fails, they will suffer an irreparable loss of prestige. . . . Meanwhile, we assemble on the Bülowplatz. One really risks one's life to get through. But everything goes well. The square looks like a military camp. The Communists are making an uproar in the side streets. Armored cars and machine guns are everywhere to be seen. The police have posted themselves on the roofs and at the windows facing the Platz, waiting the course of events. Punctually at two o'clock the Führer arrives. The S.A. marches to the Karl Liebknecht House. . . . Outside the Karl Liebknecht House the S.A. is posted, and in the side streets the Communists are shouting with impotent rage. The S.A. is on the march and overawes the Reds on their own ground, Berlin. The Bülowplatz is ours. The Communists have suffered a great defeat."[89]

Papen, who was a frequent visitor at the Hindenburg household, sensed that the moment he had been waiting for had come. In his conversations with the President he mentioned, for the first time, the meeting he had had with the leading members of the Ruhrlade on January 7 in Dortmund. The industrialists, said von Papen, had complained to him about the disastrous effects on business of Schleicher's economic policies.[90] The ex-Chancellor discreetly avoided mentioning that the men of the Ruhrlade had rejected his own appeal for financial support, but he undoubtedly lost no opportunity to exaggerate the complaints of heavy industry in order to shake President von Hindenburg's confidence in Schleicher.

Although heavy industry apparently played no direct role in the fateful political events at the end of January 1933, their attitude toward the Schleicher cabinet indirectly determined the course of events. On the one hand, they refused to support the Schleicher government because it favored the interests of light industry and commerce, and on the other, they declined to join the agrarian reactionaries in their attempts to overthrow it. Thus Schleicher was too weak to stay in power and von Papen was too weak to take power—too weak to take power without Hitler's help, that is. Having no suitable candidate of their own to support, the heavy industrialists decided to do nothing for a while in the hopes that economic conditions would soon improve and provide a better climate for positive action. In case von Papen and the reactionary Nationalist forces were successful in toppling the

Schleicher cabinet, the heavy industrialists were secretly encouraging a plot led by Robert Lehr, the mayor of Düsseldorf and
a spokesman of heavy industry, to unseat the proagrarian
Hugenberg as the leader of the Nationalist Party.[91] But in all their
calculations and plans, the heavy industrialists failed to recognize the crucial fact of the political crisis: Hitler was the only one
with real popular support and a determined movement behind
him. They continued to underestimate the Nazis, thinking of
them only as a mass following to be won over either by Schleicher
or von Papen.

From January 22 on, the Nazis continued to negotiate with von
Papen. As the end of the month approached, Schleicher's position
was becoming desperate. He had failed to win over the National
Socialists or divide them by his offer to Strasser. The Social
Democrats and Center Party, whom he had counted on, never
gave him their full support. Amazingly, the Social Democratic
Party, the second largest party in the country, exercised little or
no influence on the course of events during the winter of 1932–
1933. There were several reasons for this. The leaders of the
Social Democrats were middle-aged bureaucrats whose first concern was to protect their own jobs and the status quo. Moreover,
they had a general feeling of apathy and impotence from their
years of failure while in power and had lost faith in their own
socialist solutions for the depression. Schleicher was the only
man who still would have been capable of wielding them into an
effective political force against Hitler, but they did not trust him.

At last Schleicher recognized the impossibility of assembling a
majority in the Reichstag, so he called on the President demanding its dissolution and the emergency powers to rule by decree
under Article 48 of the constitution. Schleicher finally found
himself in the same position von Papen had been in early December, when von Papen had wanted to rule by decree and
Schleicher had wanted to form a government with the support of
the Nazis. Now the roles were reversed. The General was asking
for a dictatorship while von Papen assured the President that he
could form a coalition government with Hitler which would secure a majority in the Reichstag. The old President received
Schleicher coldly and refused him the decree of dissolution.
Why?

Hindenburg undoubtedly understood little of the economic

conflict between heavy industry, light industry, and agrarian interests; however, Schleicher's threatened investigation of the Osthilfe scandal was a definite indication that he intended to destroy the privileged economic and political position of the East Prussian landlords and the Junker class; this the old President understood. The large East Prussian estates were seen by Hindenburg as the indispensable producers of foodstuffs in wartime. This was one of the few economic convictions the old Field Marshal held, and since it was related to the military sphere, he was not about to let his advisors change his mind on it. But above all, he saw these estates as the homes of the old Prussian families that to him were the country's backbone. If they lost their properties, they would be destroyed as a class, and the nation would be deprived of that social elite which alone could recapture its greatness.

Faced with Hindenburg's opposition, Schleicher had no choice but to offer his resignation. However, the General was not yet ready to give in completely and remarked to his friend General von Hammerstein, "I shall not allow myself to be plucked to pieces."[92] At noon on January 28, when the Schleicher cabinet officially resigned, von Papen was still hesitant. He was torn between the desire to establish a "great" Hitler-Papen-Hugenberg coalition and the desire to double-cross Hitler at the last moment and become Chancellor himself in a Papen-Hugenberg cabinet. In doubt, von Papen sounded out his former colleagues who were still ministers *ad interim* in the Schleicher cabinet. Confronted with a choice of either compromising with Hitler or facing the masses during a harsh winter with another government supported only by the Nationalist Party, the majority reluctantly preferred the former.

It must not be thought that von Papen was operating alone during the last crucial intrigues before Hitler was appointed Chancellor. Just as Schleicher sought the advice of liberal industrialists and conferred with the moderates, so too von Papen had his confederates. The principal supporters of von Papen were the members of the exclusive Herrenklub. Outwardly the organization resembled the typical gentlemen's club. But in addition to its libraries, quiet lounges, fine dinners, and social advantages, the club had definite political objectives. One of the founders of the club openly acknowledged its political goal "The Herrenklub gathered its members together with the intention of making the conservative connections among them effective in the political field. It claims to be representative of a conservative upper class in Germany."[93]

Although some conservative industrialists and a few professional men belonged to the club, the landed aristocracy predominated. Because of the wealth of its members, the influence and power of the Herrenklub was great. It was not just a coincidence that Baron von Schröder was a prominent member of the club. Shortly before Hitler was appointed Chancellor, a young banker, Dr. Ernst Plesser, was talking with one of von Papen's close confidant's and one of the founders of the Herrenklub, Baron Gleichen. Plesser asked the Baron why von Papen and his associates were cooperating with Hitler. The Baron hesitated for a moment, and then in a low sincere voice said: "Hitler is like a man with a candle leading the way through a dark forest."[94] The implication was obvious: Papen and his colleagues did not know how to solve Germany's problems and Hitler seemed to be the only one in whom the common people had any confidence. If the people were robbed of their faith in Hitler, the one man they still believed could lead them through the forest of economic difficulties, the alternative would be chaos and Communism.

Old President von Hindenburg was bewildered, tired, and able to concentrate on the complex situation for no more than half an hour at a time. He was still thinking of a Papen cabinet with Hitler as Vice-Chancellor. But now von Papen himself was suggesting that Hitler be appointed Chancellor. In his confusion, Hindenburg consulted the leaders of the moderate parties. All of them had finally turned against General von Schleicher. They, too, suggested that the time had come to give Hitler the Chancellorship, with all the appropriate guarantees of course. They believed that once the Nazis were in the government they could be tamed and exhausted. The grueling day-to-day work would dull their glamor; they would be forced to pass unpopular laws signed by Hitler and Goebbels instead of by Brüning or von Papen. From their own years of experience, the moderate party leaders were certain Hitler would be unable to fulfill all his vague promises. These professional politicians knew what an unthankful role it was to be in power during a depression. They hoped that Hitler, like all the Chancellors before him, would be broken by the responsibilities of office.

Sunday, January 29, was an important day for the various intriguers making their last desperate attempts to secure power. Hitler later said: "The twenty-ninth, naturally, was buzzing with conferences, in the course of which I succeeded in obtaining Hugenberg's agreement to the dissolution of the Reichstag in return for the promise to give him the number of seats in the new government which he had originally demanded for his Party, convincing him that with the Reichstag in its present form, it would be impossible to achieve anything."[95] Berlin was full of rumors, conspiracies, and counterconspiracies.

Meanwhile, General von Schleicher had been seeking advice from his influential friends and business leaders throughout the country. Among those whom he telephoned was Otto Wolff, "the steel king" of Cologne, who told him some shocking news. Without the knowledge or consent of Schleicher, who was the Minister of Defense, General von Blomberg, the chief German military delegate at the Geneva Disarmament Conference, who was known as a pro-Nazi, had been ordered to report immediately to President von Hindenburg. He was to leave Geneva at once. Wolff advised Schleicher to make use of the powers still left to him as interim Chancellor and Minister of Defense to proclaim a state of emergency, declare martial law, and establish a military dictatorship for a limited period. Once this was accomplished, the General should move old Hindenburg and his son under "protective detention" to Neudeck and have von Blomberg arrested as soon as his train crossed the Swiss border.[96]

Both Schleicher and General von Hammerstein, the commanding General of the Army, were furious with the President's recalling von Blomberg behind their backs. But Schleicher hesitated to take the forceful measures advised by Otto Wolff. In the moment of crisis, a general was not willing to act as decisively as an industrialist.

Schleicher decided to try to divide his opponents by sending General von Hammerstein to negotiate with Hitler. Their meeting took place at Charlottenburg, in the home of Hitler's patron Carl Bechstein. Hammerstein warned Hitler that von Papen still might leave him out in the cold and they would wake up the next morning to find a Papen-Hugenberg cabinet a fait accompli. Still believing that certain compromises would have to be worked out with the Nazis, Schleicher had instructed von Hammerstein to suggest a Hitler-Schleicher coalition to rule with the united support of the Army and the National Socialists. As instructed, General von Hammerstein exerted all his influence in this direction.

It was then four o'clock in the afternoon, and Hitler still did not know whether or not Göring's negotiations with von Papen were being used as a screen for a double-cross by the latter. The Nazi Führer found himself confronted with a difficult decision; both Schleicher and von Papen were now offering him the Chancellorship. But could he trust them? With whom would he align himself: Schleicher whose offer was more direct, or the Papen-Hugenberg interests with whom the negotiations were more complicated? Here Hitler showed himself to be more than just an ambitious power-seeker. He was not concerned so much with becoming Chancellor as with becoming Chancellor in a way that would permit him to carry out the revolution he had planned. He declined the easy path, to unite with Schleicher, who really had more force behind him. Hitler chose his partners for their weaknesses, and chose them well. Already he was thinking ahead to the day when he could dispense with them.

For the moment, however, Hitler promised to let the General know as soon as he had any definite news and added an assurance of his willingness to retain Schleicher as Minister of Defense when he should become Chancellor.

A few hours later that afternoon Hitler was having coffee and cakes with his lieutenants when Göring burst in with the news: "Tomorrow the Führer is to be appointed Chancellor!"[97] A deal had finally been agreed upon with von Papen and his allies. None of this information was conveyed to General von Hammerstein as promised.

As he waited at Goebbels's apartment on the long night of January 29–30, Hitler was well aware of the possible complications that could still arise on the part of the Papen-Hugenberg group. He was still adamant in his demand for an immediate dissolution of the Reichstag, and it was not yet certain that President von Hindenburg would yield on this matter. But also disturbing Hitler was the possibility that the Army under Generals Schleicher and Hammerstein might try at the last moment to prevent the formation of a Hitler-Papen cabinet. Schleicher, as interim Minister of Defense, was the only man among Hitler's rivals who actually had any force behind him, but that force, the Army, could be decisive.

Suddenly Werner von Alvensleben, a leading figure in the Herrenklub and formerly one of Schleicher's chief liaison men with the Nazis, arrived at Goebbels's apartment with a startling piece of news. According to von Alvensleben, generals Schleicher and Hammerstein were planning to call out the Potsdam garrison and settle things by force.

This was what Hitler had been afraid might happen. Göring left immediately to warn von Papen and Hindenburg. Hitler quickly summoned the commander of the Berlin S.A., Count von Helldorf, ordering him to put his men in a state of alert. Then he called Major Wecke of the police who was a known Nazi sympathizer and advised him to prepare six police battalions to close off the area around the Chancellery and presidential palace if the Army should attempt to move in. The wildest panic spread through the government quarter of Berlin. Meissner was awakened at two o'clock on the morning of the thirtieth by a telephone call and was informed that Schleicher was preparing to transport the President and his son to Neudeck "in a lead-lined truck" and that he, von Papen, and Hugenberg were to be arrested.

Was Schleicher really planning a coup? The Army had always regarded itself as the ultimate source of power and security within the Reich. Both Schleicher and Hammerstein were convinced, after their recent interviews with the elderly Field Marshal, that he was no longer in possession of his mental powers. He might embark upon any folly with the intriguing von Papen as his trusted confidant. To the generals it seemed that now, if ever, it was the duty of the Army to protect Germany.

The night of January 29 passed slowly for the Nazi leaders assembled at the Kaiserhof. "We sit up till five o'clock in the morning," wrote Goebbels in his diary, "we are ready for everything, and have considered the thing from all angles. The Führer paces up and down the room. A few hours' sleep and the decisive hour will strike."[98]

That night in Geneva General Werner von Blomberg was boarding the express train for Berlin in response to the summons that he had received from Hindenburg and von Papen, ordering him to return to Germany at once to become the Defense Minister in a

Hitler-Papen government. Blomberg had first been introduced to Hitler's ideas by Ludwig Müller, the Protestant chaplain of the East Prussian Army, who was himself an enthusiastic National Socialist. At the Disarmament Conference this aristocratic general had shocked the bourgeois German representatives when he advised them to read *Mein Kampf* and even quoted passages to them. When the night train from Geneva brought Blomberg into the Berlin station shortly after dawn on the morning of January 30, he was met at the boarding platform by two officers who had conflicting orders for him. One was Major von Kuntzen, General von Hammerstein's adjutant, who ordered him to report to the Commander-in-Chief of the Army; the other was Colonel Oskar von Hindenburg, his father's adjutant, who commanded Blomberg to report to the President. Blomberg went to President von Hindenburg who immediately swore him in as Defense Minister, thus giving him the authority to suppress any putsch. But the General was warned not to go to his new ministry without an armed escort lest he be arrested.

The fear of a possible putsch by Schleicher forced von Papen and Hugenberg to carry through with the agreement they had made with the Nazis. On the cold wintry morning of January 30, Hitler received the long-awaited summons from the President. In spite of a sleepless night, he was fresh with excitement as he got into the car which would take him the short distance to the Chancellery.

In his memoirs von Papen described the last-minute difficulties and disputes before the new government took office. "At about half-past ten the members of the proposed cabinet met in my office and walked across the garden to the presidential palace, where we waited in Meissner's office. Hitler immediately renewed his complaints about not being appointed Commissioner for Prussia. He felt that this severely restricted his power. I told him . . . the Prussian appointment could be left until later. To this, Hitler replied that if his powers were to be this limited he must insist on new Reichstag elections. . . .

"This produced a completely new situation and the debate became heated. Hugenberg, in particular, objected to the idea, and Hitler tried to pacify him. . . . By this time it was long past eleven o'clock, the time that had been appointed for our interview with the President, and Meissner asked me to end our discussion, as Hindenburg was not prepared to wait any longer.

"We had had such a sudden clash of opinions that I was afraid our new coalition would break up before it was born. . . . At last we were shown in to the President and I made the necessary formal introductions. Hindenburg made a short speech about the necessity of full cooperation in the interests of the nation, and we were then sworn in. The Hitler cabinet had been formed."[99]

Papen was quite satisfied with his own cleverness, for the National Socialists made up a small minority of the new government, which he was sure he could dominate. Only three of the eleven cabinet posts were held by Nazis, and with the exception of the Chancellorship these were positions of lesser importance. Frick was the Minister of Interior but he did not control the police, as that office did in many European countries; in Germany the police were under the authority of the individual states. Göring was made Minister without Portfolio, with the understanding that he would become Minister of Aviation as soon as Germany had an air force. However, Göring was also named as Minister of Interior of Prussia, an office that received little notice but controlled the Prussian police.

The important posts in the cabinet went to the gentlemen of the Right. Baron von Neurath, a career diplomat, continued as Minister of Foreign Affairs, while the aristocratic General von Blomberg became Minister of Defense. Count Lutz Schwerin von Krosigk was Minister of Finance. The Ministry of Labor was given to Seldte, the leader of the monarchist Stahlhelm. True, Hitler had the Chancellorship, but the real power, as von Papen had planned it, rested in the hands of the Vice-Chancellor, von Papen himself. It was the Vice-Chancellor, not the Chancellor, who enjoyed the special confidence of the President. In fact, Hindenburg had promised never to receive the Chancellor unless he was accompanied by the Vice-Chancellor. It was also the Vice-Chancellor who held the key post of Minister-President of Prussia, and who could command the loyalty of all but two of the other ministers.

The German press devoted several leading articles to pointing out that Hugenberg was really the new dictator of Germany. By his stubborn negotiations with Hitler, the Nationalist leader had achieved his goal: he had become both Minister of Economics and Minister of Agriculture. He issued a public statement saying that he was sure the Reichstag would give the new government one year in which to work undisturbed, During that time he would "remold" the economy along "sounder" lines. The implication was clear. Hugenberg and his party of Junkers intended to enact a reactionary economic policy for the benefit of the big agricultural interests and let industry and labor be damned.

So far things had worked out just as von Papen had planned them: Hitler would play his role of "drummer"; his name would be first, but the real decisions would be made by those who outnumbered him eight to three in the cabinet and held most of the key posts. After countless detailed explanations of his plan, von Papen had overcome President von Hindenburg's reluctance to appoint Hitler Chancellor. Thus, von Papen had finally succeeded in winning the mass support of the Nazis for the government, something Schleicher had been trying in vain to do for several years. Little did the new Vice-Chancellor know how badly he was underestimating Hitler and the forces he controlled. Yet as dusk began to fall over Berlin that night a spectacle began to unfold that should have been a warning to von Papen and Hugenberg.

From about seven o'clock until far past midnight Nazi Storm Troopers in brown shirts marched past the Chancellery in a massive torchlight parade to celebrate Hitler's triumph. Out of the Tiergarten they came by the tens of thousands in disciplined columns. Their boots thundered a mighty rhythm on the pavement as they passed under the Brandenburg Gate and down the Wilhelmstrasse. Their bands blared out old martial airs. The torches they carried formed a ribbon of flame that illuminated the cold January night. From a window in the presidential palace, old Hindenburg looked down on the marching columns, beating time to the military marches with his cane, pleased that at last he had picked a Chancellor who could arouse the people in a traditional patriotic way.

Goebbels had organized this massive demonstration in just six hours. Papen and Hugenberg could not have assembled as many men in six days or even six weeks. Hitler would not be so easily controlled as the Nationalists thought. For the Nazis this was just the beginning of their revolution. "We shall still have a hard struggle to endure," Goebbels wrote in his diary the next day.[100]

Appendix

Dollar Quotations for the Mark:
1914 and 1919–1923 (Monthly averages)

July 1914	4.2 marks = $1.00
January 1919	8.9
July 1919	14.0
January 1920	64.8
July 1920	39.5
January 1921	64.9
July 1921	76.7
January 1922	191.8
July 1922	493.2
January 1923	17,972.0
July 1923	353,412.0
August 1923	4,620,455.0
September 1923	98,860,000.0
October 1923	25,260,208,000.0
November 15, 1923	4,200,000,000,000.0

(Source: Statistisches Jahrbuch für das Deutsche Reich, 1921–22 to 1924–25)

On November 15, 1923, the mark was stabilized at the rate of 1,000,000,000,000 paper marks for 1 gold mark (1 rentenmark).

Reichstag Elections
June 6, 1920—March 5, 1933

Number of seats in the Reichstag
held by each party

Date of election	June 6, 1920	May 4, 1924	Dec. 7, 1924	May 20, 1928	Sept. 14, 1930	July 31, 1932	Nov. 6, 1932	Mar. 5, 1933
Nazis	—	32	14	12	107	230	196	288
Nationalists	71	95	103	73	41	37	52	52
Small and splinter parties	9	29	29	51	72	11	12	7
People's Party	65	45	51	45	30	7	11	2
Bavarian People's Party	21	16	19	16	19	22	20	18
Center	64	65	69	62	68	75	70	74
Democrats	39	28	32	25	20	4	2	5
Social Democrats	102	100	131	153	143	133	121	120
Independent Social Democrats*	84	—	—	—	—	—	—	—
Communists	4	62	45	54	77	89	100	81
Total number of seats	459	472	493	491	577	608	584	647

*The Independent Social Democratic Party ceased to exist after 1924. Some of its members went back to the Social Democrats and the rest joined the Communists.

REICHSTAG ELECTIONS FROM JUNE, 1920 TO MARCH, 1933

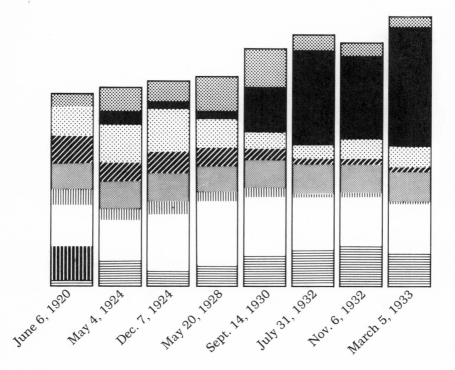

 Small and splinter parties

Nazis

Nationalists

People's Party

Center

Democrats

Social Democrats

Communists

Independent Social Democrats

Credit: *Deutschland, 1870 bis heute*, Christian Zenter, Sudwest Verlag, Munchen, 1970 (p. 207).

Footnotes

CHAPTER ONE

[1]Hjlmar, Schacht, *Confessions of the "Old Wizard"* (Boston, 1956), p. 257.

[2]*Ibid.*

[3]*Ibid.*

[4]Leonard Mosley, *The Reich Marshal: A Biography of Hermann Goering* (New York, 1974), p. 123.

[5]Alan Bullock, *Hitler, A Study in Tyranny* (New York, 1964), p. 372.

[6]Hermann Rauschning, *The Voice of Destruction* (New York, 1940), p. 60.

[7]Bullock, *op. cit.*, p. 372.

[8]William L. Shirer, *The Rise and Fall of the Third Reich* (New York, 1960), p. 125.

[9]Adolf Hitler, *Mein Kampf* (New York, 1940), pp. 50–63.

[10]See: H. R. Trevor-Roper's introductory essay, "The Mind of Adolf Hitler," in *Hitler's Secret Conversations* (New York, 1953).

[11]Hitler, *op. cit.*, pp. 291–293.

[12]*Ibid.*, p. 294.

[13]*Ibid.*, pp. 296–297.

[14]*Ibid.*, p. 300.

[15]See letter of Nauhaus to Ruttinger, April 9, 1919, *NSDAP Hauptarchive* (Hereafter referred to as *HA*), Stanford University, Hoover Institution, Microfilm Collection, no. 886.

[16]Rudolf von Sebottendorff, *Bevor Hitler Kam: Urkundliches aus der Fruhzeit der national-sozialistischen Bewegung von Rudolf von Sebottendorff* (Munich, 1934), pp. 53, 62.

[17]Robert Cecil, *Myth of the Master Race* (New York, 1972), p. 22.

[18]Sebottendorff, *op. cit.*, pp. 57–60.

[19]Sebottendorff tried to give the impression that Harrer acted on his own. See: Sebottendorff, *op. cit.*, p. 81.

[20]For Drexler's account of the event, see: Anton Drexler, "Der Beginn meines politischen Denkens," typescript of speech, *HA,* no. 78.

[21]See: Sebottendorff's letter to Hering, Dec. 7, 1922, *HA,* no. 1229.

[22]The London *Times*, May 5, 1919.

[23]Hitler, *op. cit.*, pp. 297–298.

[24]*Ibid.*, p. 492.

[25] Harold J. Gordon, *Hitler and the Beer Hall Putsch* (Princeton, N.J., 1972), pp. 93–99, 270.

[26]Sebottendorff, *op. cit.*, pp. 115–120. Also see: Alfred von Seyffertitz, untitled typescript, pp. 225–237, *HA,* no. 1372.

[27]Reginald H. Phelps, "Before Hitler Came: Thule Society and Germanen Orden," *Journal of Modern History* 35 (September 1963), p. 250.

[28]Werner Maser, *Hitler: Legend, Myth and Reality* (New York, 1973), pp. 113–115.

[29]Konrad Heiden, *Der Fuehrer* (Boston, 1944), p. 89.

[30]Bullock, *op cit.*, p. 67.

[31]Heiden, *op cit.*, pp. 26–33.

[32]Joachim C. Fest, *Hitler* (New York, 1974), p. 127.

[33]Kurt Lüdecke, *I knew Hitler* (New York, 1938), p. 245.

[34]Heiden, *op cit.*, pp. 26–33.

[35]*Hitler's Secret Conversations*, p. 267.

[36]*Ibid.*, p. 268.

[37]*Ibid.*, p. 180.

[38]Lüdecke, *op. cit.*, p. 92.

[39]Robert Payne, *The Life and Death of Adolf Hitler* (New York, 1973), p. 152.

[40]Ernst Hanfstaengl, *Unheard Witness* (Philadelphia, 1957).

[41]Georg Franz-Willing, *Die Hitler bewegung: Der Ursprung 1919–1922* (Hamburg, 1962), p. 186.

[42]Told to the author by Ernst Hanfstaengl.

[43]Konrad Heiden, *Hitler: A Biography* (New York, 1936), p. 90.

[44]All other German parties were funded by big business or organized labor. See: Louis P. Lochner, *Tycoons and Tyrants* (Chicago, 1954), p. 91.

[45]Bullock, *op cit.*, p. 74.

[46]Hitler, *op cit.*, pp. 59–62.

[47]Norman H. Baynes, ed., *The Speeches of Adolf Hitler, April 1922–August 1939*, 2 vols. (London, 1942) pp. 1–87.

[48]Hanfstaengl, *op cit.*, p. 71.

[49]Franz-Willing, *op cit.*, p. 179.

[50]Lüdecke, *op cit.*, p. 98.

[51]See: Dietrich Eckhart's letter to Max Amann, May 10, 1923, *HA*, roll 54, folder 1317.

[52]Cecil, *op cit.*, p. 23.

[53]Heiden, *Hitler*, p. 45.

[54]Fest, *op cit.*, pp. 132–133.

[55]Hanfstaengl, *op cit.*, p. 57.

[56]Cecil, *op cit.*, p. 24.

[57]*Ibid.*, p. 30.

[58]*The Protocols of the Learned Elders of Zion*, trans. Victor Marsden, privately printed. For the historical background of the *Protocols*, see: Norman Cohn, *Warrant for Genocide* (New York, 1966).

[59]Heiden, *Der Führer*, p. 19.

[60]R. J. Minney, *Rasputin* (London, 1972), pp. 74–75.

[61]Phelps, *op cit.*, p. 246.

[62]Louis Pauwels and Jacques Bergier, *The Morning of the Magicians* (New York, 1963), p. 193.

[63]Hitler, *op cit.*, pp. 506–514.

[64]Gottfried Feder, *Hitler's Official Program* (New York, 1971).

[65]John W. Wheeler-Bennett, *The Nemesis of Power* (New York, 1954), p. 46.

[66]Alan Bullock, for example, mentions Frau Hofmann in the same category as Frau Bechstein and Frau Wagner, both of whom were socially prominent and wealthy. Bullock, *op cit.*, p. 391.

[67]David Schoenbaum, *Hitler's Social Revolution* (London, 1969).

[68]Lüdecke, *op cit.*, pp. 74–75.

[69]Wheeler-Bennett, *op cit.*, p. 79.

[70]Hans Hofmann, *Der Hitler putsch* (Munich, 1961), p. 55.

[71]Franz-Willing, *op cit.*, pp. 186, 192.

[72]Oron J. Hale, ed., "Gottfried Feder calls Hitler to Order: An Unpublished Letter on Nazi Party Af-

fairs," *Journal of Modern History* 30 (1958), p. 360.

⁷³Told to author by Hanfstaengl.

⁷⁴*Hitler's Secret Conversations*, pp. 179–180.

⁷⁵Hanfstaengl, *op cit.*, p. 46.

⁷⁶Hitler, *op. cit.*, p. 736.

⁷⁷Johannes Hering, "Beitrage zur Geschichte der Thule-Gesellschaft," typescript from 1939, *HA*, No. 865.

⁷⁸Sebottendorff, *op cit.*, p. 192.

⁷⁹Of the list of stockholders, Bierbaumer, Feilitzsche, Kunze, and Eder could be said to have represented the Thule Society. Feder, Gutberlet, and Heuss were members of the Nazi Party and Braun was a Party sympathizer.

⁸⁰National Archives, Micro-copy T-84, fr. 9692 and R-25 frs. 9695 Ff.

⁸¹*HA*, No. 514.

⁸²*Hitler's Secret Conversations*, p. 282.

⁸³*Ibid.*, p. 376.

⁸⁴Jean Michel Angebert, *Hitler et la Tradition Cathare*. Published in English as *The Occult and the Third Reich* (New York, 1974).

⁸⁵*Hitler's Secret Conversations*, p. 179.

⁸⁶*Ibid.*, p. 509.

⁸⁷*Ibid.*

⁸⁸John Toland, *Adolf Hitler* (New York, 1976), pp. 85–86.

⁸⁹Col. Truman Smith, *Hitler and the National Socialists* (Yale University), pp. 25–27.

⁹⁰Sebottendorff, *op cit.*, pp. 171–182.

⁹¹*Ibid.*, p. 53. Also: *Hitler's Secret Conversations*, p. 189.

⁹²Hering, *op. cit.*

⁹³Maser, *op cit.*, p. 253.

⁹⁴Adolf Hitler Verrater, *HA*, roll 2, Folder 45.

⁹⁵Hitler to the NSDAP Parteileitung, July 14, 1921, *HA*, roll 3, Folder 79.

CHAPTER TWO

¹*Hitler's Secret Conversations*, p. 223.

²*Ibid.*

³*Ibid.*

⁴Fritz Sternberg, *Capitalism and Socialism on Trial* (New York, 1968), pp. 191–194.

⁵Kurt Lüdecke, *I Knew Hitler*, pp. 101–108.

⁶*Ibid.*, p. 101.

⁷The fact that the head of the Munich police, Dr. Pöhner, was a member of the Thule Society helped the Nazis in this respect.

⁸Lüdecke, *op. cit.* p. 103.

⁹*Ibid.*, pp. 103–104.

¹⁰*Ibid.*, p. 104.

¹¹*Ibid.*, p. 107.

¹²*Ibid.*, p. 108.

¹³*Ibid.*, p. 58.

¹⁴*Ibid.*, p. 100.

¹⁵For example, see: Alan Bullock, *Hitler, A Study in Tyranny*, p. 68.

¹⁶Ernst Hanfstaengl, *Unheard Witness*, p. 54.

¹⁷*Ibid.*, p. 55.

¹⁸*Ibid.*

¹⁹*Ibid.*

²⁰*Ibid.*

²¹*Ibid.*

²²*Ibid.*, p. 57.

²³*Ibid.*, p. 56.

²⁴Quoted in Konrad Heiden, *Hitler: A Biography*, p. 96.

²⁵Hanfstaengl, *op. cit.*, p. 44.

[26]Sternberg, *op. cit.*, pp. 258–260.

[27]Fritz K. Ringer, ed., *The German Inflation of 1923* (New York, 1969), pp. 82–83.

[28]Dr. Ernst Boepple, ed., *Adolf Hitler's Reden*, (Munich, 1934), pp. 64–79.

[29]Konrad Heiden called him an actor by profession. (Heiden, *op. cit.*, p. 95) H. H. Hoffman said he was an elderly East Prussian (H. H. Hofmann, *Der Hitler Putsch* Munich, 1961).

[30]Aktenvermerk, State Ministry of Exterior, date cir. Nov. 15, 1923.

[31]Georg Franz-Willing, *Die Hitler bewegung: Der Ursprung 1919–1922*, p. 133.

[32]The Kaiser permitted Gustave von Bohlen to take his wife's name when he married the only child of the Krupp family.

[33]Max Boehm, "Baltische Einflusse auf die anfänge des Nationalsozialismus," *Jahrbuch des baltischen Deutschtum*, XIV (1967), 58.

[34]Lampe to Wrangel, August 5, 1921, Lampe Archive, folder 53, Hoover Library.

[35]*Aufbau*, September 12, 1923.

[36]Walter H. Kaufmann, *Monarchism in the Weimar Republic* (New York, 1973), pp. 103–104.

[37]"Bericht veber die russische monarchistische Organisation in der emigration," October 18, 1935 in National Archives. EAP 161-b-12/139 folder 148.

[38]William H. Chamberlain, *The Russian Revolution* (New York, 1935), vol. II.

[39]Walter Laqueur, *Russia and Germany: A Century of Conflict* (Boston, 1965), pp. 105–108.

[40]*Ibid.*, p. 106.

[41]For example, see: *Munchenen Zeitung and Münchener Neueste Nachrichten*, June 4–14, 1921.

[42]*Aufbau*, Sept. 29, 1923.

[43]*Ibid.*, Sept. 29 and Oct. 25, 1923.

[44]Auswartiges Amt. Bonn. Polotosches Archiv IV Russland Politik 2, Vol. 3 (Oct–Dec. 1921), pp. 256–257 (Scheubner-Richter's report); Vol. 4 (Jan–Apr. 1921), pp. 46–53 (report on émigrés).

[45]*Münchener Neuste Nachrichten*, June 6, 1921.

[46]Gen. I. A. Holmsen (Kholmsen), unpublished memoirs in Columbia University Russian Archive "Na voennoi sluzhbe v Rossii: Vospominania ofitsera general nago shtaba." (Mimeo, New York, 1953), pp. 70–71. For Deterding's financing of Hoffmann, see: G. Roberts, *The Most Powerful Man in the World* (New York, 1938), pp. 304–311.

[47]Robert C. Williams, *Culture in Exile: Russian Emigrés in Germany, 1881–1941* (Ithaca and London, 1972), p. 22.

[48]*HA*, reel 53, Folder 1263.

[49]Walter Laqueur, *Russia and Germany: A Century of Conflict*, p. 108.

[50]Williams, *op. cit.*, p. 216.

[51]Hanfstaengl, *op. cit.*, p. 44.

[52]Interview with Hanfstaengl.

[53]*Hitler's Secret Conversations*, p. 291.

[54]Friedeland Wagner and Page Cooper, *Heritage of Fire: The Story of Richard Wagner's Granddaughter*, (New York, 1945), p. 30.

[55]Interview with Hanfstaengl.

[56]Quoted in Werner Maser, *Hitler: Legend, Myth and Reality*, p. 199.

[57]*Munich Post*, April 3, 1923.

[58]Quoted in Maser, *op. cit.*, p. 199.

[59]*Ibid.*, p. 200.

[60]Lüdecke, *op. cit.*, p. 96.

[61]*Ibid.*, p. 56.

[62]*Ibid.*

[63]Quoted in Konrad Heiden, *Der Fuehrer,* p. 127.

[64]Ringer, *op. cit.,* pp. 101–102.

[65]Quoted in Heiden, *Der Fuehrer,* p. 131.

[66]*Hitler's Secret Conversations,* p. 264.

[67]Interview with Hanfstaengl.

[68]Hanfstaengl, *op. cit.,* pp. 57–58.

[69]Interview with Hanfstaengl.

[70]See: Leon Jick, *A Story of Betrayal: Hitler and German Business,* A Rabbinical thesis (Hebrew Union College, 1962).

[71]Harold J. Gordon, *Hitler and the Beer Hall Putsch,* p. 47.

[72]*Hitler's Secret Conversations,* p. 179.

[73]*Ibid.,* p. 230.

[74]*Ibid.*

[75]Quoted in Heiden, *Hitler,* p. 221.

[76]*Verhandlungen des Reichstags.* Vol. 444, speech by Helmut von Mücke, p. 138.

[77]Quoted in Heiden, *Hitler,* p. 122.

[78]*Hitler's Secret Conversations,* p. 498.

[79]*Ibid.*

[80]*Ibid.*

[81]*Ibid.,* p. 180.

[82]*Ibid.,* p. 527.

[83]Gordon, *op. cit.,* p. 105.

[84]Richard Hanser, *Putsch!* (New York, 1970).

[85]*Ibid.,* p. 267.

[86]Hanfstaengl, *op. cit.,* p. 79.

[87]Gordon, *op. cit.,* p. 62.

[88]Ringer, *op. cit.,* p. 113.

[89]Bullock, *op. cit.,* p. 99.

[90]Gordon, *op. cit.,* p. 64.

[91]Dr. Pöhner, head of the Munich police and Thule Society member, provided Commander Ehrhardt with false identity papers after the Kapp putsch. Hanser, *op. cit.,* p. 262.

[92]*National Archives,* T84,4, p. 3183.

[93]Lüdecke, *op. cit.,* p. 150.

[94]This view was confirmed in an interview with Otto Strasser.

[95]The S.A. made up about one-fourth of the total strength of the Kampfbund.

[96]Leonard Mosley, *The Reich Marshal: A Biography of Hermann Goering,* p. 90.

[97]Lüdecke, *op. cit.,* p. 131.

[98]Mosley, *op. cit.,* pp. 67–71.

[99]*Ibid.,* pp. 70–71.

[100]Fritz Thyssen, *I Paid Hitler* (New York, 1941), p. 82.

[101]*Ibid.,* p. 80.

[102]*Ibid.,* p. 54.

[103]*Ibid.,* pp. 80–82.

[104]*Ibid.,* pp. 82–83.

[105]See: Letter from Ernst von Borsig to the *Berliner Tageblatt,* 1926.

[106]Hanser, *op. cit.,* p. 361.

[107]Hanfstaengl, *op. cit.,* p. 108.

[108]Gordon, *op. cit.,* p. 309.

[109]*Ibid.,* p. 354.

[110]For example, see: Arthur Schweitzer, *Big Business in the Third Reich* (Bloomington, Indiana, 1964); and Franz Neumann, *Behemoth: The Structure and Practice of National Socialism* (New York, 1941).

CHAPTER THREE

[1]William C. Richards, *The Last Billionaire* (New York, 1948), p. 89.

[2]*Ibid.,* p. 95. One of the "two very prominent Jews" later revealed himself by filing a $200,000 damage suit against Ford because of

the nasty accusations; he was the well known journalist Herman Bernstein, who wrote a book in 1921 about the *Protocols* entitled *History of a Lie.*

³*Ibid.,* p. 5.

⁴Prince Louis Ferdinand, *The Rebel Prince* (Chicago, 1952), p. 155.

⁵David L. Lewis, *The Public Image of Henry Ford: An American Folk Hero and His Company* (Detroit, 1976), p. 135.

⁶*Ibid.,* p. 136.

⁷Raymond L. Stebbins, *Henry Ford and Edwin Pipp: A Suppressed Chapter in the Story of the Auto Magnate,* ed. C. L. Holt (typed manuscript, Hebrew Union Library, xy1/S81, Cincinnati, n.d.), p. 4.

⁸Richards, *op. cit.,* p. 90.

⁹Lewis, *op. cit.,* p. 139.

¹⁰*Ibid.,* p. 140.

¹¹Allen Nevins and Frank Ernest Hill, *Ford: The Times, The Man, the Company* (New York, 1954–63), 3 vols, vol 2: *Expansion and Challenge,* p. 311).

¹²Keith Sward, *The Legend of Henry Ford* (New York, 1948), p. 159. Also Norman Cohn, *Warrent for Genocide: The myth of the Jewish world-conspiracy and the Protocols of the Elders of Zion* (New York, 1966), p. 162.

¹³Lewis, *op. cit.,* p. 148.

¹⁴*Ibid.,* p. 143.

¹⁵*Ibid.*

¹⁶*Ibid.*

¹⁷Quoted in John Roy Carlson, *Under Cover: My Four Years in the Nazi Underworld of America* (New York, 1943), p. 210.

¹⁸Cohn, *op. cit.,* p. 138.

¹⁹Lewis, *op. cit.,* p. 148.

²⁰Sward, *op. cit.,* p. 160.

²¹Lewis, *op. cit.,* p. 143; Hitler, *Mein Kampf,* editors' fn., p. 929.

²²*Hitler's Secret Conversations,* p. 228.

²³Cohn, *op. cit.,* p. 183.

²⁴Hitler, *op. cit.,* p. 155.

²⁵*The International Jew: The World's Foremost Problem,* abridged from the original as published by Henry Ford, in the *Dearborn Independent,* ed. Gerald L. K. Smith (Los Angeles, 1964), p. 40. All following quotations from *The International Jew* are cited from this edition, which is more available than earlier editions.

²⁶*Ibid.,* p. 46.

²⁷*Ibid.,* p. 50.

²⁸*Ibid.,* p. 30.

²⁹Hitler, *op. cit.,* p. 74.

³⁰Norman H. Baynes, ed., *The Speeches of Adolf Hitler, April 1922–August 1939,* 2 vols., 1:8.

³¹Hitler, *op. cit.,* p. 413.

³²*The International Jew,* pp. 191–192.

³³*Ibid.,* introduction by Gerald Smith, p. 9.

³⁴Hermann Rauschning, *The Voice of Destruction* (New York, 1940), p. 238.

³⁵Hitler, *op. cit.,* p. 424.

³⁶This material is a summation of the ideas of Ford and Hitler on the Jewish Conspiracy as presented in *The International Jew* and *Mein Kampf.*

³⁷*The International Jew,* p. 63.

³⁸Henry Ford, *Today and Tomorrow,* in collaboration with Samuel Crother (Garden City, N.Y., 1924), p. 27.

³⁹Hitler, *op. cit.,* p. 427.

⁴⁰*Ibid.,* p. 73.

⁴¹Baynes, *op. cit.,* p. 22.

⁴²Richards, *op. cit.,* p. 88.

⁴³Henry Ford, *My Life and Work,* in collaboration with Samuel Crowther (Garden City, N.Y.,

1922; reprint ed., New York, 1973), pp. 250–252. Also: Ford, *Today and Tomorrow*, p. 27.

44Ford, *My Life and Work*, p. 10.

45*The International Jew*, p. 23.

46*Hitler's Secret Conversations*, p. 304.

47*The International Jew*, p. 171.

48Richards, *op. cit.*, pp. 90–91.

49*Ibid.*, p. 93.

50*The International Jew*, p. 157.

51*Ibid.*, p. 167.

52Ford, *My Life and Work*, pp. 4–5.

53Richards, *op. cit.*, p. 376.

54Hitler, *op. cit.*, pp. 436–437, fn.

55*The International Jew*, p. 126, p. 159.

56Hitler, *op. cit.*, p. 960.

57*The International Jew*, p. 128, pp. 206–207.

58Joseph Nedava, *Trotsky and the Jews* (Philadelphia, 1971), p. 147.

59Nedava, *op. cit.*, p. 24.

60*Ibid.*, p. 143.

61*Ibid.*, p. 144.

62*Ibid.*, p. 163.

63*Ibid.*, p. 162.

64*Ibid.*, p. 61.

65*The International Jew*, pp. 22–31.

66*Dearborn Independent*, May 29, 1920.

67*Ibid.*

68Hitler, *op. cit.*, p. 251.

69*Dearborn Independent*, May 29, 1920.

70Ford, *My Life and Work*, p. 10.

71Baynes, *op. cit.*, p. 787.

72Ford, *My Life and Work*, p. 11.

73*The International Jew*, p. 63.

74*Ibid.*, p. 75.

75Baynes, *op. cit.*, p. 23.

76*The International Jew*, p. 118, and *Mein Kampf*, (Reynal & Hitchcock edition), pp. 66–81.

77*The International Jew*, p. 118.

78*Ibid.*, p. 194.

79*op. cit.*

80Jonathan N. Leonard, *The Tragedy of Henry Ford* (New York, 1932), pp. 203–204.

81Historians who have investigated Ford's anti-Semitism agree that *The International Jew* was written under his specific direction. One of his biographers, William C. Richards, wrote: "He caused to have published a series of articles in which he set up the major postulate that there was a Jewish plot to rule the world by control of the machinery of commerce and exchange—by a super-capitalism based wholly on the fiction that gold was wealth." (Richards, *op. cit.*, p. 87). In his book, *Warrant for Genocide*, Professor Norman Cohn came to a similar conclusion. "There is no real doubt that Ford knew perfectly well what he was sponsoring. He founded the *Dearborn Independent* in 1919 as a vehicle for his own 'philosophy' and he took a keen and constant interest in it; much of the contents consisted simply of edited versions of his talk." (Cohn, *op. cit.*, p. 162).

82Lewis, *op. cit.*, p. 144.

83Ford, *My Life and Work*, pp. 250–252.

84Lewis, *op. cit.*, p. 145.

85*True Magazine*, October 1951, p. 125.

86*The International Jew*, introduction by Gerald Smith, p. 7.

87Konrad Heiden, *Hitler: A Biography*, p. 221.

88Upton Sinclair, *The Flivver King: The Story of Ford America* (Pasadena, Calif., 1937), p. 109.

89Georg Seldes, *Facts and Fascism* (New York, 1943), p. 122.

90Konrad Heiden, *A History of National Socialism* (New York, 1935), p. 109.

[91]*New York Times,* December 20, 1922.

[92]Mira Wilkins and Frank E. Hill, American Business Abroad: Ford on Six Continents (Detroit, 1964), p. 96.

[93]Cohn, *op. cit.,* p. 161.

[94]Walter Laqueur, *Russia and Germany: A Century of Conflict,* p. 120.

[95]Norman Hapgood, "The Inside Story of Henry Ford's Jew-Mania," *Hearst's International* (a six part series from June–November, 1922), October, 1922, part five.

[96]Carlson, *op. cit.,* pp. 206–207.

[97]Hapgood, *op. cit.,* July issue.

[98]Lüdecke, *op. cit.,* p. 217.

[99]*Ibid.*

[100]Williams, *op. cit.,* p. 350.

[101]Lüdecke, *op. cit.,* pp. 565–566.

[102]Lacquer, *op. cit.,* p. 111.

[103]Leonard, *op. cit.,* p. 208. Also: Michael Sayers and Albert E. Kahn, *The Great Conspiracy: The Secret War Against Soviet Russia* (Boston, 1946), p. 148. *New York Times,* February 8, 1923.

[104]Nevins, *op. cit.,* p. 169.

[105]*Automotive Industries,* February 3, 1921, p. 243.

[106]Lüdecke, *op. cit.,* p. 191.

[107]*Ibid.,* p. 192.

[108]Lüdecke, *op. cit.,* p. 201.

[109]Robert W. Gutman, *Richard Wagner: The Man, His Mind, and His Music* (New York, 1968), p. 413.

[110]Bryan Magee, *Aspects of Wagner* (New York, 1968), p. 52.

[111]Gutman, *op. cit.,* p. 171.

[112]*Ibid.,* p. 405.

[113]*Ibid.,* p. 426.

[114]Geoffrey Skelton, *Wagner at Bayreuth: Experiment and Tradition,* with Foreword by Wieland Wagner (London, 1965), p. 140.

[115]*Ibid.,* p. 8.

[116]*Ibid.,* p. 13.

[117]Lüdecke, *op. cit.,* p. 194.

[118]*Detroit News,* January 31, 1924.

[119]Author's interview with Frau Wagner, October 1977.

[120]*Ibid.*

[121]*Ibid.*

[122]Lüdecke, *op. cit.,* p. 194.

[123]Detroit Concert Reviews, *Detroit Free Press,* February 1, 1924.

[124]Friedelind Wagner, *op. cit.,* p. 14.

[125]Lüdecke, *op. cit.,* p. 195.

[126]*Ibid.,* p. 200.

[127]Skelton, *op. cit.,* p. 34.

[128]See Chapter 7.

[129]*Detroit News,* July 31, 1938.

[130]Lewis, *op. cit.,* p. 150.

[131]*Ibid.*

[132]*Ibid.,* p. 151. Although Ford kept the medal, he was urged by his family and friends to give the public and especially the American Jews a statement explaining his actions. His excuse appeared in the New York *Times* on December 1, 1938: "My acceptance of a medal from the German people does not, as some people seem to think, involve any sympathy on my part with Naziism. Those who have known me for many years realize that anything that breeds hate is repulsive to me."

CHAPTER FOUR

[1]Lüdecke, *I Knew Hitler,* p. 182.

[2]*Polizeidirektion Nürnberg-Furth,* "N/No. 54," 4 February 1927, p. 18, in files of *Bayerisches*

Geheimes   Staatarchiv,   M.A. 101251.

[3]Walter H. Kaufmann, *Monarchism in the Weimar Republic,* p. 160.

[4]Albert Krebs, *The Infancy of Nazism: The Memoirs of Ex-Gauleiter Albert Krebs, 1923– 1933,* ed. and trans. William Sheridan Allen (New York, 1976), pp. 225–226.

[5]Max H. Kele, *Nazi and Workers: National Socialist Appeals to German Labor, 1919–1933* (Chapel Hill, N.C., 1972), p. 75.

[6]Strasser, *Hitler and I* (Boston, 1940), p. 92.

[7]Dietrich Orlow, *The History of the Nazi Party, 1919–1933* (Pittsburgh, 1973), pp. 68–70.

[8]Joseph Goebbels, *The Early Goebbels Diaries, 1925–1926,* ed. Helmut Heiber (London, 1962), p. 67.

[9]For a biographical account of Kirdorf, see: Emil Kirdorf, *"Erinnerungen,* 1847–1930," privately printed, 1930. Also see: Henry Ashby Turner, Jr. "Emil Kirdorf and the Nazi Party," *Central European History* 1 (December 1968), pp. 324–344. And Walter Bacmeister, *Emil Kirdorf, Der Mann, Sein Werk* (2nd ed., Essen 1936).

[10]Rudolf Hess to Walter Hewel, March 30, 1927, translated in: Gernard L. Weinberg, "National Socialist Organization and Foreign Policy Aims in 1927," *Journal of Modern History* 36 (1964), pp. 430–431.

[11]Hitler also met many other important people at Frau Bruckmann's house on different occasions, such as Professor Müller, Ludwig Klages, Geheimrat Domhöfer, director of the Pinakothek, and Ludwig Troost. See: Werner Maser, *Hitler: Legend, Myth and Reality,* pp. 127–128.

[12]*Preussische Zeitung* (Konigsberg), January 3, 1937.

[13]It is not known how many copies of the pamphlet were printed or how many industrialists received it. The F. Bruckmann K.G. of Munich, the successor of the Hugo Bruckmann Verlag, has denied any knowledge of the pamphlet's existence.

[14]Adolf Hitler, *Der Weg zum Wiederaufstieg* (Munich: Hugo Bruckmann Verlag, 1927). For an English translation, see: Henry Ashby Turner, Jr., "Hitler's Secret Pamphlet for Industrialists, 1927," *Journal of Modern History* 40 (1968), pp. 348–374.

[15]*Ibid.*

[16]Author's interview with Dr. Ernst Wolf Mommsen, former president of Krupp. Dr. Mommsen explained that the effect of foreign protective tariffs and restrictive trade agreements was particularly severe on German heavy industry.

[17]*Akten zur deutschen auswartigen Politik, 1918–1945,* Archiv des Auswartigen Amts, Ser. B.I., Pt. I (Gottingen, 1966) pp. 727–753.

[18]See: *National Archives,* Record Group 238: Nuremberg Documents, NI-635, statement by Wilhelm Tengelmann.

[19]Because he was an early member of the Nazi Party, Kirdorf later qualified for the shiny gold Party badge awarded to the first hundred thousand who joined the Nazis. On his ninetieth birthday, he was given the highest civilian award in Germany—the *Adlerschild.* See: Turner, "Emil Kirdorf and the Nazi Party," p. 339.

[20]Kirdorf, *op. cit.,* p. 182.

[21]Otto Strasser, *Flight from Terror* (New York, 1943), p. 109.

[22]Most historians portray him as a totally committed, fanatical Nazi. See Bullock, Hitler, *A Study in*

Tyranny, p. 149 and 175; William L. Shirer, *The Rise and Fall of the Third Reich,* p. 203; and John Toland, *Adolf Hitler,* p. 326.

[23] A copy of the letter was printed in Kirdorf, *op. cit.,* p. 200.

[24] *Völkischer Beobachter,.* August 27, 1929.

[25] Strasser, *Flight from Terror,* p. 120.

[26] Ernst Poensgen, "Hitler und die Ruhrindustriellen. Ein Rückblick," Nuremberg Documents, Case X, Bulow Dokumentenbuch I, copy in *National Archives,* Record Group 238.

[27] *Berliner Tageblatt,* August 24, 1930. This statement has been overlooked by historians who report that Kirdorf remained in the Nazi Party from 1927 on. See: Konrad Heiden, *Hitler: A Biography.*

[28] Turner, "Emil Kirdorf and the Nazi Party," fn. p. 341. Since Kirdorf continued to actively use his influence in Hitler's behalf even after he resigned from the Party, there is no reason to believe that he did not also continue to give donations to Hitler and Party representatives favorable to industry such as Terboven.

[29] Konrad Heiden, *Der Fuehrer,* p. 340.

[30] Louis P. Lochner, *Tycoons and Tyrants,* p. 100.

[31] See Chapter 8.

[32] See Chapter 5.

[33] Rudolf Hess to Walter Hewel, March 30, 1927, translated in: Weinberg, "National Socialist Organization and Foreign Policy Aims in 1927."

[34] Friedrich Bucher to Hitler, July 20, 1919, *Reichsleitung, Personalakte Hüttmann,* Berlin Document Center.

[35] For a description of the financial problems of *GAU* Hanover-South

Brunswick in 1928, see: Jeremy Noakes, *The Nazi Party in Lower Saxony 1921–1933* . (London: Oxford University Press, 1971), pp. 143–144.

[36] Other sources say that 9,473 copies were sold during the first year. Sales dropped to 6,913 in 1926 and to 3,015 in 1928. The second volume was published at the end of 1926. For more about number of copies of *Mein Kampf* sold, see: Bullock, *op. cit.,* p. 133, and Shirer, *op. cit.,* p. 121.

[37] O. J. Hale, "Adolf Hitler, Taxpayer," *American Historical Review* (July 1955):830–842.

[38] *Ibid.,* p. 834.

[39] Author's interview with Dr. Gangolf Weiler, a Thyssen executive.

[40] For an account of the development of the November revolution of 1918, see: A. J. Ryder, *The German Revolution of 1918.*

[41] Fritz Thyssen, *I Paid Hitler,* pp. 50–51.

[42] *Ibid.,* p. 52.

[43] *Ibid.*

[44] *Ibid.,* p. 53.

[45] John W. Wheeler-Bennett, *The Nemesis of Power, 1918–1945,* pp. 123–124.

[46] For a brief description of the Stinnes-Legien Agreement, see: Lochner, *op. cit.,* pp. 126–127.

[47] Thyssen, *op. cit.,* p. 55.

[48] *Ibid.,* p. 57.

[49] For a detailed economic analysis of why it was impossible for Germany to make the payments demanded by the Versailles Treaty, see: John Maynard Keynes, *The Economic Consequences of the Peace* (London, 1919).

[50] Theodore Abel, *Why Hitler Came Into Power* (New York, 1938) p. 72.

[51] Heiden, *Der Fuehrer,* pp. 162–169.

[52] Thyssen, *op. cit.,* p. 68.

[53]See Chapter 2.

[54]U.S. Group Control Council (Germany, Office of the Director of Intelligence, Field Information Agency, Technical). Intelligence Report No. EF/ME/1, 4 September 1945. "Examination of Dr. Fritz Thyssen," p. 13.

[55]Thyssen, *op. cit.*, p. 98.

[56]Lüdecke, *op. cit.*, p. 434.

[57]*Ibid.*

[58]Thyssen, *op. cit.*, p. 100.

[59]*Ibid.*

[60]R. G. Waldeck, *Meet Mr. Blank*, (New York, 1943) p. 49.

[61]For the Communist point of view, see: Albert Norden, *Lehren deutscher Geschichte: Zur politischen Rolle des Finanzkapitals und der Junker*, Berlin, 1947.

[62]Kirdorf, *op. cit.*, p. 196.

CHAPTER FIVE

[1]William Manchester, *The Arms of Krupp, 1587–1968* (Boston, 1964), p. 249.

[2]Louis P. Lochner, *Tycoons and Tyrant*, p. 32.

[3]Herbert Hoover, *The Ordeal of Woodrow Wilson* (New York, 1958), p. 234 and pp. 241–242.

[4]Theodore Abel, *Why Hitler Came Into Power*, pp. 30–31.

[5]For the best analysis of the Versailles Treaty, see: John Maynard Keynes, *The Economic Consequences of the Peace*.

[6]Ludwell Denny, *America Conquers Britain* (New York, 1930), p. 351.

[7]*Ibid.*, p. 363.

[8]Paul Douglass, *The Economic Dilemma of Politics: A Study of the Consequences of the Strangulation of Germany* (New York, 1932), p. 26.

[9]See: Sir Josiah Stamp, *The Financial Aftermath of War* (London, 1932), p. 102.

[10]International Military Tribunal Document, D-64.

[11]The National Association of German Industry, of which Gustav Krupp was one of the leading members, repudiated the Kapp putsch.

[12]International Military Tribunal Document, D-96.

[13]Walter H. Kaufmann, *Monarchism in the Weimar Republic*, p. 18 and pp. 21–23.

[14]Carl Duisberg to Dr. E. A. Merck, October 17, 1918, *Autographen-Sammlung von Dr. Carl Duisberg, Werksarchiv*, Farbenfabrik Bayer, Leverkusen.

[15]Carl Duisberg to Professor Fritz Haber, November 22, 1918, *Autographen-Sammlung von Dr. Carl Duisberg, Werksarchiv*, Farbenfabrik Bayer, Leverkusen

[16]John W. Wheeler-Bennett, *The Nemesis of Power*, p. 25.

[17]Quoted in: Calvin B. Hoover, *Germany Enters the Third Reich* (New York, 1933), pp. 43–44.

[18]In Germany, political parties had traditionally been based on economic interests and social class. See Kaufmann, *op. cit.*, pp. 13–29.

[19]Max Weber, *The Theory of Social and Economic Organization* (New York, 1947), pp. 278 ff.

[20]Hugo Stinnes, July 16, 1919.

[21]General Hans von Seeckt, *Die Reichswehr* (Leipzig, 1933), p. 16.

[22]Friedrich von Rabenau, *Seeckt, aus seinem Leben* (Leipzig, 1940), ii. p. 347–348.

[23]Manchester, *op. cit.*, p. 324.

[24]Henry A. Turner, *Stresemann and*

the Politics of the Weimar Republic (Princeton, 1963), pp. 69–70.

25Manchester, op. cit., p. 354.

26Ibid., p. 352.

27See: Carl Severing's account of a cabinet session on October 18, 1928: Nuremberg Record, XIV, 255.

28Gustav Krupp, "Objectives of German Policy," Review of Reviews, November 1932.

29Geheimes Staatsarchiv, Munich. Translated in: Joachim Fest, Hitler, trans. Richard and Clara Winston (New York, 1974), pp. 253–254.

30Hitler, Mein Kampf, (Boston: 1971), p. 610. Italics are Hitler's.

31Norman H. Baynes, The Speeches of Adolf Hitler, April 1922–August 1939, vol. 1, pp. 43–44.

32Hitler, op. cit., pp. 609–610.

33Ibid., pp. 617–618.

34Ibid., p. 619.

35Ibid., p. 665.

36Ibid., pp. 653–654.

37Ibid., p. 649.

38Ibid., p. 654.

39Helmut Heiber, Goebbels, trans. John K. Dickinson (New York, 1972), p. 68.

40Theodor Eschenburg, Zur politischen Praxis in der Bundesrepublik (Munich, 1968), pp. 110–141 and pp. 204–245.

41See: Wiskott to Bergbauverein, March 18, 1924, Historische Archiv, Gutehoffnungsütte, Oberhausen, No. 400106/83. Also see Turner, op. cit., p. 130.

42Wheeler-Bennett, op. cit., p. 79.

43Lochner, op. cit., p. 176.

44Ibid., pp. 176–177. Also: Turner, "The Ruhrlade. Secret Cabinet of Heavy Industry in the Weimar Republic," Central European History, 3(September 1970), p. 196; and Gottfried Treviranus,

Das Ende von Weimar (Düsseldorf, 1968).

45This had led some modern historians into the error of thinking that the Ruhrlade was no more than an exclusive social club, but the surviving records of the members leave no doubt as to the economic and political goals of the organization or the power it wielded. For example, see description of the Ruhlade by Franz Mariaux in the introduction to: Paul Silverberg, Reden und Schriften (Cologne, 1951).

46Edgar Bissinger, "Das Geheimnis der Ruhrlade," Manner un Machtean Rhein und Ruhr (Essen, 1951).

47For a detailed account of the financial activities of the Ruhrlade, see: Turner, op. cit.

48Konrad Heiden, Der Fuehrer, p. 340.

49Ibid.

50Treviranus, op. cit., pp. 308–309.

51For a report of the meeting, see: Reusch Papers, Historisches Archiv, Gutehoffnungshütte, Oberhausen, 40010124/11.

52Before the war such funds had been managed by the Central verband Deutscher Industrieller which was completely dominated by heavy industry. However, its successor organization, the Reichsverband (The National Association of German Industries) was of a more heterogeneous composition, including representatives of both light and heavy industry. See: Harmut Kaelble, Industrielle Interessenpolitik in der Wilhelminischen Gesellschaft Centralverband Deutscher Industrieller, 1895–1914 (Berlin, 1967).

53Manchester, op. cit., p. 358.

54Turner, op. cit., pp. 203–205.

55Reusch Papers, Historisches Ar-

chiv, Gutehoffnungsütte, Ober-
hausen, 40010124/11. Karl
Haniel to Reusch, March 6, 1928.
Also see Turner, *op. cit.,* p. 207.

[56]Papers of Carl Friedrich von
Siemens, Werner von Siemens In-
stitut, Munich, No. 4/Lf 519.

[57]Fritz Fischer, *Germany's Arms in
the First World War* (New York
1967), p. 169 ff.

[58]For a detailed account of Hugenberg's career from 1914–1918,
see: John Leopold, "The Election
of Alfred Hugenberg as Chairman
of the German National People's
Party," *Canadian Journal of History* 6 and 7 (1972). Also see:
Ludwig Bernard, *Der Hugenberg
Konzern* (Berlin, 1928).

[59]Leopold, *op. cit.,* pp. 155–157.

[60]For the background of anti-
Semitism among the German
conservatives, see: Georg Mosse,
*The Crisis of German Ideology:
Intellectual Origins of the Third
Reich* (New York, 1964).

[61]Mosse, *op. cit.,* p. 242.

[62]Alan Bullock, *Hitler, A Study in
Tyranny* pp. 121–250; Shirer, *The
Rise and Fall of the Third Reich,*
pp. 211–262.

[63]Turner, *op. cit.,* pp. 207–208.

[64]Rudolf Olden, *Hitler* (New York,
1936), p. 227.

[65]Wyndham Lewis, *Hitler* (New
York, 1931), p. 6.

[66]Fritz Thyssen, *I Paid Hitler,* p. 90.

[67]*Ibid.,* p. 88.

[68]*Ibid.,* p. 89.

[69]*Ibid.*

[70]*Ibid.,* p. 87.

[71]*Der Angriff,* September 23 and October 13, 1929.

[72]See: Hilble, Ortsgruppe Schwabing, December 31, 1929, *HA,* roll
2A, folder 224.

[73]George W. F. Hallgarten, *Hitler,
Reichswehr und Industrie*
(Frankfurt, 1962), p. 96.

CHAPTER SIX

[1]Alan Bullock, *Hitler, A Study in
Tyranny,* p. 136.

[2]Official Party Manifesto: On the
position of the NSDAP with regard
to the farming population and agriculture, Munich, March 6, 1930.
Also see: *Hitler's Official Programme and its Fundamental
Ideas* (London, 1938), pp. 29–37.

[3]See: Fritz Dickmann, "Die Re-
gierungsbildung in Thüringen als
Modell der Machtergreifung,"
Vierteljahrschefte für Zeitgeschichte, XIV (October, 1966), pp.
461–462.

[4]Quoted from Rudolf Heberle, *From
Democracy to Nazism: A Regional Case Study on Political
Parties in Germany* (New York,
1970), p. 86.

[5]Theodore Abel, *Why Hitler Came
Into Power,* pp. 159–160.

[6]Fritz Sternberg, *Capitalism and
Socialism on Trial* (New York,
1968), pp. 277–213.

[7]Fritz Thyssen, *I Paid Hitler,* p. 87.

[8]Wladyslaw Kulski (a.k.a. W. M.
Knight-Patterson), *Germany
from Defeat to Conquest* (London,
1945), p. 431.

[9]Thyssen, *op. cit.,* p. 87.

[10]At Thyssen's request, Hitler met
several times with Düsterberg for
negotiations, *HA,* roll. 69, folder,
1509.

[11]John W. Wheeler-Bennett, *The
Nemesis of Power,* pp. 182–184,
198–199.

[12]Gordon A. Craig, *The Politics of the*

Prussian Army, 1650–1945 (New York, 1968), pp. 436–437.

[13]Strasser, *Hitler and I*, pp. 109–117.

[14]Dietrich Orlow, *The History of the Nazi Party, 1919–1933*, pp. 210–211.

[15]Turner, "The Ruhrlade," pp. 209–210.

[16]Told to the author by Otto Lang, September 1976.

[17]For more information on Schwarz's able administration of Nazi funds, see Orlow, *op. cit.*, pp. 59–60, and p. 137. Also see *Hitler's Secret Conversations*, p. 376.

[18]Orlow, *op. cit.*, p. 186.

[19]Gordon W. Prange, ed., *Hitler's Words* (Washington, 1944), p. 42.

[20]*Hitler's Secret Conversations*, p. 388.

[21]*Ibid.*, p. 145.

[22]*Ibid.*, pp. 113–114.

[23]*Ibid.*, p. 267.

[24]*Ibid.*, pp. 267–268.

[25]Thyssen, *op. cit.*, p. 91.

[26]*Ibid.*, p. 92.

[27]Konrad Heiden, *Der Fuehrer*, pp. 403–404.

[28]Hitler's complete statement is not recorded in the transcript of the trial. The quotations given here are taken from several press reports. See Peter Buchter, *Der Reichswehrprozess: Der Hochverrat der Ulmer Reichswehroffiziere 1929/30*, Boppard, p. 237. Also: *Frankfurter Zeitung*, September 26, 1930.

[29]After the trial Hitler's speech was given extensive coverage in the press. A European correspondent for the Hearst newspapers, Karl von Wiegand, asked Hitler to write two or three articles for the Hearst chain. Hitler was given three or four thousand marks for each article. See Ernst Hanfstaengl, *Unheard Witness*, p. 160.

[30]Leonard Mosley, *The Reich Marshal: A Biography of Hermann Goering*, p. 110.

[31]*Ibid.*, p. 111.

[32]*Ibid.*, p. 112.

[33]*Ibid.*, p. 113.

[34]Wheeler-Bennett, *op. cit.*, p. 342.

[35]Mosley, *op. cit.*, p. 114.

·*Ibid.*, pp. 115–116.

[37]Curt Riess, *Joseph Goebbels* (New York, 1948), p. 38.

[38]Roger Manvell and Heinrich Fraenkel, *Dr. Goebbels* (New York, 1960), p. 77.

[39]*Der Angriff*, no. 13, March 26, 1928.

[40]Abel, *op. cit.*, p. 88.

[41]Aufzeichnungen Wageners über Magda Quandt, Institute for Contemporary History, Munich, ED/60/25, 1539–47.

[42]Bella Fromm, *Blood and Banquets: A Berlin Social Diary* (New York, London, 1942), pp. 63–65.

[43]Mosley, *op. cit.*, p. 117.

[44]*Ibid.*, p. 122.

[45]Fromm, *op. cit.*, p. 163.

[46]Mosley, *op. cit.*, p. 124.

[47]Unfortunately the Reichsbank did not show sufficient understanding of the situation. A central bank can cope at anytime with a run on the part of its creditors by issuing more notes, thus tiding the banks over the difficulty and enabling them to meet all payments. However, in the case of a run on foreign currency payments, the central bank is entirely dependent on its reserves in foreign exchange. The Reichsbank curiously took the view that all foreign demands must be met as promptly as possible and then the run would cease. The exact opposite happened. The more other countries realized the dwindling of the Reichsbank's foreign reserves, the more they

hastened to get their money back before the reserves were completely exhausted—and the devil take the hindmost!

⁴⁸Bullock, *op. cit.*, pp. 160—161.

⁴⁹For a description of the Ruhrlade's control of the *Deutsche Allgemeine Zeitung*, see Turner, *op. cit.*, pp. 212—213.

⁵⁰Fromm, *op. cit.*, p. 327.

⁵¹Quoted in *ibid.*, pp. 26—27.

⁵²*Nazi Conspiracy and Aggression*, Vol. II, p. 716, (Nuremberg Document).

⁵³*Nazi Conspiracy and Aggression*, supplement A, p. 1194, (Nuremberg Document), EC-440.

⁵⁴Heiden, *op. cit.*, p. 420.

⁵⁵A description of the Harzburg Rally was given to the author by one of the leading participants, Friedrich Christian Fürst zu Schaumburg-Lippe.

⁵⁶Amos E. Simpson, *Hjalmar Schacht in Perspective* (The Hague, 1969), pp. 70—71.

⁵⁷*Ibid.*, p. 71.

⁵⁸Kulski, *op. cit.*, pp. 508—509.

⁵⁹Otto Dietrich, *With Hitler on the Road to Power* (London, 1934), p. 12.

⁶⁰Flick Trial, Exhibit no. 679.

⁶¹Emil Helfferich, *Ein Leben*, vol. 4, (Jever, 1964), p. 15.

⁶²National Archives, Record Group 238, NI-635.

⁶³Wheeler-Bennett, *op. cit.*, p. 232.

CHAPTER SEVEN

¹Kurt Lüdecke, *I Knew Hitler*, p. 68.

²*Ibid.*, p. 70.

³*Ibid.*, p. 135. Although Italy had been an enemy of Germany in World War I, there was no feeling of bitterness between the two countries that would have precluded the Italian Fascist government from giving to a German political party. Italy saw Austria as her primary enemy during the war and after the war the Italians, especially the Fascists, felt that Italy had been betrayed at Versailles. Hence, Mussolini and other Fascist leaders considered Italy along with Germany to be a have-not power. Interview with Senator Giovanni Lanfre, September 1973.

⁴Lüdecke, *op. cit.*, p. 138.

⁵*Ibid.*, p. 139.

⁶See the section on Hungary in this chapter.

⁷Most of the leaders of the Fascist Party, with the exception of those close to the Foreign Office, did not have extensive knowledge of the Nazi Party. They regarded it simply as a German copy of the Fascist Party, a nationalist, anti-Communist movement with a strong paramilitary organization. Interview with Senator Giovanni Lanfre.

⁸Lüdecke, *op. cit.*, p. 144.

⁹Adrian Lyttelton, *The Seizure of Power: Fascism in Italy, 1919—1929* (New York, 1973), p. 428.

¹⁰*Ibid.*

¹¹Alan Cassels, *Mussolini's Early Diplomacy* (Princeton, New Jersey, 1970), pp. 161—162 and p. 261.

¹²Lyttelton, *op. cit.*, p. 428.

¹³Colin Cross, *The Fascists in Britain* (London, 1961), pp. 90—93. Also see: Robert Skidelsky, *Oswald Mosley* (New York, 1975), p. 463, and Sir Oswald Mosley, *My Life* (London, 1968), pp. 350—351.

[14] Sir Ivone Kirkpatrick, *Mussolini, A Study in Power* (New York, 1964), p. 168.

[15] Cassels, *op. cit.*, p. 167.

[16] Quoted in *Ibid.*, p. 153.

[17] Renzo De Felice, *Mussolini: Il fascista, 1921–1929* (Turin, 1965), p. 234.

[18] Cassels, *op. cit.*, p. 174.

[19] Lüdecke, *op. cit.*, pp. 111–119.

[20] Filippo Anfuso, *Da Palazzo Venezia al Lago di Garda* (Rocca San Casciano, 1957), p. 34.

[21] *Berliner Tageblatt*, May 7, 8, 14, 1929; February 4, 5, 6, 1930.

[22] Cassels, *op. cit.*, p. 172.

[23] Gaetano Salvemini, *Prelude to World War II* (New York, 1954), p. 45.

[24] André Francois-Poncet, *The Fateful Years: Memoirs of a French Ambassador in Berlin, 1931–1938*, trans. *Jacques LeClercq* (New York, 1949), p. 238.

[25] According to Braun, the cost of the Nazis' first electoral success was about 20 million marks, of which 18 million had come from Italy. He stated that "Hitler is receiving enormous sums from Italy. They come to Munich through a Swiss bank." *Saturday Evening Post,* July 31, 1941.

[26] Raffaele Guariglia, *Ricordi, 1922–1946* (Naples, 1950), pp. 76–77.

[27] Cassels, *op. cit.*, p. 161; and Salvemini, *op. cit.*, p. 44.

[28] Cassels, *op. cit.*, p. 354.

[29] Correspondence between Göring and Negrelli from the Ben E. Swearingen collection. Quoted in John Toland, *Adolf HITLER*, P. ¼?⅛.

[30] *Ibid.* Also quoted in Toland, *op. cit.*, p. 202.

[31] Quoted in Leonard Mosley, *The Reich Marshal: A Biography of Hermann Goering*, p. 125.

[32] Quoted in Lyttelton, *op. cit.*, p. 432.

[33] Lüdecke, *op. cit.*, p. 190.

[34] *Ibid.*, p. 202.

[35] Quoted in Sander A. Diamond, *The Nazi Movement in the United States, 1924–1941* (Ithaca, 1974), pp. 96–97.

[36] *Ibid.*, p. 97.

[37] Frederick W. Winterbotham, CBE, Chief of Air Intelligence of the Secret Intelligence Service 1930–1945, *Secret and Personal* (London, 1969), p. 25.

[38] *The Times*, May 8, 1920.

[39] Glyn Roberts, *The Most Powerful Man in the World: The Life of Sir Henri Deterding* (New York, 1938), p. 312.

[40] Brian Johnson, *The Politics of Money* (New York, 1970), p. 59.

[41] Andrew Boyle, *Montagu Norman: A Biography* (London, 1967), p. 174.

[42] *Ibid.*, p. 194.

[43] *Ibid.*, p. 198.

[44] *Ibid.*

[45] *Ibid.*

[46] Hjalmar Schacht, *Confessions of the "Old Wizard,"* p. 185.

[47] *Daily Herald*, September 30, 1933.

[48] John Hargrave, *Montagu Norman* (New York, 1942), p. 220.

[49] Roberts, *op. cit.*, p. 312. Also: James S. Martin, *All Honorable Men* (Boston, 1950), pp. 51–52.

[50] Anthony C. Sutton, *Wall Street and the Rise of Hitler,* (Seal Beach, California, 1976), p. 80.

[51] Andreas Dorpalen, *Hindenburg and the Weimar Republic* (Princeton, N.J., 1964), p. 70.

[52] See Chapter 6; also Amos E. Simpson, *Hjalmar Schacht in Perspective*, p. 69.

[53] Strasser, *Hitler and I*, p. 139; Alan

Bullock, *Hitler: A Study in Tyranny*, p. 243; Oswald Dutch, *The Errant Diplomat: The Life of Franz von Papen* (London, 1940), p. 169.

[54]Quoted in A. J. P. Taylor, *Beaverbrook* (London, 1972), p. 322.

[55]Louis P. Lochner, *Tycoons and Tyrant*, p. 111.

[56]After the September 14, 1930, election, Rothermere's article appeared in the *Daily Mail* and the *Völkischer Beobachter*. For excerpts of the article, see: Konrad Heiden, *Der Fuehrer*, pp. 354–355; Lüdecke, *op. cit.*, pp. 344–345.

[57]Franklin R. Gannon, *The British Press and Germany, 1936–1939* (Oxford, 1971), p. 25.

[58]*Hitler's Secret Conversations*, p. 551 and pp. 375–376. Also see: Sir Oswald Mosley, *op. cit.*, p. 343 and p. 346.

[59]*Daily Mail*, July 10, 1933, p. 10.

[60]*Daily Mail*, September 21, 1936, p. 12.

[61]*Daily Express*, May 12, 1938, p. 12.

[62]*Sunday Times*, March 26, 1939, p. 7.

[63]*Hitler's Secret Conversations*, p. 557.

[64]*Ibid.*, p. 556.

[65]Frances Donaldson, *Edward VIII: A Biography of the Duke of Windsor* (Philadelphia and New York, 1974), p. 207.

[66]Sir Henry Channon, *Chips, The Diaries of Sir Henry Channon* (London, 1967), p. 35.

[67]*Ibid.*, p. 84.

[68]Quoted in Donaldson, *op. cit.*, p. 217.

[69]Mosley, *op. cit.*, pp. 265–266.

[70]*Hitler's Secret Conversations*, p. 551.

[71]Brian Inglis, *Abdication* (New York, 1966), p. 122.

[72]Donaldson, *op. cit.*, p. 219.

[73]Ralph G. Martin, *The Woman He Loved* (New York, 1973), p. 390.

[74]Donaldson, *op. cit.*, p. 215.

[75]Roberts, *op. cit.*, p. 319.

[76]*Ibid.*, p. 266. Also see: Willi Muenzenberg, *Brown Book of the Hitler Terror*.

[77]*Wall Street Journal*, March 27, 1928.

[78]Ludwell Denny, *America Conquers Britain*, p. 230.

[79]Roberts, *op. cit.*, p. 307.

[80]*Ibid.*, pp. 307–308.

[81]*Ibid.*, p. 311.

[82]Johannes Steel, *Escape to the Present* (New York, 1937), p. 191.

[83]Roberts, *op. cit.*, p. 317.

[84]*Ibid.*, p. 305.

[85]Edgar A. Mowrer, *Germany Puts the Clock Back* (New York, 1933), p. 145.

[86]Roberts, *op. cit.*, p. 322.

[87]Lochner, *op. cit.*, p. 111.

[88]Hitler, *Mein Kampf*, (Boston, 1971), p. 660.

[89]Winterbotham, *op. cit.*, p. 80.

[90]Roberts, *op. cit.*, p. 322. Other reputable sources have cited Deterding as a support of the Nazis. See: Walter Gorlitz and Herbert A. Quint, *Adolf Hitler—eine Biographie* (Stuttgart, 1952), p. 279; Hitler, *Mein Kampf* (New York, 1940) editors' fn, p. 822; Carroll Quigley, *Tragedy and Hope: A History of the World in our Time* (New York, 1966), p. 514.

[91]M. De Bourrienne, *Memoirs of Napoleon Bonaparte*, 4 vols., (London, 1836), 2:351.

[92]Walter H. Kaufmann, *Monarchism in the Weimar Republic*, p. 82.

[93]Richard M. Watt, *The Kings Depart: The Tragedy of Germany* (New York, 1969), p. 492.

[94]*Ibid.*, p. 170.

[95]*Neues Volk*, no. 14, November 2, 1920. Also see Kaufmann, *op. cit.*, p. 82.

[96]Harold J. Gordon, *Hitler and the Beer Hall Putsch*, pp. 34–35.

[97]Ernst Hanfstaengl, *Unheard Witness*, p. 94.

[98]Gordon, *op. cit.*, p. 234.

[99]Konrad Heiden, *Hitler: A Biography*, p. 222.

[100]Gordon, *op. cit.*, p. 210.

[101]Lüdecke, *op. cit.*, pp. 114–115.

[102]Heiden, *op. cit.*, p. 223.

[103]Nandor A. F. Dreisziger, *Hungary's Way to World War II* (Toronto, 1968), pp. 24–25.

[104]Nicholas M. Nagy-Talavera, *The Green Shirts and the Others: A History of Fascism in Hungary and Rumania* (Stanford, Calif., 1970), p. 56.

[105]*Ibid.*

[106]*Ibid.*, p. 52.

[107]*Ibid.*, p. 71 and Lüdecke, *op. cit.*, p. 126.

[108]C. A. Macartney, *October Fifteenth: A History of Modern Hungary, 1929–1945*, 2 vols. (Edinburgh, 1957), 1:112.

[109]Nagy-Talavera, *op. cit.*, p. 72.

[110]Lüdecke, *op. cit.*, p. 128.

[111]Macartney, *op. cit.*, 1:72.

[112]The most detailed account of these events is found in J. Levai, *Horogkereszt, Kaszakereszt, Nyilaskereszt* (Budapest, 1945).

[113]Nagy-Talavera, *op. cit.*, p. 72.

[114]John F. Montgomery, *Hungary: The Unwilling Satellite* (New York, 1947), p. 30.

[115]Macartney, *op. cit.*, 1:456.

[116]Archduke Otto, quoted in Macartney, *op. cit.*, 1:456. Also see: G. E. R. Gedye, *Heirs to the Habsburgs* (Bristol, England, 1932), p. 153.

[117]Nagy-Talavera, *op. cit.*, p. 72.

[118]Montgomery, *op. cit.*, p. 31.

[119]Lüdecke, *op. cit.*, p. 263.

[120]*Ibid.*, p. 264.

[121]*Ibid.*, p. 265.

[122]Quoted in Nagy-Talavera, *op. cit.*, p. 90.

[123]Lüdecke, *op. cit.*, p. 401.

[124]See Chapter II.

[125]Personal correspondence with Terry Elsberry, author of *Marie of Romania* (New York, 1972); and Bella Fromm, *Blood and Banquets*, p. 238.

CHAPTER EIGHT

[1]Otto Dietrich, *Hitler* (Chicago, 1955), p. 171.

[2]*Ibid.*

[3]Otto Dietrich, *With Hitler on the Road to Power*, p. 12 (Hereafter referred to as *With Hitler.*)

[4]*Ibid.*

[5]*Ibid.*, p. 13.

[6]*Ibid.*, p. 36.

[7]Dietrich, *Hitler*, p. 17.

[8]*Ibid.*, p. 23.

[9]*Ibid.*, p. 121.

[10]Konrad Heiden, *Der Fuehrer*, p. 431.

[11]*Ibid.*, p. 433.

[12]Dr. Joseph Goebbels, *My Part in Germany's Fight*, trans. Dr. Kurt Feilder (London, 1935), pp. 16–17.

[13]Dietrich, *Hitler*, p. 4.

[14]Goebbels, *op. cit.*, p. 15.

[15]*Ibid.*, p. 39.

[16]Fritz Thyssen, *I Paid Hitler*, pp. 101–102.

[17]Dietrich, *With Hitler*, p. 14.

[18]G. Ward Price, *I Know These Dictators* (London, 1937), p. 102.

[19]For English translation of the speech, see Norman H. Baynes, ed., *The Speeches of Adolf Hitler, April 1922–August 1939*, vol. 1, pp. 777–829. The German text of the speech appeared in pamphlet form under the title: *Vortrag Adolf Hitlers vor westdeutschen Wirtschaftlern im Industrie-Klub zu Düsseldorf am 27. Januar 1932*. (Munich, 1932).

[20]Dietrich, *With Hitler*, p. 14.

[21]Konrad Heiden, *A History of National Socialism*, p. 63.

[22]Louis P. Lochner, *Tycoons and Tyrant*, pp. 85–86.

[23]William Manchester, *The Arms of Krupp, 1587–1968*, p. 360.

[24]Thyssen, *op. cit.*, p. 101.

[25]Dietrich, *Hitler*, p. 230.

[26]Goebbels, *op. cit.*, p. 46.

[27]*Frankfurter Zeitung*, January 19, 1932.

[28]August Heinrichsbauer, privately printed manuscript, *Heavy Industry and Politics* (Essen-Kettwig, 1948), p. 56.

[29]George W. F. Hallgarten, *Hitler, Reichswehr und Industrie* (Frankfurt a. M., 1955), p. 106.

[30]H. R. Knickerbocker, *Germany: Fascist or Soviet?* (London, 1932), p. 20.

[31]*Ibid.*, p. 75.

[32]Author's interview with Dr. T. Geer, Chief Economist of Krupps.

[33]Knickerbocker, *op. cit.*, pp. 164–165.

[34]Goebbels, *op. cit.*, p. 58.

[35]Dietrich, *With Hitler*, pp. 18–19.

[36]Goebbels, *op. cit.*, p. 63.

[37]Dietrich, *With Hitler*, p. 21.

[38]The Commerz und Privatbank (which probably gave Hitler more support than most other large banks) had a large percentage of its money tied up in the poverty-stricken industries of Saxony and Thuringia. From author's interview with Dr. Christian Franck, Director of the Commerzbank.

[39]Lochner, *op. cit.*, p. 106.

[40]Reusch Papers 400101290/39, letter to Wilmowsky, March 20, 1932. Also see Turner, "The Ruhrlade," p. 218.

[41]Goebbels, *op. cit.*, pp. 73–74.

[42]*Ibid.*, p. 57, 70.

[43]Alan Bullock, *Hitler: A Study in Tyranny*, p. 184.

[44]Goebbels, *op. cit.*, p. 76.

[45]For police report of the first Berlin S.A. mutiny, see *HA*, roll 73, folder 1551.

[46]Otto Strasser, Flight from Terror, p. 165.

[47]For an account of the Stennes rebellion, see: *Völkischer Beobachter*, April 4, 1931.

[48]Colin Cross, *Adolf Hitler* (New York, 1973), p. 159; Bullock, *op. cit.*, p. 184.

[49]Strasser, *op. cit.*, p. 183.

[50]*Ibid.*

[51]Reusch Papers, 400101290/5, Bücher to Reusch. Also see Turner, "Big Business and the Rise of Hitler," p. 64.

[52]Lochner, *op. cit.*, pp. 64–69.

[53]*Rheinisch-Westfälische Wirtschaftsbiographien*, Band 9, (Münster in Westfalen, 1977), "Paul Silverberg," pp. 104–131, Dr. Hermann Kellenbenz, p. 109.

[54]Paul Silverberg, *Reden und Schriften*, with an introduction by Franz Mariaux, pp. 80–81.

[55]Kellenbenz, *op. cit.*, p. 116.

[56]According to Helmut Müller, executive of the Cologne Chamber of Commerce, Silvergerg was thought of as the most popular president of the Chamber in the prewar period. Author's interview

with Helmut Müller, October 1977.

[57]Otto Meynen, "Dr. Paul Silverberg," *Der Volkswirt,* v. (1951), pp. 9–11.

[58]Gregor Strasser was certainly a sincere Nazi and it is even doubtful if he was ever attempting to usurp Hitler's position. See Dietrich Orlow, *The History of the Nazi Party, 1919–1933,* p. 269.

[59]Orlow, *op. cit.,* p. 264.

[60]August Heinrichsbauer, *op. cit.,* (Essen-Kettwig, 1948), pp. 39–52.

[61]Werner Maser, *Die Frühgechichte der NSDAP: Hitlers Wegge bis 1924* (Frankfurt a. M., 1965), pp. 396–412. Also see: Ernst Lange, "Die politische Ideologie der deutschen industriellen Unternehmerschaft," unpublished doctoral dissertation, University of Griefswald, 1933, pp. 36 and 80.

[62]These small and medium-size businessmen cannot possibly be included in the ranks of "big business" or "monopoly capital" as Marxist historians contend. For the Marxist point of view, see: Eberhard Czichon, *Wer verhalf Hitler zur Macht? Zum Anteil der deutschen Industrie an der Zerstörung der Weimarer Republik* (Cologne, 1967).

[63]Orlow, *op. cit.,* p. 177.

[64]Kurt Hesse, *Die politschen Anklagen gegen die deutschen Industrieführer* (Frankfurt a. M., privately published paper).

[65]Orlow, *op. cit.,* pp. 81–82.

[66]*Völkischer Beobachter,* November 27, 1928; Walter Oehme and Kurt Caro, *Kommt "Das Dritte Reich"* (Berlin, 1930), p. 92.

[67]Krebs, *op. cit.,* p. 225.

[68]Theodore Abel, *Why Hitler Came Into Power,* p. 90.

[69]*Ibid.,* p. 91.

[70]Jeremy Noakes, *The Nazi Party in Lower Saxony 1921–1933,* p. 94.

[71]*Ibid.,* pp. 94–95.

[72]Orlow, *op. cit.,* p. 109.

[73]Quoted in Noakes, *op. cit.,* p. 158.

[74]Author's interview with Peter Müller, October 1977.

[75]Abel, *op. cit.,* p. 91.

[76]Peter Drucker, *The End of Economic Man* (London, 1939), p. 105.

[77]Dietrich, *With Hitler,* p. 29.

[78]*Ibid.,* p. 29.

[79]Kurt Lüdecke, *I Knew Hitler,* p. 363.

[80]Bella Fromm, *Blood and Banquets,* p. 323.

[81]Nuremberg document XII, p. 419.

[82]Quoted in Amos E. Simpson, *Hjalmar Schacht in Perspective,* p. 68.

[83]*Nazi Conspiracy and Aggression,* Vol. II, p. 741.

[84]Goebbels, *op. cit.,* p. 124.

[85]Noakes, *op. cit.,* p. 186, fn.

[86]Pünder, *Reichskanzlei,* entries of September 14, 16, 1930, pp. 59–60.

[87]Most of the executives of heavy industry thought Brüning was not a strong enough Chancellor and had an unrealistic approach to economic problems. Author's interview with Dr. Ernst Wolf Mommsen, former president of Krupps.

[88]The chemical industry regarded Brüning as the only hope to escape the radicalism of both the Left and Right. Author's interview with Dr. Helmut Albert, executive of Bayer Chemical Co.

[89]See this chapter.

[90]Goebbels, *op. cit.,* pp. 88–89.

[91]*Ibid.,* p. 93.

[92]*Ibid.,* p. 99.

[93]Bullock, *op. cit.*, p. 191.

[94]Goebbels, *op. cit.*, p. 102.

[95]Turner, "The Ruhrlade," p. 220.

[96]*Hitler's Secret Conversations*, p. 84.

[97]Abel, *op. cit.*, pp. 116–117.

[98]Quoted in Lüdecke, *op. cit.*, p. 371.

[99]Goebbels, *op. cit.;* pp. 121–123.

[100]Lüdecke, *op. cit.*, p. 377.

[101]George W. F. Hallgarten, "Adolf Hitler and German Heavy Industry, 1931–1933," *The Journal of Economic History* 12 (Summer 1952):237 fn.

[102]Fromm, *op. cit.*, p. 47.

[103]*Hitler's Secret Conversations*, p. 376.

[104]*Ibid.*, p. 377.

[105]Quoted in Bullock, *op. cit.*, p. 196.

CHAPTER NINE

[1]Author's interview with Friedrich Christian Fürst zu Schaumburg-Lippe, November 1977. He has written several books: *Zwischen Krone und Kerker* (1952), *Damals Fing das Neve an* (1974), *War Hitler ein Diktator?* (1976), and *Den Ewig ist das Gesetz der Natur* (1977).

[2]*Ibid.*

[3]*Ibid.*

[4]Letter from Fürst zu Schaumburg-Lippe to author.

[5]Author's interview with Fürst zu Schaumburg-Lippe.

[6]Bella Fromm, *Blood and Banquets,* p. 215.

[7]*Ibid.*, p. 97.

[8]*Ibid.*, p. 62.

[9]*Ibid.*, p. 329.

[10]Curt Reiss, *Joseph Goebbels,* p. 43.

[11]Wladyslaw Kulski, *Germany from Defeat to Conquest,* p. 379.

[12]Reiss, *op. cit.*, p. 43.

[13]Klaus Jonas, *The Life of Crown Prince William* (Pittsburgh, 1961), p. 178.

[14]*Ibid.*, p. 182.

[15]*Ibid.*, p. 181.

[16]*Ibid.*, p. 182.

[17]*Ibid.*, p. 176.

[18]Fromm, *op. cit.*, p. 56.

[19]Fritz Thyssen, *I Paid Hitler,* p. 110.

[20]Dr. Joseph Goebbels, *My Part in Germany's Fight,* p. 133.

[21]*Ibid.*, p. 136.

[22]Dietrich, *With Hitler,* p. 40.

[23]Goebbels, *op. cit.*, p. 142–143.

[24]William L. Shirer, *The Rise and Fall of the Third Reich,* p. 239.

[25]The transaction, which was concluded in March, was supplemented by a final agreement on June 1. The double date indicates that the incoming Papen cabinet approved it. See; Flick Trial, p. 3630. Also: *Frankfurter Zeitung,* July 28, 1932.

[26]*Frankfurter Zeitung,* July 6, 1932.

[27]*Ibid.*, July 28, 1932.

[28]See: Flick Trial.

[29]Flick himself was a member of the German People's Party.

[30]Flick Case VI, pp. 227, 382–383. Many scholars exaggerate Flick's contribution of 50,000 RM to the Nazis by not making it clear that his contributions to the moderate parties supporting Hindenburg were at least twenty times greater. See: Arthur Schweitzer, *Big Business in the Third Reich,* p. 102.

[31]Karl Lüdecke, *I Knew Hitler,* p. 534.

[32]Colin Cross, *Adolf Hitler*, pp. 190–191.

[33]Goebbels, *op. cit.*, p. 157.

[34]*Ibid.*, p. 172.

[35]*Ibid.*, p. 182.

[36]*Ibid.*, p. 181.

[37]Schleicher Papers, Bundesarchiv, Koblenz, H08-42/22: Otto Wolff to Vögler, November 17, 1932.

[38]Goebbels, *op. cit.*, p. 184.

[39]Daniel Guerin, *Fascism & Big Business*, with an introduction by Dwight Macdonald, trans. Frances and Mason Merrill (New York, 1939), p. 24, fn.

[40]*Hitler's Secret Conversations*, p. 182.

[41]Shirer, *op. cit.*, p. 243.

[42]The executives of the chemical industry generally considered Hindenburg to be unfit for the office of the presidency due to his age and his lack of experience in political and economic matters. Author's interview with Dr. Helmut Albert, Bayer Chemical Co., October 1977.

[43]Shirer, *op. cit.*, p. 174.

[44]Nuremberg, Part XVI, p. 272.

[45]The speech aroused hostility only among the heavy industrialists and Junkers. See: Speech of Gustav Krupp to the *Hauptausschuss* of the Reichsverband der Deutschen Industrie, December 14, 1932.

[46]See favorable articles on Schleicher during this period in the *Frankfurter Zeitung*.

[47]Louis P. Lochner, *Tycoons and Tyrant*, p. 90.

[48]Goebbels, *op. cit.*, p. 189.

[49]*Ibid.*, p. 206.

[50]*Ibid.*, p. 207.

[51]*Ibid.*, p. 209.

[52]The financing of political parties was not seen as incompatible with democracy by the executives of the chemical industry; in fact, the financing of the moderate parties was seen as the only alternative to dictatorship. Author's interview with Dr. Albert, Bayer Chemical.

[53]Since Kalle was a Reichstag deputy of the German People's Party, I.G. Farben probably made only certain contributions through him. Other intermediaries most likely handled their contacts with other parties.

[54]The figures given in this list are only approximate. See: Lochner, *op. cit.*, p. 113.

[55] I.G. Farben also financed other newspapers during the depression. See: Lochner, *op. cit.*, p. 223.

[56]See statement of Max Ilgner, Microcopy T-301 (Records of Office of U.S. Chief Counsel for War Crimes, Nuremberg), roll 13/NI-1293.

[57]I.G. Farben Case, Vol. 1, Nuremberg, NI-8788.

[58]Carl Bosch made a public statement against a policy of economic autarky in the spring of 1932. This view was reaffirmed at a meeting of I.G. Farben's "Working Committee" by Director August von Knieriem later in the year. See: National Archives, (War Crimes Records), Record Group 238, Case 6.

[59]Kurt von Schuschnigg, *Farwell Austria* (London, 1938), pp. 165–166.

[60]Goebbels, *op. cit.*, pp. 209, 214.

[61]*Ibid.*, p. 215.

[62]Papen claimed that Schröder suggested the idea. See: Franz von Papen, *Memoirs* (London, 1952), p. 226.

[63]*Nazi Conspiracy and Aggression*, Vol. II, pp. 512–513, (Nuremburg Document), EC–456.

[64]Schröder was a member of the Keppler Circle. See: Lochner, *op. cit.*, p. 106.

[65] Otto Strasser, *Hitler and I*, p. 139.

[66] In mid-December, a "financial council" was reported to have been held at von Papen's request to investigate the possibilities of arresting the decline of the Nazi Party. See: Oswald Dutch, *The Errant Diplomat*, p. 167. This meeting was undoubtedly held in preparation for the agreement with Hitler. Participants included Thyssen, Vögler, Springorum, Krupp, and other Ruhr industrialists. See *ibid.*, p. 167.

[67] IMT case no. 10, "The U.S.A. against Alfred Krupp *et al.*" (Nuremberg, 1947), testimony of Kurt von Schröder, p. 690.

[68] For Funk's testimony, see: Nuremberg Document EC-400. Also see: Alan Bullock, *Hitler: A Study in Tyranny*, pp. 173–174. Although there is no concrete evidence that all these firms participated in the Schröder deal, it is logical to assume that many of them did because they had not contributed to the Nazi Party up to this time and Funk's list was only of those who had supported Hitler *before* he was in power.

[69] Baron Schröder himself was rewarded for his efforts by being made one of the most powerful bankers in the Third Reich. See the listing of Schröder's business affiliations by 1940 in United States Congress, Senate Hearings before a Subcommittee of the Committee of Military Affairs. *Elimination of German Resources for War.* Washington Government Printing Office, 1945, p. 871.

[70] See: Fromm, p. 136, and Martin, pp. 94–95.

[71] Martin, p. 129.

[72] Goebbels, *op. cit.*, p. 228.

[73] Meissner, *Staatssekretär*, pp. 251–262.

[74] Karl Dietrich Bracher, *Die Auflösung der Weimarer Republik* (Stuttgart, 1957), p. 695.

[75] Letters from Papen to Springorum, January 14, 20, and 24, 1933. Bia 82, Springorum Papers.

[76] Trial of Major War Criminals, IMT Nuremberg, November 14, 1945–October 1st, 1946, XXXIII, pp. 531–533.

[77] Schacht to Hitler, November 12, 1932, exhibit no. 773, IMT.

[78] Heinrich Brüning, "Ein Brief," *Deutsche Rundschau* (July 1947): 13–14.

[79] Schweitzer, p. 77.

[80] Dorpalen, p. 377. For the willingness of Catholic Center Party leaders to give Hitler governmental responsibility also see: Lochner, pp. 15–16.

[81] *Der Angriff*, November 17, 1932.

[82] IMT case no. 10, The U.S.A. Against Alfred Krupp *et al.* (Nuremberg, 1947) Testimony of Kurt von Schröder, p. 690.

[83] *Deutscher Volkswirt*, November 25, 1932.

[84] Hermann Pünder, *Politik in der Reichskanzlei—Aufzeichnungen aus den Jahren 1929–1932*, ed. Thilo Vogelsang (Stuttgart, 1961), p. 149.

[85] About 55 percent of the rural population was small peasants owning about five hectares of ground. See: Guerin, *op. cit.*, p. 42.

[86] For minutes of the Hindenburg-Landbund conference of January 11, 1933, see: Graf Henning von Borcke-Stargordt, *Der ostdeutsche Landbau zwischen Fortschritt, Krise und Politik: Ein eitrag zur Agrar und Zeitgeschichte* (Würzburg, 1957), pp. 176–180.

[87] Meissner Affidavit, November 28, 1945 (3309–PS) Nuremberg.

[88] Goebbels, *op. cit.*, p. 229.

[89]*Ibid.*, pp. 230–231.

[90]Franz von Papen, *Vom Scheitern einer Demokratie 1930–1933* (Mainz, 1968), pp. 339, 343.

[91]See letters from Reusch to Vögler, January 10 and 18, 1933; Reusch to Lehr, Reusch Papers 400101290/37.

[92]Hammerstein Memorandum.

[93]Dutch, *op. cit.*, p. 90.

[94]Author's interview with Dr. Ernst Plesser, Director of the Deutsche Bank, October 1977.

[95]*Hitler's Secret Conversations*, p. 404.

[96]Hammerstein Memorandum.

[97]Goebbels, *op. cit.*, p. 234.

[98]*Ibid.*, p. 235.

[99]Papen, *Memoirs*, pp. 243–244.

[100]Goebbels, *op. cit.*, p. 239.

Selected Bibliography

The following bibliography comprises only works in English which are available to the public. Documents and German sources are cited in the footnotes.

Abel, Theodore. *Why Hitler Came Into Power.* New York, 1938.

Absagen, K. H. *Canaris.* London, 1956.

Allen, William Sheridan. *The Nazi Seizure of Power: The Experience of a Single German Town, 1930–1935.* Chicago, 1965.

Angebert, Jean-Michel. *The Occult and the Third Reich,* trans. Lewis Sumberg. New York, 1974.

Angress, Werner T. *Stillborn Revolution: The Communist Bid for Power in Germany, 1921–1923.* Princeton, 1963.

Bewley, Charles. *Hermann Göring and the Third Reich.* New York, 1962.

Boyle, Andrew. *Montagu Norman: A Biography.* London, 1967.

Bracher, Karl. *The German Dictatorship.* New York and Washington, 1970.

Bramsted, Ernest K. *Goebbels and National Socialist Propaganda, 1925–1945.* East Lansing, 1965.

Brasol, Boris. *The World at the Cross Roads.* Boston, 1921.

Bullock, Alan. *Hitler, A Study in Tyranny,* rev. ed. New York, 1962.

Burdick, Charles B., and Ralph H. Lutz, eds. *The Political Institutions of the German Revolution 1918–1919.* New York and Washington, 1966.

Carlson, John Roy. *Under Cover: My Four Years in the Nazi Underworld of America.* New York, 1943.

Carsten, Francis L. *The Reichswehr and Politics: 1918 to 1933.* Oxford, 1966, and Berkeley, 1973 (paperback).

Cassels, Alan. *Mussolini's Early Diplomacy.* Princeton, 1970.

Cecil, Robert. *The Myth of the Master Race.* New York, 1972.

Chamberlain, William H. *The Russian Revolution.* 2 vols. New York, 1935.

Channon, Sir Henry. *Chips, The Diaries of Sir Henry Channon.* London, 1967.

Cohn, Norman. *Warrant for Genocide: The myth of the Jewish World-Conspiracy and the Protocols of the Elders of Zion.* New York, 1966.

Craig, Gordon A. *The Politics of the Prussian Army, 1650–1945.* New York, 1968.

Cross, Colin. *The Fascists in Brit-*

ain. London, 1961.

_____. *Adolf Hitler.* New York, 1973.

Dahrendorf, Ralf. *Society and Democracy in Germany.* New York, 1969.

Davidson, Eugene. *The Trial of the Germans: An Account of the Twenty-two Defendants Before the International Military Tribunal at Nuremberg.* New York, 1966 (paperback).

Denny, Ludwell. *America Conquers Britain.* New York, 1930.

Diamond, Sander A. *The Nazi Movement in the United States, 1924–1941.* Ithaca, 1974.

Dietrich, Otto. *With Hitler on the Road to Power.* London, 1934.

_____. *Hitler.* Chicago, 1955.

Dodd, William. *Ambassador Dodd's Diary, 1933–1938.* London, 1941.

Donaldson, Frances. *Edward VIII: A Biography of the Duke of Windsor.* Philadelphia and New York, 1974.

Dorpalen, Andreas. *Hindenburg and the Weimar Republic.* Princeton, 1964.

Douglass, Paul. *The Economic Dilemma of Politics: A Study of the Consequences of the Strangulation of Germany.* New York, 1932.

Dreisziger, Nandor A. F. *Hungary's Way to World War II.* Toronto, 1968.

Drucker, Peter. *The End of Economic Man.* London, 1939.

Dutch, Oswald. *The Errant Diplomat: The Life of Franz von Papen.* London, 1940.

Eschenburg, Theodore, et al. *The Path to Dictatorship, 1918–1933,* trans. John S. Conway. New York, 1963 (paperback).

Eyck, Erich. *A History of the Weimar Republic.* 2 vols. New York, 1970.

Feder, Gottfried. *Hitler's Official Program.* New York, 1971.

Fest, Joachim C. *The Face of the Third Reich: Portraits of the Nazi Leadership.* New York, 1970 (paperback).

_____. *Hitler.* New York, 1974.

Fischer, Fritz. *Germany's Arms in the First World War.* New York, 1967.

Ford, Henry, with Samuel Crowther. *My Life and Work.* Garden City, 1922. (Reprint edition, New York, 1973.)

_____. *Today and Tomorrow.* Garden City, 1926.

_____. *The International Jew: The World's Foremost Problem,* ed. Gerald L. K. Smith. (Abridged from the original publication in the *Dearborn Independent.*) Los Angeles, 1964.

François-Poncet, Andre. *The Fateful Years: Memoirs of a French Ambassador in Berlin, 1931–1938,* trans. Jacques LeClercq. New York, 1949.

Fromm, Bella. *Blood and Banquets: A Berlin Social Diary.* New York and London, 1942.

Gannon, Franklin R. *The British Press and Germany, 1936–1939.* Oxford, 1971.

Goebbels, Dr. Joseph. *My Part in Germany's Fight,* trans. Kurt Fiedler. London, 1935.

_____. *The Early Goebbels Diaries.* London, 1962.

Goodspeed, D. J. *Ludendorff.* London, 1966.

Gordon, Harold J. *Hitler and the Beerhall Putsch.* Princeton, 1972.

Granzow, Brigitte. *A Mirror of Nazism: British Opinion and the Emergence of Hitler, 1929–1933.* London, 1964.

Grunberger, Richard. *Germany 1918–1945.* London, 1964, and New York, 1967.

Grunfeld, Frederic V. *The Hitler File: A Social History of Germany and the Nazis, 1918–45.* New York, 1974.

Guerin, Daniel. *Fascism & Big Business,* trans. Frances and Mason Merrill. Introduction by Dwight Macdonald. New York, 1939.

Gun, Nerin. *Eva Braun.* New York, 1969.

Gutman, Robert W. *Richard Wagner: The Man, His Mind, and His Music.* New York, 1968.

Hale, Oron J. *The Captive Press in the Third Reich.* Princeton, 1964.

Halperin, S. William. *Germany Tried Democracy: A Political History of the Reich from 1918 to 1933.* New York, 1946.

Hanfstaengl, Ernst. *Unheard Witness.* Philadelphia, 1957.

Hanser, Richard. *Putsch!* New York, 1970.

Hargrave, John. *Montagu Norman.* New York, 1942.

Heberle, Rudolf. *From Democracy to Nazism: A Regional Case Study on Political Parties in Germany.* Baton Rouge, 1945. (Revised edition, New York, 1970.)

Hedin, Sven. *Germany and World Peace.* London, 1937.

Heiber, Helmut. *Goebbels,* trans. John K. Dickinson. New York, 1972.

Heiden, Konrad. *A History of National Socialism.* New York, 1935.

———. *Hitler, A Biography.* New York, 1936.

———. *Der Fuehrer.* Boston, 1944.

Heinz, Heinz A. *Germany's Hitler.* London, 1934.

Hitler, Adolf. *Mein Kampf.* New York, 1940.

———. *The Speeches of Adolf Hitler, 1922–1939,* ed. Norman H. Baynes. 2 vols. New York, 1942.

———. *Mein Kampf.* Boston, 1943.

———. *Hitler's Secret Conversations, 1941–1944.* Introduction by H. R. Trevor-Roper. New York, 1953.

———. *Hitler's Secret Book.* Introduction by Telford Taylor. New York, 1961.

Hoffmann, Heinrich. *Hitler Was My Friend.* London, 1955.

Höhne, Heinz. *The Order of the Death's Head.* New York, 1970.

Hoover, Calvin B. *Germany Enters the Third Reich.* New York, 1933.

Inglis, Brian. *Abdication.* New York, 1966.

Jenks, William A. *Vienna and the Young Hitler.* New York, 1960.

Johnson, Brian. *The Politics of Money.* New York, 1970.

Jonas, Klaus. *The Life of Crown Prince William.* Pittsburg, 1961.

Kaufmann, Walter H. *Monarchism in the Weimar Republic.* New York, 1973.

Kele, Max H. *Nazis and Workers: National Socialist Appeals to German Labor, 1919–1933.* Chapel Hill, 1972.

Keynes, John Maynard. *The Economic Consequences of the Peace.* London, 1919.

Kirkpatrick, Clifford. *Nazi Germany, Its Women and Family Life.* Indianapolis and New York, 1938.

Kirkpatrick, Sir Ivone. *Mussolini, A Study in Power.* New York, 1964.

Klemperer, Klemens von. *Germany's New Conservatism: Its History and Dilemma in the Twentieth Century.* Princeton, 1957.

Knickerbocker, H. R. *Germany: Fascist or Soviet?* London, 1932.

Krebs, Albert. *The Infancy of Nazism: The Memoirs of Ex-Gauleiter Albert Krebs, 1923–1933,* ed. and trans. William Sheridan Allen. New York, 1976.

Kulski, Wladyslaw (Knight-Patterson, William). *Germany from Defeat to Conquest.* London, 1945.

Lebovics, Herman. *Social Conservatism and the Middle Classes in Germany, ,1914–1933.* Princeton, 1969.

Leonard, Jonathan N. *The Tragedy of Henry Ford.* New York, 1932.

Lewis, David L. *The Public Image of Henry Ford: An American Folk Hero and His Company.* Detroit, 1976.

Lewis, Wyndham. *Hitler.* New York, 1931.

Lochner, Louis P. *Tycoons and Tyrants: German Industry from Hitler to Adenauer.* Chicago, 1954.

Louis Ferdinand, Prince. *The Rebel Prince.* Chicago, 1952.

Lüdecke, Kurt. *I Knew Hitler.* New York, 1938.

Lyttelton, Adrian. *The Seizure of Power: Fascism in Italy, 1919–1929.* New York, 1973.

Macartney, C. A. *October Fifteenth: A History of Modern Hungary, 1929–1945.* Edinburgh, 1957.

Magee, Bryan. *Aspects of Wagner.* New York, 1968.

Manchester, William. *The Arms of Krupp, 1587–1968.* Boston, 1964.

Manvell, Roger, and Heinrich Fraenkel. *Dr. Goebbels: His Life and Death.* New York, 1960.

———. *Hess: A Biography.* London, 1971.

Marie, Queen of Roumania. *The Story of My Life.* New York, 1934.

Martin, James S. *All Honorable Men.* Boston, 1950.

Martin, Ralph G. *The Woman He Loved.* New York, 1973.

Marx, Karl. *A World Without Jews.* New York, 1959.

Maser, Werner. *Hitler: Legend, Myth & Reality,* trans. Peter and Betty Ross. New York, 1973.

———. ed. *Hitler's Letters and Notes.* New York, 1974.

Merkl, Peter H. *Political Violence Under the Swastika: 581 Early Nazis.* Princeton, 1975.

Mitchell, Allan. *Revolution in Bavaria.* Princeton, 1965.

Montgomery, John F. *Hungary: The Unwilling Satellite.* New York, 1947.

Mosley, Leonard. *The Reich Marshal: A Biography of Hermann Goering.* New York, 1974.

Mosley, Sir Oswald. *My Life.* London, 1968.

Mosse, George L. *The Crisis of German Ideology: Intellectual Origins of the Third Reich.* New York, 1964.

Mowrer, Edgar A. *Germany Puts the Clock Back.* New York, 1933.

Nagy-Talavera, Nicholas M. *The Green Shirts and the Others: A History of Fascism in Hungary and Rumania.* Stanford, 1970.

Nedava, Joseph. *Trotsky and the Jews.* Philadelphia, 1971.

Neumann, Franz. *Behemoth: The Structure and Practice of National Socialism.* New York, 1941.

Nevins, Allan, and Frank Ernest Hill. *Ford: The Times, the Man, the Company.* 3 vols. New York, 1954. (See Vol. 2: *Expansion and Challenge, 1915–1933.*)

Nicholls, Anthony J. *Weimar and the Rise of Hitler.* New York, 1968.

Noakes, Jeremy. *The Nazi Party in Lower Saxony, 1921–1933.* Oxford, 1971.

Nolte, Ernst. *Three Faces of Fascism.* New York, 1966.

Nyomarkay, Joseph. *Charisma and Factionalism in the Nazi Party.* Minneapolis, 1967.

Olden, Rudolf. *Hitler.* New York, 1936.

Orlow, Dietrich. *The History of the Nazi Party, 1919–1933.* Pittsburgh, 1969.

Papen, Franz von. *Memoirs.* London, 1952.

Pauwels, Louis, and Jacques Bergier. *The Morning of the Magicians.* New York, 1963.

Payne, Robert. *The Life and Death of Adolf Hitler.* New York, 1973.

Prange, Gordon W., ed. *Hitler's Words.* Washington, 1944.

Price, G. Ward. *I Know These Dictators.* London, 1937.

Pridham, Geoffrey. *Hitler's Rise to Power.* New York, 1973.

Pulzer, P. *The Rise of Political Anti-Semitism in Germany and Austria.* New York, 1964.

Rauschning, Hermann. *The Revolution of Nihilism.* New York, 1937.

———. *The Conservative Revolution.* New York, 1940.

———. *The Voice of Destruction.* New York, 1940.

Ribbentrop, Joachim von. *Ribbentrop Memoirs.* London, 1962.

Richards, William C. *The Last Billionaire.* New York, 1948.

Ringer, Fritz K., ed. *The German Inflation of 1923.* New York, 1969.

Rivkin, Ellis. *The Shaping of Jewish History.* New York, 1971.

Roberts, Glyn. *The Most Powerful Man in the World: The Life of Sir Henri Deterding.* New York, 1938.

Rosenberg, Alfred. *Memoirs,* eds. S. Lang and E. von Schenck. New York, 1949.

Ryder, A. J. *The German Revolution of 1918.* Cambridge, 1967.

Salvemini, Gaetano. *Prelude to World War II.* New York, 1954.

Sayers, Michael, and Albert E. Kahn. *The Great Conspiracy: The Secret War Against Soviet Russia.* Boston, 1946.

Schacht, Hjalmar. *Account Settled.* London, 1948.

———. *Confessions of the "Old Wizard."* Cambridge, 1956.

Schoenbaum, David. *Hitler's Social Revolution.* London, 1969.

Schuschnigg, Kurt von. *Farewell Austria.* London, 1938.

Schweitzer, Arthur. *Big Business in the Third Reich.* Bloomington, 1964.

Seldes, Georg. *Facts and Fascism.* New York, 1943.

Shirer, William L. *The Rise and Fall of the Third Reich.* New York, 1960.

Simpson, Amos E. *Hjalmar Schacht in Perspective.* The Hague, 1969.

Sinclair, Upton. *The Flivver King: The Story of Ford America.* Pasadena, 1937.

Skelton, Geoffrey. *Wagner at Bayreuth: Experiments and Tradition.* Foreword by Wieland Wagner. London, 1965.

Skidelsky, Robert. *Oswald Mosley.* New York, 1975.

Sombart, Werner. *The Jews and Modern Capitalism.* New York, 1913.

Stamp, Sir Josiah. *The Financial Aftermath of War.* London, 1932.

Stebbins, Raymond L. "Henry Ford and Edwin Pipp: A Suppressed Chapter in the Story of the Auto Magnate," ed. G. L. Holt. Typewritten manuscript, Hebrew Union College Library, Cincinnati, n.d.

Steel, Johannes. *Escape to the Present.* New York, 1937.

Stern, Fritz. *The Politics of Cul-*

tural Despair: A Study in the Rise of the Germanic Ideology. Berkeley, 1961.

Stern, J. P. *Hitler: The Führer and the People.* Berkeley, 1975.

Sternberg, Fritz. *Capitalism and Socialism on Trial.* New York, 1968.

Strasser, Otto. *Hitler and I.* Boston, 1940.

——. *Flight from Terror.* New York, 1943.

Struve, Walter. *Elites Against Democracy: Leadership Ideals in Bourgeois Political Thought in Germany, 1890–1933.* Princeton, 1973.

Sutton, Antony C. *Wall Street and the Rise of Hitler.* Seal Beach, 1976.

Sward, Keith. *The Legend of Henry Ford.* New York, 1948.

Taylor, A. J. P. *Beaverbrook.* London, 1972.

Thyssen, Fritz. *I Paid Hitler.* New York, 1941.

Toland, John. *Adolf Hitler.* New York, 1976.

Turner, Henry A., ed. *Stresemann and the Politics of the Weimar Republic.* Princeton, 1965.

——. *Nazism and the Third Reich.* New York, 1972 (paperback).

Wagner, Friedelind, and Page Cooper. *Heritage of Fire: The Story of Richard Wagner's Granddaughter.* New York, 1945.

Waite, Robert G. L. *Vanguard of Nazism.* New York, 1952.

Watt, Richard M. *The Kings Depart: The Tragedy of Germany.* New York, 1969.

Weber, Max. *The Theory of Social and Economic Organization.* New York, 1947.

Wheeler-Bennett, John W. *The Nemesis of Power: The German Army in Politics, 1918–1945.* New York, 1954.

Wilkins, Mira, and Frank E. Hill. *American Business Abroad: Ford on Six Continents.* Detroit, 1964.

Williams, Robert C. *Culture in Exile: Russian Emigres in Germany, 1881–1941.* Ithaca and London, 1972.

Winterbotham, Frederick W. *Secret and Personal.* London, 1969.

Zeman, Zbynek. *Nazi Propaganda.* London, 1964.

Articles

Chanady, Attila. "The Disintegration of the German National People's Party, 1924–1930." *Journal of Modern History* (March 1967).

Feldman, Gerald D. "The Social and Economic Policies of German Big Business, 1918–1929." *American Historical Review* (October 1969).

Franz, Georg. "Munich: Birthplace and Center of the National Socialist German Workers' Party." *The Journal Of Modern History* (December 1957).

Gerth, Hans. "The Nazi Party: Its Leadership and Composition." *American Journal of Sociology* (1940).

Hale, Oron James. "Adolf Hitler: Taxpayer." *American Historical Review* (July 1955).

Hallgarten, George W. F. "Adolf Hitler and German Heavy Industry, 1931–1933." *The Journal of Economic History* (Summer 1952).

Heyl, John D. "Hitler's Economic Thought: A Reappraisal." *Central European History* (March 1973).

Jones, Larry E. " 'The Dying Middle': Weimar Germany and the Fragmentation of Bourgeois Politics." *Central European History* (March 1972).

Lenman, Robin. "Julius Streicher and the Origins of the NSDAP in Nuremburg, 1918–1923." *German Democracy and the Triumph of Hitler,* eds. Anthony Nicholls and Erich Matthias. New York, 1971.

Lerner, Daniel, et al. "The Nazi Elite," in *World Revolutionary Elites: Studies in Coercive Ideological Movements,* eds. Harold Lasswell and Daniel Lerner. Cambridge, 1966, pp. 194–318.

Nicholls, Anthony. "Hitler and the Bavarian Background to National Socialism," in *German Democracy and the Triumph of Hitler,* eds. Anthony Nicholls and Erich Matthias. New York, 1971.

Phelps, Reginald H. "Hitler and the *Deutsche Arbeiterpartei.*" *American Historical Review* (July 1963).

———. "Before Hitler Came: Thule Society and Germanen Orden." *The Journal of Modern History* (September 1963).

Stern, Howard. "The Organization 'Consul.'" *Journal of Modern History* (March 1963).

Turner, Henry Ashby, Jr. "Hitler's Secret Pamphlet for Industrialists, 1927." *Journal of Modern History* (September 1968).

_____. "Emil Kirdorf and the Nazi Party." *Central European History* (December 1968).

_____. "Big Business and the Rise of Hitler." *American Historical Review* (October 1969).

_____. "The *Ruhrlade,* Secret Cabinet of Heavy Industry in the Weimar Republic." *Central European History* (September 1970).

Weinberg, Gerhard L. "National Socialist Organization and Foreign Policy Aims in 1927." *Journal of Modern History* (December 1964).

Index

Kiel

Hamburg

Bremen

Weser River

Elbe River

Hannover

Berlin

R U H R

Essen

Düsseldorf

Bad Harzburg

Leipzig

S A X O

Cologne

Bonn

Weimar

Dres

Chemnitz

Rhine River

Frankfurt

Coburg

Bayreuth

SAAR

Nuremberg

B A V A R I A

Stuttgart

Augsburg

Munich

Bad Reichenhall
Berchtesgaden

0   50   100 Miles

0   50   100   150 Kilometers